P9-AFC-634

DATE DUE

AP 1 ~~98~~		
~~NO 19 '98~~		
DEC ~~14 1998~~		
~~MY 19 '99~~		
~~MY 27 '99~~		
~~OC 1 '00~~		
~~JE 1 1 '03~~		
~~DE 1 7 '04~~		
MY 2 4 '07		
AG 9 '07		
JE 2 3 '09		
FE 1 0 '10		

DEMCO 38-296

Dangerous Pleasures

A

Philip E. Lilienthal

.   .   .

BOOK

The Philip E. Lilienthal imprint
honors special books
in commemoration of a man whose work
at the University of California Press from 1954 to 1979
was marked by dedication to young authors
and to high standards in the field of Asian Studies.
Friends, family, authors, and foundations have together
endowed the Lilienthal Fund, which enables the Press
to publish under this imprint selected books
in a way that reflects the taste and judgment
of a great and beloved editor.

Dangerous Pleasures

Prostitution and Modernity
in Twentieth-Century Shanghai

Gail Hershatter

UNIVERSITY OF CALIFORNIA PRESS

Berkeley   Los Angeles   London

Riverside Community College
Library
·97
SEP
4800 Magnolia Avenue
Riverside, California 92506

HQ 250 .S52 H47 1997

Hershatter, Gail.

Dangerous pleasures

fully acknowledges the
bution provided by
tion Subventions.

Permission to reprint material published elsewhere has been granted as follows:

"The Hierarchy of Shanghai Prostitution, 1919–1949," *Modern China* 15.4 (October 1989): 463–97, © 1989 Sage Publications, Inc.

"Prostitution and the Market in Women in Early Twentieth-Century Shanghai," in Rubie S. Watson and Patricia Buckley Ebrey, eds., *Marriage and Inequality in Chinese Society*. Berkeley, Los Angeles, and Oxford: University of California Press, 1991, 256–85, © 1991 by the Regents of the University of California.

"Courtesans and Streetwalkers: The Changing Discourses on Shanghai Prostitution, 1890–1949," *Journal of the History of Sexuality* 3.2 (October 1992): 245–69, © 1992 by The University of Chicago.

"Regulating Sex in Shanghai: The Reform of Prostitution in 1920 and 1951," in Frederic Wakeman, Jr., and Wen-hsin Yeh, eds., *Shanghai Sojourners*. Berkeley: University of California Institute of East Asian Studies, 1992, 145–85, © 1992 by the Regents of the University of California.

"The Subaltern Talks Back: Reflections on Subaltern Theory and Chinese History," *positions: east asia cultures critique* 1.1 (spring 1993), 103–30, © 1993 by Duke University Press.

"Modernizing Sex, Sexing Modernity: Prostitution in Early Twentieth-Century Shanghai," in Christina Gilmartin, Gail Hershatter, Lisa Rofel, and Tyrene White, eds., *Engendering China: Women, Culture, and the State*. Cambridge: Harvard University Press, 1994, 147–74, © 1994 by the President and Fellows of Harvard College.

University of California Press
Berkeley and Los Angeles, California

University of California Press, Ltd.
London, England

©1997 by
The Regents of the University of California

Library of Congress Cataloging-in-Publication Data

Hershatter, Gail.
    Dangerous pleasures: prostitution and modernity in twentieth-century Shanghai / Gail Hershatter.
        p.   cm.
    "A Philip E. Lilienthal book"—
    Includes bibliographic references and index
    ISBN 0-520-20438-7. (alk. paper). —ISBN 0-520-20439-5(pbk.: alk. paper)
        1. Prostitution—China—Shanghai—History—20th Century. 2. Women—China—Shanghai—Social Conditions. 3. Women—China—Shanghai—Economic conditions. 4. Shanghai (China)—History—20th century. 5. Shanghai (China)—Social conditions. I. Title.
    HQ1250.S52H47   1997
    306.74'0951'132—dc20   96-5357
                                                                        CIP

Printed in the United States of America
9   8   7   6   5   4   3   2   1

The paper used in this publication meets the minimum requirements of American National Standards for Information Sciences—Permanence of Paper for Printed Library Materials, ANSI Z39.48-1984.

For Sarah and Zachary

CONTENTS

ILLUSTRATIONS
(following page 177)

ix

ACKNOWLEDGMENTS

I have accumulated many debts of gratitude during the decade in which this book took shape. My field research in Shanghai, where I was hosted by the Shanghai Academy of Social Sciences, was facilitated by Xue Suzhen, Zhao Nianguo, Wang Dehua, and the staffs of the Shanghai Municipal Archives and the Shanghai Municipal Library. Time for research and writing was supported by grants from the National Endowment for the Humanities, the Harvard University Fairbank Center for East Asian Research, Williams College, the American Council of Learned Societies, the Bunting Institute at Radcliffe College, the University of California President's Research Fellowship in the Humanities, the American Association of University Women Educational Foundation, the Pacific Cultural Foundation, and the University of California Humanities Research Institute. Much of this largesse was obtained with the help of Susan Mann, Frederic Wakeman, Jr., and Marilyn Young, who repeatedly recommended this project. I received additional funds for research assistance from the Academic Senate Committee on Research and the Division of Humanities at the University of California at Santa Cruz.

Shanghai prostitution is discussed in a massive number of diverse and widely scattered places. Erika Elvander, David Roberts, and David Schillmoeller helped me retrieve and organize sources in English; Guo Xiaolin, Max Ko-wu Huang, Jiang Jin, Pan Hangjun, Wang Xiangyun, Wang Yufeng, and Yu Yuegen assisted me in surveying and puzzling out early-twentieth-century materials. Max Ko-wu Huang also saved me from egregious errors in poem translation; any remaining howlers are not his fault. Timothy Brook, Merle Goldman, Nancy Hearst, Elizabeth Perry, Michael Schoenhals, and Jeffrey Wasserstrom called important sources to my attention. Emily Honig and Wang Zheng accompanied me on my fieldwork trip to the Hongqiao Hotel in 1993.

Sheila Levine at the University of California Press was an encouraging and engaged editor; I thank her for swallowing her dismay at the length of the final manuscript. Laura Driussi and Rose Anne White helped speed production of the book. Carl Walesa provided skillful copyediting; Cheryl Barkey prepared the Chinese glossary and wrested it from the maws of a recalcitrant piece of software. The China Publication Subventions Program eased production costs.

My greatest debt is to the many readers who offered encouragement and criticism as this project evolved. Bina Agarwal, Wendy Brown, Judith Butler, Sankong Fang, Carla Freccero, Christina Gilmartin, Nona Glazer, Carma Hinton, Grace Laurencin, Susan Mann, Sonya Rose, Janet Seiz, Michael L. Smith, and Christine Wong read and commented on portions of the manuscript. Colleagues on the Board of Studies in History at the University of California at Santa Cruz—Maria Elena Diaz, Lisbeth Haas, Martha Hodes, Cynthia Polecritti, and Marilyn Westerkamp—provided useful reactions to the chapters dealing with contemporary China. Members of the University of California Humanities Research Institute residential research seminar on "Colonialism and Modernity in East Asia"—Yoko Arisaka, Chungmoo Choi, James Fujii, Tak Fujitani, Ted Huters, Julie Park, Amie Parry, Lisa Rofel, Shumei Shih, Miriam Silverberg, and Lisa Yoneyama—lent their critical expertise to the shaping of the introduction. Emily Honig and Lisa Rofel listened, raised questions, read, and reread during the years in which the book was put to paper; one could not ask for more generous and tough-minded colleagues and friends. The thoughtful and detailed responses of Luise White and Marilyn Young, who read the manuscript for the University of California Press, forced me to sharpen the argument. Randall Stross commented with characteristic perspicacity and ire on every paragraph and endnote; he should be credited with helping to produce a leaner and more tightly organized book, but absolved of responsibility for its continuing sprawl.

Finally, I thank my daughter and son, to whom this book is dedicated, for pleasure, engagement, and a sense of balance.

PART I

Histories and Hierarchies

CHAPTER 1

Introduction:
Knowing and Remembering

This book is both less and more than an imaginative reconstruction of the lives of Shanghai prostitutes from the late nineteenth century to the present.[1] Less, because prostitutes, like every other nonelite group, did not record their own lives. It is extremely rare to find instances where prostitutes speak or represent themselves directly (although, as I will argue later, they are not entirely silent, either). Rather, they entered into the historical record when someone wanted to appreciate, castigate, count, regulate, cure, pathologize, warn about, rescue, eliminate, or deploy them as a symbol in a larger social panorama. The sources that document their existence are varied, and include but are not limited to guidebooks to the pleasure quarters; collections of anecdotes, portraits, and poetry to and by high-class courtesans; gossip columns devoted to courtesans in the tabloid press; municipal regulations prohibiting street soliciting; police interrogations of streetwalkers and those accused of trafficking in women; newspaper reports of court cases involving both courtesans and streetwalkers; polemics by Chinese and foreign reformers arguing the merits of licensing versus abolition; learned articles by Chinese scholars commenting on the world history of prostitution and analyzing its local causes; surveys by doctors and social workers on the incidence of sexually transmitted disease in various Shanghai populations; records by relief agencies of kidnapping and trafficking cases in which women were sold to brothels; and fictionalized accounts of the scams and sufferings of prostitutes. Each of these sources has its uses; as a group, they are most informative about how prerevolutionary elites constructed and sought to contain categories of the subordinated "other." In short, they tell us much more about the classificatory strategies of the authors than about the experiences of prostitutes. As the reformer Zeng Die commented sardonically in 1935:

3

Actually, these are prostitutes as they exist in the brains and ears of the writers. If you ask such a writer, "What, after all, do these women eat, what do they wear, are they willing to lead this type of life or not?" he is unable to answer.

Whether one perused the tabloid gossip columns, reformist fiction, or racy descriptions of Japanese and White Russian prostitutes in Shanghai, Zeng complained, one could not find a single straightforward statement by a prostitute.[2]

The very rich historical record on prostitution, then, is not spoken in the voice of the prostitute. And the much-sought "voices of prostitutes themselves," if we could hear them, would not be unmediated, either; their daily lives, struggles, and self-perception were surely constructed in part by these other voices and institutions. It is impossible, then, for even the most assiduous historian to apply the retrieval method of history making, where energetic digging in neglected documents can be made to yield up a formerly inaudible voice. The impossibility of such an enterprise, in fact, calls into question the retrieval model itself. It directs attention to the ways in which all historical records are products of a nexus of relationships that can be only dimly apprehended or guessed at across the enforced distance of time, by historians with their own localized preoccupations.

Yet if this study is a humbling meditation on the limits of history-as-retrieval, it also aims at more than a transparent exercise in reconstruction. Prostitution was not only a changing site of work for women but also a metaphor, a medium of articulation in which the city's changing elites and emerging middle classes discussed their problems, fears, agendas, and visions. In Shanghai over the past century, prostitution was variously understood as a source of urbanized pleasures, a profession full of unscrupulous and greedy schemers, a site of moral danger and physical disease, and a marker of national decay. It was also discussed as a painful economic choice on the part of women and their families, since it was sometimes the best or only income-producing activity available to women seeking employment in Shanghai. The categories through which prostitution was understood were not fixed, and tracing them requires attention to questions of urban history, colonial and anticolonial state making, and the intersection of sexuality, particularly female sexuality, with an emerging nationalist discourse. Every social class and gender grouping used prostitution as a different kind of reference point, and, depending on where they were situated, it meant something different to each.

The shifting and multiple meanings assigned to the prostitute demand that we move beyond transhistorical references to "the world's oldest profession," or dynasty-by-dynasty catalogs of written references to courtesans,[3] and begin instead to historicize and localize sex work. Prostitution is always about the sale of sexual services, but much more can be learned from that transaction: about sexual meanings, about other social relations, about sex as a medium through which people talked about political power and cultural transformation, about nationhood and cultural identity.

In some respects China's modern debates about prostitution echoed those of Europe and the United States. Recent feminist scholarship has explored the ways in which prostitution illuminates

> a society's organization of class and gender: the power arrangements between men and women's economic and social status; the prevailing sexual ideology; . . . the ways in which female erotic and procreative sexuality are channeled into specific institutional arrangements; and the cross-class alliances and antagonisms between reformers and prostitutes.[4]

Although this literature is far too complex to summarize here, several recurrent themes have implications for the study of Shanghai. First is the difficulty of working with sources generated largely by regulators, reformers, journalists, fiction writers, and others while trying simultaneously to hear "a language that comes from the work and experiences of prostitutes themselves."[5] Second is the attention to prostitution's powerful use as a symbol. "What was written and said about prostitution," writes Alain Corbin of nineteenth-century France, "was then a focus for collective delusions and a meeting point for all manner of anxieties."[6] For France such anxieties included fear of "venereal disease, social revolution, and 'immorality,' however defined,"[7] as well as a more generalized sense of threat to male mastery.[8] For the United States in the early twentieth century, the list of anxieties also encompassed "unrestricted immigration, . . . the anonymity of the city, the evils of liquor, the growth of a working-class urban culture, and, most important of all, the changing role of women in society."[9]

A third theme common to much of this scholarship is the insistence on regarding prostitution as a form of labor, even if not always one freely chosen, rather than (as many reformers believed) a state of degradation or a moral failing.[10] Some scholars argue that prostitutes themselves saw their activities as a form of work.[11] Prostitutes' labor, and the earnings that accrued from it, could both facilitate independence from the constrictions of family (as it did in nineteenth-century New York) and help to maintain the economic health of the women's families (as it did in colonial Nairobi).[12]

A fourth theme in recent scholarship is the attempt to move beyond characterizations of prostitutes as victims and to find the historical agency, however limited, exercised by women in the sex trades.[13] This requires attention to the entrepreneurial talents of madams,[14] as well as critiques of the polarized image of the prostitute as "the innocent victim or the sinister polluter."[15] In spite of considerable public hysteria about the traffic in women in both Britain[16] and the United States, Ruth Rosen writes that "the vast majority of women who practiced prostitution were not dragged, drugged, or clubbed into involuntary servitude."[17] Rather, as Christine Stansell comments, "[p]rostitution was one of a number of choices fraught with hardship and moral ambiguity."[18] Under certain conditions, it offered women a limited degree of control, as Judith Walkowitz explains:

> Superficially, prostitution seemed to operate as an arena of male supremacy, where women were bartered and sold as commodities. In reality, women often controlled the trade and tended to live together as part of a distinct female subgroup. Prostitutes were still not free of male domination, but neither were they simply passive victims of male sexual abuse. They could act in their own defense, both individually and collectively. They negotiated their own prices, and they were as likely to exploit their clients as to suffer humiliation at male hands.[19]

A final theme that dominates much of the recent scholarship on prostitution is the heated debate that raged between state authorities and reformers in a variety of nations during the nineteenth and early twentieth centuries. Crudely summarized, state functionaries, bolstered by medical authorities, argued that prostitution was a necessary evil to be regulated through the registration and medical inspection of prostitutes. Reformers of many types, including Christians and women's-rights activists, countered that prostitution was a social evil that should be abolished. Variations on the regulationist approach shaped the organization of prostitution in nineteenth- and early twentieth-century France, England, Scotland, Italy, and Russia.[20] When exported to the colonies, regulationism had a racial edge as well, stigmatizing native prostitutes and seeking to protect the colonizers (particularly soldiers) from the menace of disease and the purported uncleanliness of women of color.[21]

Neither regulation nor abolition was beneficial to prostitutes. Under regulationist regimes, women were subjected to intricate registration requirements that isolated them from the working-class communities of which they had been a part, increased clandestine prostitution, and led to police harassment of all working-class women on suspicion of being prostitutes.[22] Ironically, the upper-class women reformers who opposed regulation, on the grounds that licensing and inspection degraded women, did little better by their "fallen sisters." Many feminist groups saw themselves as striking a blow against the sexual exploitation of women and the larger problem of male domination. All too often, however, abolitionist laws made the lives of working-class women more difficult. State repression of prostitutes increased. Driven into clandestine prostitution and harassed by the police, for instance, many women turned to pimps as a source of protection, only to pay dearly—in loss of income, control, and personal safety—for the arrangement.[23]

Each of these themes was important in the course of Shanghai prostitution as well. But in China, prostitution was also invoked in urgent public discussions about what kind of sex and gender relationships could help to constitute a modern nation in a threatening semicolonial situation. China was never completely colonized by a single power. Rather, from the mid-nineteenth century European powers, the United States, and Japan established themselves in treaty-port cities and larger spheres of influence that encompassed both urban and rural territory. Mao Zedong coined the term "semifeudal, semicolonial" to describe this situation, in which a weak national government exercised limited authority over rural elites while foreigners dominated the modern sector of the economy and intervened in regional and national politics. Direct foreign political control, economic activity, and intellectual influence were most concentrated in the concession areas of treaty-port cities.

From the mid-nineteenth to the mid-twentieth century, Shanghai was a treaty port—a place where Westerners governed part of the city, where Western and Japanese businessmen, sailors, industrialists, and adventurers made their homes and sometimes their fortunes. Shanghai was also China's biggest industrial and commercial city, a magnet for merchants from around the country and for peasants of both sexes seeking work, and the birthplace of the Chinese Communist Party. Shanghai embraced populations from various nations, regions, and classes, and harbored political agitators ranging from Christian moral reformers to Marxist revolutionaries—all presided over by three different municipal governments (International Settlement, French Concession, and Chinese city). The International Settlement and the French Concession were governed by councils elected by foreign ratepayers; foreign investors were active in commerce and light industry; foreign educators dominated many of the city's new educational institutions.[24]

In this volatile and virtually colonized Shanghai environment Chinese elites, themselves undergoing profound economic and political transformations, keenly felt the instability of China's semicolonial situation, the fragility of China's sovereignty. The very incompleteness of China's colonization generated particular anxieties, different from those of fully colonized territories. The situation could always get worse (and frequently threatened to do so); conversely, perhaps purposeful human activity could stave off further political disaster. Many varieties of nationalism flourished in Shanghai. Most nationalists took as their goal the establishment of a strong, modern nation that could appropriate and adapt the methods of the colonizers to thwart the colonial enterprises, to keep "semicolonialism" from deepening and ultimately to roll it back.

The modernity sought by this heterogeneous lot of reformers and revolutionaries was not clearly delimited. It was a shifting and receding target, one that encompassed economic and military strength but would also, many felt, require a thorough overhaul of cultural practices. Debates over prostitution, sexuality, marriage, and public health were inseparable from attempts to define a Chinese modernity that could irreversibly consign semicolonialism to the past. And yet these conversations, incited and shaped by the significant foreign presence in Shanghai, seldom made direct reference to that presence. When Chinese writers invoked foreigners, they usually did so to make a comparative point about prostitution or marriage in Europe, the United States, or Japan. The foreign prostitutes who worked in Shanghai, their foreign patrons, the foreigners who sought out Chinese prostitutes, and the larger operations of semicolonial power that provided so much of the city's shape and history received only perfunctory mention in most of the literature on prostitution. This was a determinedly domestic conversation about modernity conducted in the urban interstices of a semicolonized space.

What it meant (to participants and observers) for a woman in Shanghai to sell sexual services to a man changed across the hierarchy of prostitution and over time, as understandings of prostitution were shaped, contested, renegotiated, and appropriated by many participants: the prostitutes, their madams, their patrons, their lovers and husbands, their natal families, their in-laws, the police, the courts, doctors, the city government, missionaries, social reformers, students, and revolutionaries. Studying prostitution and its changes thus illuminates the thinking and social practices of many strata of Shanghai society. And since the debates about prostitution often took place in regional or national publications, such a study also suggests the contours of conflicts about gender and modernity in twentieth-century Chinese society.

Across the century I am investigating here, the changing figure of the prostitute performed important ideological work in elite discussions.[25] Elite men (and occasionally elite women) wrote a great deal about prostitution, but the types of attention they devoted to it changed over time. In the late nineteenth and early twentieth centuries, the upper-class prostitute[26] appeared in elite discourse as the embodiment and arbiter of sophisticated urbanity. Guidebooks, memoirs, and gossipy tabloid newspapers known as the "mosquito press"[27] devoted themselves to the appreciation of beautiful courtesans and the depiction, often in titillating detail, of their romantic liaisons with the city's rich and powerful. This literature also contained warnings about the capacity of courtesans to engage in financial strategizing at the expense of the customer. Embedded in such writings was a highly detailed set of instructions on how the sophisticated customer should display knowledge and power to courtesans and other customers; guidebooks became primers for the production of elite masculinity. Side by side with this literature of appreciation, the local news page of the mainstream dailies and the foreign press carried accounts of the activities of lower-class streetwalkers, who were portrayed as victims of kidnapping, human trafficking, and abuse by madams, as well as disturbers of urban peace and spreaders of venereal disease.

One might conclude that there was one discourse on upper-class prostitution and another on lower-class prostitution. But as Shanghai moved
through the second quarter of the twentieth century, the themes of victimization and sexual danger gradually increased in volume, all but drowning
out the discourse of pleasure by the 1940s. During the 1920s and 1930s, the
prostitute was widely represented as a victimized, disorderly, dangerous embodiment of social trouble. Reformers regularly decried prostitution as exploitation of women and a national shame, indeed as one of the keys to
China's national weakness, since it was argued that a system that permitted
the treatment of women as inferior human beings would inevitably give rise
to a weak nation.[28]

At the same time the press and popular-fiction writers began to pay more
attention to the less privileged and protected sectors of the trade. This was
part of a more general development of muckraking reportage and fiction
targeted at an emerging middle-class urban audience. Such writings paid attention to a wide variety of social ills that included but were not limited to
begging, public sanitation, the mistreatment of domestic workers, and prostitution.[29] During the same period, the police and the courts, extending their
authority into new realms in urban life, undertook to regulate prostitution,
at least at the margins where it involved the sale into prostitution of "women
of good families," or street soliciting that was seen as a threat to public order. By the 1940s, prostitutes were clearly marked off from respectable people, particularly the respectable "petty urbanites."[30] They had been relegated
to the category of urban disorder.

This set of transformations was less orderly than the neat schematic account given here implies. The portraits of prostitution as sites of pleasure
and of danger overlapped and coexisted in time. Nevertheless, the increasing attention to disorder and danger, and the development of regulatory
regimes to contain them, had multiple consequences for the daily lives, identities, and actions of Shanghai prostitutes. Indeed, they even helped to determine who was considered a prostitute. Changes in migration patterns and
economic opportunities might have increased the number of prostitutes and
the alarm over them. But changes in elite notions about the link between
women's status and national strength helped create the language through
which a rise in prostitution acquired meaning—even gave it the most commonly used modern term for prostitute, *jinü* (prostitute female), which displaced the earlier *mingji* (famous prostitute).[31] And the elite shaped the institutions that emerged to classify, reform, or regulate prostitution—all of
which in turn became part of the material environment in which prostitutes
lived. Shanghai prostitution is a rich venue in which to explore the interlocking of material and ideological changes, since neither alone can be regarded as determinative of the conditions of prostitutes' lives.[32]

THE KNOWING HISTORIAN

Central to this study is the investigation of how things are known and later remembered, and how, later still, they are simultaneously apprehended and reinvented by the historian. Here the writer of local and national history must confront larger questions of contemporary historical practice. Just when the epistemological crisis engendered by poststructuralism appears to be waning in many academic fields, it has been taken up by that most curmudgeonly of disciplines, history. Historians wonder, with an agony no less heartfelt for being so belated: How can we let go of the belief that there is an objective, knowable, recoverable past out there, and still write history? If there is no there there, then what is it we spend our scholarly lives creating? Is history, ultimately, no more than a collection of the representations we fashion in the present, forever constrained by the limits and the politics of our contemporary concerns?[33]

This set of questions, important as it is, still assumes that the past—although no longer sitting out there waiting to be discovered—somehow awaits our touch to bring it into being as history, as a set of textual representations. Yet if we try to imagine the conditions under which the textual traces of the past were themselves produced, we realize immediately that before we ever take them up as the raw materials of our trade, they are already sedimented into historical conversations of their own.

To take an example from the subject being fashioned here: I come to the history of sex work in recent China with a particular set of questions informed by Marxism, feminism, poststructuralism, the late-twentieth-century demise of revolutionary regimes, and assorted political and intellectual commitments of both the coherent and the fragmentary variety. To summarize crudely: Marxism has shaped my interest in the historical workings of power, the centrality of material life, the analysis of capitalism and colonialism, the history of nonelites, and labor history. Feminist writings by scholars and activists have insisted that gender is central to the workings of all societies and that prostitution is sex work, a form of labor. In addition, feminist historians of European and American prostitution have raised many issues about female agency, resistance, sexuality, and the state; this book enters an ongoing conversation about those issues. From poststructuralist critics I have learned to pay attention to to the instability of all categories and to language as constitutive, not merely reflective. I have become suspicious of seamless narratives in the sources and less eager to create a seamless narrative myself; I have learned to hear silences in the historical record as more than simple absence. And yet I remain unwilling to give up the weaving of historical narratives. No longer sure that it is feasible, ethical, or wise to give order to the stories of others, suspicious as to whether historians can move beyond sophisticated ventriloquism on behalf of the oppressed, I am still unwilling to contemplate a world in which histories are unwritten or denied outright. Such a possibility takes on particular poignancy in the postsocialist period, in the wake of regimes that claimed to speak for the oppressed even while silencing history and reordering collective memory. The demise of revolutionary regimes has raised anew the question of what modernity might mean for China, a question articulated by several generations of reformers and revolutionaries described in this book. But the end of revolutionary socialism raises questions as well for those of us living in late capitalism. How do we know that capitalism is "late," for instance, rather than middle-aged or just coming into its own? What visions of equity, what workings of power, what deployments of gender and sexuality will animate postsocialist subjects on both sides of what used to be called, in a simpler time devoted to the enforcement of binaries, the Iron Curtain?

Such is a partial catalog of one historian's current preoccupations. But the writings about Chinese courtesans that were produced by cultivated gentlemen of the late Qing and early Republican eras, although they may yield answers to my questions, tell me a great deal more than what I might ask if left to my own limited contemporary devices. Many of these men were themselves writing about their own recent past—were lovingly, poignantly, nostalgically recalling the courtesans of twenty years before their own time. What we are reading, then, is not a transparent recording of the "facts" of a particular woman's native place, work history, physical charms, major liaisons, poetic talents, and so forth, but rather a story already rendered nostalgically. Courtesans here are brought into the written record—and become accessible to my own contemporary musings—only because men a century ago recalled them with longing and sadness as part of a world that they, and China, had forever lost.[34]

A similar process of sedimentation characterizes the writings about lower-class streetwalkers. Concerned about the health and strength of the Chinese nation in a world dominated by imperialist powers, many elite Chinese from the 1910s on called for an end to prostitution. Creating origin stories in support of the reform cause, they assembled a radically dichotomized, even incoherent, portrait of streetwalkers: innocent, passive adolescents torn from their families and communities by evil traffickers, or aggressive harridans purveying disease in a new and dangerous urban environment. Rather than looking nostalgically to a cherished past, the reformers gazed with apprehension at a degenerate present and an imperiled future. Streetwalkers entered into history as emblems of national disaster.

This is not merely a question of the aesthetics of nostalgia or the trajectory of particular reform campaigns. The narrativized traces that form the historical record of courtesans and lower-class prostitutes are also a set of congealed relations of power. Men defined themselves in relationship to each other by performing and then creating in textual form certain social rituals with courtesans, or by asserting themselves as advocates for reform of prostitution. In the act of writing about prostitutes, they captured, even created, their connections with other elite men by situating themselves with respect to a nostalgically recalled Chinese past, an unsatisfactory present, and a range of imagined national futures. As figures through whom such concerns were spoken, prostitutes were not marginal on the twentieth-century urban scene. Rather, they were key elements in the stories that men told about pleasure, danger, gender, and the nation—stories in which the shifting fields of power between women and men were sometimes made to stand for the equally unstable power relationships between families and the nation, or the nation and the outside world. Prostitutes are brought into history embedded in the histories and the contests for power of those who first fashioned their stories.

"Embedded" here does not imply "immobile," however. What appears to us as a concrete, examinable textual trace is in fact part of a movable past, a shifting set of relationships between historicized and historicizer, in which my entry as historian is only the latest ripple. And the fact that these gentlemen authors would not have called their appreciative or cautionary writings "history"—but would rather have labeled them memoirs, belles lettres, remonstrations with government authorities, or even historical romance— only alerts us to the important role that shifting boundaries of genre play in constituting what we now, in the inclusive mood of the late twentieth century, broadly call the historical record.

The new, improved, reflexive historian, sensitive to contested meanings and polyvocal perspectives, then, has more to worry about than how she and her contemporary concerns enable the telling of certain stories while occluding others. She must always remember that everything in the historical record itself bears the traces of earlier contests and concerns. This is certainly true in the case of self-conscious nostalgic or cautionary writing, where the authors are putting a subject into history in particular ways. But it is true as well of less obviously crafted pieces of the historical record. Statistics, for instance, can be read as the attempts by particular entities to count, classify, tax, suppress, ameliorate, or otherwise shape that which they are bringing into being by the act of counting it. Police interrogations of street prostitutes can be read as highly formulaic encounters (and in the case of 1940s China their repetitive nature virtually compels this kind of reading) in which law-enforcement officials organize prostitutes into particular categories— classifying them by motivation, for example—and prostitutes quickly learn which type of self-presentation will bring them the most lenient treatment. The historian reads such fragments as immutable "fact" at her peril—not because numbers inevitably lie, or because detained streetwalkers routinely dissemble, but because what we are seeing is not in any simple sense a set of "facts" but the itinerary of their creation, and we need to attend to both (never forgetting, of course, who "we" are and what historical baggage we carry, but not bludgeoning the reader to death with reminders, either).

In crafting this story of prostitution over the last century or so in China, I attempt to map the shifting connections between facts, fact makers, and fact interpreters, always bearing in mind that facts are constituted, not discovered, in the human process of making meaning. Whether there is such a thing as extralinguistic experience that remains outside this process does not concern me here. Historians, by definition, get to work only with discursive traces, with texts broadly defined. As a historian, I am grateful for the efflorescence of writing about prostitution that has left such a rich textual record. Nevertheless, I must ask why the record is shaped the way it is, and what its bumps, twists, configurations, and cavities can tell us about the people who made that record, their preoccupations, and their sense of place in the world.

This is both less and more than what Robert Berkhofer calls "ethnocontext," the placing of "matters within the context and terms of those living and experiencing it."[35] I have no hope of re-creating categories of meaning exactly as late nineteenth-century literati (much less prostitutes) understood them; at the same time, I have neither the desire to relinquish, nor the possibility of relinquishing, agendas and questions of my own. But if poststructuralist theory has made those of us who are historians more attentive to the process of our craft in producing historical narrative, we should also attend to the trace of craft, as well as the crafty presentation or concealment, that permeates every text we peruse. Rather than search for the past "out there," we need to triangulate the shifting relationship between what was recorded, who was recording it, and ourselves.

Perhaps this process is best described by resorting to a culinary metaphor. If we think of the process of writing history as an onion-peeling exercise, where the historian concentrates on stripping away layer after layer in search of some imagined essential core, she is apt to find herself with nothing left but compost and irritated eyes. On the other hand, if what interests her is the shape and texture of the onion, the way it is constituted by the layers and the spaces between them, the way it appears as a unified whole but breaks apart along initially invisible fault lines, the process by which investigating its interior actually alters the shape of the whole onion, the smell it produces under various circumstances, and the effects that the investigation produces in the person doing the peeling—well, then the onion approach to history can be very productive. Onions are, arguably, prediscursive and "out there" waiting to be peeled, so perhaps the metaphor is not flawless. Yet historians are, after all, examining a *something*. And it could be said that onions are not prediscursive either; they need to be recognized as food in order for peeling to become a worthwhile activity.

This chapter first describes the ways in which prostitution was "known" in various sources. Second, it discusses the way prostitution has been "remembered" in state-sponsored histories since 1949. Third, it sketches certain contemporary historical concerns that animate the reinvention of history in this study: the pursuit of elusive subaltern voices, the quixotic search for agency and resistance, and the exploration of semicolonialism as a social field. Finally, the chapter concludes with a guide to the strategy of storytelling adopted in the remaining fourteen chapters. The reader would do well to remember that these divisions among history-making activities are enforced by an act of will (mine) and a suspension of disbelief (yours): there is no clean line between knowing and remembering, remembering and reinventing, reinventing and storytelling.

KNOWING

Two sets of sources are helpful in thinking about how Shanghai prostitution was known to contemporary observers. Travel essays, guidebooks, and the so-called mosquito press dealt primarily but not exclusively with courtesans as social companions. The mainstream press reported on prostitutes of all ranks, usually as victims of oppressive social relations or threats to social order.

Among the richest sources on Shanghai prostitution are travel essays and guidebooks written by elite authors, devoted either wholly or in substantial part to descriptions of prostitution. Travel essays by visitors to Shanghai offered poetic images of prostitutes as an integral feature of the Shanghai scene. At dusk, one visiting official noted in an 1893 memoir, women, "their powder white and their makeup black and green, all lean on the balustrades and invite in passing guests." Near the end of an opera performance, he added, "the latecomers from the courtesan houses" would make their entrance, "just like the enchantment of summer orchids and musk-scented mist, elegant silk gathering like clouds. Truly it is a fragrant city that knows no night."[36]

The guidebooks derive from a much older genre of reminiscences about prostitution but appear to have been published for a growing urban audience. They have titles like *Precious Mirror of Shanghai, A Sixty-Year History of the Shanghai Flower World, Pictures of the Hundred Beauties of Flowerland, A History of the Charm of the Gentle Village,* and *A Complete Look at Shanghai Philandering,* the last by an author who took the pseudonym Half-Crazy One.[37] Guidebooks included biographies of famous prostitutes; anecdotes about famous customers; directories of courtesan houses and their residents; exhaustive glossaries of the language of the trade; meticulous mappings of brothel organization; descriptions of the proper behavior required of customers when a prostitute made a formal call or helped host a banquet or gambling party; descriptions of fees, billing procedures, and tips; lists of festivals and the obligations of a regular customer at each season; accounts of taboos and religious observances; and tales of various scams run by prostitutes to relieve customers of extra cash.

Guidebooks were one venue where elite men could display their erudition, refinement, and wit to one another. Their accounts were larded with classical references; even their name for the courtesan quarters—*Beili*, or "northern lanes"—was derived from the name of the brothel district in the Tang dynasty capital of Chang'an.[38] Their descriptions of courtesan beauty were lodged in a rich horticultural vocabulary, and in their prefaces they engaged in extended discussions about whether the lotus that grew from the mud unstained (a common trope for courtesans) was more beautiful than all other flowers.[39] Writing prefaces for each other's work, they gently mocked their fellows for devoting attention to women rather than using their talent to help the emperor rule,[40] or imagined that the songs of Shanghai prostitutes sounded grieved and touching in a time of national weakness and failed diplomacy.[41] At the same time these authors also registered appreciation of each other's profound emotions and their attachment to equally emotional courtesans.[42]

Guidebooks, in spite of the prevailing tone of appreciation, occasionally included denunciations of madams, remonstrations with customers to shun the dissolute atmosphere of the courtesan houses, or hortatory pieces aimed at persuading courtesans to leave the profession. These pieces, too, were self-conscious displays of erudition, not only in their refined moral sentiments but in their poetic form. One attack on madams was labeled as "written in the style of the Tang dynasty poet Xu Jingye's attack on [the usurping empress] Wu [Zetian]," while poems directed at customers and courtesans were "written in imitation of a poem by [the Tang poet] Li Bai."[43]

But the writers were equally apt to turn their mastery of literary styles to the production of jokes, producing a counterfeit government order to the effect that underwear and socks not be hung out to dry in the brothel districts, constructing imaginary letters from a courtesan to her customer, even crafting sly sexual jokes such as the following:

> A man named He from Jiangxi was an expert at poetry from his youth. He had the look of a handsome scholar. He visited Shanghai and stayed in a certain inn. An old man in the same inn, from Nanjing, liked most of all to play with words. One day, He and the old man saw the courtesan Xie Shanbao. Because Xie had long since ceased work as a courtesan, they did not speak to each other. But she turned her head and glanced at them in an extremely lingering manner. Because of this, He, borrowing words from the *Suiyuan Poetry Talks*, said to the old man, "The sight of a beauty can nourish the eyes, the poetry of a poet can nourish the heart. This is well said." The old man liked to fabricate vulgar literary allusions and pretend to be cultured. So he said with a straight face, "These two sentences are from the *Records of Qidong*. Following them are four more sentences." [The man named] He clearly knew that he was deceiving him, so he asked about it. The old man said, "I remember the next four sentences as 'Traveling on a

green plain can nourish my feet. Yang Guifei's breasts can nourish my hands.'"[44] [The man named] He laughed heartily and said, "So you have also seen this book. There are still two more sentences that you have forgotten." The old man was startled and said, "What are they?" He laughed and said, "The mouths of Daiyu and Lanfen [Lin Daiyu and Lu Lanfen, two famous late-Qing courtesans in Shanghai] can nurture my . . . " He hadn't yet said the next word and was already laughing uncontrollably. The old man asked more and more persistently. He told him, "Try to guess. If you can't guess, let me go back and look it up in the book to show you."[45]

These notes of sexual innuendo were rare in the guidebooks, which provided entertainment not through explicit erotic description but through literary allusions and puns:

> The twenty-fourth day of the sixth lunar month is said to be the birthday of Leizu [the thunder spirit]. On that day a certain guest was drinking at the home of a certain courtesan. The place was full, with double banquet tables. Many people were drinking and playing the finger game. Many prostitutes [literally, "flowers"] were around. Among them was a courtesan who usually drinks a lot, but that night no cup wet her lips. When others asked, she said, "Today is Leizu's birthday. For a day and a night we shouldn't eat cooked food [*shi yanhuo*]." Even though others urged her repeatedly, she steadfastly refused. When the feast was over, a guest still wanted some fun. He went to her house. She didn't receive him. Her servant told him that she had drunk too much, that she was nauseous and had gone to bed already. In fact she had asked a patron to stay for the night and had "long ago gone to sorcery mountain." The next day they met at another feast table. He asked her, "If you can't eat cooked food, how can you keep a guest for the night? Is it not very irreverent?" The courtesan couldn't answer. Her face turned red. After a while, she said bashfully, "Is it possible that there is cooked food [*yanhuo*, which also has the literal meaning "fireworks"] in his thing?" All the people at the table choked with laughter.[46]

By describing, appreciating, and putting words in the mouths of courtesans, writers established a fellowship of repartee among themselves.

The guidebooks can be read in conjunction with the mosquito press—tabloid newspapers that typically devoted a page or more to gossip about courtesans.[47] The final decade of the nineteenth century saw a proliferation of many types of newspapers in Shanghai, including tabloid papers. Among the earliest of these were Li Boyuan's *Youxi bao* (Recreation news) and Wu Jianren's *Xiao bao* (Laughter news). Both of these editors were well-known writers of "castigatory novels" (*qianze xiaoshuo*), a genre popular in the first decade of the twentieth century. The utterly permeable boundary between journalism and literature shaped much writing about courtesans.[48] *Youxi bao* sponsored elections for Shanghai's most beautiful and talented prostitutes from 1897 to 1909 (see chapter 6), a move that increased its sales and helped establish a favorable climate for the establishment of other tabloids devoted to brothel news.[49]

Perhaps the most famous of the tabloids was *Crystal* (in Chinese, *Jingbao*), published every three days beginning in 1919 for more than two decades.[50] *Crystal* overlapped with the guidebooks in content, but devoted a great deal of column space to tracking relationships between courtesans and the city's elite, as well as personality quirks and quarrels among courtesans, business successes or reversals, reminiscences about famous courtesans of earlier times, and lists of courtesan-house names and phone numbers.[51] Most of the detailed descriptions concerned courtesan brothels, but many also included substantial attention to the configuration of an elaborate hierarchy of prostitution.

Little was said in the guidebooks or tabloids about women being sold outright into prostitution, or entering into contracts against their will. For an elite audience, precise mechanisms of entry into the profession were not of interest. Not only with respect to the brothel, but also in matters of national significance, the women were portrayed as agents, not victims. During the May Fourth movement of 1919, for instance, students and other urban dwellers all over the country protested the negotiations at Versailles that ceded German rights over Chinese territory to Japan rather than returning control to China. Courtesans closed down their establishments for a day to protest the "national shame," leafleted in support of a citywide strike, set up a refreshment stand for protesting students, and joined the boycott of Japanese goods.[52] In short, courtesans were written into the civic and national drama as legitimate actors, not victims. The overwhelming picture that emerges from a reading of the guidebooks and mosquito press is a world of women with a great deal of room to choose their own companions and arrange their own working conditions, although obviously within many constraints, living lives of occasional penury but not serious material deprivation. Such women might break the heart of a son of the Shanghai elite, but their existence would not cause him any serious moral, political, or legal problems. Courtesans were seldom objects of pity.

But a survey of Shanghai's earliest and most respected Chinese newspaper, *Shenbao,* yields a very different picture. True, in the late nineteenth and early twentieth centuries *Shenbao* devoted some attention to cultivated, autonomous, upwardly mobile, romantically active courtesans, printing occasional poetry about them. But far more space was allocated to poor, oppressed, exploited, often battered prostitutes. They were not courtesans, but were usually of the "pheasant" class—streetwalkers. The term "pheasant" was a general one in Shanghai, used to refer to anything or anyone transient, including rickshaws and steamships on irregular runs.[53] Pheasant prostitutes were streetwalkers whose name described both their gaudy dress and their habit of "go[ing] about from place to place like wild birds."[54] They were often barely out of childhood, although occasionally they were married women. Stories about them stressed their rural origins and the fact they they were either kidnapped and sold into prostitution or else pawned by destitute parents. No embodiments of urbanity they. In either case, the reports emphasized that they did not wish to be prostitutes, a sentiment reinforced for the reader by the repetition of a standard litany of oppression. They were most often seen in one of two situations: fleeing from a cruel madam and being sent by the municipal authorities to a relief organization; or being hauled in by the police for aggressively soliciting customers, fined five or ten yuan, and released, presumably to ply their trade again. The coverage of their activities lacked the loving detail lavished on courtesans. A typical article read in its entirety: "Pheasant Dai Ayuan, from Changzhou, was arrested on Nanjing Road by Patrolman #318 from the Laozha police station and fined five yuan."[55]

In the 1920s and 1930s, these types of sources—guidebooks, mosquito papers, the newspapers of record—maintained their coverage of prostitution, but with marked changes. Some voices grew louder; others became muted. Although the courtesan did not completely vanish, and appeared in the literature of nostalgia and in classificatory lists through the 1940s, she was no longer the emblematic figure of the sex trades. She was replaced by the disease-carrying, publicly visible, disorderly and victimized "pheasant."

During and after the May Fourth movement, with rising concern about sexually transmitted diseases and their effect on the health of the "Chinese race," discussions of prostitution became medicalized, and its persistence was increasingly described as a public-health problem. Parallel to the medicalization of prostitution was the emergence of a legal discourse on prostitution, one that did not deem it illegal but regulated it in a way that offered protection to "women of good families." A woman of good family, legally speaking, was one whose family did not intend to sell her and who found herself in a brothel without a contract that legalized her presence there. Frequently cases were reported in the press where a woman or members of her natal or marital family would go to court asserting that she had been sold into prostitution against her will. Only a woman who could prove that she had been forced into prostitution could hope to get legal help in fleeing the brothel system.[56] Prostitutes of any rank could and did sue to be released from an illegal contract or alter their status. By the late 1920s prostitution, both high-class and low, was a litigable sphere, one that was no longer a matter only of pleasure or money, but of contestable contractual obligations and legal regulation as well.

Beyond indicating the emergence of a legal discourse, these accounts also treated relationships between prostitutes on the one hand, and madams or traffickers on the other, as points of conflict, regardless of whether the sex worker was a courtesan or a pheasant. Prostitutes were almost invariably portrayed as victims in these relationships. More generally, prostitutes increasingly appeared in written sources as victims of a variety of oppressors: the madam, inconstant patrons and lovers, the labor market, a society that devalued daughters, and occasionally the state.

Another theme of increasing prominence, sounded both by reformers and by government agencies, was the need for regulation of the sex trades as a whole, usually without regard to rank in the hierarchy. Because of their threat to public health and order—and also, no doubt, because of their increasing numbers and potential for generating revenue—prostitutes in the Republican period attracted the intensified interest of a state that was itself growing increasingly intrusive and tutelary.[57] The state—in this case, the multiple municipal governments of Shanghai—began regularly to regulate, tax, or attempt to eliminate prostitution. As early as 1920, the International Settlement government, pressured by foreign missionaries to abolish "commercialized vice," licensed all brothels and then progressively withdrew the licenses; the result of this foreign-run campaign was, as predicted by its opponents, an upsurge in unlicensed prostitution. Frequent and equally unsuccessful campaigns followed, until the comprehensive drive by the new Communist government in the 1950s eliminated prostitution. Its resurgence in the market economy of the 1980s occasioned, once again, fervent debate about whether and how state power should be deployed to frame and adjust the relationship between sexuality and social order.

The mosquito press and the guidebooks mainly described women at the top of the hierarchy of prostitution, and *Shenbao* and other newspapers mainly described women at the bottom. Both types of women sold sexual services, but there the similarity ended. Streetwalkers, unlike courtesans, worked in miserable and dirty circumstances, under duress, for cash, in the process posing both a danger to social order (dealt with by the police) and a danger to public health (as hinted at in the accounts of venereal disease). If we take these wildly differing accounts at face value, we have to question whether the single category "prostitute" assumes a uniformity where one should not be assumed, whether we should in fact stop talking about "prostitution" as a unitary occupation and instead use categories like "courtesan" and "streetwalker."

Ultimately, however, I would argue to abandon attempts at reconciliation and to look instead at the dissonance. Prostitution was an extraordinarily flexible signifier for many different kinds of Chinese engaged in many different conversations. The dissonant chorus they produced raises questions both about the contemporary meaning of the category "prostitution" and about the concerns of the patrons and the wider urban population. Above all, we must approach with caution the notion that we can retrieve from history a single set of descriptive or explanatory "facts" about prostitutes.

The perpetual reconfiguration of the discourses on Shanghai prostitution certainly reflected the changing occupational structure of Shanghai, where commercial and industrial sectors grew in tandem with a deepening rural crisis, encouraging the migration, both voluntary and coerced, of peasant women and girls. These interlocked phenomena led to a swelling of the lower ranks of prostitution, changing the sexual-service structure such that alarmed reformers came to regard it as more disruptive of social order, more dangerous to social and physical health.

Yet this change in the representation of prostitution was not an unproblematic reflection of social change in the sex trades. One must also look at the eye of the beholder,[58] considering the changing self-definition of urban elites, the effect of the May Fourth movement and the growing revolutionary movement, the development of reformist conversations on the position of women in general and prostitutes in particular, and the effect of language and categories drawn from Western missionary sources as well as Chinese radical politics. The discourse on prostitution should also be counterposed to parallel and intersecting struggles over the meaning of marriage. It is interesting, for instance, that courtesans were initially regarded as social as well as sexual companions, and portrayed as offering a range of companionship and choice not to be found in arranged marriages. In the social ferment that followed the May Fourth movement, however, intellectuals began to articulate, if not to practice, a notion of marriage as a companionate partnership between equals. If marriage was companionate and desired as such, then courtesans were no longer important as educated women with great skills, as a means for relieving the tedium of an arranged marriage, or as entertainers. All that was left for the world of the prostitute was sex. Simultaneously, prostitution was redefined as an exploitative transaction where the main connection—an oppressive one at that—was between the prostitute and her madam, not the prostitute and her customer. Because of these connections, prostitution must be looked at as one of a range of subjects of discussion about what sorts of gender and sexual relations should be considered modern and therefore desirable.

REMEMBERING

As though to illustrate the futility of the historian's boundary making, many of the authors engaged in "knowing" prostitution presented their works as products of the conscious act of remembering. Most guidebooks, as mentioned earlier, were engaged in a literature of nostalgia. Guidebooks written in the 1920s located the golden age of prostitution a quarter to a half century earlier. Some of the main guidebook authors explicitly said in their prefaces that they were recording the definitive historical account of a world that was about to disappear because of reform movements to abolish prostitution. Several authors even compared themselves with the famous Han dynasty historians Ban Gu and Sima Qian.[59] And like classical historians of the Han and later, many of these authors reprinted almost verbatim (and without citation) material from earlier guidebooks.[60]

Contemporary concerns were not absent from the prefaces written by guidebook authors. Writing in 1907, Zhan Kai worried that poverty was growing in the interior while courtesan houses in coastal cities such as Shanghai grew ever more splendid, nourished by the coffers of the rich. After castigating the heartlessness and lack of patriotism of his wealthy fellow citizens, he went on to state that he decided "to write down what I have seen and heard, and finish this book, not only in order to record these women in Shanghai, but also to show the fact that China is strong in appearance but weak in reality."[61] Fifteen years later, writing in a political and literary world forever altered by the end of imperial rule and the rise of a variety of vernacular literary movements, Wang Liaoweng nonetheless echoed some of these sentiments. In the preface to his lengthy *Sixty-Year History of the Shanghai Flower World,* which covered the period from the 1860s to the 1920s, he lamented that educated students were wasting their time reading popular magazines rather than attending to serious intellectual activity. Nevertheless, he continued, he had decided it was worthwhile to go through materials he had been collecting for several decades in order to publish a book about the history of courtesans. Rather than proceeding directly to put an end to prostitution, he said, he preferred to investigate how it had come to be. To this end he had set out to determine which stories about courtesans were factual, picking and choosing to achieve what he saw as definitive historical accuracy.[62]

In spite of their apparently modern concerns with national strength and facticity, guidebook authors resembled classical Chinese historians in their predilection for comparing the current age unfavorably with the past. Just as historians frequently mourned the failure of contemporary rulers to measure up to the sagacious rulers of yore, guidebook authors mourned the decline in entertainment skill, refinement, and classical training of upper-class prostitutes. In his 1919 series on turn-of-the-century courtesans, for instance, Zhang Chunfan warned that beauty and artistry among them had of late been replaced by a lascivious, disorderly veneer covering lives of hidden misery.[63]

This literature of nostalgia and decline emerged at a time when urban China, and Shanghai in particular, were undergoing rapid and disquieting change. As many China historians from Joseph Levenson on have noted, the question What is Chinese about China? became a serious and troubling problem for members of the elite in the face of the Western assault in the nineteenth century.[64] Part of their answer was to glorify Chinese cultural practices (now seen as particular rather than universal). And part of that glorification was to meticulously explicate the cultivated and refined social practices of courtesans (as in "the West has prostitutes, but we have courtesans"). The production of this literature peaked in the years immediately af-

ter national civil-service exams were abolished in 1905—years when definitions of elite membership, as well as elite understandings of China's place
in the world, were both in flux. Seldom mentioned in this literature, the West
was nonetheless a kind of unspoken standard against which these authors
produced an account of the world they had lost.[65]

A different problem of remembering is presented by the stories of pre-
1949 prostitution collected by the government of the People's Republic of
China (PRC) since 1949. The dominant historiography of China (indeed,
the only historiography generated within China between 1949 and the early
1980s) has taken as its major task the articulation and glorious defense of
subaltern interests. The term "subaltern" is borrowed from the South Asian
historian Ranajit Guha, who defines it as connoting a person "of inferior
rank," one who possesses "the general attribute of subordination in South
Asian society whether this is expressed in terms of class, caste, age, gender
and office or in any other way."[66] Historians of the Subaltern Studies Group
in India and the Indian diaspora have consciously attempted to write subalterns ("the people") back into a history dominated by elite historiographies.
These scholars of South Asia share a set of interests, although not necessarily a set of historical practices, both with Chinese historians writing in China
and with participants in assorted "people's history" movements in North
America, Europe, Japan, and elsewhere. I use "subaltern," rather than the
term "oppressed classes" more common in recent Chinese historiography,
because its inclusion of gender and other factors more accurately reflects
the groups actually targeted for the "voicing" of their stories by officially sponsored history movements in China.

After 1949, teams of historians worked assiduously all over China to collect and publish oral histories of worker and peasant resistance to feudal and
imperialist authorities. They called forth enormous amounts of material—
songs, stories of strikes and riots, accounts of daily life during and between
moments of struggle—that otherwise never would have been textually "spoken." The process of enabling subaltern speech in China was clearly marked
by its state sponsorship. When subalterns (typically, workers and peasants)
spoke in post-1949 China, they did so in a vocabulary provided by the state
in the process of revolution. The process of speaking in that vocabulary, in
an ensemble with other, similar (although not identical) voices, in turn
helped to form the speakers as particular kinds of subjects in a socialist state.[67]

This was a complex process that cannot be dismissed as sinister Newspeak.
What emerges in post-1949 historical work is not only the creation of language by the state, but also its adoption by "the people" to name an oppression that previously could not have been articulated. When a peasant
woman in the documentary film *Small Happiness* refers to her husband as an
"old feudal," she is appropriating a term from state discourse to name, and
justify, a rage that formerly had no language and hence no power to re-

proach.[68] The ability to articulate that rage creates palpable political forces that are easy to applaud. Nevertheless, at best the official language of revolt is homogenizing, unilinear, flattening in its inattentiveness to any categories other than those of the official class structure. At its worst, as in Cultural Revolution–era historiography, it is overblown, with resistance inflated to the point of heroic caricature or downright falsified. For a China historian, this legacy of official subaltern-speak complicates enormously the search for subversive voices,[69] since those we might call subalterns spoke (and often came to understand their own experience) in the language of the state, which simultaneously recognizes their suffering, glorifies their resistance, and effaces any aspect of their history that does not clearly fall into the categories of suffering and resistance.[70]

For a China historian, then, the attempt to recuperate subaltern experience always follows in the wake of an enormously powerful state project that has already traversed, and irreversibly marked, much of the territory (and been marked as well by its journey through that territory). This demands at least that we recognize the tremendous resonance that a Marxist language of liberation has had for several generations of Chinese, while simultaneously interrogating the terms and usage of that language. Nowhere is this process more evident than in researching the history of prostitution in early twentieth-century Shanghai, where virtually all accounts collected after 1949 are spoken (and arguably remembered) in the language of class oppression. Nevertheless, the ubiquitousness of such language should not lead historians to assume a "natural" identity of subalterns with revolutionary interests. In China, at least, prodigious efforts were required before and after 1949, at the level of organization, ideology, and even language, to bring the two together. As a high-ranking 1950s municipal official described the frantic and hostile reactions of prostitutes when they were taken in by the government to be reformed, "Not a single one of them thought that the Communist Party had come to save her."[71]

For the historian, one of the unexpected benefits of prostitution's resurgence in the post-Mao era was that by the early 1990s it was regarded in China as a subject with a history, one that could be a legitimate topic for research. When I first began work on Republican-era Shanghai prostitution in the mid-1980s, my requests for help from Chinese research institutions were met with polite compliance and tolerance for the odd proclivities of foreign historians, but the subject itself was regarded with an embarrassed reticence. By the time I completed my research in 1995, I had many direct interlocutors, as well as a variety of opportunities to listen in on official, scholarly, and popular conversations. While devoting most of their attention to the contemporary situation, all these commentators in some degree reached consciously for the past as a storehouse of information, lessons, and policy options. And yet if there is one lesson I have learned from my years of research for this book, it is that reaching for the past is an interactive process that constitutes even as it purports to retrieve. At the close of the twentieth century, the "remembering" of prostitution's recent and more distant history encompasses themes that jostle uneasily. These include nostalgia for an idealized 1950s, when the state and the people were one in their desire to eliminate prostitution; arguments that courtesans should be recognized for their historical contribution to Chinese literature and art; and tabloid hunger for detailed stories of derring-do in prerevolutionary courtesan houses. I return to these themes in the final chapter of the book.

REINVENTING

Elusive Subaltern Voices

The complexity of remembering under the aegis of the state is only one aspect of the search for the elusive subaltern voice of prostitutes. More broadly, the study of prostitution raises the problem of how we simultaneously retrieve and create a historical past. Because the sources on prostitution are so thoroughly embedded in discourses of pleasure, reform, and regulation, they cannot be used in any straightforward way to reconstruct the lived experiences of these women. The voices of a variety of men—the patron, the reformer, the lawyer, and the doctor—are far more audible than the voices of the prostitutes. These male voices provide a gender-bounded discourse of pleasure (male) and danger (to males). In the writings of female reformers, representations of prostitution were shaped by the intersection of gender solidarity and class difference. They employed the rhetoric of social purity and pity for fallen sisters who were said to suffer extreme degrees of victimization by men of all classes. (This sort of testimony was later expanded upon, shorn of its gender solidarity, and given official approval by the PRC government.) At the same time the female reformist voices provide a class-bounded discourse of redemption (with prostitutes as the redeemed and their upperclass sisters as the redeemers). Continually obscured in all of this are the voices of the prostitutes themselves—voices that, although they surely would not have been unified, given the variety of arrangements under which women sold sexual services, would certainly have sounded different from what we are able to hear at a safely historical distance today.

How can sources generated in circumstances of intense public argument about the "larger" meanings of prostitution be read in multiple registers for clues to the lived and mediated experiences of prostitutes, who were subordinate and relatively silenced on almost any axis the historian can devise? Addressing herself to the Subaltern Studies Group as well as to Euro-American intellectuals, the literary theorist Gayatri Spivak has suggested that "First World" and postcolonial intellectuals may unwittingly replicate imperialist relations of power when they "give" voice to subaltern experience. "Subaltern consciousness," she writes,

> is subject to the cathexis of the elite. . . . [I]t is never fully recoverable. . . . [I]t is always askew from its received signifiers, indeed . . . it is effaced even as it is disclosed. . . . [I]t is irreducibly discursive.[72]

This entanglement leads Spivak to flatly dismiss the possibility of an autonomous subaltern recounting of history. She bluntly asks, "Can the subaltern speak?" and as bluntly answers, "The subaltern cannot speak."[73] Spivak is particularly pessimistic about the possibilities of "hearing" female subalterns:

> Within the effaced itinerary of the subaltern subject, the track of sexual difference is doubly effaced. The question is not of female participation in insurgency, or the ground rules of the sexual division of labor, for both of which there is "evidence." It is, rather, that, both as object of colonialist historiography and as subject of insurgency, the ideological construction of gender keeps the male dominant. If, in the context of colonial production, the subaltern has no history and cannot speak, the subaltern as female is even more deeply in shadow.[74]

What Spivak calls "information retrieval" about subalterns via the humanities and social sciences is in her view also both welcome and suspect. The retriever is never just a transparent conveyer belt for information, but makes assumptions (about the existence of subaltern consciousness, about the subaltern as subject) deeply rooted in contemporary power relationships. At worst such retrieval will "cohere with the work of imperialist subject-constitution," she warns. "And the subaltern woman will be as mute as ever."[75]

This muteness is particularly profound for the formerly colonized ("Third") world, given the role that colonizers have played in constituting the Other as an object of knowledge and classification. In a phrase that reduces even an energetic historian to despair, Spivak asserts that "in the case of the woman as subaltern, no ingredients for the constitution of the itinerary of the trace of a sexed subject can be gathered to locate the possibility of dissemination."[76]

I cannot argue with Spivak's claim that any subaltern voices I hear are partly a product of where I choose to listen, enabled and enjoined as I am to do so by a mixture of privilege and political commitment that is contemporary, feminist, "First World," and embedded in a history of its own. Nevertheless, I want to resist her negative answer to the question "Can the subaltern speak?" In some measure subalterns both literally speak (that is, make utterances that enter the historical record as texts recorded by others) and represent themselves (that is, craft their explanations of their own experiences and activities in particular ways, in order to secure what advantages they can).

What a historian sees and hears in the surviving historical records is movement of various sorts. Here I want to argue for the broadest possible understanding of "speech." An intellectual making an impassioned case for the banning of prostitution in 1930s China, for instance, is certainly speaking in a way that can be apprehended later by the historian, and I argue later on that such a person should be considered a subaltern in the context of semi-colonial China. *That* subaltern speaks. The issue becomes more complicated, however, when we consider the role of prostitutes themselves in generating discursive traces. As in the case, for instance, of a courtesan who never sets pen to paper, but whose strategizing and working of the system we can infer from the vast cautionary literature that tells her customers how not to be defrauded by her. Or the courtesans and streetwalkers who sued in court for release from brothels on the grounds that they had been sold there against their will. Or the hundreds of streetwalkers whose arrests and brief court testimonies are reported in the Shanghai papers. One might expect that "the constitution of the itinerary of the trace of a sexed subject" would be even more difficult to locate in this type of case, given the illiteracy and poverty of streetwalkers and the fact that any particular one is seldom mentioned twice. Yet these records let us glimpse not only the circumstances that brought these women to prostitution, but also the regulatory regimes of the local government and the way that prostitutes positioned themselves to get the most they could from the legal system. Without recourse to direct speech, these prostitutes have nevertheless left an audible trace.

The subject positions occupied by subalterns in historical records were not simply assigned by the elites who kept those records, but were shaped to some degree by the interventions of subalterns themselves. Whether a subaltern—or anyone else, for that matter—has a constant and autonomous subjectivity is not the question here. It is a *relationship* that we are tracking, one in which we can indeed hope to see "the constitution of the itinerary of the trace of a sexed subject."

If we replace "The subaltern cannot speak" (or, what I take to be closer to Spivak's actual argument, "The subaltern cannot represent herself in discourse") with "Many subalterns making cacophonous noise, some hogging the mike, many speaking intermittently and not exactly as they please, and all aware to some degree of the political uses of their own representation in that historical moment," we probably have a closer approximation of the situation confronting historians. If we are lucky, we also have a way out of the "disappearing subaltern" impasse, in which any subaltern who speaks loses the right to that status. Finally, we have a chance to complicate the picture of one overarching discourse, in which subalterns appear only as positioned by their elite spokespersons. This picture might be fruitfully replaced not with a conception of "competing discourses" (with its overtones of free-market bonanza and may the best discourse win) but with a recognition that some discourses can be seen only *in relation to* each other. In the case of Shang-

hai prostitution, it is not only impossible but also undesirable to try to rec-
oncile them in order to produce a single seamless account. The dissonances
between them are arguably where the most interesting mapping can be done.

The Quixotic Search for Agency and Resistance

The search for female agency and resistance is something between an article
of faith and a cottage industry in the women's-history corner of the North
American historical profession in the late twentieth century, and it permeates the present study. The worlds of Shanghai prostitutes were circumscribed
by legal, medical, moral, and political regimes that must have affected how
they saw themselves, what alliances they sought inside and outside the brothel,
what options they had. Prostitutes appear to have engaged in everyday practices that helped them improve their own living and working conditions—
arranging to be taken as concubines in return for large payments to themselves, for instance, or suing their madams in court—in ways that belied their
portrayal as victims or as threats to the regulated social order.

In each of these representations of prostitutes, whether through the particular cautionary lens of the guidebooks or in prostitutes' direct (although
certainly mediated) speech to legal authorities, a historian who is so inclined
can find instances of agency, even resistance. A courtesan who worked to collect tips and gifts directly, rather than allowing all remuneration to go to the
brothel, was challenging the authority of the madam over her income and,
in a certain sense, over her body. A courtesan who left the brothel with an
attractive but impoverished young man, or a courtesan who chose handsome
actors and drivers as her companions rather than the free-spending merchants preferred by the madam, was doing the same. A streetwalker who represented herself in court as the victim of traffickers resisted being classified
as a bad woman, a threat to social order, or a spreader of disease.

It is important not to overread such activities, not to participate in what
Lila Abu-Lughod has called "the romance of resistance."[77] These acts, so easy
to read as subversion, can also be thought of as "working the system" in a
way that ultimately legitimates dominant norms. They not only leave un-
challenged, but actually reinscribe, a larger ensemble of social arrangements
in which prostitutes are multiply subordinated. In order to collect tips and
private gifts, for instance, a courtesan had to cultivate the patronage of customers in ways that could perpetuate her dependence on and vulnerability
to them. When a prostitute won release from a brothel on grounds that she
was illegally brought there, she helped to legitimize the court's authority to
determine circumstances in which women could be placed in brothels
legally, or more generally have claims on their sexual services transferred.
Furthermore, in order to leave the brothels, many of these women averred
a desire to be returned to patriarchal family authority, a desire they may well

not have felt (given their family circumstances), but one that represented their best chance of being seen by the courts as victims rather than offenders. Certainly these acts of resistance would not score well if mapped on the "virile" continuum of full-scale worker insurgence and peasant revolt;[78] yet we must also resist the temptation to construct a "separate sphere" of feminine resistance. It is important that we recognize instances of women's agency, resist the desire to magnify or romanticize them, and admit that, finally, our readings of them are limited by the many silences and irreducible ambiguities in the historical record.

Nested Subalterns: The Problem of Semicolonialism

"Subaltern" is not a fixed and unitary category. In semicolonial Shanghai, virtually every Chinese was a subaltern with respect to someone else. Even the locally most powerful warlords were subject to territorial and political assaults by would-be colonizers, whose presence was intermittently more intrusive and disruptive than the more stable foreign presence in outright colonies. If we leave out those who directly wielded state power, the ubiquity of subaltern status becomes even clearer. One set of people who were simultaneously privileged and subordinated (Chinese intellectuals in semicolonial Shanghai) used an even more subordinated group (prostitutes) as a metaphor through which to articulate their own subordination. In the 1910s and 1920s, intellectuals attempted in their writings to specify the causes of China's weakness in the international arena; often they looked to domestic cultural factors, including the widespread patronage of prostitutes. Chinese intellectuals of the 1920s and 1930s often took it as their project to voice the grievances (and plan for the welfare and control) of workers, peasants, prostitutes, and other candidates for subalternity. It is important to remember that these intellectuals were writing to and against a world in which they felt themselves to be (and were seen to be) profoundly subaltern with respect to Western governments and Western intellectuals. Their sense of their own subordination shaped the rhetorical uses that intellectuals made of subaltern groups. Rather than acknowledging their own social power over these groups, their complicity in oppression, they used that oppression as evidence for their indictment of Chinese politics and culture. They also employed women in general and prostitutes in particular as metaphors for their own oppression in a warlord society and China's sufferings in a hierarchical world order. Even the Communist Party, after 1949 the dominant shaper of discourses, had many subaltern moments, beginning as a subordinate entity in the international Communist movement and a tiny endangered group in the larger Chinese polity. After its accession to power, it continued (and intermittently still continues) to characterize itself as an embattled subaltern in the context of the global political economy.

If we categorize these intellectuals by their ability to speak, write, print, and circulate—by their ability to generate discursive traces, and in the process to distinguish themselves from subalterns by speaking on their behalf—they appear as elites. If we situate them within a semicolonial framework (which is how many of them understood themselves), their status becomes more complicated. For most groups in China, it is important to keep in mind the possibility of multiple, relational degrees of subalternity. One might label these "nested" subaltern statuses, in which some groups go to great pains to distinguish themselves from and speak for those "below," while allying themselves with and speaking to those "above." The problem with nesting, of course, is that it is too sequential an image to convey all of the crosscutting, overlapping, unstable ways in which subalternity can be constituted and dissolved in particular historical times and places. At least, however, it frees us from the monolithic category of "*the* subaltern."

Such an inclusive definition of the subaltern has its dangers. The category may become enlarged to the point where it is no longer useful (if everyone is a subaltern, what good is the category?) or politically relevant (if everyone is a subaltern, how does a politically engaged historian assess the possibilities for coalitions and liberatory actions?). Worse, is this just another way for a historian writing from the metropolis to assert an easy and unearned comradeship with those who have borne the brunt of imperialism ("We're all subalterns here")? While acknowledging the danger that a more inclusive concept may be blunted, I want to argue for it nonetheless.

What happens if we highlight the extent to which people were constituted as subalterns only in relation to others (sometimes several sets of others)? First, the workings of gender become easier to figure all across the class spectrum. In saying this I do not posit a class-free unity of all women. Rather, I suggest that gender is deployed in a variety of ways: in the case of prostitution, by elite women reformers, themselves conscious of gender hierarchy, who assert their responsibility for their sisters across class lines; and by semicolonized indigenous male elites to suggest that they are subordinated internationally just as "their" women are domestically. Second, the workings of semicolonialism in China become more visible. The indigenous oppressions of the class structure do not disappear, but they are altered in important ways by the subordination of native elites under colonizing regimes. This inclusive definition of *subaltern* is emphatically not meant to suggest that all oppressions (or resistances) are equal, that everyone is a subaltern in the same way. My hope is not to render oppression uniform and thus somehow less onerous, but rather to trace the ways in which oppressions can be stacked, doubled, or intertwined.

STORYTELLING

Any book about the past has a heft and materiality that makes it look substantial and authoritative. Regardless of how experimentally it is organized, it has a beginning and an ending. It is useful to remember that choices about where to begin and end a history are just that: choices. The decisions made by the author may be very different from those that would seem reasonable to those who made, observed, or commented on events in the past.

The boundaries of this story are, like all boundaries, arbitrary, although not completely random. *Dangerous Pleasures* begins in the late nineteenth century with a spate of colonial memos, elite memoirs, and travel writings. It does so because that is where the paper trail thickens and where particular kinds of debates about the entanglement of sex and gender with modernity in China become audible, at least to my contemporary ears. The story could equally well begin half a century earlier, with the opening of Shanghai as a treaty port.[79] An account more thoroughly grounded in the nineteenth century would have a different heft.

The book ends in the late twentieth century because prostitution once again engendered great controversy in the 1980s and 1990s, because contemporary issues and their historical resonances concern me, and because I am not a clairvoyant or a policy maker with expertise to offer in the realms of prediction or recommendation. Unlike the handful of Chinese scholars who have written about prostitution, I do not attempt to fix the origins of prostitution in early Chinese history, although I recognize that those historical resonances shape the context within which many Chinese understand prostitution in more recent times. Unlike contemporary Chinese officials and social workers, I do not take the 1950s campaign to eradicate prostitution as an end point, although I discuss it as an important moment in state regulation of urban society and family relationships. I do, however, take note of where Chinese participants and commentators locate themselves with respect to a shifting historical past, paying close attention to the lessons they draw for themselves or recommend to others, and how those lessons are reiterated or altered over time. Thus this book, although it has a fixed beginning and ending, is meant to suggest other possibilities, themselves enmeshed in other histories, for shaping a story on this particular subject.

This study traverses the (usually heavily guarded) border between fictional and nonfictional writing.[80] Literary sources are legitimate and fertile grounds for historical rummaging, perhaps particularly in tracing discussion about courtesans, since many writers of guidebooks and memoirs were also newspaper editors who produced novels set in the courtesan houses, some of them featuring famous courtesans by name.[81] So freely did authors such as Zhang Chunfan, Bi Yihong, Sun Yusheng, Zhou Shoujuan, and Bao Tianxiao cross genres that their work could certainly be used to examine how representational norms for courtesans and customers were changed—how the historical record was shaped—by the conventions of genre. The present study makes some attempt at this, mostly across nonfictional genres; its use of fiction is fragmentary rather than comprehensive. I have drawn upon short stories and scandal fiction,[82] but make only passing mention of the major courtesan novels for no other reason than that I feel insufficiently skilled to interpret them. I do, however, forage with great enjoyment in the writings of literary scholars about courtesan literature and the popular stories of love, crime, and scandal known as "mandarin duck and butterfly" fiction, to the benefit of this study.[83]

Except when I am tracking national reform debates in the 1930s and the 1990s, I confine this study to Shanghai. Shanghai, as both its boosters and detractors are fond of intoning, is not China, and this history of prostitution is a localized and limited one. Other histories could be written: of Beijing,[84] Guangzhou,[85] Tianjin,[86] and a host of other cities.[87] With the relief and nostalgia engendered by finishing a study that has taken the better part of a decade, I commend these cities to others.

This book is divided into five parts: Histories and Hierarchies, Pleasures, Dangers, Interventions, and Contemporary Conversations. The reader who has gotten this far is already halfway through part 1. Its second chapter, "Classifying and Counting," takes up the creation of a hierarchy of prostitution in Shanghai, explicating types of prostitutes and asking what was at stake for those who constituted and inhabited such a hierarchy, especially as it became "modernized" in the 1930s and 1940s.

Part 2, "Pleasures," talks about the lives of courtesans as they were recounted by men primarily concerned with exhibiting their own urbanity. Each of the chapters is concerned with a different aspect of the relationships between courtesans, servants, customers, and madams. Chapter 3, "Rules of the House," examines courtesan houses as complex social and commercial institutions where interactions among men were governed by an elaborate set of ritualized proprieties, with courtesans as the arbiters of behavior. Chapter 4, "Affairs of the Heart," takes up the negotiations and emotions involved in sexual encounters between courtesans and their customers, many of which culminated in concubinage, divorce, return to courtesan life, and concubinage again. Chapter 5, "Tricks of the Trade," highlights the cautionary note embedded in directions about correct behavior, warning of the multiple perils awaiting the insufficiently sophisticated customer. Chapter 6, "Careers," looks at courtesans as public figures about whom stories circulated across urban classes, and also traces networks among courtesans. Taken as a whole, this section maps an economy of elite pleasure, much of it recorded in a nostalgic vein, and attempts to situate courtesans in that economy as both powerful and subordinated actors.

Part 3, "Dangers," turns to writings in which prostitutes, usually of less than courtesan rank, were portrayed as both victims and embodiments of social danger. Chapter 7, "Trafficking," describes the literature on the kidnapping and sale of women. It asks why kidnapping was the most common theme in stories told about Shanghai prostitutes, given the extensive evidence that many prostitutes maintained close connections with, indeed helped support, their natal and marital families. Chapter 8, "Law and Disorder," traces quotidian regimes of regulation (as opposed to episodic campaigns to register or eliminate prostitutes). It pays attention as well to the uses prostitutes made of the courts. Chapter 9, "Disease," examines the increasing linkage that writers noted between prostitution, sexually transmitted disease, and the health of the Chinese body politic.

Part 4, "Interventions," looks at attempts by twentieth-century reformers and regulators to link prostitution to an ebbing of national strength and their efforts to ameliorate its effects. Chapter 10, "Reformers," discusses theories of reform from the late Qing through the Japanese occupation, some influenced by Christianity, all nationalist in orientation. It looks briefly as well at the practice of reform agencies that anticipated later state efforts to reeducate prostitutes. Chapter 11, "Regulators," describes campaigns to license, eliminate, and inspect prostitutes from the 1920s through the 1940s. Chapter 12, "Revolutionaries," examines the successful state-sponsored campaign of the 1950s that caused publicly visible prostitution to disappear from Shanghai for almost three decades. In each of these efforts, a tension is visible between the desire to strengthen the nation by raising the status of women through education and employment, and a desire to stabilize the nation by returning women to the (putatively protective) embrace of family authority.

Part 5, "Contemporary Conversations," turns to the furious public debate engendered by the reappearance of prostitution in China in the 1980s and 1990s. Chapters 13 and 14, "Naming" and "Explaining," track the proliferation of new forms of prostitution while simultaneously looking at how prostitution is framed with respect to China's prerevolutionary and Maoist past and its hoped-for modern future. The final chapter, "History, Memory, and Nostalgia," looks at the reemergence of prostitution as a historical topic, a focus for pre-Liberation memories, and a subject of literary and artistic representation.

Historians being order-making creatures (in contrast to our gleefully disruptive literary cousins), I have tried to tell an orderly story here. An orderly story, but not one that is unilinear or that marches forward from darkness into light (or even back to postsocialist darkness again). Instead, I have tried to encourage the reader to loop back over the material, to consider alternative readings, to imagine the messy process by which the historical record has been known, remembered, reinvented, and retold. By reading and listening in multiple registers, perhaps we can begin to understand the voices and actions of prostitutes *in relation to* those who were more visible and audible. In the process perhaps we can learn where the voices of prostitutes formed a chorus, where a counterpoint, where an important dissonant note, in the changing configurations of prostitution. At the same time, we can trace the discursive uses that others made of the prostitute. These are most apparent in arguments about the shifting meanings of urbanity, respectability, government, even nationhood, as elites and less exalted city dwellers sought to define for themselves what it meant to be an urban Chinese in the twentieth century.

CHAPTER 2

Classifying and Counting

Drawn mostly from the daughters and wives of the working poor and déclassé elites, prostitutes in Shanghai were near the bottom of both contemporary and retrospective hierarchies of class (if not always status) and gender.[1] Yet their working and living situations, as well as their individual standing and visibility in Shanghai society, were strikingly diverse, so much so that use of the single term "prostitute" to describe all of them seems inappropriate. Shanghai's hierarchy of prostitution was structured by the class background of the customers, the native place of both customers and prostitutes, and the appearance and age of the prostitutes. Guidebooks and reformers depicted a continuum of arrangements under which a woman might become a prostitute: she might be sold or pawned to a brothel owner, enter an arrangement in which she split income with the madam, or completely control her own labor.[2] Women who had been sold outright or pawned to a brothel had less leeway to refuse customers than "free" prostitutes who owned themselves.[3] Courtesans provided social companionship and artistic performances; sexual intercourse, although available, was not always linked to the direct payment of a fee. The main service offered by women lower in the hierarchy, in contrast, was frequent and unceremonious sexual intercourse. The hierarchy changed dramatically over the first half of the twentieth century, as courtesan houses and streetwalkers alike faced competition from newly established institutions such as tour-guide agencies, massage parlors, and dance halls. Any account of prostitution in this period must track a variety of working situations across classes and over time.

The hierarchy of prostitution was not a palpable structure occupying a clearly delineated space. It was, rather, the product of the shared or overlapping imaginings of a series of authors, the result of (mostly) men knowing, remembering, classifying types, and counting. For many of these authors, particularly those who wrote about courtesans, the act of classification was itself a form of nostalgia, of cataloging what they felt had been lost or was in danger of being lost. These men expressed their nostalgia by detailing life in the upper reaches of a hierarchy, at the same time expressing their disdain or alarm at the proliferation of the lower reaches. Other authors, particularly those who wrote about streetwalkers, took up the task of classification as an act of muckraking exposure, a call to fellow citizens to become aware of a social problem and take action to solve it.

To say that the hierarchy of prostitution was a shared imaginary is not to deny that courtesans were "really" divided into distinct grades. They were, and much evidence indicates that they themselves were conscious of these grades and sometimes policed the boundaries between them. In characterizing the hierarchy as an imaginary, I mean to suggest that the men who depicted prostitution were constituting it as they described it. To them, hierarchy meant order, achieved not merely by naming categories but by clarifying relationships of superiority and inferiority. By establishing hierarchical categories, fixing their importance, constructing and discursively patrolling the borders between different ranks, they helped to bring the hierarchy into being as a feature of Shanghai life. They did so through certain standard narrative moves, picked up and repeated, often verbatim, from one author to the next. Four of the most important were spatial mapping, counting, classifying, and regionalizing. Even the most exhaustive set of classifications, however, could not contain all the varieties of Shanghai sex work. Women of many backgrounds moved in and out of sex work, composing a form of casual labor, while new forms of prostitution proliferated in massage parlors and dance halls. Dismay at the undermining of the hierarchy was a persistent theme in late Republican writings. This chapter explores the hierarchy as a shared, if not stable, set of understandings that had real social force in the lives of Shanghai prostitutes.

The question of audible subalterns emerges here. The categories of the hierarchy cannot be stripped away to reveal the "real" daily working and living conditions of prostitutes, because such conditions were almost always presented as predetermined effects of the hierarchy. For instance, although in writings about courtesans madams were sometimes portrayed as strict or controlling, the figure of the evil madam was much more common in writings about lower-class prostitutes. Her cruelty was most commonly linked to greed; memoirs, glossaries, news reports, guidebooks, and scandal fiction all described madams who beat or tortured prostitutes when they failed or refused to attract sufficient business.[4] The combination of forced frequent sexual activity and ill-treatment led one guidebook author to imagine low-class prostitutes ranged along descending circles of hell.[5]

Undoubtedly the physical and emotional well-being of prostitutes varied depending upon whether the madam was cruel or kind, whether they had to entertain many guests, whether they became ill or pregnant. References to their physical and emotional states, however, were almost always made in the service of arguments about reform or laments about the unrestrained sexuality of Shanghai's disorderly urban milieu. Social workers reported that some prostitutes articulated feelings of depression, inferiority, and suspicion.[6] Relief workers who interviewed such women reported that they were "as though anesthetized . . . numbed to the conditions of their existence."[7] A guidebook commentator was most dismayed that prostitutes in such situations, "man-made instruments for the release of sexual desire," grew accustomed to their circumstances, moving "from pain to pleasure."[8] If a prostitute's status was portrayed as falling when her frequency of intercourse rose, then the ultimate measure of debasement, in the eyes of many observers, was whether a woman grew numb to selling sex or even appeared to enjoy it. Such statements were far more telling about the preoccupations of modernizing reformers and nostalgic literati than about the lives of prostitutes.

SPATIAL MAPPING: "THERE GOES THE NEIGHBORHOOD"

The hierarchy of prostitution was expressed partly through the organization of space; certain districts were associated with particular grades of sex work. Most guidebook histories of prostitution published in the Republican period, as well as some tabloid stories from the same period, lavished a great deal of attention on the the spatial organization of prostitution. Authors compiled exhaustive lists of the streets and lanes where each rank of brothel could be found, as well as the move of particular grades of prostitute from one neighborhood to another.[9] For these authors, the pleasure of cataloging space appears to have lain not in the mere collection and reproduction of place names, but in the evocation of a lost world by the recitation of those names.

Writing in the 1910s and 1920s, the authors of these works recalled that in the early nineteenth century, courtesans had operated on boats in the Huangpu River. Cruising alongside the merchant ships moored in the harbor, the boatmen would shout for customers and take on board any merchant who seemed interested. Descriptions of these pleasure boats mentioned the beauty of the women on board, their fine clothes, and the sound of musical instruments drifting across the water.[10] In the mid–nineteenth century, for reasons left unspecified, the courtesans came ashore and located themselves in the Hongqiao area of the old Chinese city, entertaining merchants from Guangdong and Fujian.[11] In 1860, when the environs of Shanghai were occupied by the Taiping army, many courtesans moved from the area of the walled Chinese city into the foreign concessions (the International Settlement was established in 1845, the French Concession in 1849).[12] The migration of courtesan houses to the concession areas continued throughout the century, and was linked by some sources to the increasing prosperity brought by the foreigners.[13]

The last quarter of the nineteenth century was conventionally labeled the "golden age" of Shanghai courtesans by nostalgic Republican-era authors. In that era, said one 1917 author, wealthy men spent generously in brothels and business was good. He contrasted this to his own era, when brothels and prostitutes had proliferated but business had declined as, by his account, China's profits flowed abroad.[14] In bygone days, men had purportedly gone to brothels to listen to music and join in socializing; sexual intercourse, although available, was not yet the major focus of activity, and was portrayed as part of a romantic encounter rather than as a thoroughly commodified activity.[15] Late-nineteenth-century courtesan houses were located on lanes just inside the northern perimeter of the old Chinese city, where authors described gardens, fences, "red skirts and green sleeves" glimpsed through bamboo curtains, and eyes alight with emotions.[16] Courtesan houses of the highest rank were also clustered in the lanes off Si Malu (now Fuzhou Road) and Baoshan Street (now Guangdong Road) in the International Settlement, lanes whose names were listed lovingly in many accounts.[17] In the Republican period this was the heart of the Settlement's commercial district, where fabric and clothing stores, pharmacies, newsstands and bookshops, opera houses, movie theaters, restaurants, and hotels lined the streets near the courtesan houses.[18] Several blocks away were lower-ranking courtesan houses, which had their own history of migration: from the old city to the Xiao Dongmen area, where many were destroyed in a massive fire, and to International Settlement streets like Henan Road, Beijing Road, East and West Chessboard Streets, and Chicken and Duck Lane.[19] After 1920, when the International Settlement began to close brothels, courtesan houses gradually moved to the French Concession, lining both sides of Avenue Edward VII (now East Yan'an Road).[20] Authors constructed enticing descriptions of the courtesan houses, characterizing them as quiet, tasteful, concealed places where beauty met wealth to the accompaniment of music. They depicted the women in these houses as properly dressed, self-respecting, and aloof from the exposed activities of common prostitutes.[21]

From the late nineteenth century, the Nanjing Road area of the International Settlement was described as a gathering place for aggressive streetwalkers (excoriated in one account as "hags unworthy of a glance from persons of refinement"), while outlying areas along the river were full of mud-walled brothels with bamboo fences where "those with the slightest self-respect" would not go.[22] North Sichuan Road, in the Hongkou district north of the International Settlement, became a center for Cantonese, Japanese, Korean, and (after the October Revolution) White Russian brothels, side by side with the dance halls, movie houses, teahouses, restaurants, bathhouses, beauty shops, and massage parlors where many casual prostitutes worked.[23]

In the twentieth century, amusement halls like the Great World (opened in 1917) and rooftop gardens atop department stores like the Wing On (Yong'an) began to feature women playing *pipa* and singing opera selections while tea waitresses offered companionship and sexual services for extra fees.[24]

Courtesans were reportedly so concerned with maintaining their distinction from streetwalkers that they would move from one district to another in order "not to associate themselves with undesirable elements."[25] Whether or not the courtesans themselves actually made decisions on this basis, the spatial mapping of several generations of writers shows that Fuzhou Road, for example, once the major preserve of courtesans, had by the 1930s become a mixed district containing brothels of every rank. Even the storytelling houses where skilled courtesan performers sang opera selections began to double as places where streetwalkers moved among the audience soliciting customers.[26] The decline in older courtesan districts over time—their tumble down the hierarchy of prostitution—allowed for a recurrent lament of "There goes the neighborhood" in the guidebook accounts. Authors commented lugubriously that one neighborhood off Zhejiang Road, formerly full of courtesan houses, had become a streetwalker area,while the famous Hongqiao district had evolved into a place where "those who haul vegetables and fuel" pursued their low-class pleasures.[27] Such comments established nostalgia for disappeared glory as a major theme in writings about courtesans.

COUNTING

Shanghai prostitution is important to the historian at least in part because of the numbers of women involved. Yet it is impossible to say with any certainty how many women worked as prostitutes in Shanghai. The profession was alternately forbidden and tolerated in the International Settlement, and brothels were licensed in the French Concession. The inconsistent attitude of multiple municipal governments meant that no systematic statistics were collected. Brothel owners often had an interest in concealing the nature and scope of their business, if only to avoid paying bribes to the authorities. Counting, like classifying and regulating, is not a neutral activity. The creation of statistics, in Shanghai as elsewhere, was part of a state-building process, an intrusive aspect of the project of modernity, often resisted by the people it sought to incorporate. Numbers that give the impression of precision were collected by an inconsistent group for changing reasons from a population that had every reason to lie.

The fragmentary statistics available indicate the unsteady secular growth of prostitution. A foreign health official in the International Settlement counted 1,632 Chinese prostitutes there in 1871, while the French authorities estimated that their concession had 2,600. Most of the brothels in these two districts were said to be establishments patronized by Chinese rather than foreigners.[28] A 1908 guide listed 1,219 women (969 top-ranking courtesans, 146 of the second rank, 42 from Canton, and 62 from Japan). No lower-ranking prostitutes were included, perhaps because the author was more concerned with providing directions to courtesan houses than with monitoring public health.[29] As International Settlement authorities grew more concerned about prostitution in the late 1910s, they found increasing numbers of prostitutes, alarm and assiduous counting propelling each other in an upward spiral. A 1915 survey by the Morals Correction Unit of the Shanghai Municipal Police found a total of 7,791 prostitutes, almost four-fifths of them streetwalkers.[30] A 1920 report of the Special Vice Committee appointed in the Settlement counted 4,522 Chinese prostitutes in the International Settlement alone, or one out of every 147 Chinese residents of the Settlement. If the greater population of Shanghai was taken as 1.5 million, the report added, and if prostitutes in the French Concession were figured in, then one in three hundred Chinese residents of Shanghai was a female selling sexual services for a living.[31] These figures did not include what the report referred to as "sly" prostitutes,[32] and in fact another set of statistics collected at around the same time found more than sixty thousand prostitutes at work in the two foreign areas, most of them streetwalkers known as "pheasants," or even lower-ranking sex workers.[33]

Virtually every observer of the Shanghai scene commented that licensed brothels were outnumbered by unlicensed ones and by disguised forms of prostitution. In the twentieth century, taxi dancers in the dance halls, masseuses in the massage parlors, waitresses in the vaudeville houses, guides in the tourist agencies, female vendors of newspapers, cigarettes, and fruit, and itinerant menders of sailors' clothing all engaged in prostitution, either because their jobs required it or because their precarious incomes needed augmenting.[34] Although they were seldom counted among the ranks of prostitutes in contemporary surveys, these part-time or "disguised" prostitutes must be considered in estimating the size of the sexual-service sector and understanding the employment alternatives for women.

Figures published in the 1920s and 1930s were less the result of counting than of broad pronouncements by social scientists and reformers. The numbers they produced tended to be big, round, and elastic, leading the reader to imagine an ever-growing and fundamentally uncountable number of prostitutes working the streets of Shanghai. One 1927 estimate of licensed and unlicensed prostitutes reached 120,000, and by 1935 estimates ran to 100,000, with much of the increase attributed to rural disaster and Depression-related factory closings.[35] An English-language report published in 1937 on the eve of the Japanese invasion estimated that 25,000 women in the International Settlement, or one of every fourteen women there, practiced prostitution. One-fifth of the prostitutes "were known to be professionals," but the authors were most concerned about the 80 percent who engaged in casual prostitution, soliciting customers on the roof gardens of department stores, in hotels, parks, tram cars, and movie theaters, and on the streets.[36] A postwar study put the number of full-time prostitutes at 50,000, but suggested that the figure should be doubled to take account of women "whose activities approach those of prostitutes."[37]

These figures suggest that Shanghai, China's largest industrial city, at some points had more prostitutes than cotton spinners.[38] The 1935 figure of 100,000 prostitutes would make approximately one in every thirteen women a prostitute, whereas the postwar figure varied from one in fifteen to one in twenty females, more if the cohort under consideration was confined to younger adult women.[39] When the authors of these surveys devised explanations for the rising numbers, they most often mentioned Shanghai's growing population, the high number of migrants (both rich and poor) from other regions of China, and the imbalance in the numbers of men and women. The population of Shanghai, including the International Settlement and the French Concession, almost tripled between 1910 and 1930. At the conclusion of World War II its population was roughly the same as in 1930, but between 1945 and 1947 it again grew by one-third.[40] Migrants from other parts of China made up more than 82 percent of this population in 1910, and more than 90 percent in 1930.[41] Women migrants to Shanghai found work in manufacturing, particularly cotton textiles; as household servants or wetnurses; as itinerant peddlers; and as entertainers or prostitutes.[42]

But far more men than women migrated to Shanghai. In the Chinese-governed sector of the city in the early 1930s, men typically outnumbered women 135 to 100, a ratio that dropped to an average of 124 to 100 in the three years after World War II.[43] The ratio was even more skewed among Chinese adults in the International Settlement (156 to 100 in 1930) and the French Concession (164 to 100 in 1930).[44] Republican-period social reformers were fond of pointing out that the predominance of unattached men in the urban population increased the demand for commercial sexual services. Although this may have been so, in both the International Settlement and the French Concession the adult male-to-female ratios grew steadily more balanced throughout much of the first half of the twentieth century, during precisely the same period when the reported number of prostitutes was steadily rising.[45]

Ultimately, the numbers are less useful as a precise indicator of growth in prostitution than as a guide to the changing ways and purposes of counting. What was being counted, why, and by whom changed frequently in Shanghai. When social-science investigation succeeded memoir as the principal genre of writing about prostitution, and reform supplanted appreciation as the authorial agenda, surveys replaced listing as the chief means of counting prostitutes. The apparent precision of survey figures was quickly supplanted by the invocation of large, vague numbers that conveyed the sense that prostitution was an uncontrollable, multifaceted, and increasingly dangerous phenomenon. Counting was one technique used by the state and reformers alike to assert control over prostitutes; the statistics thus generated are better read as a trace of growing elite concern than as a successful attempt to delimit prostitution.

CLASSIFYING TYPES

Virtually all extended descriptions of Shanghai prostitution from the late Qing through the 1940s, including those in travelogues, guidebooks, tabloids, and the reformist press, were organized around a recitation of the various types of prostitutes and the arcane terms by which the women and their services were named. Prostitutes' clientele ranged from literate scions of the elite to transient foreign sailors. Many of the terms for these prostitutes were specific to Shanghai; other cities had their own localized typologies, sorted and recited in similar fashion. Yet these accounts were not mere taxonomies; they were told as histories. Usually they were embedded in a narrative that alluded to three themes: that prostitution in China had a long history, that this history was intertwined in numerous ways with the history of scholar-officials, and that its contemporary growth was a story of decline from civilization to oppression and danger, a story that paralleled the recent history of China itself.

Traces of earlier histories, as well as ironic commentaries on officialdom, pervaded the terminology of prostitution in early twentieth-century Shanghai. *Guanren*—literally, "official person"—was one term used to refer to courtesans. An 1891 guidebook author could not fix an origin for this usage, but suggested that perhaps courtesans were called *guanren* because, presumably like officials, they were regarded as "public things" (*gonggong zhi wu*). Alternatively, he ventured, the term was derived from the "official prostitutes" (*guanji*) of the Yuan and Ming dynasties.[46] Another common term for storyteller courtesans was *xiansheng*, an appellation used for scholars, elders, and other respected persons, which over time also became a trade term for storytelling performers. It was most frequently translated into English as "singsong girl."[47] After searching for the meanings of *xiansheng* in the *Book of Rites*, the *Analects* of Confucius, the writings of Mencius, and other classical works, the compiler of a 1935 dictionary of Shanghai slang wryly concluded that in the ancient books one could not find a case of a woman being called a *xiansheng*. Like the prostitutes of Shanghai themselves, the usage was unprecedented (and, by implication, irregular or even illegitimate).[48] The terms *guanren* and *xiansheng* were both appropriated from the respectable male world of officialdom and scholarship; the result was an ongoing commentary on the devolution of both scholar and courtesan in the twentieth century.[49]

Shuyu: The Descent from Performance to Sex

Almost every twentieth-century rendition of the hierarchy of prostitution began by wistfully invoking a class of high-ranking courtesans that no longer existed: the *shuyu*. *Shuyu* were singers and storytellers who had entertained the local literati in the latter half of the nineteenth century. They were commonly addressed by terms such as *shushi* (storytelling official), *cishi* (poetry official), and *xiansheng*. The public spaces where they performed were known as *shulou* (storytelling houses), their private residences as *shuyu* (storytellers' residences). The last term was also used to refer to these courtesans as a group.[50]

Guidebook authors traced the entertainer pedigree of *shuyu* prostitutes back a thousand years.[51] In Shanghai, they reportedly had once been used by male storytellers to attract audiences, eventually becoming more popular than the men, who moved to the back of the stage and began to accompany the women on musical instruments. They were most popular in the 1860s and early 1870s. When a woman storyteller performed, her name was inscribed on a large piece of red paper and hung high outside the storytelling house. A man attained the status of intimate guest by requesting a song for one yuan. After their performances, some storytelling prostitutes also entertained callers in their private residences.[52] In the early nineteenth century, *shuyu* had to renew their performance credentials every year (some accounts say twice a year) by demonstrating their singing, storytelling, and *pipa*-playing abilities in a special examination.[53] Famed for their beauty, their extravagant dress, and their elaborate opium and tobacco pipes, they were equally renowned for their refined artistic sensibilities.[54] Unlike lower-ranking courtesans, they were not expected to drink with guests or accompany them at banquets.[55] Their professional names (chosen at the time of entry into the *shuyu*) were meant to invoke both sensual pleasure and literary associations.[56]

According to all the nostalgic accounts of these women, written after their disappearance, members of the *shuyu* class regarded themselves as skilled entertainers rather than providers of sexual services. They prided themselves on "selling their voices rather than their bodies." One Republican-era description of them reported that the *shuyu* had such high moral principles that if one was discovered having secret relations with a sweetheart, her bedding was burned and she was driven out.[57]

Other accounts say that the *shuyu* did "sell their beauty" in their residences, but kept this practice secret and made their reputations as singers.[58] Later the popularity of this type of artistic performance declined. Sources hint that the cause of its downfall was the unwillingness of the women (who were "excessively reserved and rose above vulgarity"[59]) to have sexual relations with their customers. By the 1920s the *shuyu* had been completely absorbed into a less exalted group, the *changsan* class of prostitutes, women who by several accounts "made themselves very accessible to pleasure seekers."[60] The term *shuyu* was used intermittently as late as 1948, mostly to refer to *changsan* courtesans, who also inherited the respectful appellation *xiansheng*.[61]

Twentieth-century authors told the story of the *shuyu*'s disappearance as a paean to a bygone time when artistic skill, not sexual intercourse, was said to have been the nexus between prostitute and customer. The *shuyu* thus became the vehicle for an origin story about a more refined and civilized past. In contrast, one guidebook author denounced his own time, the 1930s, as an era when "desire flows violently, following the trend of the time, and people in the brothels cannot help but loosen the belts on their pants, for there is no other way to attract business."[62]

Whether *shuyu* really did limit sexual contact with customers is not a retrievable fact; still less can one ascertain how they understood the connections between their art, their business, and their sexual activity. What is audible in these sources is the dismay expressed by male authors that vulgar and commercialized sexuality, which anyone with money could purchase, had supplanted a more ineffable set of pleasures that only a man of refinement and knowledge could hope to enjoy. What was being mourned here was not only the disappearance of the discriminating *shuyu*, but also the attenuation of shared masculine pleasures among a vanishing class of literati.

Changsan *and* Yao Er *Courtesans*

Courtesan-house practices and relationships, which are treated in detail in part 2 of this book, received far more space in the taxonomies than did the work of lower-ranking prostitutes; the former were at once a medium for the production of nostalgia and a venue for the production of masculinity. The term *changsan* (long three) is derived from a domino with two groups of three dots each. Traditionally, *changsan* prostitutes charged three yuan for drinking with guests and three more for spending the night with them; the name remained long after the fee structure changed. Throughout the Republican period, *changsan* women were at the top of the hierarchy of prostitution. Like *shuyu*, they performed classical songs and scenes from opera, although the range of pieces they performed was not as broad.[63] *Changsan* courtesans dressed in elaborate costumes, specializing in hosting banquets and gambling parties for merchants and well-placed officials. In the era before taxis became common, women rode to these parties in horse-drawn carriages or were carried on the shoulders of male brothel servants, providing live advertisement for the services of their house.[64] In the latter years of the Republican period the *changsan* brothels in Huile Li, a lane off Fuzhou Road, were the most famous. Sometimes wealthy customers would request that a woman accompany them to a dramatic performance or other entertainment.[65] The woman's brothel charged a set fee for all such services.[66]

As a group, *changsan* courtesans were young. Many prostitutes in courtesan houses first entered the brothels as children, purchased by the madams as "foster daughters" (*yangnü*). If a woman had already passed adolescence, no upper-class house would want her; madams reasoned that such a woman was already untrainable or that she would not be able to work enough years to pay back the investment.

It was difficult to make the acquaintance of a *changsan* without an introduction from one of her regular guests. *Changsan* courtesans, even those who had been sold outright to a madam, entertained daily but were not routinely expected to have sexual relations with customers.[67] Although gaining access to her sexual services was an elaborate process, a patron who went through a long "courtship" process and paid elaborate fees to the woman and her madam could hope for sexual favors.[68] Unlike the *shuyu*, *changsan* courtesans did not hide the fact that they had sexual liaisons, in the Republican period often going to hotels with customers for the night.[69] *Changsan* houses remained a feature of Shanghai life into the 1940s.[70]

Next in the hierarchy were the *ersan* and *yao er* prostitutes, also named for dominoes ("two three" and "one two," respectively). The *ersan* group was absorbed into the *changsan* class sometime during the Republican period,[71] but the *yao er* maintained a separate identity. Their standard Republican-era fees were quoted as one yuan for providing melon seeds and fruit (called a "dry and wet basin") and two yuan for drinking companionship (hence "one two"). Although their actual fee structure in a time of changing currencies remains obscure, it is clear that an evening in the company of prostitutes cost considerably more by the Republican period than the domino names indicate. Sources agree that the singing of *yao er* prostitutes was not as good, nor their sexual services as expensive, as those of the *changsan*. *Yao er* houses tended to be much bigger in size than those of the *changsan*, each house subdivided into many smaller establishments.[72]

In the *yao er* houses, customers were accepted readily whether they were regulars or strangers.[73] "As long as you have six dollars in your pocket," ran one candid commentary, "you can make her tumble under your iron hoof. The coin changes hands, and she'll let you dispose of her at will."[74] One guidebook described women who left the ranks of *changsan* to become *yao er*, or who were forced to do so by whoever controlled their labor (often an adoptive parent), because it was easier to make quick money from the sale of sex than from the protracted entertainment rituals in the *changsan* houses. The author commented that women who had lived as *changsan* found it both emotionally and physically difficult to make the transition to ready sexual availability.[75]

In the recitation of courtesan types, authors pinpointed as an indicator of tragic decline those moments when courtesans were pressured by economic factors to make themselves more sexually available. In 1922, for instance, one chronicler of courtesan life reported that a Courtesan Relief Group (*Qinglou jiujituan*) had suddenly appeared. Observers assumed that it had been formed to pressure the Shanghai Municipal Council to discontinue its ban on prostitution (see chapter 11), but they soon discovered that the group was actually a cover for an establishment where courtesans would secretly sell sex to carefully selected customers for high prices. The report on this organization lamented that with the rising cost of living, only a handful of famous courtesans could survive without engaging in sexual relations for pay.[76]

Trysting Houses and Salt-Pork Shops

If sexual intercourse was a secondary and sometimes hidden activity in the courtesan houses, the trysting house (*taiji;* literally, "stage foundation"), which catered to wealthy merchants, was devoted exclusively to clandestine sexual liaisons. The lure as well as the menace of the trysting house, as portrayed in memoirs, news reports, cautionary tracts, and historical romances, lay in its breach of closely guarded household boundaries: within its walls a man could sleep with another man's concubine or the daughter of a respectable family. Only in a chaotic yet enticing urban environment, authors implied, could such transgressive behavior be regularized in an institutional context.

Trysting houses flourished from the mid–nineteenth century until the 1910s.[77] In addition to concubines and respectable daughters, some of whom used the houses to meet lovers of whom their families did not approve, the trysting houses contained a certain number of prostitutes who could be hired by the night, the month, or even longer. They divided their fees with the female owners of the houses, who played an active role in soliciting both women and their customers.[78] Descriptions of the houses struck an ironic note by portraying men and women as members of the "new party" who scheduled their sexual encounters just like "classes arranged at a new-style school."[79] The trysting houses declined with the development of the hotel industry, which provided an alternative venue for illicit liaisons.[80]

In the twentieth century, trysting houses were gradually replaced by the more public brothels known as "salt-pork shops" (*xianrou zhuang*).[81] Like the various grades of courtesan houses, salt-pork shops were public establishments that paid taxes and received licenses in the Republican period;[82] but like the trysting places, they were devoted exclusively to the on-demand satisfaction of male copulative desires.[83] Guests who came to call were given a cup of tea, not the assortment of snacks proffered in the courtesan houses, and social preliminaries were few.[84] Salt-pork shops, said a 1932 guide,

> completely take sexual desire as their premise, so they are the most popular type among sex maniacs. They don't have the hypocritical complexities of

the brothels. Without mincing matters, you pay a certain price, and then can satisfy your desire.[85]

Women were the "salt pork," and guidebooks played endlessly with the trope in their descriptions, referring to the "inexpensive home-cooked ham" of the smaller shops, the relationship between price and "the flavor of the meat," and the cost of "cutting a slice" (three yuan in the 1930s, in contrast to the all-night price of five to eight yuan).[86] In a more ominous reference to sexually transmitted disease, one 1930s guidebook referred to the "salt-pork stink" of the meat,[87] and another reminded its readers that "meat eaters value freshness. Salt pork has not only lost the true flavor of meat, but always smells foul to a greater or lesser degree. Friends without strong stomachs don't dare to encounter it in person."[88] Salt pork was linked metonymically to Shanghai's status as a city of sojourners:

> Although salt pork is not fresh, still it can be stored. When travelers carry food on the road, it is most appropriate. . . . You can carry the whole piece with you and eat it at any time, cut off a piece and send it to your mouth. It is very convenient. Shanghai is a living dock, with many people away from home, so "salt-pork shops" have been constructed for the convenience of travelers.[89]

United by their focus on sex rather than socializing, salt-pork shops were in other respects a heterogeneous lot, ranging from beautifully decorated "aristocratic butcher shops" to rudimentary facilities.[90] In the latter, prostitutes received customers in cubicles called "pigeon sheds" (*gezi peng*), each one just big enough for a bed. The women spent a certain amount of time with each customer, depending on the size of the fee, then went on to the next one.[91] The madams were described unflatteringly as "warlike brutal old lower-class hags" or "man-crazy sharp-tongued middle-aged women,"[92] marking this type of establishment as relatively low class, since the keepers of courtesan houses were never depicted in such crude terms.

Perhaps because they began to proliferate just as the International Settlement was attempting to ban prostitution,[93] most of the salt-pork houses were located in the French Concession, in the vicinity of Eight Immortals Bridge (*Baxian qiao*).[94] By the 1930s, guidebook authors were commenting on the rapid growth of the "salt pork" business, along with the move of prostitutes to hotels; both types of facilities came vastly to outnumber the courtesan houses.[95] Such descriptions were part of the pervasive theme that the hierarchy of prostitution, and with it the orderly arrangement of society as a whole, was collapsing in a massive downward slide from a trade centered on courtesan houses to one devoted to straightforward sex for money. Nostalgia for courtesans and disdain for "salt pork" prostitutes were linked themes in this literature.

Pheasants

By far the largest group of prostitutes in late Qing and Republican Shanghai were the "pheasants" (*yeji* or *zhiji*).[96] To the pervasive messages about disease and commodified sex in the salt-pork houses, the literature on pheasants added dire descriptions of physical danger to the customer. A man who sought out these streetwalkers was said to be "hunting pheasants," but in fact most accounts made it clear that the women were the hunters.[97] Every evening groups of them could be seen on both sides of the main streets in the International Settlement and the French Concession,[98] aggressively seeking customers among the small-scale merchants, peddlers, and servants who traversed the Shanghai streets.[99] (See figure 1.) Guidebooks of the period repeatedly warned visitors to Shanghai to beware of the pheasants, whose eager assaults on passersby could shade over into pickpocketing. Rural folk were particularly vulnerable:

> If the guest is a country bumpkin who looks like he has money, then they hook the fish, finding ways to make his heart confused so that he is not his own master. Normally he regards even one cash as worth his life, but at this time he doesn't mind spending a thousand pieces of gold.[100]

Mixing his ornithological metaphors, one author warned that pheasants fastened onto their prey "like an eagle seizing a chick."[101] Another described pheasant methods as a form of gang assault:

> When pheasants solicit on the street, they usually do so in threes. . . . On a street they may be somewhat polite, but if a man is persuaded by them to enter a dark lane, a beehive of pheasants and madams will come forward and besiege him, and if he still is stubborn about it, they will use the kidnapping method. . . . Country people are often manhandled by them to the point where they cry out for help.[102]

Worse yet, this author added, pheasants also used the method of dragging a customer into a darkened lane and "lifting up the flax cake" (flax cakes resembled a penis in shape) in order to "stimulate sex mania on the part of men."[103] Pheasant prices as reported in 1932 ranged from one yuan for what was euphemistically called "one cannon blast-ism" (*yipao zhuyi*) to seven yuan for a night.[104]

Pheasants, like most other types of prostitutes, were not a uniform group, and not all of them were described as voracious. Some specialized in soliciting as they rode rickshaws along Nanjing Road; others went to teahouses or the theater and responded with feigned shyness to overtures from men; still others, known oxymoronically as "stay-at-home pheasants" (*zhujia yeji*), never solicited outside the brothel at all.[105] As styles of female garb changed in the twentieth century, pheasants began to mimic the current dress of female students: leather shoes, wire-rimmed glasses, bobbed hair.[106] As a group, however, their defining characteristic was their visibility; they spent more time on the street than full-time prostitutes of other ranks.

Pheasants and other low-class prostitutes were conventionally described as either very young and "not yet fully grown," or aging, "of fading beauty," and "badly nourished."[107] "Aging" in this case often meant between the ages of twenty and thirty; few courtesans but many pheasants were in that age range.[108] Fragmentary evidence indicates that as the ranks of lower-class prostitutes increased, so did the average age of the prostitute population.[109]

Although they worked the streets, pheasants were by no means independent of the brothel system. The social rituals in pheasant brothels were far less elaborate than those in *changsan* or *yao er* courtesan houses, but a customer could pay a nominal fee and be offered two plates of snacks and the opportunity to sit and joke with the pheasants.[110] Such interludes were brief: one guidebook reported that after fifteen minutes of repartee a pheasant would ask the customer to spend the night, and "if you refuse, she will unceremoniously order you to get out. This is truly a bore."[111]

Pheasants were presented as the quintessential victims of the madam in virtually all sources on prostitution. Neither their freedom from the physical confines of the brothel nor the fact that as a group they were somewhat older than upper-class prostitutes guaranteed them greater control over their working lives. Brothel attendants or madams supervised them as they went about finding customers, who were then brought back to the brothel.[112] (See figure 2.) Ernest Hauser recalled the prewar scene in his 1940 book *Shanghai: City for Sale:*

> At night, when you came home from the movies, you could see them in pairs, all along Nanking Road: young, poorly dressed Chinese girls, strolling hand in hand with their elderly amahs. They were not a happy-looking lot, and one could not help thinking that some of them might have found ways and means of going back to the village, if it had not been for those nasty amahs.[113]

A 1923 survey of prostitution by a foreign group of reformers was more explicit:

> No matter the weather, hot or cold, rain, frost, or snow, when evening came they must stand in groups and call out to men and on the least response they must take hold of them and cajole them to respond. If not successful, the girls were beaten.[114]

Such comments were not limited to foreigners of reformist bent. Because of pressure from their madams, a guidebook reported, by three or four in the morning pheasants no longer asked passersby to spend the night but rather entreated them desperately: "Excuse me, please help me out!"[115]

In the writings of reformers and social scientists, a further sign of the debased status of pheasants was the higher number of customers with whom they had sexual contact. A 1948 survey of five hundred prostitutes of various ranks found that most women had ten to thirty sexual encounters per month, with some women reporting as many as sixty.[116] Even higher figures appeared in articles by reformers, who reported that madams forced pheasants to have sexual relations with anywhere from four to twenty men a night.[117] Reformers also complained that lower-class prostitutes were the chief cause of venereal disease, since they spread it more widely and quickly than others.[118]

In at least one other respect, pheasants were certainly worse off than other prostitutes: because they did not remain in brothels, they frequently came into conflict with the local police who enforced municipal ordinances against street soliciting.[119] One guide advised Shanghai visitors that the only way to shake off a determined pheasant was to drag her into the street, because then she would become fearful of police intervention and desist in her efforts.[120] By the 1930s, an almost uniform tone of pity pervaded writings about pheasants, no matter what the genre. If they were insufficiently aggressive, one guidebook author wrote, the madam would beat and curse them; if they solicited more actively the patrolmen would give them "a few blows of the nightstick." If they snared customers successfully, they avoided beatings but never got to sleep because the men were "relieving their sexual urge" all night.[121] Seen in this light, their overbearing behavior looked less threatening, wrote a 1935 guidebook author, his formulation converging with that of reformers: "Their demeanor, as fierce as tigers and wolves, is actually hateful and pitiful, because they are controlled by their environment and forced by life."[122]

Flophouses

Lowest of all in the hierarchy of prostitution were the employees of those brothels called "flower-smoke rooms" (*huayan jian*) and "nail sheds" (*dingpeng*).[123] Flower-smoke rooms were places where a customer could smoke opium and visit prostitutes ("flowers") simultaneously. Like the higher-ranking establishments, they were initially centered in the Chinese city (in this case near Xiao Dongmen), but they later moved to various locations in the foreign concessions. The longest-lived brothels of this type were those near Beat the Dog Bridge (*Dagou qiao*).[124] The writer of an 1893 memoir commented that unlike pheasant houses, which cost three to four yuan and did not admit customers who were raggedly dressed, flower-smoke rooms would allow even a peddler to smoke an opium pipe and fondle women, all for one hundred cash.[125]

Guidebooks generally did not describe the clientele in courtesan houses, perhaps because they were written as though directly addressed to those patrons. In contrast, the lower-class brothels like pheasant houses and flower-smoke rooms were often depicted in pejorative terms that painstakingly distanced the authors from the clientele. The flower-smoke brothels were described as small, filthy, barely furnished, and equipped with smelly quilts.[126] They were distinguished from surrounding buildings by a ladder leaning in the doorway, which acted as their "special banner."[127] The "flowers" would stand or sit in the doorway singing lascivious songs like "Ten Cups of Wine," and when they saw someone approaching they would call out to him, make eye contact, and then rush over and pull him up the stairs "like a prisoner of war."[128]

Visiting a flower-smoke brothel was colloquially known as "jumping the old bug," a term that lent itself to various explanations. One guidebook explained that the "jump" referred to the women's habit of jumping down the ladder if they saw a customer approaching.[129] Another guide alluded to a more explicit definition:

> This is also a pictorial noun. The old bug naturally symbolizes a kind of organ. This bug doesn't have a great deal of physical strength. One jump and it's finished. "Jumping old bug" refers to its being especially quick.[130]

A daytime sexual encounter, known as "closing the room" (*guan fangjian*), cost twenty to thirty cents in the 1910s, whereas "staying in the night room" (*zhu yexiang*) cost two yuan.[131] Some accounts say that after 1933, when opium was banned, the flower-smoke establishments disappeared; others aver that they kept the name and the prostitutes but discontinued the opium.[132]

Nail sheds, scattered throughout the northern city districts of Zhabei and Hongkou,[133] were brothels housed in shacks, patronized by "simple-minded laborers of limited economic means."[134] The prices ranged from ten cents for quick sex to one yuan for the night.[135] Intercourse in such places was baldly referred to as "driving a nail," with none of the courtesan-house obligations on the part of customers to provide tips or know the social rules.[136]

Foreign Prostitutes and the "Paradise of Adventurers"

Foreign prostitutes came to Shanghai from all over the world, recruited by the shadowy traffickers that reformers called "white slavers."[137] Drawing most of their clientele from among the foreign community and transient sailors, some of them entertained Chinese customers as well.[138] Shanghai's reputation as the "paradise of adventurers" was partly based on lurid descriptions, in European-language travel writings, of the pleasures and dangers to be found in houses of prostitution staffed by European and American women.[139] These supposedly eyewitness accounts borrowed freely from one another, just as the Chinese guidebooks did, embellishing with each retelling. Many foreign writers constructed tales of horror around the imagined despoiling of white women at the hands of Chinese men:

The man between the shafts of our ricksha grinned when he was ordered
to take us to Scott Road. It is a notorious quarter where there are said to be
three hundred houses of prostitution, each sheltering from ten to fifteen
girls of every nationality. . . . These houses are managed chiefly by foreign
prostitutes. There are Jewesses from Russia and Poland, and many Roumani-
ans. It is a well-spring of evil, the hunting-ground and headquarters for
Chinese murderers, hordes of foreign cut-throats and procurers, who are
mostly escaped criminals. From hand to hand and from house to house they
pass, hundreds of girls. And among them—among the prostitutes—are
many Americans. Those fellows could tell tales of girls taken in American
cities, by hook or by crook or by the girls' own devilment, and transported
here to earn the high prices that an Oriental will pay to have his pleasure
with a white woman from that far-off country.[140]

Such encounters, according to one author, would invariably result in tragedy
for the woman, played out against the backdrop of a peril-ridden and un-
caring metropolis:

The end, of course, will be disease and death; this is inevitable. The most
stringent precautions cannot protect the prostitute from acquiring at last
the disease that makes her useless in the house and results in her departure,
either to a pitiful return to her far-away home, broken and spoiled for life,
or to a death whose misery cannot be recorded because it occurs in the
darkness and filth of a city that has no interest in her fate.[141]

If foreign portrayals of European prostitution in Shanghai focused on
threats to white women from diseased people of color, Chinese portrayals
were more mixed. Seldom were foreign prostitutes portrayed as victims. One
1905 account described white prostitutes in distinctly unflattering terms as
women with "rotten teeth and disheveled hair, no different from ferocious
demons. They look like the king of the lions in disguise. As soon as they roar
the observer's heart runs cold."[142]

Later reports were much more favorable, perhaps reflecting the shift in
public attention to questions of hygiene and economics. Accounts from the
1930s and 1940s spoke favorably of the disease-free state of foreign women
in high-class brothels, their favorable working conditions, and their ability
to accumulate a tidy sum while charging about fifty yuan per night.[143]

Among Euro-American prostitutes, the most numerous and least privileged were the Russians. An early group of them arrived in Shanghai after
the Russo-Japanese war of 1904–1905, prompting an indignant blast from
the missionary journal *Chinese Recorder*. The writer, a foreigner, appeared fearful that an onslaught of white prostitutes would upset the social order of semicolonial Shanghai and perhaps demean the status of all white people:

If nothing is done, then the good name of our civilization, yes, the very
safety of our homes, is imperilled. . . . Since the Japanese captured the

southern provinces of Manchuria and expelled all the courtesans from those territories, the open ports on the China coast have been infested by these vultures.

In spite of attempts by "public-spirited citizens" to organize "vigilance committees" and have the women deported, thus ridding the streets of "the insulting demeanor of the *femme galante*,"[144] the number of Russian prostitutes continued to grow, particularly after the October Revolution.[145] In the 1930s one observer estimated that eight thousand Russian prostitutes, but only two thousand white prostitutes of other nationalities, resided in Shanghai.[146] Many were brought in from the northern city of Harbin, and either worked openly as prostitutes in "Russian houses" (*Luosong tangzi*) in the French Concession and the Hongkou area or became taxi dancers who sold sexual services for an extra fee.[147] Of the Russian women who worked in Hongkou cabarets, and who were paid a dollar for every ten-dollar bottle of wine bought by a patron, one foreign observer wrote:

> The women may not be prostitutes, but few men who have come in contact with them will deny that most are willing amateurs under the influence of the liquor, and drinking liquor is their trade. . . . Better have these poor women decent prostitutes (if one may use the expression), getting the full financial benefit of their dealings, rather than have them getting one dollar a bottle, ruined health and ultimate descent to something lower than the lower animals.[148]

Customers were recruited for the Russian houses by persistent Chinese pimps who offered passersby a peek at a foreign "hundred-beauties picture" and guided them through back lanes to the brothels.[149] Chinese and foreign writers alike portrayed these women as figures of pity, more prone than other foreign prostitutes to becoming the victims of exploitative traffickers, less attractive (one Chinese guidebook described them as foul smelling and "heavy as a fat pig"), more likely to be diseased. For quick sex, advised one author, it made more sense to buy a "cannon blast" from a Chinese prostitute than to spend a night with a Russian woman while struggling with the language gap.[150]

Japanese prostitutes also worked in the Hongkou area, particularly on North Sichuan Road, which was known in the twentieth century as "Mystery Street" because of the Cantonese, Japanese, and Russian brothels, gambling dens, and massage parlors that lined it.[151] Among the Japanese women were some geisha, described in a nineteenth-century source as "more colorful than peaches and plums and as cold as ice," who were sometimes compared with *changsan* and *yao er* courtesans in their degree of inaccessibility.[152] The same sources also described Japanese prostitutes who were more sexually available. Some doubled as maidservants, teahouse waitresses, and small-restaurant owners; others depended upon street hawkers and rickshaw pullers to solicit business for them, charging several yuan for a "cannon blast."[153]

Descriptions of Japanese prostitutes in Shanghai were shaped by political tensions between China and Japan. In an article about geisha published in late 1919, for instance, the tabloid *Crystal* remarked that since May Fourth students had been "investigating dead [inanimate] Japanese products" (in order to boycott Japanese goods) but ignoring the live ones.[154] North Sichuan Road was described as looking like a Japanese colony. (The literal phrase was "xx colony," since during the early 1930s it was intermittently forbidden to mention Japan in the context of anything that might be construed as critical.)[155] Japanese geisha houses in Shanghai were said to be part of a Japanese policy of invasion that "uses sexual desire to numb other peoples." At the same time, they were mocked as uninteresting because "Japanese Japanize [literally, "dwarf-ize"] everything," decorating rooms simply and charging a great deal of money. The only good thing about sex in a Japanese brothel, one 1930s writer opined, was that there was no danger of contracting a sexually transmitted disease there. Prior to sexual intercourse, all prospective customers were given a shower and washed by a woman servant who checked them for signs of infection. Chinese were warned that they would be regarded as greenhorns if they were too uncomfortable to sit there naked and flirt with the servant. Additionally, they were advised that since they would be required to remove their shoes when entering the house, they should avoid wearing socks with holes in them or risk the laughter of the Japanese women.[156] The cautionary comments here had an edge of nationalist sentiment, wherein Japanese prostitutes were simultaneously derided and recognized as arbiters of cleanliness and sophistication.

Ultimately, Chinese who wrote about prostitution paid little attention to foreign prostitutes in China, beyond acknowledging their existence and linking their status to that of their home nations (hence demeaned Russians and powerful Japanese). The "paradise of adventurers" stories that so fascinated foreign writers and readers depended on a depiction of Shanghai as an exotic metropolis peopled by a motley collection of sinister Euro-Americans and unknowable Others. Such a world had little cachet for Chinese writers and readers, whose main concern was the enumeration and ranking of social types, the naming of social problems, and the prescription of correct behavior. Literature for and by Chinese represented Shanghai as large, complex, and full of dangers—but not unknowable. In this context, foreign prostitutes lay outside the hierarchy of prostitution and off to the side of Chinese concerns.

REGIONALIZING AND NATIVE-PLACE HIERARCHY

Like workers in other sectors of the Shanghai economy, most prostitutes were not of local origin.[157] In part this reflected the fact that Shanghai was an expanding city that attracted peasants with the hope of work at the same time that rural crisis and war were pushing them out of the countryside. In part it reflected the presence in Shanghai of powerful merchant and official cliques from Guangdong, Ningbo, and the cities of the lower Yangzi; men from all these regions apparently preferred prostitutes from their own native places. And in part it reflected the particular nature of the traffic in sexual services; those who bought women preferred to resell them far enough from home so that their families would not clamor for the return of the goods or a share of the profits.[158] For the brothel owners, buying women from other regions increased their ability to control them, since "[i]f the prostitute [was] removed from her home community she [was] absolutely at the mercy of her keepers."[159] For the same reason, "Shanghai girls, as a rule, when sold or mortgaged, are shipped off to some far away place," as one contemporary account noted.[160]

As with most occupations in Shanghai, the hierarchy of prostitution was structured by regionalism. Women in the *shuyu* and *changsan* houses were said to come mainly from cities in the Jiangnan, notably Suzhou (famed for its beauties), Wuxi, Nanjing, Hangzhou, and Changzhou.[161] Suzhou dialect was the language of the *changsan* brothels.[162] Even those courtesans who came from Shanghai proper did their best to speak it, or at least affect a Suzhou accent and claim Suzhou as their native place.[163]

So pervasive was Suzhou hegemony that writers linked a Suzhou pedigree with female beauty. One small but prosperous brothel in Huile Li, a former resident of the neighborhood recounted, had two prostitutes, one from Suzhou and one from Shandong, but "the second one was so beautiful you couldn't tell she was from Shandong."[164] Prostitutes of the grade of *yao er* and below were said to be of more mixed origin, some from the lower Yangzi and others from Yangzhou, various parts of Subei, and the provinces of Jiangxi, Hubei, Tianjin, and Guangdong.[165] Pheasants and flower-smoke-room prostitutes were purportedly from Yangzhou and Subei, like the laborers who patronized their brothels.[166] Subei prostitutes also carved out special niches for themselves in the sexual-service market; for example, some specialized in rowing out to the junks moored on the Huangpu River and soliciting among the Chinese sailors.[167] This intersection of class and regional divisions, with Subei people at the bottom, mirrored the larger occupational structure of Shanghai.[168]

Regional divisions shaped prostitution in other ways as well. In the 1920s, warlord conflicts drove many wealthy Cantonese to migrate to Shanghai, where they opened large businesses like Sincere and Wing On; the ranks of Cantonese courtesans increased accordingly.[169] Cantonese in Shanghai had their own intricate terminology for sexually active women, virgins, and banquets; their own styles of room decoration; their own self-accompanied musical performance style; and their own district along North Sichuan Road.[170]

Cantonese courtesan houses were part of an intricate network of Cantonese commercial interests in Shanghai: the women ordered their banquet food from Cantonese restaurants and accompanied guests to Cantonese-owned restaurants and hotels.[171] Unlike many of the women in the Suzhou houses, Cantonese prostitutes had not been sold to the brothel owners, and they generally had control over their own labor.[172] Over the course of the Republican period, access to such women became less exclusive, as did access to all courtesans. Whereas early in the century a customer needed to be introduced by a regular guest before a Cantonese courtesan would sit and drink with him, by the 1930s a man could pick her name from a colored sign in front of a Cantonese restaurant and summon her out on call.[173]

Ningbo prostitutes were featured in Republican-era tabloids and guidebooks. Supervised by Ningbo madams and attended by Ningbo servants, they lived in and worked out of hotels in the Wu Malu and Da Xinjie area.[174] Although they did business openly, Ningbo houses did not pay taxes or obtain licenses, and so technically they were illegal. Like courtesans, Ningbo prostitutes hosted banquets at home. But guests had to take the women out to another location for sexual relations, since their quarters were small, crowded with cooking equipment, and redolent of chamber pots and the pungent odor of Ningbo-style salted fish and crabs, which were offered to guests as snacks. At least one Shanghai author commented that the food in Ningbo brothels was offensive to the nose and the musical performances noxious to the ear.[175] The high-status Cantonese and Ningbo prostitutes kept to their own communities and generally did not welcome guests from other regions, at least partly because of the language barrier.[176] Aficionados of Suzhou and Yangzhou courtesans, in turn, reportedly looked down upon Cantonese prostitutes.[177] Guidebook accounts of both Cantonese and Ningbo prostitutes engaged in regional exoticizing; authors described their dress, food, and artistic performances as faintly odd and quaint.

Another group of Cantonese women from eastern Guangdong province,[178] who traced their presence in Shanghai to the early nineteenth century, specialized in entertaining foreign sailors in the Hongkou area and the French Concession.[179] At dusk and nighttime in these districts, according to one description, "sailors with white clothes and white hats [would] pace and loiter about," while women used "licentious voices, lewd talk, and sidelong glances to seduce them."[180] On the last day of the month, when sailors were paid, business was particularly brisk.[181] The women were known as *xianshui mei,* or "saltwater sisters," which was variously explained as a reference to their maritime patrons, their own origins as boat dwellers, or a transliteration of "handsome maid" into Cantonese (*hansui mui*).[182] Chinese sources describe them variously as outlandish in dress, ugly, elegantly coiffed, and beautiful.[183] A late Qing memoir mentions that they went about "bareheaded, with big feet,"[184] presumably in contrast to the elaborately dressed, bound-footed courtesans of the same period.

Until the 1930s, saltwater sisters serviced foreigners exclusively.[185] Perhaps for that reason, their potential to transmit disease came to the attention of foreign writers almost as soon as they appeared in Shanghai. Edward Henderson, public-health officer of the International Settlement, in 1871 simultaneously condemned the brothels visited by foreign sailors as filthy and cast aspersions on the foreign but nonwhite clientele. These establishments, he wrote, were "dark, dirty, and unfurnished, the worst in every way being those where Malays, negroes, &c. are the principal visitors."[186] Conversely, proximity to (white) foreigners, according to a later foreign account, conferred cleanliness: saltwater sisters were reputed to be "more hygienic than some others, partly because of the Cantonese love of cleanliness, and partly because they wish to attract foreigners."[187] Nevertheless, their solicitation of foreign sailors, and the resultant spread of sexually transmitted diseases, attracted the attention of the British Admiral, who in 1877 requested that Shanghai open a lock hospital (that is, a hospital for the treatment of venereal disease) to examine and register Cantonese prostitutes. Undaunted, the women proceeded to use their hospital registration cards, each with a photo identification, as advertisements for their services. Examinations continued until 1920, when prostitution was officially (if ineffectively) phased out in the International Settlement.[188]

Foreign writers regarded saltwater sisters as dangerous to foreigners unless duly inspected, the implication being that their Chineseness contributed to their diseased state. Chinese writers took the opposite stance, saying that the women were diseased because they slept with so many foreigners. According to one guidebook, saltwater sisters sometimes serviced twenty to thirty customers a night.[189] Another writer broadened the language of infection to encompass not only sexually transmitted diseases, but also bad moral habits, "because they are constantly in contact with foreign sailors, and so have become infected with foreign ways." Saltwater sisters, he warned, would trick any customer who was not conversant with both English and Cantonese slang, steal from sleeping customers, and foster or at least permit brawls between foreign sailors and Chinese. Always know where the exit is, he advised.[190] In guidebook descriptions, saltwater sisters provided a foil to the Chinese courtesans, who presided over refined social pleasures for the pleasure of Chinese patrons who appreciated opera and conversation as well as gambling, banqueting, and the potential for a sexual liaison. Proximity to foreigners did not enhance the status of saltwater sisters in the hierarchy of prostitution.[191]

PATROLLING THE BORDERS

Guidebook authors presented the hierarchy of prostitution not as their own exclusive creation, but as a system understood and enforced by prostitutes themselves. In the many courtesan novels set in Shanghai and consumed by the local reading public, authors represented prostitutes themselves as acutely aware of the hierarchy and concerned about maintaining their place in it. A study of these novels characterizes the "class consciousness" of these fictional courtesans as follows: *changsan* courtesans looked down on *yao er* courtesans as "unrefined in company;. . . . vulgarly eager and greedy." The *yao er*, returning the compliment, considered the *changsan* "a sham, their elaborate customs merely a scheme for extracting money from the clients." Streetwalkers, for the same reason, considered *yao er* "shams and deceitful." And all looked down on Cantonese prostitutes.[192]

In his memoir of prewar Shanghai life, Chen Dingshan tells of a beautiful pheasant named Suzhen, known as the "pheasant king" (*yeji dawang*). A "stay-at-home" pheasant, Suzhen had a courtyard residence to herself and rode the streets soliciting customers in a vehicle decorated with silk and copper, taking care to avoid the areas frequented by ordinary pheasants. The tabloid *Crystal* reported on her activities with the type of attention it usually reserved for high-ranking courtesans. The painter Zheng Mantuo took up with her, using her as a model for the portraits of beauties he painted for use in commercial calendars. The paintings sold extremely well, making him famous and raising public curiosity about the identity of the woman he portrayed. Previously most of his models had been courtesans. When the tabloids published news of his affair with Suzhen, and revealed the fact that he was using a pheasant as his model, not only young women of good families but also *changsan* and *yao er* courtesans refused to sit for his paintings, rebuffed his visits, and boycotted his calendars. Merchants stopped buying his portraits for their calendars and turned to two of his students instead. Frustrated, he switched to painting landscapes, and his income dropped precipitously. In this case, according to Chen, courtesans felt that they would be insulted if their portraits were displayed in the same publications in which appeared portraits of a prostitute of much lower rank, no matter how beautiful or well-off she was.[193]

As with other aspects of prostitute life, it is impossible to separate the concerns of the teller from those of the told. In guidebook accounts, courtesans held high status precisely because they knew how to enforce distinctions—between the knowledgeable patron and the bumpkin, between witty repartee and doltish chattering, between exquisite self-presentation and garish display. Their reported zeal to distinguish themselves from lower-class prostitutes may have emerged from a heartfelt concern about preserving their own declining status, or it may have been a rhetorical conceit employed by nostalgic literati to give voice to their own concerns about a world in which old distinctions could no longer be fixed, in which hierarchies of all sorts were destabilized. Whether or not courtesans joined their customers in patrolling the borders of the hierarchy of prostitution, that hierarchy was increasingly undermined by casual and modernized prostitution.

CASUAL AND MODERNIZED PROSTITUTION

Attempts to encompass the varieties of Shanghai prostitution in a single hierarchy were always less than complete. Many women worked outside the confines of the brothel system. They were the casual laborers of the sexual labor market, entering or leaving it as necessary to supplement their income from other jobs. Their sex work was illegal, because they were not licensed by any of Shanghai's municipal administrations. All observers agreed that the authorities were unsuccessful in registering many of the women who sold sexual services both inside and outside the brothels. The ranks of licensed prostitutes, from courtesans to pheasant streetwalkers and beyond, were equaled or outnumbered by these unlicensed prostitutes, who were known by such terms as "private prostitutes" (*sichang*), "secret prostitutes" (*anchang*), "secret nests" (*si wozi*), or "half-open doors" (*bankai men*).[194] Among casual prostitutes, as among all other groups of prostitutes, heterogeneity reigned. Some were women who lived at the fringes of the peddler economy; some were seamstresses; others, like the trysting-house women, dressed as members of respectable upper-class families and made contact with men at the theater.[195] In addition, servants hired through employment agencies were often understood to be available for a relationship of "master and servant by day, husband and wife by night—a thing with two uses."[196]

With respect to courtesans, guidebooks taught customers how to conduct themselves appropriately to avoid ridicule (see chapters 3 and 5); with respect to pheasants and other lower-class prostitutes, the message shifted to avoiding unwanted advances and disease. When part-time and casual prostitutes were incorporated into the classificatory scheme of guidebooks, the theme shifted again; authors used them to warn that in a complex environment such as Shanghai, things were seldom what they seemed. Social status was ambiguous; appropriate social behavior required an urban insider's ability to see through appearance and discern reality. Guidebook authors positioned themselves to dispense this crucial knowledge.

The hierarchy of prostitution required constant updating, particularly in the 1930s and 1940s, to take account of the proliferation of ancillary occupations such as that of tea hostess, taxi dancer, masseuse, female guide, and striptease performer. (See figure 3.) As paid companions, entertainers, and sex workers, the female practitioners of these new professions presented women in Westernized dress, mimicking a different, newer elite from the one that shaped courtesan practice. Theirs was a "modern" form of prostitution, with emphasis on functional and efficient delivery of services to members of the commercial and industrial classes.

Tea hostesses, known as "glass cups" (*bolibei*) in reference to the beverage they served, provided companionship to tea-drinking guests in the lower-class amusement halls in the 1930s and 1940s.[197] (See figure 4.) This particular job opportunity opened up for women when the management of one amusement hall on Fuzhou Road discovered that female waitresses were useful in attracting customers. Competing amusement halls soon fired their waiters, replacing them with women.[198] In the 1930s tea hostesses charged a dime or two for a cup of tea, earning a tip of an additional dime. Most guests, noted the guidebooks, did not have their minds on the tea,[199] and the women were described as experts at winking, joking, flirting, "selling romance," and being fondled. One writer for a women's magazine indirectly pointed to the gap between such women and the reformers who decried their situation. After midnight, she said, the lights were turned off and "the women who are fondled go off to be fondled. We third parties who observe from the sidelines of course do not understand the state of mind of those who are fondled."[200] One account stated that most tea hostesses had a dozen or more regular customers, and in the 1930s could net a monthly income of several hundred yuan. When business was slow, they earned additional fees by spending the night with customers.[201] Less sanguine accounts, however, described tea hostesses who earned no salary, who had to pay the cashier's office for the first six cups of tea they sold, whose jobs required them to spend money on clothing or makeup, and who were thus under enormous economic pressure to sleep with men in return for a few dollars, silk stockings, high-heeled shoes, or fabric for a traditional cheongsam (*qipao*).[202] Similar descriptions appeared in reports about coffee-shop waitresses and bar hostesses.[203]

Several articles about tea hostesses noted that since they were not under the protection of a brothel, but rather worked in a public space, they had to maintain good relations (including sexual ones) with local hoodlums or "husbands" who directly controlled their labor.[204] An additional theme in stories of tea hostesses was that some were forced into this work when the factories that had previously employed them were destroyed during the early years of the conflict with Japan. The result was exposure to men who wanted only to defile and then abandon them. This type of story linked personal and national debasement, although it did not always make the connection explicit.[205]

As dance halls became popular in 1930s Shanghai, many women began working as taxi dancers. Their job was to dance with patrons who bought tickets for the privilege, and to persuade guests to purchase expensive bottles of champagne, for which the women received a small percentage of the price.[206] From their inception, the dance halls attracted a diverse group of women as dancing companions, including courtesans who went to the dance halls to earn extra income after completing their nightly round of calls, and lower-ranking prostitutes who took the dance halls as their main location for soliciting.[207]

Themes of hardship and debasement were common in the literature on taxi dancers. Dancing itself was characterized as an activity that had no evil connotations in the West but that when imported to China gave "those with mad sexual desires and greedy merchants a kind of sex business."[208] Many accounts noted that dancers were often from families that had experienced hardship because of the unstable economy or the war, and that they were supporting parents and siblings through this work. They were depicted as humiliated by exposure to sexual harassment from dance-hall patrons, desperate to obtain an education and leave the dance halls, and constantly at risk of descent into outright prostitution.[209] Like some of the other "modernized" sex workers, they were sometimes portrayed as under the domination of madams or contractors who treated them brutally, so that their situation did not appear to differ greatly from that of women who were unambiguously prostitutes.[210] Sometimes the rhetorical devices used to describe them managed to suggest their low status by indirection, as in the article that declared: "Dancers and night-soil collectors seek existence in different Shanghai environments. The former concludes Shanghai's night, the latter begins Shanghai's morning."[211]

The masseuse was another type of service worker routinely described as a prostitute in disguise. The first massage parlors in Shanghai were staffed by French and Russian women in the French Concession, in the International Settlement, and on North Sichuan Road. Chinese guidebooks informed their readers that the massage administered there was "completely a type of sex skill. They differ from those who make their living by the flesh only in that one uses the hand to touch you, and the other uses ? to touch you" (question mark in original). The massage parlors offered a hygienic environment because "it is in the nature of Westerners to love cleanliness," and some Chinese customers could hope for "unexpected love and fortune": "If you are handsome, and we want to taste a foreign flavor, why shouldn't they be wanting to taste a Chinese flavor?" Yet the guidebook concluded that to wallow in such pleasures was to become "the plaything of licentious Western women," vulnerable to deception, ridicule, and enforced passivity because of the language barrier.[212] As in much of the "paradise of adventurer" writing about foreign prostitutes, the West was discussed through attention to the bodies of its sex workers. Euro-American masseuses were represented simultaneously as models of cleanliness and as sources of danger and humiliation, with whom a Chinese might enjoy pleasure only by giving up the capacity to initiate and control activity.

Chinese massage parlors were modeled on the Western houses, often featuring women who had been trained in foreign establishments. The parlors were advertised in the tabloid press under names such as "Crystal Palace" and "Enchantment Palace." The masseuses also picked beautiful professional names not unlike those of *changsan* courtesans. Touted as "domestic products," those "most suited to the national taste,"[213] Chinese massage parlors offered a selection of massage styles, including Turkish, Russian, Parisian, and Chinese. Their main business, however, was sex. Attendants were said to offer two types of massage: "clear" (*qing*) and "muddy" (*zhuo*), the latter including either "cannon blast" intercourse (*kaipao*) or a hand job (*shouyin*). One guidebook wryly noted that "a small minority of massage parlors actually do only massage."[214]

Massage parlors were the subject of vociferous cautionary messages. One guidebook warned that massage would merely take the customer's illness and pain and move it to another region of the body, infecting him with "a romantic illness,"[215] while another accused the parlors of "hanging up a sheep's head in order to sell dog's meat."[216] In contrast to the putative cleanliness of the European-staffed massage houses, the mainstream press reported that the massage implements in Chinese places were filthy and the white uniforms worn by the masseuses had turned "an earthen color."[217] An article in a women's magazine denounced the "loathsome and deformed social system" of capitalism and imperialism for making masseuses into "disguised prostitutes." Women who worked in the parlors, the article explained, were less well off than licensed prostitutes, because they were paid no salary and had to depend on tips. Masseuses were described, in terms similar to those used for pheasants, as under the control of cruel madams who beat them if they did not attract sufficient business.[218] In contrast to the literature on foreign masseuses, the writings about Chinese establishments alternately characterized both masseuses and their customers as potential victims.[219]

Yet another form of ancillary prostitution was supplied by female guides, employed by guide agencies (*xiangdao she*) beginning in the mid-1930s.[220] By the 1940s Shanghai had several hundred such establishments.[221] Although the first tabloid descriptions of them stressed their "proper" nature and the refined appearance of their male and female guides, by 1937 a guidebook was stating flatly that the guides knew nothing about Shanghai, were not as beautiful as their advertising promised, and were simply another form of prostitute.[222] Because the proprietors of dance halls and brothels regarded them as competition, and apparently pressured the municipal authorities, guide agencies were not permitted to advertise in newspapers, so they printed their names and phone numbers on paper napkins in restaurants and bars.[223] They also publicized their services by sending salesmen into restaurants and hotels, where they passed out advertisement cards and cajoled patrons with pictures of the guides. Once called, a woman would "sit across from you or at your side, and silently wait for you to make a move. Then she follows your conversational lead. . . . They are not as skilled at conversation and laughter as the popular taxi dancers." Of the ten yuan per day a guide might earn in the 1940s, she was able to keep about one-third; the rest went to waiters, salesmen, and the agency owner. Like the tea hostesses, female guides could not meet their expenses for basic necessities, clothing, makeup, and hair unless they slept with customers for additional money. Many of the guide agencies were owned by small-time hoodlums, who were described as mistreating their employees in the same way that madams and brothel owners abused low-class prostitutes. Prior to the Japanese occupation, guide agencies in the International Settlement were required to register with the Municipal Council and obtain permits.[224]

Among the crowds thronging to the amusement halls, movie theaters, and department stores of the 1930s were women known as "flowing rafts" (*tangpai* or *tangbai*); such a woman was so named because "she flows back and forth on the street, a bit like a raft without a captain. She will follow the current and float to you; this is called 'fishing for a flowing raft.'"[225] Unlike pheasants, who were restricted in their street soliciting by municipal ordinances, flowing rafts drifted through these new public spaces without official interference.[226] Guidebooks warned that the main danger in seeking out flowing rafts was that they looked just like women students, in fashionable clothes and high-heeled shoes, their faces powdered and lipsticked. Most worked on their own, although some were accompanied by a telltale attendant.[227] Without inside knowledge, it was easy for "a sex maniac [to] hook a married woman by mistake" and "suffer slaps or a beating." Guidebooks offered tips to the unwary: if a woman was circulating in such places by herself, she was probably a flowing raft, since "good married women absolutely do not go out alone; they always have a relative with them." The most difficult to judge were women traveling in pairs: men were advised to watch whether they glanced behind them when they walked and to pay attention to whether they responded to suggestive looks. If a woman seemed interested, the man could follow her to a quiet place like a rooftop garden of one of the many department stores, talk, and arrange an assignation.[228] Just as flowing rafts worked the amusement halls, other groups of prostitutes roamed the corridors of hotels, collaborating with the attendants to locate interested customers. "Mobile masseuses," described in one guide as "beautifully dressed women in leather shoes," also visited the hotels, offering full-body massage and hand jobs.[229] Female fortune-tellers could be summoned by hotel attendants for purposes of foretelling the future or providing intercourse in the present.[230] After World War II, a new group of prostitutes nicknamed "jeep girls" specialized in servicing the Allied army, working the vehicles in which American soldiers cruised through the city.[231]

Another new form of ancillary sex work was striptease performance in dance halls. As theatrical performance, the striptease numbers were nominally organized around stories set in places like the guide agencies. One performance, for instance, was entitled *A Visit to a Girl Guide Agency by a Foreigner.* The piece depicted a foreigner speaking pidgin Chinese who indicated his desire to inspect the bodies of the guides he hired to check for syphilitic infection. This then became the occasion for a striptease performed by spotlight. Just as Shanghai was rendered exotic by foreign observers, Shanghainese took foreign locales as exotic backdrops for these sketches. One was set in the Hawaiian islands, while another, a 1938 piece called *The Attack on a Beautiful Woman by a Savage,* was advertised in Chinese tabloids as featuring bonfires, as well as appearances by "Red Indian savages and girls in the nude."[232] A dance revue performed the following year included the following numbers: "Open-Air Bath in a Summer Night," "I Want to Do It," "A Dull Spring," "A Sacred Body," "Four Lively Horses," "The Breasts of a Virgin," "Peach-Colored Underwear," "The Night Life of Paris," "Her Belt," and "Let's Undress Ourselves."[233] Each of these performances was advertised or reported in a variety of Chinese tabloids,[234] where their descriptions appeared side by side with the gossip columns recording the doings of famous courtesans and movie starlets. The stories themselves, which were detailed and explicit, constituted a form of erotic writing that aggravated the International Settlement authorities to the point that they periodically confiscated the newspapers or withdrew their publishing licenses.[235]

The authors of the 1930s and 1940s who enumerated the new forms of sex work wrote with dismay of their proliferation and the undermining of hierarchies that had given order to the sex trades.[236] The sexualizing of Shanghai life, they implied, not only blurred the boundaries between prostitutes and other women, but threatened to unfix male and female identities as well. One of the few sources to discuss homosexuality, a 1935 guidebook, attributed its appearance to the fact that "the atmosphere of licentiousness is hotter and more flourishing in Shanghai, and hence these sexual abnormalities appear." In the interior of China, he argued, such phenomena were less common. He saw this "licentious atmosphere" as intensifying over time: twenty years earlier, "the sex wind in Shanghai" had not been "as hot and flourishing as it is now, and there were not as many forms of prostitutes as there are now." But by the 1930s, one could find not only an expanded variety of female sex workers, but also male homosexual prostitutes known as "human rabbits" soliciting in amusement halls and gardens: "Their dress is almost completely feminized, and they wear makeup. They are lewd and strange in appearance. At a glance it is indeed not easy to tell male from female." In language that offered striking parallels to reformist writings about female prostitution, the author concluded that men were being "forced by life" and by the evil environment of Shanghai to engage in such practices.[237] Increasingly, writers moved to associate prostitution, particularly in its newer and rapidly expanding forms, with China's national ills.

Life as a prostitute could be insecure and harsh, but it was probably not the worst of all situations for impoverished women in Shanghai. When 1930s commentators looked at the employment possibilities for women, they found that the display and sale of sex generally enhanced income:

> Speaking frankly, in China among real occupations for women, only women
> factory workers trade their blood and sweat for food. Others, like women

shop attendants, are partly "human signboards," and prostitutes "hang a signboard and sell sexual desire." Silk workers work twelve hours a day and earn only a few dimes. But the cheapest "miss" in a "shop," who spends the night with a guest, will get three or five dollars. Comparing the two, the woman worker is much worse off than the prostitute!

And yet, the same author continued with the ambivalence that character-ized most 1930s writing on prostitution, the profession could not be evalu-ated with respect to income alone:

> Although in terms of material reward, the woman worker cannot match
> the prostitute, in terms of spiritual happiness, the prostitute cannot nearly
> match the worker. Because the woman worker doesn't have to endure the
> painful irritation of old beards, doesn't have to receive drunken kisses,
> doesn't have to pretend to smile and go entertain someone she doesn't wish
> to see, doesn't have to endure the beatings of the madams, doesn't have to
> be examined [and licensed] by the Municipal Council.[238]

As sexual rather than social intercourse became the main work of prostitutes, and as sexual debasement became a more prominent category in the writ-ings of Chinese observers, prostitution was increasingly represented as a phys-ical and emotional hardship.

Nevertheless, within that hardship inhered a great deal of variety. Prosti-tutes at the very top of the hierarchy sometimes had considerable control over their own working conditions, and were often able to move from the brothels into marriages with powerful men. They were seldom autonomous, since at every point their power derived from associations with powerful male patrons. Yet with skill and luck they could achieve a standard of living and a degree of mobility that compared favorably with those of women workers, and with those of many wives as well. At the bottom of the hierarchy, pros-titution was not a rigidly segregated occupation, but a form of casual labor that enabled women in critical economic circumstances to survive. Here pros-titution was often combined both with other work and with marriage. As a social category, it was both permeable and impermanent.

Those with the least autonomy and mobility, whether their customers were of high class or low, were the women most entangled with the brothel sys-tem. Madams or bosses controlled their labor and their persons, and in some respects their status resembled that of slaves.[239] But acknowledging that they were often treated as commodities should not divert attention from their complex struggle, detailed in later chapters, to assert some control over their working lives.

As Shanghai became a major economic, political, and cultural center dur-ing the first half of the twentieth century, the market in prostitutes grew and changed in nature. What had been essentially a luxury market in courtesans became a market primarily geared to supplying sexual services for the growing numbers of commercial and working-class men of the city, both those who were unmarried and those who had left wives in the countryside. The increase in demand was apparently accompanied by a boom in supply, fed by a burgeoning population of refugees and peasants in distress who had daughters they could not support. The "popularization" of prostitution was accompanied by degenerating conditions of work for the individual prostitutes, with more and more women participating in the less privileged and more vulnerable sectors of the trade, including unlicensed prostitution of all types and the "modern" forms of disguised prostitution. This trend, combined with the growth of various distinct reform currents among foreigners and Chinese in Shanghai, led to a series of loud, if largely ineffective, calls for the regulation or abolition of prostitution. The prostitute, in all her guises, became recognized as a social category and a social problem. But not until the early 1950s did the municipal government succeed in abolishing this particular market in women.

This change in the political economy of prostitution was reflected in the changing discourses on prostitution, but those changing discourses cannot be understood as a simple response to growing numbers of lower-class and disguised prostitutes working the streets and amusement halls. They must be read simultaneously as a kind of road map to the changing concerns of a changing elite, concerns that shaped the daily environment of prostitutes, and their possibilities for response, in multiple ways. These concerns are explored more fully in the remainder of this book.[240]

PART II

Pleasures

CHAPTER 3

Rules of the House

In the early twentieth century, courtesan houses commanded far more attention in elite writings than any other form of prostitution. These sources place the courtesan house in multiple contexts: as a place of business that supported many commercial interests, as a site for the production of urban masculinity, and as a social space in which a courtesan constantly had to negotiate her standing with respect to the madam, the servants, and the clientele.

Courtesan houses were highly visible, intricately organized business establishments whose operations involved many suppliers of goods and services. Usually in the company of other men, customers would summon a courtesan to entertain and attend them at public occasions, inside and outside the courtesan house. Commercial and political contacts among men were formed and renewed in the presence of courtesans. These relationships among men helped to make the courtesan house a venue where elite men displayed a refined version of masculinity, one less sexual than social. The production of this masculinity was a perilous enterprise, and the literature on courtesan houses offered guidance to neophyte readers on how to obtain respect from other men and avoid ridicule from courtesans. Guidebooks proffered detailed knowledge about the business practices of the brothels, for a customer needed to know such things in order to demonstrate his own sophistication. At the same time, they described the aesthetics and etiquette of frequenting courtesans. Whether or not a man sought physical intimacy with a courtesan, he had to negotiate an intricate matrix of social and financial obligations to her and her house in order to appear urbane, knowledgeable, and wealthy to his fellow revelers and to the women of the house. Encounters not only with her, but with her madam and the brothel servants, were portrayed as transactions that required the customer to have inside knowledge of the brothel.

The guidebooks were minutely prescribed handbooks of the ritualized behavior required of both courtesans and clients.[1] They focused on the elaborate, large, and visible houses, and on the formal aspects of brothel organization. Interim and informal arrangements were probably more common in Shanghai than they are in the surviving sources. Manuals of how things were supposed to be, or perhaps had been in a nostalgically remembered past, courtesan-house guidebooks give little hint of the fluidity, strategizing, and deviations from the rules that probably characterized courtesan-house encounters. Rather, they tell us what men felt they needed to know about, as well as how they wished to order and remember, an elite practice situated in the rapidly changing commercial environment of a foreign treaty port. As the world around them shifted, often in ways they found distressing, guidebook writers and readers attempted to fix a set of ritualized practices meant to establish hierarchy and ensure pleasure.

In addition to conveying a sense of how they wished the world to be, their attention to detail also allows us to read their works for answers to questions that concerned them less—the configurations of power between madams and courtesans, for instance, or the possibilities and constraints of courtesan life. Such readings often suggest surprising configurations of power that confound any attempt to create a linear hierarchy of subalterns. Privileged by virtue of both gender and class, customers were nevertheless vulnerable to humiliation by courtesans. Madams had to be skilled at negotiating a wide range of business transactions, and they often wielded near-absolute power over their younger courtesans; nevertheless, it was possible for a courtesan to frustrate her madam's efforts at control. Female brothel servants, at first glance the lowliest inhabitants of a courtesan house, sometimes had a controlling financial interest in the establishment and dictated the activities of their putative employers. These arrangements complicate, without completely undermining, our commonsense understandings of who made the rules in the courtesan house.

OWNERS AND MANAGERS

By the late Republican period, and certainly after 1949, the brothel madam had become a stock figure of cruelty and exploitation: a capitalist in the realm of sexual labor. Yet her appearances in the historical record are not reducible to this single image.[2] Police registers, where they survive, tell us nothing more than the names of a few brothel owners.[3] Guidebooks and glossaries eschewed the histories of individual madams in favor of generic lists of nomenclature and duties. Scandal fiction and tabloids, in contrast, offered entertaining and sometimes repugnant details of the greed, craftiness, and coquettishness of madams. To assemble a coherent "portrait of the madam" from this pastiche would blur differences among a range of types and the changes in those types over time. Just as important, it would conceal part of what interests a late twentieth-century historian: the effect of genre on the creation of "fact," or, to put it more provocatively, fact as an effect of genre.

The terms used to refer to madams in memoirs, guidebooks, and newspaper reports ranged from the directly pejorative to the ironically respectful. The most common cluster of terms employed the character for "bustard," a species of game bird: "old bustard" (*laobao*), "bustard mother" (*baomu*), or "bustard woman" (*baofu*). Recent commentators have explained that the bustard was a licentious bird and that the term was meant to evoke the "greediness and ruthlessness" of madams,[4] but this characterization is probably retrospective; such linkages of meaning were not explicitly made in the Chinese sources. A number of more refined terms for female proprietors circulated as well. "The one who sets the room in order" (*pu fangjian zhe*) was used generically to refer to any courtesan or madam who established a house.[5] "This house" (*benjia*), used in other contexts to refer to members of a family or clan, was neutral in its connotations.[6] "Chief administrator" (*zhuzheng*) was apparently a term coined by literate brothel patrons. It was explained as an attempt either to prettify the madam's job, or to poke fun at both madams and the government by using a borrowed bureaucratic term in a decidedly unbureaucratic realm.[7]

Running a brothel did require certain administrative and political skills. A madam had to pick an advantageous locale for her establishment, rent the building and furnishings, arrange interior decorations, hire (or sometimes purchase) courtesans, attendants, and servants, obtain a license (in places and times when licensing was in force), hang out a sign, and answer requests for business.[8] By the late 1910s and 1920s, a madam also had to be skilled in making alliances to resist extortion by hoodlums. After investigating which brothels were making money, the tabloid *Crystal* explained, a group of hoodlums would create a disturbance there. Several days later they would send one of their number to pose as a customer, spend money freely, and profess fondness for one of the courtesans. At this point the initial troublemakers would return and their disguised colleague would heroically fend them off, earning the gratitude and perhaps the sexual favors of the madam. In return for sexual and financial compensation, he would then agree to become the brothel's permanent protector.[9] Alternatively, madams would seek out "playboys" (*boxiang ren*) or "backers" (*kaoshan*) who were powerful in the wider society, whose connection to the house would discourage incursions by random hoodlums and help to resolve difficulties if something untoward happened. Such a supporter was known colloquially as the "brothel prop" (*changmen chengtou*).[10] Whether or not her establishment had a "prop," a skillful madam also had to build connections to restaurants and theaters where her courtesans performed, inns that might send customers her way, and a variety of other business establishments.[11] Opening, running, and protecting a brothel, particularly a successful one, took both money and experience. Therefore, one guidebook explained, madams tended to be "middle-aged women who have fully tasted the flavor of the life of prostitution" (*baochang fengchen ziweide banlao xuniang*)—that is, ex-courtesans or perhaps former brothel servants.[12] (The contemporary reader should be reminded that the phrase "middle-aged" was often used to refer to women in their thirties.) Successful madams were businesspeople who presided over a trade that garnered income "large enough to pay huge taxes to the government, higher rents than other property, and yet leave profits for those in the business."[13]

In an attempt to equip potential customers with an insider's knowledge, guidebooks outlined in detail the business organization of brothels. Courtesan houses in the early twentieth century were organized either as great hall houses (*da changhu*) or residence brothels (*zhujia*). Great hall houses were the larger and more complex type, but even they usually had only four or fewer courtesans.[14] The madam (or sometimes a group of female investors who worked as brothel servants; see the discussion later in this chapter) would rent a house, the wing of a house, or part of a multistory building from a male property owner. The rental agreement was sealed when the madam sent him a four-dish banquet. If he accepted it, he could not rent to others without returning the deposit and a sizable penalty fee "if the madam is really fierce."[15] The madam then acted as a secondary landlord, renting out individual rooms to courtesans and charging them for meals, servants, and furniture. She provided electricity, sometimes requiring the courtesans to pay extra if they used more than a specified number of light bulbs. She supplied furniture (always ugly, according to one guidebook, so that a courtesan usually bought some of her own). She hired a chef who prepared meals for brothel functions in a common kitchen. In return for all these services, courtesans in 1922 were said to pay sixty to seventy yuan per month.[16] A portion of the proceeds from every banquet held in the house was remitted to the brothel's general accounting office, and periodically redistributed as shares to courtesans, servants, and madams.[17]

The residence brothels were smaller establishments. Some were opened by a single famous courtesan (*mingji*) with an established clientele of high officials and wealthy businessmen.[18] Residence brothels were richly decorated by the courtesan herself, who often provided her own coterie of attendants and servants. Other residence brothels were run by madams who sublet to courtesans but did not provide any services other than (by the late 1910s) a telephone. Although their organization was simpler than that of great hall houses, customers reportedly preferred residence brothels because they were not required to pay for so many banquets or miscellaneous expenses,[19] and because the food, ordered from a restaurant, was better.[20]

Courtesan houses were publicly visible institutions; their existence was not furtive or stigmatized. When a new brothel opened or a courtesan changed houses or professional names (see the discussion later in this chapter), it was often announced in the tabloid press.[21] In 1919 *Crystal* published a running list of courtesans' names and phone numbers, explaining that although Shanghai's Huayang *delüfeng* (a transliteration of "telephone") company did list courtesans' phone numbers, it did so by the brothel name, or required that one consult a complicated and incomplete index in order to correlate a courtesan with a brothel address.[22] By 1929 some enterprising soul had compiled a little book exclusively devoted to brothel phone numbers, which was sold in courtesan houses and tobacco shops.[23] Brothels also advertised in the newspapers, using elegant-sounding titles for their establishments and associated courtesans.[24]

COURTESANS: HIRE, PAWN, PURCHASE

Courtesans generally appeared in the historical record as powerful rather than victimized. Of all the decisions a madam made to ensure the success of her business, none was more important than the hiring of courtesans. A well-established courtesan brought with her a coterie of regular customers and could be relied upon, if properly managed, to attract more. "Courtesans are the main personages in the brothel. They must be skilled enough to attract guests, gentle and bewitching, and solicitous at entertaining," wrote a 1939 guidebook. Houses fought over popular courtesans, regarding them as "money trees."[25] Securing the services of such a woman required both clear financial arrangements and a ritual display of welcome and respect. A madam who wished to hire a courtesan went through a procedure not unlike that for arranging a marriage: she depended upon an intermediary who negotiated terms with the courtesan's intermediary, and then paid both introducers a sum.[26]

According to the guidebooks, a courtesan's arrival at the brothel was an occasion marked by rituals meant to express respect for both her person and her earning power. At no other time was her value to the courtesan house more ostentatiously displayed. Elaborately dressed and made up, she waited "decorously and properly" in her private residence for the receiving brothel to send a vehicle for her. When she arrived at her new house, she alighted holding sprays of burning herbs, was greeted with strings of firecrackers in a ceremonial salutation, and stepped over a burning torch, said to denote prosperity, on her way in the door. No one was permitted to speak until she entered a room decorated with burning candles, placed her incense there, and accepted a cup of fragrant tea from the servants. Any violation of this procedure was considered inauspicious, because receiving a courtesan was "comparable to receiving the god of wealth"—that is, her presence was considered essential to the prosperity of the entire establishment.[27] A popular courtesan immediately moved to display her value to the brothel by inviting her regular guests, who had been informed of the move in advance, to give a feast in her honor.[28] Although the arrival of the courtesan in a conveyance provided by the house, along with the firecrackers, had obvious parallels to the arrival of a bride at the family residence of her groom, there was no equivalent of the ceremonies by which a bride expressed respect to her husband's family and lineage. The emphasis here was on honoring the courtesan as a valuable resource, not incorporating her as a subordinate member of a household.

A courtesan was hired for a season of about four months, marked by three lunar-calendar festivals: the Dragon Boat Festival in the fifth month, the Mid-Autumn Festival in the eighth month, and the Spring Festival at the lunar New Year.[29] This arrangement allowed her to negotiate for better terms with the house if she brought in a great deal of business, but it also left her vulnerable to humiliation and business reverses. In the late nineteenth century a courtesan brought some of her own money as an investment in the house, and kept slightly less than half of what she earned, the remainder going to the madam.[30] In the early twentieth century, the financial arrangements began to change; the courtesan was hired for a fixed fee of two to three hundred yuan per season, fifty of it payable in advance, and all the income from the business went to the madam.[31] The remainder was disbursed to the courtesan at fixed intervals during the season, during which period the madam kept a running account of room and board charges. As the end of the season approached, a courtesan could find herself in a variety of situations. If she was popular, other houses would send intermediaries to woo her, and she might decide well in advance to move elsewhere. If, on the other hand, she found herself in debt to the madam for meals and rent, she had to give up her room at the end of the season to a newly hired courtesan, who was welcomed with great fanfare. Yet the discarded courtesan was not permitted to leave without clearing her debt. Staying on under these circumstances was regarded as a shameful fate known as "falling into the accounting department" (*luo zhangfang*).[32] Courtesans who changed brothels or became concubines were referred to as "transferring" (*diaotou*), while those who were driven out by the madam because they were ill or unprofitable were said to be "taking the sedan chair" (*tijiao*, possibly a homonym for *tijiao*, "to kick out"). A joke told at the expense of one ignorant customer described how he unwittingly insulted a courtesan by innocently asking her when she intended to "take the sedan chair."[33]

Whereas guidebooks and tabloids dwelled on the process by which madams hired sought-after courtesans, less visible in these genres were the often shadowy arrangements by which women and young girls were pawned or sold. Pawning, a common arrangement in lower-class houses (see chapter 7), was mentioned only infrequently with respect to courtesans. In pawning (*bao shenti* or *zuo baozhang*), a woman from a poor family would be turned over to the brothel for a period of several years. Alternatively, a courtesan's biological or adoptive mother would sign a contract with the madam, essentially hiring her daughter out for a season or a year.[34]

A sold woman (*taoren*) belonged either to the madam or to an owner (*taozhu*) who had purchased her specifically to be a courtesan. Whether she had been kidnapped, was sold by her parents, or sold herself, she belonged indefinitely to the madam or owner, who either closely supervised her or made sure that an older servant did so. Guidebooks and glossaries rarely mentioned mistreatment in *changsan* courtesan houses, but they reserved a rare note of opprobrium for the owners of sold women, describing them as abusive.[35] Because pawned and sold prostitutes did not transfer elsewhere at the end of a season, they had far less opportunity than "free" courtesans to negotiate improved conditions for themselves.[36]

Purchase was intimately linked to kinship in the courtesan houses, for many of the sold women were children who had been purchased and raised by the madams.[37] Not all children in the brothels were sold women; some were the daughters of courtesans whose "homes have been from the first in the brothels."[38] For instance, Li Shanshan, a famous courtesan of the 1880s, was the daughter of a Shanghai courtesan; her grandfather, who never acknowledged her, was the Qing official Li Hongzhang (see chapter 6).[39] An 1876 poem, reprinted in at least one twentieth-century source, expresses sympathy for these girls:

> The stuck-up madam is called the *benjia*.
> She spares no expense to buy sweet young things.
> Pitiful girls of twelve and thirteen
> Dance and learn singing until the moon sets.[40]

At least some of the girls who trained to be courtesans were referred to by the madams as their adoptive daughters (*yangnü*)[41] or "little madams" (*xiao benjia*),[42] while one source says that sold women "regarded the madam as their mother."[43] One memoirist noted that they suffered the most, scurrying around to serve guests with tea and tobacco.[44] A 1939 guidebook explained that by adopting these girls, madams saved themselves the hiring fee and acquired girls who were easy to control and direct. When the madam decided that a young woman was old enough to begin sexual relations, she charged a defloration fee, which helped compensate for the cost of raising the girl.[45] Like boy apprentices in ironworking shops, adoptive daughters in the brothels were paid no salary; they were being taught a skill and groomed for future earnings.[46] Unlike apprentices, however, sold women were not indentured for a fixed term. Instead, their perpetual servitude was deemphasized, if not concealed, by their classification as kin. In this respect they had more in common with "little daughters-in-law," who were adopted by the family of a future husband so that the husband's family could secure their present labor and save the future cost of purchasing a grown bride.[47]

Relationships between adult courtesans and their madams were also entangled with kinship. Many adult courtesans addressed their madams as "mother," and often the sources do not specify whether the madam was the biological or adoptive mother, or whether the term was just a conventionally courteous form of address. In 1924, for instance, *Crystal* printed a short article about Sao Muma (literally, "Licentious Mother"), referred to as the mother of the Shanghai courtesan Bao Lin. Sao Muma was described as a coquettish woman of thirty-eight who looked as if she were in her twenties.[48] Sao Muma might have been Bao Lin's biological mother, but she equally well might have been an aging courtesan who had hired, adopted, or purchased Bao Lin to take over her business. In the tabloid gossip columns, "mothers" were sometimes reported as attempting to control their courtesan "daughters." One "mother" expressed displeasure that her "daughter" spent her time going to the opera with another courtesan rather than tending to business, and it was reported that the two often quarreled.[49] Was this a mother reining in her wayward daughter, a madam demanding more work from her employee, or both? The language of kinship makes it impossible to distinguish, or perhaps points to a nexus between kinship and labor deployment.

The power of the madam with respect to "her" courtesans, then, varied enormously. Although the historical record says little about the career of any individual madam, these fragments suggest that madams could be both eager supplicants for the services of famous courtesans and exacting taskmasters toward the girls they purchased, trained, and deployed for their own profit. Kinship ties might have softened the contours of this latter relationship. Such ties between madams and their daughters may have been "fictive" if calibrated in terms of shared genes, but they were no less enmeshed in shared livelihood, bonds of obligation, affective ties, and abuse than were "blood" relationships.[50] The connection between madam and courtesan was probably ameliorated as well by the fact that the madam was making a long-term investment in a purchased girl, and could not hope to secure a favorable return if she abused her excessively. Nevertheless, calls for brothel reform from the nineteenth century onward often stressed the plight of children under the control of madams. This portrayal may be read in a number of ways. Perhaps children were the most abused and vulnerable group in courtesan houses and other brothels. Perhaps reformers found it easier to organize public indignation around the situation of children than around a group of adult courtesans who had considerable control over their own work arrangements. Perhaps the tale of reform needed a villain, and madams were easier to castigate than customers, among whom were numbered many of the city's elite. Madams clearly had serious and not always benevolent effects on the lives of courtesans. To read their power as absolute, however, is to simplify the field of social relationships in the brothels in a way that reflects the interests of long-ago reformers better than those of present-day historians.

THE POWER THAT SERVES: COURTESAN-HOUSE ATTENDANTS

The relationship between courtesans and their servants, like that between madams and courtesans, was not a clear-cut one of master and subaltern. Just as "subordinated" courtesans exercised partially concealed power over their madams, so brothel servants had a surprising degree of control over courtesans. From the perspective of customers, brothel servants appeared much like clerks and runners in government offices—low-status persons who nevertheless controlled access to important resources and had to be treated with respect.

Some servants were young, attractive women, known variously as "big sisters" (*dajie*), "sisters" (*ajie*), "followers on call" (*genju*), or "work hands" (*zuoshou*), who accompanied the courtesans out on public calls or to performances.[51] "*Xiansheng* are the flowers and *ajie* are the leaves," one guidebook explained; the job of the "sister" was to assist the courtesan, make sure that nothing untoward happened as she made her rounds, and supervise her, particularly if she was a virgin courtesan.[52] Sisters, like courtesans, had their own intimate customers, and were said to be somewhat more sexually accessible than courtesans, if not as high in status.[53] Some worked closely with a particular independent courtesan and the two split the income; stories of the scandal-fiction genre also imply that courtesans and sisters were sometimes involved in sexual relationships with the same customer.[54] Sisters were not hired for a fixed seasonal fee, and the sources of their income were various. Some sisters, apparently of lower status, received a fixed monthly wage, augmented by tips.[55] Others were expected to host social occasions as courtesans did, and were given a share of the house's profits in return for hosting a certain number of banquets.[56]

Less intimate with the courtesans and customers, but more powerful within the brothel, were the older women servants known as maidservants (*niangyi*). Although the term originally referred to a married woman brothel servant,[57] maidservants were distinguished from sisters not so much by marital status as by financial involvement in the courtesan house. Just as courtesans were often compared to officials, maidservants were likened to the retinue of private retainers that officials employed. Reflecting the vulnerability of customers to high-handed servants, an 1891 source sardonically noted that a maidservant was similar to the family servant of an official who paid to become a hanger-on, expecting to profit from squeezing the people. Young and pretty maidservants received gratuities from customers, and sometimes accumulated enough wealth to become madams themselves. They also might use their connections to help a courtesan borrow money from others, a practice known as "brokering accounts" (*qianzhang*).[58]

A maidservant's most common financial role, however, was as direct investor in a particular courtesan or house. In this arrangement, known as *daidang* (literally, "carry and ward off"), a number of people, often brothel servants, would loan several hundred yuan to support a courtesan. Sometimes the courtesan herself also invested a share.[59] The investors were entitled to a share of all the courtesan's fees and tips, and she owed deference to all of them.[60] One 1919 tabloid story speaks of a maid who controlled all the affairs of the house and slept in the courtesan's bed when no customers were present, while the courtesan slept on the floor.[61] If a *daidang* maidservant lent money to a madam, the madam assigned her lighter housekeeping tasks and did not dare to defy her.[62] In many small residence brothels where no madam was present, it is possible that the *daidang* maidservant controlled many of the decisions.[63] A maidservant might be demanding or even brutal in order to protect her investment, for *daidang* transactions were risky. If a courtesan's seasonal earnings were low, the maidservant got little return on her investment, and if a courtesan went off with a customer, the entire *daidang* sum might be lost.[64] On the other hand, maidservants who were lucky or skillful in the management of their investments accumulated enough funds to open bank accounts and provide for their old age.[65] One piece of scandal fiction described a servant in her mid-twenties known as Gold Tooth Old Three, who had networks of connections with rich men, arranged for the deflowering of virgin courtesans (making substantial sums for the house and collecting hefty tips), made high-interest loans to courtesans, and at the end of a year used her earnings to open a new brothel with herself as manager.[66]

Perhaps because they were relatively powerful figures in courtesan houses, maidservants, like madams, came in for their share of condemnation and mockery. A 1917 guidebook described them as

> often older than twenty-four, decrepit in appearance, fierce in form, extremely dislikable. When they fawn and flatter it adds to their loathsomeness. They rush about and are just detestable. One uncongenial chat and they'll drive you out the door. It is best to keep one's distance from them.[67]

Maidservants were unfavorably compared with the more pliable and agreeable sisters, although sometimes both types of servant were accused of using vulgar or violent language (for example, cursing men who offended them as "deserving of one thousand cuts").[68] Maidservants were rendered more repulsive by what commentators saw as their uncontrolled sexuality, which was implicitly contrasted to the restrained and properly channeled sexuality of the courtesans themselves. Maidservants were said to have sexual relations with male brothel servants (a practice that was regarded as adulterous if the madam's daughter engaged in it)[69] as well as private liaisons with guests. Curiously, in one nineteenth-century source they were blamed for social disorder in a way that courtesans never were: it was said that their habits of sexual promiscuity had spread to the general population "to the point where people turn their backs on their husbands and abandon their wives, and cases of quarrels and suicide appear everywhere."[70] In 1930s scandal fiction, they were portrayed as greedy for customer tips. If a courtesan complained that these demands were driving customers away, the maidservant would threaten to ask for the immediate repayment of her *daidang* loan with interest.[71] These stories suggest that the combination of sexual and financial autonomy on the part of a "servant," a positioning that destabilized both gender and class hierarchies, made male observers of the courtesan scene profoundly uneasy.

Courtesan houses also employed male servants who announced the arrival of customers with a shout, served tea and proffered towels, cleaned, prepared banquets, delivered invitations to customers and call tickets to courtesans (see the discussion later in this chapter), and transported courtesans out on call.[72] Formally known as "helpers" (*waichang* or *xiangbang*), they were also called by less flattering names such as "turtle melon seed" (*gui guazi*), "turtle" or "cuckold" (*wugui*), or "turtle slave" (*guinu*).[73] The origins of this term cluster are no more clear than are those of "bustard" for madams, but most of the implications of "turtle" were not flattering, as the "cuckold" appellation suggests. (A 1919 guide mused that they did not really qualify as cuckolds [*wugui*]; after all, the prostitutes were not *their* wives and daughters.)[74] Unlike maidservants or the male brothel bosses of the 1930s and 1940s, male servants were portrayed as relatively powerless, even debased. Guests were advised to treat them politely so that they would not move slowly in the performance of their tasks,[75] but they appeared not to inspire the kind of distress that powerful female servants did. Nor did guidebook writers regard them as particularly clever. A 1935 glossary of Shanghai slang explained that rural men from the countryside came to Shanghai along with the women who made their living in the brothels (literally, "ate brothel rice" [*chi tangzi fan*]). The literate men kept accounts for the courtesan houses, the brighter men became musicians, the strong men pulled brothel rickshaws, and "the most useless stayed in the hall as helpers."[76]

Although male servants may have been regarded as lowly and stupid, their presence in daily intimate contact with beautiful and sexually available women did inspire a certain amount of sly commentary. Most of it centered on the late Qing practice wherein helpers carried on their shoulders the courtesans going out on call. Originally the women who were summoned by customers to sing for them at music houses arrived by sedan chair, but in the late Guangxu period (1875–1908) the International Settlement began to tax sedan chairs.[77] At first only the younger (and lighter) child prostitutes (*chuji*), whose services were limited to singing, rode on the shoulders of helpers. The man would spread a white handkerchief on his shoulders, and the young girl would hold on to his head. Later the custom spread to courtesans in their late teens and early twenties, who "rode on the shoulders of the brothel servants like a Buddhist pagoda."[78] The practice of clinging to the servant's head in order not to fall off his shoulders as he moved rapidly through the streets led to the mocking aphorism "The virgin prostitute nightly strokes the turtle's head [slang for penis]."[79] It also inspired one of the few public references to menstruation among prostitutes, in the form of a four-line poem published in 1905:

> The turtle's back is hard to mount; his shoulders do instead.
> In demand, she rides strong shoulders on her round of calls.
> Modestly: "Be careful, last night my period came,
> Take care that drops don't stain my pants in back or in the front."[80]

This poem is as striking for its lack of erotic content as for its rare mention of the body of the courtesan. Courtesan beauty was usually depicted through similes rather than direct description, and reference to bodily functions virtually never entered the written record in either a bawdy or a scientific vein. Yet sexual innuendo about the behavior of male brothel servants persisted into the era when rickshaws replaced shoulder transport.[81] A 1935 cartoon depicted a courtesan and her "sister" riding in a rickshaw pulled by a "turtle slave." The iconography of the cartoon was extremely unflattering to courtesans: two upside-down black hearts on the back of the rickshaw, and a license plate with the number 606, which was also a brand name for salvarsan, a medication used to treat syphilis. After describing the perfidy and physical danger of courtesans, the caption writer went on to comment that the rickshaw-driving brothel servant was leering at the sister because it was not unknown even for courtesans, let alone sisters, to take the servants of their own house as lovers.[82] The implication in some of the literature directed at brothel patrons was that they, not the "turtle heads," were the real cuckolds, paying for services that the brothel servants enjoyed for free.

Some of the hostility expressed toward servants in these sources was probably linked to the fact that they had and controlled access to courtesans whose company was coveted and expensive. Another potential source of friction was the continuing requirement that patrons tip every level of brothel servant, who depended on this source of income. Guests were required to pay tips (*xiajiao*; literally, "leftovers") to the servants whenever they hosted a banquet in a brothel, spent the night with a courtesan, or took a courtesan as a concubine.[83] Some of the amounts were as small as several yuan, but they rose substantially if a customer had an ongoing sexual relationship with a prostitute. Tips were also required at the lunar New Year and other festivals, where they were known as "handkerchief money" (because the male servants presented customers with handkerchiefs when they arrived to have a banquet or gamble) or "eating the sacrificial rice group" (*chi zifan tuan*). At the New Year regular customers were presented with a fruit plate (*kai guopan*) and were expected to pay a generous sum, which was divided among all of the brothel servants.[84] If a customer took a courtesan as his concubine, the room attendants would present him with various silver pieces, which he could either accept (for several hundred yuan) or politely refuse (for forty or fifty yuan). Since it was rare for a customer to accept these gifts, servants usually rented or borrowed them from a silver dealer.[85] When all the courtesan houses in Shanghai jointly raised their banquet rates one yuan in about 1908, a newspaper commented that the real cost of frequenting brothels lay not in the banquet or gambling fees, but in the tips required whenever the customer banqueted, gambled, spent the night, ate an informal meal, or called on holidays.[86] Although customers sometimes bridled at the endless round of gratuities, and sought to avoid brothels at high-cost times like the lunar New Year, guides to brothel etiquette advised against such stinginess. One author upbraided patrons who were willing to meet a courtesan's every request for presents but were reluctant to pay even a coin of handkerchief money to these "small people." He admonished customers that it was a wiser strategy to spend money publicly where everyone could see it, the better to display one's generosity and sophistication[87]—and presumably to keep the "small people," with their ability to impede access to the courtesan, happy.

DECORATED OBJECTS: THE COURTESAN IN THE HOUSE

Courtesan houses were important to the Shanghai economy. They directly supported a large population of owners, managers, courtesans, and servants, and the process of decorating and presenting courtesans in an attractively appointed environment involved a wider commercial network of suppliers as well. The artifacts on and around the courtesan's body were part of her self-presentation, far more prominent in guidebook descriptions than her body itself. For a customer, the ability to discriminate among such trappings and to describe them eloquently was an act of connoisseurship, a practice that defined him as a member of the elite. A courtesan without her jewelry and her elaborately decorated room lost her appeal; a customer who could not appreciate such trappings lowered his own status.

"In the vicinity of her residence are numerous tailoring shops, hair dressers, makers of silk and satin shoes, embroidery shops, whose trade is enriched by her patronage," wrote a foreign observer in 1929.[88] Women jewelry sellers regularly visited the brothels, their cases brimming with expensive hairpins of jadeite, gold, pearl, and coral in the shape of jasmine flowers.[89] Courtesans, one author wrote, had once decorated themselves with fresh flowers: chrysanthemums in spring, sweet-scented osmanthus in summer, plum blossoms in autumn, and orchids in winter. But by the late nineteenth century these had been replaced by pearl flowers, which might cost several hundred yuan but had the advantage of retaining their shape and color indefinitely.[90] A foreign aficionado of courtesans who observed a group of them performing songs at a dinner party noted "the enormous display of jewellery [*sic*] which adorns their ears, fingers, necks or clothes: diamonds of hazel-nut size, *perles baroques* of all forms and shapes, precious pieces of mysterious jade."[91] A courtesan carried expensive accessories as well: a silver case that held a mirror and nutmeg to clear the heads of tipsy customers, folding fans inlaid with ivory and adorned with pictures drawn in gold dust. Waved slowly by delicate hands, such fans became an expression of the courtesan's bodily refinement and an extension of her attractiveness.[92]

These accessories were worth a great deal of money, attested to by the frequency with which courtesans were robbed. In the 1910s and 1920s, the mainstream newspaper *Shenbao* carried regular reports of courtesans who were assaulted by armed gunmen when they went out on call or as they entertained in the brothels.[93] One enterprising pair of robbers used more indirect methods, paying to spend the night with prostitutes, then drugging them as they slept and robbing them.[94] The items most frequently stolen were gold bracelets, pearl hair accessories, and diamond rings, although clothing was sometimes taken as well.[95] In keeping with their status as visible figures on the urban scene, courtesans were not reluctant to involve the police, and when a successful arrest was made the robbers often received sentences ranging from six months to several years.

In January 1920, for instance, the courtesan Zhen Zhuhua was on her way late one night to a restaurant to accompany customers at drinking. As her rickshaw slowed at the corner of Hankou and Tibet Roads in the International Settlement, a robber jumped aboard and grabbed her hat, which was decorated with fifty-one diamonds worth 3,080 yuan. Zhen reported the robbery immediately. Three Chinese detectives from the International Settlement police solved the case at the end of March. Their break came when the mother of one of the robbers rented out a gold butterfly pin from the stolen hat to an unknowing courtesan. When the two courtesans met, Zhen recognized her own pin. The two men and the mother were convicted in spite of the protests of one robber that he had been on his way home from buying dumplings when he heard someone cry out, saw a robber run away, and picked up the butterfly pin.[96] In a story with a less happy ending, the famous courtesan Lian Ying was murdered in 1920 for her jewelry, and her body was dumped in a field outside of Shanghai; the murder and subsequent trial inspired newspaper reports, fiction, and even a stage play (see chapter 6).

The fact that courtesans wore expensive jewelry, however, was not necessarily an indication of their personal wealth. Sometimes their accessories were assembled to give the appearance of prosperity in order to attract and keep a rich patron; in such cases the maidservant was sent to rent diamond rings and pearl head coverings from concubines and daughters of rich households. (The visit of a courtesan-house maidservant to a respectable household for this purpose was subversive, since her payments gave the women of that household an independent source of income.) If the hoped-for patron did not materialize or was inconsistent in his expenditures, both the courtesan and her attendants might find themselves hard put to pay the accessory rental fees.[97] Conversely, a customer would give expensive pieces of jewelry to a courtesan whose favor he coveted, then demand them back when the relationship cooled. If she had pawned the jewelry in the interim to pay for her living expenses, he might threaten her legally or physically. This was the predicament faced by the popular courtesan Pan Anzhen in 1929, when *Shibao* reported that she had thrown herself off a sampan into the Huangpu River. After the sampan operator fished her out and turned her over to the police, she explained to them that she had pawned a customer's gifts to meet medical expenses, but he, suspicious and enraged, had demanded the jewelry back by a specified time. Unable to meet the deadline, she saw no way out but suicide. (The detective on the case released her to the ministrations of two other courtesans and two maidservants from her brothel.)[98]

Another indication of the open, relatively unstigmatized participation of courtesans in urban life was their role in setting fashion standards in Shanghai. Tabloids commented on their habit of changing the colors they favored from one year to the next, so that, for example, rose and purple, despised a few decades earlier, would become de rigueur for fashion-conscious women.[99] Collections of photographic portraits suggest that by the early twentieth century, Western fashions had been added to the repertoire of self-presentation. Photography, itself an import, was eagerly accepted by famous Shanghai courtesans in the late nineteenth century. It may have supplanted the tradition in which courtesans painted self-portraits using mirrors and gave them to favorite customers. Women decorated their own quarters with their portraits or gave prints of them to customers; it was also possible to buy copies directly from Shanghai studios.[100] Such photographs were widely circulated, increasing the scope of courtesan visibility (if not intimacy) and the precision and variety of images.

Many courtesans experimented with different settings and costumes in their photographic portraits. In a 1917 collection (see figures 5–14),[101] Lan Yunge, dressed in brocaded robes, hair covered by strings of jewels, sat decorously among potted plants, bound feet peeping out from under floor-length skirts. Shen Baoyu, photographed in a similar setting, held an ostrich-feather fan. Qin Yu appeared in a Chinese-style satin gown covered with embroidered and pearl-bedecked flowers. Several women in full Chinese operatic costume struck dramatic poses, while others appeared in simpler Chinese dress, their surroundings replete with refined accessories: a book, a tea set, a musical instrument, a game of Chinese chess. Less common but not unusual were the Victorian dresses worn by Qin Lou, Hua Sibao, and Xiao Qinglou, which featured an assortment of elaborate flowered straw hats, high-button shoes, lace, bows, and fur-trimmed collars. Several of these women held books bound in the Western fashion, and one group posed in an early-model automobile. (Although none of the portraits shows it, courtesans were said to have taken up the Western game of billiards as well.)[102] In many of the portraits, Chinese and Western accessories were mingled: a Western overcoat over a high-collared Chinese gown; flat caps of the sort sported by working-class Englishmen, worn with Chinese tunics; a woman in snood, tunic, and Chinese slacks seated at a clavier. One year the favored winter garb would be Chinese embroidered silk cloaks lined in white fox or snow weasel; the next year they would be replaced by Western coats, which (wearers were instructed) did not have to be removed at table.[103] Although it was not prominent in these portraits, cross-dressing was apparently also practiced by some Shanghai courtesans, who occasionally dressed as men onstage (where they wore Chinese dress) or offstage (where Western dress was more common).[104] The male costumes they adopted were generally those of the scholar or cultivated gentleman, a form of self-presentation that accentuated their own appreciation of refinement. Western clothing added to rather than displaced the options considered attractive for courtesans, giving them a new set of props with which to display not only refinement, but also knowledge of the modern.

The only signifier of femininity that did not cross cultures was footbinding: small-footed women, numerous in these pictures, always wore Chinese-style clothing. One of the capsule biographies included in the 1917 portrait collection indicated that with the influx of Western styles, it was no longer fashionable to bind one's feet; customers now judged courtesans by their tiny waists instead. Nevertheless, it said, some courtesans continued to bind their feet daily, and some customers continued to seek out such women.[105] The relative silence about footbinding is part of a more general lack of description of women's bodies in the courtesan literature. Rather, the descriptive passages concentrated on clothing, fineness of features, gracefulness of movement, and whether a woman was lively or reserved.

An integral part of courtesan self-presentation was choosing a professional name. Like elite men, courtesans adopted new names at important junctures in their professional careers: when they entered a courtesan house, changed locations, opened their own establishment, or returned to life as a courtesan after a stint as a concubine. For instance, a Shanghai courtesan in the 1920s named Xiao Linglong Laoqi (Small Exquisite Old Seven) moved to Tianjin, where she changed her name to Aiwen (Loves Gentleness). On her return to Shanghai, she chose the name Nian Nian Hong (Popular Year after Year).[106] Courtesans who achieved particular fame under a particular name sometimes decided to keep it, as with the famous turn-of-the-century courtesan Lin Daiyu, who named herself for the frail and temperamental heroine of Cao Xueqin's early Qing novel *Dream of the Red Chamber.* A 1923 English-language article explained that courtesan names frequently featured the characters for rouge, peach blossom, jade, peony, moonlight, and other delicate, beautiful, or fragrant objects, adding that "these kinds of names are not given to respectable women." Alternatively, a woman might "choose characters representing the period they entered their calling, such as Shih san tan [*shisan dan*], 'An Actress at Thirteen.'" In spite of the author's assertion that aesthetic names were "vulgarized because they are bestowed upon demimonde women," many of them sounded more like the pen names assumed by elite gentlemen poets and painters. In some cases these were "studio" (*zhai*) names meant to evoke a sense of place, such as "Fragrant Nest" or "Drunken Flowers Retreat." Women who were masters of their own residence brothels might even adopt a literati-style pseudonym such as "the master of the lodge wherein verses are hummed."[107] One tabloid commentary warned against taking these place names too literally: the courtesan Gold Silver Mansion (*Jin Yin Lou*), it warned, did not necessarily have piles of gold and silver, nor did Flower Moon Chamber (*Hua Yue Ge*) resemble flowers and the moon. Conversely, a young courtesan named Humble Room (*Lou Shi*) was not necessarily plain, nor were her dwellings spartan; rather, the name was meant to suggest polite refinement.[108]

Often a courtesan's name situated her in a network of other courtesans, linked by kinship (blood or adoptive) or genealogical ties. An aging courtesan who acquired or adopted an assistant might name the newcomer after herself, adding the prefix "Small" (*xiao*). Thus Li Shuangzhu's foster daughter was called Xiao Shuangzhu Lao Er (Small Double Pearl Old Two),[109] and Shen Yuying's new assistant was Xiao Shen Yuying. ("Although her name is 'small,' her ability to flirt is not," commented an article about the latter.[110]) In another common arrangement, women who were associated with a single courtesan house over a period of years would take a single name, adding the suffix "Eldest," "Old Two," and so forth down to "Old Nine."[111] Sometimes women of a single house adopted a single surname (Zhang Suyun, Zhang Baobao, Zhang Laoyun) or shared one character of their personal names (Zhang Laoyun, Zhang Suyun, Zhang Yayun).[112] The tabloids then referred to them in clusters: the three Chens,[113] the two Phoenixes (Gao Feng and Qing Feng).[114] One guidebook complained that the proliferation of courtesans with the same name led to confusion among customers, who would walk into the wrong courtesan's room by mistake.[115] A shared name indicated a business relationship; it might or might not denote a close personal tie.

Writings about the courtesan houses generally focused on a universe of elaborate social activities conducted by beautiful, cultivated women. Yet when the authors of these writings turned to the naming question, their narratives hinted at tragedy. When a courtesan adopted a glamorous trade name, they explained, her own surname disappeared. Some speculated that behind this act lay a woman's desire to keep her present life from reflecting on her family. Alternatively, they suggested, she might not know much of her own past.

"Shanghai prostitutes mostly conceal their original surnames," explained a 1917 guidebook.

> They choose personal names as they please. . . . Women singers number in the thousands and tens of thousands, but one who looks for their banner using their real names will not find one in a hundred. Perhaps this is because if one is a prostitute, why use one's original surname to let people know? . . . Or perhaps they carefully conceal it and don't wish to let it leak out. Furthermore, some were kidnapped by bandits in faraway places when they were young, brought here, and sold into courtesan houses. They themselves do not actually know what family they come from.[116]

These dark comments indicate that life as a courtesan might have carried a burden of shame and loss, a note rarely sounded in the literature of appreciation. Yet it is not entirely clear exactly who was entangled in the romance of the lost patronym, with its overtones of filial piety and women tragically ripped from the bosom of the family: the courtesan, or her literary admirers? As with so much else about courtesan lives, the sources convey an emotional charge without indicating who felt it.

Appropriately decorated, dressed, and named, the courtesan was showcased in the exquisitely appointed setting of the courtesan house. The larger establishments were in buildings several stories high, with a foyer and banquet spaces downstairs, and small rooms with curtained doorways on the lower and upper floors.[117] Each house hung a lamp from a window above the front door, taking it down when the house was full.[118] Nineteenth-century travel records devoted almost as much attention to the rich decorations of the brothels, and the pleasurable sensations produced by such opulence, as to the women who inhabited them. "Their buildings are furnished like those of kings and noblemen," wrote Chi Zhicheng in 1893,

> with beds, night tables, and wardrobes, made of marble or fine hardwood. Aside from silk curtains, there are also dressing mirrors, chandeliers, small round pedestal tables, flowers with glass covers, paintings made of coral and jade, Western clocks, fancy plates, silver water pipes, all flickering in the light of the red lamps, making one feel intoxicated.[119]

An individual courtesan's room might be decorated with a sleeping chaise ("it is comfortable for the guest to have a nap there") or an elaborate opium couch, made of two cabinets, called the "bodhisattva's bed." Styles of decoration varied from year to year, with the preferred form of lighting moving from pearl-bedecked lamps to hand-painted lamp shades of white silk. Foreign patterned wallpaper was popular. A well-appointed room required that four big bowls of fruit be on display, as well as a silver or gold water pipe for each courtesan. (The pipes were later replaced by expensive cigarettes.)[120] As with a courtesan's jewelry, her room furnishings were often contributed by a patron who wanted the room where he spent the night to be as well decorated as the companion with whom he spent it.[121] And just as a disgruntled patron might demand that a courtesan return "his" jewelry, so a brothel's elaborate decorations could be smashed by unhappy customers or the hoodlums they hired. Guidebooks and the mainstream press mentioned brawls instigated by jealous or otherwise dissatisfied guests, mêlées in which signboards, furniture, vases, and mirrors were destroyed; madams had no hesitation about taking such customers to court for payment of damages.[122]

Although much courtesan activity took place in public or semipublic spaces such as restaurants, storytelling houses, theaters, and the banquet rooms of the larger brothels, the courtesan's own room was an important place not only for sexual activity, but also for intimate social entertaining. The importance of "the room" (*fangjian*) as a unit of negotiation in brothel transactions is indicated by the cluster of associated terms that appear in guidebooks, terms that a sophisticated brothel customer was expected to understand and deploy when appropriate. A courtesan had first to rent a room (*bao fangjian*) in a residence brothel or great hall house, then wallpaper the room (*biao fangjian*), set it in order, and decorate it (*pu fangjian*). "Lead to a[nother] room" (*ling fangjian*) was a phrase called out by a courtesan if a brothel servant mistakenly began to usher one customer into a room where she was entertaining another. It meant that the newcomer should be taken elsewhere until she could come out to greet him. In such a case the customer could elect to "borrow a room" (*jie fangjian*) belonging to another courtesan until the first courtesan was free. But if the first and second customers were on friendly terms, they could "share a room" (*bing fangjian*), engaging in pleasant conversation with a single courtesan. If a jealous customer heard that others were arriving, he might declare a "sickroom" (*bing fangjian*), which meant refusing to vacate until dawn. An astute courtesan tried to avoid such awkwardness by means of "making space in the room" (*teng fangjian*), graciously clearing the first man out so that the second one could visit. If she handled such situations skillfully and acquired a regular clientele, she could "change the room" (*diao fangjian*) in favor of one in a better brothel; the term was also used if she was obliged to move to worse quarters. If her customers were dissatisfied, they might come to "vandalize the room" (*da fangjian*). After musicians played at a newly opened house or accompanied at New Year festivities, they came to each courtesan's room to play a piece of music and collect a tip; this was called "sweeping the room" (*sao fangjian*) and was intended to inaugurate a season of good business.[123]

All this room-centered activity was social rather than explicitly sexual. Only two terms referred to more intimate encounters, and these took place outside the courtesan house. To summon a prostitute to sing, drink, or play mahjong (*majiang*) in a hotel room was known as "to open a room" (*kai fangjian*). Since hotel calls lasted longer than restaurant calls, the customer could take the opportunity to "seek pleasure, increase the degree of familiarity between the two parties, and observe the emotions of one's partner." Once this type of connection was initiated, a guidebook advised, it could lead to a regular sexual relationship. A step beyond opening a room was to rent a small room (*xiao fangzi*) in a quiet place, where the couple could meet every day in relative privacy; the author encouraged aspiring customers to decorate such a room beautifully, though it need not be too elaborate.[124]

For both courtesan and customer, "the room" was a complex site of social negotiations. A successful courtesan moved to better and better brothel rooms, regulated the flow of customers satisfactorily, and sometimes was successful in establishing her own residence brothel. A successful customer, in contrast, hoped to use his mastery of the room-based rituals to extricate her from the business and social obligations that life in a courtesan's room entailed, and install her in a space to which only he had access.

COURTESAN-HOUSE SERVICES

Sexual relations were a relatively small part of a courtesan's daily activity, which was governed by invitations to go out on call or accompany groups of men as they ate, drank, and gambled. Her day began at about noon and was organized around encounters in graded degrees of intimacy. She might spend the afternoon in the courtesan house, smoking, napping, sewing, knitting, painting, and drinking tea; she might meet an intimate guest and go shopping or repair to a rented room outside the brothel with him. At dusk she had lunch and put on her makeup, preparing for the round of calls and banquets that would occupy her at least until midnight, or even later if she was popular. Her evening might end in a sexual encounter, a drive around town with a favored customer, or (in the 1920s and later) a visit to a dance hall. At dawn she went to sleep.[125]

The Call

"If we are to trust the evidence of Chinese books," a Western commentator has written,

> it seems that it was impossible for a party of officials, or men of letters, to meet on any social occasion without summoning a contingent of girls to keep them company. . . . Never at any time in the past had the singing-girl enjoyed greater prestige than during the last days of the Empire and under the early Republic—say from 1870 down to the Nationalist revolution of 1926.[126]

The "social occasion" could take place in a restaurant, wineshop, teahouse, theater, or courtesan house, where the courtesan's attendance was meant to provide an entertaining and pleasurable backdrop to other activities: drinking, watching a play, gambling, or conversation among a party of men.

Both propriety and pleasure for the men involved depended on the appropriate performance of their parts in such rituals, as well as the courtesan's correct response. Summoning a prostitute to an occasion outside the brothel was known as "calling" (*jiaoju*)[127] and was accomplished by sending a red call ticket (*jupiao*) by messenger from the theater or wineshop to the courtesan house.[128] Places of entertainment employed someone specifically for this purpose, and the sight of such a person rushing through the street delivering call tickets was a familiar feature of life in turn-of-the-century Shanghai.[129] The courtesan would respond by coming out on call (*chuju* or *chu tangchai*, "going out on hall business"), traveling in a sedan chair owned by the brothel, on the shoulders of male servants as described earlier, or in later decades by rickshaw.[130] If she was very young, or had been pawned or sold to the courtesan house, a servant would accompany her; if she was a famous older courtesan, she might well be accompanied by several younger attendants.[131]

One essay in a collection of humorous literati pieces on brothel life suggested that the phrases "to go out on call" and "going out on hall business" had originally referred to Song dynasty officials and Qing dynasty members of the Hanlin academy who went out on official tasks.[132] This was one of many instances where literati engaged in witty self-mockery by applying the terminology and hierarchies of official government service to courtesans. Courtesan houses themselves also appropriated this terminology. In the early twentieth century, courtesans traveling out on call in sedan chairs were accompanied by male servants carrying a lamp on which was written "official business" (*gongwu*).[133] One author writing in the 1930s even recalled seeing in his youth lamps that said "chief magistrate on public business" (*gongwu zhengtang*). He went on to ruminate about the hubris involved in using such official language:

> According to the system of officials of the Qing dynasty, only magistrates of the seventh grade and above could call themselves *zhengtang*. The district chief of police [*dianshi*] and the county magistrate [*xiancheng*] merely called themselves "left and right halls" [*zuoyou liangtang*]. Yet prostitutes at this time dared to call themselves "main halls" [*zhengtang*]. It was not only a strange situation [*duoduo guaishi*], but also a foolhardy thing to do [*danda wangwei*]. Furthermore, going out to assist at drinking and going to the storytelling houses are types of prostitution [*yinye*]. If it were called the "prostitution business" [*yinwu*], that would be reasonable. But to call it not the "prostitution business," but rather "public business," means the name does not match the reality. Is it possible that prostitutes selling sex are engaging in a type of proper public business?[134]

By the 1930s such appropriation had become an occasion not for playfulness, but for high-decibel moralizing. This was part of a larger shift in the meanings of prostitution (see parts 3 and 4).

A somewhat more frivolous note was struck by a foreign observer of the courtesans:

[T]hey went from restaurant to restaurant, hotel to hotel, jazzing up parties for the hosts, always in touch with headquarters like radio-controlled taxis. Their glossy private rickshaws dashed around the brilliantly lit central area of Shanghai, among the scores of hotels and restaurants, dazzling head-lamps fore and aft, with often a hidden spotlight on the floor lighting up their fascinating little faces, the lotus blooms in their ebony hair and last but not least their glittering jewellery [*sic*]. To protect the gems from possible snatch-thieves, an extra runner always trotted behind, a hand clutching a corner of the pneumatic-wheeled, swift, softly gliding vehicle.[135]

A network of interlocking small-business interests was activated each time a customer filled out a call ticket. The messenger who delivered the ticket to the brothel collected a fee (sixty-three cash in 1891). The restaurant or hotel where the call ticket originated kept a notebook where the date and name of each courtesan who made a call were recorded. At the end of every month, someone from the restaurant went to the brothel to collect seventy cash per call, a fee classified as "carfare." The brothel also kept detailed records of each call, to make sure that restaurants did not charge for calls that had not taken place.[136] In the late nineteenth century the fee for a call was three yuan (this was one meaning of the "three" in *changsan*, "long three"—the most common name for courtesans).[137] By the 1920s, in an attempt to attract more business, the cost for a *changsan* visit dropped to two and then one yuan, of which "the girl has to pay ten cents to the servant, ten cents to the fiddler who accompanies her songs, five cents to the house for a cup of tea."[138] (Unlike *changsan* courtesans, the slightly lower ranking *yao er* did not lower their fee of two yuan per call until the 1930s; hence the saying "Loose *changsan*, stiff *yao er*.")[139] By the late 1930s, payment for a call was no longer an on-the-spot transaction; accounts were kept by the courtesan house and settled at the end of a season.[140]

A courtesan's comportment when on call depended upon the venue, her popularity, and her degree of familiarity with the customer who had summoned her. Originally all courtesans had been expected to sing a song, accompanied by a musician, but as they moved farther from their origins as opera performers, and hotel rooms became a common site of calls, many courtesans replaced the song with a few minutes of conversation. One guidebook suggested that courtesans, exhausted from as many as thirty calls a night, deliberately avoided bringing musicians with them so they would not have to sing.[141] Another way in which courtesans exerted some control over their call schedule was by "substituting a sedan chair" (*dai jiao*). If a courtesan was summoned by a customer whom she did not like but dared not refuse, she would ask one of her fellow courtesans to replace her. The customer would be told that she was ill or on another call.[142] For all but the most favored patrons, a popular courtesan on a hectic schedule would stay for several minutes and then move on to answer the next summons, even if the customer had been waiting an hour or two for her arrival. Until about 10 P.M., courtesans usually made restaurant calls, and after that were available to make hotel calls (again for conversation, but in a less public and rushed environment).[143]

The call was governed by elaborate rules of etiquette that shaped the standards of elite behavior among men, and guidebooks devoted much attention to instructing customers on how to meet those standards. If one did not have a previous acquaintance with the courtesan one wanted, a guidebook advised, it was best to have a recommendation from one of her regular customers, and to write on the call ticket that you were substituting for him. That way the courtesan might be willing to sit and chat for a while. "Otherwise," the author warned, "she will seem rather socially aloof." For his part, the customer was advised to conduct himself in a carefully considered manner. This was a "trial call" (*dayang ju*), described by one guidebook as "like looking at the goods in a store,"[144] but the admonitions made it clear that the customer was as much on trial as the courtesan. Those who had no one to introduce them could find the names of courtesans in the small telephone books sold by cigarette shops.[145]

In a lugubrious tone common to many accounts, a 1936 guidebook bemoaned the fact that because of hard economic times, access to courtesans had become easier, and a personal introduction was no longer necessary because "prostitutes have become willing to accept a lower position on cheaper terms."[146] Even in these circumstances of relatively easy access and impersonal introduction, however, customers were warned not to presume too much. "If you read the history of a particular prostitute in the newspaper and then ask her out on a trial call, you cannot speak of her secrets, in order to avoid making her unhappy and having her speak coldly to you," scolded one author, who went on to caution against dissolute or immoderate behavior.[147] After the trial call the customer was free to summon a courtesan in his own name. Guidebooks recommended that he call one courtesan often, noting that even if he called the same woman every day it would not cost more than about one hundred yuan per season. A man who kept making "trial calls," it was argued, would never establish a relationship with any particular courtesan, and a man who called more than one courtesan at a time would be derided as a "garbage cart" (*laji mache*) and would not receive their undivided attention.[148]

Courtesans, like guests, were expected to behave in stylized and predictable ways when on call. The rules governing courtesan conduct were presented by the guidebooks as a standard for customers to use in judging courtesans. Such rules reinforced the public nature of the call as an occasion where a woman's actions were supposed to give the customer "face" in front of his companions. On arrival she was supposed to greet her regular customers. If a particularly close customer was present she should ask permission to transfer her current call (*zhuanju*), sit by his side, and sing a song. If she was unaccompanied by a musician, she should make polite excuses for not singing so that the guests would not be angry. She was instructed to sit by a guest's side but not to drink with him, in order to maintain the distinction between guest and prostitute. If he insisted that she drink, she must say "excuse me" to the assembled guests. If he further insisted that she substitute for him at a drinking game by drinking his penalty cups of wine, she was permitted to drink but not eat. A courtesan who did not wish to drink should refuse politely, but yield and drink a bit if the guests were drunken or insistent. Before leaving she should excuse herself in a courteous manner.[149] Courtesans who did not exert themselves to make the guests feel comfortable, but rather let their attendants entertain while they sat "like a clay figure of a beauty," were derided as arrogant.[150] By the accretion of such detail, guidebooks taught customers how to judge whether they were being treated with due deference.

Aside from the standard brief call in a restaurant or hotel, customers could also request that a courtesan call on them to drink with a group of friends in a wineshop (a "wine call"), go with them to the theater (a "play call"), accompany them at gambling and take a cut of the winnings (a "card call"), or stay with them to gamble or engage in other activities until the sun came up (a "dawn call").[151] In the late nineteenth century, another popular form of amusement was to invite a courtesan to go for a ride in a fancy horse-drawn carriage. This had once been counted as a call, but eventually became a way for customers to display themselves in company with a beautiful courtesan, who might dress in Western, Japanese, or even Manchu-style garb for the occasion. "It is a pleasure for pedestrians to watch them passing along the streets, dressed to attract attention," said one guidebook, while a travel memoir recalled people going by in "a cloud of dust, a whiff of perfume, a flash of red and green garments and hair ornaments."[152]

Opening the Teacup

After summoning her out on call, the second step in becoming familiar with a courtesan was to go to her brothel for tea, cigarettes, snacks, and conversation. This type of encounter was known as "opening the teacup" (*da chawei*).[153] "It is a step more pleasurable than a call," explained one guide, "because calls all take place where the eyes of others are on you, and it is easy to feel awkward, but when you go for tea, you can talk and laugh in a somewhat more unrestrained fashion."[154] Once a customer was ushered into a courtesan's room for tea, her door curtain was drawn and the electric lamp was lit to highlight the room's elegant furnishings and signal other guests to stay out.[155]

Unlike the call, tea in a *changsan* house was free, occasioning financial losses for the establishment, but it was understood that after "opening the teacup" several times a customer would incur an obligation to host a banquet or gambling party that would bring income to the house. This was in keeping with the genteel performance of masculinity required of upper-class customers; they were expected to spend time establishing a relationship with the house and a particular courtesan, and to understand their long-term obligations without the constant reminder of interim financial charges.[156] A customer who visited often for tea without hosting a banquet risked mockery and cold treatment by the courtesans, and even a banquet-giving guest who showed up too often for tea might be cursed by the madam as miserly. Yet most guides opined that teatime was the best time to build an intimate connection with a courtesan, and that if customers "managed it skillfully and with face," they would soon have courtesans pursuing them rather than the other way around.[157]

The scale on which growing intimacy was measured was a finely calibrated one. On their first call, guests were advised to go in a group of two or three late at night, when the courtesans had returned after their round of calls. (If they went earlier, they were told, "only the maidservant will be able to receive you, which is not very interesting.")[158] On the other hand, if they arrived too late at night, they might find the desired courtesan already ensconced with another customer.[159] It was recommended that they stay not more than ten minutes on the first call.[160] More-established guests could try to visit in the afternoon, when the rooms were quiet and the courtesans had more leisure. Tea guests were advised to graciously withdraw if a courtesan was hosting a banquet or was summoned out on call, presumably since these were income-generating activities.[161]

Many features of the tea-drinking ritual itself were designed to remind the customer of exactly where he stood with a courtesan. In describing these rituals, guidebooks emphasized that the courtesan and her servants had the power to honor or humiliate the customer through small gestures. A stranger entering a courtesan house would be announced by the male servants with the shout "A guest has arrived," but a rich or well-known man would be greeted with the cry "Courtesan so-and-so, Mr. so-and-so is here to see you." This initial sorting of guests disappeared when electric doorbells replaced personal announcements in the 1910s, an example of a technological innovation leading to a weakening of status distinctions.[162] A guest who was not known to anyone in the house would be served tea in a small or worn teacup, whereas a favored guest got an additional, larger teacup from the courtesan's personal stock. Policemen, petty officials, or new guests who had a previous relationship with the courtesan or madam would also be favored with extra cups. A courtesan involved in a sexual relationship with a customer would provide him with special tea leaves, and the servants would add the water. The call "Hot water!" from a courtesan's room thus meant that a favored patron, one who merited the courtesan's own tea, was visiting. When two customers sat in a room and chatted with their favorite courtesans, each woman was supposed to provide teacups for her own guest, or he would be humiliated. A courtesan who was angry with a regular customer would refuse to serve him from her personal cups, a rebuff known as "dismissing the teacup." The hapless customer could either seek another courtesan or drink out of the cup provided by the house.[163] All these elaborate distinctions had apparently disappeared by the twentieth century, when courtesans became less the arbiters of refinement and more the objects of openly expressed sexual desire.

If tea-drinking rituals in *changsan* houses reminded the customer that he had continually to earn his status, procedures in the lower-ranking *yao er* houses put him firmly in control. There the encounter was known as "calling moving tea" (*jiao yicha*). When the brothel servant announced a new guest's arrival, all the women in the house who were not already occupied lined up so that he could choose one. He indicated his choice by asking her professional name, and then "moved the tea" to her private quarters. A guidebook explained, "You can then go to her room to sit and talk. Those who want to joke around do so, and if one wants to be a bit romantic there is nothing to stop one." The usual charge for "moving tea" was one yuan. As in the *changsan* houses, customers used tea drinking as a way to establish an ongoing connection with a courtesan, one that might result in a subsequent sexual encounter.[164] With greater familiarity and generous spending, customers moved up in social status within the courtesan house, which served as a venue for demonstrating their status for an audience of courtesans and other customers. Yet although these preliminary rituals might be as protracted as they were for *changsan,* the symbolism entailed in a call for moving tea was one reminder that *yao er* had less control over choice of customers than did *changsan.*

Banquets and Gambling

Customers hosted banquets in courtesan houses for many reasons: to drink and joke with male friends in a congenial environment; to enjoy the conversation and performances of attractive courtesans; to validate their own standing as a person of stature in the eyes of the madam, the courtesans, and their fellow revelers; to win the favor of a courtesan (and sometimes her madam) by spending lavishly. Banquets and gambling parties were the main sources of income for a courtesan house. In a formal banquet, the host paid a set amount for each table of eight people, plus additional fees for the food and tips for the servants.[165] To give a banquet was known as "setting a feast table" (*bai taimian*) or "setting flower wine" (*bai huajiu*), the "flowers" referring to the courtesans.[166] Mahjong was referred to as *penghe* (*penghu* in Shanghai dialect), the phrase called out by a player at the conclusion of a round. Along with the card games *yaotan* and poker, mahjong brought in the most income. Madams were said to favor customers who liked to gamble and drink.[167]

Banqueting, drinking, and gambling were collectively known as "celebrating the flower" (*zuo huatou*). Two types of occasions were common: several rounds of mahjong followed by an informal meal, or a more elaborate occasion where mahjong was followed by a banquet, often with additional guests.[168] The "flower" (*huatou*) was actually an accounting unit, equal in the 1930s to twelve yuan.[169] A round of mahjong, for instance, in 1939 cost anywhere from two to four *huatou* (twenty-four to forty-eight yuan).[170] A two-table banquet and ten rounds of mahjong at one *huatou* each equaled a dozen flowers (*yida huatou*), a veritable bouquet of pleasures.[171] Tips for servants and musicians added to the total expenditure.[172] Costs for a single night of drinking and gambling could run as high as several hundred yuan in the 1930s. (In the moralizing tone that had become typical of guidebooks by that time, the author of one such book pointed out that this was "enough to provide a half year of relief grain for a poor person").[173] The cost was shared between host and guests by having each invited guest buy tickets worth a half, one, or two *huatou;* in addition, the host might ask them to contribute if they ran up a large drinking bill.[174]

Banquets were conducted with a certain amount of ceremony. Guests arrived in sedan chairs; the bearers (and later their successors, rickshaw pullers and cab drivers) were given metal tokens issued by the brothel, exquisitely carved in the shape of peaches, flowers, or ancient bronze vessels. These were known as "sedan-chair food tickets," which could be redeemed (in the brothels and later in tobacco shops) for cash.[175] (The fact that these tokens were accepted citywide in lieu of petty currency indicates just how many small commercial transactions involved the courtesan houses.) Once the guests had arrived, a waiter set the banquet table, then shouted, "Warm the wine!" in order to summon the courtesans to attend to their guests. "His voice is so loud that guests who have come to Shanghai for the first time from far-off places don't know what's happening and often are startled when they hear it," wrote a guidebook author, reinscribing Shanghai's role as the source of strange and confusing experiences for newly arrived bumpkins.[176] After the guests sat down and took up their wine cups, a servant called more softly, "Bring up the cooked dishes!" Appetizers were followed by main dishes and a concluding course of rice or rice porridge. When the main dishes were served, each courtesan sang, accompanied by musicians playing flutes, drums, and stringed instruments.[177] These performances were followed by songs during which the courtesans accompanied themselves on the *pipa*. Throughout the meal, the servant called for refills of wine, which (the guidebook asserts) was watered down by the courtesan house as soon as the guests were too drunk to notice. The drinking might occasionally result in a guest becoming angry and overturning the table, but it was more likely that guests would attempt to settle petty conflicts and enhance their own reputations by moving on to another house for another feast as soon as the first one concluded, in order to stage competing displays of largesse.[178]

As with summoning a prostitute and opening the teacup, hosting a feast or gambling party was entangled with issues of obligation and face on the part of both customer and courtesan. Regular guests were asked by the courtesan or her madam to "celebrate the flower" whenever a brothel started a new season, a courtesan changed houses, the winter solstice arrived, a house prosperity ritual was enacted, or the madam or courtesan celebrated a birthday. It was considered humiliating for a courtesan not to have a party hosted by her regular guests on any of these occasions, and one guidebook suggests that a madam who felt thus humiliated was apt to despise the courtesan who failed to attract business.[179] This was an occasion when an enterprising guest could earn the gratitude, and perhaps the future favors, of a courtesan whose business was not booming.[180] When dealing with a more successful courtesan, a customer had to be prepared to host parties on demand if he wished to win the courtesan's favor and successfully display his own wealth.[181] Initiating a party himself, without her urging, gave him more face.[182] The cost of becoming a favored customer rose steadily over time, causing one guidebook to lament in 1939 that formerly a three- or four-*huatou* man had been considered a good guest, but that now he would be a laughingstock. The author hinted at the dangers of hosting a party but waxed lyrical about the pleasures of the occasion:

> Celebrating the flower is a difficult performance [*zhongtou xi,* "a difficult opera to play or sing"] for the brothel customer. It is also the time where he demonstrates that he has face. . . . On the day when he celebrates the flower, people in the brothel will be especially attentive. A single call will bring a hundred responses, and they will do everything just right, even the unimportant details. You call a flower to accompany you, there are songs to please the guests, and the sound of the party can be heard outside. With hugs to the left and embraces to the right, you can enjoy beauty and good fortune to the fullest. When the drinking is over and the banqueters disperse, you may also have the opportunity to tuck the prostitute you like under your arm, and follow the pleasant dream of the full moon. So those who travel there often forget that time is fleeting ["a white colt passes swiftly by"]. One can imagine the happiness and pleasure of the host.[183]

Even if he did not succeed in gaining access to his favorite that night, the host would thenceforth be treated as a valued guest. As Wang Dingjiu put it in his 1932 *Key to Shanghai* (*Shanghai menjing*), "they will curry favor with you, and you can gradually have a taste of unimaginable fascination."[184] Of course, a customer who had a regular sexual relationship with a courtesan was under a special obligation to host parties, particularly if he had bought a period of exclusive rights to her sexual services.[185]

Settling Accounts and Getting Paid

In the larger courtesan houses, so many financial transactions took place in the course of calls, banquets, and gambling parties that a separate accounting department was required to keep track of them. Accounts were settled at the Dragon Boat Festival, the Mid-Autumn Festival, and the Spring Festival, the same time when new courtesans were hired. As the holidays approached, the house would send presents to regular customers as a reminder that they should clear their bills. A good customer would then send a servant to the courtesan house to get the bill and would pay it in cash. Alternatively, a man who was summoning a prostitute out on call could write on the call ticket, "Bring the bill along." When the bill was paid, the brothel would issue a receipt written in formal honorific language and pay the carfare of the servant who had come to hand over the money. It was considered unusual, even inauspicious, for a customer to pay his bill before the end of the season. This usually happened if he had come into conflict with a courtesan or another customer, and it signified a rupturing of his ongoing relationship with the courtesan house. In such a case, the house might try to mediate the conflict, or might decide that the customer was "a nail in the eye" and let him go.[186]

If a customer overeager to settle his account indicated the severance of an ongoing commercial relationship, defaulters meant trouble of a different kind. When a guest failed to pay his seasonal bill, he was said to *piaozhang*—literally, "float accounts"—which one guidebook explained as a reference to the way something drifted away on the water's surface.[187] This practice was common enough that it gave rise to a Shanghai jingle:

The loquat is ripe.
The maids [brothel servants] put things right.
The ladies [courtesans] take fright.
The lords [customers] out of sight.
Default's at a height.[188]

A house in this situation had several methods of recourse. It could refuse to have any further contact with the customer; one guidebook said that an effective way to stop a man from visiting brothels was to convince him to default at several houses, after which he would be unwelcome at every brothel.[189] A courtesan or her maids could place a notice in the newspaper, attempting to embarrass the defaulter publicly, threatening to publish his name, or offering a reward to anyone who located him. One such notice from about 1908 read:

OLD MUDDLED ZHU. Last year I sent A Xiaomei to your residence to ask for payment of your account, but you slapped her face and hustled her out the door. At the end of the year I had to pawn everything down to my quilt and blanket to meet expenses. Now the 16th of the first lunar month has already passed. You still haven't shown your face. One might say that your muddle-headedness has reached an extreme. I hereby publish this in the newspaper to search for you. A public notice by Jin Yu of Shangren Li.

Such notices sometimes produced results, as the following pair indicates:

SOUGHT. A certain lord from Shaanxi held banquets, gambling parties, and calls at the house of a lady [*xiaojie,* here denoting "courtesan"] during the past season. He owes more than 384 yuan. He has not even paid the servants' tips yet. He has absconded. If a compassionate gentleman should locate this lord, we will send him 10 yuan. We will definitely not eat these words. Posted jointly by A Geng, A Zhao, A Qiao, and A Jin [apparently maids in the house].

FOUND. Previously we published a public notice to the effect that a certain lord from Shaanxi owed 384 yuan in brothel fees and tips, of which he had not paid a penny. Now this lord has presented himself and volunteered to pay in full within three days. Therefore, honest and tolerant as we are, we still keep his name secret. If he does not pay by the deadline, we will again publish it in the newspaper. Let it not be said that we did not give fair warning. A Geng, A Zhao, A Geng, and A Zhu.[190]

Although commentators excoriated such deadbeats for behaving "like a worm among books,"[191] ultimately houses could not do much to stop defaulters. Often the house did not know the occupation or address of a delinquent customer and had no means to pressure him for repayment. Houses resorted to the ritual practice of turning the account books upside down and throwing them on the floor at the end of each season, in the belief that this would cause customers who had not paid up to come forward and do so.[192] To limit their own losses, houses customarily held courtesans and their attendants responsible for the amount their guests had not paid. Some categories of servant tips were not paid until festival time, and if the guest defaulted, the courtesan had to make up the difference here too.[193] The extent of courtesan liability depended upon a number of factors, the most important of which was a courtesan's balance of power with the madam. An attendant might have the amount deducted from the share she was owed at the end of the season; a courtesan would have it deducted from the amount she was given to finance her season's expenses, and might also be watched closely by the accounting office and not freed until the debt was cleared.[194] But a good madam, or one who wanted a courtesan to stay for another season, might allow her to pay at a discount or forgive the debt altogether.[195] Delinquent customers added to the danger that courtesans would find themselves ever more deeply in debt, and probably contributed both to their caution in picking intimates and the urgency with which they pressed them for private gifts. More generally, decreasing their debt while maintaining the financial outlay associated with an elaborate wardrobe and a full schedule of banquets required considerable strategizing and luck on the part of courtesan, madam, and customer.

Many people depended upon the fees collected at the end of each season by the courtesan house. The madam first paid the wages of the cleaning maids and male servants. The remainder of the revenue was divided according to predefined shares. Attendants and *daidang* maidservants received one or two shares, agreed upon in advance. The remainder went to the madam (or the courtesan if it was a residence house). Hired courtesans received no shares, since they were paid a fixed amount per season. With this type of income, it was the madam and the senior female servants who benefited most if the business prospered and who suffered if it declined.[196] Courtesans also suffered when banquets declined or guests defaulted, but for them the reward structure was dependent upon a series of more personal transactions wherein they asked favored customers for extra money, clothes, jewelry, and loans. Intimate customers were also expected to present "their" courtesans with gifts and tips at festivals.[197]

RITUAL SOLIDARITY

Like other small businesses, brothels observed periodic rituals intended to enhance their prosperity as a house. Each month and before the three festivals, as well as when a new courtesan arrived or the god of wealth's birthday was celebrated, a courtesan house would conduct a ritual known as "burning the road" (*shao lutou*). On this day the god of wealth was welcomed with offerings of incense, paper money, and food. Each courtesan lit a pair of candles and bowed to the god's image. Male servants poured a cup of liquor onto the charcoal burning in the god's "spirit stove"; if the burning alcohol emitted a high flame, it was considered an auspicious sign. At the end of the day, the courtesans took their candles and a share of the charcoal back from the house's shrine to their rooms. At the end of every month, brothels burned paper ingots sprinkled with salt, saying that this would allow them to predict the flow of cash into the business ("salt" being a homonym for "cash" in Shanghai dialect). Paper ingots were also placed under the beds of the courtesans to assure a supply of "small change" tips. In conjunction with these spiritual measures, the madam also took immediate concrete action to bring in wealth by hosting a feast and a gambling party for which guests were expected to pay. These feasts were elaborate occasions; musicians played all night long, and food was plentiful. As with every social occasion in a courtesan house, "burning the road" was fraught with obligations. Guests understood that they must attend and finance these festive displays in order to remain in good standing, give a courtesan face, and win sexual access to her; courtesans understood that they must bring in rich guests in order to remain valuable to the madam. For this reason, observed a 1891 guide, "at times like this, courtesans who do not have many wealthy guests are as anxious and sorrowful as if some great disaster had occurred."[198]

Other house rituals also combined holiday observance with moneymaking. At the three major festivals, courtesans served special foods to their customers: loquats and sticky-rice dumplings for the Dragon Boat Festival, moon cakes and fresh lotus root at Mid-Autumn, snacks such as pig's feet and deep-fried fish at all three holidays. For meals on such occasions, the courtesan was expected to pay gratuities to the cook and servants, then seek the same from her guests. Attendance at such a meal could cost anywhere from twenty to seventy yuan, and a customer who hosted a banquet during the holiday season paid twice the regular price.[199] During the first two weeks of the lunar New Year, courtesans also provided a special fruit plate to regular customers. In the late Qing the platter was presented with a flourish by male servants wearing red-tasseled hats who uttered auspicious phrases; later this ceremony fell into disuse. The substantial amount of money that customers paid for this platter was divided between the madam, the courtesan, and all the house servants. The platter and other New Year's gratuities made a holiday visit so expensive that all but the richest customers tried to stay away. Absent guests were derisively known as the "lords of the sixteenth" because they would reappear in the brothels only on the sixteenth day of the first lunar month.[200]

One famous observance conducted only in *yao er* houses was the Chrysanthemum Festival, held every autumn since the late nineteenth century. In the central courtyard of the brothel, workers piled up several hundred dishes of chrysanthemums to form a mountain, framed by rocks and hills made of blue and green paper. They also fashioned human figures of chrysanthemums and grass, and constructed an arch of flowers outside the main gate. During the festival, which lasted two months, banquets took place outside at the foot of the chrysanthemum mountain rather than in the rooms of the *yao er* courtesans. Wealthy men who would normally find it embarrassing to enter a *yao er* house took pride in hosting banquets at such places during the festival, reserving a night far in advance. These patrons in turn invited *changsan* courtesans to sing and accompany at drinking. A banquet at this time consisted of five tables: four for human guests and one in the middle with people and animals made of chrysanthemums. A single event would net the *yao er* house more than one hundred yuan.[201]

If some of these rituals were closely associated with lucrative services to guests, others appear to have been performed solely by or for the residents of courtesan houses. In the late nineteenth century, itinerant troupes of storytellers were hired to perform ten-day cycles of Buddhist retribution tales for courtesans. Other groups chanted religious texts of a syncretic nature, which incorporated Buddhist and Daoist elements, when a courtesan was ill or had a birthday.[202] On the first and fifteenth day of each lunar month, prostitutes went to a number of Shanghai temples to burn incense.[203] On the afternoon of New Year's Day, courtesans burned incense at the Hong Miao temple on Nanjing Road in the International Settlement, wearing red gowns hemmed with golden bells and riding in horse-drawn carriages.[204]

One temple that initially was frequented by pheasant streetwalkers and flower-smoke-room opium prostitutes, but that later became popular with *changsan* and *yao er* courtesans as well, was the temple of the Pissing Bodhisattva (*saniao pusa*), actually a shrine built into a wall on Yanghang Street in the Xiao Dongmen Wai area. The unusual name, one guide explained, derived from the odor emanating from a nearby public urinal:

> Every day until nightfall red candles burn, altar incense lingers in the air, and male and female believers go there to respectfully burn incense and prostrate themselves [*koutou*]. There are many of these. But business at the neighboring urinal is too good. So stink and fragrance blend mistily. Passersby smell an unusual smell that is both stinky and fragrant.

The place was reportedly cherished by prostitutes because of a local legend:

> It is said that this bodhisattva was formerly a brothel customer who did not begrudge paying ten thousand pieces of gold at a throw as tips to singers. Later his money was used up and his clothing was tattered. He did not have the face to return home, and hanged himself and died here. After he died, several prostitutes who had received money from him remembered with fond regret the bodhisattva who tired himself out in official duties, with no release until death. They all mourned their lost friend, and together they carved a temple for him in the corner of a wall as a memorial. Now most popular courtesans come together on the first and fifteenth day of the lunar month to burn incense. They say that if they burn incense, the sex business will be good. Also, low-class prostitutes, if they have no customers on a given day, will come the following day to burn incense and pray silently. It may sound strange, but after they pray and return home, customers appear. Because of this the incense business in front of the Pissing Bodhisattva has remained brisk until the present, with no decline.[205]

These collective rituals were explicitly dedicated to improving a courtesan's business and that of her house.

In addition, courtesans undertook a number of individual rituals to guide their business decisions or improve their prospects. They practiced a form of divination, burning incense while asking about their future, inquiring when a customer would visit, or pondering a move to another courtesan house.[206] They scrupulously observed a number of taboos. Some of these were clearly connected to questions of prosperity: it was forbidden to snuff a candle that had been lit to the god of wealth before it had burned down, or to talk to a customer while on the way to and from the temple.[207] Others were more obscure: a prostitute answering a call at another courtesan house, for instance, was not permitted to urinate there, no matter how urgent her discomfort.[208] Seasoned customers of the courtesan houses also knew that they should avoid certain types of behavior. Practices that were regarded as damaging to the business included snooping in the house's account books, placing chopsticks on top of one's bowl after eating, standing on the threshold, resting one's chin in one's hand, walking barefoot, breaking the vinegar pot, presenting a courtesan with a belt or a mirror, talking to prostitutes who were burning incense to the gods, and laughing at any of the house's religious rituals.[209]

Most of the sources that described courtesan houses were intended as guides to correct behavior for patrons; these guides established knowledge and attention to detail as two characteristics of successful masculinity. As a genre, guidebooks described and prescribed the ritualized self-presentation required of all participants in the social world of the courtesan house. As many of these practices were disappearing in the twentieth century, they reappeared in guidebook accounts—no longer as directions for correct behavior, but rather as instances of nostalgia for the world such rituals had once held in place.

Yet the guides can be read in a number of other registers as well. They indicate that the positions of madams, servants, courtesans, and child courtesans-in-training differed from house to house and across the span of a courtesan's career. A madam could be an aging ex-courtesan with a retinue of adopted daughters, a shrewd businesswoman renting out rooms in a great hall house, a beleaguered employer of an unpopular but expensive courtesan, an abusive procurer of young girls, or a number of combinations and permutations of all of these. Similarly, a courtesan could be a closely owned and controlled property or a calculating entrepreneur. Women servants, superficially subservient to the courtesan, might also be her chief creditors and wield substantial power over both her and her madam.

Male servants, in spite of the sexual innuendo surrounding them, appear to have had dead-end jobs and relatively low status in *changsan* houses. The careers of all the women—from sold women to madam to *daidang* maidservant—were far more variable. With strategy and luck, a woman could free herself from pawn or purchase, start her own house, or bankroll a rising star and earn substantial interest. Most improvements in status, however, required money, and it was usually through a relationship with a doting and wealthy customer—or through managing such relationships as a madam or "banker" maid—that such resources were acquired. The possibilities and perils of such relationships for both courtesan and customer are detailed in the next two chapters.

CHAPTER 4

Affairs of the Heart

When Westerners who lived in or studied treaty-port Shanghai wrote about courtesans, what struck them was the absence of a visible sexuality as they knew it. In his 1929 master's thesis for the University of Chicago, the sociologist James Wiley explained to his Western readers that Chinese courtesans were trained musicians and opera performers, "singing classical songs for which they have taken a long and difficult training. . . . [S]o skilled are they that in Shanghai they often have the term S'en Sen [*xiansheng*] or "teacher" applied to them."[1] Chinese men sought out courtesans in order to enjoy conversations in which their own cloistered wives could not engage: "A game of cards, a few light refreshments and the bantering back and forth of sprightly conversation constitute the evening's entertainment. Or, if other rewards are sought, they are in the background."[2] Wiley quotes a Chinese man as telling an American writer:

> We do not ask our wives to behave like sing song girls who are trained in
> the art of entertaining men and when we go to a sing song house, we do not
> brutally demand immediate physical satisfaction which seems to be the only
> interest of half the white men in the East. We ask that they give color and
> grace to a life that is infinitely boring . . . and they do.[3]

Other explicators of courtesan life for a Western audience stressed the reserved demeanor of these female performers,[4] and one warned that foreigners sometimes "[take] for granted their bewitching smile, think that the *rencontre* will not stop there, and are frequently surprised at the cool reception of any familiarity."[5] Charming, refined, subtle rather than bawdy in her sexuality, provider of a colorful interlude in the supposedly monotonous languor of Chinese life, the courtesan was a recurring component in Western representations of China as timeless, exotic, refined, and fundamentally *other* in the subtlety of its sexual desire.

Chinese writers, too, stressed the sexual inaccessibility of courtesans, but in their writings it was not exoticized. In Chinese texts, as we have seen, sexual intercourse was less important than the self-presentation of the customer, the way he defined himself through encounters in the courtesan house. An integral part of that self-presentation, however, depended on knowledge of sexual categories and rules of access.

Perhaps the most fundamental distinction in courtesan houses was that between "dry," "wet," and "beloved" customers. A "dry" customer (*gan xianghao*) might summon a courtesan out on call and drink with her, but whether because of "family values" (*jia jiao*), a sense of his own status, or fear of disease, he did not spend the night with her.[6] Brothel patois also included the phrase "to borrow a dry bed" (*jie gan pu*), which meant to stay overnight in a courtesan house after an evening of drinking and gambling, without sexual intercourse.[7] A "wet customer" (*shi xianghao*) was one with whom a courtesan had sexual relations (whether once or a hundred times), and from whom she demanded more financial involvement. A "beloved customer" (*en xianghao*) was one with whom the courtesan had both a sexual and an emotional bond.[8]

The division between "dry" and "wet" relationships was in part paralleled by a distinction between "small" and "big" courtesans. Small courtesans (*xiao xiansheng*) were virgins who were studying or had mastered the arts of singing, conversation, and hosting banquets, but who had not yet begun to have sexual relations with customers. Their virginal state was not expected to be permanent, and after defloration they would become big courtesans (*da xiansheng*).[9] Big courtesans were not sexually accessible on demand. The ultimate goal of access to a courtesan, particularly a famous one, was facilitated if the would-be patron was a liberal spender. Gifts to the prostitute herself were important, but just as crucial was the man's ability to bring business to the house. If he dropped by frequently with his friends to drink, if he hosted a banquet for his associates and paid without complaint for the food and the company of the women, he could request a night with the courtesan he favored.[10] It was, of course, also possible for a customer to have a "dry" relationship with a big courtesan.

Relationships between courtesans and patrons were usually described by men writing for an audience of customers, would-be customers, or reform-minded crusaders. Depending upon the point of view these men adopted, sexual relationships with courtesans were configured as pleasurable or dangerous for the courtesan, her customer, and the madam. "Dry" relationships were presented as relatively uncomplicated. "Wet" relationships, in contrast, were variously described as perilous for the customer, who was exposed to demands for money and gifts, and demeaning for the courtesan, who had to meet sexual demands whether the man interested her or not. Only the madam invariably appeared as the beneficiary here. Nor was a liaison with a "beloved customer" necessarily a story of happily-ever-after. The relationship might generate pressures that the customer take the courtesan as his concubine, creating conflicts between the man, his family, and his "beloved." Even if the man was happy, one guidebook suggested, his "beloved" might not be: a steady liaison with one customer limited a courtesan's appeal to other men, and she might even end up lending him money or going into debt.[11] For the madam and brothel servants, a "beloved" guest could present either the opportunity for a lucrative buyout or the loss of a courtesan's moneymaking capacity.[12]

These concerns made a sexual relationship between a courtesan and her customer anything but private. For the customer, sexual pleasure in a courtesan house entailed financial transactions with the madam, the servants, the accounting department, and the courtesan herself. Like the round of calls, tea, and banquets, it presented social situations that had to be dealt with properly in order to avoid ridicule and achieve satisfaction. For the courtesan, sexual contact with a customer enabled negotiations that could free her from a madam and provide her with substantial financial resources, but it could also frighten away other customers, ruin her business, and drain her savings. In some cases, a courtesan had the possibility of involvement with a lover who might or might not be a customer. For a courtesan a sexual liaison was fraught with problems of negotiation and strategizing, yet it offered a chance of control over her own time, income, and emotional life that was rare for her "respectable" sisters. Since all liaisons were described in the historical record from the perspective of customers or reformers, addressing their place in the lives of courtesans requires acts of risky historical imagination.

VIRGIN PROSTITUTES AND THE MADAM'S CONTROL

Of the sexual liaisons a courtesan might make in the course of her career, the one over which she had the least control was the first. The sale of her virginity to a wealthy customer was the culmination of years of investment and training, and the madam typically chose someone who could pay enough to allow a substantial return on that investment.

Chinese sources have relatively little to say about the training of young courtesans; perhaps they assumed that readers already knew or were not interested in the details. Young women who had been purchased or adopted by a madam at a young age were educated by hired tutors in chess, poetry, and music. They learned to write, to play the *pipa,* and to sing classical songs one phrase at a time.[13] In general, the madams treated these young women well, gave them enough to eat and wear, and made sure that they were strictly supervised by female servants. During the day the "daughters" of the madams dressed like any other girls in the narrow lanes off of Shanghai's main streets.

Only their habit of sleeping until noon, and the resplendent costumes they donned in the evening, distinguished them from the neighbors.[14] In some respects they appear to have been as sequestered as their counterparts who were being prepared for marriage to upper-class men. Madams in the higher-grade brothels took care that their virgin "daughters" did not go out unchaperoned; they worried about the girls, recalled a resident of one brothel district, "just like parents worried about their children." Courtesan-house owners did not want to risk a casual sexual encounter with a local hoodlum, or a love affair, and the loss of the lucrative first-night fee.[15] Within the house, a "family law of the brothels" was respected: male brothel servants were forbidden to have sexual relations with the young women. To do so was regarded as "no different from raping a woman of good family."[16] In a 1922 autobiographical sketch intended as a reformist attack on prostitution, a young courtesan portrayed this close supervision as virtual imprisonment:

> When business was busy, A Zhu [her adoptive mother] did not allow me to go to operas. When there was not much business, I could go to operas, but had to be accompanied (even going to temple, eating and going to the bathroom, always supervised).[17]

Once she reached early adolescence, the girl would begin work as a virgin courtesan. She was summoned out on call like her older "sisters," riding to restaurants or teahouses on the shoulders of male brothel servants. Her virginity was signaled by her hairstyle, which was that of an unmarried woman,[18] and the fact that she never made calls unaccompanied. An American sociologist in the 1920s imagined her experience as akin to the social whirl of a debutante:

> For the next four or five years they live a life of continual excitement. Her evenings and nights are busy flitting from place to place and from person to person. If a girl is popular she is on the go from late afternoon until late at night, making short calls at places of entertainment, stopping for a few minutes at the table or chair of friends.[19]

In spite of the breezy queen-of-the-prom tone of this description, a virgin prostitute had little control over the pace and personnel involved in her social schedule, and if she developed an attraction for a particular customer, the madam and maids watched her closely in order to prevent an unauthorized sexual encounter.[20] To guarantee that she brought in enough income to support herself and her attendants, some houses permitted customers to sleep with the virgin courtesan's maids, in return for banquet fees, gifts, and tips. Maids who performed this service were called "hit-bottom maids" (*dadi niangyi*); one account of Shanghai customs referred to them sardonically as a "necessity for sex maniacs" (*ji se er zhi xuyao pin*).[21]

For customers, the pleasures of spending time with virgin prostitutes were described in one guidebook as subtle but not incomprehensible. Perhaps a customer was interested in becoming the one to deflower a particular virgin—either paying for the privilege or stealing it. Perhaps he went to courtesan houses not to satisfy his physical desires, but to pass the time, smoke a bit of opium, and enjoy conversation and gambling. Virgin courtesans were usually attractive and suitable for such purposes. Nevertheless, the guidebook author concluded bluntly, spending time with such women was like "raising golden carp in a jar; they are just good to look at, not to eat."[22]

Many of the terms and rituals of a virgin courtesan's first sexual encounter resembled those of marriage. Daughters in most Chinese families had little to say about the choice of their marriage partner or the timing of the match. At marriage, they passed from the control of their natal families to the control of their husbands, who had claims upon their labor and their sexual and reproductive services. Similarly, prostitutes exercised no autonomy over when and to whom they would begin to sell their sexual services. A "daughter" in one of these houses was carefully groomed for her first night with a customer, which usually happened sometime after she turned fourteen. The occasion was variously known as "lighting the big candles" (*dian da lazhu*), "comb cage" (*shulong*, referring to the fact that a woman would change her hairstyle after she began sleeping with customers), "defloration" (*kaibao*; literally, "opening the calyx"), or, more graphically, "breaking the melon" (*pogua*). Like marriage, defloration was preceded by extensive negotiations between the purchaser and the adult who had authority over the young woman—in this case, the madam. The prospective deflowerer usually hosted several expensive banquets or gambling sessions in the brothel prior to beginning negotiations, thus establishing himself as a valued customer.[23] In addition, he supplied the woman with clothing and jewelry, and paid several hundred gold dollars to her biological or adoptive mother.[24] The occasion itself was a solemn one, again likened to marriage:

> This is the most memorable day of a woman's life; it is truly her time of marriage. People in the brothels regard the *shulong* ceremony as not inferior to [that of] marriage in a respectable house, with drinking from the nuptial cup on a beautiful day.[25]

It was customary for the courtesan house to invite musicians and to burn incense and candles. The male servants, ceremonially dressed, presented the virgin and her deflowerer with banquet dishes and formal congratulations.[26] In 1939, the total cost of defloration, with the required goods and festivities, was estimated at between five hundred and one thousand yuan.[27]

Given the financial importance of this transaction to the madam, the choice of partner was up to her. By the 1930s, adopting the critical tone of reform writings about prostitution, guidebooks routinely noted that virgin courtesans were seldom pleased with the wealthy older men selected by the madams. Defloration "uses money to triumph over sexual desire. It is inhumane," commented one guidebook,[28] while another noted that a courtesan usually intensely disliked the man who deflowered her, and would get through the occasion by "blowing out the lamp, gritting her teeth, closing her eyes, and bearing the pain." Waxing eloquent, the author continued:

> When a woman has her "melon broken," even if the two are in love she doesn't understand what is interesting about it, and it is as tasteless as chewing a candle. Not to mention a situation where she is forced by money and threatened by the madam into participating. . . . This is one of the least interesting and human-hearted things in the world, and yet many rich and lascivious "evil and arrogant" people love to seek pleasure in this way. . . . Although she cannot but go through the motions of waiting on him, in her heart she wishes that he would instantly contract typhoid, go out the door, and drop dead [*qiao bianzi,* "curl up his queue"].[29]

The cartoon accompanying this vivid description showed a woman dressed in chemise, slip, and slippers, holding a watermelon and looking away in distaste as an older, bald, portly, grinning man cut into the melon with a cleaver.[30] (See figure 15.) The coercive nature of this encounter, warned the guidebooks, made intercourse with a virgin an expensive and unwise investment because "from the point of view of the need for sex, [it] is actually not worth the cost," and because the women, resentful of men "who used money as a tool to trample on them," would end the relationship as soon as possible.[31] Thus guidebooks, whose purpose was to describe and ease access to courtesans, ended by condemning sexual relationships whose basis was money rather than emotion. In doing so they acknowledged, if only indirectly, that courtesans themselves might possess sexual desire that was thwarted by their enforced liaisons with older customers.

The historical sources were not explicit about why a man would want to pay substantial amounts of money to have sexual intercourse with an inexperienced, frightened, and often hostile woman. Nothing was said about the erotic pleasures entailed in such an encounter. Desire for youthful sexual partners was apparently a factor; it was the custom for prostitutes to tell customers that they were sixteen years old, regardless of their age. One madam explained that they felt constrained to answer in this way because their guests all wanted sixteen-year-olds.[32] The pleasure of possessing a closely guarded object was at best ephemeral, since the deflowerer was not laying claim to the woman's reproductive labor or to permanent rights of access. Only one motivation for seeking out virgin courtesans was directly articulated in the guidebooks: sleeping with a virgin was thought by some, particularly northerners, to be an auspicious act that could banish disaster or bring good luck. "Striking the red," an apparent reference to the blood of defloration, was said to reverse business losses and guarantee prosperity.[33] Older men reportedly also believed that it could replenish their vitality.[34]

MATURE COURTESANS: ACCESS AND CHOICE

Once a courtesan was definitively and by general agreement no longer a virgin or a recent virgin, sexual access to her entailed winning her favor as well as the madam's approval. Nonvirgin courtesans might be sexually active, but they were not available on demand. Difficulty of access was an important part of their self-definition, and it was crucial as well to the self-understanding of their customers, who saw themselves as members of a courtesan-house elite by virtue of their ability to achieve intimacy with well-known and much-sought women.[35]

The conditional nature of sexual access sharply distinguished *changsan* courtesans from lower-class Chinese prostitutes and from reportedly lascivious Western prostitutes. A 1929 article in *Crystal* described American prostitutes, apparently in the United States, as "doing business only in lascivious physical desire, like the salt-pork shops and jumping old bugs." American prostitutes were said to be meticulous about hygiene, and strong and healthy enough to sleep with a dozen men per day, "like a wheel in motion." They were further said to routinely smear lipstick on their genitalia, which were darkened from overuse.[36]

It was precisely in counterdistinction to these explicitly described vulgar practices that twentieth-century Chinese courtesans were defined by their admirers. Exclusivity defined them, and by extension their customers, as more civilized and refined. Among *yao er* courtesans, a customer who called on a woman once and then expected to spend the night was disliked ("a prostitute with a bit of status won't consent"), and a customer who had a single sexual encounter and never returned was considered to have violated a serious taboo.[37] Among *changsan,* a customer who prematurely blurted out a wish for intimacy was regarded as boorish or even mentally unbalanced.[38] *Changsan* who sold their sexual services for a direct fee reportedly did so only when business was bad, and were referred to as having two occupations: the proper *changsan* occupation of singing and social accompaniment, and the faintly disgraceful business of "selling themselves retail."[39]

For a *changsan* who was behaving as *changsan* were expected to behave, sexual intercourse was portrayed as the culmination of a protracted and somewhat mysterious process:

> The lofty ones among the Shanghai prostitutes do not lightly consent to
> spend the night. Yet there are also customers who without spending half a
> string of cash attain a night of love. Their achievement has its reasons . . .
> but if one asks about the Way of frequenting prostitutes, they will say that
> it cannot be clearly explained. The enlightened mind can understand it.[40]

Ironic references to the (Daoist) Way and the (Buddhist) enlightened mind aside, the sources do comment on the criteria by which a courtesan chose intimate favorites from among her customers. A late nineteenth-century guide suggested that, just as when a customer picked out a courtesan, good looks and youth were major criteria. Old and ugly customers were told that they would find themselves at a permanent disadvantage.[41]

This theme persisted in twentieth-century writings. A 1920 compilation of Qing anecdotes, for instance, told of a Guangxu-era courtesan named Dexian (Virtue Fairy) who disdained the attentions of a rich customer named Jin, most likely because "his face was dark and pockmarked, and his appearance was truly ugly." She agreed that he could stay overnight, only to break her promise when a guest arrived. Unmoved by Jin's offer to pay her twenty taels of silver in "cosmetics fees," she told him to return another day. But when he did so, he found that she had just arranged to spend the night with a man ambiguously described as a "beautiful youth, a handsome and attractive beau of the immoral world" (*mei shao nian, pianpian zhuoshi jia gongzi*). After taking only one look at this young man, Jin understood why Dexian was not interested in him. Telling her that he felt as though he were "awakening from a dream of luxury," he offered her additional tips for the servants in addition to the fee for spending the night. Dexian took the money and asked for an additional four yuan of "flirting money" (*niaojin*). He refused; she insisted; he finally lost his temper, saying: "You pledge your love to another, yet chase me for profits as small as the head of a fly."[42] Significantly, Dexian's madam was compelled to offer a feast as an apology to Jin, but the story does not say that she could compel Dexian to have sexual relations with him.[43]

Stories like this led to the saying "The sisters like good lookers; the madams like big spenders."[44] A 1939 guidebook was even more explicit about the attraction courtesans felt for comely young men (known in Shanghai slang as *xiao bailian*, "small white faces"):

> Another type likes to flirt with good-looking young men, and if they go out
> on a call and see one, their feet are like an iron mold and they refuse to
> move no matter what, flirting until they get what they want.

"What they want," in this case, was explicitly delineated: a sexual relationship.[45] And although the guidebook's point was that courtesans were treacherous and flighty in their attachments, this description also suggests that courtesans exercised choice over customers, and that they both felt and acted upon some degree of sexual desire.

Good looks, however, were not the only requirement stressed in guidebooks on how to win the attentions of a mature courtesan. Money was also a factor. Mature courtesans were more expensive than virgins to summon out on call because they were experienced, attentive, and sought out by many intimate customers.[46] To have one's way with a virginal courtesan, the guidebooks said, one had to be tricky. With big courtesans, one could be open and aboveboard about one's desires, but it was necessary to meet certain obligations: to drink or host parties on the first and fifteen of the month, to receive and pay for special dishes on holidays, to pay hat money at the winter solstice, fan money at the summer solstice, and fruit-plate money at the lunar New Year. Stinginess was not advisable here: "If you evade these, you will undermine what you are trying to do. It is not permissible not to give her face."[47]

If the first requirement of frequenting a courtesan was to enhance the income of her house and her standing within it, the second necessity was to present her with gifts that went into her own coffers rather than those of the house. Popular courtesans did not easily consent to keep a guest overnight, and their preconditions might include several gold bracelets or a diamond ring, as well as payments for gambling and drinking and twenty to forty yuan in tips. If an especially rich man desired an especially famous courtesan, he might find himself paying a thousand pieces of gold for the privilege.[48]

Even more disconcerting for the customer, money was not the only variable. As one guidebook lamented, "Many are those who spend ten thousand pieces of gold and never get to touch her."[49] A 1932 guide to Shanghai, in a section entitled "Key to Brothel Hopping" (*Piao de menjing*), elaborated on this theme. Addressing the customer directly, it said that after hosting parties and becoming a regular guest, "the toad dreams of eating the swan's flesh. Having completed your duty, you enjoy certain rights. This should be the natural order of things. But there is no fixed rule about this matter." It explained that some patrons could not "get into the water" (that is, have sexual relations) even after hosting several expensive banquets, while others "tasted the flavor" without hosting even one. The key, explained the author, lay in the behavior of the patron. He should be careful to exhibit not only wealth, but good taste in dress. He should go to the courtesan house in the company of powerful male companions, so that the courtesan would not dare to play tricks on him. If he was "foolish when appropriate and serious when appropriate," even the most popular prostitute would eventually become a "prisoner of war at [his] feet."[50] Another author elaborated upon this point, saying that the two key words were "small" and "leisure." "Small" meant paying attention to details, such as helping her into her coat and seeing her off to the elevator (this particular account, published in 1939, incorporated both imported notions of chivalry and imported technology). "Leisure" meant making sure to see her every day so that the customer's attention to details and solicitiousness would make an impression on her. Otherwise, he was advised, his success at establishing a liaison would be based on money and power rather than love. If the woman had no faith in him, she would not love him, and it was advisable to avoid such a liaison. Here, as with virgin courtesans, the customer's goal was not merely sexual access, but the development of "mutual love," which was described as "full of flavor."[51]

As reform-minded portraits of courtesan lives appeared in the 1930s, a subtle shift occurred in the representation of courtesans. Still portrayed as women who had an almost charismatic ability to "work" a customer and convince him to spend his money, they were nevertheless seen as not motivated by money alone. Rather, they were presented as emotionally damaged goods who were desperate for love:

> Society despises prostitutes; at least, prostitutes give society the impression of being "base" (*jian*). Prostitutes themselves feel this if they have spent several years in the "wind and dust" [world of prostitution]. The prostitutes written about here are not those who use their sexual organs alone to make a living. They are a so-called high-status, relatively elite group: those who use their language and singing to make a living, the so-called ones who sell their mouths and not their bodies. . . .
>
> [If you, the customer, win a courtesan's true love] she will give you a great deal of emotional and material help, and furthermore this help in actuality far surpasses that which ordinary women in the family can give.
>
> Unlike ordinary good wives and wise mothers, they do not take money seriously. For them, money is merely something used to bring pleasure. They are happy to spend lavishly. . . . They need to make a living, but aside from material things, it is hard for them to make up for the emotional deficiencies in their lives. As for sex, they have ample opportunities to meet this need, just as a rich man has ample opportunity to dispose of his riches. Therefore, contrary to what one might think, they are indifferent to it. . . .
>
> What person is without a soul? The souls of prostitutes who have fallen into the courtesan houses are more troubled and depressed than those of other people. It is just that they conceal it more deeply, that's all.[52]

A customer who read these guidebooks carefully would be told how to gain and keep a courtesan's favor through the skillful deployment of financial and emotional rewards. But regardless of his money and good looks, the guidebooks warned him that a mature courtesan could match him in knowledge of human desires and ability to manipulate others to her own advantage.

Such accounts tell us little, of course, about what kinds of affective or sexual ties courtesans might have sought. They are quite informative, however, about what 1930s guidebook writers and readers found desirable: affirmation of their own savoir faire, and a sexual liaison "flavored" by strong mutual feelings. The fact that money was often the medium of access to such emotions, acknowledged elsewhere in the guidebooks, was here downplayed.

Curiously, in the guidebooks sexual acts themselves commanded none of the poetic language characteristic of novels. Late-nineteenth-century sources spoke not of sex but of deep mutual feelings, expressed in cultured correspondence between a courtesan and her customer.[53] They described the subtle ways in which a courtesan might express her devotion to a particular man: by giving him a scarf or jewelry case, wrapping a strand of his hair as a ring around her finger, or sending one of her attendants to substitute for her in making calls while she secretly went to see her lover (a so-called stolen call).[54] Nostalgic twentieth-century gossip columns recounted tales like the one of a love-struck customer who wrote more than one hundred letters to the courtesan he desired.[55] The language of these sources sometimes gently mocked sexual activity between customers and courtesans with phrases like "frozen from top to bottom" (*lian di dong*), which meant to spend several nights in a row together, or "quilt wind" (*beitou feng*), which meant to catch a cold from a sexual partner.[56] Guidebooks also explicated some of the crude sexual slang employed among twentieth-century customers. Pursuit of a prostitute in the 1930s, for instance, was known as "attaching to a shell" (*daqiaozi*, where "attach" also meant "copulate") or "nailing the tail end" (*dingshao*).[57] Yet even these suggestive references did not speak directly of sexual encounters. Given the richly developed genre of explicit erotic writing in late imperial China, this silence cannot be explained as part of a more general cultural reticence.[58] Rather, it seems related to the genres of guidebooks and tabloids, whose writers concerned themselves with questions of nostalgia and status anxiety more than with physical pleasure.

Both themes were evident in the rare instances when sources did refer directly to the sexual prowess of courtesans. A late-nineteenth-century guidebook mourned the fact that the sexual skills of courtesans, like their literary and musical skills, had declined in recent times.[59] A 1917 guidebook went further, implying that in contrast to the situation in western Europe and China's own past, sexual knowledge and sexual desire were not valued among Chinese courtesans. Under the heading "Charming Language of the Courtesan Houses," the guidebook printed the following story:

> In the early Qing, before he rebelled, Geng Jingzhong lived luxuriously and lasciviously in Fujian. He had a female servant called Linzhi, who was suddenly possessed by a fox spirit and liked to be close with men. Geng got angry and ordered twenty young men under his command to strip naked, pursue her, and have intercourse with her in turn. After she had encountered each of them once, Linzhi was still tireless. Geng laughed and said, "A trench can be filled, but this woman cannot grow tired of men." I told this story to my friend and said, "If she were in the courtesan houses, she would have a gutter reputation [*fangming saodi*; literally, "her professional name would sweep the floor"]." My friend said, "I have been to Western Europe. I saw that those who made their living from skin and flesh there all had secret picture books in their mirror boxes, and what went on between pillow and mat was extremely unrestrained. If a prostitute was capable of this, she was considered a leader, and many customers came to her, regarding her as famous. Otherwise, her doorway was cold and deserted." His meaning was that people value prostitutes for their sexiness [*yin*]. If a prostitute is not sexy, she has nothing with which to engage in prostitution. His words sound reasonable.[60]

Implied in this anecdote was that Chinese courtesans were no match in erotic knowledge or appetite either for early Qing servant girls or for Western prostitutes. In most guidebook writing, sexual inaccessibility was a sign of refined civilization, but here lack of sexual interest marked courtesans as effete and lacking in vitality, a critique often made of Chinese culture more generally in the 1910s and 1920s.

In the guidebooks, sexual intercourse was referred to variously as "staying with an intimate" (*luo xianghao*), "falling into the water" (*luoshui*), "a true melting of the soul" (*zhenge xiaohun*), or "turning the idea" (*zhuan niantou*).[61] A regular sexual relationship with a courtesan was presented as a desirable goal, but the bodily enactment of desire was not part of the guidebook discourse. Rather than providing pleasure through explicit erotic description, guidebooks briskly laid out for customers, in language late twentieth-century readers of self-help manuals would find familiar, instructions for assessing their chances of success. A customer was advised to be realistic about his own appeal in relationship to the courtesan's popularity.[62] If a customer concluded, after rigorous self-evaluation, that his qualifications would not enable him to win the woman he desired, the advice books were ready with alternative strategies. He could, for instance, attempt to "light a cold stove" (*shao leng zao*)—visit a courtesan whose business was not thriving and who was apt to be grateful and responsive to his attentions.[63] (Of course, guidebooks advised, it would also be prudent to investigate *why* her business was in trouble.)[64] Shifting the metaphor, one author called this practice "burning incense in a desolate temple," where the neglected bodhisattva would notice even a modest offering:

> Usually, with well-known courtesans and attendants, if you tactlessly try to "turn the idea," they keep their eyes on the ceiling, and it's hard to get their attention. With less well known courtesans and attendants whose business is terribly slow, if you go to light the cold stove you need have no fear that they will deceive you even if your "face" and methods are not up to snuff.[65]

This principle applied not only to sexual contact, but to summoning a woman out on call or calling on her for tea. "Cold stove" courtesans would have more time to talk with a customer, whereas more popular women would quickly leave to make their round of calls, leaving the hapless customer to "fool around with the Jiangbei [Subei; that is, low-class] maids who clean the rooms. How uninteresting!"[66]

Another strategy for increasing his chances of sexual access was for a customer to take up with one of the courtesan's attendants, whose status was less exalted and whose services were less expensive. An attendant knew the techniques of self-presentation and graceful entertaining. Like a courtesan, she could be expected to give her customer face before his male companions. If a customer spent the night with her, he did not have to tip the servants (since she was one of them) as he would with a courtesan. She would, however, expect him to give her gifts and to host banquets, particularly if her contract entitled her to a share of the house's seasonal earnings. If he found experienced and high-class attendants to be too demanding, the less discriminating customer was advised to patronize the young maids who cleaned the room. They might be receptive to his blandishments, he was told, because, surrounded as they were by the luxurious possessions of the courtesans, they longed for beautiful clothing and jewelry of their own.[67]

If a customer was willing to take high risks in order to enjoy high returns, he could attempt to establish a sexual relationship with the madam. The madam's customer could eat what he wanted, do what he pleased, and never worry about incurring her ire, as the courtesan's customers might, if he smoked an extra cigarette or stayed an extra fifteen minutes. A customer who had intimate relations with the madam enjoyed the status of a boss, and everyone, from the courtesans to the lowest maids, would do his bidding. Furthermore, a madam had money and could help out a customer who needed a spot loan. Many of the same advantages would accrue from a relationship with a madam who also acted as a courtesan in a residence-type brothel. The only problem with such women was that they had to make calls and manage a business, and had limited time to spend with intimate customers.[68]

A customer's obligations increased once he had successfully "stayed with an intimate." Aside from tips to servants and madam, he was expected to provide a continual flow of gifts to the woman herself and continue to bring his friends to the house for drinking, eating, and gambling.[69] Some of these expenses, notably the endless round of tips, could be avoided by taking the courtesan to a hotel rather than staying with her in the brothel. Initially this practice, known as "opening a room" (*kai fangjian*), was considered disreputable, but it became more widespread after the Municipal Council forbade brothels to keep guests overnight in the 1920s.[70] At first, brothel patrons regarded the new prohibition as an empty bureaucratic regulation, but they soon found out that the police intended to enforce it through periodic raids. At the same time, Shanghai's hotel sector grew larger and more elaborate, with rooms "even more lavish and beautiful than the chambers of prostitutes." This allowed most sexual encounters between courtesans and their customers to move to hotels. A waggish comment in one guidebook made sly use of the fact that the International Settlement was also known as the Special Municipality:

> Brothels don't permit men and women to stay together, yet in a hotel one can truly fall in love. This is truly contradictory to the point of being funny. Things that happen in the concessions are all according to foreign rationality. It cannot be explained using a Chinese mind. If the means of organization were not special, it would not be a "special municipality" worthy of the name.[71]

The gradual move of sexual encounters out of the courtesan house contributed to its decline as a comprehensive institution for social and sexual services. At the same time, the move to hotels also isolated sexual relations from the web of social and financial obligations that had previously characterized courtesan-house encounters. Meeting a courtesan in a hotel room for sex differed little from taking a lower-class prostitute there, and guidebook writers often mentioned such encounters in conjunction with a more general rise in hotel-based adulterous affairs.[72]

Actors and Other Lovers

Even the most romantic liaison with a customer generally involved some modicum of financial calculation on the part of a courtesan. Lovers, in contrast, might not overlap with clientele or even with husbands. When they chose sexual partners for love, rather than material advantage, courtesans were said to prefer actors or their own drivers to well-heeled literati and merchants. This was true even if their business was flourishing and they had many prominent customers.[73] Lin Daiyu, the famous courtesan named after the heroine of the Qing novel *Dream of the Red Chamber,* in her late forties began a liaison with an opera singer who was not yet twenty, laughingly telling friends, "I take it as a drug for my health."[74] The social status of theater performers, like that of courtesans, had historically been regarded as "base" (*jian*). Whether it was their shared stigma, the fact that actors were well-known and popular figures, or their fashionable taste in dress, cigarettes, and brandy, courtesans found them attractive enough that such relationships became a standard theme in the guidebooks.[75] One memoirist quotes a courtesan as explaining:

> We have sunk into the wind and dust [that is, have become prostitutes]. We have known many people. Only someone with the same tastes and inclinations is worthy of making a mutual pledge of body and heart. We are not like the average rich customers of modern times. Although perhaps they have rather an illustrious rank in the nation, and lay special claim to riches and honor, unfortunately if you look at their external appearance, you will dislike their money-grubbing air, and if you look at their inner quality, you will dislike their [character unclear]. They are frequently inferior to actors. Therefore we can crave their money and silks, but cannot stand to unite our hearts with them.[76]

Actors and drivers were also said to be even tempered and much nicer to the courtesans than paying customers.[77]

Taking an actor as a lover (*pin xizi*) was derided by some guidebooks as shameful,[78] but it was also said that courtesans who did not form relationships with opera singers or drivers would not become famous.[79] If the gossip columns and guidebooks are any indication, the practice was widespread in the early twentieth century: one Beijing newspaper in 1918 published a list of famous courtesans, including the Shanghai luminaries Hu Baoyu, Lin Daiyu, Lu Lanfen, and Zhang Shuyu (see chapter 6), who had taken actors as lovers.[80] Another tabloid list of forty-seven such liaisons showed some courtesans as having more than one relationship with an actor.[81] A local wag commented on this situation: "There is a saying that most of the famous mountains of the world are occupied by monks. Today one can modify this to say that most of the famous courtesans of Shanghai are occupied by actors."[82]

Whereas courtesans deployed considerable skill to induce their regular customers to spend money on them and their house, the mark of their relationship with actors and other lovers was that the women spent money on the men, giving them expensive presents and even borrowing money to clear their debts. This was known as "raising a small devil" (*yang xiaogui*). Guidebooks warned customers not to spend money in courtesan houses where the women were involved with actors, or they might find that their largesse was lining the pockets of other men.[83] One courtesan was reportedly embarrassed when she gave her lover a piece of fabric that a customer had given her. The lover had a garment made, wore it publicly, and was seen by the customer, who angrily withdrew his attentions from the courtesan.[84] The famous courtesan Zhang Shuyu also liked to dress her carriage driver in silk clothes with colorful trim and a woolen hat with gold braid, leading to rumors that she was in love with him. Upset by the gossip, she then asked him to dress more plainly, warning that otherwise the police might haul him in for impropriety in dress.[85]

Guidebooks and tabloid authors found these liaisons alternately disturbing and amusing. One writer saw in them a chance for courtesans to even the score with men: "[T]hey often are toys for men, playthings, and so if they have some money they want to take revenge, and find several young and beautiful men to use as playthings."[86] Here the power attributed to courtesans in social encounters and choice of customers reached an extreme. In these representations the women were not only controlling their choice of sexual partner—an option that no respectable woman could claim—but were using that occasion to deprive the chosen men of their autonomy, in effect feminizing them. "Small devils" were described as materially comfortable, but extremely constrained in their personal freedom: they could have no ambitions of their own, had to show up on time each night to meet the courtesan after her round of calls, and appeared to be virtual slaves of their women keepers.[87] One sardonic tabloid account described a self-employed courtesan named Wendi Laosi who was constantly accompanied in public by a tall, handsome, athletic college student. He followed her every instruction, waiting quietly beside her while she played cards, sitting silently in a corner while she smoked. Wendi Laosi's fellow courtesans referred to him as the "aide-de-camp," saying that the chief administrator (*zhuzheng*) of a courtesan house needed an aide just as China's head of state did.[88] Each of these accounts focused on the inversion of "normal" power relationships that occurred when a woman paid for and controlled a man, presenting a direct if unstated challenge to conventional gender arrangements.

Another type of liaison in courtesan houses, conventionally designated as an "oddity" (*guai*), was sexual relationships between courtesans. Until Western sexological terminology came into use in the Republican period, the common term for such relationships between women was not "same-sex love" (*tongxing lian* or *tongxing ai*) but "mirror polishing" (*mo jingzi*). A 1935 slang dictionary explained that the term derived from the old custom of using a smooth copper mirror to polish another copper mirror, with no protrusions on either surface. Sex between women was also known as "spreading out slippery noodles" (*tan fenpi*).[89] Among the early-twentieth-century courtesans whose lives are delineated in short biographical sketches was one known as Hong Nainai (Grandma Hong), described as a *ren yao*, which can mean variously a human devil, a person with abnormal sexual characteristics, or one who is fond of adornment. Hong lived in Enqing Lane in the International Settlement. It was said that her guests were few but her spending lavish; one account added cryptically that "her supply is taken from among women, not from among males."[90] More explicit accounts explained that Hong was "very seldom intimate with men, but she likes to be on intimate terms with women," dubbing her the "leader of the mirror-polishing party." It added that Hong had relationships not only with other courtesans, but also with concubines and daughters of rich families, all of whom came to regard men as a "nuisance."[91] As with the other sexual relationships entered into by courtesans, little is said directly about the emotions or sexual practices associated with these liaisons, but several sources mention intense possessiveness and jealous quarrels between women who were sexually involved. One source names Hong Nainai as an arbiter of such disputes, adding that other women accepted her authority.[92] It was also reported that members of the "Hong party" had begun inviting small audiences, for a fee, to watch them have sexual relations at various restaurants.[93] It seems unlikely that courtesans engaged in floor shows of any variety, although public performances of lesbian sexual acts by prostitutes (featuring a dildo stuffed with wood-ear fungus, which swelled up when soaked in hot water) were described as an attraction in 1930s hotels.[94]

The production and circulation of stories about the noncommercial sex partners of courtesans were themselves a kind of voyeurism. These stories seem to have been intended mostly to give readers a vicarious sense of being in the know about the intimate lives of famous courtesans and customers. But they can also be read as delineating an arena within which a woman could choose her own companions—space most definitely not open to women outside of prostitution. The choices to which commentators devoted attention were those in which the "normal" male prerogative of initiating and controlling a sexual encounter was most attenuated. Every encounter of a customer with a courtesan contained within it the possibility that she would reject him. But stories of liaisons with actors, drivers, "small devils," and other women went beyond rejection to destabilize the gendering of power altogether.

MISTRESSES, CONCUBINES, AND EXIT STRATEGIES

The fickle, autonomous, sexually aware courtesan, who knew what kind of lover she wanted and actively pursued him, had a less sinister discursive twin: the loyal, loving, faithful courtesan. Stories about such women had many variations. An 1870s story reprinted in 1920 told of Lin Aiguan, an orphan sold to a brothel by her relatives. Described in terms befitting her respectable family origins ("gentle and serious in style, of few words, and not fond of adornment"), she fell in love with a customer named Yong and secretly became engaged to him, although he was too poor to buy her out. Several years later, Yong's friend Chen took an interest in Lin Aiguan and had the madam order her to have sexual relations with him. When they entered her bedroom, the story goes, she drew a knife and knelt before him, saying:

> "I have an unlucky fate. It does not matter whether I live or die. The reason I have just barely managed to stay alive is because although I belong to the smoke and flowers [prostitution], I still admire chastity and loyalty. You have many beautiful women at home [literally, "at home you can embrace flowers and hug willows"]; you can find a beautiful one anywhere. Why do you force me to entertain you? If you want to defile my body, please defile my blade first." Her speech finished, she put the knife on her dressing table. Chen guffawed and said, "I knew you were in love with Mr. Yong, but he has no power to succeed. What can you do?" Lin said, "If we do not succeed, I will carry on our union in death. Otherwise, why would I carry this blade?" Mr. Chen was moved, saying, "You understand Yong. How could I not understand him?" He left abruptly and brought Yong back to Lin's residence that very night. As he left the residence he gave two gold bars to the madam, saying, "Lin does not belong to you. Give her up and take the gold. You should look at the situation. If you don't agree, look at this blade!" The madam had no other choice but to give her to Yong.[95]

In other stories, one loyal courtesan nurses her lover through a bout of tuberculosis, then changes her name after his death so that her return to courtesan life will not besmirch his family reputation.[96] Another refuses to sleep with a rich businessman, although she is forced to host banquets for him, but exchanges declarations of patience and constancy with her poor yet appreciative lover.[97] In each of these cases, the virtuous courtesan is emotionally constant, knows her (lowly) place, and is as chaste as possible under the circumstances.

If the courtesan was rendered less threatening when she practiced standard female virtues, her potential for danger was even more contained when she stated her desire to become the concubine of a respectable man. Capsule biographies of courtesans in guidebooks and the mosquito papers frequently included a statement that a particular courtesan did not wish to be a prostitute and wanted to find a lover and become a family dependent.[98]

Principal wives were usually acquired for a man by his family on the basis of matched backgrounds, with the aim of enhancing family assets and status. A courtesan could not contribute much on any of these counts. Concubines, in contrast, were usually picked by the men themselves with an eye to sex, romantic attraction, and good conversation, as well as the production of male heirs. Given her background and history, a courtesan could not aspire to the status of principal wife, but the terminology used for concubinage was virtually identical to that for marriage.[99] Only one commonly used term, "to follow the respectable [partner]" (*congliang*), indicated that a courtesan was not herself coming from a respectable natal home. For wealthy men, choosing a courtesan as concubine was "not considered at all disgraceful," according to a foreign observer writing in 1871. Even high government officials, who were legally forbidden to consort with courtesans, entered such arrangements.[100] (Attempting to explain this practice to a Western readership, one foreign commentator invoked the Western notion of companionate marriage. He argued that since courtesans who became concubines knew more of the world than sequestered principal wives, they were "logically and spiritually nearer the type of a foreign wife than his first wife."[101])

An interim arrangement that might lead to a more permanent union for a courtesan was for her to be "rented" by a single patron. The man would pay a monthly fee to the madam, and would either visit the woman regularly or take up residence in the brothel. Alternatively, he might install the woman in quarters of her own. Men who could not yet afford to redeem a prostitute's pawn pledge or buy her outright, or who were not yet prepared to do so, made use of this arrangement. In the late 1920s, monthly rental fees could run as high as fifty yuan.[102] Some accounts suggest that courtesans who had been rented by a wealthy man felt satisfied with the arrangement, since it left them with more leisure time (and possibly more income) than did a regular courtesan schedule.[103] Renting, like concubinage, assured a man more or less exclusive access to a particular woman,[104] and reduced the possibility that he would be humiliated by a rival or rejected by the courtesan herself.

A man who wished to acquire a courtesan as concubine had to pay a "body price" to the madam (in the case of a woman who had been pawned or sold to the courtesan house) or to the courtesan herself.[105] Selling a courtesan into concubinage could be lucrative for a madam.[106] Nevertheless, madams opposed the departure of courtesans who were bringing significant profits to the house. In cases where the woman wished to leave but the madam would not consent, the customer might hire gang members to kidnap the courtesan. Alternatively, the courtesan might go to a government official and petition to redeem herself for the original price of purchase. These desperate actions were sometimes preceded by a period of ill-treatment by the madam.[107] Scandal stories of the 1930s had as a staple character the cruel madam in a *changsan* house who demanded exorbitant prices, refused to let courtesans continue to see suitors who couldn't pay such sums, and even locked up or beat courtesans who would not comply.[108] Such stories sit uneasily beside the more common portrayal of mature courtesans as women with an unusual degree of control over their working lives, but they were an insistent subtheme.

If a madam's stake in a courtesan marriage was mainly financial, the stories about why courtesans themselves agreed to become concubines were more complex. Emotional attraction to a particular man may well have been a factor, but it is little mentioned in the written sources, aside from passing declarations that a courtesan and her customer had fallen in love and decided to marry. A second possible reason to leave the courtesan house—this one also voiced by men who wrote about courtesans—was the attractions offered by the roles of wife and mother. In a 1905 collection there appeared a prose poem titled "Encouraging Prostitutes to Get Married," apparently written by a literati male, that was composed in the style of a piece by Tao Yuanming (365–427 C.E.). Tao, a former government official, had hated the corruption of public life and went into seclusion at the age of forty. His original poem described the pleasures of an idyllic life after resigning from office. Through its stylistic resonances, "Encouraging Prostitutes to Get Married" made an implicit comparison between marriage for a courtesan and retirement for a government official. The poem extolled the virtues of domestic respectability for a weary (but apparently skeptical) courtesan. The poem reads in part:

> Marry a good man! You are getting old; why not marry a good man? Since you know that you are the master of your own body, why do you feel regret and hatred? Why suffer sorrow alone? You know that an old one is dependable, while a youth cannot be pursued. Becoming a principal wife is not something we can attain. You can see that today [marriage] is right and the past [prostitution] is wrong. . . . Leaving the madam, you are given in marriage. You are happy to share your life with your beloved guest. . . . On the beautiful morning of an auspicious day, slaves and servants welcome you, maids wait at the gate. You will throw away your face powder, but your personal charm will remain. Joining hands with the groom, you take your seat. Together you pour the wine. You are happy that the plain clothes of a wife suit you. What is there to dislike about needlework [the task of a wife]?

By your boudoir you use smiling words, and know the leisure of returning to a proper way of life. The days pass in entertaining games of chess. Although the room is quiet, life is peaceful. You are fortunate to have a good mate as your companion. It is lucky that you have a spouse with whom you can always be together, lingering in a friendly manner. No one comes to ask recklessly about the willows, no customer frivolously attaches to the flowers.[109] The days can pass in a leisurely way. What would be difficult about relying on him for life?

Marry a good man! Please leave the courtesan house behind. . . . Enough! How long does the beauty of a woman last? Why not sincerely decide whether to go or stay? Why do you aimlessly go with the flow? The brothel is not what you want. . . . Marry a good man and have a child. Soon you will raise a son to empathize with you. When he grows up and becomes successful, you receive the royal edict sealed with purple wax [celebrating the son's appointment as an official]. Celebrate growing old with your husband in mutual respect. Enjoy your husband's official status. How can you still hesitate?[110]

The message is mixed. Stability, respectability, affection, financial security, leisure, sons, and status are all invoked as the rewards of becoming a concubine. Yet the poem also indicates that the woman is less than satisfied at being married to an older man rather than a youth she could not catch (or perhaps one her madam would not let her keep). It hints as well that she would have preferred to become a principal wife.

The gossip columns of the tabloid press suggested that immediate financial advantage was the most common reason that courtesans became concubines. A pawned or sold courtesan hoped to find someone who was willing to pay off her "mortgage" or, if she had been sold outright, to reimburse the madam for her purchase price plus interest and expenses. "Free" courtesans entered a relationship so that the suitor/husband could clear their debts, pay them a "body price," and equip them with jewels and other valuables. Debt was endemic in the courtesan houses, fueled by conspicuous consumption, high-interest loans, rising prices, and defaulting customers. It inspired gloomy political comparisons: a tabloid described one popular courtesan as having "a debt as big as that of China, and no sovereignty or freedom."[111]

The process of marrying in order to clear debts and start anew was called "taking a bath" (*xizao*[112] or *huyu*[113]), a term probably meant to suggest a cleansing of the "wind and dust" of courtesan life. The tabloid accounts are quite clear about what sort of man courtesans found attractive for bathing purposes: one who had abundant money and personal connections.[114] Even famous courtesans whose business was flourishing found such alliances at least temporarily useful. A single gossip column in September 1919 gave details of the following nuptials between famous courtesans and their suitors: Lin Daiyu with a wealthy mining-company executive; Bao Qin with a man who was in a position to influence the outcome of the annual beauty/talent contest for courtesans; Jin Shuyu with a man who had already rented a house for her; Hua Yunyu with a Cantonese who had the ability to pay off her considerable debts; and Jian Bing with a rich army officer.[115] Stories were told of famous courtesans, including Lin Daiyu, who "bathed" many times in the course of their long careers.

Difficulties

In spite of the allure of such marriages, and the frequency with which they occurred, the course of concubinage seldom ran smooth. Courtesans were often impatient with the confinement and the emotional discomfort of being a concubine. If a man installed his new concubine in the same residence with his principal wife, the wife might forbid him to visit the concubine's quarters. Daily friction between husbands, wives, and concubines was reportedly a standard feature of such living arrangements, souring even the most loving liaison.[116] Some found that life as a concubine was in some respects less secure than life as a prostitute, depending as it did on the continuing favor of one man. Courtesans who had led active social lives sometimes found family life too sequestered, and left their new husbands to seek a less constraining situation.[117] Kui Qingyun Laowu, for instance, nicknamed "Gang Bandit" because of her wild behavior, left her new husband after a month when he objected to her opening her own bank account. (She reportedly followed her favorite opera singer to Hangzhou.)[118] Hong Ruyu chafed when her husband objected to her smoking and going out late to enjoy herself with groups of other courtesans. (Their compromise: he agreed that she could smoke at home; she agreed not to go out with other women.)[119]

The stormy breakups of many of these relationships can be read as testaments to the emotional volatility, independence, or coldly calculating nature of courtesans. In breathlessly reported detail, *Crystal* followed the case of Bao Qin, a courtesan originally from a poor family in Changshu. Adopted by a neighbor and then pawned into a Shanghai courtesan house at age thirteen, she later redeemed her pawn pledge and enjoyed a successful career, eventually winning the title of vice president of the Flower World in an annual courtesan contest (see chapter 6). After a short-lived first marriage and a return to professional life, she decided in September 1919 to become the concubine of a man named Gu Er, in return for a body price variously reported as five thousand or fifty-four hundred yuan. Her mother came from Changshu to Shanghai to supervise the festivities. Even before the marriage took place in mid-October, however, Bao Qin reportedly became dissatisfied with her status as Gu's fifth wife (or fourth concubine). (A later account said that she had been forced into the arrangement by creditors and did not wish to marry Gu at all.) Within a week the paper reported that Bao Qin had been screaming and crying day and night, expressing her discontent at ranking fifth in a hierarchy of women, and threatening to leave. Gu Er coolly replied that he regarded his payment of the body price as a philanthropic act. He appreciated her favoring him by "taking a bath," he said, but he would not restrain her if she wished to leave. By October 24 she had done so, returning two thousand yuan of the body price. Bao Qin's mother, disturbed by reports that Bao Qin had stopped eating and drinking and was talking nonsense all day long, escorted her back to Changshu. *Crystal* first suggested that Bao Qin had been feigning insanity in order to avoid having to return any of the body price, but later it reported that her motives might have been even more devious. The night before her marriage, the paper said, she was seen with her old customer Mr. Tang, a government official. The next day, already married, she had a sudden craving for duck gizzards and liver, bought five of them, and sat in front of Gu Er chewing and smacking her lips. When he asked her to stop, she reacted rudely. He then paid her two thousand yuan and sent her away. She subsequently returned to Mr. Tang, who rented her for a few months at four hundred yuan a month, then took her as his wife (*furen*). This, however, was not the end of Bao's marital vicissitudes. Ten years later, the indefatigable gossip columnists reported that she had scolded and even beaten Mr. Tang, and that he had ended the liaison. She then reappeared on the courtesan circuit, habitually sporting a student uniform and a leather coat. After relationships with a number of famous men, she settled down for a time with the secretary of the warlord Bai Zhongxi, then dumped him when his career suffered some reverses.[120] One account presents Bao Qin as "innocent, ingenuous, simple, and candid" when she entered courtesan life, but adds that she later became dissolute under the influence of her fellow courtesans, and later still "wild and untractable."[121] Expressive and sensual, she was at the same time attentive to questions of status and financial gain. In each of her marital decisions, she apparently took care to assess her chances of access to wealth and power, and made her decisions accordingly, resorting when necessary to subterfuge and extreme behavior to achieve calculated ends. She did so, however, in an environment in which it was all too easy for courtesans to accumulate debts but difficult to clear them; her choice of partners was always made in the context of difficult financial pressures.

As Bao Qin's departure from Gu Er indicates, often the biggest financial obstacle to leaving concubinage was a disputed claim to the body price. If a marriage was not successful, the man could demand that the woman repay the body price, thereby reducing whatever financial assets she had built up by agreeing to the marriage. Such cases sometimes wound up in court. In 1929, for instance, one Xu Shaoqian sued the courtesan Huiran Laojiu for breaking their marriage contract. Xu's complaint said that in 1928 he had paid Huiran five hundred yuan in cash and five hundred yuan by check, as well as five hundred yuan to a madam or maidservant to whom Huiran owed money. In return she was supposed to take down her signboard, stop work-ing, and move into a house Xu had rented for the two of them. After a few days of cohabitation, Xu became suspicious when Huiran began to return home late, and discovered that she was still going out on call. In reply Huiran filed a countercomplaint, stating that Xu had taken back gifts of clothing and furniture, as well as running up a debt for drinks and meals at her cour-tesan house. Her lawyer argued that she was entitled to the money she had been paid "in exchange for flesh," but his lawyer retorted that no regulation or law covered cases of cohabitation. Ultimately the court decided that Huiran should return the check and the payment to the madam (the cash payment was excluded, since Xu had no written proof that he had paid it). For his part, Xu was ordered to pay his debt to the courtesan house. In this case, the courtesan emerged from a liaison with no significant financial gain.[122]

After ending a marriage,[123] a courtesan's most common option was to use her newly acquired resources to open her own establishment. The tabloids eagerly recounted the details of courtesans who had "come out of the moun-tain" and returned to their rounds of calls, tea, and banqueting.[124] Not all liaisons were short-lived: some women returned to courtesan life after bear-ing several children; one did so when her husband disappeared after seven years of marriage and turned up months later deeply in debt.[125] These women appear to have been no more stigmatized as formerly married courtesans than they had been as unmarried ones; the fact of previous marriages did not deter new customers from seeking them as concubines.

For customers, the successful pursuit of a particular courtesan demon-strated their elite status and helped establish their exclusive access to desir-able women. The persistent cautionary note in accounts of concubinage at-tests to the frequency and ease with which courtesans slipped out of such arrangements. For a courtesan, acquiring a steady customer and entering a long-term liaison or marriage with him presented certain possibilities to max-imize her income and control vis-à-vis both madams and customers. Presents and tips to sought-after courtesans went into the pocket of the courtesan, not the owner. When a courtesan became a concubine, the madam was usu-ally paid a fee, but so was the woman herself, and she might use a marriage as an interim measure to terminate an unsatisfactory relationship with the madam and accumulate financial resources. More broadly, the historian hears another message, although it is perhaps not exactly what the tabloid and guidebook authors intended: that life in the demimonde, for a woman with an established clientele and acute business skills, allowed more space than conventionally respectable marriage for a woman to arrange her own time and control her own income, and that women in the profession of pros-titution recognized this, valued it, and acted accordingly.

If entering a marriage was advantageous, under certain circumstances so was leaving one. The sources say little about the emotional tenor of such liaisons, but the actions of the women suggest that emotional and material interests quite possibly intertwined. We cannot disentangle these interests in the historical record, nor should we assume that they were experienced in a disentangled fashion by the courtesans. Affairs of the heart among Shanghai courtesans were profoundly marked by their struggles for financial security and personal control.

CHAPTER 5

Tricks of the Trade

Embedded in writings about Shanghai's courtesan houses was a muted but persistent cautionary note. Courtesans were never represented as the stark figures of danger and social decay that their streetwalker sisters became in the 1920s and later. Yet guidebooks and tabloids portrayed the courtesan houses as places of subtle menace where a man might lose, if not his health, at least his money or his pride. There he risked exposure in front of his fellow customers as a country bumpkin, one whose behavior was insufficiently knowledgeable and sophisticated for the world of Shanghai manners. Shanghai courtesan houses were an important venue for the creation and exhibition of urbane masculinity—a serious business conducted in quarters superficially dedicated to play. In guidebooks and tabloids, readers were apprised of the rules, requirements, and pitfalls of frequenting courtesan houses. Encounters with courtesans provided occasions for the demonstration of urbanity, while courtesans themselves became arbiters of urbane performance, women whose services and affections were not completely under the control of the customer.

Extravagant Caution

The most detailed guidebooks to the courtesan houses, those that provided meticulous catalogs of pleasure and guides to etiquette, were prefaced by statements that the purpose of assembling such detail was didactic. Books that persuaded people to avoid brothels were generally too boring to read, one 1891 author reasoned, and so their hortatory message was never heard. By providing more than two hundred specific pieces of information about brothel customs, he hoped to keep people reading long enough to warn them that they could lose their money or even their lives in brothels, and to "reveal in detail the means by which people are cheated." His purpose, he said, was to make it clear "that the wonderful realm is in fact a phantasmagoria filled with dim shapes," so that people would find it as devoid of flavor as chewing on wax.[1] Almost half a century later, the guidebook author Sun Yusheng focused on the emotional dangers to an unwitting customer who was unfamiliar with the guile of experienced courtesans:

> The sweet talk in the brothels, the seductive and bewitching forms found there, can excite the brothel visitor. The false emotions and fake love of the prostitute, which resemble the beautiful relations between lovers, in actuality will lead one to lose one's soul and break one's heart. Young people who enter this door without knowing the conditions within the trap will become confused and suffer great losses. This book completely exposes all the secrets of the brothels and the dark plots used by prostitutes to bewitch people. If philanderers read it, they will not fall to the bottom, and if young people read it, they can develop their judgment.[2]

Sometimes the message included a reference to the suffering of prostitutes. The cover of Sun Yusheng's 1939 guidebook depicted a portly middle-aged woman in a black cheongsam (*qipao*), evidently a madam, brandishing a stick over a kneeling, cowering younger woman in a long sleeveless gown and high heels, evidently a prostitute. Over the lintel of the doorway in which the two stood, the figure of a woman lying spread-eagled could be seen in outline. Two of the calligraphic dots in the title (on the character *huo* in *shenghuo*, "life") were rendered as hearts rather than dots. The subtitle of the book was *Boxiang menjing*, or "Guide to Being a Playboy." The cover sent a mixed message about the suffering of prostitutes and the pleasure (and possibly love) to be found in visiting them.[3] (See figure 16.)

Having duly established their credentials as detached educators, guidebook writers could then proceed to a poetic evocation of the world they had set out to criticize. This double message of lavish attention and warning led to abrupt discontinuities in the narrative. Sun Yusheng's warning about emotional traps in the courtesan houses was followed almost immediately by the following passage:

> The lives of these prostitutes generally speaking are leisurely, unburdened, and spoiled. They eat rich foods and wear silks, doing nothing in the daytime, living a quiet and leisurely life in their dove-cage-like rooms, cultivating their spirits. At night they rush about on the streets bright with electric lights, as numerous as a school of silver carp moving downstream, each powdered and rouged, wearing red and green, delicate and graceful, selling their beauty—seductive, lascivious, good-looking women, most making a specialty of hooking youth.

It is likely that a reader would be less impressed by the phrases of warning than by the captivating descriptions of courtesan life. In fact, most guidebook writers assumed that their readers would be drawn inexorably to the courtesan houses. It was impossible, argued the author of the passage just given, that a man in search of a broad range of experience would choose not to go to places of pleasure. Because one could find in the brothels every type of problem one might meet in life, the author continued, he had decided it was necessary to teach people how to frequent brothels correctly. Such instruction would enable them to "understand everything about dealing with the world." The key maxim for the worldly gentleman to keep in mind, he concluded, was "[T]hink it through, see through it, let it go" (*xiangdechuan, kandepo, fangdeluo*).[4]

Blockheads and Epidemic Victims

The guidebooks described in chapter 3—books that explained the details of summoning a courtesan out on a social call, going to the courtesan house for tea, hosting a banquet, and celebrating festivals—can be read as a kind of collective etiquette guide to correct behavior for the uninitiated guest. The production of this sort of advice apparently peaked in the 1930s, when navigating the shoals of Shanghai life was represented as requiring particular types of knowledge, and ignorance invited humiliation. Correct behavior necessitated but was not limited to the formal fulfillment of financial duties. It also included the ineffable art of self-presentation. A successful customer enjoyed two benefits: he increased his likelihood of winning a courtesan's favor, and, equally important, he avoided ridicule by the group of courtesans who observed him in the brothel. Someone who failed to meet the requirements by not spending enough money, by spending too much money, by dressing inappropriately,[5] by assuming intimacy too quickly[6]— generally, by saying or doing the wrong thing—would be ridiculed, significantly, as a country bumpkin.[7]

The term of disparagement commonly used to mock a rube was "blockhead" (*amulin*; literally, "wood forest"), intoned with the clear implication that the person was as stupid as a block of wood.[8] The term for a man who allowed himself to be cajoled into unnecessary expenditures, or who betrayed his ignorance by not spending money when he should, was "epidemic victim" (*wensheng*).[9] Frequenting a courtesan house could cost a customer as much as one thousand yuan annually, according to a 1932 guide, but an epidemic victim could easily pay twice that amount.[10] In order to decide whether a particular expenditure put him at risk for "infection," a man had to be able to correctly assess his degree of intimacy with a courtesan. To host a banquet with a woman with whom he had a sexual relationship was not high-risk behavior, for instance, but if she had another intimate customer, it was foolish. Even without sexual involvement, it was appropriate to host a banquet with a particularly attentive courtesan.[11] A man who did not maintain control over the flow of resources from himself to a courtesan, but handed over presents on demand, was an epidemic victim.[12] Inviting a courtesan to a restaurant was a smart move, but taking her to the theater was foolish, because there she would not only see old acquaintances, but perhaps have the opportunity to watch her opera-singer lover perform onstage at her customer's expense.[13]

Experienced customers were told to develop a repertoire of practices to avoid the status of epidemic victim. For instance, guidebooks advised them to summon courtesans out on call rather than hosting expensive banquets; to avoid excessive drinking or gambling; to follow other customers to a courtesan house and drink at their expense (such a person was called a "great lord of the border"); and to stay away on holidays, when tips and gifts were required.[14] A truly skilled guest could actually make a living by going to courtesan houses. By positioning himself to bring new business to the brothel, and by helping new customers to arrange liaisons, he could enjoy a discount from the house, and drink or gamble at the expense of those customers for whom he was, in a subtle way, pimping. Some swindlers prospered in the courtesan houses as well, by cheating at mahjong.[15] In general, writers opined, it was better for courtesans to curse one as wily rather than mock one as an epidemic victim.[16]

Although guidebooks made it clear that one could not frequent brothels without spending money, lavish expenditure was not a guarantee of success with the courtesans. As one writer of a customer memoir commented in the dark political days of 1919, one could become a senator by spending money, but some hapless customers spent money in the courtesan houses all their lives and were still cheated, because courtesans preferred young and handsome visitors over old and ugly ones.[17] In addition to concrete advice about wise expenditures, some guidebooks also offered discussions on how a customer could encourage a courtesan to become emotionally attached to him by talking in a lively manner, fanning her if the room was hot and asking after her comfort if it was cold, taking her to the theater and the movies, and plying her with expensive candies. These were limited expenses that were said to yield more gratitude and affection than would the hosting of ten banquets.[18]

With respect to both blockheads and epidemic victims, the guidebooks pointed to courtesans as the sources of mockery, the judges of whether a man understood local practices well enough to pass muster. The audience for this judgment, however, was a man's fellow customers in the courtesan house, those with whom he drank tea, banqueted, and gambled. One of the best ways to ensure a favorable reception by courtesans, in fact, was to arrive at the house in the company of powerful friends who were already regular customers. Such friends, advised the guidebooks, could introduce a man to popular courtesans, thus giving him face. They could also act as mediators for a man seeking to arrange a sexual liaison with a courtesan. Perhaps most important, they could communicate by example and direct advice the appropriate means of comportment. But an experienced customer who brought a neophyte to the courtesan houses took the same risk as a guarantor who introduced an apprentice to a craft; the newcomer's unruly behavior could damage his own reputation.[19]

In practice, of course, customers could retaliate against women who they felt had humiliated them. In about 1908, for instance, a customer published in a local tabloid a denunciation of the courtesan Jin Hanxiang, accusing her of lowly background (she had started her career as a pheasant streetwalker) and arrogance because she had failed to appear when he summoned her to a restaurant on call. Stung, Jin Hanxiang wrote back to explain that she had been late because of an overbooked call schedule, and that the customer should have come to her with his complaint rather than going to the press. Denying the charge of arrogance, she concluded, "It is not worth it for Master Yan to be nickel-and-diming people who make their living in the courtesan houses." The newspaper's editorial staff here entered the fray, chastising Yan for his impatience and Jin Hanxiang for failing to send a maid to apologize for her tardiness.[20] Here the customer possessed the power to denigrate the courtesan's background and character, accuse her of not conforming to appropriate standards of behavior, and force her into a defensive position. This argument, conducted in the public venue of the tabloid press, suggests that courtesans were not all-powerful in the social world of Shanghai, and that even within the brothels their behavior had to conform to certain standards of submissiveness.

It is thus all the more striking that the guidebooks invested courtesans with so much power to judge urbane masculinity. In a sense, the courtesans themselves were positioned as bodies of knowledge about urban sophistication. A man's capacity to "master" these bodies of knowledge helped determine his standing in the eyes of his fellow customers, both those who observed him directly when he visited courtesan houses and those who heard him spoken of admiringly or mockingly by other courtesans. In the rapidly changing Shanghai environment, positioning oneself favorably in the urban hierarchy, and being validated by both courtesans and other customers, was not merely a matter of entertainment.

Sexual Expenditures

As chapter 4 suggested, when and how to initiate a sexual liaison with a courtesan involved complicated calculations on the part of the brothel customer. The guidebooks offered advice on how a man might get the most value for his money. Once a woman was no longer a virgin, they explained, she was able to exercise a modicum of control over who purchased her sexual services. Having fulfilled her duty to bring in a large sum of money for the madam, immediately subsequent to her defloration she might arrange for a customer she liked to spend the night with her. The cost, while only half that of "lighting the big candles," was still several times more than an ordinary sexual encounter.[21] This practice was known as "jostling through the city gate" (*ai chengmen*). A 1932 history of the courtesan houses explained that this expression originated in the late nineteenth century, when the north and east gates of Shanghai's Chinese city (Xin Beimen and Xiao Dongmen) were closed after 9 P.M. An official who came back to the city after that hour would approach the gate in his sedan chair, and his servants would shout that he wished to present an official document (*zhaohui*), actually a wooden tablet cut in half, which had to match the half held by the guards at the gate. But as soon as the guards checked his tablet and opened the gate, unauthorized persons who wanted to enter the city after hours would push their way through as well. Sometimes an enterprising soul would pretend to have a wooden tablet, and when the gate opened a crack he would slip the guards a bribe and fly through, accompanied by several "jostlers." The historical account was explicit about the symbolism in the appropriation of this term by the brothels: "The genitals of the prostitute are taken as the city gate."[22]

Advice to customers on becoming a jostler was mixed. On the one hand, they were warned that jostling involved paying more than they should for a woman who was no longer a virgin, and that experienced customers should not let themselves be talked into such a transaction.[23] On the other hand, they were told that they were much more likely to derive pleasure from jostling than from defloration:

> It is as though the evil and arrogant one [who deflowers a virgin] is a petty laborer opening up a road, spending his blood, sweat, and spirit, constructing a flat, wide road, on which someone else then drives a car and shows off, spending very little but getting substantial benefit. Guests who are sharp about business don't want to light the big candles, but rather wish to jostle through the city gate.[24]

Although the purpose of such accounts was not to explore the scope of courtesans' control over their own sexual activity, many of them made it clear that a jostler could expect greater pleasure because his partner had affective ties to him and engaged in sexual intercourse willingly.[25]

The pleasure was even greater, but so was the peril, if a customer who was emotionally or sexually attracted to a virgin courtesan succeeded in "stealing defloration" (*tou kaibao*). Unlike formal defloration or jostling, such an encounter did not have the approval of the madam, and in fact denied her the payment she expected for having raised and trained the young woman. Here the guidebooks hinted at the possibility of mutual passion on the part of customer and courtesan:

> The first time a virgin is trampled, there is no feeling, so how can one comfort or bring happiness to one's partner? Stolen defloration is different.

> Both parties are burning with deep feelings. If the prostitute is willing, one
> need not ask whether the madam permits it.[26]

The dominant theme of guidebook explanations, however, was not mutual-
ity but male skill. "Stolen" sexual relations were represented as a prize that
could be won by good-looking young men who simultaneously sweet-talked
the courtesan and hoodwinked her madam. In these degenerate times of
unrestrained sexual desire, wrote a 1939 author, when even women of respectable families were easily stained with bad habits, virgin prostitutes felt
the stirrings of desire early, and could be convinced to surrender their virginity for a handkerchief, two pairs of shoes, and twenty yuan.[27] From the
skilled customer's point of view, virginity was a prize to be wrested from both
madam and courtesan as cheaply as possible, preferably with the enthusiastic participation of the virgin herself. If the madam discovered the liaison,
however, the consequences for both courtesan and customer could be grim.
The young woman could expect cruel treatment and pressure to have a fully
paid first-night encounter with a rich, unwitting customer who was unaware
that another had already seized his prize.[28] The customer who "stole defloration" could expect demands for reparations from the madam, with the
amount approaching the price of a "legitimate" defloration.[29] Worse, a really crafty madam might outwit the customer by playing dumb as the illicit
liaison unfolded, then refusing to let him leave until he either paid in full
or bought the courtesan outright.[30]

If stealing defloration was a scam perpetrated by a customer with some
degree of collusion by the courtesan, as the guidebooks would have it, then
passing off a nonvirgin courtesan as a candidate for defloration was a scam
perpetrated by the madam, again with the courtesan's collusion. Because first-
night fees were so high, enterprising madams often attempted to sell a young
woman's virginity as many times as possible. Such recycled virgins were known
by the term "sharp" or "clever" courtesans (*jian xiansheng*). This was a visual
pun: the character *jian* is written with the character for "small" on top of that
for "big," implying that such a woman was not virginal ("small") but rather
sexually active ("big"). As early as 1919, tabloid writers were sardonically describing cases of false advertising with queries such as this:

> Zhen Zhuhua of Minhe Li said to people that she was a *xiao xiansheng*, and
> had never broken her melon. But I remember she had quite an affair with
> the opera singer Bai. How could she say she is a *xiao xiansheng?*[31]

By the 1930s, guidebook writers routinely bemoaned the decline in virginity, which they saw as part of a more widespread degeneration in brothel
mores. Sexually wanton behavior, they complained, had replaced the strictly
observed codes of an imagined past.[32] When a customer paid to deflower a
"sharp" courtesan, the sly madam would use unspecified artifice to make the

young woman "flow red a full measure of drops just the same," while the customer, "in a muddle," was unable to tell the difference.[33] This new situation, the guidebooks advised, called for increased vigilance on the part of the customer. Most of what went under the rubric of defloration was merely

> taking someone for a fool and tricking a fathead. According to normal biology, the first time a girl engages in sexual intercourse, the hymen must be blood red and stain the outside. So everyone takes this as proof. But there are many who fake it. So when a defloration guest is doing his work, he must carefully inspect this "flower" to see whether or not there are contraband goods.[34]

Failure to notice the deception would cause the customer to be secretly laughed at by the courtesans,[35] and indeed the deceived customer became a standard figure of fun in 1930s scandal stories. In one tale, two courtesan sisters (one "big" and one "small") convinced a rich young man that he could sleep with one and deflower the other upon payment of two gold bars and two pearls. After he handed over the goods, a friend from Suzhou (the women's native place) told him that both women were well-known there for their love affairs with actors.[36] If courtesans were caught in a virginity deception, the angry patron might lead his friends to vandalize the brothel.[37] Similarly, since virginity was prized as an asset by the madam as well, a woman who had been sold to a house as a virgin might suffer physical abuse from both customer and madam if the claim turned out to be false.[38]

Competition

Relationships between customers and courtesans, like any other business encounter, were marked by competition. Courtesans maneuvered to secure the attentions of customers they found desirable,[39] while patrons, as suggested earlier, had to best numerous rivals to win famous courtesans. Like so much else in courtesan houses, both types of competition were governed by elaborate codes of etiquette and encoded in specialized language.

For both courtesan and customer, this etiquette was based on variations of serial monogamy. When a customer summoned a courtesan out on call, for instance, she owed him her full attention for the duration of the call, even though it might last only several minutes. During that period, she could greet other customers but could not act in an overly familiar manner with them. When it came to hosting guests for tea and banquets, the exclusive loyalty of both parties was expected to last as long as the social encounter. If a courtesan's relationship with a customer developed to include physical intimacy, however, the rules tightened. In such a case she was not supposed to begin a sexual relationship with one of his associates, or she would be cursed by guests as a low-down woman of easy virtue. (In this case, the interloping man was also apt to be ostracized by his friends.)[40] The sources do not state clearly whether a courtesan could ever have more than one sexual relationship at a time, but they were clear that she should do nothing to humiliate a regular male patron in front of others in his social circle.

For his part, a customer was expected to have a sexual relationship with only one courtesan in a brothel for the duration of one season, or about four months. Prior to sexual intimacy, courtesans competed for desirable customers and quarreled with each other over the results, providing endless material for tabloid gossip columns.[41] After a customer began sleeping with a courtesan, however, each had claims upon the other. If a second courtesan attempted to steal him from the first, it was known as "pressing" or "hitching up" with him. Guidebooks warned that he might be caught between two feuding courtesans, haplessly singing a phrase from the musical drama *Story of the Western Chamber:* "I'm stuck in the middle and cannot move!"[42] More often, changing courtesans was portrayed as an act initiated by the customer. A man who took up with a second prostitute before the season changed was said to be "jumping troughs" (*tiaocao*) or "building a road outside legitimate territory" (*yuejie zhulu*).[43] A man who "jumped troughs" was usually angry with his courtesan because she was receiving attentions from another customer. He might then vent his spleen by ostentatiously hosting banquets and parties with one of her fellow courtesans in attendance.[44] In one 1919 gossip item, a customer known as "Monkey King" even invited local newspaper writers to witness his trough jumping, saying that he wanted to humiliate his former favorite.[45]

In the late Qing, custom demanded that a man who wished to change partners pay a fee to the first courtesan in order to secure his release; after that she would regard him as a stranger. This fee was known as the "door-passing call" (*guomen ju*).[46] If a man had gone so far as to buy a courtesan to be his concubine, and later separated from her and took up with another, the first courtesan was considered to have a claim on him and could legitimately marshal her allies to demand negotiations with her potential successor.[47]

By the twentieth century, however, the details of such formal procedures had disappeared from the historical record. They were replaced by elaborate descriptions of jealousy in a highly competitive environment. In keeping with the themes of status anxiety and emotional fickleness in the guidebooks, most such accounts portrayed men as being at a disadvantage in keeping a courtesan loyal and true. A customer's worst nightmare was to find himself in a "white-board face-off" (*baiban duisha*),[48] where he was competing with another man for a courtesan's sexual favors. The term derived from a mahjong play. A mahjong set included four blank tiles, nicknamed "small white faces" (*xiao bailian*).[49] (It cannot have been coincidental that this was also the term for the handsome young men reportedly favored by courtesans.) A team needed three of the four tiles to make a set; if each team held two of the tiles, neither would give one up to let the opponent complete the set, resulting in a stalemate. The more popular a courtesan, the more likely that two or more men would be simultaneously vying for her attention. One guidebook used a colorful, if dubious, extrapolation to emphasize the scarcity of courtesans relative to the "small white faces" who desired them. Of 136 mahjong tiles, he said, four (or one in thirty-four) were small white faces. Applying this ratio to the Chinese population, there must be more than 13 million small white faces among the Chinese population of 400 million. In Shanghai alone, this would mean 100,000 handsome young men seeking the favor of a mere several thousand courtesans. Of course, in this situation, white-board face-offs were inevitable. The accompanying cartoon depicted a richly dressed woman chewing pensively on her finger as she stood between two seated, smoking, handsome young men, one happy and one sullen.[50]

Given this situation, the skillful prostitute was one who could entertain several customers without provoking them to anger.[51] More commonly, one or more customers would become wildly jealous—"eating vinegar," in common parlance.[52] In 1875, the newspaper *Shenbao* reported that a frustrated courtesan caught between two jealous customers had tried to commit suicide, a situation summed up in the phrase "Madmen drink vinegar and a charming courtesan swallows opium."[53] According to the tabloid gossip columns, however, most courtesans were more calculating. Some abandoned moderately rich customers in favor of very rich ones. One particularly noted member of a politically active circle of courtesans, Hua Yunyu, reportedly consorted with a Mr. He in order to advance her career and a Mr. Tao because she appreciated his good looks. When other courtesans remonstrated with her, she answered that no one had the right to interfere with her freedom of love. Another courtesan, Gao Yayun, kept a fiancé to support her financially and a lover known for his good looks, and was reported to be quite distressed when the opium-besotted fiancé affably told the lover that he could have her. (She subsequently went to Hankou to begin her career anew.)[54]

Although courtesans often had to struggle to become well known and popular as entertainers, in discussions of competition they were portrayed as possessing considerable power to choose among customers. In doing so they were said to consider both good looks and money, hesitating only when several potential customers possessed both.[55] Sexual intimacy increased the obligations of both courtesan and customer, but where a well-known mature courtesan was involved, the favor was hers to bestow. The guidebook language of striving to show oneself at best advantage was largely addressed to the men, not the courtesans.

Scheming Businesswomen

Beyond their cautionary statements about the risks of appearing coarse and inexperienced, the guidebooks were also a repository for warnings about the capacity of courtesans to relieve customers of their money. With and without the collusion of the brothel owner, courtesans were said to perpetrate various scams. If a courtesan found a customer who was trying to conceal his brothel visits from his family, she would engage in activities bordering on blackmail.[56] Prostitutes of all ranks, customers were warned, were experts at requesting clothing or jewelry from a close customer.[57] The terminology for such transactions, "grabbing small change" (*chao xiaohuo*)[58] or "the ax chop" (*kan futou*),[59] made explicit the customers' fear of being bilked, and this became the theme in much of the cautionary literature about courtesans. They were said to be as skillful in matching their requests to the customer's resources as a doctor writing a prescription of exactly the appropriate strength. The prescription was "flavored" with rice soup[60] (a slang term for flattery), tears, vinegar (slang for jealousy), and sweet sugar syrup. A 1935 guidebook carries an illustration of a woman reclining under a quilt while a mustachioed man sits next to her on the bed. She is ticking off on her fingers items depicted in a cartoonlike balloon above her head: a fine house, a car, and a diamond ring.[61] (See figure 17.)

One purpose of the guidebooks was to apprise potential customers of these acquisitive practices and the special terminology that described them, so that the customers could experience the pleasure of being in the know about Shanghai customs. Often this pleasure was conveyed through humor. In one story, for instance, a Shanghai man traveled to Canton on business and visited an inexperienced courtesan. Her madam had cryptically instructed her, "Tonight you must do the ax chop." The terrified young woman took the instructions literally and feared that she was being ordered to commit murder. Concealing the kitchen ax under her bed, she broke down and wept in front of the customer, and confessed that she could not bear to kill him. Laughing, he instructed her in the secret meaning of the term "ax chop," thus allowing readers of the story to experience vicariously the sweet sensation of teaching a courtesan the language of her own trade.[62]

In efforts to increase the "take," guidebooks said, a woman might practice the "bitter-meat stratagem" (*kurou ji*) of pretending to be at odds with her madam or arranging for bogus creditors to dun her in front of a customer. She would then beg the customer to buy her out as a concubine. For a customer to succumb to pity without thoroughly investigating the truthfulness of a woman's claims was to become, once again, an epidemic victim.[63] Customers used a particularly disparaging name, "old centipede," for both madams and experienced courtesans. Meant to denote their poisonous nature, the term also evoked a hundred appendages outstretched (for cash?) or poised for intrusion.[64]

Just as customers had unflattering names for madams and experienced courtesans, women in the brothels developed terms by which they classified guests behind their backs. A "beancurd" guest, for instance, was one who would do the woman's bidding. A "melon seed" guest required one bite and a "walnut" guest one hard knock before he would "put out." A "soap" guest or a "stone" guest needed time and energy, but would eventually yield something. The worst were "flea" and "fly" guests, who buzzed around the brothels but vanished as soon as one "swatted" them for contributions.[65] Guidebooks routinely listed these terms, by way of warning customers that the hospitable and affectionate demeanor of courtesans was only a cover for their calculating and deceptive nature.

The essence of this nature, commentators said, was that although courtesans might pretend to deep emotional attachments, they were incapable of sincerity. A customer might spend a great deal of money to rent a courtesan by the month, receiving assurances of exclusive sexual access to her, "but although that is what they say, actually people in the brothels are all women of easy virtue" who might well sleep with others in return for extra income. He who spent money to "taste this piece of meat, and not permit others to have a finger in the pie," could well find himself played for a fool or a "big greenhorn."[66] A writer for Shanghai's most prominent courtesan tabloid stated that any man who visited courtesans long enough would inevitably be "cuckolded" by them, implying that customers hoped for fidelity in the brothels even as they required it in their families.[67] Guidebook authors argued that this hope was unreasonable, because courtesans were not like respectable women:

> Why would a good woman want to become a prostitute? If not for money, then why? . . . So a prostitute's love rises and falls with the financial power of the customer. Their so-called love is sold for money, temporary and not everlasting.[68]

Lack of sincerity, these authors felt, was actually produced by the environment of the courtesan houses. Required to be sincere with one guest today and another tomorrow, courtesans reportedly lost the capacity for genuine emotion and replaced it with a survival instinct that enabled them to feign sincerity.[69] By the late 1930s, this analysis had been appropriated by feminist writers who agitated for the elimination of prostitution. They argued that courtesans had both an excruciating sense of their own low social status and an unlimited capacity for manipulation:

> Society despises prostitutes; at least, prostitutes give society the impression of being debased. Prostitutes themselves feel this if they have spent several years in the "wind and dust" [world of prostitution]. . . . Most of them, from the time they are young in the brothels, develop into character types that are lively, licentious, forthright, and outstanding. The result of social contact with every type of customer is that the depth and thoroughness of their knowledge of people rivals that of certain statesmen. They depend completely on their skill and technique in dealing with guests in order to get

hold of "epidemic victims" who will provide them with the means of consumption. Brothels seldom actually lose money.[70]

White Pigeons, Fairy Jumps, and Half-Open Doors

The wily courtesan, endlessly resourceful in pursuit of material gain, became a standard figure in 1930s scandal fiction. Scandal stories often took women from many walks of life as central figures of danger, describing in collections of brief vignettes how even an apparently innocent schoolgirl or nun was capable of deceiving and cheating unwary men. With respect to prostitution, scandal-fiction anthologies repeatedly elaborated several themes. The first was that courtesans were capable of turning seemingly heartfelt emotional encounters into opportunities for gain. In one story a courtesan pledged to become a man's concubine, collected a substantial sum of money from him to clear her debts, then absconded to Tianjin with the funds. Another fictional courtesan had sexual relations with a magistrate and stole two of his diamond rings as he slept. Knowing that he would not risk his reputation by making the circumstances of the theft public, she refused to return them. In a third story, a pregnant courtesan and her swindling husband convinced a merchant that their child was his, collected monthly payments from him for a year, then disappeared.[71]

Scandal-fiction stories also described the exploits of lower-ranking prostitutes. Like the courtesan stories, these pieces developed the theme that in Shanghai's complex environment, things were seldom what they seemed, requiring inside knowledge of urban ways in order to avoid personal disaster. Behind many prostitutes, they implied, lurked a gang of con artists (*chaibaidang*) who deployed the women as decoys. One much-described scam was called "freeing a white pigeon" (*fang baige*). Described in late-nineteenth-century sources as well as twentieth-century scandal stories, the scam had several variations, each of which involved selling a woman under false pretenses. In one version, traffickers posing as relatives would bring a young woman to Shanghai and pawn her into a brothel. After a few days one of the traffickers would go to the police, claiming that the woman was his unlawfully abducted wife. The madam would be detained by the police and punished according to the law that forbade purchasing women of unclear origin to engage in prostitution. Here the brothel was victim rather than perpetrator (a circumstance that suggests alternative readings of the standard trafficking stories told in chapter 7, in which madams were usually evil incarnate). In a second version of the scam, women were sold as wives, and after the bride-price was paid they fled back to the "white-pigeon gang." The third variation involved prostitutes who found suitable "epidemic victims" to spend money on them, allowed themselves to be purchased as concubines for a hefty price, then disappeared with the goods.[72] Guidebooks waxed eloquent about the dangers of these birds:

The birds of Shanghai, aside from old bustards [*laobao*—madams] and
pheasants, also include this white pigeon. Furthermore, all these birds are
female. Everyone knows about the fierceness of the bustard and the poison
of the pheasant, but the white pigeon tastes especially sweet, and only when
it has reached the stomach and the poison has been emitted do one's
innards ache. . . . So the harm done by white pigeons is even greater than
that done by old bustards and pheasants. . . . Beware!

The cartoon accompanying this particular warning depicts a man with
hands extended over his head and a surprised and distressed expression on
his face, while just above him a richly dressed young woman flies off with
what looks like a cash box dangling from one ankle.[73]

A related confidence trick was the "fairy jump" (*xianren tiao*), whose details always hewed closely to a single formula. A beautiful, well-dressed woman
would catch a man's eye at the theater or on the street. Telling him that her
husband or father was out of town, she would lure him to her well-appointed
home and into her bed. Just as the two began sexual activity, one or more
men would burst into the room, announce that they were the woman's relatives, abuse the victim verbally and physically for seducing a respectable
woman, and extort cash or a substantial promissory note before letting him
go.[74] What made the "fairy jump" so dangerous as a ploy, one guidebook
warned, was that the women decoys were modestly dressed as "modern girls"
from respectable families. Therefore, "blockheads" who knew enough to stay
away from pheasants, lest their noses fall off from a sexually transmitted disease, could find themselves entrapped when they least expected to be.[75] Perhaps because their occupation or social status was not immediately obvious,
or perhaps because they were deployed as a lure, the women in these scams
were also known as "half-open doors" (*bankai men*).[76]

The interplay between who the con artists appeared to be and what they
actually ended up doing—the act of imposture—accounted for much of the
humor of the scandal stories.[77] One common plot twist was to have the beautiful decoy replaced in midseduction (usually in the dark) by an ugly woman
("with teeth falling out and hair half gray, and a face as wrinkled as chicken
skin").[78] In another standard narrative, the seductress was revealed at a crucial point to be a man.[79] Or, in a reversal of the standard arrangement of victim and trickster, the customer might be revealed as an experienced member of a con-artist gang (*chaibaidang*). When the enraged male "relatives"
banged at the door, he would say calmly, "We belong to the same family. Why
don't we meet?" signaling that he knew exactly what the intruders intended
to do. In the stories, the knocking would abruptly disappear at this point, allowing him to have sexual intercourse with the "half-open door."[80] The most
complicated tale combined all these elements—gang members, half-open
doors, and cross-dressers—into an extended comedy of mistaken and revealed identities. A half-open door attempted to lure a (female) swindler

who was cross-dressing as a man in order to attract and cheat women. The half-open door thought the swindler was a man; the swindler thought the half-open door was a rich and respectable woman. When the two got into bed together, the half-open door summoned her "relatives" and complained that the swindler had forced himself on her. But she was bested when the "relatives" looked in the bed and saw the swindler, who had removed her male attire and was revealed as a woman. The swindler burst into tears, saying that the half-open door was a friend who had asked her to spend the night. She then threw some furniture around and walked out, leaving the crew of "relatives" dumbstruck and outsmarted at their own game.[81] In wildly exaggerated form, this story encapsulated many of the dangers enumerated in the guidebooks: that in Shanghai peril wore an alluring face, humiliation was one misstep away, and wits and specialized knowledge were required of men who wished to frequent the world of prostitution.

The exhaustive attention to scheming courtesans, a theme that spread from the guidebook genre into both reformist literature and scandal fiction, is perhaps best understood as a warning about the dangers of the urban environment, where some women were unconstrained by the financial and social controls of respectable marriage. Each of the schemes described in this literature centers on a moment when the prostitute slips beyond the control of the customer, taking his assets with her. Chinese writings did not always equate fidelity with marriage or disloyalty with prostitutes; novels and memoirs provide numerous accounts of both scheming wives and virtuous courtesans. But in the early twentieth century, the inability of a customer to secure the loyalty of a courtesan, even by becoming a regular patron or making her a concubine, signified an anxiety-provoking dissolution of conventional gender arrangements. Guidebooks and memoirs posed the modern brothel, whose rules were dominated by tricks of the trade, as a counterpoint to the nostalgically recalled older world of the courtesan, a world more orderly and fixed, a place where affection had not yet been commodified.

CHAPTER 6

Careers

Shanghai courtesans had "careers" in at least two senses of the term. First, they were publicly visible figures about whom stories circulated through a variety of popularly read publications. Sometimes these stories took the form of complete life narratives, many pages long, printed and reprinted in guidebooks and collectanea of courtesan miscellany. Other tales were more fragmentary and fleeting: guidebooks published pithy anecdotes about individual liaisons, arguments, or other exploits, while day-to-day changes in life circumstances (a new customer, a move from one courtesan house or city to another) were reported in the gossip columns of tabloids like *Crystal*. Some stories took groups of women, rather than individual figures, as their subjects: the widely followed "flower list" elections of prominent courtesans that became a recurrent ritual in the first two decades of the twentieth century, or the reports of courtesan political groups that organized (albeit fleetingly) around issues of national concern.

As with all historical traces, these stories point in two directions. They provide a catalog of incidents in the life of a courtesan, from which one can glean the elements of a "life and times of" narrative. They also lead back to the eye of the beholder and recorder, usually an erudite man, offering sections of a map to the concerns and pleasures of the community that consumed the services and images of courtesans. In circulating across the genres of early-twentieth-century tabloids, guidebooks, and fiction, the courtesan stories became a medium through which a broader urban reading public was called into being.

Courtesans had "careers" in a second sense as well: their working lives moved through overlapping and variable phases of virgin entertainer, popular performer, hired employee, protégée of powerful men or ambitious madams, intimate companion, concubine, divorced and reemergent social figure, petty proprietor, madam, aging doyenne, and pitiable hag. Not every courtesan appeared in all of these incarnations. And it is also likely that what we know about this aspect of courtesan "careers" is irreducibly marked by generic categories of reporting. The déclassé, down-on-her-luck old woman, for instance, bereft of beauty, love, and customers, was a powerful literary trope that may not have had much to do with a courtesan's understanding of her own life course.

Nowhere is the gap between retrospective curiosity about courtesan lives and available historical material more aggravating than in the virtual silence about menstruation, contraception, pregnancy, childbirth, and mothering among courtesans. Because the birth of a child was a reportable gossip item, we know that courtesans had children. Because male writers paid intermittent attention to aging courtesans, many of whom depended upon their biological or adopted children for support, we know that such relationships were ongoing. And that is virtually all we know. When contraception is mentioned at all, it appears as an artifact of courtesan oppression, recited by later reformers and revolutionaries in a narrative of coercion and control by evil madams. As distorted and partial as such stories may be, it would be no less a form of colonizing violence to presume that current categories of reproductive rights, mother-child bonds, or female agency and resistance had any particular currency among early-twentieth-century courtesans. (If a tree falls in the forest, and no one records it in a way that can be subsequently accessed, it would be unwise to carry on about the quality of the noise it might have made. And before indulging in a high feminist rage about the unsatisfactory quality of records about women compiled by men, perhaps we should recall that our own contemporary children, viewed retrospectively through particular sets of historical data, might appear principally in the form of unexplained gaps in a woman's curriculum vitae.) The final section of this chapter takes up the scattered traces of reproduction and mothering in courtesan careers, even though such exploration sits uneasily beside the much richer information available about courtesan rivalries, love affairs, house affiliations, and political alliances.

BAD GIRLS, GOOD GIRLS, AND DEAD GIRLS

Courtesans as represented in popular stories fall loosely into two categories: bad girls and good girls. Readers familiar with madonna/whore constructions of female behavior may be surprised to find this particular dichotomy contained *within* tales of prostitution, although this encompassment is not unique: Western narratives do often feature the "hooker with a heart of gold." Yet the variety of individual courtesan circumstances provided rich material for any number of framings, and ultimately it is surprising not that the stories feature one of these two themes, but that authors limited their choices only to two. This circumscription of choices required what appear to the contemporary reader as strenuous interpretations of "fact." "Bad girls," for instance, were represented as salacious in character almost from birth, even when the events of their early lives included rape at seven, sale into marriage at eight, and sex for pay (under the supervision of a mother-in-law) at ten. Although redeemed by occasional acts of heroism, "bad girls" usually embodied other disagreeable characteristics as well: they were bad-tempered, scheming, greedy, and inconstant. "Good girls," in contrast, were almost inevitably educated, refined, reserved, quiet, and filial. These biographies and biographical fragments did not sort the women by physical appearance; women in both groups were described as attractive or plain. But the beautiful "bad girls" put their beauty to immoral uses and were thus rendered repulsive, while the plain features of a "good girl" were taken as external manifestations of her modest and virtuous heart. Very seldom did these stories present a courtesan of complex or contradictory character; rather, the life course of each woman, no matter how full of reverses, was read as an unfolding of her "bad" or "good" character. As biographies, then, they were not in any sense comprehensive accounts of a life, but strings of anecdotes intended to illustrate and judge the personality of a courtesan.

A much smaller group of stories concerned women who became celebrated victims of spectacular crimes. My use of the term "dead girls" to label such stories is partly facetious—not all of the victims actually died—but it is meant to illustrate another way in which courtesans were featured as visible urban actors whose lives, and deaths, were of interest to a wider public.

The particular readings authors gave to the "facts" of courtesan lives tell us a great deal about the authors' preoccupations and the categories of meaning through which they understood events. Precisely because these readings often seem so strained, they direct attention to the culturally specific, even idiosyncratic nature of all interpretation. Where they saw lewd and improper female sexuality, a contemporary reader may see child abuse, coerced sexual intercourse, and other forms of victimization. Where they saw calculated greed, a contemporary reader may discern resourcefulness, resilience, even resistance. (One might observe that victimization/resistance is no less a limiting dichotomy than madonna/whore.) The point here is not to argue that all readings are equally "true," or equally constructed and therefore "untrue." Rather, it is to call attention to the ways in which cultural mediation (then and now) constructs experience, shapes moral judgment, and constrains or enables action. By counterposing the two readings of courtesan lives available to me (those of male authors and my own), and making as visible as I can the creaky and cobbled structure of representation that supports each of them, I also hope to raise questions about something the historical record does not directly tell us: the ways in which courtesans understood the events of their own lives.

Bad Girls

"Bad girls," as indicated earlier, embodied a lasciviousness that appeared inappropriately early and persisted long after a courtesan should have become a concubine or a madam. The most famous "bad girls" violated another expectation of proper behavior as well: they crossed class lines, sometimes spectacularly, in their rise from humble and dubious backgrounds to the relatively exalted rank of courtesan. Su Yuanyuan, for instance, the daughter of a stonemason, began work as a child silk laborer nicknamed Little Spinach (*Xiao Bocai*). After having sexual relationships with her foreman and factory manager, she became a prostitute when her filature went on strike. Even at the advanced age of forty, it was said, she still needed to sleep with three or four men a day, and was known as the Old Hero among her fellow courtesans.[1] Luopeng Ajin was the daughter of a widowed boatwoman on the Huangpu River. Her mother's paramour ran a low-class flower-smoke room (an opium brothel). Luopeng Ajin was known as Five Fall Down because she would have sex with local boatmen and casual laborers in return for five cash, the price of a snack-sized pack of peanuts. Through a customer in the opium brothel, she found work as an attendant (*genju dajie*) in a courtesan house, an experience that reportedly made the low-class customers of her past look like a "dusty leftover meal." At various points in the late Qing and early Republican periods, she became the concubine of two wealthy customers and then had an affair with a famous actor. If meteoric rise was a common feature of such stories, however, so was degradation and poverty in old age. Luopeng Ajin's actor lover beat her badly, then left her; she grew old and unattractive and sank again to the status of attendant.[2]

The themes of sexual transgression, class trespassing, and retribution were all present in the story of Shanghai's most famous late Qing courtesan, Lin Daiyu. Basic biographical facts about Lin are difficult to pin down. She was born sometime around 1865;[3] her hometown was variously given as Yunjian, Songjiang, or a small town named Zhang Lian Tang between Suzhou and Songjiang.[4] The most extensive guidebook biography of her says that she was the daughter of a poor plasterer named Lu and a mother who liked to make herself up and keep company with local rascals. Named Jinbao (Golden Treasure) at birth, she was disavowed by her father, who said she was not his daughter and he did not know "whose seed" she was. The account did not suggest that his outburst had anything to do with a preference for sons over daughters; rather, it impugned her mother's sexual behavior: "So the salacious impression she left throughout her life was half received from the upbringing her mother gave her."[5]

Jinbao's lewd behavior was said to date from early childhood.[6] After a series of childhood mishaps (she fell off a wall and hurt her arm at three, contracted smallpox and almost died at five), at age seven she reportedly had sexual relations with a rich neighbor twice her age. "It is said that young girls who lose their virginity will die, but Daiyu remained in good health," comments the biography, stopping just short of calling this proof of her lasciviousness. At eight she was purchased as a daughter-in-law by the family of shoemaker Li, who lived outside of Shanghai. Li's mother was a crafty woman who waited until Jinbao was ten and then turned her out as a secret prostitute. But local ruffians so disrupted the family peace by "salivating when they looked at her" that the Li household was forced to move. Before long, Jinbao's mother-in-law took her to Shanghai, where she was hired as a servant in a wealthy household. Zhu, another woman servant in the house who dabbled in trafficking, lured Jinbao away, and Jinbao became Zhu's "money tree." Zhu hired a teacher to train Jinbao to perform, and the following year took her to Tianjin,[7] placing her in the brothel of a well-known madam. Here Jinbao became known as Xiao Jinling (Small Golden Bell). As a new young prostitute, she could not compete with the famous courtesans in the house. She tried mightily to attract guests, using what the biography sardonically labeled the "entertainment method of donating her body."[8] Thus she contracted syphilis. When her entire body erupted in sores, she was dismissed from the Tianjin brothel and returned to Shanghai, broke off with Zhu, and after she was cured hung up a signboard with the name Lin Daiyu. Lin Daiyu, of course, was the moody and talented heroine of Cao Xueqin's early Qing novel *Dream of the Red Chamber,* which was popular among courtesans.[9] But Jinbao had a more proximate reason for choosing Lin Daiyu as a professional name: it had previously been used by another Shanghai courtesan, Hu Baoyu, whom Jinbao admired.

Lin took the Shanghai courtesan world by storm. She did this not by dint of her beauty, but by following a customer's advice: to attract attention in the prosperous city of Shanghai, one must appear extravagant. Her face was scarred from syphilis and her eyebrows had fallen out; she learned to apply makeup artfully and became known for her trademark eyebrows penciled in charcoal. Gradually, one biographer says, "every stinking man who talked of the courtesan quarters [*Beili*] was saying Lin Daiyu, Lin Daiyu."[10]

Soon thereafter Lin Daiyu began the pattern of twin behaviors for which she became best known: "taking a bath" (becoming a concubine in order to clear her debts; see chapter 4), and having affairs with actors.[11] She first became the concubine of a cloth merchant named Huang; this liaison was short-lived. (One version of the story has her refer to Huang as her "bathtub.")[12] Over the next year she was seen nightly with the prominent Beijing opera actors Li Chunlai and Heier Chen Jitai. She began a relationship with the Nanhui County magistrate, Wang Hengfang, who installed her in a house and paid off her debts. Wang's official duties often took him away, and as soon as he was gone Lin promptly invited Li Chunlai to live with her.[13] At least ten years her senior and Shanghai's most prominent performer of martial roles in opera,[14] Li may have been the recipient of her most deeply felt attraction, or he may merely have been her most celebrated partner. Wang heard of their affair but decided to ignore it, until one day he found Li in Lin's bedroom. Furious, he reportedly said, "If today I don't punish an actor, what kind of man am I?" Li, undeterred, was equally enraged. At this point, Lin Daiyu coolly suggested to Li that Wang's official career would suffer if it became known that he drank and consorted with prostitutes. Li quickly got the idea; grabbing a knife, he ordered Wang out, saying, "This is my house. Who dares to take me to court?" (Here and at many other points in biographies and anecdotes about Lin Daiyu, the juxtaposition of factual details with imaginatively reconstructed descriptions of dialogue and inner thoughts create an appearance of verisimilitude.) Intimidated, Wang left and no longer bothered Lin and Li. But Lin was not through with him yet. When her funds again ran out, she moved to the county where he was an official and put up a sign on her house that said "Private Residence of Government Official Wang, Chief Magistrate of Nanhui County." Then she rode a sedan chair through the streets with the name Wang inscribed on her carriage lamp. Desperate to disassociate himself from her, Wang paid her a handsome sum to leave town. Soon she broke relations with Li Chunlai as well.

By the last decade of the nineteenth century, Lin Daiyu had a retinue of regular customers that included scholars, wealthy merchants, and high-ranking officials. In return for a body price of eight thousand yuan, she became the concubine of a rich man named Qiu and moved to Nanxun, but throughout her brief marriage she secretly transported various possessions back to Shanghai in preparation for her divorce. During this time she also had affairs with Qiu's tailor and one of his relatives. Qiu contrived to get her addicted to opium, but it did not decrease her "lustful thoughts," and he angrily locked her up. Later she made a deal with her guard and escaped to Shanghai, where she enjoyed all the property she had removed from Qiu's residence. (Somehow the retelling of this episode is remarkably neutral about the actions of Qiu, who could certainly be portrayed as a drug dealer and wife abuser. Lin, on the other hand, comes across as conniving, lewd, and generally uncontrollable.)[15]

Back in Shanghai, Lin Daiyu took up with an opera singer named Lu Sanbao who specialized in female roles, and reportedly so distracted him that he lost interest in his family, even failing to attend his father's funeral. ("Her tricks can be said to be clever beyond compare.") Tiring of him, she left and set about to enjoy her wealth, only to fall victim to a thief who took all her goods, forcing her back into courtesan life. Over the next few years her lovers reportedly included the leader of the Boxer movement in Tianjin, whom she aided in escaping from the authorities; a rich official in Tianjin whom she seduced away from her sworn sister; and a military man in Wuchang.[16] In 1905, when she was about forty, she almost succeeded in entertaining the Manchu official Duan Fang when he stopped in Shanghai on his way to go abroad, but his advisers dissuaded him from such unseemly activity. Disappointed, she reportedly said that she had hoped to rely on him later to attain what she wanted. In this series of liaisons she was, variously, an impediment to filial behavior, a disloyal friend, and a schemer. Only her protection of the Boxer rebel was categorized by the biographer as one good deed among many evil ones.

Many of the most popular anecdotes about Lin Daiyu were told and retold in guidebooks and historical romances. One group of stories concerned her hubris in dealing with customers. She reportedly decided that she would like to add scholars to her retinue of admirers, which was composed mostly of rich merchants. Inviting four famous scholars to a banquet, she presented them with food and wine, then confined them in a room full of musical instruments, books, pens, and ink, all of the best quality. They could enjoy themselves, but were not permitted to leave, a prohibition that Lin enforced by locking up all of their shoes for a month. When one scholar tried to escape in a pair of borrowed slippers, she chased him and brought him back. One collection in which the story was recounted compared her actions with those of "Westerners who excel at opening up new colonies,"[17] implying that her desire for control knew no bounds.

A second type of anecdote made fun of her advancing age. An 1898 poem ostensibly in Lin's honor used elliptical references to mock her scanty eyebrows (which were compared to a remote mountain and a new moon), her big feet, her age (it was suggested that she should be addressed as Saosao [elder sister-in-law]), and her marriages, which were said to number seven or eight.[18]

A third set of Lin Daiyu stories centered on her relationships with other courtesans. On one occasion in 1899, a famous storytelling house invited Lin and four other famous courtesans to perform. The other women were either too busy, deterred by a heavy rain, or miffed at the order in which the performers were listed. Only Lin, described as more open-minded and generous than the others, showed up. (The tone of this anecdote is in sharp contrast to the sardonic and even condemnatory tone of most of the writing about Lin.)[19] Apparently, however, her relationship with fellow courtesans was not completely immune from rivalry and friction. One long anecdote that appeared in several versions recounted her feud with another famous courtesan, Lu Lanfen,[20] whose age and performance skill were roughly equal to her own. The two became rivals over the affections of the opera singer Lu Sanbao, and according to one version, Lu Lanfen succeeded in winning him from Lin.[21] Another account told in great detail of how Lu and Lin, while attending guests at the same banquet, refused to speak to each other directly but made elliptical barbed comments about each other by way of skilled repartee with the guests. Their conflict became a hot topic in all the local tabloids, which gave details of vain attempts at mediation by their customers. Finally the editor of *Youxi bao* commented that both Lu and Lin were talented women fallen into the "wind and dust," who had to serve different men every day, and who were not in control of their own fate. As pitiful creatures, the editor opined, they should learn to be more open-minded in their dealings with each other.[22] This characterization of Lu and Lin as demeaned victims was unusual in the literature about them, which usually focused on their appeal to powerful men. Yet the public attention accorded to this feud delivered another message as well: that courtesans were witty and visible public personages whose every foible was subject to public consumption.[23]

A fourth group of stories described Lin Daiyu's lifelong attraction to drivers and actors. It was said that every marriage she made became strained when she began to flirt with the servants. At one point she was reportedly arrested by an Indian policeman when he found her embracing an actor named Zhao in a hired carriage parked at a secluded spot. One longtime patron finally abandoned his plans to marry her when she refused to break off her contact with drivers and opera singers; he even fled to his hometown in Jiangxi, where she followed him in pursuit of gratuities. On an occasion when she reopened her courtesan house and celebrated with a banquet, one actor who had had an earlier affair with her reportedly refused to leave because he did not want another man to be the first to sleep with her this time.[24]

In the early years of the Republic, the aging Lin became the lover and sponsor of the actor Long Xiaoyun. She provided him with clothing and food, hired teachers to tutor him in Chinese and English, and persuaded the military governor of Jiangsu to give him a sinecure, which he eventually lost when other officials protested that he was an actor and his sister a prostitute. Long then took up with another courtesan and sold Lin (the biography gives no details of his claim on her). This event is referred to as "the most regrettable event in her life."[25]

After this Lin made another of the intercity moves that characterized her long career, going to Beijing for a time. There she continued to attract the attention of powerful men. Tang Hualong (a former Qing official, political associate of Liang Qichao, and supporter of Republican President Yuan Shikai[26]) reportedly paid three thousand yuan to establish a relationship with her but was able only to shake hands with her. When she returned to Shanghai in 1914, she was popularly called "Elder Uncle" (*Da Bobo*) because of her advanced age (about fifty) and vast experience. Tabloid accounts of the same period also called her the "old hero" (*lao yingxiong*), one of Shanghai's "two olds" (the other being her ex-lover Li Chunlai), and one of the Five Ancients (when she and some other older courtesans had a gambling party with a seventeen-year-old customer).[27] At this point in the biography, the theme of Lin's lifelong salaciousness and perfidy was supplanted by another, that of the aging courtesan:

After all, because she was aging and her beauty had faded, she could not draw a capacity crowd [as an actress]. Before long, she hung up her sign-board once more in San Malu. In old age, to apply powder and paint, and compete with fledgling maidens for the prize in love's drama—this was also a great pity.

The tabloids augmented this theme, describing Lin as "lonely" and suffering from "miserable conditions" even as they enumerated her many jewels, gifts from powerful men of the Qing and the Republic.[28]

In spite of her reported decline, Lin continued to attract attention and suitors. She and another famous courtesan appeared as guest stars in an opera and were enthusiastically received by army officers and wealthy young men, who threw packets of money onto the stage.[29] She was the subject of a titillating unauthorized biography entitled *Record of the Old Crab Walking Sideways,* with chapters devoted to each of her many marriages and love affairs. (She was referred to only as "Old Crab," while the men's names were replaced by a blank square.) Lin was reportedly furious at inaccuracies in the account; her parents were from a respected family, she said, and had never run a bean-curd store as the biography claimed.[30]

In 1919 *Crystal* reported that Lin, then fifty-four, had agreed to marry an official of the Beijing Mining Company for a price of three thousand yuan. The man was about ten years her junior, and the columnist (whose pen name was Old Gourd) archly suggested that he probably had no siblings and regarded "Old Lin" as an elder sister. This marriage, the writer continued, would probably not last too long.[31] (In fact it may never have taken place, since it is not mentioned in more detailed accounts of her life.) More extended was her dalliance with a parvenu merchant named Xue, known in Shanghai as the Great King of Dye because he had made a fortune speculating in dyes during World War I. Xue was reportedly determined to marry Lin Daiyu even before he laid eyes on her. He pursued her assiduously, overcoming her initial reluctance (he was over sixty; Lin thought that an official would provide a more reliable income stream) by offering her 300,000 yuan for her support in old age. In spite of Xue's incomparable wealth, however, apparently his household contained a person more powerful than he: his wife. Learning of Xue's engagement to Lin, she locked him up, and Lin broke off the engagement. At Mid-Autumn Festival in 1919, Xue reappeared and continued to court her throughout the autumn and winter, finding a house for her in the French Concession and setting a marriage date for spring 1920. But after the marriage the expected sum of money never materialized, and a few months later even Xue's monthly payments of several hundred yuan ceased. In early 1921 he appeared again, but Lin Daiyu reproached him with his broken promises and he vanished once more. Furious, she threatened to sue him. Fearing the damage to his reputation that such a suit would entail, he pleaded with his wife to allow him to save face and do the right thing, and finally extracted fifty-five hundred yuan from her. (The biographer had fun with this scene, with an elaborately reconstructed speech in which this wealthy man entreated his wife to have pity on guiltless Lin Daiyu.) This sum became Lin Daiyu's divorce payment.

Once again Lin hung out her signboard, but both the courtesan environment and her own physical health took a turn for the worse. By 1920 the Municipal Council had already begun a campaign to eliminate brothels in the International Settlement, and Lin was forced to borrow the sign of a courtesan house that had not yet been banned. In 1921 she suffered a bout of paralysis in her right side.

Before her illness Lin took up with one last male partner, a merchant named Wang, who made valiant efforts to find people who could cure her. This part of her story is told separately from the rest of her biography. Under the title "Lin Daiyu, in the Midst of Illness, Catches a Ghost," one guidebook recounts the following harrowing tale of physical decay and retribution.

Lin lay paralyzed; neither Chinese nor Western medicine seemed to help. Finally she sent for a well-known witch. The woman put on a Daoist robe and began to mumble. She said that the room was filled with nine of the most powerful ghosts she had ever encountered, who demanded not only Lin's life, but her own as well. Lin begged her to catch them, and she resumed her mumbling. Suddenly a black shadow spoke, revealing itself as a *huqin* player named Second Dog, a former companion who had died after Lin abandoned him to take up with the actor Long Xiaoyun. Lin burst into tears as the witch pursued the figure of the ghost, who disappeared after saying that he would come back to take revenge in two years. The next day, Lin was able to move her limbs, and her mouth was no longer twisted.

Later Lin's condition deteriorated again, and her husband summoned another witch to expel the evil. But she never fully recovered, and toward the end of her life she spent an enormous amount of money on medicine and opium. Because her right arm was lifeless, she hired an attendant who had formerly worked in an opium den to light her opium pipe for her. She suffered from bouts of insomnia; her courtesan house closed; she was forced to sell her jewelry; it was rumored that her husband, exhausted and financially strapped, was preparing to leave her.[32] Lin Daiyu died, poor and sick, at the age of sixty.[33]

The dominant tone of this account, like that of her biography by the same author, was condemnation of Lin's past perfidy. In this representation, hers had been a lifetime of scheming and planning, in which respectable men were acquired for their wealth, betrayed and humiliated by Lin's liaisons with low-class men, and discarded when she no longer found them useful. Her reward for this transgressive behavior was a lonely and vulnerable old age, unprotected by the family networks and social rewards available to aging respectable women. Yet this account of just deserts was interstitched with something else as well: nostalgia for a world that was disappearing as famous turn-of-the-century courtesans passed from the scene one by one.

Good Girls

The opposite of Lin Daiyu, in narrative if not necessarily in life, was the courtesan who provided a perfect complement to the male literati ideal—educated, quiet, reflective, and modest in comportment. A common feature of stories about these "good girls" was that they had become courtesans not because of low birth or lasciviousness, but because their otherwise decent and sometimes high-born families had fallen on hard times, and they had to pay for the burial of a parent, or help a bankrupt father to support the household.[34] Whether or not particular events actually happened is less important here than the frequency with which they were featured, indeed used to encapsulate the courtesan's personality, in biographical sketches. "Good girls" were often described in tabloid gossip columns as preferring solitude and study to the endless round of entertaining duties required of courtesans. Zhu Xiaofang, for instance, reportedly did not like to show herself in public, preferring to sit at home in front of a burning stick of incense, drinking Longjing tea and painting watercolors.[35] Zui Chun, a bespectacled courtesan adept at foreign languages and good at arithmetic, had been forced to become a courtesan because of some unspecified bad luck, although she was tormented by the knowledge that her activities were disgracing her family.[36] Chen Xiaofeng was the daughter of an aging courtesan and a civil servant; her grandfather had once been governor of Sichuan. In keeping with her noble birth, she was said to read a great deal, write well, and be familiar with foreign languages and Shakespeare. (By 1919, when these descriptions were written, Western icons of cultivated life were an accepted part of courtesan self-presentation.) Like most "good girls," she was presented as longing to leave courtesan life for marriage to a respectable man.[37]

One of Shanghai's more prominent "good girls" was Jin Xiaobao, a member of a group of courtesans known as the Four Guardian Spirits (see discussion later in this chapter). She was said to be literary, interested in education, skilled at painting orchids, and "honest and respectful like a virgin."[38] Although one biography said that she came from a family of women who entertained on painted pleasure boats in Suzhou, another maintained that she was from a poor but respectable family in Suzhou, forced to sing for a living when her family fell on hard times.[39] During one period of her career, she arranged to attend school by day and entertain by night.[40] The anecdotes about her are punctuated with dramatic and erudite speeches in which she expresses her love of learning and her high moral standards. When she heard that a group of Shanghai gentry was planning to establish a women's school, she reportedly offered to contribute, saying:

I am like a flying carpet that has fallen into a pigsty [*fei yin duo hun*]. I drift aimlessly year by year. The sea of evil has no shore. There is no place where I can find repose. If the prominent personages of your organization do not regard a courtesan as demeaned and base, and reject me completely for life, then I humbly gather all my hairpins and rings and donate them, following you and offering my tiny contribution. My contribution is very small, and cannot be of much help. Rather take it as my effort to merit a better lot in the next life. It also shows that I did not sink into the bitter sea of my own will.[41]

On another occasion, a boorish customer with the inauspicious nickname of Pockmarked Nitwit (*Shoutou Mazi*) offered to compensate her for a lost earring if she would give him an "explanation" (*shuofa*)—that is, sleep with him. Her reply, delivered with an icy smile:

I do not dare ask my lord to compensate me in full. If my lord wishes to compensate me, I will be very grateful. But what "explanation" can there be? If you desire an "explanation," in my life I have come into contact with countless rich young lords. They all need an "explanation." I have but one body, and I fear it cannot be divided up.[42]

In stories of courtesan lives, as indicated earlier, "bad girls" usually came to no good end, outliving their beauty and good health like Lin Daiyu and suffering a descent into a tormented old age. "Good girls," on the other hand, were extended the possibility of living happily ever after. As befitted a woman of her virtue and scholarly leanings, Jin Xiaobao offered to support one of her customers so that he could study in Japan. After his return to China, he took her as a concubine.[43] (Although a scholar has recently produced evidence that he later deserted her,[44] this is not mentioned in any of the contemporary biographical accounts, whose happy endings it would surely disrupt.)

Li Pingxiang, often known as the "poet courtesan" (*shi ji*), was by virtue of her education and literary talent an exemplar of the "good girl" genre, although in her romantic attachments and means of entry into prostitution she departed somewhat from the ideals of modest behavior. She was born Huang Jingyi, probably in the 1880s.[45] Her birthplace is variously reported as Jiaxing[46] or Songjiang, although some sources say that her family was originally from Anhui[47] (which stood lower in the hierarchy of native-place origins in Shanghai). She was said to be the daughter of a Suzhou tax official (*lichai*), one of a long line of Confucian scholars, who personally taught her writing and poetry.[48] Her father bragged to others of her erudition, calling her the family's "uncombed *jinshi*" (*bujie jinshi*, a *jinshi* being someone who had passed the metropolitan level of the imperial examinations, which were not, of course, open to women).[49] At the age of fourteen she was betrothed into the Liu family,[50] but before she could be married her father died, and the responsibility for the family's livelihood fell upon her mother. Near the Huang family lived the Pan family, whose son Pan Qingyuan[51] was about the same age as Huang Jingyi and had been her close friend since childhood. He is described as handsome, although of humble origins. Huang had secret sexual relations with Pan, and did not want to marry into the Liu household. She argued with her mother, who reportedly spoiled her and let her continue to see Pan, although she went ahead with the Liu marriage. Less than three months after the marriage took place, she fled to Hangzhou with her mother and her lover Pan, on the pretext that she was going there with her mother to worship. While the fugitive lovers took up residence in a temple, Huang's mother wrote a letter to Liu, saying that her daughter had died of a sudden disease. Liu sent people to fetch her coffin and buried it at Tianma Shan. Pan and Huang continued to live in Hangzhou and take care of her mother there.[52]

Unfortunately, Pan apparently had little to recommend himself aside from good looks; he had no skills with which to support the household. The three of them drifted to Suzhou, where Huang made some money inscribing poems on fans and selling them at a street market.[53] In the spring of 1901 they went to Shanghai. There Huang "fell into" prostitution in a *yao er* brothel, where she took the professional name Li Jinlian (Golden Lotus). (One of the biographical accounts states that she was lured to Shanghai by a swindler, making invisible her choice to run away with her lover Pan. A later memoir says that Pan sold her into prostitution.)[54] In a few months, sympathetic admirers who knew her poetry arranged for her to move to a *changsan* house, into the highest rank of courtesans, and changed her name to Li Pingxiang.[55] Many customers knew that she could write poetry; she became famous for matching guests line for line in quoting and composing poetry. She was also known for her calligraphy.

Four of Li Pingxiang's poems are frequently quoted. It is not clear exactly when she wrote them, or whether her poetic sensibilities were in any way shaped by her experiences as a courtesan. Some biographies introduce them when talking of her childhood talent for poetry, while others quote them after explaining how she became a courtesan. Nor do the accounts make clear how the poems were circulated; did she read them aloud? give them to customers in written form? Were the texts published in guidebook collections just as she wrote them, or are we reading a version of her poetry as remembered and written down by one or more customers?[56] A group of her works known as *The Poems from Heavenly Charms Chamber* (*Tianyun ge shi*) was published at some point by the Wenming Book Company (*Wenming shuju*), in an edition arranged by her admirers.

Poem on Choosing Chrysanthemums

Slanting and straight, slanting and straight, the leaves climb up the branch.
Nourished all alike, they each grow differently.

Even though they are decorative in appearance, in the end they are free
 from vulgarity.
I have my own way of looking at them and don't care whether others regard
 me as stupid.
The best chrysanthemums of the bunch are pricey like a fine horse.
They are like a beautiful woman, without peer, who ranks first among the
 masses of ugly women.
It is a pity that chrysanthemums, loved by Tao Yuanming,[57] have a cool
 character.
What man will consent to pick them before they have bloomed?[58]

Poem on Losing a Cat

All day you loved to lie on the messy pile of books.
What made you penetrate the clouds and not come back?
Under the lamp he gradually saw the hungry mice appear.
I suspect that the shadows of flowers forced them to come out.
Just as slaves of bad character turn their backs on their benevolent masters
Or like a worthless general who eats his fill and then runs away
The cat might have laughed at his master and thought me too stupid.
My face to the wind, I loiter around waiting for you.[59]

Poem at Mid-Autumn

Mid-autumn moon, the best of the year.
Most of the time I view it from my sickbed.
Tonight the wine cups are filled to overflowing.
Which families are having a reunion, their images reflected in the wine
 cups?
Nearby frost, the garden fruits sit in profuse abundance.
Flakes of snow, the river fish suddenly leap onto the fishing rod.
In the lonely boudoir there is no companion.
Late at night, my chanting of poems encircles the flowered fence.[60]

Poem Crying for a Younger Sister

The hibiscus has withered and died, the chrysanthemums have decayed.
The past eleven years are like a dream from which I have awakened.
I work hard to embroider the curtain, I am diligent with pen and ink.
It is a pity that when the doctor treated her, he delayed the use of ginseng
 and cocklebur.
She was modest and considerate in understanding the intentions of our
 parents.
Her clever hands often opened a volume of the sutras.
Today I lovingly recall memories of her.
Sadly the cold moon enters the distant window.[61]

Each of these poems combines the themes of elite connoisseurship—the appreciation of flowers, the chanting of poems—with themes of fleeting time

and relationships lost and longed for. Although a discerning ear might hear a woman's voice in the choice of subjects and use of poetic conventions, nothing marks these pieces as courtesan poetry, other than their means of circulation and their audience. They were passed around and read aloud among courtesan customers in Shanghai, and the city's "men of talent" competed for the attentions of Li Pingxiang. Some even compared her with the famous Song dynasty poet Li Qingzhao.

It was said that Li Pingxiang preferred literary customers and had no use for vulgar people. Nevertheless, her popularity drew her into at least one compromising situation that gave rise to an oft-repeated story suggesting the humiliations that even the most cultivated courtesan might encounter. An old man[62] became very enamored of her, and his sons and even grandsons also had intimate relations with her. One grandson visited her so often that his attachment became known to his family members. Li Pingxiang was summoned to the family residence, either by the family patriarch or by his wife, and was forced to kneel for a long time. Extremely distressed, she reportedly said that as a prostitute, she received all customers who came to her. She should not be blamed, she said, for the fact that members of this household had visited prostitutes. It was not possible for her to investigate three generations' worth of the family background of each customer. This story became a publicly circulated joke, and her reputation was said to have been slightly tarnished by the incident.[63]

Meanwhile her lover, Pan, spoiled and dependent upon her support, heard that a customer wished to take Li Pingxiang as a concubine. (One account says that by this time Pan was addicted to opium.)[64] Fearful of losing his "money tree," he reportedly began a lawsuit (whether he sued her or her customer is not entirely clear), posing as her father or uncle and opposing her "secret romance."[65] Eventually a judge issued an order that she could not return to work as a prostitute. She left for Ningbo, where she did not do well, and then returned to Shanghai, living at 1 Shantou Road, where she opened a painting and calligraphy studio known as the Xie Wenyi Studio, selling her paintings and calligraphy to support herself. Several literati, including Meng Yuesheng, Wang Yuanruo, Li Yunshu, and Wang Yiting, were among her admirers and customers for her artwork. In 1906 she married a district superintendent (*guancha*) named Huang Xiubo, and thereafter was reported to be living in Malishi.[66]

None of these accounts condemns Li Pingxiang for actions inappropriate to a virtuous woman or a loyal wife. Rather it is her lover, Pan, who is portrayed as irresponsible for being unable or unwilling to support her. Li herself is represented as filial to her mother, loyal to Pan, and stunningly skilled in her literary interchanges with customers. She may be unwise in love, but unlike Lin Daiyu she is never salacious. Her story ends with her departure from prostitution into an apparently stable marriage. Even before the marriage, however, the basis on which these authors evaluate her lies outside the realm of prostitution; she is held up as a model solely because of her literary skill. It is through literature, not sex, that she mediates relationships with customers, and for a courtesan this is apparently sufficient to merit "good girl" treatment in biographical sketches.

Dead Girls

Whether they were bad girls or good girls, courtesans were never rendered in biographical or press accounts as part of the seamy or furtive side of Shanghai life. Always they were visible, their colorful dress, career moves, and alliances with powerful customers grist for the tabloid gossip columns. Public discussion of courtesans granted them, or perhaps took for granted that they had, a certain status in Shanghai social life. Even when terrible calamities befell them, the reporting was restrained, almost dignified in its treatment. In April and May of 1929, for instance, two courtesans in succession were splashed in the face with sulfuric acid by an unknown assailant. Tabloid articles on these incidents described the women's injuries and medical treatment in great detail, but the tenor of the reporting was polite and concerned rather than lurid. The articles mentioned that neither of the women had any known enemies; any suggestion that the attacks might have been precipitated by conflicts over sexual matters was completely submerged.[67] Although written commentary on courtesan activities sometimes contained an arch or critical tone, and although potential customers were warned that their wallets might be lightened and their masculine pride wounded in encounters with courtesans, seldom were their individual lives condemned as dangerous either to themselves or to public health and morality.

Nowhere is this more evident than in the reporting of the robbery and murder of the courtesan Lian Ying in 1920. In contrast to the coverage of, for instance, the Jack the Ripper murders of prostitutes in London in 1888,[68] the Green River murders in 1980s Seattle, or the Miami murders of 1994–1995, Lian Ying's violent death was not the occasion for public reflection on the debased condition of prostitutes, their vulnerability to assault, or the need to return women to familial protection and control. Rather, it was reported as unwarranted violence against a well-known figure, which brought forth a vigorous response from her family, friends, customers, and the municipal authorities. Although the conditions of the murder were linked by many commentators to Lian Ying's courtesan status, only in the foreign press was there even a hint—and it was only a hint—that Lian Ying's demise was somehow *the fault of* that status.

Lian Ying's full formal name was Wang Lianying.[69] She was the daughter of a Hangzhou bannerman who died when she was young; her mother remarried a teahouse owner named Wang Changfa. The family's financial situation worsened after the 1911 revolution. Lian Ying attended a girls' school in Hangzhou, but did not graduate. The details of how she first became a courtesan have not been preserved, but in 1916 she came to Shanghai with someone referred to in all sources as her mother, who appears to have been her birth mother rather than her madam. She took up residence with a popular courtesan from Shanghai who had more customers than she could handle and was happy to have Lian Ying as an assistant. Soon, however, either Lian Ying herself (who was said to have a temper) or her mother developed conflicts with the mother of the other courtesan, and after a series of quarrels Lian Ying moved out and set up her own house. The breakup was acrimonious; the other courtesan made widely known her belief that Lian Ying was not qualified to operate her own courtesan house. Yet by all accounts, Lian Ying was beautiful and sang well, and many of the other courtesan's customers followed her to her new establishment. Elected Premier of Flower Affairs (*huawu zongli*) in the winter 1917 courtesan elections (see discussion later in this chapter), in the autumn of 1918 she began to work together with Xu Di, a courtesan who had also won an official title.

In 1919 Lian Ying became an assistant to two other courtesans, saying that she was too weak to meet customer demands and feared for her health. *Crystal* commented that she was apt to move again soon, adding that she had a "strange temperament" and was in the habit of suddenly breaking off relations with people who annoyed her. It also said, however, that Lian Ying was extraordinarily patient with her mother, and that she took offense if anyone was rude to the meddlesome old woman. It may be that the reason for Lian Ying's "weakness" was pregnancy; in 1919 she temporarily retired and bore a daughter, the result of a relationship with a customer named Yang. One account says that she became addicted to opium at around this time. After the child's first-month ceremony Lian Ying returned to work,[70] moving to Xiao Huayuan, one of the main courtesan districts. Slightly more than a year later, on June 9, 1920, she was murdered. At the time of her death she was twenty years old.

The story of the murder was reported in great detail in both the Chinese and foreign press, and verbatim accounts of the confessions and trial proceedings were reproduced in Wang Liaoweng's 1922 collection of courtesan lore. The level of detail reflected both the rarity of such a lurid crime and the prominence of the victim; in turn, the reporting itself helped to constitute the murder as an event for public consumption.

The man who masterminded Lian Ying's murder was an unemployed white-collar worker named Yan Ruisheng, described as twenty-six years old and almost six feet tall.[71] He lived with his widowed mother in a rented house on Guangdong Road; neighbors told the police that he had once had a wife but that she had long since left him.[72] He had studied at Zhendan University in Shanghai (he was "a man of decidedly superior education. It was understood he could speak English very well and also French," reported the *North-China Herald*), and he worked for a time as a translator and calligrapher, but in early January 1920 he became unemployed and fell ever deeper into financial trouble. His money troubles did not, however, curtail his taste for the company of courtesans and the city's gilded youth. He was friendly with his former college classmate Zhu Yajia, a son of the Shanghai merchant Zhu Baosan, and he was reportedly in love with the courtesan Ti Hongguan, to whom he owed money for a season of entertainment costs. In May or June, still unemployed and knowing that he had to pay his seasonal debt at the Dragon Boat Festival, Yan borrowed a diamond ring from Ti Hongguan, pawned it for six hundred yuan, bet on the horses at Jiangwan, and lost. Desperate to locate some money to redeem the pawn, on June 4 he used a friend's calling card to summon Lian Ying out on call. Why he chose Lian Ying is unclear; the *North-China Herald* accounts referred repeatedly to her fondness for "adorning herself with expensive jewellery [*sic*]," and so she may have seemed to Yan to be a likely candidate for robbery. She responded to the call summons wearing expensive clothing and a large diamond ring. On June 5 Yan tried to call Lian Ying out again, but she did not respond; on June 7 he borrowed yet another customer's calling card, summoned her, and used the encounter to estimate the worth of her diamond ring at two thousand yuan. On June 8 he invited Zhu and his friends to go to Lian Ying's house to gamble, hoping to establish his credentials with her as a man with wealthy friends. At the conclusion of the party, Yan invited Lian Ying to come the following day to the house of Xiao Lin Daiyu ("Little Lin Daiyu," adoptive daughter of the famous courtesan) to play mahjong. He then proceeded quite deliberately to set up the conditions for a robbery and murder.

First he arranged to borrow his classmate Zhu's car, saying that he wanted to take a courtesan for a ride the following day. (Later he would confess that he had involved Zhu partly because he held a grudge against him for refusing to help Yan secure an earlier job opportunity; he hoped to get Zhu into trouble.) On the morning of June 9, Yan purchased chloroform from a drugstore and contacted an acquaintance, an intermittently employed thirty-year-old tea-store clerk named Wu Chunfang. He told Wu that he needed one thousand yuan for holiday expenses, that he planned to kill a courtesan to get it, and that Wu could have any goods worth more than one thousand yuan if he would help. When Wu consented, Yan gave him money to buy the murder weapon, a hemp rope (the *North-China Herald* says a silk sash). The two arranged to meet at a teahouse at 3 P.M.

At 1 P.M. Yan went to Zhu's house and borrowed his car, paid off Zhu's chauffeur, and went to meet Wu and his assistant, an opium addict named Fang Rishan. He left them waiting at a teahouse near Xiao Lin Daiyu's establishment and summoned Lian Ying out on call. When she did not arrive at the house of Xiao Lin Daiyu by 4:30 P.M., he went to her house and rousted her out of bed, then returned to consult with his accomplices. At this point the chauffeur unexpectedly reappeared. Yan disposed of him by telling him that Wu was his servant and must accompany him, and that the car was too small to hold all of them. Once again he sent the chauffeur away and returned to Xiao Lin Daiyu's house. According to *Crystal,* while waiting for Lian Ying he engaged Xiao Lin Daiyu in conversation, asking her why she was not wearing her two-thousand-yuan diamond ring. The paper reported that she had put it away because there was a shortage of food at that time in the city and she did not wish to conspicuously flaunt her possessions. But she despised Yan, and to him she said only that the ring was slightly loose and she was having it fixed. He asked which shop was fixing it; she told him that an old customer was arranging the repair and she did not know where the work was being done.[73]

At 6:30 P.M. Lian Ying finally showed up at Xiao Lin Daiyu's house, wearing her trademark jewelry: a pair of diamond bracelets, two diamond rings, one large diamond brooch, and a gold wristwatch. Yan lied to her, saying that his friends had broken their appointment to play mahjong, and suggested that they go for a drive instead to take the country air. (The *North-China Herald,* with charming attention to colonial detail, added, "He told her, it is alleged, that, as he had studied abroad, he was very particular about his health.") After much persuasion he prevailed. (*Crystal* adds that Xiao Lin Daiyu tried to pull Lian Ying aside and warn her that Yan was an evil person, but Lian Ying paid no heed.)[74] Yan drove out into the wheat fields in the Xujiawei area with Lian Ying at his side and Wu and Fang in the back seat.

By this time it was dusk. Yan stopped the car, and the three men got out on the pretext that they had to light the car lamp. They retrieved the chloroform from the trunk, and Wu stuffed a cotton ball soaked in chloroform over Lian Ying's mouth and nose. Terrified, she begged the three men for her life, but they only poured more chloroform onto the cotton. At this point, Yan went off to distract a passing peasant from the scene by offering him a ride in the car. Wu and Fang robbed her of all her jewelry (later itemized by her parents as two diamond rings, a pearl necklace, a diamond bracelet, earrings, an ear pick, two pins, a gold watch, and a small gold mirror), strangled her, and threw the body into a field. Yan returned from giving the peasant a ride, and with the other two loaded Lian Ying's body into the car in order to move it to a more isolated spot. As they drove along dividing their loot, Yan took his eyes off the road and hit a tree, damaging the mudguards. Before the three men unloaded the body, Yan noticed that Lian Ying was still breathing. He ordered Wu and Fang to make sure she was dead, handing them the bottle of chloroform to finish the job. Yan then drove off to return the car, promising Wu and Fang he would return for them at midnight. He returned the car to the chauffeur, promised him money to repair it, told him not to say anything to Zhu about the damage, and asked for the car back at midnight. By the time he got back to the field, his accomplices had disappeared (Fang, the opium addict, reportedly got a craving for the drug and left).

Meanwhile, Lian Ying's mother and stepfather, learning that she had gone out for the evening with Yan and not returned, became worried and sought out Zhu. Knowing nothing, but assuming that Lian Ying and Yan were having an affair, he reassured them that she would soon be back. The next day, he happened to mention to his chauffeur that he thought Yan had hidden Lian Ying away somewhere. When the chauffeur told him about the damage to his car, Zhu began to suspect that something was wrong. On June 11, two days after the murder, Zhu and his chauffeur spotted Yan on his way to the pawnshop to redeem Ti Hongguan's ring. Zhu stopped and asked where Yan had hidden Lian Ying, and Yan denied all knowledge. When Zhu suggested that they call on Lian Ying's worried parents, Yan panicked and jumped out of the car in the middle of the road. That evening, Yan sought out Wu and asked him to bury Lian Ying's corpse, a request he ignored. Yan fled the city on June 12.

On June 15 (the *North-China Herald* says June 17), Lian Ying's badly decomposed body was discovered, along with the hemp rope (or silk sash). Her hair was bound with an ornament that her parents recognized as hers. The corpse was identified by Lian Ying's stepfather, and the International Settlement police offered a reward for Yan's capture. In subsequent days, Settlement detectives worked steadily on the case. They retrieved a diamond-inlaid gold pin that the murderer had pawned, visited the murder scene, and publicized a reward of one thousand yuan offered by Lian Ying's family for the capture of the criminal. (According to the *North-China Herald,* the reward was offered by the keeper of Lian Ying's house, and amounted to five hundred yuan for information leading to the body and an additional five hundred yuan if the jewelry was recovered.) At the same time, Settlement authorities sought to prevent other such crimes by prohibiting restaurants and hotels from summoning "sing-song girls" out on call after midnight. Several weeks passed; the case remained unsolved.[75] Then, in mid-July, as Yan waited on a platform in Xuzhou for a train to take him north, a Chinese policeman recognized him as the man on a "wanted" circular and arrested him, remanding him to Shanghai. The Chinese press reported that he was found with a one-thousand-yuan diamond belonging to Lian Ying concealed in his mouth. Police recovered on his person a large diamond ring, a pearl necklace, an earring, and a pin, which were returned to her parents. When interrogated, he supplied the names of Wu and Fang; the former was captured, but the latter eluded the police. Wu had received as his cut a diamond ring, a pin, and at least one other piece, which he had asked Fang to sell for him and which were never recovered.

The two defendants were apparently tried twice: first in the Mixed Court, where a Chinese magistrate and a British assessor heard the case, and then in a Chinese military court. The Mixed Court claimed jurisdiction because "the offense was substantially committed in the Settlement," although no one disputed that Lian Ying's body had been found in Chinese territory. Throughout the trial, friends and admirers of Lian Ying filled the courtroom and jammed the surrounding streets, and the newspapers all reported the proceedings as front-page news. Based on full confessions by Yan and Wu, as well as testimony by Zhu and his chauffeur, the Mixed Court found the men guilty of robbery and murder.

For reasons that remain unclear, the two convicted men were then turned over to a Chinese military court, although a Chinese civil district court also claimed jurisdiction in the case. At this trial, according to the *North-China Herald,* Wu tried to exonerate himself by saying that Yan and Fang had actually committed the murder, and that he had neither seen nor participated in it. Yan testified, according to the *Herald,* that "his main intention was to rob the girl. He never meant to take her life." Like Wu, he claimed that the actual murder had been committed by the two other men, but took responsibility for planning Lian Ying's death. He requested that he be given a Bible, informing the court that he was a Catholic and asking that a priest be present to read the service after his execution, since he expected to be sentenced to death. The court found the two men guilty of forcible robbery and murder as defined in article 376 of the Criminal Code, and both were given the death sentence, but at that point the story dropped out of the press and their ultimate fate was not reported. Chen Dingshan's 1967 memoir says that Yan Ruisheng and his accomplices were executed at the Western Battery in Wusong, with massive crowds of spectators jamming the train to Wusong, even riding on the roof.[76]

A striking feature of the trial coverage in the press was the restrained and respectful language used to describe Lian Ying. The *North-China Herald* called her "one of Shanghai's most famous sing-song girls," "reputed to be the second best-looking of this class in Shanghai," "a girl of unusual appearance, very beautiful, and looked upon as a first class girl in her line of business." Despite the fact that during precisely this period the foreign community was engaged in an intense debate about licensing or eliminating brothels, a campaign in which sing-song houses were supposed to be included, no hint of moral opprobrium was attached to descriptions of Lian Ying's occupation. If the journalists named one failing, it was not that she was a beautiful woman who moved about in public and engaged in nonmarital relations with men, but rather that she "was very fond of adorning herself with expensive jewellery [*sic*] and would do anything to get ornaments." Twice the newspaper commented that this was probably "the direct cause of her death," but it did not use the opportunity to rail against adornment in general or courtesans in particular. The story line read as an account of the craven and horrifying murder of a beautiful professional woman, a recognized member of the Shanghai community. Yan, in contrast, was portrayed as a man who "loved philandering and was not of good character."[77] His very taste in entertainment portended instability and danger: he was "said to have been in the habit of attending moving picture shows and was extremely fond of those showing sensational plots."[78]

Throughout the trials, the plight of Lian Ying's relatives was mentioned sympathetically in the tabloid press. Lian Ying reportedly left 370 yuan in cash in a suitcase, but her burial service cost 1,100 yuan, and her mother was forced to pawn her remaining jewelry and silver utensils to pay off her debts and buy her a coffin. In addition, *Crystal* reported, Lian Ying's mother had paid a private detective 1,000 yuan to arrest Yan (an account that contradicts other reports of the arrest circumstances), and needed more money to bring suit against him. Lian Ying's old patrons helped her hire a lawyer known as the "flower-protecting lawyer" (*huhua lüshi*), presumably so called because he frequently represented courtesans in court, but nothing further was ever reported about the lawsuit.

Ten years later, *Crystal* ran a nostalgic retrospective on the death of Lian Ying. Her family, the report said, had kept her coffin in an association hall (*gongsuo*), paying an annual storage fee, and for many years had not arranged for burial. Her daughter, Hao Guan, was being raised by Lian Ying's parents and brother; she was by this time eleven years old, and was being trained in opera. On the ninth anniversary of Lian Ying's death, her mother sent out an obituary notice and summoned monks to chant the burial service. The costs were paid by two of Lian Ying's old customers, each of whom donated three hundred yuan at the request of her mother.[79] Here, as in the earlier description of the trials, Lian Ying's family appeared as a stable, caring group of people determined to see justice done, able and willing to care for her remains and to raise her daughter with due attention to all proprieties.

After her death the story of Lian Ying passed into popular legend, becoming the basis for Beijing and Shanghai opera pieces, plays, popular songs, a movie, commercial advertisements, and more than twenty years of popular discussion. Chen Dingshan reports that in one stage production of the story, actors drove a real car onstage to simulate the evening courtesan scene on Fuzhou Road. In another scene the actors ate watermelon, an expensive prop to procure in winter. In a different production, Lian Ying appeared to her sister in a dream after the murder. The part of the sister was played by a very popular actress. Her principal song, "You Tell Me Your Suffering," was made into a recording and performed by the courtesans of Shanghai, in a tight circuit of art and life. One actor who portrayed Yan Ruisheng was reportedly so moving that those in the audience who knew Yan all cried for him. Some Shanghai residents believed that Yan Ruisheng had not in fact been executed, but that Yan's friend Zhu had hired a substitute. Chen comments that Shanghai residents fixated on the case at a time of great national instability, implying that it offered them a diversion from more serious matters. He also calls Lian Ying and Yan Ruisheng "the founders of erotic news" (*huangse xinwen zhi bizu*), noting that they began a tradition of cases of love suicides and murder that were avidly followed by the public and made into plays. With just a trace of acerbity, he adds that the actresses who played Lian Ying were all more beautiful than the original, and calls it her luck to become so famous because of her death.

Chen's account itself, set down more than forty years after the events, is a fine illustration of how such a story could accumulate increasing levels of detail, most of it unverifiable, as time went on. He reports, for instance, that Yan Ruisheng first planned to rob Xiao Lin Daiyu rather than Lian Ying, because he coveted a diamond she had cajoled from a customer who had in turn "borrowed" it without permission from a client at his brother's jewelry store. When Xiao Lin Daiyu declined Yan Ruisheng's offer to go out for a drive, he turned on the spur of the moment to Lian Ying, who happened to be returning from a call wearing a jeweled tiara. In Chen's version, Yan Ruisheng did not want to murder Lian Ying, but his accomplices insisted. After her death he is said to have fallen on his knees and tearfully confessed the murder to his wife. Lian Ying's fate is thus presented as the result of a series of unfortunate accidents.[80]

Stories of individual courtesans—as objects of admiration, disapproval, or vicarious adventure and danger—were a staple of urban Shanghai life. Circulating through various journalistic and literary genres, the stories established these women as public figures about whom information could be traded and accounts embroidered. The process of circulation helped to create an urban community based on shared knowledge, a common tissue of stories. In this sense, courtesans were known far beyond the elite circle of patrons who paid for their company, vied for their attentions, and wrote down their histories. Women like Lin Daiyu, Li Pingxiang, and Lian Ying became icons to a wider urban readership who absorbed lessons about proper female behavior and urban danger from their life stories.

The contemporary reader who devours detailed accounts of their lives in search of a subaltern voice, however, is pursuing a risky strategy. These stories are replete with instances of agency, cunning, longing, talent, guile, violence, loyalty, filial piety—a virtual treasure trove of themes varied enough to satisfy the feminist researcher, the Confucian scholar, and the melodrama junkie all at once. As individual tales, they compel fascination. As a generic group, however, their utter predictability is sobering. The bad girl dies alone; the good girl makes a respectable marriage; the dead girl becomes a trope in urban cautionary tales of violence and greed. Read in this way, the stories offer little in excess of their generic messages; the piling on of detail gives each story the appearance of uniqueness without offering much clue to the self-understandings of these courtesans. Ironically, it is the famous courtesans, the ones about whom we can recover the most "facts," who disappear most thoroughly into their own stories.

RITUALS OF RECOGNITION: THE FLOWER-LIST ELECTIONS

Another means by which the community of patrons and readers created and recognized itself was the selection of courtesans for the "flower list of successful candidates" (*huabang*) in elections that took place irregularly in Shanghai from the 1860s to 1920.[81] Similar elections had been held since the mid–seventeenth century in the Suzhou area.[82] As intricate rituals of describing and judging, in some respects the elections deliberately paralleled the selection of successful candidates in the imperial civil-service examinations.[83] But whereas male candidates for government service sat for written examinations after years of preparation, courtesans did not initiate their own participation in the flower-list elections. Brothel patrons were invited to enter the names of their favorite courtesans on the "flower list," and the woman who received the most letters of recommendation was awarded the same title as the man whose exam received the highest grade (*zhuangyuan*). Other titles derived from the examination system (*bangyan, tanhua*) were awarded as well. A courtesan's chance of being selected for one of the several dozen top posts was roughly one in one hundred, significantly better odds than the one-in-three-thousand chance that the male holder of a district-level degree would pass the metropolitan exams.[84] In some years, separate lists were published for beauty and skilled operatic performance; the latter list drew its titles from the imperial examinations for military officers. A separate "leaf list" was assembled for outstanding courtesan attendants.[85]

Although women were judged on the basis of their appearance and performance skills, not unlike the criteria in contemporary beauty pageants, the flower-list elections were crucially different from beauty contests in one important respect: the object made visible to be judged was not the woman herself, but the letters of recommendation written by customers on her behalf. "Gentlemen" (*jun*) were invited to submit such letters via public announcements in the tabloid press, which then printed each letter as it arrived.[86] In the 1897 election, the winner, Zhang Sibao, received nine recommendations, while the second- and third-place holders each received seven.[87] In the testimonials that accompanied their votes, patrons marshaled their powers of eloquence to extol the virtues of their chosen favorite, in the process exhibiting their authorial skill to their fellow literati. Typically, the published list of winners reprinted the best of these descriptions, presenting as many as several dozen women for the delectation of the reader. Some lists provided the name, address, native place, and age of each woman, followed by a brief poem describing her or comments about her dress, character, and family background. Others compared the women to flowers and birds, lavishing more literary attention on the plumage and coloring of these symbols than on the women themselves.[88]

Still other letters commented on the election procedures, suggested witty new categories, gave advice about selection criteria, defended the character of their favorites, or complained about the results.[89] The sponsoring newspapers were at pains to assure readers that they added nothing to the commentary, drawing their election copy exclusively from the letters of readers.[90] The public conversation about courtesans conducted through these letters helped to forge a community of repartee within which men displayed their literary talents to one another. As the preface to a collection of biographies and pictures of the 1917 flower-list winners explained:

> The good looks of beautiful women and the articles of famous scholars are the most precious treasures in the world. . . . The good looks of beautiful women, embellished in the articles of famous scholars, appear even more pleasing and lovely. The articles of famous scholars, permeated by the good looks of beautiful women, read as even more full of talent and excellence.[91]

Yet courtesans were not merely passive objects of verbal display in the election rituals. They were eager to be elected because the titles brought prestige to them as individuals and business to their houses, while failure to be mentioned could injure their reputations.[92] The winning courtesans were usually referred to by their titles in any published item of news or gossip concerning them.[93] An elected title also increased the price a courtesan commanded when a madam rented her services for a season or a man purchased her as his concubine.[94] "Once they are listed, their reputation and price increase tenfold. Those who are not listed usually feel regret. But whether they rise or fall may depend on the likes and dislikes of one individual. Some people also obtain it through bribery," wrote Xu Ke in his 1920 collectanea of Qing courtesan customs.[95] Recognition via the elections was a process of highly politicized choices, where success was dependent upon a courtesan's ability to mobilize a network of connections to patrons and a wider public. If her efforts at self-promotion appeared crude, she could be subjected to devastating ridicule, as when Jin Qiaolin submitted a letter of self-nomination in classical style and a news commentator wondered in print how an illiterate courtesan could possibly compose such a learned piece by herself.[96] Although courtesans competed energetically for the election titles, some complained that the awards were a mixed blessing, since they brought in their wake crowds of well-wishers who expected to receive gifts of cash. In 1919, one courtesan actually gave up her title after her "mother" complained bitterly about the expense.[97]

The earliest Shanghai elections were organized by individual writers affiliated with newspapers and publishing houses, and were publicized among a small circle of literati. But in the last years of the nineteenth century, the newly established tabloid ("mosquito") press began to sponsor flower-list elections. Li Boyuan's tabloid *Youxi bao* (Recreation news) ran elections as frequently as four times a year beginning in 1897. The first election attracted such attention and boosted the paper's circulation so dramatically, selling out an initial run of five thousand copies and a reprint of three thousand, that it virtually ensured imitation by other tabloids.[98] Among the election sponsors in the first decade of the twentieth century were the *Flower Heaven Daily*, the *Flower World News*, the *Idle Emotions News*, the *Pleasure Talk News*, and the *Colored Phoenix News*. A common lament in many contemporary accounts was that these imitators demeaned the flower-list ritual by demanding payments from courtesans in return for a place on the roll. Continuing through 1909, these elections moved from imitation of the civil-service examinations to simulacrum, bestowing imperial titles even after the examinations were abolished in 1905.[99]

The turn of the century was a time of great political turmoil among elite Chinese men, who were increasingly upset about the imperial court's inability to defend China from foreign incursions. Inevitably, concerns about the fate of the nation seeped into discussion of the flower roll, as literate men employed the time-honored ploy of comparing government officials to courtesans. During the Sino-Japanese war of 1894–1895, several writers commented, court officials had ingratiated themselves with the enemy, yet were able to maintain their high salaries and status. In an era when even elite, educated men were so lacking in virtue, these authors asked plaintively, how could anyone criticize courtesans ("weak and lowly women") for having relationships with more than one patron?[100]

No elections were held from 1910 to 1917, an interval during which the dynasty was overthrown, the Republican government was established, and the country descended into political chaos dominated by feuding warlords. When the elections resumed in 1917, the organizers updated the nomenclature. Instead of imperial civil-service titles, leading courtesans were awarded titles such as president, prime minister, general, magistrate, political council member, talent minister, arts minister, appearance minister and vice-minister, military governor, special district military governor, character minister, chief of administration, troop inspector, and government consultant.[101] At first glance these elections seem little more than a feeble nod toward the glories of the past, an atavistic echo at a time when the writers of the New Culture Movement were mounting vigorous attacks on many aspects of literati culture.[102] Yet some observers of these modernized election rituals felt otherwise. The use of political terminology, they suggested, was an oblique expression of political dissatisfaction with China's weak and ineffectual government. In 1917 a commentator in the newspaper *Zhonghua xin-*

bao even suggested that the election organizers planned to permit "pheasant" prostitutes (*yeji*; literally, "wild chickens") to stand for election under the rubric of the opposition (*zaiye dang*; literally, "parties in the wilderness," written with the same character for "wild" as appears in *yeji*), perhaps in an allusive show of support for China's own parties out of power. At the same time, the commentator continued, perhaps with tongue in cheek, the appropriation of presidential terminology by courtesans would help to undermine rigid Chinese status distinctions and install a more flexible foreign-style social system, which should be taken as a sign of progress.[103]

These Republican-era elections were far larger in scale than their imperial predecessors. In late 1917, for instance, the New World Amusement Hall sponsored an open election meeting where participants paid to vote. In the 1917 and 1918 elections, several patrons bought tens of thousands of tickets in order to cast all their votes for particular courtesans, thus making a public demonstration of their own wealth as well as their courtesan preferences.[104] The 1919 elections held at the Great World Amusement Hall provided several weeks of material for the tabloid gossip columns, awarding titles such as Chang E (the mythical Chinese beauty who flew to the moon), Moon Dance Leader, and Moon Dance Fairies.[105] By 1920 even the staid *Shenbao*, Shanghai's oldest newspaper, was publishing advertisements for the elections.[106] A steadily proliferating number of competing elections and titles testified to the commercial potential of these contests for the organizations that sponsored them, which now included companies as well as amusement halls and tabloid newspapers. One of the 1920 elections, for instance, was run by the Qimei Milk Candy Company, which held a highly publicized "fragrant nation" election for the positions of president, vice president, and premier. (The "fragrant nation" label was necessary to distinguish this election from the one sponsored by the New World Amusement Hall, which had taken out a copyright on the term "flower-nation elections.") The winning courtesans received elegant sets of Western-style furniture; the first-place winner was thenceforth known throughout Shanghai as the "milk president," after the main ingredient in the sponsor's product. The purpose of the contest was to promote the sale of Qimei candy.[107] Some of these Republican-era elections, unlike the earlier ones, centered on contests where several thousand courtesans competed in the performance of opera pieces.[108]

Just when the flower-list elections reached a high point of frequency and visibility, however, the clamor for reform originating in the foreign concessions altered the environment for such rituals. The elections were abandoned after 1920, when the Shanghai Municipal Council began to draw lots and withdraw brothel licenses.[109] In subsequent years, old-style literati increasingly displayed their erudition in the production of nostalgic pieces about the glorious courtesan past. One form this nostalgia took was the creation of genealogies of flower-list elections, where the list of titles and winners from each year was carefully reproduced. In the histories of the flower lists fashioned at this time, Li Boyuan's elections were praised as models of rectitude, where courtesans were selected, just as imperial scholars had been, according to strict criteria of talent, unlike later elections corrupted by bribery and commercialized presentation.[110] (The fact that the imperial examination system itself had in its later years included generous provisions for commercial purchase of official titles was not mentioned in these accounts.) At the same time, a growing segment of the educated community began to define itself partly through public advocacy of the reform of prostitution, rather than ritualized public appreciation of it.

COURTESAN NETWORKS

Relationships among courtesans, like so much else about courtesan life, entered the historical record only when writers and reporters felt they were of interest to customers or the wider urban readership. Feuds, as noted earlier, were eagerly followed by the tabloids, which also dutifully reported instances of business cooperation or competition. If one courtesan left town to go on a pilgrimage, for instance, or her business became too much for her to handle, she might invite another courtesan in to help her out. Depending upon their experience and current popularity, the two might work as equals or in a hierarchical pair. Sometimes a small group of courtesans opened a house together. The newspapers commented that one such group "was as close as blood sisters," but usually nothing was said about the depth or duration of such relationships, much less the affective ties that might (or might not) have cemented them.[111]

A slightly more visible form of courtesan association was groups of women who formally swore a bond of sisterhood, even if they had no business dealings with each other.[112] One such group called itself the Ten Sisters (*shi zimei*), styling its forms of address after those of Shanghai hoodlums. Popular in the first decade of the twentieth century, these ten women numbered themselves Old One, Old Two, and so forth. They were each associated with different brothels and moved in and out of marriage at different times, but were said to be very close and to socialize together frequently. Some sources suggest that more than one group of women adopted this name, and that the individual titles such as Old Three and Old Four were passed on to others when a woman left the profession. Yet here, too, details are sketchy.[113]

The most famous appellation for groups of prominent courtesans was the Four Guardian Spirits (*sida jingang*), a name derived from the Buddhist figures who guarded the heavens. In local temples, these Buddhist deities were portrayed holding a sword, a *pipa,* an umbrella, and a dragon (some sources say a clam). As one collection of courtesan lore facetiously noted, the prosperous port of Shanghai, where Chinese and foreigners congregated, was in need of guardians, and therefore some had become flesh, appearing on earth in all their beauty to maintain favorable weather. The presence of courtesans was linked, if only in jest, to the prosperity and safety of the port.[114] The Guardians were frequently mentioned in the tabloids, which said that they were welcomed in the manner of high officials on their daily trips to a local garden. The four courtesans who collectively bore this name varied from one account to the next, and there was even some scholarly quibbling about the exact membership, but the four most frequently mentioned Guardians were Zhang Shuyu,[115] Jin Xiaobao, Lu Lanfen,[116] and Lin Daiyu.[117]

Unlike the Ten Sisters, the Guardians were a group created by the press and guidebook writers;[118] they did not constitute themselves on the basis of affection or shared business interests. They were a disparate collection of individuals who did not appear to share any particular personality characteristics or sense of themselves as a group. What they did have in common was fame and a prominent presence on the Shanghai courtesan scene, and the name became a shorthand way of referring to their visibility.

At the turn of the century, the Guardians were approached by a group of men who wanted to establish a cemetery for famous courtesans who had no one to claim them. The men wanted to provide courtesans with a proper burial in a place where their customers, lovers, and admirers could visit their graves. They asked Lin Daiyu to take charge of collecting donations to purchase the land, with the assistance of the other three Guardians. The four women had sixteen hundred donation booklets printed up; each took four hundred to distribute in courtesan houses for collection at the end of the month. Lin Daiyu alone collected 300 yuan on the first night, with both courtesans and customers making donations. (Elsewhere, however, it was reported that donations totaled only 428 yuan, and Lin's contribution is not mentioned. Instead, she is criticized for poor management of the fund drive.) Jin Xiaobao (the most literary, and perhaps literate, of the four) negotiated a price on a plot of land near Longhuasi and completed all the necessary paperwork. In spring 1899, the group erected a boundary stone and a memorial arch inscribed with the phrase "Public Cemetery for a Group of Women" (*qunfang yizhong*), signed by Jin Xiaobao and followed by a list of all the courtesans who had contributed. Later, because of bad management, the graveyard disappeared, and by 1928 no one knew exactly where it had been.

As interesting as the establishment of the graveyard itself is the literature it generated. A 1928 collection reprints letters written on behalf of Lin Daiyu, in her voice, entreating the other three Guardians to help her. It also contains letters on behalf of all four Guardians to the public, explaining the project and soliciting donations. The language of these letters is flowery, arcane, and suffused with a tragic sensibility. The women refer to themselves as born into an unfortunate fate, unable to communicate their pain to others, destined for early death, and conscious of the fleeting nature of time and mortality. Lin begs the other Guardians, and all of them entreat the wider public, to have compassion and work together to build the graveyard. The women also say that because this act is performed "for people of our own kind," they will take responsibility for asking people to donate. Just what the reader can infer from these letters about courtesan views of the world is one of history's conundrums. Each of the letters was written on behalf of the women, most likely by a male amanuensis. The highly stylized phrases in which the women express the sadness of their lives and the ephemeral nature of all life sounds remarkably like the linguistic repertoire of the guidebook and collectanea authors themselves. Paradoxically, the question of "voice" becomes most troubling in circumstances where courtesans appear to be speaking for themselves.[119]

This problem is even more evident in the text of an opera written by two literati at the encouragement of the tabloid editor Li Boyuan while the cemetery project was under way. Apparently performed to great acclaim, *The Jade Hook Scar* was divided into ten scenes. Some of these were devoted to straightforward renderings of the fund-raising process, but the play was lent dramatic unity by the introduction of the (fictional?) courtesan Chen Daiyu, who died after being mistreated by her madam and became the first courtesan buried in the cemetery.[120] The use of Chen as a plot device introduced a type of victimization that may well have occurred in courtesan houses, but was conspicuously absent from the biographies of any of the four Guardians. Like the fund-raising letters, this opera must be read as a recitation, by female voices, of a particular male-authored version of courtesan life.

Courtesans and the Nation

The revolutionary ferment of the late Qing and early Republican periods, with its concomitant emphasis on women's education as a key to national reform, affected the world of Shanghai courtesans.[121] Just as women in other walks of life organized and began to demand particular kinds of education, so did courtesans. In about 1906, a courtesan named Blue Bridge Villa (*Lanqiao Bieshu*) became renowned, and garnered official praise, when she donated one thousand yuan for the rights-recovery movement, in which Chinese sought to buy back foreign investments in the transportation system.[122]

Taking up the language of Darwin, in 1914 a number of older courtesans (including Lin Daiyu and Weng Meiqian) established the Courtesan Evolution Corps (*Qinglou jinhua tuan*).[123] Two of the major activists in the organization were Zhang Manjun and Zhu Ruchun. Zhang was reportedly an eager reader of revolutionary newspapers and an early spokesperson for patriotic sentiment in the brothels. She was known for making a speech at about this time denouncing a local fashion in which courtesans wore pants printed with the pattern of the national flag. Zhang pointed out that many fighters and heroes had lost their lives for this flag, and that wearing it on pants might make Chinese a laughingstock among foreigners.[124]

Some years earlier, Zhu Ruchun had been the second-place winner of the 1897 elections, and she was known for her personal attractiveness.[125] In her middle years, she became convinced that prostitutes needed an education in order to rescue them from the "bitter sea." (It is not clear whether she or the guidebook authors were the source of such phrases to describe the situation of courtesans. Other phrases included "damaged flowers" and "broken moon.") This group raised funds from a benefit performance by a women's theater troupe, publicized by the Courtesan Evolution Corps and featuring performances by many of Shanghai's most well known courtesans. The benefit raised more than one thousand yuan, which was used to rent a schoolhouse, hire teachers, and register fifty students, including courtesan-house attendants and child prostitutes. The organizers themselves also enrolled. "In a single transformation the devil-filled hell became a place of calm and order" (*xiange liyi*; literally, "rituals with stringed accompaniment"), proclaimed the guidebook history; the courtesan students learned to boycott foreign products in favor of Chinese goods. As Zhang Manjun said in a speech at the opening ceremonies, it was impossible not to feel boundless hope about the future of the courtesan houses.

All too soon, however, the enterprise foundered under the daily demands of courtesan life. Zhu Ruchun left for Tianjin, in one of the many intercity moves of a courtesan career. The students, who entertained daily until three or four in the morning, could not rise in time for morning classes. Their work required that they spend a great deal of time adorning themselves and begin to receive guests again in the late afternoon, so the fact that classes were not dismissed until after 4 P.M. was another problem. The school lacked a permanent operating fund and competent management. Attendance plummeted and the school closed, bringing an end to the history of the Courtesan Evolution Corps.

Five years later, the courtesan Jian Bing established a school on the first floor of one of her two courtesan houses. The enterprise was organized more simply than the Evolution Corps school: students attended classes one hour a day, paying three yuan tuition a month. Classes were taught by Jian Bing's brother, who had some training in literature. Courtesans and their children attended this school, but after four months it too folded, reportedly because the schoolmates spent too much time gambling and entertaining every night, to the detriment of their studies. Soon thereafter Jian Bing took up with a wealthy army officer and made plans to marry him.[126]

Short-lived as these organizations were, they marked the beginning of direct courtesan participation in national political events.[127] Such participation became standard in the first decade of the Republic. In response to Japan's Twenty-One Demands in 1915, several courtesans donated part of their call income and makeup money, totaling three hundred yuan, to a fund for national salvation. In a letter that she sent to many local newspapers, the courtesan Zang Chunge linked courtesans to other citizens and her own fate to that of China. Although she was born unlucky and now belonged to a "house of songs," she said, "those in the courtesan houses, after all, have families, and those who have families must also have a nation. For this reason, the root of life lies in serving the nation." In listening to her customers talk, she continued, she had learned that a certain country was trying to make China into a second India or Korea—that is, a colony. "Although I am a prostitute," she declared, "I am also a citizen of the nation." By placing part of her savings at the disposal of a patriotic organization, she hoped to help save China.[128]

Just before the May Fourth demonstrations of 1919 broke out in Beijing, nineteen Shanghai courtesans organized a reading group and invited Lin Daiyu to be their "Big Brother" or "Elder Uncle." ("It reminds us of the Boxer movement and makes us shudder," commented *Crystal,* failing to explain why this particular group was greeted with the opprobrium reserved for atavistic rebels, rather than the usual approval.)[129] In the wake of the May Fourth demonstrations, courtesans closed their houses to all business on May 9 to observe a day of national shame and declared their intention to use only Chinese-made goods. Early in June, courtesan houses closed again to observe a citywide strike that lasted until midmonth. Outside Jian Bing's door, a black notice board replaced her usual colorful flag, pleading for nonviolent resistance. Prominent courtesans announced the formation of a Courtesan National Salvation Corps (*Qinglou jiuguo tuan*), distributing two thousand leaflets throughout Shanghai calling for nonviolence and the release of incarcerated students. They also set up a facility to provide food and water to striking students.[130] Most courtesan declarations limited themselves to statements about the nation, usually prefaced by a comment that even those in the lowly profession of prostitution shared the more general patriotic sentiments. An organization called the National Social Reform Association, however, addressing "sisters in the courtesan houses," called for attention to their own situation. It said that they had been forced to sell their bodies because they had no other means of livelihood, and were pitiable creatures, but could improve their own future prospects as well as those of the nation by forming small groups to leaflet the city about national salvation. Here the national destiny was linked to the improvement of courtesans' lot in life.[131]

In the 1910s, concern about the fate of the nation became almost a requirement of courtesan behavior, to the point where *Crystal* reported in 1919 that a famous courtesan's business was in decline because she was not able to read and was not conversant in the vocabulary of "patriotism" and "countrymen."[132] For her part, Jian Bing made a point after the May Fourth demonstrations of refusing to entertain Japanese customers. When one of her regular customers invited a Japanese guest to a banquet in her house, Jian Bing went off to listen to opera, leaving the servants to order dishes from a nearby restaurant. Lin Daiyu sent one of her attendants over to help host the banquet, but Jian's refusal was reported in the local gossip columns.[133] Almost two decades later, shortly after the outbreak of full-scale war between Japan and China, a journalist reported on a public a cappella singing contest conducted by courtesans that raised 1,670 yuan in cash for refugee relief. The contest was attended by, among others, the head of the city's Social Affairs Bureau and the secretary of a major relief organization.[134]

With each of these stories, the place of the courtesan in public political events, as well as the place of those events in the lives of courtesans, was being incrementally enlarged. In both guidebooks and the press, stories about the Courtesan Evolution Corps, or about the closing of courtesan houses in a citywide strike, were printed side by side with news of recent liaisons, fashions, and illnesses among famous courtesans. The widening scope of what counted as courtesan news and activity in no way supplanted the major focus on the doings of "bad girls" and "good girls," and most courtesan appearances on the public scene were linked to the traditional categories of beauty and talent, not patriotism and self-improvement. Nevertheless, an insistent new subtheme appeared, in which courtesans were citizens of a threatened nation who were especially at risk because of their lowly profession. With each report linking courtesans and nationhood, a new way of understanding courtesan life took hold: one that targeted courtesans as well as other prostitutes for reform in pursuit of a strengthened and modernized China.

SILENCES: CONTRACEPTION, PREGNANCY, CHILDREN, OLD AGE

As noted at the beginning of this chapter, the peculiarities of the historical record on courtesans mean that we have more information about their efforts to save the nation than we do about how they avoided or sought pregnancy, what they did with children they bore, and how they survived past the age when they could support themselves as performers or close companions for the rich and powerful.

Sources compiled after the revolution of 1949 are heavily marked by the categories of "speaking bitterness," in which people learned to reinterpret their remembered past through the matrix of oppression and resistance.[135] From these we learn that regimes of control in the brothels, in consciously drawn contrast to regimes of control in the postrevolutionary state, showed little concern for the reproductive health of women. In some brothels, we are told, women were expected to continue to work even if they were menstruating or in the second trimester of pregnancy; such practices led to disorders ranging from menorrhagia of the uterus to frequent miscarriage. After a miscarriage, a prostitute was put back to work as quickly as possible.[136] To prevent pregnancy, madams gave their prostitutes daily doses of alum. Alternatively, they dispensed live tadpoles to eat, on the theory that the "cold element" in tadpoles would counteract the "heat" of pregnancy. The same remedy was applied as an abortifacient. Prolonged periods of tadpole consumption apparently contributed to infertility.[137]

No accessible information survives, however, about how common tadpole usage was in Shanghai brothels, who controlled or enforced its adoption, whether it varied from courtesan houses to streetwalker flophouses, or what other methods were available and effective (or not). Abortion, although apparently widely practiced in urban China, was even less discussed than contraception in writings about prostitutes, perhaps because it was illegal under late Qing and early Republican criminal law.[138] Similarly, although sexually transmitted disease was mentioned by public-health authorities as a cause of infertility, stillbirth, and miscarriage among prostitutes (see chapter 9), information here too is scanty. A 1948 survey, citing sexually transmitted diseases as the cause, found that the rate of pregnancy among a sample of five hundred prostitutes was very low. Slightly more than one-fifth of these women worked in first-class houses, and slightly more than half of the five hundred had a sexually transmitted disease, but the study did not analyze the incidence of disease among courtesans.[139]

If we know little about the factors that inhibited pregnancy, we know less about how it was regarded by courtesans, madams, or customers. Contemporary interviewees, operating in the "speak bitterness" mode, proffer a version of events congenial to contemporary feminist categories: pregnancy as a mode of resistance. In their search for a secure future, these aging interview subjects recall, prostitutes used sexual strategies, particularly their capacity to bear children, to obtain social goals. Just as married women consolidated their positions in their husbands' families this way, so some prostitutes used pregnancy as a way out of prostitution and a ticket to marriage or at least concubinage. A group of old Shanghai residents interviewed in the mid-1980s recounted the tale of Qiaonan, a young prostitute in Daqing Li, who had a liaison with the scion of a wealthy family. Because she was beautiful, her madam treated her well and guarded her carefully, and was reluctant to allow the young man to buy her out of the brothel. When Qiaonan became pregnant, she and her lover agreed that she would not have an abortion. She refused the required doses of tadpoles, and when her pregnancy became so far advanced that there was no hope of her continuing to attract customers, the madam finally permitted her lover to purchase her.[140] In cases like this, we are told, pregnancy was the occasion for struggle between prostitutes and owners over who controlled disposition of sexual services and fertility decisions.

Yet tabloid gossip entries suggest that pregnancy and children might have been perfectly compatible with continuing work, and were not necessarily regarded as a scourge by madams or an exit strategy by courtesans. One 1919 item concerned a courtesan who did not know which customer had fathered her child. When a customer named Gong insisted that the baby was his, the madam was pleased and told Gong to pay the expenses of what amounted to the courtesan's maternity leave.[141] Another entry reported matter-of-factly that a courtesan was grief stricken at the death of her infant son and would probably postpone her resumption of business for some time.[142] Children, as indicated in chapter 3, were not a rarity in the courtesan houses. Many were adopted in as entertainers in training, but others—boys as well as girls— were born and raised there. (See figure 18.) A famous 1880s courtesan named Li Shanshan was herself the child of a courtesan by the son of the prominent Qing official Li Hongzhang. When the son stopped sending Shanshan's mother money, the courtesan took five-year-old Shanshan to his house to demand support; the story goes that he promptly sickened and died the next day. Li Shanshan grew up in her mother's courtesan house, began work as a virgin courtesan at eleven, and committed suicide at sixteen when her sweetheart was murdered by a jealous rival.[143] If courtesans raised their daughters to learn the skills of an educated entertainer, some also strove to educate their sons, although the historical record is too fragmentary to be very useful on this point.[144]

Whether or not they had given birth to children, older courtesans and madams sometimes adopted and raised foster daughters, marrying them off for substantial bride-prices. A thirty-year-old madam earned enough from two such marriages to close her place of business. Another courtesan, famous for her musical skills, married off four daughters and acquired a significant nest egg, which she unfortunately squandered on opium, ending up as a stock figure: a vagrant with ragged clothes and swollen feet wandering the streets of the French Concession bemoaning her former glory.[145]

It was this figure, the aging, impoverished beggar, that appeared most frequently as the inevitable denouement of courtesan careers. How common this ending was in the lives of courtesans is not at all clear, since coverage of most women ended when they became concubines (if they stayed in these arrangement for more than a few months). It is quite likely that most courtesans did not end their careers on the streets of the French Concession, but guidebook authors were interested in the ones who did. Weng Meiqian, a celebrated performer at the turn of the century, was found more than three decades later ruined by opium addiction and selling songs on the street.[146] Hu Baoyu, born in 1853, was first among Shanghai courtesans in pleasing guests, studying English, smoking a silver water pipe, and feuding with her female rivals. Yet all her fame, and a long and prominent career, could not save her from an old age spent in desolate conditions in the Chinese city, far from the commercial areas of the International Settlement she had once dominated.[147]

Like loyal or beautiful courtesans who were repeatedly compared to officials, aging and degenerate courtesans provided a means for male writers to elaborate on two of their favorite themes: nostalgia for times past, now replaced by an ugly and obtrusive present, and sorrow at the ephemeral quality of human life.[148] Ultimately, we know what we know about these women, and can fashion an account of their careers, largely because men invoked them, indeed spoke through them, to voice their own preoccupations.

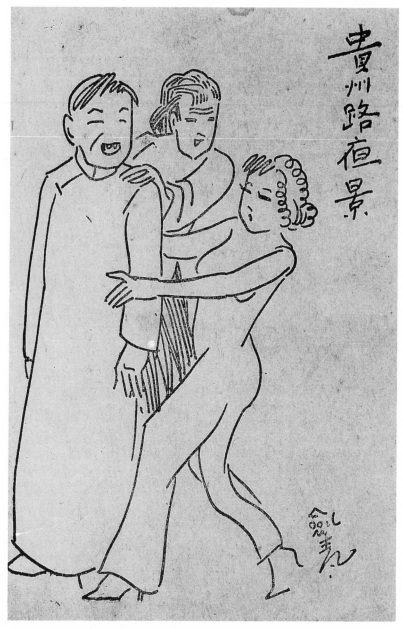

貴州路夜景

Fig. 1. Pheasants soliciting customer (Xiao Jianqing 1936)

Fig. 2. Pheasant and attendant (Xiao Jianqing 1936)

Fig. 3. "A stray lamb who has lost his way" amid the delights of Shanghai, which include, *clockwise from lower left,* performances, baths, guides, dancing, and human flesh (Xiao Jianqing 1936)

Fig. 4. Scene in amusement hall (Xiao Jianqing 1936)

蘭雲閣又名張颺

Fig. 5. Lan Yunge (Qi Xia and Dan Ru 1917)

玉　　寶　　沈

Fig. 6. Shen Baoyu (Qi Xia and Dan Ru 1917)

寓　　琴

Fig. 7. Qin Yu (Qi Xia and Dan Ru 1917)

卿　　蓮　　金

Fig. 8. Courtesan in operatic dress (Qi Xia and Dan Ru 1917)

Fig. 9. Courtesan with book (Qi Xia and Dan Ru 1917: vol. 1, front cover)

寓　　　　周

Fig. 10. Courtesan (and attendant?) with Chinese chess set (Qi Xia and Dan Ru 1917)

樓　秦

Fig. 11. Qin Lou (Qi Xia and Dan Ru 1917)

寶 四 花

Fig. 12. Hua Sibao (Qi Xia and Dan Ru 1917)

筱　青　樓

Fig. 13. Xiao Qinglou (Qi Xia and Dan Ru 1917)

留　香　　館

Fig. 14. Courtesans with automobile (Qi Xia and Dan Ru 1917)

Fig. 15. Man "cutting the melon" (Wang Zhongxian n.d.: p. 10; reprinted by permission of Sun Chau Book Company Limited, Hong Kong)

妓女的生活

白相門徑

Fig. 16. Cover of Sun Yusheng's *Jinü de shenghuo,* 1939

Fig. 17. Prostitute and list of demands (Wang Zhongxian n.d.: p. 42;
reprinted by permission of Sun Chau Book Company Limited, Hong
Kong)

是如柳名又 一其 玉寶如 卿翚林名又林媛媛洪

Fig. 18. Two courtesans with child (Qi Xia and Dan Ru 1917)

Fig. 19. Patron inspecting prostitute under supervision of madam (Xiao
Jianqing 1936)

Fig. 20. Women's Labor Training Institute (courtesy Shanghai Municipal Skin Disease Prevention and Cure Research Institute)

Fig. 21. Drawing blood for STD tests (courtesy Shanghai Municipal Skin Disease Prevention and Cure Research Institute)

Fig. 22. Attending classes (courtesy Shanghai Municipal Skin Disease
Prevention and Cure Research Institute)

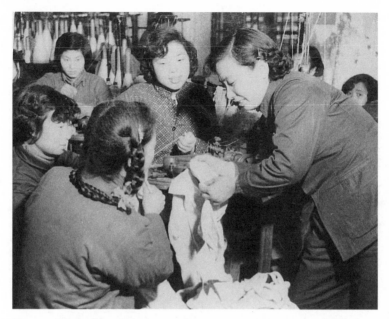

Fig. 23. Learning embroidery (courtesy Shanghai Municipal Skin Disease Prevention and Cure Research Institute)

Fig. 24. Graduation ceremonies (courtesy Shanghai Municipal Skin Disease
Prevention and Cure Research Institute)

Figs. 25, 26. Illustrations accompanying Lu
Xing'er's account of interviews with incarcerated
prostitutes (Lu Xing'er 1993a)

PART III

Dangers

CHAPTER 7

Trafficking

The literature about courtesans, as we have seen, was suffused with nostalgic longing, the risk of humiliation, anxieties about elite masculinity, and occasional worries about the nation. Nevertheless, it was predominantly a literature of male pleasure—the pleasure of encountering, appreciating, possessing, and vicariously enjoying courtesans. Yet this was not the only public conversation about prostitution in Shanghai. Discussions of danger—to prostitutes, their customers, and the wider community—ran parallel to and sometimes intertwined with conversations about pleasure. Part 3 looks at three such discussions, on the subjects of trafficking, law, and disease.

The trade in women was one site of intersection between Shanghai sex workers, their families, traffickers, and the state in the late nineteenth century and the first half of the twentieth. It involved not only the elite courtesans described in part 2, but also women in the lower reaches of the hierarchy of prostitution. Mentioned only briefly in guidebooks, tabloids, and memoirs, trafficking was ubiquitous in other types of sources: the mainstream press, reform treatises, scandal fiction, and the records of relief agencies and the police. Both foreigners and Chinese took up the topic, although in most periods Chinese voices were dominant.

Trafficking tales were quintessential victim stories. Authors across these various genres explained that women were commonly sold into prostitution either because their parents were pressured by desperate poverty to sell them to traffickers, or because they had been kidnapped and sold without the knowledge of their families.[1] In either case, entry into prostitution was said to involve a dramatic rupture of family networks, pushing women into the urban world of Shanghai brothels as atomized victims.

This representation was incomplete and misleading. Yet it had tremendous persuasive force, influenced many of the efforts to abolish prostitution, and continues to resonate in contemporary conversations about the resurgence of sex work (see part 5). This chapter examines the trafficking story not only for what it describes about the trade in women, but also for what it suggests about the preoccupations of record keepers and the strategies of sex workers in pre-1949 Shanghai.

Many of the sources stress that trafficking was an important means of entry into Shanghai sex work. This chapter first describes what we know about how trafficking worked, and how women and their families sought redress from its injuries through the legal system. When family connections were severed by the most extreme form of trafficking—kidnapping—families sometimes sought to restore their ties by suing in court for the woman's release from a brothel. The connections between prostitution, family, and the state emerge most clearly in this type of interaction.

In spite of the ubiquity of abduction stories, it is important to remember that much trafficking involved the consent and knowledge of women and their families. Many prostitutes, perhaps most, remained enmeshed in complex family networks that were a source of obligation, support, and conflict. These networks are explored in the second section of the chapter. Police and social-worker interviews with prostitutes indicate that income earned by sex workers, although often minimal, was as crucial to the economic support of their families as that earned by other types of women workers in Shanghai. As prostitutes contributed to their families, so did families come to the aid of prostitutes in trouble with their madams.

If sex workers were enmeshed in familial networks, why are they presented in contemporary sources as either disenfamilied victims or the objects of a contest between natal family and madam, played out in the courts? The final section proposes several reasons that severance from natal family became the dominant story told about prostitutes in early-twentieth-century Shanghai.

KIDNAPPING

White Ants and Items

Among the perils that Shanghai held for women,[2] contemporary authors often warned, was the danger of being abducted or tricked into prostitution. In the cautionary literature on prostitution that emerged in the twentieth century, seemingly innocent urban characters were rendered sinister:

> Many of the hotel boys, the theater ushers, the waiters in the restaurants, the flower girls, newspaper sellers, mafoos (carriage men), maid-servants, and even ricksha coolies, are aiding and abetting the trade. The most dangerous of all, perhaps, are the women hairdressers and the sellers of jewelry, because they have easy access to the household and can exercise their pernicious influence freely.[3]

News reports reinforced the impression of danger to insufficiently supervised women living in Shanghai. In November 1920, *Shenbao* reported, the eighteen-year-old servant Liang Caihua went out shopping and met Liang Deyu, a friend of her employer. He invited her to an opera, then took her to a brothel and spent the night with her. The following day, the brothel's madam testified, Deyu pawned Caihua into the brothel in return for a price of one hundred yuan for a six-month period. A relative of Caihua's learned of her disappearance and led police to the brothel; Deyu was sentenced to three years in jail, while the madam received a three-month term.[4] Stories like this one indicated that in a complex urban environment, even familiar acquaintances could imperil not only a woman's chastity, but her freedom.

Local abductions were only one aspect of the traffic in women, which extended from Shanghai through its hinterland and beyond to distant provinces. Trafficking entailed purchasing or forcibly procuring human beings, transporting them, often far from home, and selling or pawning them to an employer who acquired virtual ownership rights over them. At least three groups of traffickers were described in accounts of the trade: kidnappers, transporters, and brokers.[5] The first specialized in the abduction of people already in Shanghai. These kidnappers were said to be mostly women from Subei,[6] but anecdotal evidence indicates that both men and women from a variety of native places did this work, using a combination of blandishments and force to secure control over women already in the city.

In a 1929 court case, for instance, two women aged eighteen and sixteen brought charges that a Shaoxing woman named Zhou née Chen had tried to sell them into prostitution. According to the eighteen-year-old, Wang Lancui, Zhou had struck up a conversation with them at an employment agency where they were looking for work as servants, making use of the fact that they were all originally from Shaoxing. She spent the day with them and at night invited them to a movie, but, Wang testified in court, her attentions soon became suspicious:

> She took us to the door of a lower-class hotel. She went in first, and after
> about half an hour came out with several men, who looked us over carefully
> and carried on among themselves. I saw that the situation was not good.
> Furthermore, when we were walking around the streets with the accused,
> she said to us, "The two of you want to become servants, but it is very hard
> work, not as good as becoming a prostitute in a brothel, happy and well-off,"
> and so on. So we left her and took a rickshaw to my mother's house in Jiang-
> yuan Lane, Xinzha Road, told her about it, and afterward reported it to the
> police and had the accused arrested.[7]

Prominent in newspaper reports of the Republican era were stories in which a seemingly respectable person proved to be a trafficker. In a 1929 news item, a woman who had come to Shanghai to look for work as a servant found temporary lodging at a monastery and was pawned into a brothel by the monks. Another story from the same year reported that the owner of a rickshaw business tried twice to mortgage the wife of one of his pullers while the hapless husband was out working.[8] Although both these attempts were thwarted when the victims' relatives came to their aid, stories like these emphasized the dangers of the Shanghai streets, particularly for women recently arrived from the countryside. They proffered the lesson that women should not trust anyone outside their immediate families. The overarching issue, however, was broader: fear of the breakdown of familiar community connections, such that neither women nor their relatives could trust their own perceptions of the strangers surrounding them.

Picking up where kidnappers left off was a second group of traffickers who transported the abducted women. They either acquired women in Shanghai for sale to other provinces,[9] or traveled to famine-afflicted areas to buy both males and females for resale in urban areas as prostitutes, maids, and adopted sons.[10] As a 1940 foreigner's memoir described the trade:

> They had been bought at a rather tender age, cheaply; in flood or starvation districts, the agents could have them for a couple of dollars apiece. And if they were lucky, they could resell the choice ones for a thousand dollars in Shanghai. At the age of thirteen these children would spend their first night with one of the favorite Chinese customers of the house.[11]

Married women, as well as young children and unwed girls, were frequent targets for kidnappers.[12] Women for sale were known simply as "items" (*tiaozi*); children were called "stones" (*shitou*).[13] Among the records of the Chinese Anti-Kidnapping Society[14] now held in the Shanghai Municipal Archives are documents from the 1920s and 1930s concerning both types of cases. Some of the women whose cases are recorded lived in Shanghai with their families, and simply disappeared while out alone or with their friends; others had come to Shanghai from other areas and were working as servants when they were abducted. The archives include cases of women kidnapped in Shanghai and sold to Fengtian, Tianjin, Fuzhou, and Yantai, as well as a case of a woman from Shaoxing sold as a prostitute in Shanghai. A letter to the Anti-Kidnapping Society from a father whose daughter had disappeared conveys the pain and confusion caused by such abductions:

> I, Yunbiao, originally from Shangyu, now running a tailor shop at Gongji Helou, Sheng Cheng Li, Hankou, have a daughter, whose childhood name is Wumao [Five Hairs], and whose school name is Xiaohua [Little Flower], who lives with me in Hankou. She is fifteen, and normally comes and goes as she pleases. Last year on the fourth day of the fourth month she was kidnapped. We asked people to search everywhere, published notices in the paper, but found no traces. The day before yesterday we suddenly received a letter mailed from Shanghai. The return address said Fuzhou, Mr. Zhao,

with a chop from the Dongxing Steamboat [Company]. When we opened it, it was a letter from our daughter, briefly saying that she had been kidnapped by bandits and sold as a prostitute to the Guibao Tang on Nantaididang Jie in Fuzhou, and that she was suffering daily, just like being in jail. She begged us to find a means to rescue her from the fiery pit. When I saw this, I was so pained that I did not want to live. When I think of my young and ignorant daughter, kidnapped by people, to the extent that she must depend on others and "sell her smiles," I can imagine what kind of suffering she is experiencing. But we are far from her. If I go there to save her, I do not know the place. I am afraid that hoodlums will trick me. So I can only beg you to think of a means to save her.[15]

Like other cases preserved in the archives, this one tells a story of family connections violently ruptured by strangers, followed by painstaking attempts to reweave those connections through the good offices of the Anti-Kidnapping Society.

In some cases the records indicate merely that the trafficker was a bandit or robber, but often the kidnappers were friends of the family, and in two of the archival cases the abductors were a husband-and-wife team. Kidnapping and trafficking were enterprises in which women excelled, using their relatively easy access to other women and children to facilitate abductions.[16] In the early 1930s, a sociological study found that 28.6 percent of all jailed female criminals, many of them women over fifty, were serving sentences for kidnapping.[17] Two pieces of evidence, however, indicate that men as well as women did this work: a common slang term for traffickers, *fuxiong*, can be literally translated as "father brother," indicating that males were involved;[18] and descriptions of the trade indicate that many prostitutes were raped by traffickers between the time of their purchase and resale to a brothel.[19] In some cases the women were apparently persuaded to go willingly with their abductors, learning only later that they were to be sold.[20] In others they were taken by force while alone, as in the case of the married woman Xiao, who was grabbed in 1929 while washing clothes on a riverbank in Subei.[21] Both types of story emphasized that the world was a dangerous place for any unaccompanied woman, regardless of whether she was foolishly credulous or full of housewifely diligence.

In the sources on trafficking, the actual mechanisms of transporting women from one part of China to another remained obscure. One account indicated that to avoid detection, traffickers with kidnapped "items" in tow did not stay in inns; they hid themselves and their booty in barbershops, bakeries, and employment agencies.[22] Foreign reports asserted that traffickers were connected by elaborate networks of middlemen and hideaways, but gave no specifics.[23] Various sources refer to the involvement of the Green Gang (*Qing Bang*) in Shanghai prostitution, and gang connections may have helped to provide an organized network for the transfer of women, but again the details were not recorded.[24] Frequently news reports would indicate that a woman had been sold multiple times, often being moved from city to city with each sale, but also sometimes changing status with each transaction: from maid or worker to prostitute to adopted daughter to daughter-in-law.[25] This indicates that trafficking was closely linked to contiguous or overlapping markets in women's labor: factory and domestic work, marriage, and prostitution. In spite of these glimpses, however, the silence surrounding the logistics of trafficking rendered the stories more terrifying; what the reader saw was a sudden, unexplained, and often irreversible disappearance.

The third group of traffickers, usually women residing in Shanghai, were brokers known as "white ants" (*bai mayi*) or "worldly feet" (*shi jiaozi*).[26] One source comments that the term "white ants" indicated that female traffickers were regarded as a pestilence and a threat to social health,[27] but it is not clear that this explanation was widely shared. A 1920s guidebook to prostitution listed the most famous white ants in Shanghai by their nicknames, Pockmarked Ah XX and Aunt X from Nanjing.[28] White ants might personally engage in kidnapping, but they also had connections with long-distance traffickers and potential employers in Shanghai, including brothel owners.[29] A white ant would pick out an appropriate prospect, take her to a brothel, bargain for the best sale price, and leave the woman there for a day and two nights. Then the white ant and the madam would sign a contract, with the broker receiving a 20 percent commission, known as yellow-head money (*huangtou qian*).[30] White ants were active at every level of the hierarchy of prostitution, selling women to high-class courtesan houses as well as "pheasant" houses and opium brothels.[31] As prostitution "modernized" in the 1930s, becoming entwined with new establishments such as massage parlors, dance halls, guide agencies, and bars, traffickers were reported to be working through these new institutions as well.[32]

The message of news reports and guidebooks to Shanghai—that traffickers were ubiquitous in both city and countryside, and that ruination awaited a woman and her family if she fell into their grasp—was elaborated in collections of short fictional pieces aimed at a popular audience. One such collection, entitled *One Thousand Scandalous Stories of Shanghai,* included a section entitled "Scandalous Stories of Women Kidnappers."[33] The kidnappers portrayed in this volume, of both the local and long-distance variety, were patient, conniving, and ruthless. One posed as a mother seeking a bride for her "son" (himself an innocent youth looking for a bride) in order to kidnap the daughter of a respectable family. Another woman, who worked with a gang of kidnappers, married a widower in order to abduct his daughter and sell her to a Beijing brothel. In the section's most poignant story, a young wife and mother from the suburbs of Wuxi was approached by a female abductor while washing clothes (this is a recurring scenario in both fictional and nonfictional sources) and was persuaded to go to Shanghai to find work.

After her departure her two children became ill and died, and her husband went to Shanghai to find her. One night he stayed at a small inn where many travelers shared a room. He heard a couple whispering in another bed; the woman sounded like his wife. He called out his own name in a low voice and heard his wife sob. The next morning, when he was unable to pay for his lodging, his wife came forward and identified him as her husband, but the manager beat her, saying, "I spent money to buy you. Who is your husband?"[34] The ubiquity and apparent popularity of this genre of story, in both fiction and the press, suggests that it articulated shared fears about the dangers and dislocations of the urban environment, fears embodied by the figures of the kidnapper and his or her victim.

In Search of Redress

Prior to 1949, the police and the courts periodically undertook to regulate prostitution, at least at the margins where it involved the sale into prostitution of "women of good families," or street soliciting that was seen as a threat to public order (see chapters 8 and 11). Prostitution per se was not illegal in Republican China,[35] but trafficking was. Article 288 of the 1923 Provisional Criminal Code of the Republic of China stipulated imprisonment and fines for "whoever for lucrative purposes induces any woman belonging to a respectable family to have illicit intercourse with any person for hire," with stiffer penalties for "whoever makes the commission of the offense under the last preceding section a profession."[36] The 1935 Criminal Code, while omitting a specific reference to respectable families, likewise made it criminal to remove "any person who has not completed the twentieth year of his or her age" from family or other "supervisory authority." The punishment was more severe if the person was removed without his or her consent or if the person was taken away "for the purpose of gain or for the purpose of causing the person who has been taken away to submit to carnal knowledge or to do a lascivious act." Lesser penalties were provided for those who "receive[d] or harbour[ed] such person or cause[d] such person to be concealed," and unsuccessful attempts to commit any of these offenses were punishable as well.[37] Both versions of the code called trafficking criminal insofar as it involved removal from a family or other nexus of authority for purposes of sale, sexual activity, or sale for sexual activity. In addition, local regulations issued by the Public Security Bureau in November 1928, writes Frederic Wakeman, "stipulated the death sentence for kidnappers; confiscation of property used as a safe house; [and] prison sentences for relatives of the victims who negotiated with kidnappers without telling the police," although the degree of enforcement is unclear.[38]

Police were responsible for enforcing the prohibition on trafficking, turning cases they discovered over to the courts,[39] but according to foreign observers, enforcement of the antitrafficking law appears to have been spotty at best. This was routinely cited as evidence of the ineffectualness of Chinese justice.[40] In 1925 a foreign commentator on the Shanghai legal scene criticized what he implied was a hypocritical gap between statute and practice:

> In spite of . . . the solemn declaration of the fundamental law of the Republic of China concerning the freedom of her citizens, and respective provisions of the Criminal Code, punishing very severely every violation of this principle, trafficking in children and women for the purpose of prostitution is an event of daily occurrence. Chinese society displays generally great leniency towards this kind of case and criminal proceedings of that nature are comparatively rare.[41]

Before World War II, antitrafficking enforcement was further inhibited by the existence of three different municipal governments in Shanghai, each of which applied different local regulations to trafficking cases.[42] In the Chinese-controlled section of the city, 1928 police statistics recorded 223 cases under the category of "rape and kidnapping," involving 482 perpetrators—less than 10 percent of the total number of crimes or criminals.[43] Regulations jointly passed by the Public Security and Social Affairs Bureaus in 1928 required police to help kidnapped women and children reunite with their families, or to remand them to charitable organizations if no relatives could be found. The regulations also provided for publishing pictures and descriptions of recovered victims, and required charitable organizations not to release women to "relatives" unless they could produce a guarantor and an accurate description of the kidnapped person's speech, actions, appearance, and special characteristics. In the International Settlement, the number of Chinese charged in the Mixed Court with breach of trafficking laws was typically several dozen a year between 1912 and 1934, occasionally ranging upward of one hundred. Compared both with the overall population of the International Settlement and with the estimated number of prostitutes, this was a minuscule number.[44] It conformed to the pattern in China as a whole, where only 566 cases of trafficking were discovered and 935 people convicted between January 1932 and June 1933.[45] Given the laxity of enforcement, Shanghai police often learned that women had been illegally sold into prostitution only after arresting them for street solicitation, which was forbidden under local ordinances.[46] Yet although it was not aggressively suppressed by the police, trafficking did carry potentially serious penalties.[47] A selection of forty-five traffickers whose sentences were recorded in the Chinese press from 1916 to 1925 were jailed for terms ranging from one month to nine years; almost half were sentenced to one year or more in prison.[48]

Most news reports of kidnapped women focused on dramatic moments when the victim herself called attention to her plight, leading to the apprehension of the traffickers. In one such instance, Gong Fangzi, an eighteen-year-old from Danyang, was abducted in April 1920 by two traffickers. They tried and failed to sell her to a pheasant brothel in the French Concession. Gong's loud crying as she was led through the streets attracted the attention of a Chinese police detective, who took all three into custody. The traffickers were sentenced to one and two years in jail, respectively. Gong was sent back to Danyang after the magistrate of her home county sent a letter saying that her parents were too poor to finance the trip to Shanghai to get her.[49] Similarly, the woman named Xiao whose riverbank abduction was described earlier saw one of her kidnappers on a Shanghai street while she was out soliciting one night, grabbed him, and shouted until two police detectives arrived and arrested him.[50] Such incidents, apart from the intrinsic reading pleasure afforded by their high drama, reinforced the larger story of victimization by highlighting cases in which women managed to escape.

Another common story of intervention and rescue involved relatives of abducted women who learned of their plight and either sought police intervention[51] or took matters into their own hands. Mothers, aunts, great-aunts, uncles, sisters, brothers, fathers, and husbands trooped to the police with a steady stream of complaints about women who had disappeared and were subsequently discovered in the company of suspected traffickers or in Shanghai brothels.[52] Sometimes the relatives captured the kidnappers themselves and hauled them in to the authorities, and a few energetic county officials from areas where women had been abducted also went to Shanghai to participate.[53] When they were presented with a specific abduction complaint and the location of the victim, the police usually managed to send detectives to take the traffickers and madams involved to court.[54] Newspaper reports framed these situations as stories of dramatic discovery and family reunification. In one 1880 incident, a man attended a dinner party at which prostitutes were entertaining and discovered that one of them was his niece, kidnapped several years earlier.[55] In 1936, *Shibao* reported that Wang Suzhen of Hangzhou was tricked by two neighbors into accompanying them to Shanghai, where they sold her to a brothel. Her mother sent relatives to look for her. One of Wang's male relatives bumped into her on the street in front of her brothel, spent the night there in order to establish his credentials as a good customer, and the next day filled out a call ticket requesting her presence at a social occasion. Thinking that he was Wang's customer, the unsuspecting madam let her go; she escaped, and the two trafficking neighbors were arrested.[56]

A 1929 story was presented as a case in which family virtue triumphed over the betrayal of strangers. The victim was a woman from Jurong County, betrothed at age eight, orphaned at sixteen and sent to live with relatives who coveted the land she had inherited. Suffering from their ill-treatment, she succumbed to the sweet talk of a man who was a pedicurist in a bathhouse in Shanghai, and at seventeen went off with him to Wuxi, where he slept with her for half a year and then sold her into an unlicensed brothel for three hundred yuan. When prostitution was forbidden in Wuxi, the madam resold her to a brothel in Shanghai for six hundred yuan. Meanwhile her childhood fiancé had come to Shanghai and was working in a Japanese firm while looking for her. After four years, when he was invited by a friend to a banquet in that brothel, he discovered his fiancée, bought her (the madam wanted one thousand yuan, but they agreed on a price of eight hundred), and married her. The newspaper report praised his sense of moral integrity in saving his wife.[57] As a genre of crime and human-interest reporting, these stories emphasized the heroic lengths to which families would go in reclaiming an imperiled member.

When prostitutes were brought before the courts or questioned by the police for street soliciting or operating without a license, one of the arguments they commonly made on their own behalf was that they were working as prostitutes against their will. For instance, in 1929 an eighteen-year-old named Tan Yuxi was picked up in a sweep by Chinese plainclothesmen aimed at clearing the streets of prostitutes. Facing a court-imposed fine, she testified that she had been kidnapped in Suzhou two months before and sold into a pheasant brothel. Although the trafficker had long since disappeared, the brothel owner was charged with buying a good woman and forcing her to become a prostitute (*po liang wei chang*). The owner was detained pending investigation in spite of his argument that Tan had willingly signed a contract and was entitled to half of what she earned.[58] The newspapers also reported cases in which women claimed to have been kidnapped and forced to become prostitutes in order to justify escaping from a madam,[59] and occasionally reports surfaced of a woman accusing a man of trafficking because she held a grudge against him and wanted to get him into trouble with the law.[60] In all of these cases, a woman's assertion that she had not entered prostitution of her own free will, which might well have been accurate, was also strategic, serving to shift the attention of the authorities from her to others.

One enterprising group of con artists made ingenious use of the trafficking laws, posing as kidnap victims and suing for redress to relieve brothel owners of their money. In this type of scam, a woman would be sold to a white ant either by a relative or someone posing as one. After the woman was pawned into a brothel, her husband would report to the police that he had just located his abducted wife, and the woman would corroborate his story. The brothel owner would often be jailed for six months for buying a woman of unclear origin to engage in prostitution, losing both the new prostitute and the money paid for her. The scam was a variation of the ruse known as "letting a white pigeon go," apparently in reference to the habits of homing pigeons. In cases like this, the charge of trafficking itself became a weapon of extortion. Conventional arrangements of predator and prey were given

an ironic reversal, strengthening the portrayal of Shanghai as an unfath-
omable den of iniquity full of people unrestrained by any standards of ethical behavior.[61]

FAMILIES, SEX WORKERS, AND THE STATE

Cases of abduction appeared to be the form of trafficking in which the bond
between a woman and her family was most dramatically broken. Yet sometimes a kidnapping case would be thrown out of court when the alleged victim testified that in fact she had volunteered to become a prostitute in order to clear family debts.[62] Like kidnapping, trafficking as a whole was more
complex than a cursory reading of reform treatises and the press might indicate. For one thing, abductions were a minority of trafficking cases; most
involved the sale or pawning of a woman at the behest of her family.[63] Furthermore, abductions involved a severing of family networks, whereas police and social-work sources indicate that women often became prostitutes,
with or without family knowledge, precisely in order to maintain—and maintain contact with—their families.

News reports from the late nineteenth century through the 1920s, although they give few details of any given case, offer ample indication that
families often knew exactly where their missing women had gone. Women
were sold to brothels not only through the mediation of anonymous traffickers, but also directly by their relatives or other intimates of the family: fathers, mothers, stepfathers, foster mothers, foster fathers, mothers' lovers,
aunts, uncles, future mothers-in-law, mothers-in-law, husbands (when the
woman was a principal wife and when she was a concubine), sisters-in-law,
lovers, friends, and acquaintances from the same native place.[64] Some of these
sales involved perfidy: the married man who took his married lover's daughter home to be turned out as a prostitute by his own wife, who was herself a
prostitute in a flower-smoke opium brothel; the woman who was brought by
her sister-in-law from a rural area under false pretenses and sold to a brothel;
the fellow townspeople who offered to find women jobs in Shanghai and then
sold them.[65] Other sales may have entailed attempts at revenge by getting
someone into trouble with the law: the woman who accused her ex-lover of
selling her daughter, only to have him retort that she herself had agreed to
sell the girl and had then reneged when she took a new lover.[66] Accounts in
which parents were the sellers usually mentioned dire family poverty or the
recent death of one parent, rather than deception or strained family relations.[67] In other cases, women fleeing unhappy marriages or mistreatment
by stepmothers fell into the hands of traffickers.[68]

A substantial number of cases that came to the attention of police or the
courts hinted at deep conflict between the natal and marital families of
women who were sold: the man who accused his mother-in-law of selling his

wife (her own daughter) to a brothel,[69] the father who complained to the police when his married daughter was sold to an opium brothel by her mother-in-law,[70] the brother who went to the police to regain custody of a sister who had been sold to a flower-smoke room by her husband.[71] Most frequently, a parent or sibling came to the rescue of a woman who had been sold or pawned by her husband or in-laws.[72] Sometimes the courts granted a divorce in such situations; sometimes they returned her to her husband; often they turned her over to the Door of Hope, a philanthropic organization (see chapter 10), where she was to stay until a suitable spouse could be found for her.[73]

The more intractable the parties and the more complex the competing claims, the more likely the court was to remand the woman to a welfare organization. In one case in which a woman sold her married daughter and the daughter's husband assembled a group of riotous friends to take her back by force, the mother and the husband were both sentenced to one-month terms in jail, his friends received two-week jail terms, and the woman was sent to a philanthropic organization to find a new spouse.[74] In another case, a married woman claimed that she had been kidnapped and sold by her elder brother's wife. Her husband's brother asked to take her back to her husband, who was ill in the countryside with a foot disease that left him unable to travel, and the madam claimed that the woman's own father had pawned her. In spite of the woman's expressed desire to go home to her footsore husband, the court officials in the French Concession sent her to the Door of Hope until the case could be transferred to her home county of Funing.[75] The courts appeared to favor the reinsertion of women into family networks, or the creation of new families for them through marriages arranged by welfare organizations. Yet in spite of this preference for families, judges did not automatically return women to the custody of their natal families, although the judicial reasoning behind this pattern was not made explicit in the news reports. Judges may not have been sure that the "family members" who stepped forward to claim "their" women were really who they said they were, particularly if the woman in question had been previously sold.[76]

This range of circumstances is a reminder that many varieties of economic arrangements and emotional commitments fell under the rubric of "family," which was not a standard set of idealized relationships or a zone free of conflict. Many women entered brothels because of conscious decisions by their families, decisions in which they sometimes participated. The League of Nations Commission of Inquiry into the Traffic in Women and Children conceded as much when it reported in 1932 that a majority of prostitutes had been "put into the profession originally by those who exercised parental or quasi-parental control over them."[77]

Streetwalkers sometimes testified that they had reluctantly chosen prostitution in order to support dependent relatives. On February 27, 1947, for instance, the Shanghai police arrested a madam and three prostitutes and fined them for violation of police licensing regulations. The confessions of the four are a rare instance in which the voices of sex workers are conveyed directly, albeit structured by the protocols of police interrogation. Their statements illustrate the permeable boundary between prostitution and other types of urban work available to young women, and the ongoing connection of sex workers with their families. The madam, a Shaoxing native resident in Shanghai, had run a small foreign-goods store with her husband. When inflation and capital shortage cut into their business, she switched to running a small brothel in which profits were divided with three prostitutes. Her three "girls" (*guniang*) were Tang Xiaolong, Zhang Xiuying, and Chen Abao.

All three women gave dire economic necessity and the need to support dependents as their reasons for taking up sex work. Tang Xiaolong, thirty-two, who came from Suzhou, told the police: "My mother recently died, my father is old, and we have many debts. Forced by the situation, in February of this year I came to Shanghai, and willingly placed myself at the above address, the home of Shen and Sun, as a prostitute. . . . As soon as I clear my father's debts I plan to change occupation, either becoming a servant or returning home. The above is the truth." Whereas Tang apparently had no husband, one of her coworkers, twenty-five-year-old Zhang Xiuying from Yangzhou, found that marriage was no guarantee of financial security: "I have an old mother at home and one son. My husband joined the army four years ago and has not returned. I had no means of livelihood, so on January 14 of this year I left home and came to Shanghai, looking for a former companion, Zhang Yuehua [a woman], and asked her for an introduction to a job. For a while I could find no regular work. The friend, with my agreement, introduced me into this brothel to be a prostitute in order to survive. Fees were split evenly with the madam, and room and board were provided by the brothel owner. I was definitely not tricked or forced into becoming a prostitute, but actually was driven to it by family poverty. The above is the truth. I ask for understanding in your judgment of this case and will feel very lucky."

Twenty-six-year-old Chen Abao, unlike the other two, had previously done other work in Shanghai: "I was formerly a wet nurse. . . . After February I returned home, because my husband in the countryside was very ill. At the end of last year my husband passed away, leaving an old father at home, and a young son and daughter. Life was difficult in the countryside, so I recently came to Shanghai, borrowed a room at 7 Furun Li, and entered into a system of dividing the profits with the madam, becoming a prostitute in order to live. This is the truth." Reviewing the testimony of the three women, the chief of the Morals Correction section of the police concluded that "the reason they became unlicensed prostitutes was because all were forced by life circumstances. They were not kidnapped or forced into it by others."[78]

These stories suggest that many women entered prostitution without encountering any traffickers, much less the kidnappers emphasized in so many of the sources. Some were older than the archetypal kidnapping victims; they had filial obligations to marital as well as natal families, and were often the sole support of children or elderly dependents. The decision to take up sex work was sometimes made by the prostitutes themselves, within the context of family as well as individual economic needs, and they often earmarked income for the support of their families. Under arrest, they could have won lenient treatment by arguing that they had been abducted. Instead they situated themselves in a different nexus of respectability, one in which filial obligations required that they temporarily take up a distasteful occupation.[79] The circumstances under which their confessions were made caution us against reading them as unproblematic "fact." But their statements do complicate the portrait of women violently abducted and forced to sell sexual services. And the particular ways in which they formulated their statements suggest that they were not innocent of the craft of representation, or its immediate practical uses in deflecting the attempts of the state to categorize them either as victims or as disorderly elements. They became participants in their own representation, if not under circumstances of their own choosing, in the process leaving at least a trace of a subaltern voice.

Two surveys of prostitutes, conducted just before and after the establishment of the PRC, reinforce the picture of economic necessity intertwined with family obligation. A 1948 survey of 500 licensed prostitutes found that only 4 percent had been tricked or seduced into prostitution; the remainder gave their reasons for taking up sex work as poverty (60 percent), sudden unemployment or bankruptcy (18 percent), family pressure (5 percent), or an affinity for the work (13 percent).[80] As the researchers put it, "they were brought up in such an environment and liked this type of life."[81] A survey of 501 prostitutes done by the Shanghai municipal government in 1951, when brothels were being closed, found that 43 percent of the women had taken up sex work because their parents or husband were dead, unemployed, or underemployed. Another 27 percent had left home because of intolerable family situations or divorce, though no details are given about their situations. Only 11 percent had been sold or pawned by their parents or husbands, and a mere 9 percent had been kidnapped.[82]

Family and community networks affected not only the decision to enter prostitution, but the point of entry for doing so. When women looked for any type of work in Shanghai, they typically relied on networks of relatives and people from the same native place to serve as introducers and guarantors.[83] Prostitution was no exception. Police interrogations of prostitutes from the 1940s include cases where women found employment in brothels through sisters or other female relatives, and interview data suggest that women from a single village often brought one another to particular brothels in Shanghai.[84] It seems probable that such networks did not cease to function once women became prostitutes, but rather provided a social context partly rooted in kinship and native-place connections.

Women took work where they could find it, and the particular nature of sex work did not automatically make it the least desirable job available. A 1941 news article on lower-class prostitutes, after reporting that one woman might service twenty-five men in one night, nevertheless observed that most of the women were not dissatisfied with their fates, because survival in the brothels was easier than in the countryside.[85] As a social worker who interviewed prostitutes before 1949 remarks, "Other work was rather tiring. This kind of work made more income, and one ate well, so they did it."[86] In the late 1940s, researchers found that with the dislocation caused by inflation and civil war, many women came to Shanghai from the countryside precisely *because* they envied the life of Shanghai sex workers:[87] "The life of prostitution with its glamour and easy life has a special appeal to the hard pressed working classes of women in the neighbouring villages."[88] Although researchers noted that sex work might actually be attractive, this was not the kind of statement that was ever elicited from a prostitute in court or at the local police station; the venue itself precluded it.

Consistent with the picture of sex work as shameful rather than attractive, we are told that women often concealed the nature of their work from the very families who were supported by their income. Those who came from the countryside sometimes told fellow villagers that they were working as servants, and because they looked and acted prosperous on their visits home, the locals decided that servant work must be lucrative indeed.[89] Shao Meiting, an unmarried woman from the countryside near Ningbo, in 1947 found a job as a temporary worker at the Delong cigarette factory in Shanghai, but when the factory folded, as she told the police, "I had no way to support myself, and had to sink to becoming an unlicensed prostitute. Originally I planned to do it for several months and then return to the countryside. My parents don't know I am doing this." In spite of her belief that prostitution was demeaning, Shao declined a police offer to refer her to a relief organization: "I can't go, because my parents are old and my sisters are still young, and there is no one at home to take care of them."[90] Women with families in Shanghai often showed the same inclination both to keep their occupation secret from their families and to persist in it. Chen Ying, arrested for unlicensed prostitution in 1948, told police that she was the sole support of her mother, her brother's widow, and her nephew. "My mother doesn't know, because I work during the day and return home at night. She thinks I am working outside." Chen stated that she was unwilling to look for other work because "I can't make enough at other work to support the family. When I think of my old mother, crying day and night, I can't stand it."[91] Many women who became prostitutes because they lost other jobs, could not find other work, or judged prostitution to be the most desirable work available remained crucial to the survival of family networks.

Even for those women who were sold or pawned into prostitution, the transaction did not always mark the rupture of familial connections. True, contract language from the sale of a daughter in the late nineteenth century makes it clear that a woman, once sold, was supposed to relinquish family ties:

> The sale being effected she can be taken away, her name changed, and when she is grown up she shall abide by the will of the purchaser who may make use of her for any purpose he please, whether the same be respectable or otherwise. In case of disobedience she may be disposed of without hindrance. Having by this consignment yielded up all interest in her, intercourse between her and her relations will cease for ever, and she shall not be redeemed. In case of death, which is mutually to be regarded as the order of heaven, no complaints are to be preferred [*sic*].[92]

Nevertheless, many sales were neither so formal nor so final, and the conflicts they generated surfaced in the legal system. In 1920, for instance, natal and marital families faced each other in court when a woman named Xu Dingyi brought charges against her brother-in-law in the Mixed Court for selling her sister into prostitution. Xu raised money to buy out her sister, who asked for and obtained a divorce. (The Mixed Court then declared the case closed and set the man free.)[93] The woman's own unwillingness to be sold was apparently the legal crux of the case, bolstered by support from her natal family. But other court cases are best understood not as the individual woman breaking free of contractual obligations incurred by the family, but rather as the family reasserting claims on the individual woman.[94] In one 1929 case, a man was told by a go-between that his wife had found work as a servant. Almost half a year later, because the lunar New Year was approaching, he went looking for her so that she could go home to take care of the housework. The go-between explained that she had already sold his wife, and offered him 200 yuan to obtain a new one, but he brought a complaint in court instead.[95] Occasionally, even husbands who had willingly sold their wives asserted claims on their income; this was the case with a man named Qi, who sold his wife for 240 yuan in 1931. After five years she gained her freedom, but continued working as a prostitute on her own. In 1936 Qi saw her on the street and tried to extort 1,000 yuan from her; since she had no money, he and some other men held her captive in a hotel until they were discovered and arrested by the police.[96]

Pawned Prostitutes and Ongoing Family Claims

Unlike the sale of wives and daughters, pawning a woman into prostitution appears to have been a family decision to deploy an economic resource—a woman's body—without relinquishing it. (The dynamics of such decisions, and the extent of a woman's participation in them, by and large remain opaque in the sources.) Pawning arrangements were practiced at least through the 1930s, most commonly at the lower levels of the prostitution hierarchy, and some sources suggest that half or more of all women in prostitution were pawned.[97] The terms of the transaction were not unlike those for pawning clothes or other household valuables, also a common practice among the urban poor.[98] The most detailed account of a pawning transaction is an 1871 description by Edward Henderson, a public-health official in the International Settlement. Henderson explained that the parents or owner of a young woman might consign her to a brothel in return for a loan of half her value. If she was valued at two hundred dollars, for instance, they would borrow one hundred. They would then divide her earnings (say, twenty dollars per month) with the brothel owner (taking ten dollars) and return some of their share as 4 percent interest on the loan (four dollars). The madam provided board; the parents or owner claimed any presents she received. This arrangement could well have been essential to the support of a poor family, since it provided them with a lump sum supplemented by a small but relatively steady income, and relieved them of the need to feed one person. Henderson added that a pawned woman's family (in the case he mentioned, it was her husband) might subsequently sell her outright to the brothel in return for an additional sum of money.[99]

By the twentieth century, the pawning process had been simplified; a woman was given as collateral on a loan. During the loan period she lost her freedom and control over her income, which accrued to the brothel owner.[100] This type of pawned prostitute was called *baozhang* (literally, "to guarantee the accounts"), as distinct from a prostitute who took a short-term loan from the madam (*daidang*) that was repaid out of her earnings.[101] Pawn periods were typically two to three years, although one court news report mentions an eight-year period.[102] Pawning prices ranged from forty yuan for a "season" (about four months) in 1920 to four hundred yuan for a several-year period in 1929.[103] An investigation in 1937–1938 found that women who were pawned brought higher prices than those who were sold,[104] perhaps because the brothel owner did not have to assume indefinite responsibility; he or she could obtain control over the woman's three most productive years and then dispose of her. The brothel owner might also have been willing to pay out more at the outset in anticipation of receiving the sum back with interest. Alternatively, perhaps families who pawned their daughters were able to bargain harder for a favorable pawn price, whereas those who sold their daughters were in such desperate straits that they could not afford to bargain.

As public agitation for reform grew in the 1930s (see chapters 10 and 11), even guidebooks began to bracket their detailed descriptions of life in the brothels with language condemning prostitution, particularly the situation of sold and pawned prostitutes. In a climate of growing public disapproval of prostitution, pawned women were regarded as no less victimized than those who had been sold. News reports told of women, pawned into brothels by parents, brothers, or husbands, who escaped and were sent by the courts to the Door of Hope, effectively removing them from the control of their families.[105] Sometimes the family member responsible for the pawn transaction was jailed.[106]

In several important respects, though, pawned sex workers differed from their sold sisters. Since the transaction itself preserved the contact with families, pawned women could expect to return to their parents or husbands when the pawn period was up (although, one guidebook author noted darkly, by then most had sexually transmitted diseases "and their lives are over").[107] Parents who became aware of the harshness of their daughters' working conditions sometimes sought to have them released from the contract. In 1917, for example, the parents of a fifteen-year-old girl, who had pawned her into a courtesan house to learn singing and acting skills (apparently as a virgin courtesan), sued a madam who permitted a customer to deflower the young woman.[108] Nor was this type of suit limited to the upper reaches of the hierarchy of prostitution. A 1920 case involved a sixteen-year-old woman pawned to a pheasant brothel by her mother on the understanding that her duties would be limited to waiting on patrons. When the madam began to pressure her to engage in sexual relations with customers, the mother attempted to get her back. (She was fined fifty yuan for pawning her daughter, while the madam was fined fifty yuan for forcing her to be a prostitute.)[109] Some reports indicate that this outraged concern about the loss of a daughter's virginity may have been financially motivated. In a 1924 tabloid report, an impoverished man and his lover pawned their daughter to a madam for five hundred yuan. The agreement was that when the girl became old enough to earn a defloration fee, the money would be divided with the parents. The girl lost her virginity, but the madam failed to split the fee; the parents then took the girl back, leaving the madam who had trained her financially bereft. (Ironically, in this case it was the madam, not the family, who turned to her native-place association in Shanghai for help; eventually the parents returned half of the pawn price to her.)[110]

By the 1930s, protective families coming forward to rescue their pawned daughters had become a common subject of dramatically recounted stories printed in women's magazines. In one such piece, a mother braved intimidation and beatings by the madam and her male associates, and finally won a judgment in court in which she agreed to work as a maid for the madam if her daughter could work as a servant outside the brothel rather than remain a prostitute.[111] Her story was printed as an example of maternal love and an indictment of the system that let such contracts continue; like the kidnapping stories, it extolled the triumph of family over exploitative strangers.

For pawned prostitutes, the knowledge that they were working on behalf of parents or other family members, whether to clear a debt or pay for a parent's funeral, allowed them to construe their work as an act of filial piety. Indirect evidence suggests that women may have participated in the decision to pawn themselves. In a 1929 court case, for instance, a man pawned his wife into a brothel just outside the clothing store where he worked. When his own father brought charges against him for selling his wife, both the woman and the madam appeared in court and testified that she had been pawned, not sold. The woman showed no inclination to use the occasion to win her freedom from the madam, and since her husband worked literally next door, she cannot be viewed as one who was cut off from a family network.[112]

The ongoing family connections of prostitutes were a feature not only of the lower ranks of prostitution, where many women were married or supporting natal families; such connections were also alluded to in the elaborate descriptions of courtesans published in the 1910s and 1920s. A frequent motif in the capsule biographies of these women, as noted in chapter 6, was the déclassé courtesan from an upper-class family who had fallen on hard times, bringing her refinement and the skills of her gentry upbringing into the courtesan house with her.[113] The theme of the déclassé courtesan undoubtedly appealed to both a vanishing literati elite suffused with nostalgia for its own past and a growing popular audience interested in vicarious glimpses of that elite. Nevertheless, the frequent and concrete evidence of family origins provided about these women, the continuing presence (in some cases) of their parents in their lives,[114] and the determination of some parents to save money and bring their courtesan daughters home to a respectable marriage[115] all indicate that women at the top of the hierarchy, like casual prostitutes at the bottom, were not "disenfamilied" by their entrance into sex work.

Engendering Political Order

The most common story told about Shanghai sex workers in news reports, reform literature, police files, and the papers of welfare organizations featured a sundered family (natal or marital) and efforts by both the prostitute and the family to reestablish their connection by taking the woman out of prostitution. Yet prostitutes were situated in multiple familial networks, and even conventionally defined families often sent their daughters and wives into prostitution without relinquishing claims on their persons or their income. Tales of victims abducted and sold should have been one type of story among many; their prevalence, amounting almost to domination, demands an explanation.

Part of the explanation may lie in the issue of control over women's labor. Both family and brothel owner stood to gain materially by securing control over that labor, including the labor of sex work. Accusations of kidnapping loomed especially large when families wanted to reassert claims on the women, because an admission that they had sold their own wives and daughters would surely have weakened such claims. Conversely, under Republican laws on prostitution, women could obtain legal protection in exiting a brothel if they asserted that they had been removed from a respectable family and sold into prostitution. When leaving a brothel meant an improvement in a woman's material or emotional situation, then, she had to portray herself as a victim seeking reunification with her family in order to attain that goal. Thus abduction-and-sale was a common story told by prostitutes who brought suits for their freedom, in spite of the considerable evidence suggesting that abductions constituted a minority of trafficking cases and that most involved the sale or pawning of a woman at the behest of her family.

Accusations of trafficking in general and of kidnapping in particular were also prominent in letters of complaint written by citizens to the police in the 1940s. Such letters typically noted the existence of an unlicensed brothel in the neighborhood, adding a comment like this one from a 1946 case: "The ten or so prostitutes are all from the countryside and were tricked into coming here. Many of them don't want to be prostitutes and so they are brutally beaten by the brothel owner. Today at night we heard crying."[116] Sometimes a letter named a specific culprit as a kidnapper: "The worst among them is named Yang Er. He formerly sent his own younger sister to the countryside to kidnap three young girls to come to Shanghai, forcing them to sell sex. If they disobey they are brutally beaten."[117] The postwar municipal government was committed to eliminating unlicensed prostitution, and so the police dutifully investigated these complaints, but they never paid attention to the accusations of trafficking. In fact, it appears that what actually angered people who lived near brothels was the noise and street disputes they generated rather than trafficking, and that what concerned police was unlicensed prostitution rather than trafficking. Nevertheless, since trafficking *was* illegal, anyone seeking to build a case about the noxiousness of a neighboring brothel invoked kidnapping, leading to the impression that it was a ubiquitous feature of Shanghai sex work.

The legal system was not the only factor helping to emphasize trafficking and obscure other types of entry into sex work. Reform discourse invoked trafficking in particular ways as well. In the early 1920s, for instance, a debate erupted among foreigners in the International Settlement over whether prostitution should be regulated (that is, licensed) or abolished.[118] Proponents of regulation held that prostitution was a "social evil," but that its occurrence was inevitable. They supported their arguments either with references to human nature or with discussions of China's dire economic situation, in which families could survive only by sending their daughters out to work or selling them. Missionaries, in contrast, forcefully advocated abolition, grounding their arguments in notions of the free-willed self. They argued that no Christian could condone the sale of women against their will, regardless of the circumstances. Part of this argument rested on the assumption that women were forced to become prostitutes, and missionaries made the point vigorously.[119] A resident of inland China, using the pen name "Honor," wrote to a Shanghai paper of the traffic in women along the Yangzi, "which affords such facilities to the Chinese pimp to bring them down by the junk-load, to feed the hungry wickedness of the great ports on the river." At each port, kidnapped girls were sold at secret auctions. Honor argued that "the great majority of women in port brothels are of this kidnapped class," working as prostitutes not because of choice or economics, but because of compulsion. After having been prostitutes they could not return to their families, and only then the economic necessity began, since "[w]ho will want her for aught else—public sink of bestial passions, spawner of frightful disease." Honor went on to assert that women did not become prostitutes by "temperamental choice," but rather that men created demand for these women:

> It is beside the point to argue that these women, for the most part, are hardened, that pity is lost on them, and that they would not leave the life if they could. Once well in, doubtless they would not. The economic mesh which encircles them, not to mention the power of the *acquired* mentality and perverted psychiatry, is as chains of steel. But *they did not begin voluntarily.* [Emphasis in original.][120]

Other proponents of abolition reinforced the point, declaring:

> Possibly hardly one per cent of the girls have any real choice in the matter: it is not a case of too-confiding love such as often leads foreign girls to the life, nor pleasure in sexual excitement, which might make things more bearable. It is sordid commerce of the lowest kind, leading to kidnapping, sale by parents or husbands, and a brutal compulsion to the life, which is often accompanied by beatings and starvings.[121]

Choice and its negation, kidnapping, thus became important themes in a debate about state regulation of prostitution and its relationship to public and private morality. In the process, women forced into prostitution under the most extreme circumstances were taken as representative of all sex workers, in an effort to strengthen the case for abolishing prostitution altogether. Similar sets of images figured in the debates of the 1930s and 1940s, as well as the discussion that accompanied the 1950s campaign to eliminate brothels, all of which are discussed in part 4.

Many of the rescue and reform efforts directed at prostitutes in Republican-era China entailed moving women back into their natal or marital families, or creating a suitable family for them by locating spouses. The Chinese Anti-

Kidnapping Society, whose work was discussed earlier, the Door of Hope, which is taken up more fully in chapter 10, and other welfare organizations all made active efforts to match ex-prostitutes or kidnap victims with husbands.[122] Acknowledging that women were, in fact, *both* enmeshed in families *and* employed as sex workers would have undermined one of the main indicators of order and disorder. It was an indicator that was shared across the political and social spectrum, embraced not only by missionaries and nationalist modernizers, but by authors of popular fiction, who repeatedly portrayed Shanghai as a place of danger where innocent women fresh from the countryside encountered China's enticing but dangerous modern face. (Many of the sources of danger in these stories were female as well, suggesting that the peril of letting women out of the home was twofold: they could become prey or predators.) Victim-sundered-from-natal-family thus became the dominant story told about Chinese sex workers as part of a larger discourse on China's twentieth-century crisis, expressed in forms as diverse as reform debates, state regulation through the legal, fiscal, and public-health systems, and popular fiction. The image of the sex worker as atomized victim tells us much about the language of political crisis in Republican China, a language rich in symbols of women at risk.

CHAPTER 8

Law and Disorder

Stories of women kidnapped by traffickers and sold as prostitutes abounded in early-twentieth-century Shanghai. The image of women and children torn from their families and dehumanized by the human flesh market came to stand for a host of social dislocations that weakened China as a nation in the eyes of domestic and foreign critics alike. As we have seen, their discussion situated the women firmly as victims, in spite of rich evidence suggesting that their situations were more complex.

In legal discourse, a similar procedure of simplification was at work. When prostitutes encountered the court and police systems, they were sometimes cast as endangered victims of coerced sex or ill-treatment by madams. In other instances, such as violation of street-soliciting ordinances or accounts of fraud and robbery with sex as the lure, they were cast as dangerous perpetrators. This bipolar representation saturated popular accounts of prostitution. Yet although it offered more positionings than the stories of kidnap victims, it did not come close to capturing the range of prostitute interactions with legal and regulatory institutions.

Prostitutes went to court to assert claims on property and on their own labor, and to bring complaints against people who made competing claims. Frequently they behaved neither as disadvantaged victims nor as stigmatized disrupters of urban peace, but as aggrieved citizens pursuing various goals in a legal venue. This was true of madams as well. Prosecuted for licensing violations, they appeared as contributors to urban disorder. Charged with beating or coercing prostitutes, they contributed to the creation of the evil madam as a stock figure in scandal fiction and reformist writing. Yet their encounters with the courts and police were not reducible to these categories. Even when the courts moved to chastise a madam for exceeding the permissible limits of behavior, they often acknowledged and reinforced the legitimacy of her claim on the labor of "her" prostitutes.

This chapter examines the weaving of a legal discourse on prostitution in Republican-era Shanghai, a discourse shaped by overlapping sets of police regulations and legal jurisdictions in Shanghai's various municipalities. Whereas chapter 11 focuses on campaigns for comprehensive control and rearrangement of prostitution, the present chapter looks at quotidian regimes of regulation, tracing legal attempts to encompass prostitution, as well as the competing stances of prostitutes and madams as litigants and defendants. It examines the dual figures of victim and victimizer (the latter including madams as well as prostitutes), but simultaneously directs attention to the capacity of prostitutes, in their daily activities, to both use and exceed the confinement of these representations.

THE REGULATORY MATRIX

Criminal Law

The Qing criminal code did not explicitly forbid prostitution, although it prohibited many of the conditions that enabled prostitution to exist. It prescribed punishments for officials who frequented brothels, as well as their sons. It attempted to segregate respectable families from prostitutes, actors, and singers (all stigmatized populations in the early Qing) by forbidding the latter to buy, adopt, or marry people from respectable families and by forbidding civil and military officials from taking prostitutes as wives or concubines. Both the Qing and Republican criminal codes made procuring and trafficking illegal,[1] and as the preceding chapter noted, many trafficking cases were adjudicated in Shanghai under the Republican law. But prostitution (as well as patronizing prostitutes) was not explicitly forbidden by Republican-era criminal codes, either.[2]

In spite of the cautionary and scandal literature linking them to numerous scams and robberies, prostitutes and madams seldom ended up in prison for the commission of any type of crime. A 1932 survey of incarcerated women in Shanghai's three jails (the Haining Road jail in the International Settlement, the Xuehuali Road jail in the French Concession, and the Jiangsu #2 jail in the Chinese municipality) found 359 female convicts. None was a prostitute; two were madams serving sentences for, respectively, kidnapping and harming the family. The authors commented that in Shanghai many brothel operators committed crimes and were arrested, but madams with money and power used bribes or other means to solve their problems with the law, seldom coming to trial. Thirty-four of the women were serving time for sex crimes: adultery (*jianfei*), enticement (*heyou*), aggressive enticement (*lüeyou;* this appears to be female-on-female crime, in which a woman is lured into captivity and possibly prostitution), harming marriage, harming the moral atmosphere, and escape (from what or whom unspecified). Although the authors argued that brothels and opium dens corrupted the atmosphere and harmed local citizens, contributing to an increase in crime, the purported linkages were neither spelled out nor borne out by the survey data.[3]

Licensing and Taxation

Under all of Shanghai's governments, prostitution was routinely licensed and taxed under local rather than national regulations.[4] Through the second decade of the twentieth century, the official approach to prostitution in both the International Settlement and the French Concession focused on licensing and inspection rather than abolition. In 1877, the governments of the International Settlement and the French Concession agreed to license prostitutes, keep a registry of brothels and prostitutes, and conduct weekly inspections of brothels that serviced foreigners. Although this was primarily designed as an attempt to control the spread of sexually transmitted diseases, it was partly intended to protect prostitutes as well: the Mixed Court was empowered to close brothels if the prostitutes objected to their treatment by the owners.[5]

In 1898, brothels in the International Settlement were brought under the auspices of a licensing bylaw so inclusive that it rivaled later warlord attempts to tax everything that moved:

> No person shall keep a fair, market, Chinese Club, lodging house, music hall, theatre, circus, cinematograph, eating house, or other place of refreshment or public entertainment, hotel, tavern, billiard, bowling or dancing saloon, brothel, pawnshop, Chinese money exchange or cash shop, Chinese gold-smith's or silver-smith's shop, dairy, laundry, bakery, slaughterhouse, livery stable, public garage, pen for cattle, pigs, sheep or goats; or sell or keep a shop, store, stall or place for the sale of clothing, wines, spirits, beer or other alcoholic beverages, or any noxious drugs and poisons, proprietary or patent medicines, butcher's meat, poultry, game, fish, fruit, ice, vegetables or other foodstuffs, tobacco, lottery tickets or chances in lotteries, or hawk any goods; or keep for private or public use, or let ply or use for hire any launch, sampan, ferry or other boat, any horse, pony, mule or donkey, any motor car, motor bicycle, or other motor vehicle or, [sic] carriage, cart, handcart, ricsha, sedan-chair, wheelbarrow or other vehicle or drive any tramcar, motor vehicle or horse drawn vehicle; or pull any ricsha or keep or have in his possession any dog, within such limits without a licence first obtained from the Council and in the case of foreigners countersigned by the Consul of the nationality to which such person belongs.[6]

Infringements of this bylaw could cost the offender a one-hundred-dollar fine and a further twenty-five dollars for each day the infringement continued.[7] Clearly the Shanghai Municipal Council had to be highly selective in enforcing this bylaw, and until 1920 brothels were not in practice required to register, although "[r]egistration and inspection of certain native prostitutes [those servicing foreigners] continued as a system up to 1920."[8]

After 1920, prostitution became illegal in the International Settlement, with the important exception of courtesan houses, which were taxed both by the Municipal Council and by the provincial government of Jiangsu. Nevertheless, prostitutes of all classes remained ubiquitous. In the early 1920s, while the licenses of all prostitutes and brothels in the International Settlement were being systematically withdrawn by the Shanghai Municipal Council, reports began to mention that women were not only violating the regulations against soliciting, but were operating without licenses.[9] Police began to conduct periodic dawn raids on unlicensed pheasant brothels, arresting both madams and prostitutes.[10] Unlicensed prostitutes were created as a class of offenders, whether they plied their trade on the streets or not. Meanwhile, the number of licensed courtesan houses continued to rise; Municipal Council records show 697 brothel licenses issued in 1936, increasing to 1,325 in 1940. Brothels were charged a quarterly tax of 48 yuan per house, netting the council 68,865 yuan in revenue in 1939 and 77,092 yuan in 1940. This amount was second only to hotel and restaurant tax revenue.[11]

In the French Concession, by contrast, licensed prostitution remained legal throughout the 1920s and 1930s. Prostitutes continued to be required to submit to medical inspection.[12] A 1928 French Concession list of establishments classified sing-song houses and brothels as "Category C: establishments for the use of the public," rather than Category A, "inconvenient, insalubrious or dangerous establishments," or Category B, "establishments which can be inconvenient or unhealthy." To obtain a Category C license, the applicant had to specify the location, operational details, staffing, fire protection, hygienic measures, and floor plans of the proposed establishment and obtain authorization from the French consul general and the Municipal Administration Council.[13] At least through the mid-1930s, applications filed by would-be proprietors (mostly Chinese and female) were routinely approved.[14] Brothels operating without such licenses were, however, sometimes raided and closed down.[15] In both foreign settlements, violations of licensing regulations were discovered by police and enforced by the Mixed Court.[16] The vast majority of licensing cases handled by the courts concerned Chinese brothels and prostitutes.[17]

Under Japanese occupation, the puppet municipal administrations continued to license prostitution.[18] In 1938, the government issued revised regulations for the licensing of dance halls and taxi dancers, although the regulations expressly forbade "improper activities."[19] In November 1942, the city government reportedly lifted any prohibition on prostitution, and statistics collected by the police indicated that 5,253 women were licensed as *shuyu* storytellers, guides, prostitutes, and masseuses.[20] The postwar Guomindang government licensed and taxed brothels and prostitutes as well (see chapter 11). This ongoing attempt to control prostitution by keeping records of it—and to use those records as a basis for revenue extraction—far overshadowed the impulse to abolish prostitution in pre-1949 Shanghai.

Police Regulations

Daily regulation of the sex trades in Shanghai lay largely with the police: the Shanghai Municipal Police in the International Settlement, the French Concession police, and the Public Security Bureau in Chinese-controlled sections.[21] A 1926 list of police regulations in the International Settlement included article 23: "If prostitutes dare to solicit customers on the street, and annoy passersby, after investigation, the police will detain and send them to government offices to be punished according to regulations."[22] The corresponding regulation in the French Concession, also numbered article 23, stated in part that prostitutes were not to gather in groups, make fun of each other, or speak in a lascivious or lewd manner. Those whose clothing was improperly seductive of passersby were threatened with revocation of their licenses.[23] These provisions translated into cases pursued by the police and adjudicated, from 1864 to 1927, by the Mixed Courts in the International Settlement and the French Concession.[24]

In the Chinese-controlled territory of Shanghai, several offenses involving prostitutes were forbidden under national police regulations.[25] These regulations were enforced by the Public Security Bureau, not the courts.[26] The law of penalties for breach of police regulations was in force from at least 1915, with a revised version promulgated in 1928. Article 43 stipulated detention for up to fifteen days or a fine not exceeding fifteen yuan for "secret" (unlicensed) solicitation by a prostitute, procuring, or supplying lodgings for immoral purposes. Article 45 added that "indecent language or immoral conduct on a highway or in public places" (along with parading around naked, gambling, or "wearing curious dresses detrimental to public morals") was punishable by five days of detention or a five-yuan fine. Detention was to take place in a Public Security Bureau detention house; fines were to be paid within five days after a judgment.[27] This judgment took place entirely under the auspices of the Public Security Bureau, usually within a day of the offense. The Public Security Bureau also issued regulations for the management of hotels, which among other things forbade prostitutes to drink or spend the night there, and forbade guests to entertain prostitutes in hotel rooms.[28] As prostitution expanded into new forms, the municipal administration scrambled to keep pace with new regulations. In 1936, for instance, the Social Affairs Bureau issued a proclamation banning guide agencies, dancing-companion societies, and other "disguised organizations," with breaches to be punished by the Public Security Bureau.[29]

The intensity with which police enforced these regulations is a complex question. On the one hand, Shanghai was underpoliced; the Public Security Bureau employed about four thousand policemen in the early 1930s, while Beijing, with one-third the area and about the same population, had more than twice as many.[30] The situation was quite possibly further complicated by the fact that during this period most policemen in the Shanghai Public Security Bureau came from the northern provinces of Hebei, Henan, and Shandong, and therefore spoke different dialects from large segments of the communities they were supposed to police.[31] During the Nanjing decade, frequent personnel changes and massive corruption were also the norm among policemen.[32] All of these factors might well have meant that minor offenses such as street soliciting by prostitutes went unattended.[33] On the other hand, in 1930s Shanghai the government was perpetually short of tax revenue, and each bureau helped defray its own expenses by collecting taxes of some sort. The Public Security Bureau relied on fines paid for the breach of police regulations, which provided some incentive to enforce them.[34]

Solicitation and Its Discontents

Although many infractions of police regulations probably went undetected or unpursued, streetwalkers were apprehended on a daily basis for violating police regulations against soliciting.[35] Prostitutes charged with soliciting included pheasants, opium prostitutes, Cantonese, and Russians.[36] The women were usually fined between one and ten yuan and released, with slightly higher fines levied on Cantonese who importuned foreigners. Occasionally women jumped bail and failed to appear in court; even more occasionally, they were detained for a week if they could not pay their fines.[37] Madams and male brothel owners were also fined for permitting prostitutes to solicit or doing so on their behalf, most commonly paying a twenty-yuan penalty or serving a sentence of several weeks, particularly if they were repeat offenders.[38]

Even when the police were motivated to arrest streetwalkers, the task was not easy. Frustrated that pheasants would slip into the shadows whenever his patrolmen went by, the police chief in the French Concession went out on the streets himself in 1917 and personally arrested more than ten women.[39] In 1930, a decade after prostitution was banned in the International Settlement, the Chinese Ratepayers' Association complained to the Shanghai Municipal Council that street soliciting was still ubiquitous. Wearily, the council replied that the police were aware of the problem, and that "action is being maintained against soliciting and the use of public establishments as places of assignation, prosecutions being instituted in all cases where sufficient evidence is obtainable."[40]

As the effects of the world depression deepened in Shanghai, many observers reported an increase in the ranks of unlicensed prostitutes soliciting on the streets.[41] The early 1930s saw several organized attacks on street soliciting in the International Settlement and the French Concession. Patrolmen and plainclothes detectives on special assignment swept the areas where pheasants worked, transporting the women one by one in a black police vehicle to the police stations as a warning. But as soon as the special patrols became less frequent, a guidebook reported, the women reappeared, this time congregating off the streets in teahouses or in more deserted places.[42] In 1941, a news reporter commented that although five hundred prostitutes were arrested each month in the International Settlement, the majority still eluded the law:

> Thousands of patrolmen cannot clear them off the streets; often when patrolmen appear on a prostitutes' street, they don't see a single woman. They have already fled to another street, or are hiding in a dark place, and reappear after the policeman has gone.[43]

At the end of World War II, when a Guomindang-controlled municipal administration was installed in Shanghai, the mayor's office and the police undertook a renewed campaign to forbid street soliciting. Repeated notices in internal police files indicate that the police chief had trouble convincing his branch station chiefs and patrolmen to crack down on soliciting. Stung by his criticism of their performance, these subordinates submitted lists of all the prostitutes they had detained for soliciting. These lists were full of repeat offenders, indicating that as soon as a woman was released from detention she went right back out on the streets.[44] Up through 1948, police records show arrest of prostitutes on major streets and in department-store rooftop gardens, as well as repeated efforts by officers to persuade street patrolmen to take this task seriously.[45]

Depending on the venue where these offenses were reported, the prostitutes appeared either as undifferentiated statistics, insubordinate threats to local authority, or pathetic victims of social and legal injustice. News reports, even at their most fulsome, typically offered little information: the prostitute's name (from which we can tell that many of them were married),[46] native place, brothel address, street where she was found "forcibly soliciting" customers, badge number of the detective who arrested her, and amount of the fine. A few stories were embellished with details of pheasants who got into fights with each other over a customer, or who tried unsuccessfully to bribe the police.[47]

Beyond mention in the dry, spare news reports of arrests and fines, and the bureaucratic language of internal police memos, the soliciting pheasant was also the subject of memoirists and reform agitators. Authors in these genres fashioned wildly differing accounts from virtually identical plot elements. E. W. Peters, a policeman in the International Settlement from 1929 to 1935, recalls the nightly cat-and-mouse (or, more accurately, hunter-and-pheasant) game enacted in the main thoroughfares and alleys:

> Special plain-clothes squads, composed of several Chinese policemen with a couple of foreigners in charge, are detailed nightly to round up these girls and their *amahs*. They go off in a police raiding van at all times of the night between 9 P.M. and 2 A.M.

Chinese policemen in plain clothes waited until they were solicited, then arrested the pheasants and their attendants, who were taken by the vanload to the police station until the station was packed. Some protested innocence, while others cursed the police or made jokes at their expense, pretending intimate familiarity with them. After a night in the station, at 10 o'clock the following morning they were brought before the judge, lined up in groups of a dozen, fined ten yuan per head (both prostitutes and attendants), and dismissed. Sometimes several hundred were processed in a morning, after which "the merry throng go home to get painted up for the following night."[48]

Peters's pheasants are saucy, irrepressible, at ease with the bawdy display of their sexuality, eager to discomfit their captors and return to the streets. Tabloid reporters were less exuberant in their portrayal of the women, noting that the revolving-door system of fines set up a situation in which the police and the prostitutes each took a share of the prostitutes' nightly income.[49] Reform writers, in turn, used solicitation stories to condemn what the writers saw as the injustice of police and court regulation. A 1922 story in the magazine *Xingqi* featured many of the standard figures of prostitute fiction: the young and inexperienced pheasant, the late night on the street in wintry weather, the unsuccessful pursuit of a customer to avoid the wrath of an abusive owner. Arrested by a compassionate patrolman who thinks she would be better off sleeping in jail rather than freezing on the street, the young woman spends the night alternately fearing death and daydreaming about her first love, a shop apprentice who gave her some extra money aside from the regular fee for sex. The next day she is hauled before the judge, along with people who have been arrested for brawling and stealing. She thinks to herself, What crime have I committed? If two people exchange flesh for money, why is it that only the one who contributes the flesh is a criminal and not the one who pays? The judges enter, one Chinese and one Western, letting the reader know that the case is being heard in the Mixed Court. The pheasant has never seen an official before. She is determined to speak out when her turn comes, but when she is called to the docket she can only blush. The Chinese judge asks her why she was soliciting on the street, and before she can answer he fines her ten yuan. Emerging from the courtroom, she sees her (male) brothel owner hand a sum of money to the policeman (it is not clear whether this is the fine or a bribe), and the policeman turns her over to her owner "like a runaway dog." That night she is out on the street soliciting again.[50]

The fictional treatment creates a voice of the prostitute, but that voice speaks in the stentorian tones of a reformer. In addition to its implicit condemnation of the authorities and their collusion with brothel owners, the story invokes two themes not found in other genres: romantic love and gender justice. The pheasant is represented as young and pure, just at the age when "the flowers of love should be sprouting," but is condemned instead to "the hell of rouge and powder." For her, romantic love is attainable only in her daydreams as she waits in the holding cell. This glimpse of a world of emotional connections from which she is barred serves to deepen the reader's sense of tragedy at her fate, a tragedy marked by an inability to be loved rather than by trafficking or economic hardship. The second theme, that women are unfairly penalized for an economic exchange in which men also participate, foreshadows late-twentieth-century demands for decriminalization voiced by prostitutes from many nations.[51] Given their sense that prostitution was degrading for women (see chapter 10), it is unlikely that the writers of Chinese reformist literature, fictional and nonfictional, would have been supportive of decriminalization—certainly their literature shows no indication of such support—but they did see women as victimized by the unpunished lust of men.

As noted earlier, during the late 1940s the Guomindang government sought to tighten the regulation of prostitution as part of a campaign to reestablish control over Shanghai. In the course of this campaign, police chief Xuan Tiewu received many letters from Shanghai residents complaining that the regulations were being flouted. Like police memoirs and reform writings, such letters also engaged in a conscious process of representation, classifying both prostitutes and their customers as a source of disorder. A writer signing himself "a resident of Yunnan South Road" wrote:

I personally believe that since the victory, you have put every effort into social construction and adjustment. You have also improved social morals, and strictly forbidden prostitution, with visible results. People cannot stop talking about it. I greatly admire this. But there are also those who ignore the law and deliberately violate regulations. I live on Yunnan Nanlu, where I have run a business for many years. This district is rather quiet and isolated, yet every night I see crowds of unlicensed prostitutes soliciting by the side of the road. The small hotels in the area temporarily become the place where they meet. Most of the johns are low-class and ignorant, and are easily provoked by a single word, so conflicts and brawls often occur. I work during the day and have a hard time concentrating [from lack of sleep], and when I want to sleep at this time I find it impossible. All of the neighbors have been affected by this, and often complain about it. If this continues, not only will it violate your orders, but it also will present an opportunity for hoodlums to come and make trouble. Therefore I am reporting this situation to you, and hope that you will speedily send officials to investigate. This will be of benefit to the people and create good fortune for us. We are extremely grateful.[52]

Police plainclothes detectives filing internal reports on the extent of illegal street soliciting exhibited a similar exasperated tone. Listing the many major streets where prostitutes could be found, one detective commented that across from the Great World Amusement Hall "the prostitutes stand shoulder to shoulder. . . . There are also pimps (*mawang*) looking for customers. Although there is a police kiosk there, they act as though they see nothing." The report concluded:

> In the areas described above where prostitutes are active, one seldom sees a patrolman. These prostitutes stroke their hair coquettishly and aggressively solicit passersby without shame. This does grave damage to the public image of the city and violates decent customs. We are preparing to order each branch station to abolish it.[53]

The double encounter of prostitute with her customers and the police, then, lent itself to a variety of possible representations. Writers used prostitutes to establish the status of Shanghai as an ungovernable city, where women and much else were out of control (the experiences of Peters and the Guomindang police detectives). They used them to mourn the stolen youth and ruined innocence of young women whose sexuality, in a kinder, gentler world, would have been protected (the story that appeared in *Xingqi*). They used them to incite the police to improve street behavior and rebuild the nation in the wake of ruinous foreign occupation (letters from disgruntled residents). However, even when the prostitutes in these pieces were given "voice," what they said was fashioned by the intentions of the authors, crudely limited by the larger discursive uses to which prostitution was being put.

In the rare cases where prostitutes' words were recorded directly, as in the transcripts of police interrogations discussed in the previous chapter, it is tempting to assume the possibility of retrieving a direct, genuine, uncomplicated prostitute's "voice." When prostitutes were being detained for soliciting, however, they found themselves inserted into a particular set of power relations that called forth certain responses. Their replies to official queries took on a formulaic character where the repetition of certain phrases compels attention. As a 1935 tabloid report on unlicensed prostitutes noted: "Every arrested prostitute will be questioned as to why she wanted to be a prostitute, and each time the answer is that she was forced by life."[54] Twelve years later, as the previous chapter shows, women were still using this identical phrase to describe their motivation. Several possible factors are at work here, probably simultaneously. The women may have been describing their own sense of their individual situations, reaching for the language of economic necessity (the product of reformist and social-science discourses that most of them encountered indirectly, if at all) because it seemed to express their circumstances. They might have been consciously deploying a strategy that they knew would hasten the end of the interrogation, win them a degree of routine leniency that would allow them to pay the fine, and leave—in effect, participating in a familiar protocol governing encounters with police. It may also be that police stenographers, bored with the endless sameness of solicitation arrests and fines, themselves provided the "forced by life" shorthand as an alternative to recording the minute variations of individual histories, histories that were irrelevant for the purposes of police record keeping. Whatever the circumstances that created these historical records, the prostitute's "own voice" in police transcripts is a drone, whether it is a genuinely felt expression of hardship, a crafty exercise in self-representation, or a bored gesture in the direction of police power. Even with the addition of the prostitute's voice, the repertoire of figures in solicitation stories remains confined to the victim and the perpetrator.

Isolating Children from Brothels

One of the ways in which International Settlement authorities sought to contain the effects of prostitution was by keeping brothels away from children and children away from brothels. It was forbidden to locate brothels near schools, lest innocent children be corrupted.[55] Conversely, in both foreign settlements and the Chinese city it was prohibited for children under the age of sixteen to stay overnight in a brothel.[56] Given the young age at which many courtesans began their training, often under the rubric of adoptive daughter, as well as the youth of many pawned and sold prostitutes, violations of this regulation were common. In the early years of the Republican period, the Mixed Court heard a dozen or more cases each year in which Chinese were accused of allowing children under sixteen in brothels,[57] usually as virgin prostitutes or maids. Such cases often came to trial when a girl's relative or an anonymous tipster brought an infraction to the attention of the police. The court either remanded the girl to the custody of her relatives or sent her to the Door of Hope.[58] The madams or male brothel owners were usually fined between ten and fifty yuan, or occasionally sentenced to jail for several weeks to several months.[59]

In practice, however, it was not simple to disentangle the brothel from the skein of social relationships involving Shanghai children. Frequently the madam, the girl's relatives, or the girl herself came forward with an explanation of extenuating circumstances. One madam obtained a verdict of not guilty after she explained to the court that a group of girls were staying in her brothel for training in music, although the judge ordered her not to let them stay there again.[60] Another madam argued successfully (with her lawyer's help) that the girl she was accused of keeping was already sixteen and thus not covered by the regulations. (Madams who retained lawyers tended to fare better in such cases than madams who did not.)[61] Some girls visited brothels in the company of their mothers, who had friends employed there.[62] And in many cases, the brothel turned out to be a place where girls visited or lived with their closest relatives: some of these girls were the daughters of brothel servants;[63] others were the daughters of madams. Court practice in such cases was inconsistent. Sometimes the girl was removed from her mother's custody, sometimes the mother was ordered to close her brothel, and sometimes the court simply handed the girl back to her mother's care.[64]

In a number of cases where the court had sent a girl to the Door of Hope, family members came forward to argue for custody. In two different cases, men claimed that their daughters had merely been visiting or living with their aunts, who were prostitutes; in the case of a fourteen-year-old girl who was found selling sex, both the girl and her mother asked the court that they be reunited. The court rejected all of these claims, apparently reasoning that the parents had acted irresponsibly enough to lose custody. It did, however, let two mothers in another case take their daughters home after the two retained a lawyer to plead for them and guaranteed that the girls would not go to a brothel again.[65] Sometimes the police were even more aggressive in asserting their authority to remove children from the parent/brothel nexus, regardless of the desires of the parties involved. In 1917, for instance, the police discovered that the daughter of a paper-lantern maker had been sent to a brothel to learn to sing and act. Apparently uninterested in being rescued, she escaped while being transported to the Door of Hope, whereupon the police arrested her mother and demanded that she turn the girl in.[66] In each of these instances, the courts were the venue for a tug-of-war between families and the state over the proper place for children.

The regulation against children in brothels sought to keep the sale of sex hermetically sealed off from a clearly defined realm called childhood. Any violation of this boundary, in the eyes of regulators, not only accompanied the mistreatment of children (in the form of beatings or forced sale) but was itself a form of mistreatment. Yet the details of these cases indicate that girls *were* found in brothels—not necessarily ministering to the sexual needs of depraved customers, but perhaps learning performance skills, visiting their relatives, or simply residing in the only home they knew. And madams, far from assuming the position of wrongdoer and meekly relinquishing such children, entered the courts to actively explain the relationships that they felt justified the children's presence there.

MADAM RIGHTS AND WRONGS

The Madam as Plaintiff

As long as the business conducted there did not violate certain regulations, operating a house of prostitution was not illegal. Neither was being a madam, and such women were forthright about using the law to protect their own interests with respect to both prostitutes and customers. Madams went to court to sue prostitutes who owed them money for room and board, or who borrowed money and failed to repay it.[67]

Brothels were publicly acknowledged places of business, and the police were as responsible for keeping order there as in any other commercial establishment. When hoodlums broke in on customers drinking and gambling in a courtesan's room, attempting to extort money from the customers and stealing the courtesan's jewelry, International Settlement police arrested the hoodlums. When a customer lost his temper and inflicted a head wound on a male brothel servant, Settlement detectives took the brawler to court, where he was fined. Madams, even those in low-class opium brothels, did not behave like a stigmatized or furtive group: if customers grew rowdy or dissatisfied and began to damage the premises, they called the police.[68]

Madams were also not reluctant to bring legal complaints against customers for stealing "their" prostitutes or helping them escape, and their claims were legitimized by the courts and police. In 1880, a madam brought one of her customers to court in the International Settlement because she suspected him of helping a prostitute to leave her brothel. The customer denied any involvement, but rather than dismissing the madam's claim as legally unjustified, the judge asked her to produce additional evidence.[69] When prostitutes from cities like Hankou and Nanjing fled with their customers to Shanghai, their madams did not hesitate to follow them and report the cases to the Shanghai police as suspected abductions.[70] Madams even attempted to invoke the protection of the law when charges of kidnapping were leveled against them. In a 1936 French Concession case, a madam complained to the police when several men claimed that one of her prostitutes was their kidnapped relative, attempting to extort three hundred yuan from her as a retroactive purchase price. The police obligingly arrested the men.[71] Such stories raise the possibility that some of the kidnapping reports discussed in chapter 7 may have been carefully fabricated extortion scams. Furthermore, news reports indicate that prostitutes were abducted out of brothels as well as into them, and in such cases the French Concession courts were willing to jail the abductors, who were sometimes brothel customers, and make efforts to locate the missing women for return to "their" madams.[72] News reports do not make it clear whether the judges and police in such cases saw themselves as protecting the madams' contractual rights or the bodily safety of the prostitutes themselves. What is clear is that the authorities found nothing unusual or unseemly about being asked to keep order in houses of prostitution.

If madams were not afraid to use the law and its enforcers, they were not totally dependent on them, either. Attempting to locate a prostitute who had escaped from her pheasant house in 1920, a madam named Dai gathered her male relatives to lock up and torture the missing woman's brother, whom they suspected of concealing her.[73] In 1936, a madam hired two toughs to cruise the streets in an automobile looking for two escaped pheasants, who were spotted shopping and forced into the car.[74] As indicated in chapter 3, madams (and individual prostitutes as well) often made alliances with so-called brothel props—hoodlums or powerful paramours who could offer protection from other hoodlums. In pheasant houses, these enforcers were also known as "counterfeit trademarks" (*gaipaitou*).[75] It was said that a powerful "counterfeit trademark" could induce the police to leave "his" pheasants alone rather than arresting and fining them for street soliciting.[76]

By the mid-1920s, some reports were beginning to suggest that brothel owners and prostitutes were joining the Green Gang in order to obtain support from powerful gang elders to whom they swore loyalty.[77] Madams also established connections with private detectives,[78] who could be quite brutal in defending the interests of the house. In one 1929 case, for instance, a seventeen-year-old prostitute in a salt-pork brothel in the French Concession fled with a customer. The madam believed that she had been taken away by Chen Ayan, a bamboo artisan, so she had two detectives seize him, shut him up in the Qingjiang Hotel, and torture him until he revealed her whereabouts. Desperate to end the abuse, Chen falsely said that he had taken the woman to Pudong, but when the detectives took him to the south docks to cross the river to find her, he jumped into the river and committed suicide. The private detectives were arrested.[79] Another protection strategy employed by madams was to show special consideration for policemen and petty officials who visited the brothel, offering them services ranging from extra cups of tea to sexual favors.[80] The world of hoodlums and that of policemen overlapped considerably in Republican-era Shanghai; ties between the two were cemented by shared gang affiliations, favors, and payoffs. Successful madams incorporated themselves into this nexus of relationships.

The Madam Accused

Civil suits against brothel keepers were apparently more common than criminal charges. "Suits for declaration of freedom are very frequent and are instituted by the numerous so-called Chinese 'sing-song' girls and prostitutes against their masters and brothel-keepers," wrote a foreign observer about cases heard before the Mixed Court in the 1910s and 1920s.[81] Nevertheless, when prostitutes or their customers brought legal complaints against madams, the issue was not *whether* a madam had claims on her prostitutes—that was assumed—but rather the *extent* of those claims.

One important set of complaints involved breaking the relationship between madam and prostitute, often (but not always) so that the prostitute could marry. In the late nineteenth century, a prostitute who wished to leave a recalcitrant madam could appeal to government officials for permission to do so—once she repaid the madam the original purchase or pawn price.[82] The madam's right to this payment was not in question. But if a madam was found in violation of the regulations governing prostitution, this gave the prostitute an opening to gain her freedom. In a 1917 case, for instance, the prostitute Wang Yueying formed a liaison with a customer, Wu Jintang, and refused to sleep with other customers. When her madam forced her to do so, in violation of the regulation against forced sale of sex, Wang turned herself in to the Door of Hope. The madam was fined thirty yuan.[83] In 1921, just after the International Settlement campaign to license brothels, another madam refused to let a policeman buy a prostitute out of a flower-smoke room, and hid the prostitute by sending her to work in another, unlicensed brothel. Unhappy about this decision, and making use of the fact that the brothel was unlicensed, the prostitute turned herself in to the Door of Hope.[84] (The fact that the would-be buyer was a policeman was apparently so unremarkable as to merit no comment.)

Prostitutes of courtesan rank who wished to end the ownership or pawning relationship with their madams often chose to improve their negotiating positions by retaining a lawyer. They also made use of existing regulations against certain types of prostitution in order to pressure the madams to let them go. The journalist and fiction writer Bao Tianxiao describes a "flower-protecting lawyer" (*huhua lüshi*) named Zhu Bangsheng, active in the early twentieth century. A fifteen-year-old virgin courtesan sought his help because her madam was pressuring her to have sexual relations with an older customer she did not like. Zhu interrogated her and discovered that one of his old friends, Zheng, had expressed affection for her. Zhu then persuaded Zheng to pay the young woman's living expenses while he pursued the case. Zhu relocated the woman to a hotel, cautioning her not to take expensive clothing or jewelry when she left the brothel, lest she be accused of stealing. Discovering the girl missing, the madam was hesitant to report it to the police for fear of bringing trouble on her house. Soon after that Zhu sent her a letter saying that the young woman had accused her of ill-treatment and coercion. He invited the madam to negotiate, then informed her that she had committed two crimes: selling a respectable woman into prostitution, and selling the virginity of a minor. He threatened her with police intervention and prison; she replied that she had spent a great deal of money in raising the girl, whose future earnings she regarded as her own "burial fund." Finally Zhu arranged a settlement wherein the suitor Zheng paid the madam four hundred yuan in return for the young woman's freedom. As Zhu's reputation spread, many courtesans who wished to leave their houses sought him out.[85]

Three cases reported in the 1929 tabloid press suggest a similar pattern of courtesan litigation. In the first, a courtesan who had been pawned to a madam, and later purchased by her, became angry because the madam secretly sold the rights to her virginity to a customer. When the customer took her to a hotel and asked her to stay, she refused his advances and sought out a lawyer. Alarmed that she might lose control over the courtesan, the madam secretly took seven hundred yuan from the courtesan's drawer. At this point, the lawyer printed an official announcement in the newspaper, stating that the courtesan was breaking her relationship with the madam because the madam had induced her to have illicit relations with another party for the purpose of making a profit. It is likely that his purpose in bringing this accusation, which might have resulted in a fine, was to convince the madam not to make further demands of the courtesan.

The second case also involved defloration rights to a pawned courtesan. In this case, the madam convinced the virgin courtesan to sleep with a customer, promising her jewelry and a cash payment. Unbeknownst to the courtesan, the madam demanded substantial amounts of money from the customer and kept most of it for herself, even refusing to pay the courtesan's tailor bill when she went into debt. Furious, the courtesan left the brothel and asked a famous lawyer to represent her in a suit for her freedom; his fame was such that several of the mainstream newspapers reported the hiring. Here again, the courtesan and her lawyer accused the madam of forcing the courtesan to be deflowered by a guest against her will, implicitly threatening legal action if the madam did not release the courtesan. At the same time, they offered to negotiate and settle out of court. In a modern twist, the courtesan also announced that she planned to attend a girls' school once she obtained her freedom.

In the third case, a courtesan who had been hired by a madam and whose business was flourishing hired a lawyer to obtain her freedom from her abusive adoptive mother, who had made the hiring arrangement with the madam. The courtesan offered to compensate the mother with money provided by a sympathetic customer. The lawyer obtained an agreement that the mother should not interfere in the courtesan's daily life, but that when the courtesan got married the mother should be informed and given sufficient money to support her in her old age. The mother agreed to these terms. But when the courtesan failed to marry immediately, the mother apparently grew impatient for her money, went to the courtesan's house, and stole her jewelry. In this case the legal settlement did not accuse the mother of violating any legal regulations, but recognized her claim on compensation for the costs of raising the courtesan, to be paid at the time of marriage.[86]

In each of these cases, the issue was not the fact that madams hired courtesans to entertain and provide sexual services, but rather the extent of the madam's control over the timing and financial benefits attached to those services. The presence of lawyers in such a situation was not dissimilar to their use in other sorts of contract negotiations; the courtesans who hired them did not cringe before the law like a stigmatized population, but sought to use it to enhance their own positions. When the lawyers accused madams of violating specific regulations, they did so not in order to show that it was utterly illegitimate to be a madam, but in order to threaten and cajole the madams into making particular concessions. In short, both courtesans and madams behaved as though the law was theirs to use, not there to limit their activities.

The method of hiring a lawyer and charging a madam with violating regulations was not limited to courtesans. The 1929 case of Zhao Xiuying, reported in some detail in the press, concerned a déclassé descendant of an official family whose mother was forced by poverty to pawn her into a courtesan house in Shaoxing. After establishing her noble pedigree, the news report went on to tell how she was kidnapped by bandits and pawned again, this time into a Shanghai pheasant house. Beaten repeatedly, Zhao was illegally detained by her madam after the pawn period was up, and tricked into signing a "body-selling contract" that gave the madam ownership rights in perpetuity. (The story implied that Zhao was duped because she was illiterate, her educated background notwithstanding.) She fled with a sympathetic customer but remained fearful that the madam would use the contract to pursue legal claims against her, so she hired a lawyer to bring charges that that madam was operating an unlicensed brothel, trafficking, and forcing respectable women to become prostitutes—all violations of police regulations or the criminal code. According to the news report, the madam retained a defense lawyer and the case went to court, although the outcome was not reported.[87]

Customers, too, recognized that a madam had legal claims on a prostitute. Most customer complaints were filed when a customer wanted to buy a prostitute as a wife or concubine and met resistance from the madam. Such conflicts occurred up and down the hierarchy of prostitution. In 1875, for instance, a firewood peddler paid a madam fifty yuan as betrothal money for a prostitute he had met in a flower-smoke brothel. According to court testimony, the madam took the money but refused to let the prostitute marry him immediately. After hearing his complaint, a judge sent a policeman to tell the madam either to permit the marriage, return the money, or face prosecution. (The man's claim was compromised when both the madam and the prostitute claimed that the firewood peddler had never paid them anything.)[88] In this case, the judge's warning underlined the fact that once the madam was paid a particular sum, she had to let the woman go—but if she did not accept the money, she would continue to have authority over her. Other court cases adjudicated between madams who wanted a high body price for "their" women and customers who wanted to pay less, or customers who wanted to buy women out and madams who wanted guarantees that the women would not open competing courtesan houses.[89] The Mixed Court agreed without any reluctance to hear such cases; its role was apparently to quantify the claims of the madams, not to challenge their legitimacy.

Women who could prove that they had been forced into prostitution could get legal help in fleeing the brothel system. Many cases that came before the courts in the Republican period thus centered around the contention, made by a prostitute or her relatives, that she had not voluntarily entered the brothel and they had not voluntarily sold her there. Madams routinely contested these assertions, saying that women had been sold to them as foster daughters or pawned as prostitutes. Since pawning or sale was a contractual transaction, madams frequently produced the signed contracts in court as proof that all parties had agreed to the arrangement. Brothel owners who had acquired women by irregular means were not above forging such contracts or tricking women into signing them after the fact. The prostitutes, in turn, often contended that such documents had been signed under duress.[90]

The Evil Madam Condemned

Beginning in the 1910s, the evil madam became a stock figure across many genres of writing about brothels. (See figure 19.) Her identifying feature was the mistreatment of her prostitutes, who were locked in their rooms, beaten, or even tortured if they did not please guests, refused to service them, were unable to have sexual relations because they were ill, or were suspected of stealing from the madam. The prostitutes most vulnerable to such abuse, as indicated in chapter 2, were those who had been pawned or sold to the madam. Sometimes the battering came at the behest of the madam but was carried out by male brothel owners or servants. News reports of such incidents most frequently concerned low-class brothels such as pheasant houses or flower-smoke rooms. They came to the attention of the International Settlement authorities either when police discovered them or when the battered women turned themselves in to the Door of Hope. Egregious ill-treatment was punishable in the International Settlement by fines or short prison terms, and might cause the courts to nullify a pawning contract. The battered prostitutes were most often sent to the Door of Hope or another welfare organization.[91]

In the more lurid accounts of scandal fiction, mistreatment by madams was elaborated into detailed regimens of torture designed to force recalcitrant prostitutes into submission. A harrowing story published in 1937 told of a woman named A Jin, perhaps seventeen or eighteen years old, who was tricked by a male swindler and sold for one hundred yuan to a pheasant madam named A Mu ("mother"). A Mu allowed three ugly men to deflower A Jin, then pierced her buttocks with an iron awl and hung her by her feet from a roof beam over burning incense until she consented to have sexual relations with customers. On nights when she failed to bring in business, A Mu forced her to stand in the courtyard naked in the snow (late-night torture scenes involving snow, a meteorological rarity in Shanghai, were a standard feature of such accounts). A Jin grew thin and unattractive, earning less as time went on and suffering more at the hands of the relentless A Mu.[92] Such stories purported to reveal the "true face" of prostitution, establishing credibility by piling on details of sadism in an almost pornographic manner.

The figure of the evil madam was also featured in stories where a prostitute fled a brothel, seeking refuge on the streets or with a customer, and came to the attention of the police. One story reported in the press involved a seventeen-year-old woman whose professional name was Red Cloud. Pawned into a French Concession salt-pork house by her mother in 1928 for four hundred yuan, she was repawned to another house because the first brothel owner objected to her physical frailty. Red Cloud's new madam was reported to be exceptionally cruel. Red Cloud was compelled to solicit customers on the street until four in the morning. If she failed to bring in business she was forced to kneel on broken tiles with a pan of water on her head, was forbidden to sleep, and was whipped if the water spilled. Driven beyond endurance, Red Cloud fled the brothel early one morning and leaped into a rickshaw parked at the end of the lane. Upset to the point of incoherence, she could not tell the puller where to go, so she directed him by means of hand motions. After nine hours of running through many of the districts in Shanghai, the hapless puller lost patience and asked her where she really wanted to go. Unable to explain that she had no money to pay him, she left the rickshaw and went to a house at the side of the road, begging to be taken in. When her request was refused, she returned to the puller and offered to marry him instead. Delighted, the puller told her that he might be too old for her (he was thirty-six), but that he had three younger brothers at home, all unmarried. He took her to his house in the Chinese-controlled Zhabei district, whereupon his brothers immediately began to argue over who should have her as a wife. The tumult alerted some inquisitive neighbors, who suspected that the woman had been kidnapped, and a group of them tried to blackmail the brothers. Eventually police arrived to investigate the disturbance, bringing Red Cloud and the three brothers to the Public Security Bureau.[93] The newspaper did not report whether charges were brought against the madam or the brothers, and Red Cloud's fate remains a mystery. Yet a prostitute's suffering, in this as in many similar stories,[94] was attributed to mistreatment by an evil madam, rather than to the perils or disgrace of prostitution itself.

PROSTITUTE RIGHTS AND WRONGS

The Vulnerable Prostitute

Not all the sufferings of prostitutes were attributed to torture by evil madams; some were ascribed to love gone horribly awry, leading to suicide and occasionally murder. In 1918, a prostitute killed herself because her lover reprimanded her after a customer stole her clothing. Other women committed double suicide with favored customers, taking morphine or opium when the man could not afford to buy the woman out. It is not clear that such "suicides" always reflected the woman's wishes: in at least one case, a policeman was accused of murdering a flower-smoke prostitute because she had rejected him and taken up with another policeman, even though he claimed that her death was half of a failed suicide pact in which he too had intended to die.[95]

Such stories marked prostitutes as creatures full of inchoate feeling, capable of dramatic, even desperate emotional moves. At the same time, however, the stories reinscribed the notion that brothels were places of danger precisely because relationships there were not circumscribed by a normal sense of social restraint.

The Prostitute Accused

As chapter 5 indicated, courtesan houses were sometimes described as places of peril, where a man risked being humiliated by supercilious women or cheated by petty chiselers and con artists. This muted note of danger in courtesan-house literature was much amplified in writings about lower-class prostitution, where desperation was said to drive women to relentless scheming at the expense of customers. In 1929 Xiao Linglong (Little Sound-of-Jingling-Jade), a twenty-year-old Shanghai prostitute, was picked up by the police as she fled to the city's south station to catch a train for Hangzhou. The news report said that she had been kidnapped from Hangzhou as a child and sold into a pheasant brothel, had escaped back to Hangzhou once and been caught, and had come of age working as a prostitute in Shanghai. She caught the fancy of a customer, who paid the brothel a monthly fee of fifty yuan in order to rent her exclusive services and install her in a room outside the pheasant house. Unbeknownst to him, Xiao Linglong was unwavering in her determination to return to Hangzhou. Over a one-month period, she "tricked" him (says the account) into giving her many items of clothing and accessories, then took the goods and headed for the train station. Her plan failed only because she was waylaid by a hooligan who tried to blackmail her, and their altercation caught the attention of police.[96] Although the point of the story appears to have been her capacity to steal from a customer (and perhaps default on a brothel contract as well), the account provided enough details to support an alternative reading: that such a woman was driven to theft and flight by a desire to return to her native place, thus escaping her status as a kidnap victim and owned prostitute.

Brothels were also written about as places where men, temporarily detached from the protective nexus of respectability and kin, were vulnerable to personal disaster. Newspapers commonly reported on men who awoke after spending the night in a hotel with a pheasant or other low-class prostitute only to find their money and clothing gone.[97] Another recurring story was that of the customer who died in a prostitute's bed, leaving his relatives bereft. In a 1916 case the victim was Huang Youpeng, who spent the night with the prostitute Chen Lianbao and then (said the news report) emitted a peculiar groan. Alarmed, Chen shipped him to the Red Cross in a rickshaw, but Huang's situation was so critical that the Red Cross sent him back to the brothel, where he died. The autopsy suggested that he had committed suicide by taking opium, but his brother-in-law suspected foul play, claiming that one hundred yuan was missing from Huang's wallet.[98] The theme of suicide in the perilous company of prostitutes took a slightly different form in a 1929 report. A waiter named Wang Asan had been "renting" a prostitute named Old Three by the month. The two were devoted to one another and wished to marry, but Wang was in terrible economic straits. His father denied him permission to marry, pointing out that Wang had no job and that Old Three was a prostitute and severely addicted to opium besides. Wang also asked his maternal uncle for help and was turned down. Meanwhile Old Three was pressuring him to marry. Unbearably anxious, Wang secretly swallowed poison and went to Old Three's brothel at 4 A.M. She awoke at midmorning to find him lying next to her, pale and moaning. Old Three informed the madam, who called the police, and Wang was sent by car to Renji hospital, but attempts to revive him were unsuccessful. Wang's father requested that no autopsy be performed, and the police captain consented. Old Three arrived to view the remains and was surrounded by the relatives of the deceased, who said to her, "Asan died because of you; you should wear deep mourning." At first she did not consent, but after the relatives reprimanded her, she agreed. Ironically, after his death Wang and Old Three were granted the recognition of their relationship that his kin had denied him in life. Nevertheless, the message of the story was that liaisons such as theirs were a bodily threat to men who strayed from the family compound.[99]

The Courts Condemned

Reform writers, in addition to detailing the hardships suffered by individual prostitutes, decried the inadequate protection that the legal system offered to prostitutes. In such accounts the portrayal of the prostitute as victim appeared in its most unalloyed form. In a 1938 article in a Shanghai women's magazine, a reporter recorded the story of the prostitute Ma Ruizhen "in her own words." The story was heavily shaped by the conventions of reformist writing, beginning with the title, "After Jumping Out of the Fiery Pit," which invoked the image of brothel as hell. The point of this account was the intertwined power of both legal and illegal forms of coercion to keep women in the employ of madams, particularly if the women had been mortgaged and the term had not yet expired. Ma Ruizhen, by her own account, was a prostitute who briefly passed through a prostitute reform organization in the late 1930s. Ma was released from the reform school on a court order obtained by her mother. As they left the courtroom, her mother told her that the madam had threatened the mother's life if she did not get the daughter released immediately. On the street they found the madam and several of her male associates waiting to escort them back to the brothel. The madam wanted to beat Ma and demanded immediate compensation for the two months' income she had lost while Ma was incarcerated. If Ma did not pay her immediately, she threatened, she would turn her over to the "boss" (*laoban*), whom Ma referred to as "the highest penal official in the brothel," a man who might well kill her or sell her into another city. Then some of the madam's associates mediated. They convinced Ma and her mother to kneel in front of the madam and beg that Ma be allowed to continue to work in order to pay off the debt. Ma was sent back onto the street to solicit customers under the watchful eyes of the brothel servants.

For two days, according to Ma's story, she deliberately failed to bring in customers. The madam cut off her food and threatened to have her hung up and beaten if she did not bring in some business before midnight. Ma fled to the local police station, where a sympathetic officer took her into protective custody and put out an order for the madam's arrest. But the local patrolmen and detectives were in collusion with the madam, because both received regular payoffs taken from the earnings of the prostitutes (a daily "street-standing tax" of twenty cents to the patrolmen and a weekly six-yuan "politeness tax" to the station detective). When the police examining officer put Ma back on the street after twenty-four hours, she was immediately snatched up by one of the madam's associates and taken to the madam, who had already seized her mother. Both mother and daughter were severely beaten. Only then did a bystander intervene and help Ma drag the madam and her accomplices to the police. But when the case went to court, the judge agreed that Ma and her mother were contractually bound to work for the madam; he ordered the mother to work as a maidservant in the brothel, while Ma was permitted to work outside as a maid. In this way she could pay off her debt while avoiding work as a prostitute. Only after the debt was cleared could she and her mother hope to return to the countryside district where Ma had grown up. In the indictment offered by this reformist piece, state power intervened to legitimize and perpetuate the conditions of servitude in the brothels, overwhelming the capacity of women and their families to escape.[100]

QUOTIDIAN REGULATION

Throughout the Republican period, conflicts between prostitutes and madams erupted into visibility in the form of court cases, news reports, and reformist literature that cast the prostitute as victim. Conflicts between the activities of street prostitutes and the emerging regulatory regimes of Shanghai generated another paper trail, one that situated prostitutes as the perpetrators of danger and disruption, even when their activities were coerced by madams. The daily lives of both madams and prostitutes, however, occupied a more capacious space than that defined by either of these representations or even both of them combined. Republican law and social practice did not stigmatize madams and prostitutes as a population apart, even when some of their actions were denounced or criminalized. Between and around their dramatic appearances in suits for freedom, cries for reform, and campaigns for urban order, madams and prostitutes went about their business much like other urban residents. Brothels, like other utility consumers, were caught illegally tampering with their electric meters.[101] They were fined for creating a fire hazard by allowing customers to smoke in the rooms, or burning paper money to capture the attention of the god of wealth and attract more business.[102] Prostitutes and brothel maids went regularly to the police to report thefts of their jewelry and clothing.[103] Prostitutes were cited for beating their maids, for defaulting on sums they borrowed from their maids, and for failing to purchase licenses for their dogs.[104] Like other inhabitants of Shanghai's rickety and dangerous poorer quarters, they showed up on the list of disaster victims when boilers blew up and buildings collapsed; their relatives joined in lawsuits to determine liability for such accidental deaths.[105] When they managed to accumulate assets and then died, they were featured in court cases where their relatives battled over the estate.[106] In short, prostitutes were neither consistently stigmatized nor consistently portrayed as in need of rescue. The victimized prostitute and her mirror image, the dangerous prostitute, were powerful but ultimately impoverished representations. Legal and reform discourses constituted these figures even as they sought to regulate and rescue them. But prostitutes exceeded the capacity of a single discourse, or even a cluster of discourses, to represent them.

CHAPTER 9

Disease

Prostitutes were excoriated in guidebooks and police writings as disruptive of law and order, rifling men's wallets and undermining their attempts at urban sophistication. They appeared as far more sinister figures, however, in discussions of sexually transmitted (venereal) diseases (STDs).[1] STDs were the subject of diverse but overlapping conversations in nineteenth- and twentieth-century China. Foreign authorities in cities like Shanghai sought to protect their Euro-American residents from the public-health threat presented by a "dirty" Chinese population. Missionary doctors, both Western and Chinese, attempted to establish their own authority and medical protocols while vanquishing the competing claims of "traditional" Chinese medical practice. Guidebooks warned individual men to protect themselves against disease in dangerous urban encounters. Chinese reform writers of many persuasions—Christian, nationalist, feminist—saw venereal disease as a threat to the Chinese "race" and a menace to womanhood. In all these conversations, prostitutes were portrayed as a deadly conduit of disease. Yet the directionality of the conduit shifted in each of these different conversations, as did the larger social problems of which venereal disease was said to be a symptom.

Colonial Authority and the Question of Inspection

Warnings about the danger of sexually transmitted disease appeared in documents written by foreigners in Shanghai as early as the 1870s, and were common in Western sources by 1920, as part of a general colonial concern with the "cultural hygiene" of governed peoples. Edward Henderson, Police Surgeon and Municipal Health Officer for Shanghai from 1870 to 1898,[2] acknowledged that sexually transmitted disease might not have originated with Chinese prostitutes, but rather was linked to Shanghai's status as "a busy mercantile port." Once transported to Shanghai, often from Japan, venereal disease made inroads among a foreign population "consisting mainly of young unmarried men, [who] are particularly liable to suffer from those evils." Nevertheless, if prostitutes were not the origin of the pestilence, they were, in Henderson's eyes, the main means of its transmission.[3]

Like other foreigners, Henderson categorized the sale of sexual services as part of the native dirt and disease threatening the colonial population, a fetid tide that government had the responsibility to stem: "The question of the supervision of public women . . . demands the serious consideration of those whose duty it is to guard the interests, and care for the health of the foreign community of Shanghai." He repeatedly referred to the lack of cleanliness among native prostitutes; his comments were consonant with the foreign representation of China and Chinese as filthy, disease ridden, and potentially dangerous to Europeans. In his view the problem was exacerbated by the execrable state of Chinese medical knowledge:

> The native women who infest the settlement, and who are the chief sources
> of danger to foreigners, place themselves almost exclusively under the care
> of Chinese doctors, whose notions with regard to contagion are utterly
> vague, and whose detection or treatment of disease cannot in the least be
> relied on.

Furthermore, he continued, in the rare cases where Chinese prostitutes had the sense to seek out foreign medical treatment, they were "generally very irregular in their attendance, seldom or never continuing their visits until a complete cure is effected." In short, Chinese medicine and personal-hygiene practices lacked the science, precision, and determination that should characterize a modern nation and its citizens.

Henderson's discourse on dirt was not confined to Chinese, but was extended to other people of color; he denounced as "the worst in every way" those Shanghai brothels "where Malays, negroes, &c. are the principal visitors." Inspired in part by the 1866 Contagious Diseases Act in Britain, Henderson recommended that prostitutes be inspected and certified healthy.[4] But an attempt to convince prostitutes to appear for examination on a voluntary basis failed because the enterprise lacked funds and the women objected.[5]

In 1877 a lock hospital (one containing facilities for the treatment of venereal disease) was opened for the examination and certification of Cantonese prostitutes ("saltwater sisters") who serviced foreign sailors.[6] (Henderson proposed to confine his inspection efforts to the 223 women in sixty-two houses that catered to foreigners, since he felt that including the 1,385 other known prostitutes, whose clientele was Chinese, would be "impossible, as it would be impolitic.") Effective inspection required an elaborate procedure in which prostitutes were registered by the Shanghai Municipal Council (SMC), were issued cards with their photographs attached, and were required to appear weekly for examination and have their card validated by the doctor. The women were to pay the cost of the tickets and photographs. Diseased women were to have their cards and photographs impounded until they were cured. Treatment was voluntary, but the police were to contact brothels whose employees failed to appear. If women resisted treatment, the Mixed Court was to close their brothel down. Foreign prostitutes were exempt, since they were regarded as more apt to seek medical advice, and therefore cleaner, than their Chinese sisters.[7]

Initially reluctant to appear for inspection, the women eventually turned the examinations to commercial advantage by using their registration cards as advertisements for their services, derailing in some small way this new regime of control.[8] Henderson himself called the lock hospital a failure in 1886, saying that it had failed to keep up with the growing numbers of native prostitutes, and proposing that it be either improved or closed. In 1900 it was closed and inspections were transferred to a new isolation hospital, but the scope of examinations was significantly reduced.[9] Although the cost of operating the hospital was partially defrayed by fees and fines collected from the brothel keepers,[10] these covered only about one-third of the total, leaving the Municipal Council in 1920 with a net annual outlay of almost five thousand taels.[11] The registration and inspection of some prostitutes continued until 1920,[12] as did debates over whether examinations helped to stop venereal disease.

This was not the end of colonial-government concern about venereal disease. In 1921, the London-based Eastern Commission of the National Council for Combating Venereal Diseases submitted a report to the Shanghai Municipal Council. The report urged the SMC to provide "facilities for the free diagnosis and treatment of venereal disease." They recommended some facilities targeted specifically at Chinese patients, largely for instrumental reasons:

> In view of the extent to which close association takes place between the foreign population and the Chinese population it is essential if a permanent reduction in the incidence of venereal disease among the foreign and seafaring population is to be secured that treatment should also be made available for the Chinese in as far as possible.

The report further advocated an educational campaign aimed at the general public, including notices in public places, press advertisements, the showing of films like *Damaged Goods, The End of the Road,* and *The Gift of Life,* and distribution among foreigners of the pamphlet *How to Fight Venereal Disease.* Sailors in particular were named as a vulnerable population who should be provided with free treatment and taught wholesome ways of spending their time ashore. They should also be warned, the commission said, "as to the high rate of incidence of venereal disease prevailing in the town and that no system of license which might be in force in any way indicated freedom from venereal disease on the part of the women under license." Finally, the report recommended the total suppression of prostitution.[13]

The Municipal Council, already in the throes of an unsuccessful campaign to license and suppress prostitution, responded primarily to the public-health recommendations that affected foreigners. Replying that it could not provide free treatment to everyone, it appointed a physician qualified in venereal-disease work as an assistant health officer, and also opened a free clinic for foreign sailors and foreign indigent males with venereal disease.[14] Until at least 1940 the Municipal Council ran a venereal-disease clinic at General Hospital, dispensing free treatment to sailors and indigent Russians, keeping the European population safe from the scourge of disease spread by Chinese prostitutes.[15] Chinese prostitutes patronized by Chinese customers were not included in any of these measures.

Medical Authority and the Question of Professionalism

For the small group of Western and Western-trained Chinese doctors who worked in China's urban missionary hospitals, venereal disease was a major public-health problem. Many of these doctors published accounts of their work in the *China Medical Journal,* which was read by medical missionaries, other Westerners in China, and members of supporting churches in their home countries.[16] Typically, the journal contained several articles a year on venereal diseases, with slightly more attention given to the subject in the early 1920s and again in 1929–1930, when major initiatives were under way to ban prostitution.[17] Although many of the authors were missionaries, their primary interest as practicing medical professionals was not to denounce the social and moral conditions that permitted the spread of sexually transmitted diseases. Rather, they concerned themselves with quantifying the incidence of syphilis (and less often gonorrhea) and describing advances in treatment.

Studies conducted in Shanghai hospitals during the late Qing and Republican periods show a low rate of syphilitic infection among hospital patients in general, but a higher rate among those taking the blood test for syphilis.[18] On the basis of the *China Medical Journal* literature, Christian Henriot has estimated that 10 to 15 percent of Chinese urban dwellers had syphilis, while a higher but unspecifiable percentage suffered from gonorrhea.[19] (Those afflicted with gonorrhea, one doctor observed in 1935, were less likely to take it seriously enough to seek hospital care, particularly since no dramatic treatment existed for it at the time. Female sufferers were often unaware that they had the disease.[20]) Henriot's conclusion is consistent with postwar estimates that put the Shanghai syphilis rate at 10 to 15 percent and the rate of gonorrhea infection at 50 percent. This meant approximately half a million Shanghai dwellers with syphilis and 2 million with other venereal diseases.[21]

Some occupational groups had much higher reported rates of infection. A 1927 survey of studies from Suzhou, Beijing, and Shanghai found that soldiers and police had a venereal-infection rate of over 35 percent, while the rate among merchants was 31.8 percent, as against an average of 19.5 percent for the general population. In the case of soldiers and merchants, their high rates of infection were said to be directly connected to their frequency of contact with prostitutes.[22] Among female patients, married women were the vast majority covered in these studies, infected by husbands who had contracted the disease from prostitutes.[23]

Prostitutes were said to have the highest rates of all, and to act as the most pestilent link in the chain of transmission.[24] "All doctors agree that the number of such [venereal disease] patients is astonishingly large, and that it is rapidly increasing," warned K. C. Wong in a 1920 *China Medical Journal* article entitled "The Social Evil in China." In a moralizing note rare for the medical journal, he added, "Again, parents or guardians not only are unaware of the moral dangers which beset their daughters or wards but ofttimes exclaim increduously [*sic*] that such dangers do not exist."[25] Not only were prostitutes said to have very high rates of infection, but their disease was said to be more intractable than that of other groups. One account mentioned that out of fifty-two women who had been given a particular treatment for gonorrhea, only two had failed to respond—one of whom was a prostitute.[26] By 1941, in fact, a series of articles in *Shenbao* stated that according to local experts, at least half of the Shanghai population was infected with venereal disease; that 90 percent of it was first spread by prostitutes; and that 90 percent of the lowest-class Chinese prostitutes and 80 percent of the foreign prostitutes had venereal disease. The new forms of disguised prostitution were said to be no safer: 80 percent of the guides in guide agencies were said to be infected, while masseuses were not only diseased, but also clothed in filthy uniforms. Only in a handful of high-class brothels were the Chinese and foreign prostitutes said to employ "modern methods of hygiene" or stop work if they became infected. (Perhaps reflecting the origins of this series of articles in an English-language Shanghai paper, the author was more sanguine about the cleanliness of high-class foreign prostitutes: "They have such good knowledge of hygiene that the chance of their infecting a customer is small.")[27] Physicians wrote that most prostitutes, regardless of their place in the hierarchy, could expect to contract a venereal disease within a year or two of beginning work. But lower-ranking prostitutes were said to be the most dangerous of all, since they had more sexual partners and spread disease more widely, while both they and their clientele lacked the knowledge or the economic means to combat it.[28]

In taking up the question of treatment, Western physicians often made mention of ancient Chinese remedies. Some emphasized continuity between Chinese and Western modes of treatment—for instance, in the use of mercury.[29] Most accounts, however, disparaged and exoticized native medical practice:

> Luetic ulcers are treated with a paste made from pounded scorpions, or the moulted skin of a snake, mixed with a kind of clay. Toad soup, made from dried toads, chopped up and steeped in boiling water, is reputed to be efficacious for ulcers and open sores. Syphilitic ophthalmia is dosed with noxious pastes, and not a few cases of pan-ophthalmitis, and total blindness have resulted from a single iritis mistreated and neglected. Needling is one of the more common forms of treatment for keratitis ("to let the light in") and is used also for various inflammatory lesions of the eye. . . . Quack doctors often cooperate with the brothels, advising a visit to a certain prostitute as a sure cure for gonorrhea. Apart from this, and the application of pastes to "dry up the secretion" gonorrhea receives scant attention being regarded as [having an] inevitable and self limited course.[30]

The articles in the *China Medical Journal* discussed Western treatments as well. Standard Western-style medical protocol for syphilis in the early Republican period consisted of injections of salvarsan (popularly known by the brand name "606"), in which the active ingredient was arsenic. This was alternated with injections of mercury cream into the muscle. Later, neosalvarsan ("914") supplanted salvarsan as the drug of choice, but both 606 and 914 were expensive, and mercury remained in common use.[31] Treatment was protracted and painful.[32] Even after World War II, when penicillin and sulfa drugs provided a quick and reliable cure,[33] their cost put them out of reach of most Chinese; nor could the Shanghai municipal government afford to use them in its campaign to examine prostitutes in the late 1940s.[34] Western treatments for gonorrhea were more varied, and to the contemporary eye appear no less peculiar than scorpion paste and toad soup: injections of boiled skim milk into the buttocks to clear the eyes of gonorrheal ophthalmia, swabbing of the cervix and vagina with Mercurochrome or flavine every day for a month.[35]

Knowledge of both "traditional" and Western-style medical treatments for venereal disease was imparted to the urban reading public through advertisements in the mainstream press. Sometimes a remedy was given a patina of Western modernity, as in the following advertisement from the early 1900s:

> Newly arrived foreign insurance underwear. This is truly a necessary protective item among the flowers and willows. In the brothels many people have damp poison, and they also often take laxatives. If you are infected it will make you very tired, and you will regret it greatly. This clothing is made by foreign machines. It is effective; dirt and poison cannot infiltrate it. The price is also rather cheap: 1.50 foreign for one pair. . . . Customers who are interested in making a purchase can go to Number Three stone warehouse in the first *ya* in Fengji Li, which is found by turning north, west of the New Yamen on British Great Road. Not sold in the evening.[36]

In a 1988 study, Huang Ko-wu found that medical advertisements occupied more than one-third of all advertising space in *Shenbao* from 1912 to 1926. Advertisements for Western hospitals and clinics as well as Chinese-style hospitals listed venereal disease as one of their specialties. Common as well were advertisements touting the benefits of particular drugs. Huang points out that because sexually transmitted diseases were a taboo topic, not often treated in direct conversation, self-treatment with commercial products sold through advertisements and delivered anonymously through the mails was very common. Like the articles in medical journals, many advertisements mentioned that these diseases had been contracted through visits to prostitutes. Strikingly, the text of these advertisements was often written in the plaintive voice of an innocent visitor to Shanghai who, suffering a momentary lapse in his usual standards of probity, visited a brothel, and discovered an infection after returning home.[37] Under the rubric of a warning against quack remedies, one 1931 guidebook added to the confusion by saying that people could contract venereal disease not only from prostitutes, but also from sleeping in strange beds, sitting on unfamiliar benches, using common towels and bath items, failing to wash the head with medicated soap after a haircut, sending clothes out to be laundered, and sharing a chamber pot or living quarters with infected persons.[38] Such warnings helped to instill a fear of venereal infection in the urban reading public.[39]

These warnings and nostrums were actively disparaged as quackery by the newly ascendant medical profession. As Frank Dikötter notes:

> Posing as the guardians of public health and national vitality, [medical practitioners] clamoured for individual self-regulation and for increased state intervention under the guise of medical advice. Sex became both a cultural and a medical domain which was harnessed by the modernizing elites for social promotion and professional autonomy in the early years of the Republic.[40]

The relationship of doctors to state authority in 1920s Shanghai was not, however, a simple alliance. Doctors were jealous of governmental interference in their professional domain. After the ineffective attempt by the International Settlement government in 1920 to license and then ban prostitution, the Shanghai Medical Society urged that sexually transmitted disease be approached primarily as a public-health rather than a moral problem. Although the society's members did not approve of licensing prostitution, they stopped short of endorsing a police-enforced ban. Rather, they recommended the establishment of a Venereal Disease Department under the commissioner of public health to supervise clinics, train women inspectors, and provide support to institutions doing preventive and rescue work. Such an arrangement would "help to relieve the regular police of the undesirable function of enforcing standards of moral conduct in a highly cosmopolitan community not altogether in sympathy with such ideals."

Above all, the physicians of the Shanghai Medical Society were intent on establishing the authority of the medical profession over the control of sexually transmitted disease. This meant not only that unorthodox medical treatments by "chemists" and "quacks" should be prohibited, but also that government officials should remove themselves from involvement: "[T]he medical profession and not the administration authorities should be in charge of general prophylaxis." In short, the doctors argued that it was high time to sever the link between the issues of public health and morality, and to redefine disease as a problem best left to one set of professionals—themselves.[41]

This shared professional ethos among physicians was, however, fissured by subtle tensions between foreign and Chinese doctors, tensions that manifested themselves in arcane disagreements about the history of sexually transmitted disease in China. To sketch the division crudely, foreign doctors held China responsible for its own venereal diseases, whereas Chinese doctors blamed the foreign presence. A 1924 editorial in the *China Medical Journal*, for instance, ventured a guess that syphilis was present in ancient China because prostitution was—in short, that the origins of venereal disease were local products of a native Chinese failing (albeit one shared by the West).[42] Other foreign authors extended the connection to their own time, where the "large proportion of men . . . who patronize brothels after marriage" was taken as an indicator of current "moral conditions."[43] Perhaps the most elaborated foreign critique of the centrality of prostitution to Chinese family practices was offered by Frances Heath, a Beijing doctor, in 1925. Heath wrote, "Magnification of the sex impulse, legalized prostitution, concubinage, and slavery all were logical end-products of ancestor worship, though fostered also by ignorance and poverty." In her rendering, the widespread desire for sons to carry on ancestor worship led to early marriage and much attention to sex, so that a man found one female sexual partner insufficient. Men routinely went to prostitutes, leading to the spread of venereal disease, which in turn affected family fertility, causing sterility from gonorrhea or, in the case of syphilis, "repeated abortions, or syphilitic offspring." After some years of no male children, Heath observed, the husband would take a concubine, and the cycle would start over.[44] Prostitution, venereal disease, the devaluing of women, and ubiquitous sexuality here blended in the sort of exotic stew most noxious to beleaguered Euro-Americans abroad.

Chinese doctors writing about the history of venereal disease in the *China Medical Journal*, in contrast, had a mixed agenda. On the one hand, they were eager to show that China's ancient medical tradition encompassed knowledge about these diseases. One author found references to gonorrhea in a work dating from 2736 B.C.E. attributed to Huang Di, the mythical progenitor of the Chinese race. Chancres, Chinese authors proudly noted, were described in Chinese medical texts as early as the seventh century. On the other hand, these same authors asserted that syphilis was a foreign import, brought to Canton by the Portuguese from India in the early sixteenth century. (Among the many names for syphilitic lesions in Chinese medical texts was "Canton sores.") They took exception to the argument made by some Western scholars that syphilis had been known in China in ancient times.[45] "[I]mages of syphilis also reinforced stereotypes about foreign sexuality," Frank Dikötter notes, adding that "writers rarely failed to mention that the ports frequented by foreign sailors were the places most severely affected by the disease."[46] This formulation contributed to the portrayal of cities like Shanghai, where foreigners had a significant presence, as hotbeds of disease and social decay. After an elaborate description of Shanghai's ubiquitous panderers and prostitutes, and the ensuing spread of sexually transmitted diseases, K. C. Wong added: "The above description only applies to cities, and especially to treaty ports. In the country, moral conditions are better. Indeed, immoral women are seldom tolerated there and when found are dealt with summarily."[47] Chinese doctors used the discourse on syphilis to make a larger point about the foreign contribution to China's contemporary predicament.

For a brief period in the early 1920s, physicians writing in the *China Medical Journal* stressed the close connection of prostitution to venereal disease, and the special responsibility of the medical missionary not to confine "himself [*sic*]" to the medical side of the problem:

> [A]s a Christian missionary he is unable *ex animo* to approve of measures which seem to sanction or condone the social evil, such as the municipal or police licensing of brothels and the provision at public expense of means by which men may indulge their passions and escape the physical penalties. . . . His aim is to heal both body and soul.[48]

By the mid-1920s, however, missionary physicians had begun to devote most of their attention to emphasizing the need for prevention, public-health education, and treatment.[49] Wu Liande, a respected physician of the Manchurian Plague Prevention Service, wrote in 1927:

> I would advise that the medical profession of China join in this crusade against ignorance, and advocate without hesitation in homes, college institutions and hospitals, not only the need of control of the sexual appetite but also efficient prophylaxis.[50]

By 1937, Chester Frazier of the Peiping Union Medical College concluded that prophylaxis and education had failed; syphilis could be controlled only through treatment.[51] Articles about treatment, even when they mentioned prostitution as a source of infection, had the effect of destigmatizing prostitutes by describing customers as equally in need of medical attention.

Guidebooks and the Threat to the Individual

In addition to detailing the multiple pleasures of visiting courtesan houses, guidebooks devoted a modicum of attention to the dangers of frequenting prostitutes, the deadliest of which was sexually transmitted disease. Usually the warning about venereal disease was a code for class. Very little disease was said to be found in courtesan houses, and guidebooks that dealt exclusively with high-class establishments sometimes did not mention it at all. Occasional references to courtesan disease were thoroughly entangled with the common themes of courtesan writing explored in part 2: protocol and nostalgia. An 1891 source, for instance, described the practice of "leaping into a warm quilt," wherein a customer arrived at a brothel in the early morning in order to avoid detection by his family, occupying a bed recently vacated by another patron. By failing to observe the proprieties of elaborate courtship and sexual restraint, he put himself at risk of disease. The same source also engaged in nostalgic mourning for an imagined past in which courtesans were skilled musical performers, as well as skilled bed partners. Such women were now rare, the author mused, and furthermore it was easy to contract a fatal disease from a moment's pleasure with modern-day prostitutes.[52] Here disease became one feature in a larger picture of loss.

By the 1930s, guidebooks were opining that even with courtesans a customer could not count on immunity from infection. Warnings about disease were intertwined with cautionary tales about acting like a bumpkin on Shanghai's dangerous urban streets. One contemporary guidebook cartoon, for example, mentioned in chapter 3, depicted a prostitute and her attendant in a rickshaw pulled by a brothel servant. Hanging on the back of the vehicle were two upside-down hearts—black, rather than white and pure like those of respectable women. The number of the license plate was 606, an unsubtle reference to salvarsan. The accompanying text warned that "epidemic victims and blockheads" would foolishly offer their hearts to a beautiful courtesan, failing to notice her black heart and diseased body: "These prostitutes are unavoidably the place for introduction of 606, and epidemic victims and blockheads will certainly need several injections of 606."[53] Similarly, in scandal fiction the hapless male victim of courtesan disease was most likely to be an out-of-town visitor who was captivated by a particular courtesan, squandering his health and the family fortune until his loyal mother came to Shanghai and took him home to die of venereal disease.[54] In a 1939 guidebook, the courtesan house had become a place where physical, financial, and social dangers converged, a place that "harms the body, or wastes one's money, or interferes with one's reputation." By this time, in the wake of several decades of public medical discussion, the warnings had become explicit: brothels were "the place where syphilis begins and is spread, and if you have physical contact with [a courtesan] and become infected, not only will your own health suffer, but you will pass it on and infect your wife." In an unusually macabre description, this guidebook described courtesans as "skeletons with powdered faces, dangerous, poisonous." Yet even here the author moved quickly to redeem sexual encounters with courtesans by describing disease-free situations where a customer and a courtesan fell in love and wanted a physical relationship so that both could "achieve the satisfaction of their sexual desire."[55] Sex without love, rather than sex per se, was presented as the source of venereal infection.

As soon as guidebooks moved on to describing the lower rank of *yao er* courtesans, the warnings about disease became more graphic and pronounced. "Her body today is wanted by Zhang, tomorrow is played with by Li, and this goes on every day, without a night off, so it is impossible to avoid disease," wrote a 1939 author. "If you want to visit prostitutes, *changsan* courtesans are somewhat more reliable."[56] Insofar as venereal-disease warnings remained tied to the class of the prostitute, they could be read as indications that an elite man should seek out only courtesan houses, rather than as a generalized comment on the dangers of frequenting brothels or the wages of sin.

Prostitutes of lower than courtesan rank were typically portrayed as both victim and perpetrator. Those who were pawned or sold, because they were under the control of a madam, were reportedly forced to have repeated sexual relations until and even after they became infected. Without money for treatment, they then became "instruments of infection" themselves.[57] This note of victimization was daily amplified in the newspaper *Shenbao*. The diseased prostitute most often appeared as one who had been kidnapped or sold, was forced to have sexual relations with customers, developed venereal sores, was cruelly treated and even tortured by her madam (although one madam sent her sick charge to a hospital), escaped or was rescued by relatives, and subsequently was remanded to the Door of Hope—a tale of redemption in which venereal disease became a tangible sign of all the physical and social abuses endured by lower-class prostitutes.[58]

The victim status of these women in no way modified their characterization as dangerous to men who recklessly sought them out. The ubiquitousness of venereal disease in low-class brothels, authors warned, had earned them the name "fruit stores" because it was so easy to get "strawberries" (syphilitic lesions) there.[59] Newcomers to Shanghai were told that their noses would fall off and their bodies would decay if they visited pheasant brothels.[60] Rather than simply advising readers to avoid prostitutes altogether, many guidebooks sought to inform them about how to discern and avoid specific dangers. If a guidebook customer insisted on frequenting houses below the courtesan rank, he was advised to take a number of precautions: when paying a call on a prostitute, squeeze her hand and discreetly check whether it is inflamed; in bed, first inspect her elbow joint for lumps, and if you find one, "pull up short at the overhanging cliff." In one of the most explicit passages to be found in the guidebooks, a 1932 work advises, "When the front lines where the two armies connect are tense," you can press down on the stomach and lower regions of your opponent. If she calls out in pain, she has venereal disease, and you must "immediately throw down your spear, don't begrudge the funds for the payment of soldiers or continue to press forward with the attack."[61] In selecting a prostitute, the same guidebook said to avoid women who were short or had squat necks, because these were signs that a woman had entered the life early and failed to develop normally. "Having been through so many battles, it is difficult for them to avoid venereal disease," the author said, adding that tall, slim women were safest. Having located a willowy prostitute, the prospective customer should check her for hot hands, red eyes, bad breath, and lumps under the arms. In unusually explicit language, the passage concluded: "One can also check whether her . . . [ellipsis in original] is swollen and inflamed. If the battleground has become like paste or gruel, you should halt the attack." In addition to such fine points of inspection, men were given the kind of advice that physicians dismissed as quackery. They were told to visit streetwalkers on a rainy day, when fewer customers had preceded them, and to drink boiled water "after the battle." They were also cautioned to beware of diseased prostitutes who might be taking medicine that would cause them to pass their disease to the customer, thus curing themselves.[62]

The most graphic descriptions of disease were reserved for prostitutes in the "flower-smoke" opium dens, where sex was cheap and infection inevitable. "For about seventy cents you can go from Paris to London by water, but if you hit a reef, you must immediately open heaven's window [suffer the ravages of venereal disease on your face], suffering harm on your entire body," according to one of the more mildly worded warnings.[63] Here "winning first place in the imperial examinations" (*zhong zhuangyuan*) did not refer to being chosen in the flower-roll election, as it did for courtesans; rather, it meant to break out in syphilitic sores.[64] The sufferings of the diseased prostitute were meticulously detailed:

> After ten days, the lower body begins to rot. In a few more days, skin
> and flesh drop away. Then she is favored with a rest, and she suffers even
> more. . . . She has to use a thick solution of salty water to wash her broken
> skin and flesh. When it is nearly healed, she is forced to receive guests again.
> Then she suffers again from broken skin and flesh. Then she rests again.
> She continues with this five or six times, until there is nothing more left to
> rot. She is forced to receive ten to one hundred guests a day. Then she does
> not feel anything.[65]

Nor would her customers escape a similarly horrible fate; readers were told that most beggars on the street who were "blind, missing noses, with twisted feet and rotting legs," had contracted venereal disease in the flower-smoke rooms.[66]

The warnings about foreign prostitutes and those who serviced foreigners were spoken in the language of national power relations. European and American women were generally categorized as attentive to hygiene and relatively uninfected, but White Russians, whose status in Shanghai was much lower, were an exception: they were described as "heavy as a fat pig," redolent of body odor, and unlikely to have access to good disinfection facilities. Japan, in contrast, whose growing power was both envied and resented, was said to have disease-free prostitutes in Shanghai. In fact, one guidebook said, in Japanese brothels the customer had to take a shower and be inspected by the prostitutes to ensure that he was free of disease. Those who failed to pass muster would be refused service, no matter how much they were willing to pay.[67] This reversal of the conventional power relations between prostitute and customer mirrored the reversal of relations between Japan and China, one that rankled many intellectuals. As for the Cantonese "saltwater sisters" whom Henderson and others saw as such a threat to the white population, Chinese warnings about them concentrated on the foreign origins of their disease. Because they slept with many foreigners a day, the sources said, Chinese men who went to them "may become infected with foreign syphilitic sores. This is not a joking matter."[68]

It was because of this foreign contact, they continued, that such elaborate inspection procedures had been implemented for these women.[69] Yet these procedures were said to be haphazard, and prospective Chinese customers were advised to demand a look at a prostitute's inspection certificate before having sexual contact with her.[70] Some foreigners (sailors) were specified as the source of infection, while others (government authorities) were lauded for their ability to protect their citizens. This latter characterization led some guidebook authors to argue that the Chinese authorities, too, should be protecting their nationals by examining prostitutes whose clientele was Chinese.[71] By implication, the guidebooks defined a strong nation as one that kept its prostitutes clean and its populace healthy.

Almost as soon as they emerged on the Shanghai entertainment scene, those engaged in ancillary occupations joined the roster of dangers condemned by the guidebooks. All aspects of the "sex industry," including prostitutes, masseuses, pornographic performances, lascivious pictures, and female guides, wrote one guidebook author, preyed upon

> young people who are physically vigorous or those whose will is weak. As
> soon as you mistakenly enter their clutches, you will certainly end in total
> moral decay. The lucky ones are infected with syphilis, to the point where
> they become disabled, and it is too late for regrets. . . . [Those who] become
> bewitched by them will either have their whole bodies poisoned, or become
> crippled and die.[72]

Unwary visitors to a massage parlor, another guidebook added impishly, might be relieved of their muscular pains only to find themselves afflicted with a "romantic illness."[73]

Guidebooks usually construed disease as an individual calamity caused by characterological weakness. If a man could stay away from prostitutes, or keep the company of courtesans without becoming sexually entangled, his individual health would remain intact. If he could not muster the proper restraint, he became vulnerable to disease and decay. Here too prostitutes were conduits, but they transmitted infection through a defect in the shield of individual moral judgment rather than through openings supplied by national weakness or deficiencies in public-health policy.[74] Many guidebooks implied that a man was not born with such character defects, but developed them in the course of visiting prostitutes. Prostitutes become not merely the site, but also the cause, of moral decay, with disease as its inevitable outward sign.

Reformers and the Threat to the Race

By the 1920s, venereal disease had become a standard feature in Chinese reformist writings about prostitution. As chapters 10 and 11 will indicate, many of the twentieth-century movements for regulation and reform of prostitution were explicitly linked to the fear of venereal disease. In a discussion of Republican-era writings about venereal disease, Frank Dikötter has argued that Chinese intellectuals voiced their dual concerns about the "race" and the nation by speaking about disease in the language of military conflict. "[M]ilitary terminology of 'assault', 'invasion of the organism' and 'bodily defences' started to pervade medical representations of disease," he writes.

> . . . The gruesome consequences of venereal disease for the individual,
> the family and the "race" were spelled out in harrowing detail by popular
> writers. . . . Representations of social degeneration flourished with the rise
> of the idea of "race" in an era of rabid nationalism. . . . Cultural representa-
> tions of syphilis gave expression to the idea that China had been colonized
> by the dual force of foreign capital and fatal disease. Imperialists "violated"
> the country's territorial integrity, and germs "encroached" (*qinfan*) upon
> the urethra.[75]

Venereal disease was linked to China's struggle for survival, which was figured in the terms of Social Darwinism. Here prostitutes, themselves victims of disease, became the breach in China's defenses. Through contact with prostitutes, men brought the disease home to their wives, passed it on to their children, and damaged "the health of the nation and the future of the race."[76] By the 1930s, articles in women's magazines advised their readers to demand before marriage proof that the prospective partner was not infected, in order to protect future children.[77] As Lin Chongwu put it in 1936:

> The harm of prostitution is none other than its being a site of the spread of disease, which has serious consequences for the strength or weakness of the race. The strength of the race depends on the abundance of good elements. According to the laws of heredity, weeds cannot be sprouts.[78]

In the battle for survival of the fittest, prostitution and venereal disease diminished the chances of success, and themselves became markers of China's subaltern status with respect to stronger, healthier powers.[79]

Their conviction that sexually transmitted disease threatened the Chinese race, and that prostitutes were breeding grounds and transmission belts for this foreign menace, led many reformers to argue for the abolition of prostitution.[80] They often advocated education and treatment as important health measures, but were deeply suspicious of the approach to STDs that entailed the licensing and examination of prostitutes. One of their more pragmatic arguments was a straightforward denial of the benefits of medical examination, which purported to protect the public from diseased prostitutes but was ineffective at doing so. A 1933 article in a women's magazine denounced examinations as a way of protecting upper-class men. Syphilis was spread both by prostitutes and their customers, the writer said, yet inspections placed the burden on prostitutes alone. A licensed prostitute who was found to be diseased and forbidden to work, but who needed a means of livelihood, would move over to the unlicensed sector, there to spread her infection to the rickshaw pullers, soldiers, workers, and other lower-class men who could not afford to visit a licensed brothel.[81] In 1941, a newspaper report on prostitution attacked the false sense of security provided by inspections. Diseased prostitutes in the French Concession were given a small number of injections by the authorities, said the author, but this was not sufficient to cure them. A complete recovery would require that they stop work for several weeks or months, but this the madams generally would not permit. Even if the French Concession government were willing or able to undertake the massive expense of providing sufficient medication, the author added, venereal disease would continue to invade the French Concession via unlicensed, illegal prostitutes from the International Settlement. A final public-health complication was that more and more licensed, allegedly "clean" prostitutes were becoming addicted to drugs such as morphine. When their addictions made them useless as moneymakers, their madams evicted them or sold them to lower-class brothels, where they moved beyond the reach of licensing and examination. Alternatively, the author said, the madams sent them back to the countryside, there to marry and pass the disease to their offspring.[82] As a 1936 attack on licensed prostitution put it, "It is just as the Bible says: 'Your sins will be passed on to the third and fourth generation of your descendants.'"[83] Finally, the same author argued, a false sense of security about safety from venereal infection would increase the sale of sex and promote "male sexual superficiality," clearly not a desirable social habit.[84]

Prostitutes were a recurrent feature of the conversations about sexually transmitted disease in Republican China. For the colonial medical authorities, they were an ignorant but menacing conduit of infection to the white population. For members of the foreign and foreign-trained medical profession, they were one piece of an intricate public-health problem that, although it was resistant to treatment, could probably be made to yield to science applied by properly trained doctors. For the authors of guidebooks and tabloids, prostitutes were repositories of multiple dangers as well as pleasure—to be guarded against, as well as properly enjoyed, through self-restraint, knowledge, and judicious choice of action. For reformers they were a conduit, this time from an invasive foreign world directly to the collective Chinese body, and the body politic as well.

For all the interlocutors, the sexual activity of prostitutes was important as a means of transmission, but the fact that prostitutes were women was not an occasion for theorizing about the more general subordination of women in Chinese society. Prostitutes were prostitutes; they transmitted disease. Wives were wives; they were prone to infection by husbands who went to brothels. Although the two groups of women suffered similar physical consequences from the disease, and one might speculate about social and emotional commonalities as well, these were submerged in the dichotomy of dangerous woman/respectable victim. This was not true of other conversations about reform, in which prostitution was invoked in a litany of oppressions suffered by women.

In each of the conversations about prostitution and disease, the note of victimization was present, but muted. Prostitutes might have been an unwilling and coerced source of danger, but they were dangerous nonetheless. Whether that danger was best controlled through increased regulation or abolition was a matter of acrimonious debate, as the next chapter explains. Ultimately, the inability of the Republican state to take up either of these tasks was one of an ensemble of disappointments that caused many Chinese reformers to withdraw support from that state in favor of one that promised more success at protecting the health of the race and the nation.

PART IV

Interventions

CHAPTER 10

Reformers

In the last decades of the Qing dynasty and through the first half of the twentieth century, Chinese intellectuals with allegiance to many ideologies pondered the question of how to strengthen China. The object of their critical zeal varied across time and from one writer to another. Some focused on China's polity, while others singled out culture or social arrangements. (The content of categories such as "polity" and "culture" likewise varied across the half century of discussion.) Many of them, however, found the position of China's women, as indicated by everything from Confucian aphorisms to footbinding and illiteracy, to be a crucial indicator of China's weakness.

Some of these critics addressed themselves directly to the issue of national strength. They argued that China, which mistreated "its women" (a formulation that figured China as male), was in turn treated like a woman by stronger nations: subordinated, humiliated, with pieces of its territory occupied by force, rights to its use bought and sold with impunity. These critics set themselves in opposition to many elements of Chinese culture and politics, sometimes proposing an agenda for radical political transformation, at other times adopting the language of the social-purity campaigns taking place in Britain and the United States. Other critics organized their writings around visions of a postcapitalist society where Chinese women would no longer depend upon men for their survival, and where gender equality (albeit along with a gendered division of labor) would become an indicator of China's status as an advanced society. In reformist writings, gender, modernity, and nation were interlocked as terms of an unsolved equation. Writers hoped that this equation could be made to yield up a solution through their relentless social investigations and careful analysis, in which they compared an imagined "modern" China to its own (equally imagined) past and to the rest of the world.

Prostitution appeared repeatedly in these discussions as an important instance of women's low status. The attention focused on it increased throughout the 1920s and 1930s, when national and local governments waged intermittent campaigns to ban unlicensed prostitution. Each of these campaigns, discussed in chapter 11, generated a furious production of commentary by intellectuals associated with feminist causes, the Communist movement, or both. The present chapter takes up the shifting meanings (or values, if we maintain the equation metaphor) that these intellectuals attributed to prostitution, exploring its power as a signifier of national weakness and, more occasionally, of national modernity. The focus here is on Chinese conversations that did not directly involve state regulators, although these conversations were sometimes occasioned by state regulatory campaigns.

The chapter concludes with a brief survey of institutions for the rescue and reform of prostitutes, noting an interesting disjuncture between the big utopian schemes of the intellectuals and the fine-grained methods of social reform practiced on Shanghai streets. Theorists of reform criticized the Chinese family as an important (if not the only) source of women's oppression, and visualized a day when women would become independent. Yet practitioners of reform, even while implementing programs to teach former prostitutes a job skill, centered their operations on reinserting women into families, chiefly by locating spouses for them. In reform institutions a particular vision of family became linked to the project of saving China, whether for Christianity or for healthy nationhood.

Political Reformers and the Health of the Nation

Chinese critics often invoked prostitution as emblematic of weaknesses in Chinese culture, proposing solutions linked to nationalism. This was part of a larger argument in which gender relations were imbricated with national strength, since it was argued that a system that permitted the treatment of women as inferior human beings would inevitably lead to a weak nation.

As many scholars have noted, discussions of women's status from the late Qing onward were almost invariably linked to the urgent need to strengthen the nation. Reformers saw the low status of women as both cause and effect of China's weakness; feminism was routinely subordinated to many varieties of nationalist political agenda.[1] In this context, late Qing writers occasionally included prostitution on a list of women's problems, which they took as an indicator of the depth of China's crisis. Kang Youwei, whose utopian writings on the status of women have been discussed by many scholars, made only passing mention of prostitution, concentrating instead on the need to end footbinding, educate women, and improve China's marriage system.[2] His younger colleague Liang Qichao likewise focused on education and the employment of women, whom he felt to be, in Charlotte Beahan's words, "an important but dangerously ignored national resource."[3] In keeping with their analysis of women's subordination, the late Qing thinkers who designed the reforms of 1898 included on their agenda the elimination of footbinding and the establishment of girls' schools.[4]

An exception to the routine linkage of feminism and nationalism was found in the Chinese anarchist movement, which initially flourished among Chinese expatriates in Tokyo in the first decade of the twentieth century. Anarchists declared "absolute equality of the sexes" as one of their goals, along with the destruction of national borders and authoritarianism.[5] Some anarchists, particularly the anarcho-feminist He Zhen, explained the sexual oppression of women as rooted in economics.[6] All women were oppressed by their dependency on men, she argued, but three groups were more subordinated than others: housemaids, because they depended on their masters; factory workers, because they depended on factory owners; and prostitutes, who were beaten, stigmatized, and dependent upon the money of their customers. (Wives and concubines were also dependent upon men, but their suffering was thought to be less extreme than that of these three groups, who "had to choose immediately between subservience and starvation.") This denunciation of women's subordination was then folded into a larger anarchist critique of capitalism, which forced women to sell their bodies as workers and as prostitutes.[7] Among anarchists, as among nationalists, prostitution was usually discussed briefly as one aspect of women's oppression, to be eliminated with the success of a broader revolution.[8]

In the early years of the Republic, intellectuals of varied and overlapping persuasions—nationalist, feminist, and anarchist—sought not only to improve the status of women, but to require better behavior of men in the name of larger political goals. One aspect of such improved behavior was a willingness to forgo the company of prostitutes. Sardonic commentators in the mainstream and tabloid press commented on the propensity of high-ranking politicians to dally with courtesans when they should have been negotiating for China's interests in the international arena.[9] The feminist Society for the Reform of the Family in the Republic, founded by Lu Shaofen and other women, advocated "the improvement of women's role in the family structure" primarily via equal education and freedom of marriage, but the final point in the society's ten-point program was "the elimination of such habits as gambling, visiting brothels, viewing plays, drinking and smoking opium."[10] In 1912, the anarchist Society to Advance Morality (*Jinde hui*) was founded in Shanghai and Beijing, requiring that its members refrain from frequenting prostitutes, gambling, or acquiring concubines. Other organizations with anarchist sympathies adopted similar requirements. Feminist and nationalist writers linked such habits to China's national weakness, whereas anarchists rejected an enhanced role for the state and called instead for individuals

to improve their own moral behavior.[11] Curiously, in this respect the anarchist agenda converged with that of Chinese Christians, who also used *Jinde
hui* as the Chinese name for the Moral Welfare League, a largely foreign
group whose attempt to abolish Shanghai prostitution is described in the
next chapter.[12]

Christian Reformers and the Health of the Soul

The idea that prostitution was a national disgrace and a contributory factor
in China's national weakness gained currency early among Chinese Christian elites. In a 1913 Chinese-language guide to Shanghai that bore the didactic English title *What the Chinese in Shanghai Ought to Know,* the Christian
Huang Renjing commented on the propensity of Chinese men to conduct
business and politics with each other in courtesan houses:

> Famous persons from all over the country go to brothels. They are the
> leaders of our people. When leaders are like this, one can imagine the
> situation among industrialists and businessmen. . . . The development of
> the West is due to the skill of the craftsmen and the diligence of the mer-
> chants. They are not like the degenerates of our country, who make use of
> brothels to reach their goal [that is, who entertain business and political
> associates at parties in brothels]. I hope that our people will learn from the
> Westerners, not go to brothels, and forbid prostitution. It is possible to catch
> up with the Westerners. The reason they developed from barbarism to
> civilization at this speed is that most of them do not go to brothels. They
> have virtue; we Chinese should learn from them.[13]

Chinese Christians linked prostitution to China's political vulnerability in the
international arena. "The amount of money wasted in Shanghai on prostitution in half a year," observed one Chinese Christian acerbically, "is enough
to redeem the railroads which have been mortgaged to the Japanese."[14] Another commented that Japan's victory in the Russo-Japanese war, fought
mostly on Chinese territory in Manchuria, was attributable to the fact that
80 to 90 percent of the Japanese soldiers had had no contact with prostitutes.[15] In this conceptual "nesting" of subaltern statuses, sex work in China
was taken as paradigmatic of a social decay that was then invoked to explain
China's position vis-à-vis colonizing powers.

Like the foreign missionaries whose categories they adopted, Chinese
Christians located the ultimate cause of prostitution in individual moral weakness. Male and female sexual desire, economic need, and social custom were
powerful but secondary factors. One essay written by a Chinese member of
the Moral Welfare League, the group responsible for the 1920 campaign to
abolish prostitution in the International Settlement, was published in *Shenbao* on the eve of the campaign. The essay argued that women became prostitutes not only because they were poor but because their parents, prefer-

ring money to virtue, were willing to sell them into prostitution. Traffickers preyed on women who were both economically vulnerable and morally deficient: "Anywhere there are weak, helpless, poor, stupid, or licentious women who might be caught, the agents of prostitution will be ready to go." Commercialized sex was facilitated by all those "local evil elements" who were willing to sacrifice their scruples for the sake of profits: traffickers and madams, certainly, but also

> the landlords who ask a high price for the brothel's rent, the doctors who give prostitutes papers to prove that they are healthy, the lawyers who use clever arguments to defend the business, the pharmacy salesmen who sell forbidden drugs to prostitutes, the local officials and policemen who accept bribes, the tax collectors who have the right to reduce their tax, and other institutions they deal with that are in charge of trade and transportation.

The main driving force attracting customers to brothels, the author argued, was alcoholic drink, which was roundly condemned. Men's patronage of brothels could not be explained by reference to ineluctable sexual desire; the essay cited French and American medical authorities who held that men could live perfectly well without sex. Therefore, prostitution could not be justified by arguing that it sacrificed a few women to protect womankind from uncontrollable male sexuality. Customers went to the brothels because of their moral failings and ultimately became victims of further moral decay, financial loss, and venereal disease, which they spread to their families. Most prostitutes, for their part, could not make the transition to madam status and ended up impoverished, ill, and stigmatized. This analysis was not specific to China: the author freely interspersed statistics about prostitution in London and Chicago with comments about Shanghai. Human weakness, rather than anything particular to China's national situation, was the key.[16]

Their focus on individual moral behavior allowed some Chinese Christian writers to salvage aspects of a Chinese ethical tradition, instead of thoroughly condemning it as many foreign missionaries did. K. C. Wong, for instance, writing of the "social evil" in China, conceded that prostitution had been recorded in Chinese historical writing as early as the Zhou dynasty. Yet although individual courtesans had occupied high social positions in the past, he added, prostitution had always been condemned in China as first among the four vices (the other three being drinking, gambling, and opium smoking). Confucius had warned young people away from prostitutes, and Mencius had counseled them to "have few desires."[17] Chinese ethical beliefs were thus made to look utterly compatible with the program of, say, the Women's Christian Temperance Union, which was active in Shanghai efforts to reform prostitution.

For Wong and some other Christian essayists, the problem was not China's ethical deficiency, but rather poverty, low wages, lack of skills that would allow young women another source of livelihood, "child slavery, concubinage, the power of parents to sell their children, kidnapping, unsatisfactory conditions in factories employing female labour, and other social problems."[18] Wong was careful to distinguish the Chinese condemnation of prostitution from the purported attitude of the Japanese, who were said to believe that leading an immoral life to support one's parents was virtuous.[19] He implied that China's social practice may have been inadequate, but its potential for incorporation into a higher moral order was greater than that of its island neighbor.

Chinese Christian writings generally did not invoke international practices shaped by the colonizing powers as causes of prostitution. For missionaries and their Chinese converts, the continued existence of prostitution pointed to weaknesses in Chinese culture. These weaknesses might be ameliorated by preachers of the social gospel, but could be cured only by Christian morality, which would improve the climate for individual moral choices.[20] The need for Christianity, in turn, helped to make respectable the entire network of missionary interests supported by imperialist powers.

May Fourth Critics and the Health of Society

The May Fourth movement, which centered on demonstrations in 1919 to protest China's treatment at the Versailles conference, encompassed a much broader movement of cultural and political critique among Chinese intellectuals, and is conventionally taken by many historians of China to mark one beginning of the "modern" period.[21] In the writings of May Fourth intellectuals, prostitution, concubinage, and the purchase of maidservants were often linked as evils to be eradicated.[22] Li Dazhao, a prominent May Fourth writer and later cofounder of the Chinese Communist Party, in 1919 called for an alliance of righteous men and conscious women to eliminate all three. Linking prostitution to weaknesses in national culture, Li recounted with disgust the fact that when a Shanghai newspaper had solicited reader opinions on the status of women, no one had responded, proving that "in the ordinary psychology of Chinese there is no recognition that women have character [renge]." He gave five reasons that prostitution had to be made to disappear. It was an insult to human values, forcing women to engage in the most debased form of livelihood while suffering insults and ill-treatment. It lowered the value of love, the most important thing in life. It threatened public health through the uncontrollable spread of venereal disease; doctors also said that long-term prostitutes "degenerated" (bianxing), potentially affecting the survival of the race. It violated the freedom of persons under the law, a violation that all nations practicing popular rule would not permit. Finally, it lowered the status of women, and thus doing away with it had to be the first priority of the Chinese women's liberation movement. The specific reform measures Li advocated would later become a standard litany: forbid trafficking, limit the numbers of prostitutes, give them job skills in publicly funded relief organizations, and find them husbands. More fundamentally, provide free compulsory education for all women; more fundamentally still, "reform the social organization in which a portion of women cannot live without selling sex."[23] In his linkage of prostitution with women's status, racial health, fundamental reform, and modern state practices, as well as his disparaging comments about Chinese social attitudes, Li made it clear that prostitution was an attribute of backwardness, one that would have to be discarded as an integral step in the march toward modernity. And his emphasis on job training and marriage as the means of extricating women from prostitution anticipated, in important respects, the particular route toward gender modernity chosen by the Communists.

During the decade that followed the May Fourth demonstrations, the *Ladies' Journal* (*Funü zazhi*), a feminist magazine published in Shanghai, became one forum for an ongoing discussion of prostitution. Feminist critics of both sexes located China's "prostitution problem" firmly in the trajectory of shared human history, and used it to further develop a critique of capitalism. As their theorizing removed China from a uniquely victimized or backward status, however, it simultaneously established prostitutes (and women more generally) as victims of male economic, sexual, and moral domination.

Many of these articles followed a generic formula. They began with a denunciation of prostitution, calling it "a monument to women's subordination," "a serious blow to women's personal character and an insult to women," "a disgrace to the people of the world," and a practice that was bad for ethics, society, and the race.[24] Prostitution, itself the product of shortcomings in society, in turn contributed to a variety of social ills: venereal disease, which weakened the race and sickened the nation; a decline in popular character and morals; troubled relations between the sexes; the desecration of women's personal character; and concubinage.[25] For the sake of social evolution and the ennobling of humankind, it was imperative that it be eliminated.[26]

Having established the deleterious effects of prostitution, these authors then moved to enumerate its "root causes." They described a history of gender relations, in no way specific to China, whose most prominent feature was the decline of women's status relative to men. Early in human history, this account held, women and men had developed a sexual division of labor, with female activities mostly confined to agriculture and the home. Men, who engaged in hunting, making war, and other "important human activities," soon came to treat women as property, giving away their wives and daughters in exchange for material gain or political alliances. After they had completely subordinated women economically, men began to seek sexual satisfaction outside the family.[27]

Some authors posited that the root causes of prostitution lay in biology as well as economics. Men had a fundamental tendency toward polygyny, they asserted; male desire was biologically stronger than female desire.[28] Some authors hedged their bets as to why: "Probably males are mostly richer in the impulse of sexual desire, but whether this is innate is a question."[29] Nevertheless, they assumed that men would prefer to seek multiple sexual partners—via polygyny when economics and prevailing moral standards permitted it, via prostitution when they did not.[30] Men regarded sexual intercourse as a game rather than an act of love. Love, in turn, was linked by these writers to equal status for women.[31]

Writers commonly buttressed their argument by describing systems of prostitution in ancient civilizations, citing examples from Greece, Rome, Egypt, Babylon, ancient Israel, and early Christian society.[32] These historical accounts of prostitution in the West were supported by citations of foreign scholars and activists.[33] Often this discussion of the West would be followed by an account of Chinese prostitution, beginning with the Spring and Autumn Period (770–476 B.C.E.).[34] The *Ladies' Journal* also printed translations of scholarly articles on prostitution by Japanese and British authors, bringing China into a worldwide discussion by juxtaposing foreign and Chinese contributions.[35]

In keeping with their mission of local cultural critique, these writers did devote attention to the specific oppression of women in China. The Chinese ethical system was made for elites and men, one author commented dryly, not for demeaned classes and women. Because women were regarded as inferior to men, Chinese heaped opprobrium on some prostitutes, cursing them as she-demons and thieves, but accepted the system of prostitution as a leisure-time activity and praised the talent of other prostitutes. Throughout history, members of the Chinese gentry had patronized prostitutes while simultaneously promoting the value of chastity for their own wives and daughters.[36] This "strange and laughable" practice had persisted into the 1920s, when the Chinese government continued to offer rewards for widows who maintained their chastity, even as it permitted and taxed prostitution.[37]

If prostitution was ubiquitous in Western and Chinese history, however, it found new protection under capitalism, which exacerbated the gap between rich and poor. Under such circumstances daughters of the poor became prostitutes, while sons of the poor patronized prostitutes because they could not afford to marry.[38] In Europe and the United States, men married late because marriage required them to support a family at a high standard of living. While waiting to marry, they were obliged to visit prostitutes because they could not suppress their sex drive.[39] (Yet in China, the practice of early marriage was no deterrent to patronizing prostitutes because of the bad social habit of "playing with" women.)[40] The most common cause of prostitution singled out by these analysts was economic difficulty: women became prostitutes in order to make a living.[41] Here again the authors referred to foreign examples, including early-nineteenth-century Paris as described by Parent-Duchâtelet,[42] London as described by A. Sherwell and W. Acton,[43] Berlin,[44] Japan,[45] and Sweden.[46] August Bebel was frequently quoted to the effect that prostitution was an inevitable product of capitalism.[47] In the modern period, Chinese writers concluded, "[t]he problem of prostitution is a common problem worldwide, not a problem unique to one nation or one society."[48]

Nevertheless, some authors cautioned, prostitution was not merely the result of poverty. In times of prosperity, Chen Dezheng argued, the numbers of prostitutes increased, as did their wages. He believed that this was because the income of most working women could not keep up with their desired level of consumption, while demand for prostitutes also increased in times of prosperity.[49] Authors cited studies from Brussels, London, and New York, as well as from Italy and Russia, that showed that prostitutes had far more varied motivations than economic necessity, including their own sexual desire and pursuit of pleasure, or their history as victims of seduction.[50] Chinese prostitutes all gave economic compulsion as their reason for engaging in prostitution, one critic added, only because it was not culturally acceptable to air the family's dirty linen in public, and economic hardship sounded more respectable than many other explanations.[51]

Even while acknowledging the importance of economic factors, some analysts broadened the argument, positing a "close and direct" connection between modern prostitution and modern civilization. In addition to the familiar nostrums about economic compulsion, they pointed out that much of Euro-America was in ethical crisis. In the single-minded pursuit of improvement in material life, the new middle classes ignored the spiritual and physical costs, leading to mental illness, ethical confusion, and "illnesses of sexual desire." Because these new middle classes were a characteristic feature of modern civilization, their pursuit of prostitution was likely to be a feature of modern life until fundamental reforms were undertaken.[52]

In 1924 the national government in Beijing proposed to license prostitution nationally, touching off one of many Republican-era debates on the relative merits of licensing and abolition.[53] Feminist authors generally derided licensing, on grounds that often deepened the portrayal of women as victims. A key point of those who opposed licensing was that women did not become prostitutes willingly, but were forced to do so either by economic oppression or by moral sanctions (as when, for instance, a woman lost her virginity, was abandoned by her sexual partner, could not make a respectable marriage, and drifted into prostitution). One critic ridiculed the idea that any woman would willingly become a slave to men's sexual desire, any more than any man would voluntarily enter slavery in societies where it was practiced.[54] Developing the idea that women were victims of the prostitution system, one author quoted Ida Tarbell as saying that prostitution was the fault of the customer,[55] while another critic intoned: "The creators of the system of prostitution are men, the supporters of the system of prostitution are also men; the women are merely passive." Chastity was not required of men, who were permitted to regard women as their private property and place the shame and burden of prostitution exclusively on the women involved.[56] Prostitution also victimized women, one author argued (again citing European studies), by rendering them more like men, with thick necks and deep voices—unnatural creatures robbed of their femininity.[57]

Many May Fourth commentators linked the elimination of prostitution to a complete program of social reform, in which a strengthened Chinese government and socially conscious members of the elite would both play crucial roles. The government was enjoined to revive industry and commerce so that poor people could support themselves without selling their daughters; to ban gambling, opium smoking, and drinking so that males would not take up these habits (habits that had led them to force their wives and daughters into prostitution); to forbid trafficking; and to grant women full political rights. Other measures proposed by reformers could conceivably have involved both state and private efforts: public lectures about the dangers of prostitution, expanded charitable organizations, vocational education for women, economic equality for women, and sex-education programs. Still others seemed to rely on nonstate initiative: the promotion of proper amusements, a renewed respect for chastity for men as well as women, improvements in the marriage system so that people would not seek prostitutes because of unhappy family situations, and freedom of sexual choice for women.[58] Always implicit and sometimes explicit in such ambitious programs was the goal of a new culture that would support a strong state (and vice versa), with the elimination of prostitution helping to mark the move from backwardness to modernity.

Comprehensive as this program of social reform appeared, it was not thoroughgoing enough for some May Fourth critics, for whom prostitution was one interlocked feature of a complex social system and could not be addressed in isolation.[59] These critics advocated nothing less than the elimination of private landholding and capitalism. Li Sanwu reached for the imagined Chinese past of the well-field system in ancient times as an example of an economic system based on self-sufficiency, where no one had trouble making a living and prostitution was unknown. By the Spring and Autumn Period, Li continued, economic inequalities had emerged, and women were placed in a particularly vulnerable position, forced to become prostitutes under official sponsorship because they had no other way to survive. Drawing his contemporary examples from Beijing and Nanjing as well as Japan and most of the nations of Europe, Li named societies that permitted licensed prostitution and those in which the unlicensed variety flourished, pointing out that morals and public health were damaged under both systems. If prostitution was indeed a product of fundamental economic arrangements, Li said, trying to eliminate it through moral pressure or government fiat was pointless: "Under these kinds of circumstances, things like the movement for complete abolition of prostitution by the Women's Christian Temperance Union or the Salvation Army's pledge not to buy or sell prostitutes are truly very foolish." He compared such measures to treating a skin disturbance whose root cause was in the internal organs. Those who were confused enough to pursue such a course did not understand philosophical causality, he said. Here and throughout his argument, Li took an understanding of the "real" nature of prostitution as a means of asserting certain "modern" intellectual skills and social-science qualifications.

Li invited his readers to imagine a future society in which "the prostitute class" would vanish, but it was not a vision he was able to fully articulate. Like the reformers whose partial efforts he deplored, Li in the end turned to the same measures advocated by so many other May Fourth writers: women's education, which would lead to women's economic independence, making it possible to forbid the "commodification of sexual function" and marriages aimed at making a profit. Naming prostitution as a worldwide problem rather than one confined to China, and buttressing his arguments with quotations from Engels and the British philosopher Edward Carpenter, Li Sanwu asserted his status as an intellectual engaged in global questions, rather than an analyst of China's parochial ills. Nevertheless, he shared the May Fourth faith in a march from backwardness to modernity, in which China could catch up if enlightened intellectuals who understood the scientific laws of social change emerged to guide it.[60]

We know very little about where the May Fourth discussion of prostitution among intellectual reformers was lodged in the wider society. When the reform magazine *New Human* (*Xin ren*) published a special issue on prostitution in 1919, sales of the journal jumped from three thousand to more than twenty thousand, indicating wide popular interest in the question. But what sort of interest? One author suggests that many readers were using the journal not as a map to China's social problems but as a guidebook to the various types of brothels in Shanghai.[61] This comment, intended to cast aspersions on the seriousness of Republican-era social reform, nevertheless indicated the many overlapping varieties of public interest in prostitution, and its ubiquitousness as both issue and symbol in May Fourth–era discussions.

Discussion of prostitution in May Fourth terms, in which the status of women was linked with the health of society, was not the exclusive preserve of highbrow reform journals. It spilled over into the mainstream press as well. Even when it was not cited as a direct cause of national weakness, prostitution was linked to it by analogy or simple proximity. A *Shenbao* article entitled "The Evil of Evil Madams" editorialized in 1920:

In today's China, there are many who induce others to do evil, but each time avoid the consequences of their crime. Military officials induce the troops to harass people, while civil officials induce their underlings to harm people. As soon as these activities are exposed, the troops and underlings are condemned, but the officials are calm and in fine shape. . . . Furthermore, they shield their troops and underlings and cover up in order to avoid being implicated in the crimes themselves. . . . Evil madams who induce prostitutes to solicit customers are in the same category. They force prostitutes to do evil, and also cause people to be harmed by their evil.[62]

To read this passage as a simple rhetorical flourish intended to dramatize the "evil of madams" is to miss an important and barely subtextual message. The practices associated with prostitution are here being invoked as part of a sickness in the culture, expressed in the exploitative and self-protective activities of anyone with power. In this rendering, prostitution is not so much causative as constitutive; prostitutes take their place alongside all those harassed by civil and military authorities, and madams become part of a pervasive and nested regime of power that is manifestly bad for "the people" and the nation.

The tabloid press also cast prostitution as an issue of social and political health, even as it devoted much space to detailing the love affairs and career moves of courtesans. A writer for *Crystal* summarized three common explanations for prostitution: women lacked other employment opportunities; prostitutes were victims of madams and male brothel keepers; and prostitution was often a route up the social ladder, allowing a poor woman to become a wealthy concubine. Each of these explanations mandated a different solution: more jobs for women in the first case, abolition of madams in the second, and a lifelong ban on marriage for prostitutes in the third. Yet the author concluded that all three approaches shared a common theme; prostitution was a product of the social system, and any measure that tried to eliminate it without effecting larger social change in the status of women was of necessity superficial.[63]

Unlike many of the loftier May Fourth treatises on the need to eliminate prostitution through state intervention, some newspaper articles questioned whether becoming a prostitute was such a terrible fate. Every time state authority moved to abolish prostitution, one author sardonically noted in *Crystal,* the women protested that they were "forced by life" to enter this profession. Yet, he continued, this tale of oppression was only one of the stories in their repertoire. When their ability to work was not threatened, courtesans enjoyed an exalted social status, consorting with politicians, earning respect for their parents and wealth for their children. Any government that hoped to abolish licensed prostitution would have to find suitably comfortable work for the displaced courtesans, since they had no desire to become workers or peasants.[64] This theme was also taken up in a *Shenbao* article that attributed prostitution not to economic privation or male lust, but to female vanity and the desire to move up the social ladder:

> Colorful carriages, huge buildings, rich decorations, and beautiful clothes—all these are admired by society, aren't they? A person from a common family or a poor family doesn't even dream of having all these. But once [a woman] becomes a prostitute, she can enjoy them. If she is lucky, she can be promoted and compare with famous and rich ladies. People are amazed by her luxurious life. They don't ask where her money comes from. The prostitute is not shamed, but rather honored. When there is no other way to satisfy her vanity, what should she fear? Why shouldn't she become a prostitute? Then how can the numbers of prostitutes decrease? Therefore, I would say, it is not women's fault that they become prostitutes. The power to eliminate prostitution is in the hands of men. If prostitutes cannot get what they admire, the number of prostitutes will be fewer and fewer. This is not a matter of law, but rather a problem we have made ourselves.[65]

Yet female vanity, for these journalistic commentators, was not an isolated character flaw. Rather it was linked, in true May Fourth fashion, to larger social ills. A commentator in *Crystal* lambasted Shanghai people for defects that suggested a prevalence of sloth, vanity, and lack of shame, enumerating them as follows.

1. [They] get out of bed late in the morning.
2. Women do not work.
3. Men care only about finding sex partners.
4. Women pay too much attention to makeup.
5. [People spend] too much time . . . at play.
6. [They are] afraid of strangers.
7. Young boys are frivolous.
8. Girls are arrogant.
9. Men are not ashamed to be the slaves of foreigners.
10. Women are not ashamed to be prostitutes.[66]

In the neat gender parallelism of much of this list, a woman's position as a prostitute lent her a debased status equivalent to that which accrued to a man by virtue of his position as colonial subject; both indicated a degree of social decay that boded ill for the nation.

Popular Fiction and the Health of the Family

Discussion of prostitution in the May Fourth era also found expression in the city's burgeoning fiction magazines. Directed at a mostly male urban audience that included wealthy merchants, intellectuals, and students as well as shop employees and clerks, the fiction press flourished in the 1920s.[67] Authors such as Bi Yihong,[68] who set their stories in brothels, took what Perry Link has called "an almost sociological interest in the brothel scene," citing

"the theoretical need to reveal the sick side of society in order to heal it."
Link continues:

> The justification for brothel stories in particular was sometimes that they
> exposed the famous or powerful among the clientele of prostitutes. But
> more commonly the argument rested on sympathy for the prostitutes
> themselves, who were forced to solicit business every day, who were mis-
> treated by the brothel owners, whose family life suffered in every conceiv-
> able way, and so on.[69]

One of the many fiction magazines to publish brothel stories was *Semi-monthly*
(*Banyue*), which first appeared in September 1921. The following year it ran
a series of stories with titles such as "Infant of the Northern Lanes," "Son of
the Brothels," "Daughter of the Brothels," "Mother of the Brothels," and "Father of the Brothels," all set in courtesan houses.[70] Perry Link comments that
such stories were reprinted in collections categorized by family relationships
("The Mothers of Prostitutes," "The Daughters of Prostitutes"), "showing how
almost every family relationship was destroyed by prostitution."[71] In Bi Yihong's "Infant of the Northern Lanes," for instance, a courtesan is forced
to leave her infant son with her madam; the child contracts smallpox and
dies, whereupon the courtesan is instructed to dry her tears of maternal grief
and go off to accompany guests at drinking.[72]

"Son of the Brothels," by a revolutionary-general-turned-author who
used the pseudonym "Master of the Seeking Good Fortune Studio," follows
a similar formula, elaborating on the sufferings of apparently privileged courtesans.[73] A Zhen is a courtesan whose virginity is purchased with great fanfare by Wang Yiyong, a rich young man who promises to buy her out of the
brothel. She reassures herself that her ceremony of "lighting the big candles" is not so different from a wedding, and that having sexual relations with
Wang is not so different from the actions of a wife. After a while, however,
the fickle Wang goes off to light the big candles with someone else; he tem-
porizes and then disappears when A Zhen tells him she is pregnant. Stub-
bornly, A Zhen refuses the madam's demands that she take an abortifacient.
Still pregnant, she feels for the first time that her status as a courtesan is one
of sexual debasement:

> Pitiful creature. Before she had lost her virginity, her body was clean. She
> was a prostitute in name but not in practice. After she was sullied and
> abandoned by Wang Yiyong, she became a prostitute and began to receive
> guests. Is this not clearly a case of Wang Yiyong ruining her and making her
> into a prostitute?

After her son's birth, A Zhen resumes work as a courtesan, resisting Wang
Yiyong's attempts to claim the child and going underground when she hears
that Wang may try to take him by force. In one scene where A Zhen con-

fronts Wang, the writer describes the custom of not letting daylight or fresh air into the brothels, adding, "[O]ne can see that the brothel scenery forever lacks the slightest change." Here the brothel is made to stand for all that is stagnant in Chinese society.

Wang suffers retribution in the story's final scene, which takes place twenty years later. Now a petty legal official, he sentences a thief to death, only to find out on the execution ground that the criminal is his own son. At this point it is too late to prevent the execution. A Zhen, who after her disappearance had become a brothel maidservant, eschewing marriage for fear that a husband would not accept her son, is so grief-stricken that she kills herself by knocking her head on the city wall. Wang goes insane. Since he has no other son, there is no one to visit him and care for him.[74]

This story's message of social criticism is hardly less subtle than its hyperbolic plot. Prostitutes long for a stable family and are victimized and degraded when it is denied them; brothels are a dark and changeless environment; officials who uphold the law in public and frequent prostitutes in private will suffer for their hypocrisy. This essentially conservative message, which advocated the rectitude of officials and the chastity of women, owed little to the May Fourth agenda. Yet its denunciation of social ills and its call for justice dovetailed with May Fourth demands for family reform.

The affinity of popular fiction with May Fourth concerns is perhaps most obvious in "Daughter of the Brothels," which although it appeared in the fiction magazine *Semi-Monthly* was billed as an oral history of the courtesan Lin Biyao. Lin tells of her sale at age five to a madam named A Zhu, who beat the child when she lost at gambling and hired an evil-smelling man who also beat her while teaching her to sing. Closely supervised by A Zhu, Lin complains that she had "no more freedom than a black slave," a comparison that owes far less to conventions of popular fiction than to the concerns of early-twentieth-century political reformers. Under A Zhu's tutelage, Lin works as a courtesan first in Shanghai and then in Tianjin, where she catches the fancy of an army commander. After detailing the profligate spending habits of a courtesan's clientele, the author proceeds to a denunciation of the harm caused by such practices, spoken in the courtesan's voice:

> People say, "The rooms of the popular Beijing courtesans are a microcosm of the Republic of China." . . . Actually, popular courtesans can be counted as representatives of the debt group, so they can indirectly exert pressure on the Ministry of Finance. In other words, they add to the burden of the nation's citizens. Think of it. The crime of us "daughters of the brothels" cannot be summed up by the word "lowly." It also contains the germs of a disaster for the nation and its people.

The real target of criticism here is not the courtesans, but the men who frequent them.

A Zhu agrees to sell Lin to the commander as a concubine, although Lin is revolted by his appearance and opposed to a liaison with him. Fortunately, the commander abandons her for another courtesan and calls off the liaison. Lin's account concludes with a stirring call for liberation, not merely for prostitutes but for all Chinese women:

> I hope that the 200 million women compatriots can become politically awakened and do all we can to liberate ourselves, rather than waiting for men to liberate us. We can hope that the phrase "Daughter of the Brothels" will disappear without a trace. . . . Fellow women compatriots, let us quickly save ourselves![75]

Here, popular fiction merges with the more formal political rhetoric of the May Fourth era. Prostitutes, like all Chinese women, must liberate themselves; Chinese women, like all Chinese, must stand up and take action without relying on others to save them. "Daughter of the Brothels" is of dubious value as fiction and of doubtful authenticity as a courtesan's life story, yet it can be usefully read as a clarion call for reform.[76]

Prostitution, Imperialism, and Rural Crisis: The 1930s

Intellectuals continued their debate about prostitution after the nation was nominally unified under a new national government in Nanjing in 1928. Important themes linked discussion across the 1920s and 1930s. Prostitution was still treated as a social evil that harmed social order, women's rights, and the progress of the race.[77] Prostitution was worse for society than robbery, Tang Guozhen asserted, yet the government punished robbery more severely because its harm was more direct.[78]

Prostitution's ubiquity across time and place was still taken as a marker of China's participation in a common human history.[79] A 1936 polemic by Mu Hua against licensed prostitution, for example, began by invoking the standard May Fourth explanations for prostitution: economic difficulties, trafficking, the atrophy of moral values, the marriage system, and the low level of education. It moved quickly to universalize the problem, juxtaposing statistics on Parisian prostitutes used by Bebel with a survey of prostitutes who applied for licenses in Suzhou. Mu's conclusion to this section emphasized the primacy of economic causes regardless of geography: "'In sum, [the cause is] just poverty!' The door of the brothel is open for the wives and daughters of the poor."[80]

This narrative, like that of the 1920s, drew on notions of a transcultural biology:

> The male of the human species has a sexual desire that is not less flourishing than that of the beasts, while the biological burden and the capability of the female in sexual intercourse are very different from that of the beasts.[81]

Women's difference from beasts was not specified here as the author invoked
Bebel and echoed Engels to sketch out the establishment of private property, the rise in the status of men and the imposition of restrictions on wives,
and the establishment of prostitutes as objects of enjoyment. Then Mu Hua
returned to particular local Chinese conditions:

> Because of the immaturity of industry and the desolation of commerce, with
> most households in economic distress, women in industry and commerce
> and maids in households make a meager income insufficient to carry the
> burden of supporting the household, and only by selling sex as a sideline
> can they supplement their insufficient wages. So the supply of prostitutes
> matches male sexual needs, leading to even greater inflation in the market
> in human flesh.[82]

What is striking about this passage, which echoed many standard Depression-
era descriptions of the Chinese economy, is precisely that it was geographically unmarked and historically genericized. Coming directly after citations
of Bebel and Engels on the universal evolution of marriage systems, it pointed
away from anything that might be designated as specifically Chinese, even
as it described local problems. China was inserted into a seamless world
predicament that privileged (universal) economics over (backward local)
culture.

Like the earlier May Fourth commentators, Mu Hua indicated that a comprehensive state initiative was needed to remedy this situation.[83] His writing
showed as well a May Fourth concern for the psychological and physical rav-
aging of women under both feudal and capitalist regimes:

> At present, on the one hand Chinese women are suffering from various
> kinds of capitalist exploitation, and on the other hand they are tightly
> bound by feudal power. To allow women to sell their flesh in order to make
> a living is a type of polygamous robbery that breaks the rules of conduct,
> and of course to add unconditional recognition [via licensing] makes the
> situation worse and will make it forever impossible to eliminate or decrease
> the sale of women.

He called for thoroughgoing social change to end the harm prostitution did
to women, humankind, society, and the race.[84] Mu's narrative strategy put
across the message that Shanghai was just like Paris (indeed, as a similar essay by Guo Chongjie pointed out, Shanghai is "the Paris of the East"); both
were mired in the problems of capitalism, with China as a full participant in
capitalist ills.[85]

As they had been in the 1920s, critiques of prostitution were peppered
with legitimizing foreign names and phrases.[86] Guo Chongjie, writing in
1936, cited Havelock Ellis to the effect that prostitution is a necessary part
of the marriage system, and that if it is abolished the system will collapse.
She quoted the Swedish feminist Ellen Key as saying that prostitutes, unlike

wives, maintain some limited control over their own freedom and individual rights, whereas a wife, in signing the marriage contract, actually sells herself. Guo also cited a statement in *The Fate of Women and Prostitution* by someone identified only as Gross-Hoffinger that prostitution cannot be eliminated without first transforming marriage. Max Rubner and Franz Hugel were mentioned for their belief that prostitution was rooted in human nature (Rubner said economics was the root, while Hugel argued for biology) and would disappear only on the last day of the world. Whether the standards invoked were those of political economy or sexology, the universalizing impulse was similar.[87]

Economic pressure was still cited as the most important cause of prostitution, its effects exacerbated by the world depression.[88] Critics still proposed relief measures that ranged from developing proper production skills for women to permitting them complete sexual freedom.[89] For many authors the solution to prostitution would of necessity be the universal modern one of marriage reform and female employment. Lin Chongwu argued that both men and women should be held to identical standards of behavior:

> Responsibility for chastity should be shared equally by men and women. The abandonment of chastity should also be shared equally by men and women. . . . How is it acceptable to consign females to hell in order to provide males with pleasure, and call this fair?[90]

In similar fashion, Guo Chongjie asserted that until women had the capacity to live independently, "their means of livelihood will be, if not the retail sale of sex through prostitution, then the wholesale sale of sex through marriage." As long as women had no other way to make a living, Guo argued, there would always be prostitutes.[91]

Elite arguments against prostitution in the 1930s were not without cultural specificity. At one point in the commentator Lin Chongwu's essay, after he invoked the case of the Athenian lawmaker Solon and the authority of Parent-Duchâtelet, Hugel, Flexner, Rousseau, and Lincoln, the argument took a sudden particularistic turn. Lin exhorted the state to promote traditional Confucian virtues for women, such as honesty, honor, propriety, and justice, so that women could resist the lure of Western ways:

> The European wind assails the East, leading to female vanity, beautiful clothes and makeup, powder and perfume, a fool's paradise, the love of pleasure and the fear of labor. . . . If one can't be frugal, how can one be honest? . . . Abandoning a sense of chastity and shame . . . leads to selling sex for a living. "If this is how it is in the higher reaches of society, how much more so in the lower reaches?" So promotion of virtue should start with the families of government officials; giving up pearls and jade, turning away from gold and diamonds, with coarse dress and simple adornment . . . will promote the cultivation of female virtue.[92]

Yet in spite of the Confucian undertones, Lin's discussion was firmly grounded both in the twentieth century—where China was one nation struggling among many, rather than the undisputed repository of civilization—and in a universal moral discourse, where Rousseau and Lincoln were cited for their belief that human trafficking cannot be permitted in a civilized society. When Confucian imperatives were laid literally paragraph by paragraph with those of St. Augustine, Charlemagne, Parent-Duchâtelet, and Rubner,[93] an invocation of unique cultural values became its opposite: an application to join a human march toward a civilized, moral society, in which both prostitution and the intent to eliminate it were credentials for membership.

As it had a decade earlier, the question of whether governments should license and examine prostitutes inspired energetic and scornful polemics on the part of feminist writers. In 1933–1934 the national government in Nanjing, which had banned prostitution within that city since 1928 (see chapter 11), proposed lifting the ban to permit licensed prostitutes to do business. Government officials felt that licensing prostitution would control the spread of venereal disease and unlicensed prostitution, and thereby help restore the city's prosperity, which had been adversely affected by the world depression.

When representatives of the Nanjing Women's Association petitioned the mayor not to rescind the ban, he replied that the problem of relief work for prostitutes was more complex than they were willing to recognize. Many women became prostitutes, he stated, not out of economic need but because they were dissolute and liked to sleep with customers. Building on the assumptions about the universality of prostitution that feminist authors themselves had helped to establish, he added that prostitution was a natural social phenomenon found in every civilized nation, giving London as an example.[94]

The proposal to lift the ban, as well as these assertions by the mayor, inspired a flurry of angry ripostes in the Nanjing magazine *Women's Sympathetic Understanding* (*Funü gongming*). Venereal disease would not be stopped by licensing, said one author, because infected prostitutes who were ordered to stop working would continue to sell sex secretly.[95] Licensing would not stop unlicensed prostitution, either, added another: the example of Shanghai clearly showed that it flourished even where licensed prostitution was permitted.[96] Nanjing would not prosper by encouraging prostitution, commented a third; real prosperity required the development of industry and commerce.[97] After all, cities that permitted prostitution, such as Shanghai, Tianjin, Beiping, and Taiyuan, were also in economic trouble.[98] One critic commented caustically on the mayor's argument about the ubiquity of prostitution:

> As for the statement that prostitution is a natural product of society, and that prostitution exists in all civilized nations, it seems that those who advocate lifting the ban give as their main reason that we must become part of the

world trend. They seem to think that if a civilized nation has no prostitution it is insufficiently decked out. Alas! With such a conceptualization, how can licensed prostitution be banned? How can unlicensed prostitution fail to prosper?[99]

Finally, a sharp-tongued satirist writing under the name Suo Fei ridiculed the proposed government action in even more extreme terms. With tongue in cheek, this writer suggested that Chinese soldiers had not fought effectively to defend Manchuria (occupied by the Japanese in 1931) because they did not have dancing girls on their arms as their officers did. Japanese forces, in contrast, fought valiantly because they were well provided with prostitutes. In view of this problem, Suo said, the Nanjing government proposed to lift the ban on prostitution as a "great plan for saving the nation." Henceforth government officials would not have to spend their time taking the train from Nanjing to Shanghai to visit prostitutes. Instead they could stay in the capital and concentrate on solving national problems. In fact, Suo added, lest the demand exceed supply, not only should unlicensed prostitutes become licensed, but women of respectable families should also become prostitutes, the better to sacrifice themselves for the nation. "It is not the Three People's Principles that will save the nation, but rather the flower maidens [*hua guniang*]," Suo concluded. "Let us shout with a single voice: Long live the flower maidens!"[100]

In spite of important continuities of explanation and argument in the 1920s, new themes as well entered the discussion of prostitution in the 1930s. Authors developed more-elaborate theories of sexuality and its importance in human life. Fang Long, advocating a single standard of chastity for both sexes, noted that

> [t]he role of sexual enjoyment between the two sexes is like that of the atom in chemistry or the electron in physics, so in order to seek a harmonious life between the sexes, the first requirement is that the man who is the husband must not divide the benefit by going to frequent a prostitute, [by seeking] the love of a second woman who is not his wife.[101]

If sexual desire was a natural feature of life, however, it was generally male sexual desire that was discussed. For instance, Luo Tianwen worried that men who could not afford to marry and could not find prostitutes would engage in rape, masturbation, or homosexuality, or suffer from sex mania and mental illness.[102] Another new theme was the characterization of prostitution as an institution that consumed without producing, leading to the waste of social resources. In 1933, Yi Feng drew on a Japanese study that estimated in some detail that residents of Shanghai spent 166,400 yuan per day on licensed prostitutes alone, for an annual total of more than 60 million yuan.[103]

As China's economic crisis worsened in the 1930s and Japanese en-

croachments on Chinese territory intensified, critics began to link prostitution to this new situation. Prostitution might be a worldwide problem, Tang
Guozhen said, but it took a particularly complicated form in China, which
was economically more backward and vulnerable than other areas.[104] Zhu
Meiyu went so far as to link prostitution and the political crisis, asserting that
in China prostitution had always increased in times of chaotic politics. Prostitution and an inferior society were mutually causative.[105] If prostitution was
not just a Chinese problem, Cao Gongqi inquired, why did it feel more serious in China? His answer highlighted the centrality of prostitution to the
thinking of Republican-era intellectuals: "Because in China the prostitution
problem is not only a partial social problem, but rather through a partial
problem expresses the whole problem of Chinese society."[106]

The key to both the partial problem and the whole, some authors began
to assert in the 1930s, was the bankruptcy of the village economy, pushed to
the brink of collapse by imperialism, internal disorder, and natural disasters.
Forced into urban factories at low wages, some rural women turned to prostitution because it paid better.[107] On the fact of rural crisis there was broad
consensus among feminist writers, but they parted ways when it came to devising solutions. Some believed that the prostitution problem could be solved
through village relief work and new types of employment for rural women.[108]
Others countered that this was not enough. China's semicolonial status, the
world economic depression, and the near collapse of the Chinese economy
could not be undone by establishing a few rural relief agencies; rather, the
solution would require a new society, in both urban and rural China, to be
achieved by a struggle with imperialism and its representatives.[109] Increasingly, 1930s authors began to describe in approving terms the campaign to
eliminate prostitution in the Soviet Union.[110] Stirring calls for an overhaul
of the social system filled the women's magazines, accompanied by visions
of a society without oppression, exploitation, or class divisions.[111] Some writers on prostitution even began to quote Marx to the effect that human society thus far had been in a prehistoric state, and that the first page of real
human history was soon to be written.[112]

In the midst of this escalating rhetoric about imminent national disaster
and redemption, one writer, Zhou Shixian, took a more prosaic position on
whether women's entry into prostitution could be attributed to the collapse
of the village economy. A native of Suzhou, he noted that in a nearby village
every girl aspired to be a prostitute. At age eight or nine a girl would go to
Shanghai, where she would be placed with relatives who worked as prostitutes.
Typically she would begin as a maid, move up to attendant status, and then
become a virgin courtesan. Many people knew this to be true, Zhou averred,
and anyone who said that prostitution was a result of rural bankrupty was
just not familiar with the ways of the profession. We cannot just rely on theory,
Zhou added, observing that the reality often stuns all scholars.[113]

But Zhou's was a minor note in the ongoing chorus that linked prostitution with national crisis and the quest for modernity. Reform writers, whether they took prostitution as a mark of backwardness or understood it as a feature of modernity, sought to distinguish themselves from those who worked as prostitutes, frequented them, or wrote about them appreciatively. By establishing their superior moral habits and sensibilities, their awareness of the requirements of a modern state, and their familiarity with Western history and social-scientific inquiry, the reformers claimed for themselves the attributes of a sought-for state of modernity—and with it the hope of escape from their own keenly felt subaltern status.

Sexual Debasement and National Disgrace: The Occupation

With the threat and arrival of Japanese occupation, writers made the connection between prostitution and national weakness ever more explicit. In 1936, Jing Zhi pointed out that the Japanese threat to the nation in the Northeast and North China was not just a matter of military attacks and smuggling; it also entailed "using the policy on prostitution, drugs, and gambling" to poison and murder the Chinese race. Jing argued that the immediate task for all those concerned about prostitution was "to demand national independence and freedom" and to resist Japan.[114]

The Japanese occupied much of China in 1937–1938, leaving the concession areas of Shanghai as a "solitary island" in an ocean of enemy territory. As Poshek Fu has documented, writers on the "solitary island" saw themselves as facing a series of moral dilemmas about how to aid the Chinese cause, dilemmas that only intensified after Japan occupied the foreign-concession areas in December 1941. Many of these writers produced commentary on the social and political health of occupied Shanghai, and occupied China more generally. For Bi Yao, writing in 1938, "solitary island" Shanghai was a morally decrepit zone, evidenced by the tendency of its denizens to lose themselves in pornographic writing and reading and to purchase aphrodisiacs. These activities numbed the masses rather than awakening them at a moment of national crisis. A "cave of immorality" (yinku)[115] ever since its establishment as a treaty port, "solitary island" Shanghai had now become even more immoral with the influx of refugees—including, the author added darkly, many women. Bi Yao argued that pornography and social disorder, along with drugs, were elements in an enemy plot to render people useless and amenable to control. He concluded with a saying popular several years earlier: "The vanguard of Great Britain's expansion of power was the military flag; for France, it was the clergy; for Imperial XX [Japan, unmentionable in this context because of censorship], it is prostitutes."[116]

If some writers treated prostitutes as a sign of moral decay and a tool of the enemy, others found in them a source of heroic symbols. In his study of intellectuals in occupied Shanghai, Poshek Fu discusses Wang Tongzhao's wartime novel *Shuangqing* (The two virtues), in which the protagonist, a virgin courtesan in North China during the warlord era, "suggests the symbolic resister" to Japanese occupation:

> This choice was an obvious one. The post–May Fourth literary construction of women as weak and helpless and usually pure figures victimized by men's social and sexual abuses matched in symbolic terms the dismal situation of passive resistance under Japanese domination. By creating the figure of a "chaste" prostitute, therefore, Wang connotes committed patriots striving to maintain their moral integrity in the face of extreme danger.[117]

To characterize courtesans as the embodiment of female fidelity in a time of national crisis was not an innovation of occupation-era intellectuals: it was common as early as the Ming dynasty.[118] Some occupation writers consciously evoked these historical resonances by setting their dramas of loyal courtesans in the late Ming period, when China was facing invasion by the Manchus.[119] In turn, Chinese writers more sympathetic to collaboration attacked the image of the chaste prostitute as an impossibility under conditions of "poverty, misery, and distress." As the author He Zhi commented, "It is . . . sheer nonsense to remind a starving man of integrity or to discuss chastity with a prostitute."[120] Although discussion of the social practice of prostitution was so muted during the war that tracing its most rudimentary social history is difficult, the prostitute as flexible symbol was repeatedly invoked as both source of national decay and embodiment of possibilities for resistance.

The Practice of Reform: Rescuing Prostitutes

Many of the same reformers who wrote so eloquently about the need to effect large-scale social change before prostitution could disappear also addressed themselves to the immediate practical problem of rescuing prostitutes. Their writings anticipated, in almost every particular, the program of reform that was actually followed by the Communist government when it eliminated prostitution in the 1950s. In 1936, for instance, Lin Chongwu wrote of the need for an institution where prostitutes could be forcibly confined, educated, taught job skills, and guided to a concept of morality that would "restore their original sense of shame." In such an institution, diseased prostitutes could be cured and helped to find a suitable marriage partner. Lin recommended that women whose illness was difficult to treat, whose thinking remained unstable even after education, or who did not wish to return to society should remain in the institution and support themselves. Coercion was very much present in Lin's program, which recommended that recidivists be returned to the institution permanently, losing citizenship rights and all hope of reentering society.[121]

The rescue institutions founded in Shanghai throughout the first half of the twentieth century incorporated most of these features: confinement, education, medical treatment, job training, and marriage. Such institutions were sponsored by an intriguing mix of state and private (often foreign) authority, while the vision of how prostitutes should be reintegrated into society via work and marriage reflected an eclectic collection of missionary, May Fourth, Victorian, and reinterpreted Confucian social schemes.[122]

Chief among these institutions was the Door of Hope.[123] Founded in 1900 by a group of foreign missionary women, the Door of Hope consisted of what was known as the Receiving Home, in an alley off Nanjing Road, and a larger residential facility on the outskirts of the city, "far removed," as Mary Ninde Gamewell put it, "from the crowded, dangerous district with which the girls have grown too familiar."[124] A woman fleeing the brothels went first to the Receiving Home. In 1917 Gardner Harding described one such flight that he had personally witnessed:

> I can still see a little crowd of furiously hurrying people that broke across my path one evening.
>
> In front of them was the flying figure of a girl, her little silken coat torn and hanging by one shoulder. She was ten paces ahead of her pursuers as she passed me, her little face drawn and blanched with terror and exhaustion.
>
> Fortunately, her pursuers were not agile. A stout madam hobbled along on little feet; two burly men in blue peasant clothes lumbered along beside her, apparently the major-domos of her establishment. And all too apparently, the scudding little miss ahead was a very recent inmate of that establishment, launched on a gallant and desperate break for freedom.
>
> The crowd parted like sheep. A few heads turned around out of curiosity, but none out of sympathy. The pursuers swept by. Suddenly the girl turned under a bright street light and began to pound with both fists against a kind of matchboard doorway. A tall Sikh policeman started across the street from his traffic post on the opposite corner. Then the crowd closed in and it was all blur.
>
> When I got to the fragile doorway under the light the girl was gone and the Sikh policeman was dispersing the crowd. They scattered quickly, all but the stout woman and her two strong men. The woman scolded vehemently and viciously shook her fist at the sign above the doorway through which her victim had escaped. Then the policeman "moved her on" in true Occidental fashion, and the incident seemed to be closed.[125]

The girl so eloquently portrayed in this colonial drama may have known of the Door of Hope because a municipal regulation required each brothel to post the Receiving Home's address in a prominent place, along with an assurance that anyone who tried to stop a woman from seeking refuge would be prosecuted. After the Mixed Court heard her case, a woman was committed to the residential facility, where she would spend the morning in study and the afternoon in handicraft work, making her own clothes and doll clothes for sale.[126]

By the Republican period the Door of Hope was partially funded by the Municipal Council, depended upon by the police, used by the Mixed Court, and regarded as an "almost public institution."[127] Women who had been abducted or sold into brothels, or who had conflicts with their madams, were sent there by the police or the Mixed Court, or "rescued" by Door of Hope workers. Some turned themselves over to the institution voluntarily. (Women in this last category were usually sent for a hearing to the Mixed Court, which then formally turned them over to the institution.)[128] The Door of Hope provided a safe house, taught literacy and handicraft skills, and ultimately helped to arrange marriages for most inmates. Most of the inmates became Christians after a few months, reported Mary Gamewell with satisfaction in 1916, and went on to marry Christians.[129] From 1901 to 1918, more than twenty-two hundred women were taken in to the Door of Hope.[130] Even after the demise of the Mixed Court in 1927, the Chinese courts continued to remand women there.[131]

The difficulty of convincing prostitutes that a good life was possible for them after leaving the brothels was forthrightly discussed in the reform literature. This problem of motivation was regarded as most acute among prostitutes who were remanded to institutions like the Door of Hope, rather than those who entered voluntarily. During the 1920 campaign to eliminate prostitution in the International Settlement, for instance, the feminist reformer Hu Huaichen wrote that the Door of Hope was unlikely to be successful in teaching formerly licensed prostitutes a job skill. How could they be taught a skill in a short period of time? Who would pay for it? Would women who had been leading a prosperous life in courtesan houses really want to learn sock weaving? As for finding spouses for these women, Hu warned that they would be unhappy with husbands of middling income, preferring to dream of prosperity. Nor were the husbands likely to be satisfied with wives whose childbearing capacity was questionable and who were discontented with their lot.[132] Foreign critics of the 1920 campaign echoed these reservations, noting that rescue work had not been successful because "the environment of rescue homes is intolerably dull. A girl snatched from the streets is very much in the position of a convalescent from a severe illness, who needs dainty food and continual humouring."[133] Sometimes the boredom and hostility of prostitutes confined to the Door of Hope and other institutions took the form of violating regulations, stealing, petitioning the court for release, random yelling, arson, and digging escape tunnels.[134]

This discussion about the intransigence of prostitutes continued throughout the Republican period. Liao Guofang, writing in the *Ladies' Journal* in 1929, warned:

This kind of woman has been degenerate for too long. . . . [I]f one speaks to them of liberation, not only will one fail to get their sympathy; one may even be mocked by them. They believe that their own lives at present are very free, they feel no oppression, so they understand nothing about what liberation is.[135]

In the "solitary island" period of occupation from 1937 to 1941, the number of pheasant prostitutes soliciting in the International Settlement began to alarm the authorities. Initially planning to send arrested prostitutes back to their native places, the police quickly found that the women were crafty about revealing any personal information. Exasperated, Chinese officials of the Municipal Council in the Settlement secured the cooperation of various women's groups to interview detained prostitutes. The interviewers found that the women were "as though anesthetized, and no longer hoped for any other kind of life. . . . [They were] numbed to the conditions of their existence," as well as diseased. In order to make possible a new life for these women by sending them back to their native places or finding them spouses, the interviewers said, it would first be necessary to educate and provide medical treatment for them. Thus was founded the Municipal Council Temporary Women's and Children's Relief Station.

The Relief Station's educational director described the difficulty of educating prostitutes. "Prostitutes are not ordinary women," she wrote. "They have deeply rooted vulgar practices, know no shame in their behavior, assume airs of importance, are lazy with many ailments, like to sleep and to cry, and are especially good at trickery." Presented with a schedule that required them to rise at 6 A.M. for exercise, cleaning, and housework, followed by an afternoon of study and meetings and a brief evening period of wholesome amusements, many prostitutes tore up their books and asked: "Why should we chew yellow bean sprouts [suffer hardship] here when in our 'own homes' [the brothels] servants will address us as 'Miss'?" This particular article conformed to the usual pattern of successful reform stories later made popular by the Communists: gently prodded by understanding teachers, the women learned to make their own clothes, reinterpret their life stories as narratives of suffering and exploitation, and develop a desire to contribute to the war effort as factory workers, maids, or cooks for the army. Like their sisters in reform in the 1950s, they referred to themselves as having "leaped out of the fiery pit."[136] Yet in spite of the cheerful forward-march ending to this report, convincing prostitutes to cooperate in their own reform remained difficult in the late 1940s, when the Guomindang government ran a reform institute. Such difficulties were a common feature of the Communist reform campaign in the 1950s as well. Government-sponsored reform efforts before and after the 1949 revolution are taken up in the next two chapters.

CHAPTER 11

Regulators

At several points in the history of treaty-port Shanghai, members of the foreign and Chinese communities initiated intense campaigns to regulate or ban prostitution.[1] Taking up these campaigns, government officials sought to implement their visions of the modern state: clean, moral, and orderly in its regulation of prostitution. Health officers of the International Settlement government were concerned primarily with the spread of sexually transmitted disease among the foreign population. Foreign missionaries and women reformers deplored the spread of "commercialized vice" and its effect upon prostitutes, customers, and foreign children growing up in Shanghai. In the 1920s and 1930s, groups of Chinese activists sought to abolish prostitution as part of their drive to modernize China and improve the status of Chinese women. Finally, in the late 1940s the Guomindang-run municipal government of Shanghai undertook the registration of prostitutes with an eye to eventual abolition.

Although these groups of reformers and regulators differed in their aims and methods, they had one thing in common: they all failed to significantly affect prostitution in Shanghai. Not until the establishment of the People's Republic did any municipal government succeed in closing brothels, punishing traffickers, and reeducating prostitutes. The repeated failure of state campaigns was linked to the instability and weakness of "the state," which was not a steady entity. The Shanghai Municipal Council (SMC), which ran the 1920 campaign, was merely a local authority, albeit one with ties to powerful foreign powers. Less than a decade later, a spate of abolition edicts originated upriver in the national capital of Nanjing. Their dim echoes in Shanghai were a measure of the gulf between national proclamations and local configurations of power. The 1940s municipal government, energetic in generating a prostitution policy, was fatally weakened by local economic pressures and the national civil war. Yet these efforts, however ineffective, indicate the scope of state efforts to link prostitution with the moral, political, and physical health of the body politic. An examination of attempts to regulate prostitution also suggests the limited extent of state authority over contested social terrain in the Republican era.

ABOLITIONIST DREAMS, 1920–1937

The Abolitionist Argument

Almost from the beginning of their tenure in Shanghai, public-health authorities in the International Settlement expressed concern about the growth of prostitution and its effect on the health of the European population.[2] In 1869, when Dr. Alex Jamieson conducted a survey of public-health problems in the International Settlement, his classification scheme grouped together dirt, pollution, disease, and commercial sex, naming as health hazards the city sewage system, the condition of the river, the water supply, vaccination, and brothels.[3] Some foreigners saw prostitution as one among many threats to their own health and well-being in an environment where the white population was surrounded and outnumbered. The late nineteenth-century lock hospital described in chapter 9 was one reflection of this concern.

Some residents of the International Settlement were profoundly uneasy about the allocation of public funds for the lock hospital, as well as the involvement of municipal organizations like the police and the courts in licensing and inspecting prostitutes. One unhappy taxpayer objected in 1877 that government regulation of prostitution condoned immorality, asking:

> There was always one test for a Christian man by which he could tell
> whether he ought to support an undertaking and that was, Could he ask
> the blessing of God on it? . . . Could any one ask that blessing on a scheme
> countenancing and protecting fornication, in fact making provision for the
> flesh to fulfill the lusts thereof?[4]

Yet in spite of the problems involved in inspecting prostitutes, municipal authorities before World War I apparently rejected the alternative of abolition. Jamieson, while denouncing the "baneful" effects of prostitution on families, women, and public health, felt that it would exist as long as human nature "is constituted as at present." He argued that "attempts to abolish this form of vice can never prove successful, and therefore that rational men will direct their energies towards limiting the extent and lessening the severity of the inevitable effects."[5]

Half a century later, as World War I drew to a close, Shanghai prostitution became the subject of sustained public debate among foreigners and some of the Shanghai elite. The worldwide movement of troops during the war was accompanied by the spread of sexually transmitted diseases, which became a frequent subject of discussion in Chinese medical journals, as well as in what the *North-China Herald* called "newspapers and periodicals of the highest possible class."[6] Many of these articles explicitly linked disease to prostitution.[7] In the International Settlement of Shanghai particularly, the menace of sexually transmitted disease was heightened by what observers saw as an alarming expansion of prostitution.[8]

The dual concern with increases in disease and in commercialized sex, in turn, dovetailed with the agenda of foreign Christians, many of them missionaries by profession, who were increasingly turning their attention to medical, educational, and industrial reform in China.[9] In 1916, Mary Ninde Gamewell published a heartfelt description of the nightly traffic in women that took place in teahouses along Nanjing and Fuzhou Roads:

> In and out among the square tables, filling the brilliantly lighted rooms, trail slowly little processions of young girls. Nearly all are pretty and very young. Clad in silk or satin, adorned with jewelry, their faces unnatural with paint and powder, they follow the lead of the woman in charge of each group. She stops often to draw attention ingratiatingly to her charges and expatiate on their good points. When one is chosen she leaves her to her fate and passes on to dispose of others. Multitudes of victims, innocent of any voluntary wrong, having been sold into this slavery when too young to resist and not uncommonly in babyhood, are kept up hour after hour in the close atmosphere of the tea-room awaiting the pleasure of their prospective seducers. Out on the street, by ricsha [*sic*] and on foot, women continue to hurry to the tea-houses with their living merchandise, and still they keep arriving till the night is far advanced and business at a stand-still.[10]

Perhaps because of the religious impulse behind much social reform, the discussion of prostitution among the foreign community in Shanghai was conducted in the language of morality. The prostitute was cast as both embodiment and victim of immoral behavior, a danger to respectable women and an agent of contagion. The Women's Christian Temperance Union (WCTU) in late 1916 appealed to the SMC to deal forcefully with street solicitation. When the council demurred, saying that brothels were "as a rule restricted to definite areas," the *North-China Herald* asked sarcastically:

> For example, is the region of the Nanking Road all about the Town Hall "a definite area" such as ought to be tolerated? From an early hour in the evening immoral women appear quite openly in this part of our main street. There is an alleyway next door to the entrance to Louza police station which nightly sends forth a number of them. . . . If the community likes its daughters to push their way by these women in going to the Town Hall dances, there is no more to be said.[11]

Writing to the *North-China Herald* in 1917, a reader using the pen name Pride's Purge asserted that Shanghai had no right to call itself a model settlement as long as "palaces of vice and extravagance" continued to exist there. "What might give food to whole families in devastated countries or should have gone to the help of our defenders goes to help in swelling an immoral woman's revenue to enable her to have motor cars and bedeck her unfortunate carcase with jewels," the letter exclaimed.[12] Developing the image of a small, clean community threatened by an engulfing tide of dirt, the same writer added a week later:

> Of course, if the city authorities and the public here are absolutely indifferent as to where such houses are located, whether within a stone's throw of a church, or in the proximity and facing dwelling-houses with respectable families and public offices, or on a road where school children have to pass, then there is nothing more to be said about the matters: but if, on the other hand, it is an acknowledged disgrace to have houses of such resort in the centre of the city and it is only a question of stirring mud, then it is high time that public opinion should compel the removal of that mudheap lying in front of them.[13]

Adding warnings about disease to those about dirt, Dr. Margaret Polk observed in a lecture to the local chapter of the WCTU that "prostitutes themselves immune from the disease at the time may nevertheless be the vehicle for carrying the contagion." In a sardonic aside about women's lack of suffrage rights, she went on to suggest that women should use the vote, if they could get it, to make prostitution a penal offense for both parties.[14]

Among many missionaries and female Christian activists, however, the prostitute was less a figure of immorality and disease than an outlet for unacceptable male desires. They combined moral arguments with an appeal for women's rights. The Reverend Isaac Mason, for instance, argued that "commercialized vice" should be abolished "to make women free, and give them a chance to choose their own moral path, and not be thrust down as slaves to men's lusts and harpies' greed, without any regard to their own wishes."[15] Miss Laura White, an activist in the WCTU, was quoted as saying that "the matter was such as to demand the attention of the whole of the women of Shanghai. . . . [T]he women could handle the matter better than did the men."[16] Adopting the rhetoric of compassion for one's fallen sisters, Mrs. Evan Morgan told the WCTU, "Girls with no work, no friends, find the path of prostitution not only easy but necessary. There should be some sort of institution to which such people might go, that they might be kept from temptation."[17]

In spite of these broad linkages between prostitution, morality, sexual desire, and gender equality, the largely foreign movement that emerged from this discussion opted for a narrowly focused approach to the problem. In May 1918, missionaries, doctors, and women activists representing seventeen philanthropic and religious organizations met to form the Committee on

Moral Improvements, later known as the Shanghai Moral Welfare Committee and still later as the Moral Welfare League. The committee's express purpose was to investigate ways of eliminating prostitution in the International Settlement.[18]

The newly formed committee was soon at loggerheads with the SMC, criticizing its patchwork approach to the control and remediation of prostitution. The Moral Welfare Committee opposed state medical examination of prostitutes, which by this time had been practiced for several decades, because it gave clients a false sense of security, encouraged vice, and involved the ratepayers in a system of approved prostitution. Furthermore, the committee criticized the fact that inspection was limited to prostitutes who serviced foreigners: "Are the Chinese of our community not worth taking equal care about . . . ? We take equal care about the whole community with regard to other contagious diseases; why not with these . . . ?"[19] The committee asked that the SMC remove the word "brothel" from licensing bylaw 34, so that brothels would no longer be legitimated by the issuance of government licenses.[20] Supervision, argued the committee, "meant implied official sanction,"[21] and government licensing of prostitution was "a positive hindrance to any progressive policy in the interests of the moral welfare of Shanghai."[22] The committee ridiculed the argument that if prostitution was eliminated in the Settlement it would just move elsewhere in Shanghai:

> Strange that we do not hear the argument that it is no use trying to put down robberies in the Settlement, as they would still go on just over the borders; or that it is useless to practise hygiene on our side of the line as the other side is still insanitary![23]

A meeting of the female membership of the committee sounded the note of women's rights with a resolution that declared: "Believing that the existence of brothels always involves the degradation and exploitation of women, we women of Shanghai call upon the ratepayers to take steps to abolish all known brothels in the Settlement."[24] Finally, the committee accused the SMC of being willing "to leave conditions as they are, to cover things up and to preserve a prudery which ill-becomes the practical gentlemen who form the governing body of this Settlement."[25]

The SMC, for its part, opposed the Moral Welfare Committee's publicity campaign and defended bylaw 34. It argued that the bylaw had "proved a means whereby such houses can be shepherded into certain areas and generally kept under better control than would otherwise be possible."[26] But the SMC's argument was weakened by the fact that licenses had never actually been granted to brothels under this bylaw, because the authorities considered it impractical for the police to enforce it.[27]

After a year of agitation by the Moral Welfare Committee, the Ratepayers' Meeting of 1919 voted to establish a committee to investigate "vice conditions" in the International Settlement.[28] One letter writer to the *North-China Herald,* signing himself "Mid-Victorian," worried that the presence of two women on the committee would inhibit frank discussion, and recommended instead that an auxiliary ladies' committee prepare a separate report. Replying to this suggestion, a writer using the pen name Post-Victorian called him "far too squeamish," recounting an old tale of how a woman refused to take off any of her clothes even though it might have saved her from drowning. "Does 'Mid-Victorian' admire this sort of thing? I imagine that most sensible women of this generation . . . would rather part with a few superfluous garments than be drowned." Women, the writer continued, could "discuss with men the miseries and wrongs which many of their sex suffer . . . without surrendering in the least their modesty and dignity." Still, this writer did approve of the idea of a separate committee of women, because men were apt to regard the problem

> wholly from the masculine point of view. . . . Why not give women with
> their quick intuition and keener sympathies the opportunity to deal with
> the evil? . . . The social evil is mainly for the women to solve, as the conse-
> quences of it fall more heavily on their sex than on the other. They may not
> be able to eradicate the evil entirely, but much can be done to improve the
> hard lot of thousands of wretched women and perhaps a great many can be
> rescued.[29]

The final report of this Special Vice Committee, submitted in March 1920, was considerably more moderate than the initial abolitionist positions espoused by the Moral Welfare Committee, and more modest than the sweeping vision of social reform articulated by women activists. Although it advocated the ultimate elimination of brothels, the Special Vice Committee concluded that immediate suppression was impossible. Instead, it recommended that bylaw 34 be strictly enforced so that every brothel had to obtain a municipal license. Licensing, however, would be an interim measure. Each license would be assigned a number, and every year one-fifth of the numbers would be selected at random and the licenses withdrawn. In that way, prostitution could be eliminated from the International Settlement within five years. During the five-year period, brothels were to be restricted: they had to submit to police and health inspections, they were forbidden to sell opium or alcohol, and they could not not allow their prostitutes to solicit customers.[30] Every brothel would be required to exhibit the address of the nearest police station and other places where prostitutes could get help and free medical assistance, as well as display a statement that no woman could be detained against her will. Medical examinations of prostitutes were to be discontinued. In addition, the Vice Committee recommended strengthening institutions such as the Door of Hope.[31]

Modified though this report might have been from the original agenda of the Moral Welfare Committee, it was still too radically interventionist for the municipal government. The SMC continued to favor regulation rather than elimination of brothels. Council members argued that if licenses were withdrawn from brothels, brothel owners would just move their businesses outside the Settlement and beyond the reach of regulation; unlicensed brothels would proliferate in the Settlement and require more police to suppress them; street soliciting would increase. Aside from this major caveat, though, the SMC endorsed many of the report's provisions and added a few of its own.[32] Undaunted by the SMC opposition, the Special Vice Committee brought a resolution to accept the report before the Ratepayers' Meeting in April, where it passed over the objections of SMC members.[33]

Licensing and Enforcement

Once the resolution was carried, the SMC was obliged to implement it. In May 1920 brothels of every rank, from courtesan establishments to flophouses, were required to go to the International Settlement's tax bureau to register and pay for their licenses. The police were ordered to ascertain where brothels were located and how many prostitutes resided in each one.[34] Licensing fees were a modest dollar per half year. No licenses were to be issued to any brothel located near a school, a provision that made several of the city's most famous courtesan houses ineligible for licensing. If a brothel violated any of the stipulations in the Vice Committee report (solicitation, serving alcohol, and so forth), its license could be revoked.[35] In any case, all licenses were to be withdrawn permanently within five years.

Although this was a far stronger measure than that initially favored by the SMC, it remained a compromise resolution that fell short of a serious effort at abolition. It was designed to render commercial sex invisible by gradually withdrawing brothel licenses, rather than undertaking a comprehensive campaign to eliminate trafficking, provide for displaced prostitutes, or penalize customers.

The abolition plan was supported by some sectors of the Chinese elite. Letters from individuals, educational and student associations, and Chinese Christian groups endorsed the findings of the Special Vice Committee and called for an end to prostitution.[36] But those who wrote for the city's burgeoning tabloid press were more skeptical. One essayist in *Crystal* wryly observed that in abolishing licensed prostitution, municipal authorities were limiting their own revenues in what amounted to an act of social charity. The writer implied that this self-sacrificing act would be wasted if social relief was not provided for the unemployed prostitutes. In a revealing comment on social hierarchy, he noted that they certainly would not want to become industrial workers or peasants, and that even though they might be happy to become concubines, new social conventions called for monogamy.[37] Another

Crystal commentator called attention to the gendered power differential inherent in the ban. Banning prostitutes without banning customers, he believed, had the effect of abolishing selling while continuing to permit buying. It was the opposite of the Chinese campaign to boycott Japanese goods, which prohibited the act of buying. The ban on prostitution, he mused, reflected the fact that men had power relative to women, just as Japan did relative to China.[38]

As the licensing regulations began to take effect, another reaction emerged among Chinese residents of Shanghai: panic in the commercial sector of the population that made its living by providing services to upper-class brothels. A group of shopkeepers wrote a letter to the Chinese General Chamber of Commerce, arguing

> that 1st class brothels serve as places of meeting and entertainment of
> prominent merchants and gentry, [that] these houses are very different
> from the 2nd and/or low class bawdy houses, and that 1st class brothels have
> a great deal to do in the matter of promoting the prosperity and develop-
> ment of local commerce.

Were these brothels to be closed, argued the merchants, "the writers [of the letter] will suffer greatly." They asked that licensing of first-class brothels be canceled and that some other measures be adopted instead. The Chinese General Chamber of Commerce forwarded their letter to the SMC with an endorsement.[39]

At the same time, the sing-song girls or courtesans joined the chorus of opposition to licensing. Although they did not approach the SMC directly, they entreated a local French resident, J. E. Lemière, to speak on their behalf. Sing-song girls, explained Lemière in a June 23 missive to the SMC, were not prostitutes:

> The singing girls are really artists; they earn their living by entertaining
> guests, receiving a regular fee for each attendance. They may be likened to
> actresses. . . . [T]hey never considered themselves to be prostitutes and as a
> matter of fact a great number never departed from the path of morality.[40]

In another article about courtesans, Lemière stated his belief that it was slander to label them as prostitutes, reiterating their motto: "We only sell our songs (literally 'our mouth'), we do not sell our body!"[41]

Like the Chinese merchants, Lemière made a strong case for the commercial importance of the sing-song houses and their connections to the larger urban economy:

> [I]t is customary for the Chinese of the best classes to meet daily in those
> houses of entertainment, where they receive their friends and discuss
> business matters. To oblige the singing girls to register as prostitutes, to
> oblige a house of entertainment to register as a house of prostitution, will

compel both of them either to close their houses in this settlement or emigrate somewhere else, a measure which will not only cause strong disaffection amongst the best Chinese classes, but will also cause a lot of shopkeepers, like tailors, shoe-makers, embroiderers, Jewellers [*sic*], piece good retailers, musical instrument merchants, restaurant keepers, etc., to follow those girls where they will decide to fix their new abode, thus causing a very serious loss to the Revenue Department and it appears to me that both loss of revenue and the annoyance caused to the Chinese Ratepayers can be and ought to be avoided.[42]

Even the Moral Welfare League (the former Moral Welfare Committee) passed a resolution that "sing-song houses" not be required to register as brothels. At a league meeting in April 1923, S. J. Calder had argued that sing-song girls should not be censured since they "did not sell their bodies to first-comers, and since the sing-song girl's history was so closely linked with the history of China herself. . . . Sing-song girls were entertainers and not corrupt beings." Although many courtesans had been persuaded or compelled to register as prostitutes, Calder said, sing-song houses were like gentlemen's clubs in other countries.[43] This position was supported and given a nationalistic twist by Y. S. Ziar, chair of the Chinese Advisory Committee to the SMC, who expressed distress that Japanese geisha houses were being treated differently from Chinese sing-song houses. Ziar felt that this inequity

will very likely be considered by the Chinese community as one of the instances of the unjust discriminations shown to that community as a whole and will form the germ of ill feeling and dissatisfaction, especially in view of the present spirit of the Chinese people.[44]

To these cries of distress, the SMC could only reply that the resolution adopted by the Ratepayers' Meeting obliged them to license all brothels. The SMC did leave a loophole, however: sing-song houses that did not operate as brothels would not be required to conform to the regulations.[45] Here legal necessity reinforced tradition in encouraging the courtesans to downplay the sale of their sexual services.[46]

The licensing procedure generated a new set of encounters between brothels and the police. A detective team of one Chinese and one Westerner patrolled the brothels to make sure that each had obtained a license and was displaying it prominently. Unlicensed operators were taken to the Mixed Court, where they could be fined as much as fifty yuan or jailed for six weeks, while those who failed to display their licenses were assessed smaller penalties. Licenses were not supposed to be transferable, and owners who obtained them improperly were fined and their licenses revoked. Brothel owners who employed unlicensed prostitutes were penalized, as were the individual women. Violations of multiple regulations sometimes led to jail sentences of as long as one year for owners. Frightened, some brothel owners took pains to conceal evidence of license violations such as keeping young girls or opium implements on the premises.[47] Others sought patrons who could provide protection from the authorities, in the process making themselves vulnerable to fraud. *Shenbao* reported several cases in which Chinese men were sentenced to a year in prison for posing as government officials. These scam artists offered to "help" prostitutes regain their licenses or to bribe the police in return for a hefty protection fee.[48]

Still other owners moved their establishments to the French Concession or the Zhabei district in Chinese territory, where they made it known to municipal authorities that they were willing to pay taxes if allowed to operate.[49] Individual prostitutes whose houses had been closed developed their own subterfuges, as a Chinese guidebook to the brothels explained in 1922:

> Even though there is only one name on the sign [outside a brothel], inside there is not just one prostitute. Those whose licenses have been withdrawn still operate, writing their names on a piece of red paper that is stuck on the door at dusk so that seekers can find it. It is taken down during the night and put up again the next day. Also, guests do not stay in the brothel; instead they rent a room. So although the police strictly inspect, they cannot easily discover the secret.[50]

Finally, many brothels went underground in the International Settlement, continuing to operate without licenses. Ningbo prostitutes in Shanghai began to operate out of hotels.[51] One group of courtesans formed a secret operation to sell sexual services out of unlicensed "salt-pork shops."[52] Unlicensed brothels began to use male pimps or rickshaw pullers to solicit customers for them, in order not to call attention to their operations.[53]

In December 1920, after they had been duly licensed, the phased closing of brothels began with the first drawing of licenses. The brothels whose numbers were drawn, 174 in all, were required to close their doors by the end of March 1921.[54] Similar drawings took place every year until 1923.[55] In April 1924, it was announced that the remainder of licensed brothels were to be closed on December 31, 1924.[56]

The advocates of suppression thus had triumphed, but the controversy did not end there. Throughout the campaign, the Moral Welfare League continued to act as a self-appointed watchdog over the resolution's implementation,[57] and to quarrel publicly with the formulations of the SMC about the success of the new policy. In the 1921 Municipal Report, for instance, the commissioner of police stated that the SMC's predictions about the failure of the policy had become fact: "[W]hile 218 brothels have been closed officially, prostitution and its attendant evils have in no way decreased, but have merely spread over a much wider area with the consequent impossibility of any effective police control." When questioned by an indignant Frank Rawlinson of the Moral Welfare League, an SMC official wearily replied that "police reports show that while brothels officially closed, remain closed, it is nevertheless a fact that the former occupants, having no other means of earning a living, continue a life of prostitution in private houses, where they are in no sense subject to police control."[58]

This exchange was the beginning of another acrimonious round of public debate. After Rawlinson repeatedly inquired as to what the police were doing to enforce a rigorous policy of suppression, an SMC official finally chided him publicly. Police could not take action against unlicensed prostitutes, he said, unless they were practicing in an unlicensed brothel, since prostitution itself was not illegal. "Much as the Council is in sympathy with the aims of your League, as with every other effort to promote the moral welfare of the Settlement," he continued testily,

> it is of opinion [*sic*] that, easy as it is for the Moral Welfare League and others to advocate a more rigorous policy of suppression, it is in fact practically impossible to do more than is being done at present. That your League should hold a contrary view and consider more effective suppression possible, can, in the Council's opinion, be only attributed to your League's refusal to face the real facts of the case, and to the apparent confusion existing in the minds of its members regarding brothel-keeping, which, if not under license, is an offense under a Municipal By-law, as distinguished from prostitution, which is no offence.[59]

Angry letters continued throughout the summer of 1922, with some citizens expressing approval of the Moral Welfare approach to prostitution and others criticizing its inadequacies. The *North-China Herald* was generally unsympathetic to the methods of the league, arguing that its members were not realistic about the limitations of colonial influence:

> [W]hat end can Dr. Rawlinson hope to achieve by shutting up the houses and driving their inmates over the borders of the Settlement? . . . [I]t must be remembered that Shanghai is a town chiefly filled by Asiatics whose view of these questions is quite different to ours, with the further complication of a large influx of unhappy Russian girls, who have but the one alternative to starvation. . . . [A] very comprehensive, liberal and merciful scheme of rescue work would seem indispensable before we set the terrors of the law in motion against them.[60]

In another editorial it added that the league's approach, in addition to being narrow and inhumane, was ineffective:

> [T]he plain fact of the matter is that the women are to be found in all sorts of streets where they were previously unknown. . . . So far from these women being made more inaccessible, they are more easily found than before. There is the less distance to go to find them from any residential district.[61]

Perhaps in response to these criticisms, in late 1922 the Moral Welfare League began a project of direct social work. The program was more exhortatory than practical, however. It encouraged prostitutes who lost their licenses to go to the Door of Hope, find a job, stay with Christian families, and eventually get married. It also targeted the consumers of sexual services with a leaflet saying they should stay away from brothels, avoid summoning prostitutes out on call, refrain from contact with immoral women, and refuse to rent houses to brothels or other immoral businesses. The effect of these activities was not reported.[62]

Broadening its admonitions beyond the boundaries of the International Settlement, the league and its associates also petitioned He Fenglin, the military governor of Shanghai, about brothels in the area around North Sichuan Road known as the "Trenches." Commending him for taking "official action in regard to dives and brothels in various parts of the city outside of the settlement limits," the letter requested that he permanently close these establishments, all of them owned by foreigners. Noting that many Chinese schoolchildren passed through the area each day, the letter warned, "These saloons are subversive of morality and stimulants to evil living, and act as a powerful means of education on this large body of growing youth." And in an unusual attempt at alliance making, the missionaries suggested to the warlord that the disreputable foreigners who patronized these places set a "dangerous example" of lawlessness for the Chinese population: "Prostitutes at times openly ply their trade on these public roads. In short, these dens continually disturb the peace and are a constant menace to good government, morals and life."[63] Social order in a healthy Chinese nation, the letter implied, required the abolition of commercialized sex. But the call for reform was not taken up by He Fenglin, and the abolition effort remained confined to the International Settlement.

Although some members of the league began to express doubts about the policy's effectiveness, the leadership of the league continued to defend its approach, and to dispute the assumption that prostitution was a necessary evil, bolstered by economic necessity and male desire. When one *North-China Herald* reporter argued as much, Isaac Mason retorted:

> Does your correspondent really believe that a large number of girls are of necessity doomed by a beneficent God to be sacrificed to the ungoverned lust of men in return for money to maintain an existence? That such girls, through no fault of their own, are born into a wheel of fate, and their sacrifice is necessary because of men's desire? . . . And if such a thing is thinkable, how are these girls—this maiden tribute—to be provided? . . . To call passion an "unconquerable" physical requirement is to forget the great numbers of both men and women who daily conquer, and who live chaste lives; such language only serves to encourage those who are glad of an excuse to take the easier path. . . . These diseases are the consequence of wrong-doing, and are not to be charged to those who wish to preserve a moral conscience and the decencies of civilization.[64]

Impassioned as Mason's rhetoric on this subject was, it paled beside that of one of his supporters, who wrote from the upriver town of Jiujiang:

> For good and righteous cause did the Creator put the barbed wire of abominable disease around the whole neighborhood of sexual crime, and so firmly secure it there that no device of regulation, registration, inspection, or medical treatment can pull out the stakes, and secure immunity to the trespasser. . . . The averment of your correspondent that prostitution is a necessary evil is a public insult to all decent men and women; and men who practise it are a shame and a stinking cancer on the British name in the East. The dogma is *pestilential,* and ought to be stamped out like the plague.[65]

In spite of the fervent sentiments of these gentlemen, licensed and unlicensed prostitution persisted long after their official demise. Chinese-language guidebooks and memoirs confirmed that, just as the critics had predicted, many brothels moved to the French Concession[66] or to streets in the Chinese-controlled area that bordered the International Settlement.[67]

Fifteen years later, a Chinese writer looked back and deplored the 1920 measures. "Drawing lots or expulsion are just means of 'treating your neighbor like a gutter,'" she argued, adding that when the International Settlement banned prostitution, the French Concession "hurriedly pulled on its slippers and extended a welcome." The bustling streets in the International Settlement changed from an area where the "cars were like flowing water and the horses like dragons" to one that was desolate, while the Nanyang Qiao area in the French Concession went from a "desert" to a fertile region. "In the end," the author sardonically concluded, "Mr. Morality could not triumph over Brother Cash."[68]

At the time, however, Isaac Mason of the Moral Welfare League shrugged off the move of prostitutes out of the Settlement, saying that Chinese who were disturbed about the movement into Chinese territory should try to improve conditions there. Asserting that there was no definite proof that conditions had gotten worse in neighboring territories, he concluded: "Over 90 per cent of Shanghai's prostitutes are Chinese, and practically all who move into Chinese territory as well as their patrons, are subject to Chinese law, so that is the natural place for them."[69]

Elsewhere Mason argued, by this time virtually a lone voice, that the campaign had been partially successful at stopping solicitation. He wrote in 1924:

> [P]rostitution is making less show on the streets now than it did five years ago. Conditions are totally changed in Nanking and Foochow Roads. . . .
> Over 95 per cent of our problem is Chinese, and among these, vice is much less flaunted than it used to be; the brothels are fewer, the streets show less exhibition of girls, and in fact vice now has to be sought instead of its hitting the eye every evening as one went through the city. I consider this a gain to "public morality" even if private vice remained the same.[70]

Yet according to other foreign descriptions, the abolition campaign did nothing to stop street soliciting, either. Pheasants who continued to operate illegally in the International Settlement sought the shelter of the French Concession on a daily basis:

> Donning their best paint, powder and clothes, the Chinese girls took to the streets by the hundreds. They did not rely on beauty and charm exclusively or even on slim silken legs revealed by gowns slit almost to the thigh. Congregating in bunches, they grabbed customers with the Chinese equivalent of an American football tackle. Kidnapped bedfellows were taken to small hotels around the corner. When the police appeared along the International Settlement side of Avenue Edward VII, their favorite hunting ground, the girls ran across the street into the more broad-minded French Concession until the patrol, making a pretense of duty, had passed.[71]

A blunt critique of the license-and-eliminate scheme was proffered by A. Hilton Johnson, deputy commissioner of police. "Brothels in the strictly legal sense" were fast disappearing, he said, "[b]ut if the aim of the Council was the abolition of *prostitutes* or the suppression of *prostitution* or the improvement of *public morality*, then, of course, the measures adopted by them at the instance of the Rate-payers have been a failure" (emphasis in original). Twenty of his senior police officers reported that prostitution had spread out of the former brothel districts over a wider area of the International Settlement. Solicitation in public parks and amusement places had greatly increased, with former "crudely aggressive tactics" replaced by "the 'glad-eye' method of attraction." Hotels, lodging houses, and secret houses of assignation had largely replaced the brothels, while "chauffeurs, ricksha coolies, hotel boys, lodging house employes, professional pimps and others" now enjoyed the profits formerly collected by brothel keepers. From a police point of view, he concluded, conditions were both better and worse: better because the decline of brothel districts meant less "street rowdyism," worse because no brothels meant the disappearance of news centers where police could get information.[72]

Foreign residents of Shanghai added their voices to the chorus of criticism, noting that the demise of the brothels and the increase in unlicensed prostitution presented both police and citizens with a problem. One letter to the *North-China Herald* complained, "The serio-comical situation in the International Settlement of Shanghai to-day is that prostitution cannot be driven from the streets, because the police are afraid of making a mistake and insulting a decent woman, while decent women avoid being out after dark fearing to be taken for prostitutes."[73] Continuing the rhetorical linkage of prostitution with dirt, another dissatisfied writer declared about the league:

> [T]he moral turpitude that was confined and so more under control, has been by their efforts, released from control, and now pollutes the atmos-

phere. They have done their sweeping with a dirty broom where they should
have used the latest scientific method, a suction sweeper."[74]

A third writer accused the league of "trying to drain a ditch with a sieve,"
while a Chinese observer preferred a metaphor rooted in local geography,
saying that the league's "chances of success are equal to that of anyone who
might try to mop up the Huangpu river with a bath sponge."[75]

In the International Settlement, courtesan houses were effectively rele-
galized by 1924, apparently in response to pressure from local merchants.
After several months of rumors, in June the SMC announced that courtesan
houses would be permitted to operate, "bringing to an end," as a women's
magazine disapprovingly commented, "the earthshaking enterprise of banning prostitution in the concession."[76] A 1924 addendum to the International
Settlement tax and licensing regulations laid out the procedures for proper
licensing of courtesan houses. Such houses were explicitly prohibited as sites
of sexual activity, drug use, gambling, or political meetings. Permissible activities were limited to singing, storytelling, and drinking with meals. Even
the required wattage of the lights was stipulated, in order to eliminate dim
corners where inappropriate encounters might transpire. The names of
women who assisted at drinking were to be registered on the license obtained
from the SMC. The regulations also reiterated the prohibition on permitting girls under the age of fifteen to stay in brothels of any type. These establishments were to be taxed at the rate of ten yuan per season.[77] Thus, although the government declared an end to brothels when the last licenses
were withdrawn in 1924, it collected revenue from licensing fees in a new
category, "sing-song [courtesan] houses."[78] Plainclothes detectives visited
such houses periodically to fine courtesans who were caught spending the
night with their customers.[79]

Courtesan houses were thus effectively removed as a target of abolition.
Meanwhile, much commercial sexual activity moved out of brothels and into
hotels. Regulation followed in its wake. In the International Settlement and
the French Concession, hotel owners became liable to fines for allowing unlicensed prostitutes to use the facilities, failing to register the names of customers, or actually hiring prostitutes to solicit customers and bring them to
the hotel.[80] In one such case heard by the Mixed Court in 1923 and reported
in the *North-China Herald*, Subinspector Moore testified that he found men
and women together gambling in a hotel. The foreign defense lawyer argued
that hotel keepers could not control such behavior, but the Chinese magistrate replied that

it was a bad custom which must be stopped. . . . There need not have been
actual prostitution—but men and women could not have been together in
the hotel at that time of the night, i.e., after 10 o'clock for a purpose that
was honourable. The practice was against the morals and customs of both

the Chinese and foreigners, and it was the intention of the Court to put a stop to it.

The hotel keeper in this case was fined thirty dollars.[81] In the Chinese-controlled city, 1927 police regulations threatened to suspend licenses of hotels that permitted "immoral activities," and explicitly prohibited hotel guests from inviting prostitutes to drink or spend the night, playing with prostitutes, taking opium, and gambling.[82]

Arrests for street soliciting varied from year to year, but showed no pattern of decrease after 1920. (Nor was there a massive increase, as some critics had predicted, at least until the onset of the 1930s depression.) To these arrests of individual prostitutes were added the cases of brothels that failed to obtain licenses or continued to operate after they were withdrawn.[83] The enforcement of licensing regulations had the effect of creating new classes of offenders: unlicensed brothels, unlicensed prostitutes, permissive hotel proprietors. As the campaign eliminated legally licensed prostitutes, the group of violators grew.

Although the Moral Welfare League and the licensing controversy eventually faded from view, later observers judged the league's approach ineffective both in controlling sexually transmitted disease and in eliminating prostitution. Physicians rejected government regulation as an effective approach to the problem, seeking instead to place emphasis on medical and public-health measures. In the process, they promoted detached, scientific authority (their own) as superior to moral and religious authority. Although the physicians of the Shanghai Medical Society in 1923 wrote that they preferred regulated districts to "indiscriminate promiscuity," a survey of the local situation convinced them that regulation had failed, and that "no appreciable good would be got by a superintendence of prostitution even with a much larger and more expensive organization than heretofore, particularly as the local circumstances are entirely unfavourable for success." A comprehensive approach to prostitution, they asserted, would have to involve preventive and rescue work, the improvement of employment opportunities and working conditions for women, and efforts to make prostitution less profitable.[84] Echoing this opinion, a Chinese commentator advised lawmakers to be realistic and concentrate on a medical commission that "will achieve a greater measure of real good and not work untold hardships on prostitutes; privations these poor unfortunate girls have suffered in the past at the hands of the League, the result of hounding and merciless persecution." Proposing a focus on sexually transmitted diseases, he concluded, "If we can't have a moral community, let us have a clean one."[85] Predictably, the activists of the Moral Welfare League were unconvinced of the superiority of this approach. Where Jesus said, "Go, and sin no more," commented Isaac Mason, "the voice of today seem [sic] disposed to say 'go, and be more hygienic next time, and patronize a well-conducted place.'"[86]

Ultimately, this campaign to end prostitution, like every other campaign until 1949, fell victim to a combination of factors: a weak municipal government with limited jurisdiction, a refusal to acknowledge the many vested interests that benefited from prostitution, and an inability to develop a comprehensive welfare program that could address the social causes of prostitution. In addition, the 1920 campaign was hampered by divisions in the foreign community over the most effective and the most moral strategy to pursue. Although the debate generated a great deal of heat in the foreign press, its effect on Chinese prostitutes and their clientele was minimal. And in spite of the Moral Welfare League's expressed concern about the status of women, the campaign did nothing to increase the degree of control that Shanghai prostitutes exercised over their own lives. In fact, Chinese prostitutes remained virtually invisible in the reform discourse of the 1920s; the debate was not really about them, but about the intersection of "commercialized vice" and colonial "uncleanliness" that so threatened Victorians abroad.

Abolitionist Reprise: The 1928 Ban

In 1928, the newly established Nanjing government of Jiang Jieshi (Chiang Kai-shek) banned prostitution in the cities of Jiangsu, Zhejiang, and Anhui provinces. In Nanjing, a mayoral decree in fall 1928 ended the taxation of prostitution, ordering prostitutes to change profession immediately or be driven out of the city. Several organizations were directed to take up welfare work on behalf of the displaced prostitutes. The city of Zhenjiang followed suit, and by the spring of 1929 Suzhou had banned prostitution as well. The ban, which was locally enforced by the municipal administrations, was less than completely effective, and prostitutes continued to operate illegally.[87] Nevertheless, reports circulated of prostitutes and customers being arrested in Nanjing and Zhenjiang. Conditions of detention for prostitutes in Zhenjiang were said to be particularly brutal, with food supplies so scarce that some women died from malnutrition.[88] In this uncertain environment, prostitutes of all ranks from these cities elected to move to Shanghai, particularly the International Settlement.[89] Among the displaced were some of Nanjing's most famous courtesans, whose romances with Shanghai officials were duly reported in tabloid gossip columns.[90]

The 1928 ban in the cities of the interior was quite possibly on the minds of Shanghai courtesans in early 1929, when the tabloids reported that the Jiangsu Stamp Tax Bureau, under the Nanjing Ministry of Finance, was preparing to levy a new tax on houses of entertainment. Courtesan houses in the foreign concessions were not under the authority of the provincial government, and each licensed courtesan was already paying twenty yuan in licensing fees each quarter to the SMC. Nevertheless, the provincial authorities saw an opportunity to collect revenue by charging courtesans one jiao (one-tenth of a yuan) for each call ticket they received. Since popular prostitutes made anywhere from several hundred to one thousand calls in a season, and worked three seasons per year, the tax would have been much more than the amount they were paying to the concession government.

Initially the provincial Stamp Tax Bureau used persuasion rather than coercion. Setting up a sales bureau in a Buddhist temple, officials announced that each courtesan should come to the bureau and pay three to five yuan every month in return for having her call tickets stamped. Courtesans were classified as *changsan shuyu, yao er,* or foreigners. Madams and courtesans who visited the sales office, often stopping first to burn incense at the temple, met an affable bureaucrat from the Stamp Tax Bureau who lectured them about the duty of citizens to support the government.

The taxation scheme was not without its flaws. The Settlement police were suspicious at first, and several tax collectors were actually arrested at a courtesan house in Huile Li as they were attempting to collect money. An official identified as Vice–Bureau Chief Guan subsequently secured cooperation from the Settlement authorities, but the ultimate success of this taxation scheme was not reported. The tabloids did suggest, however, that courtesans were willing to cooperate, even in the absence of any effective enforcement, because they did not want their activities banned in Shanghai as they had been in other cities.[91] The taxation scheme remained an ineffective aberration, a feeble attempt to assert Chinese authority over commerce conducted in foreign areas, taken seriously by brothel owners only because another branch of the same Chinese government was prohibiting prostitution altogether. As for the upriver ban on prostitution, it was also a failure, lifted in Nanjing and Suzhou in the mid-1930s over the vociferous protests of women's groups.[92]

REGULATIONIST NIGHTMARES, 1945–1948

From August 1945 to May 1949, for the first time in more than a century, the entire city of Shanghai was governed by a single municipal administration under Chinese control.[93] The new government spoke in the language of national reconstruction and renewal, expressing a desire to cleanse an urban landscape sullied by many years of occupation and war. For these urban planners, a rational, healthy city did not require that prostitution be immediately eliminated. While regarding abolition as a desirable goal, they portrayed themselves as pragmatic men who believed that postwar economic conditions necessitated the continued existence of prostitutes and brothels. Rather than expending their energies on what they felt would be a futile and unenforceable ban, they devised an elaborate scheme to register, license, and inspect prostitutes, while strictly limiting the geographical area in which they could operate. They brought brothel hiring arrangements formally under the rubric of labor relations by attempting to regulate the pay arrangements and working conditions in brothels, much as in any other workplace. Finally, they sought to control the proliferation of unlicensed prostitution by stepping up arrests for soliciting and by regulating ancillary occupations such as taxi dancing, massage, and working for guide agencies. This approach to prostitution represented the triumph of the regulationist rationale—and, after more than three years of effort, became the clearest indication of its failure.

The Regulationist Rationale

In reports written in the first few months after Shanghai was returned to Chinese control, police chief Xuan Tiewu discussed the work of reestablishing order in Shanghai after the occupation. He listed the elimination of prostitution, opium, and gambling as the second most important task of the police force, preceded only by hunting down traitors and counterrevolutionaries (that is, Communists), and ahead of preventing theft and improving transportation. Like many other Chinese analysts, Xuan accused the Japanese-dominated occupation government of actively fostering opium, gambling, and prostitution as part of a "policy of spreading poison and rot." Continuing a long tradition of associating a discredited regime with immoral behavior, he charged that since November 1942, when the city government had lifted the ban on prostitution, "the decadent atmosphere reached its peak," allowing unlicensed prostitutes and every kind of "disguised prostitution" to flourish. Without offering specifics, he asserted that the number of prostitutes had greatly increased during the eight years of occupation. "Since this city has already been restored [guangfu]," Xuan continued, it was an urgent task to "reregulate prostitution and clean up the public atmosphere."

While immediately banning gambling and planning to eliminate all opium sales and addiction by June 1946, Xuan was unable to be so sanguine about a complete ban on prostitution. "Although the nation has adopted a system of an outright ban on prostitution," Xuan said, Shanghai, with its treaty-port history and dense population, was "in an exceptional situation." Instead of an immediate ban, the police proposed to experiment with a policy of licensed prostitutes in designated red-light districts under unified management by the police, accompanied by a strict ban on all disguised forms of prostitution.[94]

Police Chief Xuan elaborated this approach in a "plan for putting Shanghai prostitution in order" submitted to the mayor in October 1945, accompanied by provisional regulations for managing prostitutes. The plan was based on three principles: licensing the unlicensed (*hua si wei gong*), simplifying the complicated (*hua fan wei jian*), and collecting the scattered (*hua ling wei zheng*). Brothels and prostitutes alike were to be licensed, while unlicensed prostitution was to be strictly banned.[95] Brothel owners were required to apply to the police for a license, providing rental or property-tax documents, a guarantor's letter, and a photograph. The application was also to specify the number, names, ages, native places, and residences of all prostitutes in the brothel. Brothel licenses were not transferable. In order to prevent the spread of disease, each room was supposed to have disinfection facilities, and customers were to be required to use condoms; prostitutes were instructed to refuse to sleep with any man who did not comply. Women under the age of eighteen were banned from brothels, as were customers under the age of twenty. The regulations even stipulated the type of lamp to be hung in the brothel door. Brothel owners were told that they could not mistreat prostitutes, or force women who were ill, more than four months pregnant, or less than three months postpartum to work. Soliciting was forbidden, either by prostitutes or by touts specifically hired for the purpose. Each prostitute was also required to obtain an individual license (the application was to be accompanied by six photographs), preceded by a physical examination. Licenses were good for one year. During that period the woman was expected to present herself for periodic health examinations.[96] The license fees proposed at the end of 1945 were steep (although inflation would soon make them seem negligible): five thousand yuan per brothel and five hundred yuan per prostitute.[97] Registration would also give the police a means of enforcing wage arrangements. Brothel owners who supplied room, board, and clothing were to be entitled to 30 percent of a prostitute's income.[98]

The principle of "simplifying the complicated" expressed Xuan's belief that the key to limiting prostitution lay in controlling the proliferation of its varieties. In a disgusted recapitulation of the hierarchy of prostitution, Xuan named *shuyu* and *changsan* courtesan houses; *yao er* brothels; Ningbo and Guangdong houses; and salt-pork, pheasant, *tangbai*, and foreign prostitution—with licensed and unlicensed subvarieties of each—not to mention guide agencies, massage bathhouses, "glass cups," and other types of disguised sale of sex. The variety of prostitution, he argued, made it difficult to manage. In a striking statement of faith that a "rectification of names" would lead to an ordering of social life, he declared that all of these forms should be replaced by a single type of institution: the brothel. The number of brothels should be fixed at one thousand and the number of prostitutes at ten thousand, for a perfectly consistent bureaucratic average of ten prostitutes per brothel. (If more than one thousand people applied to open brothels, the police chief proposed drawing lots.) Xuan acknowledged that this would permit an increase over the licensed number of 902 establishments and 4,982 employees recorded by the occupation regime. Nevertheless, he argued, the increase would be offset by a decrease in the numbers of unlicensed, diseased, and otherwise sub-standard prostitutes, for whom government relief and retraining would have to be provided.[99]

"Collecting the scattered" was likewise intended to bring rational order to a chaotic situation in which brothels were distributed throughout the city and prostitutes walked any street they pleased soliciting customers. In order to rid the central districts of prostitution, Xuan proposed that Tilan Qiao and two other areas be designated special prostitution districts. His proposal also stipulated that prostitutes could conduct business only in the brothels, and could not solicit customers outside, urge them to drink in restaurants, or spend the night with them in hotels.[100]

Citizen Complaints

If intricacy of procedures had been an indicator of a tightly woven net of official control, Shanghai's prostitutes would have been caught in a fine mesh indeed. But the campaign to regulate prostitution soon became mired in bureaucratic indecision and fiscal neglect. Prostitutes were initially instructed to register by the end of 1946.[101] In April 1946, months after Police Chief Xuan's initial proposals, the administration held a meeting to discuss regulation, with representatives from the police and the bureaus of health, social affairs, and engineering. They designated North Sichuan Road and several other areas as red-light districts, and divided up responsibility: the engineers were to build the brothels; the Health Bureau, to examine the prostitutes; the police, to issue permits and enforce regulations; and the Social Affairs Bureau, to provide relief to prostitutes who drew lots to give up the work.[102] In June 1946 the city government announced that it would concentrate on licensing the unlicensed, but would not yet try to limit the number of prostitutes.[103]

Frustrated with the slow pace of implementation, Police Chief Xuan petitioned the mayor for a citywide meeting of concerned bureaus, women's organizations in Shanghai, female senate members, and relief organizations, in order to discuss prostitution. But the city government turned him down, saying that measures for forbidding prostitution could be divided into three steps: licensing the unlicensed, collecting the dispersed, and banning in successive batches. Rejecting a broader approach based on mass mobilization, the city government directed police to carry out this narrower mandate.[104]

By the end of summer 1946, important aspects of the program had stalled. The draft regulations proposed by Xuan almost a year earlier had yet to be promulgated; revisions went back and forth between the police chief and the mayor.[105] The Social Affairs Bureau announced that it was still having trouble establishing a relief organization for prostitutes.[106] Meanwhile, daily police encounters with prostitutes were driven not by the police chief's expansive vision, but by secret letters of complaint written by angry urban residents about the disruption caused by unlicensed brothels. Many letters denounced the brothel owners—most of whom seem to have been male—as arrogant, rude, and in cahoots with local hoodlums.[107] Typically, in such cases the police would either close the brothel down or require the operator to purchase a license, sometimes detaining the owner and prostitutes for a week or less.[108]

Some of these letters criticized the police for insufficient efforts to close the brothels down. One group of residents wrote:

> We, the residents of lane #35 and #57 (Hongxiang Li), Xinzhalu, all live and work in peace, and have never interfered with anyone else. The low-class licensed and unlicensed prostitutes in these lanes have gradually increased, and six to seven establishments make a living this way. More than one hundred people are involved in this. Every afternoon from 6 o'clock until 3 o'clock the next morning, they walk the street and solicit customers, even hitting and cursing in order to get customers. They make noise all night long. They have no shame. They disturb the peace and cause the neighbors to be unable to live peacefully. The customers bang on the doors and mistake respectable people for prostitutes. . . . Activities like this poison the moral atmosphere and disturb the peace. Yet the Changsha Road police station responsible for this area surprisingly turns a blind eye.[109]

In another case of alleged police malfeasance, the citizen whistle-blower skillfully contrasted the figure of the powerless prostitute with the allied might of the brothel owners and police:

> I am reporting that the residents downstairs are operating an unlicensed brothel in order to service the Allied army. . . . The most detestable thing is that the policemen of our police department repeatedly come to take bribes. [The women] are often insulted and they kneel and beg before [the owners] will let them go. . . . This group of innocent girls doesn't dare to resist. The prostitutes will have to live in this hell without seeing the light of day forever. The above is the truth that I myself have seen and heard.

A week later the same resident wrote to Police Chief Xuan again, alleging that the local patrolman had reluctantly pulled the brothel owner out from under his bed and taken him to the police station, along with his concubine and three prostitutes, but that the owner had bailed or bribed himself out after one hour and returned to brag to the neighbors about it.[110]

Many of these citizens presented themselves as concerned not only with local order, but also with China's national health and morality. They called upon the police to defend Chinese values against those whose behavior brought disgrace to the nation. One man wrote to the mayor with particular vehemence in November 1946:

Prostitution is an insect eating at the social fabric, and the origin of evil. If prostitution is not stopped, it will only add to the evil of the urban district. Today, when we speak of democracy and humanity, we cannot permit the existence of prostitution, because everyone has individual freedom. Prostitutes are mostly women of good families. Some have been sold, some kidnapped. As soon as they enter the brothel, they sink permanently into a bitter sea, are trampled upon daily, and cannot pull themselves out. Alas! There is nothing more cruel than this under heaven. I hope that Your Excellency can keep pity in your heart, and resolutely liberate them like the American President Lincoln freed the black slaves, causing them to stand on their own and enter the correct path.[111]

Continuing the linkage of prostitution with threats to the health of the nation, some letter writers denounced brothel keepers for having collaborated with the Japanese:

I have secretly investigated the fact that the hoodlum Zeng Guozhu and others are running an unlicensed brothel at 38 Qiujiang Zhilu [branch road]. Furthermore, during the occupation the brothel boss took the enemy as his father, sold out the motherland, became a helper to the tiger, took city people as his fish and meat, and swore allegiance to Sheng, the interpreter for the enemy police of Zhabei subdistrict, acted as a fox borrowing the tiger's powers, and depended on his power to trick people. There was nothing evil he didn't do. After the surrender, he [and his cronies] disappeared for a time. Then they reappeared. Not only did they formally announce that they had opened an unlicensed brothel, but now they are operating exactly as they did during the occupation. . . . At this time of instability in our country, they should be closed down.[112]

The more common complaint in these letters from citizens, however, was that unlicensed brothels created a disturbance in the course of servicing American soldiers stationed in Shanghai. Noise and street brawls were mentioned in every letter:

After the victory the Allied army arrived in Shanghai, and Tang suddenly indulged in the wildest fantasy and decided to open a small-scale brothel in his house in order to service the Allied army and make a big profit. He hired unlicensed prostitutes and a large group of hoodlums to go to every street and solicit Allied soldiers, so his sex business flourished. Sometimes there weren't enough prostitutes and he had to hire people from other places to supplement them. In the middle of the night they disturbed the peace. They filled the lane with their noise. Most of the Allied soldiers were drunk, and after they sought pleasure and came out of the room, they would bang on the doors of the other residents. The residents were disturbed, afraid, and angry. Their voices carried outside the building, they didn't close the doors or windows, to the point where naughty children in the lane went to sneak a look at the scene. Morality degenerated because of this. National decency and social peace were all ruined.[113]

There were darker hints as well of sexual depredation and national disgrace. "One woman receives eight people. This is against human morals," intoned one writer, while another worried:

> Every day they go to the American fleet to sell sex and dancing to the American soldiers. Their strange ways of selling sex are difficult for decent women to behold. Aside from hurting the morality of our nation, it disturbs the peace of the neighbors. They only want to sell sex to the Americans in order to make a profit, and they don't care about national morality and the fact that we will be laughed at by our allied nations. . . . If we don't secretly ask to ban and forbid them, how will our nation's morality be put in order?[114]

Sometimes the letter writers had reason to fear that the rapaciousness of drunken American soldiers would extend beyond prostitutes to their own wives and daughters. "After they are drunk they pay no attention to whether the women are prostitutes or ordinary women, but hug and kiss anyone they find in the lane," observed a neighbor of one establishment, while another reported:

> There is a brothel in my neighborhood at #480, with American soldiers upstairs. In the middle of the night there is often the sound of fighting and wild firing. Ai, isn't this a danger to life and limb? The last few days the American soldiers have not paid, and the prostitutes have all fled. The American soldiers have come to my house looking for prostitutes. My wife and daughter heard that they wanted women, feared for their own safety, and fled. I said [to the Americans] that this is not a brothel, there are no prostitutes here. The American soldiers beat me, and broke my pots, stools, and tables, demanding prostitutes. I was frightened all night long.[115]

In the case of one noisy brothel for American soldiers that closed down every time the police arrived only to reopen several days later, the neighbors complained so consistently that patrolmen from the Xincheng station eventually demolished the building, accompanied by members of the American military police.[116] In all these cases, citizens linked their own immediate living environments to the health and strength of the Chinese nation, calling upon the police to act as national guardians. Controlling prostitution had become, at least in the minds of a vocal segment of the public, a test of competent government. Yet the police effort to assert control over the city's sex trades remained inconsistent and faltering.

Stalled Enforcement

Even as they attempted to implement their ambitious licensing plan, the police apparently flirted with an alternative approach to regulating prostitution. A group of men, headed by one Hui Genquan, at the end of 1945 had petitioned the police to establish a Shanghai Prostitutes' Association (*Shang-*

hai shi huanü lianyihui). The petitioners, all middle-aged white-collar workers or minor Guomindang functionaries, stated that they had run a similar organization in occupied Shanghai. They submitted their organizational charter to the police, proposing a guild organization that would help brothel owners to undertake tasks including medical treatment, burial, dispute resolution, financial assistance, and cooperation with the police. In early 1946 they asked that the city government subsidize their organizational expenses until such time as they won approval (from the same government) to formally establish themselves and collect dues from the membership.

After six months of inaction on the part of the police, Hui Genquan wrote again, plaintively noting that he was funding the organization out of his own pocket and earnestly offering "to help the government clean up bad elements, and redress all matters having to do with the improvement of brothel owners and prostitutes." Some in the police department apparently thought that a guild of brothel owners could be helpful, and in August the police wrote a letter supporting Hui's organization to the Social Affairs Bureau. More than a month later the Social Affairs Bureau sharply rebuffed the request, reproving the police:

> Selling sex is an improper occupation, and the government has not yet
> finished eliminating it, because there were no other options. If you approve
> their organizing a legal association, there is no difference between that and
> preserving their legal status. If the objective is to improve their livelihood, it
> seems that you should take charge of this, calling together the organizations
> and groups concerned with this problem, such as the municipal party orga
> nization, city government, Health Bureau, Social Affairs Bureau, Women's
> Association, and so forth, to together discuss the establishment of a supple
> mental organization to aid in the improvement of the lives of prostitutes,
> with subgroups for each grade of prostitute, to be taken charge of by people
> in that occupation. As soon as the environment improves and there is no
> need for such an organization, it should be ordered to disband.

The police dutifully called a meeting of all the groups named in this letter. On October 1, 1946, the groups decided that a prostitute organization had no legal basis and would make it even harder to abolish prostitution later. In its stead they proposed that prostitutes be permitted to form mutual help groups, since national laws did not permit prostitutes to establish longer-term organizations. Hui Genquan received an official letter of refusal in November 1946, but nothing more was ever heard of the proposed mutual help groups.[117] Regulation with an eye toward elimination remained the official agenda, even as its implementation foundered.

The project of inspecting prostitutes for disease also progressed unevenly. As soon as prostitutes began to register in 1946, some of them were given physical examinations; 85 percent of the first group were found to be suffering from syphilis or gonorrhea. A news report quoted the chief examiner as stating that actual rates were probably even higher, but that some prostitutes, desperate to obtain licenses, disguised their symptoms by taking injections or washing with medicinal liquid just prior to the examination. Penicillin, the report added, could effect a cure within a week, but its price rendered it inaccessible, while even neosalvarsan ("914") was prohibitively expensive.[118] Police Chief Xuan had earlier proposed that the Health Bureau send mobile medical teams to each brothel to give compulsory treatment for sexually transmitted diseases, but in August the Health Bureau announced that the project would be delayed because of personnel and money shortages.[119] By December, health officials ventured a sobering assessment of the work against STDs. More than 60 percent of the city's prostitutes had syphilis, a Health Bureau report said, but they could not afford to stop work for the twelve to eighteen months needed to complete a course of treatment. The report proposed relaxing the restrictions on diseased prostitutes to permit those with mild symptoms or those who had had more than sixteen injections of arsenic to continue work temporarily. The authors argued that this would make prostitutes more willing to submit to examination and treatment. At some unspecified future date, the report concluded, when supervision, social conditions, and treatment methods had improved, this measure could be eliminated.[120]

Meanwhile, concerned citizens began to hold the government responsible for the threat to public health represented by diseased prostitutes. Estimating that at least ten thousand licensed and unlicensed prostitutes were currently suffering from syphilis, a resident named Li Ping wrote to *Dagong bao* in 1946:

> These women infect men, and the latter infect their wives and children.
> The result is really a dangerous phenomenon that is terrible to consider.
> We want to ask, are the governmental authorities who keep order in this city
> going to manage to wipe out a serious disease like this that could destroy
> our nation? . . . This is a threat to the people of the whole city. We urgently
> hope that the government will engage in actual preventive work . . . not just
> go through the motions and waste the people's money.[121]

By the end of 1946 the mayor had decided to establish an Institute for the Prevention and Treatment of Sexually Transmitted Diseases, whose successful operation depended upon a veritable orgy of record keeping in several government departments. The police were to be responsible for the investigation, registration, and management of prostitutes, sending a list of registered prostitutes to the Health Bureau. The institute would then choose a day to examine prostitutes in a given establishment and have police order the women to come to the clinic. The clinic was to keep records on every prostitute inspected and issue each one an inspection certificate, which the prostitute needed to obtain a license from the police. Police were instructed to confiscate the licenses of diseased prostitutes, then order them to stop work and go for treatment. After treatment the prostitutes were to submit to re-examination, and upon being informed by the Health Bureau that they were cured, the police were to reissue their licenses. In addition to this daily exchange of records among government bureaus, the Health Bureau was to submit monthly reports to the police department, the police were to submit monthly reports to the Health Bureau on trends in prostitution, and the Health Bureau was to send a public-health nurse around to brothels, accompanied by a police officer, to interview, do propaganda, and check permits.[122]

This elaborate set of procedures bore little resemblance to the actual work of inspection and treatment. In the ten-month period from March to December 1946, city authorities gave one-time examinations to 3,550 prostitutes. Although the rules required monthly examinations, only 3 prostitutes in the entire city came close to meeting that requirement.[123] Women who did not pass the examinations often went on to work without licenses, thus removing themselves from the limited sphere of state regulation. Of the 1,310 prostitutes treated by the city in 1946, only 312 received a clean bill of health; 233 of them contracted another sexually transmitted disease while under treatment for the first one.[124] Medical professionals criticized the testing procedures as inadequate because they relied upon the Kahn but not the Wasserman test for syphilis, and a cervical smear but no bacterial culture for gonorrhea. Actual rates of disease, one doctor argued, were probably even higher than the recorded syphilis rate of almost 60 percent and the gonorrhea rate of 14 percent. As for the police requirement that customers wear condoms and prostitutes disinfect after each customer, enforcement was virtually nonexistent. Of 500 prostitutes surveyed in a 1948 study who had undergone government health examinations, 94 percent worked in brothels that did not provide such facilities, or else the women did not use them.[125] Xu Chongli, a college graduate in sociology at the Institute for the Prevention and Treatment of Sexually Transmitted Diseases who questioned the women at their monthly examinations, recalled in 1986 that public-health efforts were ineffective:

> The one or two conversations we had left no impression on them. They knew only that if they were not well, they should come in for a couple of injections, then come back for an examination.
> Some of the madams came with them. Sometimes the madam would bring in all the prostitutes in the brothel together. We didn't generally deal with the madam. Their attitude toward us was all right. When we examined the prostitutes, we called them individually into a small room, and talked casually with them. Some didn't understand why we were asking these questions. Some were not too willing to talk.
> Prostitutes with venereal disease did not necessarily stop entertaining

guests as the doctors instructed. We issued certificates and gave instructions, according to the rules, that she could not conduct business, because it could spread the disease. If she still did it, it might be discovered by the police. . . . But the police were possibly in league with the brothels and bosses. Just pass them some cash, and sick prostitutes could work as usual.

The name given to us by the Health Bureau was "Institute for the Prevention and Treatment of Sexually Transmitted Diseases." But we couldn't do a thorough job of prevention or treatment. When sick people came to the clinic, we always said, "You must do such and such, come to get injections." If she didn't come, we didn't go look for her.[126]

Police attempts to increase the rate of examination among prostitutes were not particularly successful. In 1948, police records show the central police station ordering branch stations to detain licensed prostitutes who failed to appear for exams and madams who conspired to keep their prostitutes from being examined. When the branch station received such notices, it was responsible for carrying out the sentences, filling in the forms, and returning them to the central police department. Typically, detentions were for one or two days; surviving records show eleven prostitutes and thirty madams or male brothel owners punished over a three-month period, a tiny percentage of the people involved in sex work.[127]

The campaign to "collect the scattered" brothels into designated red-light districts also encountered some snags. As of December 1946, 809 brothels scattered across all the districts of Shanghai had registered.[128] In January 1947 some indignant residents wrote to the mayor describing a brothel in their "clean residential district, right near a primary and a middle school":

The flock of these female devils is intolerable. All of the ugly forms of lovers' talk have appeared. They stand in lines by the door and tempt passersby, recruiting new customers, hoping that they will become guests at the brothel. This kind of person will take anyone as a "husband." Whether the men are old or young, all the women care about is whether they have money, and they have no shame. Therefore, the crazed bees and reckless butterflies come in groups like wild ducks. The sounds of joking and laughter can be heard in all directions, not just in the lane. Because of this, the residents are disturbed, and students entering and leaving find their eyes mesmerized and hearts confused. . . . Allowing a brothel to operate in this kind of residential district where there is also a school not only brings endless harm to the residents but also is a blot on the government.

The mayor obligingly ordered the brothel to move, only to be informed by Chief Xuan that it was in a designated red-light district, duly licensed, and had a separate entry sufficiently far from the schools. The mayor then withdrew his order, leaving the neighbors unsatisfied.[129] In the pattern of enforcement that emerged after the first flush of comprehensive planning, police periodically moved in to close down excessively noisy brothels in response to complaints from the neighbors.[130] This reactive policy was a far cry from the ambitious scheme of planned red-light districts envisioned by Chief Xuan.

Reeducating Women

Reviewing police work through August 1946, the city council praised the police for their progress in controlling prostitution but identified several key tasks as uncompleted. In addition to improving examination of prostitutes and sanitary facilities in brothels, and strictly banning soliciting, the most urgent piece of work, the council members felt, was the construction of a relief facility. There, they said, former prostitutes could be taught to sew, weave, embroider, type, and cook, learning skills that would allow them to make a living. At the same time, the council envisioned the facility as a place where women could learn to be "virtuous wives and good mothers," rather than dissipated individuals who knew only how to consume and not how to produce. Here in embryonic form was the reform program later implemented by the Communists, complete with the reinsertion of women into families.[131] All that was lacking was the organizational capability to implement it.

Responsibility for the long-delayed relief facility for prostitutes was finally assumed by the police, and the facility was opened with very little funding from the city. By September 1947 it had sixty-four inmates.[132] But in October 1947 a new police chief, Yu Shuping, reported to the mayor that the project was in trouble. His exasperated letter suggests the depth of resistance on the part of prostitutes to the city's regulation drive, noting that many unlicensed prostitutes had fled detention, or were bailed out by hoodlums and other troublemakers who posed as their relatives. Currently, he added,

> [i]n order to avoid trouble, the institute, before unlicensed prostitutes are sent there, is strictly limiting them. We have found that the facilities at this institute are rather simple and crude, and the surrounding environment is extremely bad. The women in the institute frequently collude with undesirable elements in the vicinity, waiting for a chance to flee. So the refusal of the institute to take in everybody has its reasons.[133]

The police and the Social Affairs Bureau proposed an ambitious new facility that could house two thousand women, but the records show no indication that this project was ever approved, much less begun, and well into 1948 police officials continued to complain that regulation was hamstrung by insufficient space to detain and reform prostitutes.[134]

Several years into the new regulatory regime, a conflict emerged between courtesans and the municipal government that echoed the protests of 1920. In mid-1948, a representative of the Association of Shanghai Shuyu wrote to the mayor requesting that *shuyu* courtesans be exempted from health examinations, since they "sold their mouths but not their bodies." To do otherwise, he argued, was to conflate them with low-class prostitutes, and thus indirectly to encourage them to sell sex. This petition was denied by the mayor on the advice of the police chief, who noted that *shuyu* courtesans did sell sexual services, protestations to the contrary notwithstanding. The barrier separating courtesans from common prostitutes, so assiduously maintained in the 1920 campaign, had disappeared.[135]

The hoped-for future of effective regulation continued to recede. The registration deadline for all prostitutes was extended, first to mid-1947, then to the end of the year.[136] By January 1948, 804 brothels and 5,638 prostitutes had registered.[137] Prostitution was clearly not on the wane; in the Hongkou district alone, the number of brothels had increased from about a dozen to sixty, and 401 prostitutes had registered. In addition, the district police station reported more than one hundred instances in which prostitutes had been arrested for operating without a license, operating in off-limits areas, or soliciting.[138] An article published in the journal *Shanghai Police* in 1948, grandiosely entitled "We Must Be Society's Doctors," named prostitution as one of the most intractable social ills. A thorough cure would require solving the problems of livelihood and occupation for these women, concluded the author; this was impossible under current circumstances.[139]

In March 1948, the police chief noted wearily that since registration had been formally completed, it was time to concentrate on "collecting the scattered." He proposed a much-diminished scheme in which first-class brothels would be strictly limited to Huile Li off Fuzhou Road and Chunyu Fang off Shantou Lu. Meanwhile, second- and third-class houses, which were "numerous, scattered, and not easy to collect in one district," should be eliminated by natural attrition. The city council voted to extend the registration period again, this time until the end of 1948.[140] In early 1949 Police Chief Yu petitioned for, and the mayor granted, another yearlong extension, on the grounds that because of the

> special environment of Shanghai, the large population, the social and economic circumstances not yet having turned for the better, the difficulty of a living, and the insufficiency of social relief organizations, if registration is stopped the number of unlicensed prostitutes will go up, and it will be difficult to eliminate them.[141]

In late May, well before this new extension ran out, Shanghai was taken by the Communists. According to Guomindang government materials preserved by the Communist administration, at that time 518 brothels and 3,505 prostitutes had been successfully licensed, a fraction of the people engaged in Shanghai's sex trades.[142]

Ancillary Agitation

The effort of the police to regulate brothels was accompanied by an attempt to assert control over the new venues in which prostitution was practiced.

Shortly after launching the 1945 initiative to rationalize and control prostitution, the police department also issued regulations aimed at the ancillary occupations of taxi dancers, singers, and hostesses in restaurants, coffee shops, bars, teahouses, and barbershops. A November 1945 government directive forbade the licensing of new dance halls, bars, or amusement halls.[143] In January 1946 new regulations stipulated that dancers, accompanied by their employers, were to come to the police station to obtain a license. (Chinese dancers had to provide three photographs of themselves; foreign dancers, four.) The dancer and employer were required to split the income from dance tickets in a seventy-thirty arrangement. The licensing fee was set at one thousand yuan for a six-month period. Licenses were to be denied to women who were under the age of sixteen; were not in good health; had been sold, kidnapped, or forced to become dancers; or lacked the proper citizenship documentation. Dancers were to carry their license and badge while working, remain in the dance hall, and refrain from exhibiting "attitudes and actions that offend morality." The regulations for singers and hostesses were virtually identical.[144] Not all ancillary occupations received the blessing of regulation, however; in December 1945, the mayor approved a recommendation to ban massage parlors and guide agencies, which the police chief said were "run by social degenerates who deeply damage public morals."[145] An additional motivation appears to have been pressure from the American army, which was concerned that more than sixty of its soldiers per week were contracting sexually transmitted diseases.[146]

This prohibition called forth an immediate response from the almost three thousand employees of the guide agencies, who planned a demonstration at the headquarters of the city government on January 4, 1946. Learning of the demonstration plans, the authorities called together the guide-agency managers and told them that they would be permitted to reclassify themselves as brothels, register with the police, and continue operation. Masseuses were to be similarly treated.[147] In granting this request, apparently because it would allow for health inspection of the women, the municipal government effectively acknowledged that the agencies and massage parlors provided sexual services and should be regulated accordingly. Apparently this classificatory legerdemain did not satisfy everyone, however. After guide agencies were officially shut down, the guides continued to work out of bars and hotels.[148] Massage bathhouses petitioned the city government to change their names to Turkish baths and remain open; guide agencies asked to rename themselves music and book houses. Both requests were denied.[149] Rather than being formally designated as prostitutes, however, many guides and masseuses came forward to register as taxi dancers; by early February 1946, 1,759 dancers had been licensed.[150] But in the wake of reports that dance-hall owners were continuing to exploit taxi dancers, requiring them to buy three thousand yuan's worth of dance tickets each day and to present the owners with periodic gifts, the city government threatened to prohibit taxi dancing altogether.[151]

In September 1947, the Administrative Branch of the national government banned commercial dance halls as an austerity measure, ordering them to close by the end of the month.[152] (It was considered inappropriate for people in the cities to engage in such activities at the height of a civil war.) Bars and coffee shops that employed dancers were also included in the ban. The Shanghai government moved reluctantly to implement the measure, since it feared that the closure of the city's twenty-nine dance halls would throw many people out of work.[153] Although it immediately banned new dance halls, with respect to existing establishments it decided on the (by then) time-honored method of drawing lots, this time once a month, and withdrawing licenses over a six-month period. It proposed additionally to convert the dance halls into cafeterias, to be staffed by the former taxi dancers. Predictably, neither the dance-hall owners nor the taxi dancers were pleased with this proposal, and the government found itself inundated with guild and union petitions protesting the ban.

Subsequently, the head of the Social Affairs Bureau successfully petitioned the Nanjing government for an extension of one year to eliminate the dance halls. Half the dance halls, selected by lottery, were to close by the end of March 1948, and the remainder by the end of September. At the same time the Social Affairs Bureau mounted a major effort to offer job training and help dancers find alternative employment in shops, restaurants, teahouses, factories, and other establishments. This effort was to be funded at least partially from a hefty 50 percent tax collected from the dance halls that remained open. Yet as an article in the magazine *Contemporary Woman* pointed out, in a time of such inflation and unemployment, when even university graduates had difficulty finding jobs, was it reasonable to expect that barely literate taxi dancers would be able to easily change professions? In this situation, the author lamented, dancers were truly consigned to the "eighteenth circle of hell."[154]

The loud cries of protest from taxi dancers that the ban was costing them their only means of livelihood drew an unsympathetic response from some quarters. Writing in the women's magazine *Home,* one author said that although dancing was not inherently objectionable, in the current Chinese environment it had become a dissolute practice that ruined marriage and destroyed families. In the kind of sharp language feminists usually reserved for madams and traffickers, the author denounced taxi dancers as greedy for money and unconcerned whether said money was stained with "the blood of the poor." The article concluded by suggesting that dancers take the ban as an opportunity to change their lives, break away from the embraces of dissolute and shameless people, and join in the pathbreaking work of creating proper jobs for women.[155]

The taxi dancers, and other dance-hall employees, owners, and managers, were disinclined to take up this challenge. The lottery at the end of January 1948, contrary to informal promises made by the head of the Social Affairs Bureau, included two of the largest dance halls among the fourteen chosen for immediate closure. Dance-hall employees responded with a march, led by the male guild leadership, which quickly metamorphosed into a riot at city-government headquarters. The offices of the Social Affairs Bureau were trashed in this episode: windows and door panes were broken, office furniture was smashed. The government responded by disbanding the Dance Guild, the Dance Hall Employees Union, and the Professional Musicians Association, although local officials were clearly unhappy with the national policy and the problems it posed for social peace in Shanghai. Subsequently the dance halls were closed according to plan.[156]

If the campaign to license brothels foundered because of insufficient funding, personnel, and bureaucratic will, the campaign to eliminate ancillary occupations appears at first glance to have been more successful in banning masseuses and taxi dancers. Nevertheless, its effectiveness was illusory. In an environment of increasing inflation, political uncertainty, and corruption, women banished from the dance halls and massage parlors resurfaced as unlicensed prostitutes. By 1949, the police had lost the capacity to register or control prostitution. After the flurry of ambitious plans subsided, what remained was a government that lacked the resources to eliminate social ills, and an urban populace that increasingly saw the persistence of those ills as a measure of government incompetence. In the 1950s, the Communist government repeatedly cited this link between effective government and the control of prostitution to differentiate itself from its predecessors. Eschewing the licensing campaigns to which both abolitionists and regulationists had resorted, it moved directly and forcefully to eliminate brothels in the name of national renewal.

CHAPTER 12

Revolutionaries

Although prostitutes acted resourcefully on their own behalf and for their families, municipal regimes in Shanghai from the 1920s through the 1950s continued to see them as dangerously adrift from their proper social moorings, both agents and victims of a larger social disorder. Regulation of prostitution was always part of a larger project in which state authorities extended their reach into new realms of urban life. The Guomindang regime and its twentieth-century municipal governments sought to enlarge their domain of regulation to include the family, echoing both their Confucian antecedents and the modernizing regimes of Europe. In their view, encoded in regulations on trafficking and prostitution, women in families were indicative of a well-ordered society. The sundering of family networks through trafficking and sex work bespoke a larger crisis in social order, a crisis that would entail the reinsertion of women into families as part of its resolution.

This belief about the proper place of women was not challenged in 1949. Administrators of the prostitution-reform campaign of 1951 conducted by the People's Republic of China (PRC) government shared the assumptions about the need to "renaturalize" women in the familial order and thus order society. After the revolution of 1949, the government of the PRC began a campaign to end prostitution in China, armed with organizing techniques that enabled it to successfully extend the reach of the state into realms where earlier municipal governments had failed. In Shanghai this campaign got under way in 1951, continuing with decreasing intensity until the government declared prostitution eradicated in 1958. A major feature of the campaign was the detention of prostitutes in a Women's Labor Training Institute. Although they were not permitted to leave the institute at will, neither were they treated punitively: the explicit strategy of the municipal government was to cure their sexually transmitted and other diseases, equip them with job skills, and reunite them with families or find them appropriate husbands.

For the new Communist leadership, the elimination of prostitution symbolized China's emergence as a strong, healthy, and modern nation. The language the Communists used to describe this campaign was that of reeducation, redemption from imperialism, and the creation of a new woman, free from her past shameful history as China was free from her national shame. Like earlier reformers, the Communist-government functionaries regarded prostitution as a social illness. Unlike earlier reformers, however, they had much greater control of state power, and an expansive definition of the appropriate scope of activity for that power. They appropriated some aspects of older discourses on prostitution—that of the public-health threat posed by sexually transmitted disease, for instance—and literally drowned out the rest. Using public media to discredit earlier discourses on pleasure and entertainment, the government closed brothels and forcibly altered the social environment in which they flourished. Government-mandated changes in the labor market, the law, the police, the press, the brothels, and even marriage and the family rapidly and forcibly altered the ways in which prostitution was framed in public discussion.

Key to the success of this entire project, in the view of government officials, was a more intimate intervention: teaching former prostitutes to think, and speak, as recently liberated subalterns. Their own understanding of their recent past had to be aligned with that of the state, by encouraging them to speak of that past—not in unison, but in harmony with one another—in a language provided by the state. Their words were often published in the press because they were considered to have didactic value for the larger urban population, most of which was engaged, to one degree or another, in a similar reinterpretation of the past.

In comparing this campaign with the efforts of earlier regulators, it must be remembered that "the state" was not a steady entity. The Shanghai Municipal Council, whose 1920 effort to license and eliminate prostitution was discussed in chapter 11, was merely a local authority, albeit one with ties to powerful foreign powers. The Nanjing government of the late 1920s and 1930s had difficulty asserting its authority beyond the immediate environs of the capital, while the 1940s municipal officials of Shanghai found themselves overwhelmed by fundamental economic problems. In contrast to all of these, the People's Government in 1950s Shanghai was closely integrated with the national government, carrying out policy directives in partial coordination with other cities in China. The 1920s reformers were foreigners, and their governing body made little attempt to alter Chinese institutions except as they impinged on foreign life in Shanghai. Over the next several decades reformers found fundamental social change on a national scale to be beyond their capabilities. The 1950s reformers were Chinese, and they explicitly identified themselves as agents of nationalistic renewal through the cleansing of Chinese social institutions. Whereas the SMC in 1920 acted reluctantly to ban prostitution, responding to pressure from reformers who were peripheral to state authority, the 1950s government controlled the timing, nature, and extent of reform, with no visible input from nonstate groups.

In spite of significant differences, each of these governments reached down into local society to regulate and alter the working conditions of prostitutes, and each made an attempt to regulate commercial sexuality in ways that had not been attempted by any earlier state authority. All these campaigns also evidenced a similar concern, often implicit but always discernible, with the pernicious effect that prostitutes—loose women who were also women on the loose, detached from the control of families—had on public health and morality. Without ever formally acknowledging their influence, perhaps even unaware of it, the revolutionary reformers of the 1950s built on the analyses and practices of earlier regulators.

Preparation

Even before Cao Manzhi entered Shanghai with the People's Liberation Army, he knew that eliminating prostitution was one of the tasks that awaited him as head of the Civil Administration Bureau (*Minzheng ju*).[1] He had first encountered prostitutes seventeen years earlier, as a young county secretary in the underground Communist Party organization in Shandong. There he saw madams and prostitutes going to the Commerce Bureau (*Gongshang ju*), presumably to pay taxes; he watched coastal families supplement their incomes by sending their wives and daughters aboard ships in port to sell sex to the sailors. Born in the 1910s, Cao was of the generation that grew up in the wake of the May Fourth movement, and he had been moved by May Fourth writings on the oppression of women in Chinese society. But it was the Chinese Communist Party that decisively shaped his understanding of the nature of prostitution. He read Clara Zetkin's account of her conversation with Lenin; as he recalls it, Zetkin wanted to start a magazine about how to liberate prostitutes, but Lenin admonished her that prostitutes could not be liberated unless the world proletariat was liberated. For Cao, too, prostitution was inseparable from the larger social context of feudalism and imperialism. Although the particular terms in which he voiced this connection were drawn from Marxism-Leninism, the connection itself would have been familiar to most late Qing and Republican reformers. If ordinary women were oppressed by the social system, he felt, prostitutes were ruined (*cuican*) outright by it. "Prostitutes suffered ruination not only from the harmful social relationships in China," he recalled in a 1986 interview,

> but also from the ruination of imperialism, which was quite widespread. . . .
> If China had been a strong nation, if its people had been a people with high

international standing, if we had not suffered a foreign invasion, our women would not have suffered such great ruination.

Cao also shared with many non-Communist reformers the assumption that prostitution was inevitable in a capitalist society:

> It follows commercial capital—that is to say, it follows the freedom, equality, and fraternity of capitalist society, because this so-called freedom is merely the freedom of commerce. Commerce must have many merchants moving from port to port—today in Singapore, tomorrow in Thailand, the next day in New York; today in Shanghai, tomorrow in Tianjin—not returning home for years at a time. Yet sexual needs are one of their basic biological needs (for clothing, food, housing, transportation, and sex). This gives rise to brothels, brothels then become legal, and parliaments approve them. . . .

For Cao and his fellow Communists, the conundrum was how to rescue China from its weakened state—how to make it strong and modern—without accepting the social problems that seemed to be a constitutive part of modernity. By identifying prostitution with capitalism and then positing *socialist* modernity as their goal, they redefined the framework of the 1930s debates, in which the existence of prostitution had been a lamented but inevitable marker of modernity.

Since 1938, Cao had been involved in several campaigns to eliminate prostitution in Shandong, and he knew that it could not be effectively banned in Shanghai until the urban social environment was decisively altered. This meant that the power of the Green Gang (*Qing Bang*) and the Red Gang (*Hong Bang*), whose members ran many of the larger brothels, had to be broken. It also meant that if the government was to forbid prostitutes to practice their trade, it had to be able to offer them alternative means of support. For almost two years after the city was taken over, Cao bided his time:

> When we had just entered Shanghai, we were not prepared. If we had abolished [prostitution] immediately, how would we have fed [the prostitutes]? Where would we have sent them? They had no homes to return to. So we had to harden our hearts. After Liberation, prostitutes were still on the street. Our cadres didn't like it, and the democratic parties didn't like it. They felt that in Shanghai, liberated by the CCP [Chinese Communist Party], women who had been ruthlessly and forcibly ruined should not be allowed to continue to suffer. At the time there was really nothing we could do. If you are going to use force, first of all you have to have a place to put her, a place for her to eat, and next you must prepare to treat her illnesses. And our methods for treating illness, our medicines, all had to be prepared in advance.
>
> We also had to prepare a group of cadres, but the number of cadres I had brought in was extremely limited. I had to take over all of Shanghai: the city government, the courts, the jails, the police stations, the Guomindang Administration Branch (*Xingzheng yuan*), all the administrative bodies of Shang-

hai. My organization took over altogether more than five hundred units, but I was given only twenty-eight cadres. How could we do everything? The Public Security Bureau had brought in even fewer cadres, yet they had to take charge of every aspect of public order. . . . So, we were very sad.

At the time, when I lay down to sleep, some cadres criticized me: Why do you still permit prostitution? Why doesn't the leadership solve the prostitution problem quickly? Why not arrest the hoodlums? Why not solve the problem of prostitution? I said, "You sleep well, right? I haven't been to sleep yet. Will you give me a building? I don't have a building yet. How I am going to take them in? If I take them in, for sure there will be nothing to eat on that day. Shall we make prostitutes into beggars on the street? What kind of policy is that?" So for a time we permitted them to continue, but it was because we had to, not because we wanted to. We hardened our hearts and got through that period, and later took them in.

During the two years before the reform campaign began, the Public Security Bureau continued to license brothels and prostitutes, just as the Guomindang government had done in the late 1940s. Yet in spite of this official permission to operate, the number of people involved in the trade shrank. New government regulations in August 1949 put severe restrictions on the freedom of brothel owners to run their business. Brothels were forbidden to entertain government employees or minors, sell drugs, permit gambling, host large banquets, arrange assignations between prostitutes and clients outside the brothel, allow sick prostitutes to work, or force any woman to have sexual relations or remain in the brothel against her will. Government-controlled newspapers publicized the fact that a prostitute could bring charges against any owner who tried to prevent her departure or marriage or who tried to charge her fees or keep her personal possessions.[2] If brothel owners still had any doubt that the environment was becoming inhospitable to prostitution, they could look to the fate of their compatriots in other cities: between 1947 and 1951, prostitution was successfully banned in Shijiazhuang, Jilin, Beijing, Tianjin, Nanjing, Suzhou, Yangzhou, Zhenjiang, and Hangzhou.[3]

In response to these measures, many Shanghai brothel owners closed their establishments. Some of the biggest gang-connected operators, dubbed "brothel tyrants" in the press, had fled the country at Liberation in 1949; others were arrested and executed in the April 1951 campaign to suppress counterrevolutionaries.[4] At the same time, women returned to their home districts as the rural economy began to recover from civil war, or found other jobs in Shanghai. In mid-1950, the newspaper *Dagong bao* reported that the number of licensed prostitutes in the city had declined from 1,897 (in early 1949) to 662, and the number of brothels had decreased from 518 to 158.[5] By November 1951, the numbers were down to 180 licensed prostitutes in 72 brothels.[6] Of course, licensed prostitutes were only a fraction of the women who sold sexual services, and they continued to be outnumbered by their clandestine sisters, the unlicensed prostitutes. Nevertheless, by late 1951 the city government faced a much reduced prostitute population when it finally turned its attention to closing the brothels and clearing the streets.

On November 13, 1951, police gave brothel owners one last chance to go out of business without facing criminal sanctions. The Public Security Bureau called together owners of the city's remaining brothels and informed them that they were to close their establishments and personally arrange other means of support for their employees. Most owners ignored this order, and a week later the police held a meeting with licensed prostitutes and told them that the brothels would soon be closed down. Public Security officials then decided to go to the city government for a formal decision to close the brothels, which was issued on November 23.[7]

Even before police in the busy central districts of Shanghai began preparations to arrest the owners and take in the prostitutes, across town another drama was unfolding. In early November, women who were employed as teachers, social workers, or staff of the Women's Federation were quietly taken aside by their supervisors and told to report to a large building complex at 418 Tongzhou Road, in the Tilan Qiao district. Those selected had to meet certain criteria: a high school or college degree, and experience working with people. But when they learned that the building was to be a labor and education center for ex-prostitutes, and that their new job would be to reform these women, some resisted the assignment. Recalls Yang Xiuqin:

> I didn't want to go. I was only eighteen, and I felt that I couldn't do this work. At that time everyone had the impression that prostitutes were low-class people, prostitution was a low-class business, and asking us to have contact with those people wasn't easy to accept, so I didn't want to go. I cried. I sat on the stairs and cried. After that the leaders talked to me quite a bit. They said, "These people have also been oppressed. They didn't want to do it [become prostitutes]. After Liberation our New China does not permit the existence of the system of prostitution. The work we are going to do has not been done by anyone before, and is of far-reaching significance." They talked reason to me, persuaded me, so in the end I went.[8]

For some of the staff trainees, their commitment to the project of reform entailed overcoming a class-based disdain for prostitutes and replacing it with a newfound sense of gender solidarity. As Yang Jiezeng recalled, "They had not willingly gone down that road, but had been forced by life. As a woman comrade I should rescue them."[9]

The reluctant recruits, who numbered more than fifty, were given three weeks of training. During this period they were not allowed to return home, write letters, or make phone calls, because the government did not want the timing of its planned raid on the brothels compromised.[10] The training classes, taught by a staff member of the Civil Administration Bureau, focused on what the government saw as the dual nature of prostitutes. On the one hand, trainees were told, prostitutes had been cruelly treated and deserved the sympathy of the reformers:

> They themselves didn't want to engage in prostitution. They had suffered and been oppressed. We cadres were first of all to sympathize with them, and second to be warm to them, because they had not felt warmth. They had no parents, had left their own families, and they had a madam supervising them. They called her "mama," and the only others in their lives were customers. These were all economic relationships, without human warmth. So we wanted to show them some human warmth. We were not to use hitting or cursing as methods of reform, but rather were to try to persuade and educate them, to raise their consciousness.[11]

On the other hand, the reformers-in-training were instructed, prostitutes were products of a social environment that encouraged them to be parasites, and one purpose of reform was to ensure that they broke with their old habits:

> Many of them had been in the brothels for many years, leading a life of luxury—or, as we call it, "profiting by the labor of others"—leading a life of debauchery. If you suddenly asked them to labor, they wouldn't be accustomed to it. We were to educate them to labor, to live by the labor of their own hands, not to rely on prostitution.[12]

The program of reform was to address both aspects of a prostitute's character, using three methods: education in everything from literacy to class consciousness, cure of venereal and other diseases, and training in work habits and skills.[13] The work would be conducted at the Tongzhou Road complex, which was formally dubbed the Women's Labor Training Institute (*Funü laodong jiaoyangsuo*). (See figure 20.)

Between 8 P.M. on November 25 and 10 o'clock the next morning, police moved swiftly to arrest brothel owners, round up prostitutes, and seal the doors of the brothels. In all, 324 owners were arrested and subsequently sentenced either to prison or labor reform. Strictly separated from them, and remanded by the police to the Women's Labor Training Institute, were 181 licensed prostitutes and 320 streetwalkers, a total of 501 women.[14]

The Subjects of Reform: Competing Discourses

When the prostitutes, transported by police trucks, arrived at the main gate of the Women's Labor Training Institute, the staff lined up to welcome them. For the inexperienced reformers, their first sight of prostitutes en masse was a shock:

> We had never seen prostitutes before and we always thought that prostitutes must be very beautiful—either their faces, or their makeup, or their clothes

must be good-looking. But after they arrived, we saw that they were not good-looking at all. Because the day that they came they were not working. They had their bedrolls with them, and their luggage all packed up. Many were wearing no makeup. Others had been crying and their powder was smudged and not good-looking. . . . They seemed even less attractive than ordinary people.[15]

The bedraggled and depressed state of these women was hardly surprising, given that police had forcibly removed them from their familiar surroundings, social networks, and source of income. Yet newspaper articles written at the time of the roundup describe the newly incarcerated prostitutes as eager for liberation by the state. According to the accounts prepared for public consumption—stories that quickly became the official mythology of reform—prostitutes had been brutally mistreated in their working lives. Virtually every account cited the grinding poverty of their families, the kidnap and forced sale of many women into prostitution, the sadistic behavior of brothel owners and madams, and the mistreatment and even murder of prostitutes who became too ill to work.[16] The women were portrayed as being acutely conscious of their oppression and its causes, and desperate for liberation. Many reports published the day after the roundup cited the reactions of two prostitutes, Wu Caifeng and Wang Acai, who were said to have made impromptu speeches in the police station while awaiting processing. Wu reportedly stood on a stool in the Laozha police station and declared, "Sisters, we are liberated, we are born anew! Sisters, why have our pure bodies been trampled on by others? We were all loved by our parents; why did we sink to this state? It was the Guomindang reactionaries who harmed us! Today we are excited and happy! The people's government, under the leadership of Chairman Mao, is helping us to begin anew. Today is our most memorable day, our most glorious day." On their ride to the Women's Labor Training Institute, when one woman inadvertently used the word "prostitute," another was said to have replied, "If anyone uses the word 'prostitute' again, I won't answer to it!"[17]

Such was the representation of their state of mind in the press—an account that assumed a direct causal connection between suffering and class consciousness, between oppression and the desire to be reformed. Although it made for inspiring reading, this story not only oversimplified the social relations of the prostitutes' world, but also trivialized the problems faced by the reformers. A less clear and optimistic reading was offered by an investigation of five hundred Shanghai prostitutes in 1948, on the eve of revolutionary change. Interviewing women at all levels of the hierarchy of prostitution, the investigators were surprised to find that 56 percent reported satisfaction with their occupation, mainly because it was more lucrative than other options available to them. Half expressed no desire to change occupations, while slightly more than one-quarter professed an ambition to find a wealthy husband. Their main fear was that if they came forward to be examined for venereal disease they would be reported to the police and ordered to change occupation.[18] At the same time, the investigators noted that

> the minority of them (178 cases) are indifferent to life and the majority (211 cases) took the attitude of "Eat, drink, and be happy". . . . [Another] 108 are pessimistic in their outlook. In general, they have neither faith nor trust in others.[19]

The combination of relative financial satisfaction, fear of state authority, apathy, depression, and suspicion of all outsiders did not bespeak a population hungry for transformation.

Additionally, the roundup sundered the only reliable relationship the prostitutes knew—that with the madam and the madam's paramour, who were often adoptive parents as well as employers. As exploitative as brothel life might have been, it provided both work and family for these women. Their fear was increased by the rumors that pervaded the city in the days before the brothel closings: that the women's heads would be shaved, that the women would be distributed to the People's Liberation Army as collective wives, that they would be used as live minesweepers in the military campaign to take Taiwan.[20] Given this atmosphere, the roundup scene lacked the picture-perfect class consciousness of the newspaper reports, as Cao Manzhi acknowledged many years later:

> We loaded them into cars. These people all cried. They didn't get in the cars. They all hung on to the madams, calling, "Mama, Daddy, the Communists are going to murder us, we don't want to go," and so forth. "They're going to sell us again, we want to stay with Mama and Daddy." They cried and carried on.
>
> They did not want to accept reform, and by no means did all of them wish to leave the life and marry respectably [*congliang*]. Those who did were extremely exceptional—of the ones I encountered, often not even one in one hundred. Very few among those who lived well wished to voluntarily give up the trade. In general, after a prostitute had been in the brothel half a year, her psychology changed.
>
> Vagrancy became second nature to them. Like when a pickpocket steals things, becomes habituated to it, finds that there is profit to be made. Especially for young people, aside from the ruination of one's character and body, the actual life was better than that of factory workers, because the brothels had to bring them up well so that they would be beautiful. They could not enjoy this kind of life if they left the brothels.
>
> You can't simply talk about ruining their chastity, or call it a case of smashing a pot to pieces just because it's cracked [that is, writing oneself off as hopeless and acting recklessly]. This is not the reality I encountered in my work. Rather, we should call it a case of vagrancy becoming second nature to them.[21]

Wu Caifeng and Wang Acai may indeed have made inspiring speeches to their captive sisters, but if they did so their exhortations fell on suspicious and terrified ears. When the female staff of the Women's Labor Training Institute saw the tear-streaked, sullen faces of their new charges, they knew that winning the trust of these women would be difficult and that altering their behavior might require coercion.

The reform process did not get off to a smooth start. True, the women were provided with living conditions better than those enjoyed by many Shanghai residents. Each was assigned a bed, a quilt, a wool blanket, sheets, two washbasins (for feet and face), toothpaste and toothbrush, chopsticks, and two food bowls.[22] They were permitted to wear their own clothes, and were treated courteously by the staff.[23] They were fed well and their rooms were kept warm. But when Cao Manzhi went to address them as part of their orientation, he found himself the target of an innovative spontaneous protest—a cry-in:

> I went to where they lived. There was a rather high stage, and I stood on it and prepared to give them a speech. Just as I started to talk, one of the prostitutes cried out: "Sisters, cry [*jiejie meimei, ku*]!" It was very effective: as soon as she called out, more than three hundred people began to cry simultaneously. Every single one cried in a truly brokenhearted way. At first their tears were false, but the more they cried, the sadder they became. "Now we are in the hands of the CCP. Before we could get by, but this time we don't know if we'll live or die." The more they thought about it, the sadder they became. Some cried out, "Mama, where are you? Your child can't even write to you!" They said all kinds of things. They cried without stopping for two hours.
>
> I sat there. I asked the head of the guards to bring me a stool, and I sat and watched them cry. . . . When they had almost finished crying, it was time to send in food for them. They all got their bowls filled, and then they dumped their food on the floor. All of them. Not one ate.
>
> I knew their state of mind. Later I talked with several of them, and they said, "When we began to cry, it was to put some pressure on you. But after that it was genuine. We were crying over very sad things. We didn't know where you would send us. Maybe you would execute us. Maybe you would draw our blood. When troops fight in battle, don't they lose blood?" and so forth. Their thinking was unbelievably confused. But not a single one of them thought that the CCP had come to save her.[24]

The Reform Process

In an uncanny echo of the semicolonial vocabulary of dirt and cleanliness, the head of the Women's Labor Training Institute, Yang Jiezeng, referred to the reform process as "sweeping garbage" (*sao laji*).[25] For her the garbage was not the prostitutes themselves, but rather their physical ailments, cultural ignorance, misconceived emotional ties, and misguided attitudes about work. The reform project targeted these one by one.

The first step in gaining the trust of the "sisters" (who after the roundup were never referred to as prostitutes) was to treat their sexually transmitted diseases and other illnesses.[26] (See figure 21.) This in itself was a problematic process, since many of the women believed that their blood was being drawn in order to sell it on the open market. Medical examinations began on their third day in the institute, and the group prognosis was grim: half of the 501 women suffered from venereal disease, while a full 90 percent had health problems ranging from heart disease and tuberculosis to ringworm.[27] In addition, a majority were addicted to opium or heroin, and the process of enforced withdrawal made them listless and frantic by turns.[28]

The municipal government spared no expense on the medical treatment of the "sisters," ultimately spending 180,000 yuan on the cure of venereal disease alone.[29] Doctors were brought in from the Shanghai Venereal Disease Clinic to treat the women at a specially equipped facility inside the Women's Labor Training Institute; those in need of more extended care were sent out to local hospitals and their bills paid by the city.[30] Scarce penicillin was diverted from the People's Liberation Army, gradually replacing salvarsan, which required a longer course of treatment.[31] Perhaps more than any other feature of the reform program, the medical treatment ultimately convinced the women that the reformers meant them no harm, and that if the government considered them worth the expense to cure, perhaps there was a place for them in the new society.[32]

The second step was to organize an extensive series of classes for the women, who spent half of every day in study. (See figure 22.) Since the majority of the group was illiterate, and illiteracy had often been a factor in their being "tricked" into consenting to their own sale, some of the classes focused on achieving an elementary school level of literacy.[33] But the most important task of the classes was to instill a sense of class consciousness, in keeping with the government's view of prostitutes' dual nature: they had to be made to hate the old society and recognize their oppression in it, and they had to recognize that their own past actions were less than glorious, were now in fact illegal, and must not be repeated.[34] Much of the teaching was geared to the psychological state of the individual women in the classes, as reported by their own team leaders (*duizhang*):

> Depending on what they were thinking at the time, we would educate them accordingly. There was all kinds of thinking among them. Some of them felt that it was better to be on the outside doing nothing all day, while here they had to love labor, to work and produce, so they were unwilling. We talked about this in the classes, and educated them. We told them that this was bad for their own health and a hindrance to society.[35]

Whereas small-group discussions were focused on the thinking of individual women, larger-scale activities were aimed at giving the entire group of prostitutes a shared way of understanding their past. In one intriguing instance of life imitating art, a month after their incarceration the women were shown the movie *Sisters Stand Up* (*Jiejie meimei zhanqilai*), which told the story of prostitutes undergoing reform. Along with the play *Sister* (*Zi*), performed for them by a local drama troupe, the film reportedly moved many of them to tears by reminding them of the circumstances of their own lives.[36]

Teaching the women to think of themselves as members of a single oppressed group meant minimizing the factors that divided them. Like most Shanghai residents, prostitutes could identify their place of origin and felt a special kinship with those from the same region who spoke the same dialect they did.[37] In many sectors of the Shanghai workforce, native-place kinship was accompanied by hostility to those from other regions.[38] Although prostitution was very much structured by native-place origins, individual prostitutes apparently identified each other by brothel rather than native place, and all spoke Shanghai dialect, so place of origin was not an insuperable obstacle to the creation of a shared identity. The women were also divided by the class of customers they had once serviced; the life of high-class courtesans had little in common with that of working-class streetwalkers. Nevertheless, when women from all along the hierarchy of prostitution were confined together in the Women's Labor Training Institute, the differences in status were apparently less important than the common fact of confinement and reform.[39]

A key factor in reforming the women was to break their emotional ties to the madams. Several weeks after the roundup, the institute organized a large accusation meeting at which women publicly confronted their former bosses, who in some cases had had virtual ownership rights over them.[40] At this meeting, the most extreme practices of the madams and male brothel owners were dramatically denounced.[41] Yang Jiezeng describes the careful process of preparation for this large gathering, a process in which prostitutes were taught to recognize themselves as oppressed:

> We used the accusation meetings to inspire them to hate the brothels, to
> hate this kind of life, to hate those who had oppressed them, and finally, to
> hate the old society. In order to achieve this goal we needed material, but we
> knew just a smattering of information, nothing vivid enough. So we asked
> them to speak themselves. This counted as a form of self-education. We
> acted as a close friend would. They could speak to us of their own bitter
> water, could pour out the words in their hearts. Before the meeting, we first
> sought out many typical ones, those who had suffered the most, and worked
> with them. ´. . . At the meeting, we arranged many slogans, like "The old
> society turned people into devils; the new society turns devils into people."
> The atmosphere was very angry. Some people called out slogans. When the
> prostitutes made their accusations, on the one hand they shed tears, on the
> other they were furious.[42]

This did not conclude the process of dissociation from the madams. Seven months after the roundup, when the institute began a formal evaluation of the women's progress, each woman was told to make a self-criticism. One confessed that she had remained in contact with her former madam, even leaving her child with her for safekeeping. As a result of this campaign she broke relations with the madam and took her child back.[43]

While helping to sever ties between the madam "mothers" and their prostitute "children," institute staff did everything they could to strengthen ties between prostitute mothers and their biological offspring. Seventeen of the women had brought children into the Women's Labor Training Institute with them, and subsequent births brought the number of resident children to forty-nine by August 1952. Nursing mothers were allowed to keep their children with them for the first few weeks; children were then housed in an onsite child-care center with the mothers nearby, separated from the rest of the prostitute population. Reformers recall that one breakthrough in overcoming suspicion came when the staff validated the prostitutes' role as mothers, rather than forcing them to eat tadpoles in an attempt to induce abortion, as the madams might have done.[44]

The third important feature of the reform regimen was involvement in productive labor. (See figure 23.) Women spent half of each day working in one of the institute's workshops, which produced socks and towels. In the minds of the reformers, imparting an actual skill was less important than cultivating the habit of working.[45] This was not easy:

> On the outside she wasn't even willing to do her own washing. In here she
> had to lift loads of more than a hundred catties. We had to do a lot of work
> with them to get them to consciously accept our direction.[46]

Women earned a regular wage for this work; for some of them, it was their first experience of receiving and controlling their own earnings.[47] In this respect, the institute's program built directly on less comprehensive reform efforts that had been part of the Shanghai social-welfare scene since the Door of Hope was founded in 1900.

Undergirding and reinforcing all these aspects of reform—medical treatment, education, and labor—was the establishment of regular collective routines and daily habits.[48] The women rose at 6:30 each day, spending most of their time in organized activities. They were divided into teams, subteams, and small groups, each of which had a group leader and additional women in charge of study and daily life. The small-group leaders were elected by the women themselves.[49] Although women could not leave the compound at will, they were permitted to meet regularly with their relatives, and eventually a system of asking for leave to return home for visits was established. These visits home were used both as rewards and as a means of assessing the women's progress toward release:

Their Sisters' Group (*jiemei xiaozu*) had to evaluate and examine and decide who could go out. Their family also had to work on it. We also asked the masses in the area to work on it, to help us investigate just what they did after they went out on leave. Before they went out on leave they had to say when they would be back. Some went out overnight; some went out in the morning and came back in the evening. The great majority returned on time, and voluntarily reported to the staff what had happened that day: they had helped wash clothes at home, cleaned the house, cooked, and so forth. After we listened we investigated to see whether it was true. So we made contact with their families, and asked them what they had done when they went home, and also asked the masses, was it true that after they came home they did not go out, was there any activity? In this way we knew whether they were good or not. So this system of asking for leave was very useful.[50]

Such a system, unheard of in previous reform efforts, depended for its efficacy on the mobilization of large segments of the city population under the supervision of state authority. It rewarded the women for assuming domestic roles in their families, and linked future release to the successful performance of domesticity. By means of these routines, in a transformed urban environment, the behavior of the women, and apparently their thinking as well, were gradually modified.[51]

The success of the reform was put to a dramatic test in September 1952, when a second group of prostitutes, almost twice as big as the first, was rounded up. These were unlicensed prostitutes who had continued to work the streets after prostitution was formally banned, as well as bar hostesses, masseuses, and others who sold sex regularly.[52] They were picked up in one night in a well-coordinated police sweep:

We got several hundred people to dress as customers. They were everywhere on the street in ones and twos. . . . The trucks were hidden in advance in the lanes. The method was a bit savage. One of them would "hook" her, and . . . [then] our plainclothesmen would come out and stuff a handkerchief in her mouth. Otherwise she might call out. . . . We also tied them up, [but] some jumped off the truck, and one almost died; it took two days [of treatment] to save her.[53]

From the moment of their violent arrest, these women were more difficult for the Women's Labor Training Institute staff to deal with than the first group:

The second group was different from the first—they made a lot more fuss. Among them were many hoodlums, and some who were very young. They were not like the first group, who it seemed had been sold into the brothels. These were people who engaged in hoodlum activities. Some came from homes that were not badly off, and some were even students. They willingly engaged in prostitution. So they were antagonistic at being brought in.[54]

The group tripled the resident population at 418 Tongzhou Road. Many of the new inhabitants were given to loud arguments and fighting. The staff responded by putting women from the original group in charge of the newcomers, and they repeated this procedure when a third group—five hundred women, most of them taxi dancers—was rounded up.[55] (Subsequent inmates were brought in singly, not in large groups.) This work utilized the street wisdom that ex-prostitutes could bring to bear on reforming their sisters; it also gave the earliest inmates a chance to demonstrate the extent of their personal reform.

Release

In 1953 the Women's Labor Training Institute began to release its reformed inmates. (See figure 24.) The women had three main destinations. Those with relatives in the countryside were generally released to the custody of their families. The institute contacted the local government in a woman's native place to make sure that the family could take her back, then met with the family members. Sometimes this involved reuniting women with families they had not seen since they were kidnapped; sometimes it meant sending them back to husbands who knew full well that they had been prostitutes, who had indeed sent them to Shanghai to try to make a living. In such cases the institute staff reproved the family members for their negligence:

> "If she had no relatives in Shanghai, had no one she knew, how could you feel easy in your minds letting a woman come to Shanghai? If you have difficulties, you should overcome them yourselves in the countryside, instead of telling her to go to Shanghai, depending on her to solve your difficulties."[56]

In every case, the institute staff tried to ensure that the woman would not be discriminated against, be rejected by her family, or return to prostitution.[57] This reintegration effort echoed the procedures followed by local government for kidnapped women in the 1920s and 1930s, but it was far more comprehensive. It is not known how successful this effort was in securing the full reacceptance of these women into their rural communities, but apparently few returned to prostitution.[58]

A second group of women, whose attitude and performance had been best or who had relatives in Shanghai, were assigned factory jobs in town and if possible sent home to their families. A third group, with no family to return to, were sent to state farms in Gansu, Ningxia, or Xinjiang, accompanied (apparently permanently) by some of the institute staff. For many of them, a chance at a respectable marriage was part of the deal:

> Xinjiang had no women, and most people couldn't find wives. Some of these prostitutes had no home to return to, and as prostitutes it was difficult

for them to find mates, so we introduced them [to the Xinjiang units]. The ones who went to Gansu went because they were short of labor there, and they could take their families. We explained the conditions there to them, and what they would do there. Those who wanted to go signed up; those who didn't want to go didn't have to. In 1955 more than five hundred went to Xinjiang.[59]

Regardless of where the women were sent, the staff regarded it as part of their work to see that married women were reunited with their spouses and unmarried women were married off. They were aided in the latter enterprise by unmarried men who, hearing that the institute contained a number of unmarried women, wrote requesting a wife:

Some unmarried men knew the situation at the Women's Labor Training Institute, and voluntarily wrote letters saying that they were unmarried, and had also suffered in the old society, so they sympathized with the bitter experience of these people, and wanted to find this kind of a mate. These people were workers; some were merchants. We didn't accept everyone who wrote. First we did an investigation, to find out about their work and family situation. After that we found someone about the same age, and if she was willing, we introduced them.[60]

The staff's matchmaking duties did not end when a woman was released, as a former head of the institute recalls:

Later, if they started courting a man in the factory, we sought him out for a talk and let him know about her past, in order to avoid his going back on his word after marriage, and causing problems. We also asked that the woman herself explain things to the man. Some people, after they learned about the past of these women, understood that they were victims of the old society, and loved them even more.[61]

The concern with stabilizing the lives of ex-prostitutes by installing them in a secure, ideologically acceptable family nexus bore a more than passing similarity to the policies of the early twentieth-century Door of Hope. But the breadth and depth of intervention exceeded anything attempted by private relief organizations before 1949.

It is not entirely clear how successful government efforts were at preventing discrimination and its informal twin, gossip. Although I interviewed many people involved in the 1950s reform effort, I was not able to talk to former prostitutes, even those whose identities had been made public during the campaign. The reason they gave was that although their spouses knew of their histories, their children did not. Many had moved within Shanghai several times to put a distance between themselves and neighbors who knew that they had been prostitutes. A foreigner arriving at their apartments would, they feared, start the neighbors wondering. This fear of visible contact with a foreigner could have had many dimensions that had nothing to do with prostitution. Yet it suggests that their personal histories of oppression, however acceptable in terms of state ideology, still had the capacity to disrupt their lives in the present.[62]

After 1953, more and more inmates of the Women's Labor Training Institute were juvenile delinquents rather than former prostitutes. In 1958, its original mandate fulfilled, the institute closed its doors. In all, more than seven thousand women had been the subjects of reform there.[63]

REFORMERS COMPARED

Much of the Communist reform program for prostitutes was not new: the daily curriculum and emphasis on work and marriage resembled the approach of the old Door of Hope, whereas the medical treatment and police supervision were similar to measures employed by both the International Settlement government and the postwar Guomindang regime. Nevertheless, the 1950s campaign differed in significant respects from its closest predecessor, the 1920 effort to eliminate prostitution in the International Settlement. In the 1920s, the Shanghai Municipal Council was a reluctant reformer, forced into that stance by the zealous campaigners of the Moral Welfare League. The members of the SMC preferred a regulatory approach that protected the public health by inspecting prostitutes and licensing brothels, thereby requiring them to conform to certain standards of cleanliness and order. The Moral Welfare League activists believed in suppressing prostitution, which they denounced as a form of "commercialized vice" that should not be licensed and thereby condoned by state authority (in the form of the municipal government). As the governing body of the International Settlement, the SMC was subject to decisions taken by open meetings of the taxpayers. In the 1920 case, it was required to carry out the licensing and elimination of brothels over the considered objections of many of its members. Although it had a monopoly on governmental power in the Settlement, it was subject to the consent of the governed. The members of the Moral Welfare League, because they were organized, vocal, and persistent, effectively captured a reluctant state authority and bound it to their agenda for moral reform.

No such rift was visible in the ranks of the 1950s reformers. The campaign to eliminate prostitution was carried out by organs of the municipal government with a high degree of unity and coordination. Acting on a resolution passed by the municipal Consultative Conference, various government agencies—the Public Security Bureau, the Civil Administration Bureau, the Health Bureau, the Democratic Women's Federation, and the residents' committees—each carried out their appointed tasks. The police arrested brothel owners and took in prostitutes. The Civil Administration Bureau ran the Women's Labor Training Institute, which housed, treated, and reeducated the women. The Health Bureau allocated resources for their medical treatment. The Women's Federation provided staff members for the institute and neighborhood cadres to reinforce the work of supervision of the women and their families. The residents' committees used informal surveillance to guard against any resurgence of prostitution.

Coordinating all these efforts, though largely invisible in the public record of the abolition campaign, was the Communist Party. The CCP approach to prostitution had been developed in the rural districts of the liberated areas and honed in the cities of the north, which came under Communist control earlier than Shanghai. The head of the Civil Administration Bureau, Cao Manzhi, was a veteran of abolition campaigns in Shandong and elsewhere. He understood the theoretical underpinnings of the CCP position and had the organizational skills and clout to administer an effective program. Unlike the 1920 effort, the 1951 campaign was conducted by a unified state authority with a well-developed position on prostitution—a government impervious to outside pressure (had there been any in favor of another approach) that apparently enjoyed a great deal of popular support for its efforts.[64]

Although the representatives on the SMC in 1920 came from the most powerful nations on earth, in Shanghai they were far from omnipotent. The reach of their state authority was of limited breadth and depth. So was their reform effort, which was aimed at eliminating brothels from the International Settlement rather than thoroughly abolishing all forms of prostitution and reforming individual prostitutes. Even this limited effort failed, in part because they had no authority over the area of Shanghai outside the International Settlement, and many brothels responded to the campaign by moving their operations to the French Concession or the Chinese-controlled area. It failed as well because a foreign government in Shanghai could not begin to ameliorate the social system of which prostitution was a part. The SMC could not or did not provide extensive welfare facilities for displaced prostitutes; it made no attempt to punish traffickers or discourage customers; it did nothing to quell the fears or silence the protests of the many commercial establishments that indirectly derived some revenue from prostitution. It took the brothel, and only the brothel, as its unit of regulation. Anything that happened outside the brothel walls, including unlicensed prostitution, the sale of women and children, and the interweaving of prostitution with the rest of the urban economy, was beyond the scope of the state.

In contrast, the CCP-guided government of the 1950s controlled not only all of Shanghai, but the countryside from which most prostitutes came. It could send reformed prostitutes back to their native villages or dispatch them to far-flung regions to take up new lives. It was engaged in a massive restructuring of the economy that made it possible to find employment for ex-prostitutes. It even took on the role of matchmaker in order to settle the women in stable households. In the lanes of Shanghai, it built, with popular support and participation, a network of mutual supervision linked to state authority that made it difficult and dangerous for prostitutes, madams, and traffickers to resume operations. The reach of the state in the 1950s was both wide and deep, making it a far more powerful entity in the lives of Shanghai residents than the imperialists it excoriated had ever been.[65]

Although the 1920s reformers could not agree on whether prostitution should be regulated or suppressed, they shared the Victorian assumption that it was a product of human nature—specifically, male sexual desire. They differed largely on the feasibility and practicality of controlling human nature. The regulators argued that since prostitution was natural, it could not be eliminated, and that the state should confine itself to ensuring that it was conducted in a licensed locale by hygienic practitioners. The abolitionists, on the other hand, called on men to transcend their nature with the aid of religion, to subordinate their sexual nature to the higher moral law subscribed to by religious men and all respectable women. In using legal means to enforce a moral code, they argued, the government could also strike a blow for women's rights, by helping to secure the freedom of all women from the untrammeled sexual depredations of men.

For the 1950s reformers, there was nothing natural about prostitution; it was a purely social product. They proceeded from the assumption that prostitution grew out of a distorted social system dominated by imperialists and a reactionary Chinese government linked to rural landlords and urban gangs. Imperialists had invaded China and damaged its economy, creating rural distress. The Guomindang and its warlord predecessors had worsened the rural crisis and shored up landlord power. Displaced peasants, many of them women sold by their relatives, had been forced into prostitution or had sought it as a means to support their families. Urban power brokers had controlled gangster networks that made money from procuring and brothel keeping, paying off the urban police in the process. Governments, both foreign controlled and native, had profited from the taxation of prostitution. In this rendering, the entire system of political and social power became a malignant growth that had to be excised if the Chinese people were to live. Prostitution was a small but integral part of that growth; its elimination was an essential part of the cleansing of the Chinese social system. China could then go on to build a socialist modernity in which prostitution did not have an inevitable part, as it had under semicolonial capitalism.

Both the 1920s and the 1950s reformers saw prostitutes as dually constructed creatures: victims who sometimes profited from the circumstances of their victimization. The earlier group, while acknowledging that women were victims of economic pressures that drove them to prostitution, placed far more emphasis on their sexual victimization, since they were repeatedly subjected to the exercise of a male desire they were presumed not to share. Some of the Moral Welfare writings also hinted that prostitutes were vain and greedy women who diverted money that could be spent on charity into their personal adornment. What is most striking about the 1920s discourse on prostitution, however, is that prostitutes themselves were not at the center of it. Very little time or attention was devoted to their circumstances, much less their desires. Instead the discussion focused on the deleterious consequences of "commercialized vice" to the foreign community. This may have happened in part because most of the prostitutes were Chinese, whereas the clientele of concern to the reformers was white. Racism and cultural chauvinism rendered the women opaque to the reformers, who were more concerned to save white men (and women and children) from prostitution than to save the prostitutes from their surroundings. Although foreigners ran welfare institutions like the Door of Hope—which fit nicely with the characterization of prostitute as victim—they talked very little about prostitutes themselves, compared with the amount of time they expended on discussion of "the social evil."

The 1950s reformers, in contrast, placed the prostitute as victim squarely at the center of their reform discourse. One among many unfortunates in the "old society," she was nevertheless given a prominent place in 1950s reform writings as a victim of multiple oppressions: economic deprivation, sexual assault, kidnapping, forced labor, denial of medical care, physical abuse. Sexuality and sexual desire, on the part of either the prostitute or her client, were utterly eclipsed in this discourse. In the descriptions by reformers and prostitutes alike, sex was represented either as rape (by landlords, traffickers, brothel owners) or forced labor (during menstruation, after an abortion, on pain of beatings). But as with the 1920s campaign, the characterization of prostitute as victim (certainly not as sexual actor) was tempered by dark hints of character defects. Women might easily grow accustomed to a life of luxury, the warning went, a life in which they enjoyed fine clothes and leisure that were not the fruits of their own labor. The reform process was meant not only to detach the prostitute from her exploiters and to heal her physical and psychological wounds, but also to accustom her to labor, thereby readying her for productive employment and mending any character flaws induced by her previous life. These two characterizations coexisted uneasily: if a woman supported a brothel owner through her forced and degraded sexual labor—if she was, in fact, repeatedly victimized by the exploitation of that labor—how then could she also be a social parasite? Nevertheless, the two images—victim and parasite—had something important in common: neither granted women any agency in determining the conditions of their own pre-Liberation existence. Instead agency, in the form of the opportunity to construct oneself anew, was bestowed by a prostitute's wholehearted participation in the process of reform.

Both reform discourses, then, rendered the prostitute partially invisible by portraying her as essentially passive. This characterization undoubtedly reflects, in part, the lack of control that prostitutes in twentieth-century Shanghai had over their bodies, their labor, and their sexuality. It also reflects the uneasiness that both groups of reformers felt in dealing with women cut loose from the respectable social controls imposed by the family. The 1920s reformers failed to eradicate prostitution because they could not alter the social system that had detached these women from their families. The 1950s reformers succeeded, and restored Shanghai prostitutes to the ranks of respectable wives and mothers, as part of a much larger effort to reconstitute the family system[66] and "renaturalize" women into it.

The Maoist state eliminated prostitution and a host of other practices that many urban Chinese understood as signs of sexual shame and national weakness, and simultaneously promulgated a model of socially stable monogamous marriage as the only correct venue for sexual activity. This vision of socialist sexuality, expressed in marriage-law reform[67] and 1950s writings about marital sexuality[68] as well as in the elimination of prostitution, effectively removed gender and sexuality alike from the list of Chinese practices felt to be in need of modernization. No longer did urban intellectuals agonize about aspiring to a modernity that seemed forever threatened and beyond reach, and that had to be aggressively pursued in every realm, including the sexual. In Mao's China modernity was to be measured not by prostitute-free streets or monogamous conjugal relations, both of which were now inscribed in law, but rather by rising production figures and leadership in world revolution. Some of the questions that in the Republican period were spoken through sexual discourse were now redirected elsewhere—to tractor production, improvements in public health, and an increase in the pace of collectivization. These, not sexual hygiene or well-regulated prostitution, became the hallmarks of modernity.[69] Like earlier attempts to fix the relationship of prostitution to a Chinese modernity, however, this one proved impermanent. Prostitution, and public controversy about its relationship to modernity, reemerged in the 1980s with the state's invention of market socialism.

PART V

Contemporary Conversations

CHAPTER 13

Naming

During the period of economic reforms that began in 1978, foreign reporters, tourists, and businessmen in China reported, at first occasionally and then with increasing frequency, that prostitution had reappeared in Chinese cities. Over the course of the reform period profitable networks organized themselves around prostitution, generating income for a variety of sex workers, pimps, hotel attendants, massage- and beauty-parlor owners, roadside-stall operators, underworld gangs, and the police—to name only some of the groups who became involved with the developing sex trades. Beginning in the mid-1980s, official Chinese broadcasts and publications began intermittently to discuss prostitution, usually in the course of unsuccessful campaigns to eliminate it. At the same time scholars in recently rehabilitated disciplines like sociology and sexology, as well as newly created fields like women's studies, conducted surveys of prostitutes and their clients, simultaneously naming prostitution as a social problem and beginning to proffer solutions. Prostitutes began to appear as protagonists in established socialist genres such as social reportage and in newly resurgent genres such as tabloid fiction.

As prostitution once again became a recognized feature of Chinese society, it was incorporated—as it had been earlier in the twentieth century—into a larger public discussion about what kind of modernity China should seek and what kind of sex and gender arrangements should characterize that modernity. This discussion was not a simple reprise of the beliefs and arrangements of the earlier period. Activities classified as "prostitution" differed in some respects from their Republican-era predecessors. The "modernity" invoked in this discussion was not identical to that which haunted and eluded Republican-era intellectuals. The regulatory regimes devised by the post-Mao state to control, educate, and punish workers and consumers in the sex trades did not precisely replicate the failed experiments of the 1940s or the more effective ones of the 1950s. Tracing prostitution's most recent eruption into discourse, then, requires attention to at least three things: the reform period's particular visions of modernity; the historical resonances important to Chinese interlocutors as they fashioned the terms of debate; and the shifting content of the linkages they made between sex, gender, and modernity.

The first two chapters of this section, like the rest of the book, tack back and forth between what we know about contemporary sex work and how we know it. As in the preceding chapters, no clean boundary can be drawn between looking at "facts" and at their production. Although conventional reading practices require linearity, these two chapters should probably be thought of as the two parts of a dialogue; together they convey the interplay that makes the narrative work. The present chapter, "Naming," first examines the commonsense formulation that prostitution "returned" to China in the 1980s after an absence of several decades. It then offers a sketch of life in the sex trades, asking how, where, by whom, and to whom sexual services were sold. It explores what we know about why and how women became sex workers, and traces the categories through which they understood their own experiences. Chapter 14, "Explaining," takes up official and nonofficial formulations of late twentieth-century prostitution, returning to the process by which knowledge about sex work is created. How did the state categorize and seek to regulate reform-era prostitution? State formulations dominated public discussion in China; what was the effect of those formulations on wider social understandings of prostitution? What sorts of competing, resistant, or reinforcing formulations were articulated by nonstate sources? What meanings were attributed to sexual transactions by sellers, buyers, emergent social scientists, Women's Federation cadres, women's-studies scholars, journalists, fiction and nonfiction writers? Did this cluster of apparently dissonant formulations share a set of underlying assumptions—in, for example, linking sexuality to modernity? How did these formulations differ from those created by prostitutes and feminist social critics in contemporary North America and Europe—in, for example, treating prostitution as female sexual slavery, or as sex work?

The concept of "formulation" requires some explanation. In his study *Doing Things with Words in Chinese Politics,* Michael Schoenhals argues that "formalized language and formalized speech acts help constitute the structure of power within China's political system." In addition to registering publications and controlling photocopy equipment, he says, the state "exercises direct control over political discourse" by controlling the formulation of problems.[1] A formulation (*tifa*) is a fixed way of saying something; party leaders maintain that deviation from the correct scientific way of putting a problem can lead to confusion among the masses.[2] Although Schoenhals sees the importance of formulations diminishing in the reform era, the state did not completely discard them. The process of devising them, however, was no longer utterly monopolized by officialdom. Scholars, journalists, and others were active as well, and state formulations both reacted to and incorporated unofficial ones. This section adapts Schoenhals's use of the term "formulation" to include not only the precise choice of words and phrases, but also somewhat broader acts of classification.

Paying attention to the way in which a problem is formulated is not merely a matter of linguistic politesse. It is a means of understanding the complex nexus of language, regulation, and social flux. In late twentieth-century China, the state was simultaneously naming and regulating prostitution. As the numbers of women selling sexual services grew in the late 1980s and 1990s, state authorities first characterized the problem as one of vice, evil, or harm, linked to a wider spread of bourgeois liberalization. By the early 1990s, they had added two other formulations: prostitution as a violation of women's rights, and prostitution as a crime against social order. These "formalized speech acts" and their corollaries (vice was bourgeois, the violation of rights was feudal) had immediate policy implications, and palpable effects on the daily lives of those classified as prostitutes. Regulatory language did not merely describe a preexisting phenomenon called "prostitution"; it also constituted that phenomenon and, having created it, immediately moved to alter it.

China, of course, is not the only place where classificatory strategies are significant. In English the term "prostitution" has acquired multiple connotations, most of them having to do with vice, fallen virtue, and the loss of physical and ethical integrity. Deciding that the term is irredeemable, many advocates of prostitutes' rights in the United States and Europe have adopted the term "sex work," which calls attention to the labor performed in transactions involving sexual services. Although "sex work" has become the accepted phrase in contemporary transnational discussions, I retain the term "prostitution" here, not out of any fondness for its Victorian resonances, but because it is a closer approximation than "sex work" to the way sex-for-money transactions were named in Chinese discourse.

In the 1980s, government authorities often referred not to prostitutes (*jinü*), but to "women who sell sex" (*maiyin funü*), a term that emphasized an action rather than an ontological or occupational status. This was reportedly meant to indicate that such women did not specialize in the sale of sexual services.[3] An alternative explanation offered by Wang Xingjuan, a prominent researcher on women's issues, was that "prostitute" denotes a woman who has a license and whose sale of sex is recognized as legal by the government.[4] This usage departed somewhat from pre-1949 terminology, in which "prostitute" referred to both licensed and unlicensed activity.[5] The term "women who sell sex," which Wang says connoted illegal activity, was retained in sources of all types published through the early 1990s, and was used far more frequently than "prostitute."

Yet although the term "women who sell sex" emphasized an act of exchange, sex was not designated as work or analyzed as a form of wage-earning labor. This means that an entire range of approaches to and understandings of prostitution were not invoked. A formulation does not only name; it also silences other possibilities. This section of the book examines the implications of that silencing.

While including a discussion of the particular conditions of Shanghai, this final section widens its focus to take account of other locales as well as national-level discussions. In part this reflects the geographical patterns of the new sex trades, which began in coastal zones like Guangdong and Fujian, where the economic reforms were implemented earliest and most intensively. (Shanghai, in contrast, was intentionally left out of many reform experiments of the first decade, apparently because Deng Xiaoping felt that the risks of failure were too high.)[6] In part the national focus of this final section reflects the new nature of discussion about prostitution in the reform era. Whereas earlier regulatory efforts were fundamentally local in timing and scope, state interventions in the late twentieth century often followed closely from central-government initiatives. The question of how the party and the state should deal with prostitution became part of a larger national debate about the costs of reform. Similarly, nonstate intellectuals conducted local studies of sex work in order to address social problems faced by the nation as a whole. The efforts to classify and control prostitution can best be understood by attention to both local and national frames.

Virtually everyone who commented on late twentieth-century prostitution referred back to China's past, usually to invoke the bad old days of semicolonial weakness and vice, or to make comparisons with the good old days of the 1950s when the state successfully closed brothels. Sex work came to be regarded as a topic that had a history, rather than an embarrassing or titillating subject inappropriate for scholarly attention. Nevertheless, the comparisons were illuminating less for their reconstruction of the past than for what they suggested about the refurbishing of that past to suit the needs and tastes of the complex present.

COMMONSENSE FORMULATIONS: RESURGENT PROSTITUTION

The first commentators to invoke these historical comparisons were foreign reporters in 1980s China. Ever alert for discrepancies between what the government said about socialist society and what could be observed in daily social life, reporters noted that prostitutes were increasingly visible in hotels and coffee shops patronized by foreigners. Their articles invariably classified prostitution as a resurgent phenomenon, with titles like "Prostitution Is

Back, and Peking Isn't Happy" (John F. Burns in the *New York Times*, 1985), "Prostitution Returns, Chinese Officials Say" (Daniel Southerland in the *Washington Post*, 1985), "Newest Economics Revives the Oldest Profession" (Edward Gargan in the *New York Times*, 1988), "What the Revolution in China Wiped Out, Reform Brought Back" (Adi Ignatius and Julia Leung in the *Wall Street Journal*, 1989), and "Prostitution Thriving Again in China" (Lena Sun in the *Washington Post*, 1992).[7] As background, these reporters told a standard story that typically went like this:

> Before 1949, before socialist morality became creed, prostitutes engulfed port cities from Tianjin to Canton. . . . [O]ne of the first targets of the new local governments was the eradication of social decadence. . . . Tens of thousands of prostitutes were sent to re-education centers. . . . For decades afterward, Chinese officials boasted that prostitution . . . had disappeared from the mainland.[8]

Embedded in much of the foreign writing on China was an assumption that prostitution is a "natural" feature of society that will always exist, absent tireless enforcement of state restrictions. Alternatively, foreign writers characterized it as an inevitable product of a market economy, citing the state's loosening of social and economic controls, official encouragement to make money, and "changing sexual mores and contacts with foreigners and overseas Chinese from Taiwan and Hong Kong."[9]

Chinese officials shared this characterization of prostitution as something that first disappeared, then reappeared. State propaganda had long touted the elimination of prostitution in the early 1950s as one of New China's victories over imperialism. Far from regarding its return as inevitable, however, some officials saw it as evidence that the cost of interaction with foreign industrialized nations might be too high. In 1985 foreign reporters surmised that conservative leaders like Chen Yun and Deng Liqun were commenting on prostitution to embarrass the chief architect of reform, Deng Xiaoping, and pressure him to slow the pace of economic change.[10] These efforts were unsuccessful, and by the 1990s the grounds of debate had shifted. Some officials could be heard to grumble (although not for attribution) that prostitution was an inevitable part of society and that the state should tax it rather than waste time and resources in futile attempts at suppression. Regardless of their policy differences, however, most officials, and many social scientists as well, invoked a standard four-character phrase to describe prostitution's resurgence: *sihui furan*, or "dying embers that flare up again."

On the surface, the assumption that prostitution was here, then gone, then here seemed like the most undeniable sort of common sense. Like most commonsense understandings, however, this one prevented certain questions from being asked. Had prostitution ever disappeared? Was there anything historically specific about its particular visibility in the late twentieth century, something that was not a mere replication of prostitution in pre-Communist China or the years of Mao's rule? Was there anything locally specific about the emergence of prostitution in China, something that was not an exact replication of the situation in Southeast Asia, Latin America, or the United States? Some of these questions were addressed by nonstate commentators, but they were generally ignored in state documents.

Intriguing accounts by political refugees from Guangdong, published in Hong Kong in the late 1960s and 1970s, suggested that perhaps the embers of prostitution had never died at all. A former Guangzhou teacher wrote that before the Cultural Revolution began in the mid-1960s, two types of prostitution had been practiced in Guangzhou. One was in government guest houses, where foreigners who were friendly to China were "entertained by hostesses who anticipated their every wish." The hostesses, middle school graduates who had been given six months of training in English, were reportedly kept confined and were paid nothing by the foreign guests. The other type of prostitution was found in organizations such as drama troupes, where daughters of landlords and Guomindang-government officials made off-duty income by sleeping with influential party personnel. Arrangements were not made directly with the women, but were channeled through a group leader who kept thirty yuan of the fifty-yuan fee. These reports were unverifiable, but their message was clear: prostitution was portrayed as a direct consequence of government policies, a sign that China was badly governed by hypocritical officials who claimed to have eliminated prostitution even as they enjoyed prostitutes themselves and procured them for foreign friends of the revolution.[11]

In the aftermath of the Cultural Revolution, both the volume and variety of these Hong Kong reports increased. One particularly detailed account was compiled from reports by a group of educated youth who had been held in detention centers during the 1970s, apparently for political offenses, and there had encountered prostitutes among their fellow inmates. Most of the prostitutes were young urban women whose families had been sent to poor rural districts or to May Seventh cadre schools during the Cultural Revolution, leaving the families' adolescent daughters with no one to support or supervise them in the city. These young women slept with "old men from the countryside" or with wealthy overseas Chinese who lived in special housing in Guangzhou. In one report, a married rural woman provided sexual services to village men in return for salted fish and meat, with the approval and connivance of her husband. Her sons used some of the accumulated proceeds to acquire coveted places in the People's Liberation Army.[12]

Like the accounts of pre–Cultural Revolution prostitution, these stories delineate a gap between official claims and actual social practice. They express the disillusionment of an idealistic generation raised "under the red flag" when the disruptions of the Cultural Revolution pushed them out of the classroom and brought them into contact with social problems about which they had been taught nothing. One young man recounted his aston-ishment when he heard during his imprisonment that a beautiful young woman had been locked up for prostitution. When he asked his fellow in-mates if such things still existed, they mocked him, saying, "Four-Eyes, didn't the teacher teach you? Go back and ask the teacher!" (Here his eyeglasses served as a convenient trope for his educated status and the gap that sepa-rated him from ordinary criminals, a gap "unnaturally" bridged by the up-heaval of the Cultural Revolution.) Later the woman was displayed and de-nounced before all the inmates as a "lascivious woman whose stinking name has spread far," who "admitted in writing that more than sixty men have slept with her," and who was also accused of "corrupting the revolutionary ranks" by using sex to obtain favors from cadres.[13] So common was prostitution, the narrators of these stories learned in prison, that a whole local slang existed to describe it. A prostitute was a *mada* or "motor"; the women's section of a detention center was a *mafang* (literally "horse room"), a place full of pros-titutes. Prostitutes in downtown Guangzhou solicited customers through the use of code words. If a woman approached a man and asked if he had a win-dow facing south, a phrase that usually referred to connections with Hong Kong and Macao, she was inquiring about his access to a convenient place to have sexual relations.

In many of these vignettes, through hearing the life circumstances of a prostitute, a previously sheltered young prisoner became aware that some women were desperate enough to sell themselves "for a bowl of wonton and noodles," poor enough to supplement the family diet with food given in pay-ment for sex, conniving enough to combine sex work with pickpocketing, shrewd enough to take money from overseas Chinese and then slip away "like a cicada shedding its skin" without providing sex, or shameless enough to strip off their clothes during jailhouse brawls. The stories of prostitutes were framed within two larger narratives: the loss of political innocence by the Red Guard generation, and a critique of government policies that allowed the perpetuation of poverty and created new sources of social disruption and chaos. Like the government authorities they were criticizing, these authors took the presence of prostitution as a sign of moral and political decay.

LIFE IN THE SEX TRADES

If prostitution's disappearance under Mao was apparently less than complete, the scope and visibility of sex-for-money transactions grew exponentially in Deng Xiaoping's reform economy.[14] The most striking feature of prostitu-tion in late twentieth-century China was the proliferation of venues, prices, and migration patterns. In contrast to the situation before 1949, specialized brothels were rare, and were never labeled as such. Instead, what one article called "smoke and flower women of every status" offered their sexual services in hotels, movie houses, theaters, dance halls, bars, hair salons, coffee shops, rented rooms, roadside shops, taxis, train stations, public squares, parks, and private homes.[15] By the mid-1980s, complex segmented markets for sexual services had emerged in Chinese cities and towns, drawing out-of-province women as well as local ones into sex work.

With the proliferation of sexual services came an information explosion about the working conditions, social characteristics, and psychology of prostitutes. Like the paper trail left in earlier twentieth-century sources, these data were gathered by reporters, police, social scientists, and fiction writers. Understanding how prostitution was constituted demands simultaneous attention to the conventions of the genres through which these data were selected, presented, and interpreted. Fortunately, these features of the sources are not subtle, since virtually every writer was explicitly shaping an argument about prostitution.

Numbers are particularly unreliable where illegal activities are concerned. Government statistics on prostitution typically recorded an aggregate number of prostitutes and customers detained each year (although the two groups were penalized differently, as discussed in the following chapter). These numbers were usually announced by the government either in order to justify a forthcoming arrest sweep or to announce the success of one just completed. Sometimes pimps were included in this number as well, and the number of repeat offenders was never indicated. Some types of prostitutes were more vulnerable to detention than others. National and local governments also varied in the zeal with which they pursued offenders, alternating intense waves of activity with long periods of relative inattention. The statistics thus tell us as much about government policies toward sex work as they do about prostitutes. Nevertheless, the rise over time in numbers of people detained is worth noting. (Table 2 in appendix A summarizes the available figures.) According to the Ministry of Public Security, from 1981 through 1991 authorities detained 580,000 prostitutes and customers (rendered quaintly by the translator as "whore-mongers").[16] The number of prostitutes and customers arrested in 1992 alone equaled 42 percent of the total arrests made in the previous eleven years.

How many of those detained might have been prostitutes is impossible to tell, since the authorities never said how often they detained both parties to a sexual encounter, and prostitutes might well have been arrested without a customer present. In early 1994, however, the national government announced that 1993 arrests of prostitutes alone totaled almost 250,000.[17] Qualitative evidence on the intermittent and uneven nature of enforcement suggests that this figure was only a fraction of the number engaged in prostitution.

Government officials, as noted earlier, attributed the appearance of prostitution to the influx of foreign ideas and investment along the coast in the mid-1980s. Social-science researchers also posited a pattern in which prostitution spread from the coast to the interior, and from urban to rural areas. "The hot points for selling sex are still the big southern coastal cities like Xiamen, Shanghai, Guangzhou, Zhuhai, Haikou, and Sanya," wrote Wang Xingjuan in 1990. "But it is spreading toward the west and north. Some small cities and townships, and even roadside shops in remote villages, have sex-selling activities."[18]

Yet a description that names the areas of greatest foreign investment as the initial source of prostitution may be oversimplified. Chinese researchers found prostitutes even earlier in interior cities, drawn there from the countryside as government restrictions on population movement eased in the early years of the reform era. In the early 1980s, Chinese began to change occupations and locations in ways forbidden since the late 1950s. The movement of women into sexual services was linked to larger shifts in the labor market: urban workers took up moonlighting or left their assigned jobs to start up their own businesses; farmers left the land to migrate from less to more prosperous areas; and township dwellers moved to larger urban settlements.[19] Women made up roughly a third of all transients, and transients as a group tended to be young.[20] As early as 1982, an unpublished Women's Federation investigation in Xi'an (not one of the early-developing coastal areas), based on police files and interviews, found prostitutes from rural areas working out of small hotels with a local clientele. Many were married women who had been sent to work as urban prostitutes by their husbands; in some cases the husbands acted as pimps. Others had fled unhappy family situations. Still others worked in clothing repair at the railroad station and moonlighted as prostitutes. These women charged only several yuan per encounter,[21] a price that would come to seem very low later in the decade, when inflation and a growing "luxury market" in women sent prices into the hundreds and thousands of yuan.

By the latter half of the 1980s a new type of prostitution had emerged in the coastal cities and special economic zones, appearing first in Shenzhen and Guangzhou, then in Shanghai and northern cities.[22] High-priced prostitutes, working mainly out of hotels, sought out a foreign clientele, which included both short-term visitors and long-term resident businessmen from Hong Kong, Taiwan, and Macao. Some of these women themselves lived in big hotels and maintained a group of regular customers, who contacted them by dialing their beeper numbers. Reporters for the *Wall Street Journal*, with an eye to brand-name quality, described a woman in Guangzhou named Ah Hong who worked the hotels wearing "Pierre Cardin sweaters, elegant silk pants, spiked heels." She called guests randomly from the hotel lobby, suggesting that they become friends. University-educated, Ah Hong charged each customer fifty to one hundred U.S. dollars, and reportedly earned twenty-seven hundred U.S. dollars a month, in a nation where the average monthly income was equivalent to forty U.S. dollars.[23] Prostitutes who made less money lived in hotel rooms with other prostitutes or rented rooms in private homes, but saw their customers in the hotels.[24]

A 1989 police investigation of a guest house in Humen, ninety miles north of Hong Kong in Guangdong, gives some sense of how a group of less elite hotel prostitutes worked. Police found about thirty prostitutes staying in the guest house as permanent guests. Referred to as "northern girls," they came from Hunan, Guangxi, Sichuan, Shanghai, Shenyang, Heilongjiang, Hubei, and Guizhou (but not from Guangdong; apparently prostitutes often worked outside their own provinces). Most were about twenty years old. They followed guests to their rooms and propositioned them directly, or else called the rooms. Some had been brought there under the control of pimps, who also stayed in the guest house. Some hired bodyguards. They earned one hundred yuan per encounter, five hundred if they spent an entire night. Their earnings supported pimps and bodyguards, as well as payoffs to hotel attendants and security personnel. One woman told an undercover investigator that the attendant on duty received a ten-yuan tip for each session. Attendants regularly colluded with prostitutes, letting them know when guests were in their rooms. The women also asserted that the hotel manager welcomed prostitutes as an added attraction for guests. Clients were tourists from Hong Kong and Macao, as well as Chinese managers and marketing people from various companies, cadres, and workers. The women said that the manager sent appropriate presents to the Public Security Bureau, which rarely checked the place.[25] In many cases, it appears that official collusion extended beyond the law-enforcement authorities. In Fujian, prostitutes were discovered working in a hotel run by the People's Liberation Army; in Guangzhou, similar activities were uncovered in a guest house belonging to the provincial Women's Federation; in 1994 Shanghai, both the Public Security Bureau and the People's Liberation Army were deeply involved in the operation of karaoke clubs and brothels.[26]

In addition to directly soliciting foreign hotel guests in their rooms, prostitutes worked discos, karaoke bars, and coffee shops in or near the hotels. In Shanghai's Hongqiao Hotel in 1993, I observed high-priced prostitutes in the disco and bar on the thirtieth floor. Unlike other customers at the disco, they did not pay the cover charge of eighty-five yuan (seventy-five on weekdays) upon entry. Some had permanent free-entry status as honored guests, while others deposited some form of identification and received a tag indicating that they would pay when they left. They danced with other patrons of the disco, who were foreigners from Hong Kong and other Asian nations as well as rich local men. Some accompanied guests into one of the dozen or so karaoke booths in the back, which could be rented by the hour. (These were private but not concealed from view, since all had large windows opening on the hallway.) Prostitutes were not completely distinguish-able from other women in the bar, unless one watched them over a period of time. After dancing with a man, a prostitute would move with him away from the deafening music of the dance floor and toward a tiny lounge near the karaoke booths. There prostitutes sat and conversed with their poten-tial customers in several languages or stood next to men, interspersing ne-gotiation over prices with long silences. The absence of flirtatious or overtly sexual behavior was noticeable; many of the women exhibited all the ani-mation of statues, except when they clustered in groups to talk to one an-other or joked with the attendant in the women's room. They also appeared to be on friendly terms with the waitresses in the bar area, who were dressed in military camouflage outfits and shorts. Some of the prostitutes wore beep-ers; others crowded the small bank of phones at one end of the lounge, ap-parently dialing rooms inside the hotel in quick succession. A man from Hong Kong who was accompanying two visiting Korean businessmen ex-plained that the women charged eighty-five yuan (the cost of the cover charge) to dance and converse with a man. Unlike the situation in Japan and Korea, the three men complained, the amount of time guaranteed to the purchaser was not standardized. Disgruntled customers often found that women abruptly left them in mid-chat. A woman could conduct several of these conversations in an evening and make substantial money without ever leaving the disco or agreeing to an act of sexual intercourse. In order to have sexual relations with her, a man had to offer enough money to exceed what she could make at the disco.[27]

Foreigners familiar with the bar scene observed that these women could be quite aggressive in marketing themselves. In the breathless style charac-teristic of much writing about the reform era, reporters incorporated this pushiness into a larger description of a post-Mao China on the move for money:

> With chopsticks in one hand and portable phones in the other, the entre-
> preneurs of Shanghai, this most colourful and exciting of Chinese cities, are
> engaging in a single-minded pursuit of cash—foreign cash. Shanghai is
> throwing off the constraints of communism and is on the make. . . . In its
> pre-revolutionary heyday, prostitution was an institution in Shanghai with
> celebrated singsong houses offering food, entertainment and opium in
> addition to sex. This comprehensive service has yet to return but thousands
> of beautiful young women have revived the sex and escort trades, although
> the marketing sometimes lacks a little subtlety. A worldly western diplomat
> was lost for words recently when a young woman detached herself from a
> crowd and confronted him with a blunt sales pitch. "Do you want to buy
> me," she asked in English. The woman who introduced herself as Jane in
> the Casablanca disco and karaoke club high above the Hongqiao district was
> also keen to get to the point. "Will you buy me a ticket?" she sweetly asked

the overseas Chinese businessman. "What's the ticket for?" he inquired, genuinely puzzled. "It's only 100 yen [*sic*]," she replied by way of explanation. He declined but her face tightened as she pulled his sleeve back to reveal a Rolex watch. "You can buy me a ticket," she argued much more forcefully. He refused again but offered to buy her a drink instead, which she disdainfully accepted. When the drink arrived, Jane immediately excused herself to go to the toilet. She didn't return but was soon replaced by another equally attractive woman and the cycle started again.[28]

In this back-to-the-future version of China's aspirations, the call girl was grouped with entrepreneurs in other trades, all of them engaged in a frenzy of activity that recalled pre-1949 Shanghai even as it invoked an emergent twenty-first-century modernity.

Brothels, the organizing institution of pre-1949 prostitution, were relatively rare in the late twentieth century.[29] Because brothels remained illegal, it was far more common for women to frequent bars, hotels, and coffee shops, modifying their practices to elude the intermittently attentive police. For instance, when police took to raiding hotel rooms late at night, prostitutes ceased spending the night with customers and changed their times of operation to dusk or early morning. Rather than solicit guests themselves, they sent male intermediaries to make arrangements and collect the cash in advance.[30]

Another way for a prostitute to avoid police interference was to eschew casual and short-term sexual encounters with foreigners and enter into a rental arrangement. Men from Hong Kong and Taiwan who spent several months a year in China would frequently choose a beautiful, educated woman as a companion. The man would provide housing and living expenses, sometimes completing marriage-registration procedures with the local authorities (although he might well have a spouse at home as well). These arrangements normally were not interfered with by the police. The man secured regular social, domestic, and sexual services. The woman received considerable material benefits, controlling her own time and activities when the man was not in China, perhaps even returning to the discos and karaoke bars to seek short-term patrons.[31]

By the late 1980s, a considerable domestic clientele for prostitution had emerged, comprising men who had acquired wealth or official privilege under the reforms. Police told foreign reporters in Guangzhou that "[j]ust a few years ago most of prostitutes' customers in Canton were foreigners. Today, they are mainly Chinese men."[32] In the first nine months of 1985, of three hundred men detained by the Guangzhou police for patronizing prostitutes, only one-quarter were from Hong Kong, Macao, or foreign countries; two-thirds were from Guangdong province, and the remainder from other provinces. Proprietors of individual enterprises (*getihu*), drivers, labor contractors, enterprise staff members, and cadres—all occupational groups with new opportunities for moneymaking and travel—were the customers most frequently mentioned in news reports and surveys, although university students, teachers, and retirees figured in these stories as well.[33] It appears that the women who serviced these Chinese customers were a different group from those who solicited foreigners. A writer who interviewed a number of Shanghai prostitutes found them unwilling to sleep with Chinese men, disdainful of their inability to afford a hotel room and their fear of being seen or arrested in their hometown. Rich Shanghai men went to Shenzhen and Guangdong to find prostitutes, who charged several hundred yuan per encounter.[34] By 1993, it was reported that some bars were hiring Russian and eastern European women to provide sex to wealthy Chinese customers, and by 1994, the reemergence of teenage prostitution was being reported in Shanghai.[35]

The rental arrangements employed by foreign businessmen were also used by Chinese men whose work took them away from home for long periods. Men from more prosperous coastal areas found it easy to rent women in interior cities like Xi'an.[36] These liaisons sometimes also inverted conventional social hierarchies. In Shanghai, for instance, labor contractors from the countryside hired lower-class urban women as local mates; the housing and money these women received offered more comfortable circumstances than marrying a worker, and were apparently enough to overcome the well-known Shanghainese disdain for rural outlanders.[37]

At the lower end of the hierarchy of prostitution, customers included what one social survey called "elements that have been released from labor reform or labor education, living in the lower strata of society." Echoing reformers of the Republican period, the author described them as men who "do not have the economic means to marry, do not want the trouble and effort of a household, and use visits to prostitutes to satisfy their sexual needs."[38] A larger group of lower-class customers, however, were drivers and passengers in the numerous vehicles that hauled goods on China's growing network of long-distance roads. In one district of eastern Zhejiang province, an investigation found thirty-four prostitutes working in privately run truck-stop restaurants and hostels. News items from around the country described women standing by the side of the road, leaping onto the running boards of passing trucks, and inviting drivers into roadside restaurants. After finishing his meal, a driver who decided to stay at an adjoining hostel might find the waitress in his bed.[39] These services were often organized at the behest of truck-stop owners. At a 1992 provincial-government conference in Shandong, officials noted:

> There are more than twenty-five thousand roadside stalls in the province. They have played a positive role in developing the local economy and enlivening circulation. However, to reap staggering profits, some stall owners lured, allowed, or forced female workers to prostitute themselves or employed or asked female workers to solicit customers in a pornographic way.[40]

A literary (but not necessarily fictional) account of a truck stop in the Tai-hang Mountains suggested that these roadside establishments were wild ter-ritory, patrolled irregularly by police but otherwise free from the social con-straints of nearby cities and towns. Describing the stretch of road as a place where in the past illicit lovers had abandoned their illegitimate children and residents had dumped their garbage, the story continued:

> Most people who stop here are drivers and owners of cargo. Most patrons are "big shots" in industry, commerce, and taxation. The rest are idlers from the nearby city, what Western society calls *bengke* (the English is PUNK, "a worthless thing"). Mothers of good folks advise their sons: "Don't go to the ring road!" Women say sternly to their husbands: "You're not to go to the ring road!" It is as though the ring road were a big vat of dye, and good men who walk through there would emerge covered in black. Mysterious ring road! Wildflowers in the colors of seduction and lasciviousness![41]

The story offered an imaginative reconstruction of the life of one truck-stop hostess named Er Lanzi (Second Orchid). Er Lanzi, literally the embodiment of the ring road's unrestrained mores, appeared one day at the truck stop "bringing a woman's wild nature and a woman's hope." She is reported as saying, "At the time I scared the owner of that small restaurant dumbstruck, and then he was wild with joy," presumably at the prospect of increased busi-ness. She pawned herself to the restaurant owner in return for one-third of the monthly profits. If a patron ordered food and cigarettes, he was permitted to kiss and fondle Er Lanzi, who wore a skimpy red dress even on chilly moun-tain nights. Although she did not have sexual intercourse with customers, she apparently colluded with the restaurant owner to blackmail men who wanted to sleep with her. The author reported that on March 25, 1993, she "used every possible means to tease and tempt" a driver from Yangquan into a back room. The record of his subsequent interrogation by the police is quoted (or reconstructed) verbatim in the story:

> *Question:* What were you doing there?
> *Answer:* Moving cargo.
> *Question:* Tell us what happened.
> *Answer:* After I entered the room, I locked the door. She smiled at me and took off her clothes, leaving a bra and underpants. The bra was black and the underpants were red.
> *Question:* Who asked you to talk about that? Tell us what happened!
> *Answer:* I also took off my pants. When I walked toward her she yelled, "Help! He's behaving like a hoodlum! Rape!" At that moment the owner rushed in.
> *Question:* How did he open the door? Didn't you lock it?
> *Answer:* She opened it. Then he asked me, "Public or private?" "Public" meant that he would bring a rape charge, "private" that I would hand

over one thousand kuai. I tried every possible way to persuade him, and
settled it for six hundred kuai. Otherwise, I would report it to the police.
Question: Did you know that what you did was against the law?
Answer: I knew. Whoring [*piao nüren*] breaks the law.
Question: You knew and you did it anyway?
Answer: From now on I definitely won't do it again.
Question: According to the Security Administration Punishment Act, the fine
is two hundred yuan. What do you have to say?
Answer: All right.[42]

Part legal education, part cautionary tale, part subtle humor poking fun at
the police, the story rendered Er Lanzi both enticing and dangerous. Ultimately, though, the narrative made sure that her "woman's wild nature" was
contained by a morality tale of chastity lost. She fell in love with a poor but
honest local laborer, bought him dinner every night on her personal tab,
and restrained her flirtation with customers in his presence. When he finally
spent the night with her and bit her shoulder black and blue, she cried and
said she was his, that she loved him. But when she became pregnant by him,
he accused her of not knowing who the father was and left her.[43]

Another common venue for attracting Chinese customers traveling on
business was the coffee shops near urban train stations and docks. A 1993
report in the *Xi'an Legal News* described young women in heavy makeup and
miniskirts (*mi ni duanqun;* literally, "enchant-you short skirt") who roamed
the streets convincing hapless male travelers to stop in at their establishments
for liquor, coffee, soda, or even hot milk. It depicted a coffee shop where
hostesses entertained a group of men with cigarettes, tea, and caresses:
"[S]ometimes a woman could not avoid coming into contact with a man's
sensitive parts, but luckily the lights were dim, causing everyone to avoid em-
barrassment." When the men's bill came to 1,860 yuan rather than the expected 200, the group lodged a complaint with the police. The coffee-shop
manager tried unsuccessfully to bribe the police chief, who became right-
eously angry, closed the coffee shop, locked up the manager, and fined the
guests for "sexual activities" (*seqing xingwei*). The hostesses, however, had long
since disappeared.[44] Although the standard service in these establishments
appeared to stop short of sexual intercourse, entertainment by hostesses was
described as part of a generally increasing availability of sexual services, provided by wily women who did not hesitate to entrap and fleece innocent travelers. Even while calling for increased regulation of coffee shops and detailing
the dangers found therein, however, official publications like this one appealed to their urban readership with detailed descriptions of titillating
scenes.

Most stories about prostitution depicted women soliciting their own business, whether at a bank of phones in a hotel lobby or on the running boards
of passing trucks. Nevertheless, in some regions pimps had appeared by the

late 1980s. Reporting on prostitution in Fuzhou hotel bars, Edward Gargan described young women drinking Coca-Cola while "young men in ostentatious jewelry look for clients to whom they can offer the women's services."[45] Some taxi drivers used their contact with travelers to locate potential customers. Social scientists commented that if young women wanted to establish themselves as prostitutes and avoid arrest, they had to depend on the practice of pimping (*la pitiaoke*, literally, "pull leather-strap guest"). Police intervention thus had the effect of increasing both licit and illicit male control over women's sexual services. Pimps contacted customers, delivered prostitutes discreetly, covered their tracks, collected money, and acted as bodyguards.[46]

Like "prostitute," the term "pimp" covered a variety of arrangements, from friends, relatives, or business associates who acted as simple intermediaries or protectors, to traffickers, often in league with the growing underworld, who kidnapped women or lured them with promises of employment and used physical coercion to induce them to become prostitutes.[47] In the first seven months of 1991, the government said, it had uncovered thirty-three hundred prostitution gangs with links to the underworld Triad organization; by 1994, foreign reporters were describing intricate connections in Shanghai between the Triads, prostitution rings, and government agencies.[48] Pimps were far from ubiquitous; one writer even claimed that Shanghai had no pimps at all ("Shanghai women are tough; they cannot be controlled").[49] Yet the need for women to protect themselves from police interference, as well as the increasing amounts of money to be made in the sex trade, combined to attract increasing numbers of men to pimping, even though it was a criminal offense that was sometimes punished by execution.[50] Descriptions of income division between pimps and prostitutes are scarce, but one researcher who studied gangs comprising prostitutes, gang heads (*baozhu*), and pimps found that the women gave 30 percent of their income to the gang head and 20 percent to the pimp. Alternatively, women organized themselves into groups (*tuanhuo*), often on the basis of native-place origin, which could grow to involve several dozen people.[51] The Chinese press also reported cases where women were arrested for acting as madams, arranging for sexual encounters and providing premises (typically in restaurants or rented rooms).[52]

The range of venues, clientele, and pimping arrangements corresponded to a range of prices, made even more difficult to trace by the rate of inflation and the fact that high-class prostitutes preferred payment in foreign currency or foreign-exchange certificates. In 1985 Chinese researchers found prostitutes charging one to eight yuan (35 cents to $2.75 U.S.) in Fujian; in 1986 a newspaper reported that relatively low-class prostitutes earned twenty to thirty yuan per encounter.[53] By the 1990s, fees for Beijing prostitutes reportedly ranged from fifty to five hundred yuan.[54] Such information does not take account of arrangements where women worked in cooperation with restaurant, coffee-shop, or bar owners and took a share of the profits. What is clear, however, is that prostitution proved lucrative enough either to replace or to supplement other employment options for women from a variety of regions and class backgrounds.

REEDUCATION AND ITS DISCONTENTS

Faced with a growing prostitute population of a complexity rapidly approaching that of pre-Liberation Shanghai, the government reached for the old methods of incarceration and reeducation. Increasing numbers of prostitutes were remanded to reform facilities in the late 1980s and 1990s. Prior to that time, prostitutes had been detained briefly and then sent back to their native places.[55] In turning to reform facilities, authorities recognized that many women were operating in their own hometowns, and that deporting outsiders was a temporary and partial solution. Women sometimes were sent to facilities exclusively for prostitutes,[56] but more often they were integrated into the general population of female reeducation subjects. In "mixed" facilities, prostitutes made up an ever-increasing percentage of the inmate population.[57]

By 1991, about fifty-six thousand prostitutes had passed through 103 reeducation centers nationwide.[58] In 1992 China had 113 such facilities, with a population of about fifty thousand prostitutes. Most major cities had a reform institute; Guangzhou had several, and Beijing and Guangzhou also boasted the nation's only two reeducation facilities for customers. The reform institutes (*jiaoyangsuo* or *shourong jiaoyusuo*), usually under the jurisdiction of the Public Security Bureau, held several hundred inmates serving sentences from six months to two years. In keeping with the framework of reeducation, the staff were called "teachers" (*laoshi*) and the inmates "students" (*xueyuan*). Most of the prostitutes in the reform institutes were first offenders. Recidivists were sent for one to three years of labor education (*laodong jiaoyang*) in institutions run by the judicial department (*Sifa bu*).[59]

What to do with this newly created class of offenders was by no means clear. "How to educate and reform them was a new problem for us, since prostitution and visiting prostitutes had disappeared in the early years of liberation," commented the authors of one correctional-facility work report.[60] Their first response was to fall back upon the analytical categories of the 1950s, notably the centrality of labor in the reeducation process:

> Because the inmates had been spoiled by their parents or had been poisoned by the thinking of the exploiting classes in which one does not labor but is rewarded, and in which pleasure is supreme, they commonly cultivated the bad habits of loving indolence and hating labor, and seeking after pleasure. Therefore it is very important to organize them to participate in labor. Through labor and labor education, they can be led to correctly

recognize the importance of labor; to discard the thinking of despising labor, fearing bitterness and looking down on laboring people; and to go further and correct their labor attitude; . . . [to] cultivate the cooperative spirit of collectivism and the characteristics of disciplined labor and ability to eat bitterness and labor patiently, and thus to thoroughly transform their thinking. . . . Through participating in labor they can learn a skill and in the future feed themselves through their own efforts, which is beneficial in overcoming their dependence upon men.

In addition to participating in labor, inmates were to be organized to develop "proper interests and hobbies" through small reading groups, speech contests, and physical exercise.[61]

Work reports by correctional staff, however, indicated that reform was a more complicated procedure than installing a love of labor and a healthy involvement with hobbies. In the 1950s, reformers could expect to release prostitutes into an environment newly imbued with socialist virtues, where any recidivism would be reported by neighbors, and where a work assignment and sometimes a marriage had already been arranged by helpful state authorities. In the 1990s, in contrast, women would return to a less ordered social situation, in which their work lives and their sexual activity were primarily their own responsibility. They had to be taught, as one Beijing work report put it, "to strengthen their ability to resist the sexual pollution [*xing wuran*] in the social environment, and establish a correct view of honor and disgrace, morality, and the legal system." Although the work report made use of the rhetoric of class and labor, when it came to specifying a course of study for prostitutes the focus shifted to the individual, and the language resonated with that of Western self-help movements. "In order to cause them to newly establish a woman's self-respect," the report intoned,

> correctional personnel must not, regardless of circumstances, injure their self-esteem, but must use all means possible to inspire and protect it. Because "self-esteem is the foundation of a person's character, and if one loses self-esteem, one's character will collapse."

The work report also dealt frankly with what reformers saw as the most problematic aspect of these women's personalities: their unrestrained, even depraved, sexuality. Because of their long periods of prostitution and licentious activities, reformers felt, the sexual desire of prostitutes was difficult to control, manifesting itself under conditions of incarceration in abnormal (*yichang*) forms such as homosexuality, sex talk, flaunting of their past incredible sex lives, cracking low-class vulgar jokes, and masturbation. Regardless of what social surveys said about the economic motivation of most prostitutes, and their reported ambivalent attitudes about sexual activity, in the accounts of reformers they became women who had given themselves over to sex—in fact, organized their personalities around it. Reform would require, then, a reorganization of their desires, to be accomplished by "forcibly asserting strict control over these bad sexual activities" and by organizing the women to study the textbook *The Rectification of Sex Crimes and Mistakes*.[62]

Many Chinese observers felt that the success of such methods was decidedly unimpressive. Small and crowded, the reform facilities saw their populations swell every time a new assault was made on prostitution.[63] In spite of the government's zeal in rounding up prostitutes, the reform institutes were inadequately funded: staff members received wages from the state, but utilities and other operating expenses were supposed to be paid from the proceeds of inmate labor.[64] In order to meet these expenses, many reform institutes required inmates to work extra shifts, which could be as long as twelve hours per day. Compulsory labor at menial tasks supplanted all other activities, including the education and job training that were supposed to prepare these women to refigure their desires and find useful work outside the sex trades. Compounding the problem was a shortage of staff—some institutes had only eight staff for every one hundred women—which made in-depth education impossible. If inmates fled, the institutes had no vehicles in which to chase them.[65] All these conditions left institute staff very demoralized: working at facilities far from their homes (since reform institutes were often located in districts far from the city center), ill-paid, surrounded by uncooperative inmates, fearful of contracting an STD,[66] many felt their task to be impossible. As for the prostitutes, they felt that their relatively poor and overworked keepers, who had not been to fancy hotels or owned fine clothes, understood little of life. The inmates' experience with long hours of tedious labor did nothing to convince them that labor was glorious. The main effect of reform, some observers concluded, was to expose a great number of first offenders to a small number of recidivists who taught them new ways to operate.[67] Scattered studies put the recidivism rate at about 25 percent,[68] but some correctional staff, convinced that their work was ineffective, estimated that 80 percent of the inmates would return to prostitution.[69]

CLASSIFIED SUBJECTS

A woman incarcerated for prostitution was more likely to resemble a truck-stop sex worker like Er Lanzi than a call girl like Ah Hong; high-class prostitutes did their soliciting largely out of public view, and were able to pay off hotel staff and the police. Even among lower-class prostitutes, those with experience and good local connections were more successful at avoiding arrest. Of one hundred prostitutes surveyed in a Beijing reeducation center in 1992, 90 percent were first offenders.[70] Younger, poorer, and less experienced women, as well as women who had recently migrated from the countryside, were thus overrepresented in the reeducation centers.[71]

Yet it was the incarcerated population that was accessible to corrections officials and social scientists, and it was from this group that most information about age, marriage and family arrangements, native place, education, occupation, and motivation was drawn. Like arrest statistics, such data revealed at least as much about the preoccupations and policies of the investigators as they did about the subjects. Sometimes they also suggested, albeit indirectly, how prostitutes felt about being investigated. One social scientist, herself highly critical of the questionnaire approach to social problems, reported that incarcerated prostitutes systematically lied on surveys in order to frustrate and embarrass the authorities; in one Guangzhou investigation, virtually every prostitute reported that her main customers were policemen and managers.[72] (It is also possible, of course, that these women were accurately describing their clientele. The Chinese press abounded with descriptions of Communist Party officials who were caught either visiting prostitutes or procuring them for foreigners.)[73]

Although its meaning is far from transparent, information collected from incarcerated women can tell us something about the prostitutes subjected to state rehabilitation. Data on the age of incarcerated prostitutes is summarized in table 3 of appendix A. Of 100 prostitutes surveyed in Beijing, 30 percent had begun to sell sex before the age of seventeen; in the national 1989–1990 survey, almost two-thirds of 363 prostitutes surveyed had begun sex work before age nineteen.[74] Most had some history of adolescent sexual activity before they began to sell sex, a fact that social-science researchers used to argue the need for "correct sexual knowledge and guidance."[75] Such researchers, who often conducted in-depth interviews with the women, also reported that many of them came from unhappy or neglectful homes, families where the parents were divorced, or situations where they had been raped by fathers, brothers, or neighbors.[76] Seventy percent of the Beijing women and 63.1 percent of the national sample had never been married.[77] Not all incarcerated sex workers could be classified as youth gone astray, however. Of 132 women in the national survey who reported beginning work as prostitutes after the age of twenty, slightly more than half were married, and an additional 9 percent were widowed or divorced.[78] Some career trajectories involved the knowledge or collaboration of a husband, flight from an unhappy marriage (the writer Lu Xing'er reported hearing women say, "I have to sleep with a husband I don't love—how is this different?"), or the need to replace income formerly provided by a husband now divorced, deceased, or absent.[79]

Some prostitutes, particularly those who worked the joint-venture hotels, were highly educated. Among the elite sex workers in Beijing, Shanghai, and other large cities were undergraduates, graduate students, university teachers, engineers, and researchers. Their clients were mostly foreigners: diplomatic personnel stationed in China, businessmen, tourists, and returned overseas Chinese from Hong Kong, Macao, and Taiwan.[80] Prostitutes in detention centers, however, had received much less formal schooling. (See table 4 in appendix A.) The percentage of surveyed women who had attended or graduated from junior middle school ranged from slightly more than half to three-quarters. Except in Beijing, the number who had attended senior middle school was small, and very few of those surveyed had received post-secondary schooling. Data about number of years in school reveal little about the quality or effect of the education these women received. The 1992 Beijing survey prepared by the correctional staff notes, without further comment, "Sixty-five percent had finished elementary school or attended junior middle school (without graduating), but their actual cultural level was much lower than their schooling history would indicate."[81] The implication here is that intelligent, well-educated women would not become prostitutes, an assumption not borne out by a look at the profession as a whole.

Although elite prostitutes like Ah Hong supported themselves exclusively as sex workers, many prostitutes held other jobs as well. Some were farmers who had migrated to the cities as part of the floating population. They sold newspapers or other goods on the streets all day; in the evening, their services reportedly could be bought in the parks for a box of rice or a pair of silk socks.[82] The occupational distribution of prostitutes incarcerated in several urban reeducation centers is given in table 5 of appendix A. More than a quarter of those surveyed were farmers, a figure all the more striking since most of the reeducation centers (and presumably the arrest sites) were urban. Another quarter were unemployed. If displaced peasants (some of whom had jobs in the urban casual labor force), the unemployed, and those who did not answer clearly are excluded, 45.6 percent of those surveyed had stable urban occupations, with the largest numbers being workers, service personnel, and individual entrepreneurs.[83] A small number of women with professional jobs were involved as well, a group well represented in the tabloid and cautionary literature. In one series of vignettes about women who moonlighted as prostitutes, a county librarian responded to a morning call on her beeper, grabbed a bundle (presumably of seductive clothes), raced out, and within an hour was back at her post, sedately checking out books.[84]

The native-place origins of incarcerated prostitutes, and the patterns that brought them to particular cities, were as complex as the pre-1949 networks of migratory labor. Some cities attracted women from all over China. Wang Xingjuan found that Guangzhou, which drew most of its prostitutes from within the province in the early 1980s, by the end of the decade had prostitutes from every province except Tibet and Taiwan. Seventy-two percent of prostitutes arrested in Guangzhou in the first eleven months of 1988 were from outside the province.[85] Wang noted the development of native-place gangs (*bang*) in several cities, commenting that in one unnamed city the Chengdu *bang* had cornered a sector of the sexual-service market.[86] Other sources hinted at an erotic component to native-place segmentation: customers from Hong Kong were said to like tall northern Liaoning women for variety, and some were apparently willing to pay five times more for a minority woman from Xinjiang than for a Beijing or Shanghai woman.[87]

Attempts to fix and classify the characteristics of prostitutes in detention were ultimately as revealing for what they left out as for what they included. In all the official and scholarly writings about prostitution cited in this chapter, not one mentioned pregnancy or contraception use among prostitutes, although one researcher stated in a personal interview that she knew many prostitutes who had had repeated abortions.[88] (A survey of 122 customers detained in the Second Shanghai Correctional Facility indicated that 87.7 percent of them never used condoms, and only 4.1 percent used them regularly, so clearly the responsibility for preventing pregnancy must have fallen to the women.)[89] The only mention of pregnancy in any written source appeared in an *Asian Wall Street Journal* article profiling Ah Hong, the Pierre Cardin–clad prostitute who worked the Guangzhou hotels. Ah Hong had terminated several pregnancies with the help of a "friendly and discreet female doctor." The reporters added, "She is terrified of getting pregnant again, but feels it is probably beyond her control."[90] The silence about contraception and pregnancy, similar to that about Republican-era prostitutes, was surprising in the context of recent reproductive discourse in China. In a nation that provided free and ubiquitous birth control as part of its family-planning campaign, the silence on contraception use among sex workers speaks worlds about the exclusive entanglement of birth control with marital reproductive sex. Its use in other contexts was regarded as inappropriate— certainly not a legitimate subject for promotion by the government.

THE REAPPEARANCE OF STDS

In the late 1980s and early 1990s, public-health authorities in China became increasingly concerned about sexually transmitted diseases. Just as in the Republican period, these were described as being connected to the foreign presence in China. A 1991 article states:

> AIDS is a new member in the family of venereal diseases, which are as ubiquitous as flies. Therefore, as Portuguese merchants came to trade in Guangzhou, China's important port, at the beginning of the 16th century, they brought European civilization, as well as syphilis, into China with them. So when we are enjoying the air and sunshine today, we must inevitably face the reality that VD probably is spreading.
>
> On 1 October 1949, when New China stood up from among the ruins, we came to know that what old China had left us was: 10 million VD patients, brothels everywhere, and tens of thousands of prostitutes.
>
> After 15 years of arduous efforts, in 1964, Hu Chuankui, director of the

Research Institute of Dermatosis of the Chinese School of Medicine and Sciences announced to the world on behalf of the Chinese Government that China had basically eliminated VD.

Nevertheless, perhaps no one would have expected that after approximately another 15 years, VD spread to China again. And it tends to spread from coastal areas to inland areas and from cities to rural areas. According to incomplete statistics from 1982 to 1987, on average the incidence of VD in China had a 3.13-fold increase each year."[91]

Information provided by the Ministry of Public Health in 1989 reported 204,077 cases of STDs in the country, of which women constituted one-third.[92] In 1991 alone, Health Ministry officials said, 44,100 new cases were reported, a 47 percent rise over 1990.[93] By 1993, the Ministry of Public Security was citing expert estimates of more than 3 million cases nationally.[94] Public anxiety about STDs was visible: in many Chinese cities advertisements were posted for clinics that used combinations of Chinese and Western medicine to treat them, echoing the newspaper advertisements of the Republican era. A typical poster explained that one got these diseases from sexual intercourse, and listed the symptoms and consequences. It boasted a 98 percent cure rate, promised treatment for both men and women, and guaranteed money back if the treatment was not successful, in which case the clinic would refer the patient to a hospital and cover all medical expenses.[95] The most common sexually transmitted disease was gonorrhea, with cases also reported of syphilis and acute wet ulcers (*shichuang*).[96] But officials and the press also evidenced rising concern about AIDS. By late 1992 China had 932 reported patients who were HIV-positive and 11 cases of AIDS, 2 of them prostitutes; in November 1993 the numbers were 1,159 HIV-positive people and 19 cases of AIDS; in September 1994 the figures were 1,535 and 40, respectively. In December 1994 the China AIDS Network, founded by an epidemiologist, estimated the actual number of carriers at as many as fifteen thousand.[97]

In the public discussion about the spread of sexually transmitted diseases, prostitution was named early and often as one of the culprits. A 1990 report on STDs in Beijing stated that these diseases had entered the country from abroad or from the open cities on the coast, as well as through a small number of districts where prostitution was common. Foreigners were named as the initial carriers: sample statistics from the Beijing public-health inspection bureau suggested that 2.5 of every 10,000 foreigners who came to Beijing carried an STD. But Chinese who went to other cities on business and visited prostitutes (and by implication those who did so in Beijing as well) were named as the major source of infection.[98] As one article in a legal journal stated flatly, "The main cause of the rampant spread of AIDS and other sexually transmitted diseases is prostitution and whoring."[99]

Although their role as the major agents of transmission was not verified in any study, many prostitutes themselves were infected with STDs. High-class prostitutes in Shanghai reported that they used condoms and had access to "imported medicine,"[100] and it may be that their rate of infection was relatively low, but the same was not true of lower-class prostitutes. In 1986, one report estimated that about 10 percent of detained prostitutes (mostly lower-class) had an STD, but subsequent surveys ran much higher: over 40 percent nationally, 84 percent and 65 percent in two groups of incarcerated Beijing prostitutes, an estimated 80 percent among Guangzhou prostitutes.[101] Because detention centers had limited funding, they did not routinely test sex workers for the HIV virus (test kits cost forty U.S. dollars apiece, or 150 to 200 yuan, while other STD tests cost ten U.S. dollars), and some centers reportedly could not afford to treat women whom they knew to be infected.[102] As of the mid-1990s, government concern about STDs remained at the level of condemnation and statistics collection; it had not yet been translated into a public-health policy directed at the new and multiplying means of transmission in Chinese society.[103]

THE QUESTION OF MOTIVATION

In spite of the ubiquitous "dying embers flare up again" formulation, most analysts of prostitution in the late twentieth century made an important distinction between the past and the present. Whereas pre-1949 prostitutes had been forced by poverty into a life of sex work, they said, contemporary prostitutes took up this life willingly.[104] Like the formulation of resurgent prostitution, this statement bears questioning in all of its particulars. "Forced" is a complicated construct. As earlier chapters have shown, it is not at all clear that most pre-1949 prostitutes would have described themselves as "forced by life," even if they regularly produced this formulation when interrogated by the police. But during the reinterpretation of pre-1949 experience that took place in the 1950s, as we have seen, many groups of people came to understand their personal histories through the categories of oppressor and oppressed. It became undesirable, even impossible, for them to interpret their earlier actions in terms that entailed any choice, negotiation, or strategy making. The question of motivation on the part of a particular prostitute was made irrelevant. In referring to former prostitutes, the expression "forced by life" became not just a description of economic circumstances, but a totalistic explanation of all their actions and emotions. These memories of the pre-1949 period had a public as well as an individual life, encoded in "speak bitterness" narratives, materials used to educate young people in the history of the class struggle, and official theorizations of the status of women. It became a publicly shared and frequently reiterated truth that pre-1949 prostitutes had been "forced" into sex work; endless varieties of personal and social circumstance were subsumed in that single formulation. At the same time, one defining characteristic of the new socialist society was that it was to be a place where women were no longer forced to sell sexual services.

In the reform era, although many features of Mao's socialism were interrogated and repudiated, this characterization remained virtually intact. "Forced" remained part of the indictment of the old society; absence of "forced" was one of the achievements of the new. When reform-era commentators classified late twentieth-century prostitutes as "willing" to do sex work, the term connoted their dismay that these women apparently chose to do that which a "good" society would not require of them. Their behavior also departed from established categories of good and bad for women, representing a rupture with the gender norms of the recent past and perhaps the more distant past as well. Having characterized contemporary prostitutes as "willing," investigators then asked why this was so. This focus on motivations helped to establish the individual, a discrete entity with desires and emotions, as the central subject of social-science inquiry—part of a larger move away from class as the only legitimate category of analysis.

Investigating what motivated women to sell sex entailed the same techniques as establishing their age, native place, and marital status: incarcerated prostitutes were asked to fill in questionnaires. In some cases prostitutes (usually in detention) were interviewed by researchers and reporters, and their stories were fashioned into academic or cautionary narratives and printed for consumption by scholarly and popular audiences. Accounts of "motivation," then, were heavily mediated. In at least one major national survey, for instance, respondents had to select their motivation from among a limited number of predefined choices.[105] Investigators commonly reported the following motivations: the pursuit of money, material advantage, and improved social status; the desire for revenge, usually coupled with feelings of self-contempt; and the pursuit of pleasure.

Two statistical surveys of detained prostitutes from 1989 are summarized in table 6 of appendix A. Money was mentioned as the primary motivating factor by more than half the women in each survey, but the second survey went on to argue that this desire for money was not rooted in dire economic need. More than three-quarters of the women came from households with average or better economic conditions, yet 52 percent of the entire group felt that their economic circumstances were not adequate to satisfy their demands.[106] This kind of answer led social scientists to argue that feelings of relative poverty were ubiquitous in reform-era China, where increasing access to information about life in richer countries was reinforced by a growing domestic gap between rich and poor. Although women had jobs, income, clothing, and food, rural women felt themselves poor compared with urban women, while urban women compared themselves unfavorably with foreign women.[107] Women in fixed-salary jobs such as retail, hotel, and restaurant work, as well as white-collar jobs such as accounting and nursing, found that a salary of two hundred yuan a month was inadequate in an environment where a fashionable set of clothes cost one thousand yuan.[108] And increasingly, women living on their salaries felt themselves relatively poor compared with contemporaries who were supplementing their income through prostitution.

A 1992 survey of one hundred detained prostitutes in Beijing found that ninety-three of them had been drawn to prostitution when they saw their former classmates and girlfriends becoming rich, eating well, drinking, and having fun, and felt themselves to be extremely miserable and shabby in contrast. Corrections officials reported that these women lost their psychological equilibrium; their original concept of value became distorted, and they began to believe that "money is supreme, and pleasure comes first." They were no longer satisfied with their own life circumstances, and hoped that within a short time they could also lead a life of pleasure. They believed, said officials, that selling sex was a shortcut to riches for a young and beautiful woman.[109] The investigation pointed to the case of one inmate (first incarceration, sentenced to two years), originally an attendant at the Wangfu Hotel. When she first came to work she had found it all new and interesting, and was very satisfied and enthusiastic. Later, she saw staff members whose work was not as good as hers appearing one by one adorned in beautiful clothing and dazzling jewelry. She moved from envy and puzzlement to comprehension and determination to surpass them. "Driven by strong jealousy and vanity, she began to plan and prepare her road to riches, from taking tips in violation of regulations to demanding tips; finally she began sleeping with customers and selling her flesh."[110] In this account, vanity and jealousy led inexorably to moral ruination, as they had in innumerable cautionary tales earlier in the century.

At the same time, the party's slogan "To get rich is glorious" facilitated, perhaps even created outright, a frank celebration of material pleasures that was echoed by prostitutes as well as more socially respectable citizens. One woman serving a three-year sentence in a detention center told corrections officials that she began to sell sex at age eleven, adding:

> Money is the best and most beneficial thing. For the sake of money I would pay no attention to character, pay any price. Human life consists of eating, drinking, and having fun. I often bragged that my daily living expenses [as a prostitute] were not less than three hundred yuan. There was no big hotel in Beijing that I hadn't been to.

As if to verify her sincerity, the report noted that her cosmetics, clothes, and jewelry were worth ten thousand yuan.[111] Government officials, of course, endorsed the idea that people should want material goods, but categorized prostitutes as women who were too lazy or incompetent to work for them, and who saw prostitution as a shortcut to the goal of material wealth.[112]

Sometimes sex workers sought not goods but opportunities: a different job, withdrawal from the paid labor force, a wealthy husband, an exit visa, capital for a future business venture, or generally a different kind of life. During the reform era, access to good jobs grew ever more competitive. In the market's most elite sector, women looked for joint-venture jobs that paid up to one thousand yuan a month, but these were difficult to find, and high-class prostitution paid better.[113] In less privileged urban jobs, women were a disproportionate number of those laid off as state-owned factories were streamlined, and new female job seekers found that many enterprises were unwilling to hire women.[114] When women came from the villages to areas like Shenzhen to work in the clothing, hotel, and electronics industries, some found that prostitution was more lucrative.[115] For many, the alternative to prostitution was not starvation, but long, frustrating searches for dead-end, low-wage jobs. As incarcerated prostitutes said to the writer Lu Xing'er, "Where are we going to work? And why would we, for such low wages?"[116]

The high-class prostitutes who became the legal or common-law spouses of foreign and Chinese businessmen were able to withdraw from this situation of dismal employment opportunities.[117] In doing so, they joined a small but growing group of women, many of them married to newly wealthy men, who left the paid workforce and devoted themselves to what had formerly been decried as the decadent life of a bourgeois housewife. Some analysts saw prostitutes responding to a more general social permission for women to "get close to big money" (*bang dakuan*)—that is, depend on a rich man to support them.[118] Of course, some sex workers in long-term arrangements generated their own income as well by continuing to solicit customers when their patrons or husbands were out of the country. It was also reported that some used their money to "keep" handsome young men of their own, like their courtesan sisters earlier in the century.[119] In separating sexual activity both from romantic love (with respect to their patrons) and from companionate marriage (with respect to their lovers), they flouted several sets of social conventions at once.

Women who solicited foreign customers sometimes did so in the hope of making a marriage that would allow them to leave China permanently. Five percent of the women detained in one reform facility reported to the researcher Wang Xingjuan that their motivation was to leave the country or marry a foreigner, while another group of university graduates told Lu Xing'er that they regarded sleeping with foreigners as an easier way to obtain an exit visa than taking the TOEFL (Test of English as a Foreign Language) exam required for admission to U.S. universities.[120] One of the Shanghai women interviewed by Lu was serving a two-year sentence for sleeping with foreigners (*shewai*) and indirectly causing others to sell sex. (See figure 25.) While working as a receptionist at a major hotel, she saw many of her classmates leaving China, marrying foreigners or going abroad to study, and she wanted to do the same. Eventually she jettisoned her Chinese boyfriend and took up with a series of Taiwanese and Hong Kong businessmen who gave her parents money, promised to buy her older brother an apartment, and agreed to provide various other advantages. The narrative identified two villains: the girlfriends who taught her to regard foreign men as the source of goods and privilege, and the atmosphere at big hotels, which was full of talk about money, clothes, foreign boyfriends, and economic power. When she was locked up with people who had gone to Guangzhou and Shenzhen specifically to sell sex, she saw herself as having nothing in common with them. She maintained that in strategizing to marry a foreigner and leave China she had committed no crime.[121]

Women often used the language of the market in speaking about their decision to take up sex work. Their capital, they said, was their youth and beauty, and, recognizing these as perishable assets, they intended to use them to accumulate more durable capital. Some planned to buy a taxi license, hire drivers, and secure a stable income that way; higher-class prostitutes set their sights on the purchase of a passport or a building.[122] Many not in detention expressed their desire to save money, find a considerate husband, open a small business, and live a comfortable life.[123] These strategies were not merely permanently deferred dreams: one woman took enough money back to her village to build an elaborate house, exciting the envy of all her neighbors and, the account suggested, inspiring many of them to take up prostitution themselves.[124]

Whereas some analyses explained sex work as a rational economic choice among limited options, others pictured emotionally damaged women turning to prostitution because they had been rejected or wanted revenge. Of the one hundred incarcerated prostitutes in the 1992 Beijing study, twenty were said to have met with reverses in love or marriage. They had been "played with" and abandoned by a man, or their husbands had taken up with other women (*bugui*), or they had themselves been seduced (*jianwu*) but feared loss of face (*diuren*) and did not bring a case. Not understanding how to use the legal system to protect their own proper rights, corrections officials said, they instead chose revenge as a means to relieve their internal pain, and used inappropriate sexual relations (*luangao liangxing guanxi*) to play with the opposite sex in order to achieve psychological equilibrium. Thus they took the road to prostitution.[125] The same public conversation that was silent about abortions among prostitutes included frequent mention of young women who turned to prostitution after terminating a pregnancy in a sequence of seduction and betrayal by an inconstant lover.[126] (See figure 26.) Such stories reinscribed the notion that chastity was a "natural" and socially reinforced safety zone from which women strayed at their own peril, risking loss of self-esteem and a downward spiral into crime. Yet even detention-center surveys suggested that prostitutes themselves held more varied attitudes about chastity: one national survey found that almost 40 percent found chastity "very important," but another 36 percent felt that it need not be maintained in a situation where the two parties had feelings for each other. (Only 2.8 percent stated that chastity could be ignored in order to satisfy sexual demands, perhaps indicating that most did not understand their sale of sex as having much to do with their own sexual desire.)[127]

The rejection/revenge explanation hinged upon the figure of the damaged woman who deployed sex without any sense of physical pleasure. It coexisted, sometimes in the same discussions, with a depiction of women as pleasure-crazed individuals who had a frank desire for sexual experimentation. "I want to be with [(literally, "pluck"] one hundred handsome men [*cai jun nan yibai*]," a Henan prostitute told the researcher Wang Xingjuan.[128] Curiously, most sources that reported the female interest in pleasure moved almost immediately to invoke the nation as seriously destabilized by unconstrained female desire. "Ignorance, emptiness, and intoxication with money and material enjoyment caused them to sink into places of pleasure and not to feel shame," commented one overseas Chinese newspaper, adding that prostitution should be seen as a question touching on the cultural quality of the Chinese people (*minzu*).[129] Other sources attributed the unseemly search for pleasure to the influence of Western concepts of sexual freedom, which caused women to abandon Chinese values about female virtue. One incarcerated Beijing woman confessed to watching pornographic videotapes with her husband before her divorce, adding:

> From Western movies, videos, and novels, one can understand that if Westerners feel themselves to be unhappy at home, they can take a lover and sexual partner outside as they please. I appreciated this lifestyle. Husband and wife should not have responsibility to one another in sexual relations. . . . After my divorce, under the guidance of Western "sexual freedom and sexual liberation," curiosity drove me to specially seek out foreigners to engage in sexual experimentation, to seek spiritual and physical stimulation. I also fantasized about finding a foreign husband and leaving the country, in order to achieve my wish to live a Western life.[130]

Such women were portrayed as mesmerized by the popular American slogan "If it feels good, do it." One male investigator, whose account of roadside prostitutes veered wildly between explicit sexual description and off-site moralizing, describes his argument with "Little Sichuan," a woman who never stopped smiling even after she was arrested. She referred to her work as "a way of finding pleasure and making money." When the author went to interview her in her holding cell, she began to flirt with him, saying that she would be happy to spend time with a man like him for free. When he tried to induce a more sober reaction by saying, "You must have had it really hard, to take this road," she smiled and replied, "I know what you want to hear, but you must really excuse me. I truly don't have a tragic story." She cut off his lecture on the need for shame in human life by asking, "Shame is face, right? How much is face worth a pound?" He told her that women had paid a tragic price for liberation and freedom, and that their current status was hard-won, yet it seemed that she stupidly didn't value these gains and was happy to let others use her as a plaything. Her cool reply: "I don't see it that way. I give men my body; men give me money. It's an equal exchange." Utterly exasperated, he finally invoked the nation: "Our nation clearly forbids prostitution. It is a serious ruination of a woman's body and mind, and a factor in social disorder. Prostitution will cause the spread of STDs and bring a serious catastrophe to individuals and society!" She: "Society or no society, I don't care. . . . My body belongs to me, and I'll do what I want with it. I sell my body; how does that hurt others? Arresting me, hah, it's like a dog catching mice— minding other people's business!" Fuming at her unwillingness to connect her individual conduct to the fate of the nation, he ended the conversation.[131]

Like the depictions of women driven by rejection, the portrayals of women who would sell national virtue for their own pleasure must be seen as deeply implicated in a larger conversation about the future of China. They cannot be read as a simple report of individual motivation. Neither, for different reasons, can the statements about sexual freedom and pleasure made by prostitutes in detention, a venue in which they would have every reason to deny interest in both. Perhaps predictably, when a sample of such women were asked about their attitudes toward sexual freedom, a quarter proclaimed themselves opposed to it and 58 percent adopted a carefully neutral attitude. When the same group of women were asked what they should seek in life, 29 percent advocated the pursuit of pleasure, while another 44 percent cited the venerable role of "virtuous wife and good mother" and a quarter thought it was important to pursue a career.[132]

Ultimately, the public discussion about motivation points back to those diverse groups that dominate the contemporary discourse on prostitution, to *their* motivations and desires. Whatever their specific motivation for selling sex, prostitutes have emerged in the writings of others as powerful embodiments of a more general dissatisfaction and longing. Wang Anyi, a woman fiction writer whose works have been controversial because of their explicit treatment of sexuality, has argued that a much wider group of women shared the aspirations of prostitutes. As she told an interviewer in the late 1980s:

> I have come into contact with two kinds of women in the main: intellectual women and so-called indecent women—women who have no decent jobs, who stand around in front of hotels and fool with men or prostitute themselves. Don't feel contempt for them. Most have ideals in life and dream of something higher than the sky. Last month, I went to a female prisoner's reformatory farm. Most of the women there are imprisoned for

prostitution. Lots of them did it to secure a happy life. [Interviewer: Not for money?] Money was one element. Without money you cannot live that kind of life. It's complicated. They simply do not want to fall into the fate of common female factory workers, crushed each day on the bus, with a tiny little pay packet every month and then to make everything worse, getting saddled with a baby. They don't want their lives to fall that low and that I think is very normal. Many of them are the most ambitious among us.[133]

Whether prostitutes were taken as exemplars of a "crisis of faith" (*xinren weiji*)[134] in contemporary society, or as particularly sensitive barometers of new economic social pressures, their choices, and the meanings ascribed to them by others, clearly resonated with larger anxieties in late twentieth-century China. It is to the barely submerged presence of those anxieties in the legal, scholarly, and entertainment discourses on prostitution that we now turn.

CHAPTER 14

Explaining

The previous chapter described the contours of reform-era prostitution, paying only passing attention to the assumptions and categories that shaped knowledge about it. This chapter highlights these formulations, turning first to official regulatory regimes and then to a range of unofficial but increasingly authoritative voices.

After the establishment of the People's Republic in 1949, the state was the only voice authorized to name and solve social problems, and official pronouncements about prostitution in the 1980s and 1990s continued to have weight and palpable effect. But the state's voice in the reform era was not as unified as it had once appeared to be, and official utterances about prostitution betrayed many ambivalences. Should prostitutes be regarded as victims—the formulation inherited from the 1950s—or as victimizers of the social order? Should prostitution be dealt with by strengthening the legal system—a modernizing project of the late twentieth century—or by turning to the familiar but decreasingly effective method of political campaigns? When government authorities decided to incarcerate prostitutes and some customers in reform institutes, how was state practice shaped, and limited, by the memory of past successes in eliminating prostitution?

In the reform era, unlike the Maoist period, unofficial voices were also loud and varied. These commentators were themselves produced by the same conditions that enabled the appearance of reform-era prostitution: diminished state control, relations mediated by the market, and the pursuit of imagined pleasures. An easing of state intervention into scholarship led to the rehabilitation of disciplines like sociology, the promotion of legal studies, and the development of women's-studies scholars in both academic and government settings. The topics these scholars chose to write about were no longer assigned by their work units, but were driven by a complex combination of desires: to have a significant effect on government policy, to write pieces that would be widely read, to sell manuscripts in order to supplement dwindling real salaries, to act as a voice for social improvement, and to help women. The reduction of state control over publishing, although fitful, permitted a proliferation of popular media such as tabloid newspapers and magazines, and the public appetite for such entertainment ensured their survival. The line between scholarly and popular commentary on prostitution blurred as university presses published tabloid magazines in order to make money; so did the line between fictional and journalistic accounts. The result was a cacophony of voices on prostitution that resembled that of the early twentieth century more closely than it did the unified voices of the Maoist period. Underlying the proliferation of opinions, however, was a shared belief that particular sex and gender arrangements were both a sign of and a means to modernity, even if the commentators diverged on how those arrangements should look and who should shape them.

STATE FORMULATIONS

The Legal Status of Sex Work

Government bureaus responded to the appearance of prostitution in the early 1980s with a patchwork of proclamations and local regulations. On June 10, 1981, the Ministry of Public Security issued a "Circular on Resolutely Stopping Prostitution," followed by similar documents almost every year for the next decade.[1] Local authorities, particularly in coastal areas where prostitution was most visible, responded to the problem with their own bans, often grouping prostitution with gambling and other activities.[2]

On a national level the body of law published as *Criminal Law*, issued in 1979 and amended in 1983, did not prohibit prostitution, but did forbid forcing women into prostitution (article 140), luring them, or providing accommodations (article 169). Prostitution itself could also be punished as a crime through the use of the principle of analogy (article 79), but it was virtually never invoked.[3] Rather than being addressed primarily through criminal law, prostitution and patronizing prostitutes were covered by the Security Administration Punishment Act (SAPA), which took effect in January 1987, replacing a 1957 version. Chapter 3, article 30, of SAPA said, "It is strictly prohibited to engage in the sale of sex [*maiyin*], to have illicit relations with a prostitute [*piaosu anchang*], and to introduce or provide accommodation for prostitution and illicit relations with a prostitute." These offenses were punishable by a fine of up to five thousand yuan, fifteen days of detention, and either a statement of repentance or reeducation through labor. In reeducation through labor, an offender was incarcerated for a period of one to four years in an institution similar to a prison.[4] Although the 1987 SAPA contained no precise legal definition of prostitution, it was defined in an official Ministry of Public Security commentary "as an illicit sexual act between a man and a woman involving a financial relationship in which property is transferred by one party and received by the other."[5]

Over the next few years the people's congresses in each province issued their own regulations prohibiting prostitution and patronizing prostitutes, which reiterated and supplemented the provisions of SAPA, but generally did not exceed the framework of fifteen days, five thousand yuan, labor reeducation, and the possibility of criminal prosecution for pimps, traffickers, and others. Generally, first offenses were punished by brief detention and fines, while repeat offenders were more likely to be fined and sentenced to labor education. Although the same sets of regulations covered both prostitutes and their customers, it was common for women to be sentenced to several years of reeducation, while men were generally fined and released. In both national and provincial regulations, hotels and transport vehicles were singled out as likely sites of prostitution; accordingly, hotel managers and drivers were warned that they faced suspension of licenses, fines, and other penalties if they permitted prostitution on their premises. Local levels of government were empowered to approve the construction of educational and treatment sites for prostitutes and patrons, and could require medical treatment for those with STDs, with costs sometimes borne by the patient.[6] In practice, this set of laws and regulations meant that the vast majority of prostitutes, pimps, and patrons were dealt with by the public-security organs rather than the courts, except in cases that also involved trafficking, assault, or other aggravating circumstances.

As state authorities intensified their attention to prostitution in the late 1980s, two competing legal formulations emerged, echoing those of the Republican period: prostitutes as victims whose rights were being abridged, and prostitutes as victimizers who disturbed social order and health. Just as in the early twentieth century, the portrayal of prostitute as victim was usually associated with stories about the traffic in women, a problem that drew increasing public concern during the reform era.[7] Although articles on the subject made it clear that most abducted women were sold as wives rather than prostitutes, in some highly publicized cases traffickers who had forced women into prostitution were executed,[8] and in others authorities directly linked crackdowns on abduction to prostitution.[9] This linkage became more common in the 1990s, when articles began to mention widespread prostitution as one of the practices that created a profitable market for traffickers. Authorities also expressed concern about the involvement of underworld gangs who worked across provincial and international boundaries, as cases emerged of women who had been lured or kidnapped and shipped to brothels in Hong Kong, Taiwan, and Thailand.[10]

The victim formulation eventually found expression in the 1992 Law Protecting Women's Rights and Interests. Chapter 6 of that law, "Rights of the Person," included the following articles:

> Article 36. It is prohibited to abduct and sell or kidnap women. It is prohibited to buy abducted or kidnapped women. . . .
> Article 37. Both working as a prostitute or [sic] visiting prostitutes are prohibited.
> It is prohibited to organize, coerce, lure, keep, or introduce women to work as prostitutes, or hire or keep women to engage in obscene activities with others.[11]

In one strand of national legal thinking, then, prostitution appeared primarily as a violation of the rights of the woman-as-person. The most common such violations, according to an official commentary on the law, were ill-treatment of women, sex crimes and sexual harassment, kidnapping, prostitution (*maiyin*) and visiting prostitutes, limiting women's personal freedom (*renshen ziyou*), and encroaching on women's character and reputation.[12] All except prostitution could be construed as acts done to women without their consent. The ban on "working as a prostitute" fit awkwardly within this framework, and was not elaborated in the law. It was probably included to make the law consistent with SAPA and with other regulations, discussed later in this chapter.

The second formulation, of prostitute as victimizer, was evident by late 1990 in articles holding that prostitution was a crime, and that provisions for punishing prostitutes, as well as traffickers and pimps, should be provided by criminal law rather than local regulations or administrative decrees. The most elaborated statement of this position was put forward by Chen Yehong in 1990 in a scholarly journal, the *Journal of Central China Normal University* (*Huazhong Shifan Daxue xuebao*).[13] Chen concurred with the dominant state formulation of prostitution as a recurrent "evil social phenomenon," "influenced by decadent ideas and lifestyles of the Western bourgeoisie," but went on to argue that it had to be dealt with through legislation rather than periodic campaigns. Although the current criminal code did specify prison terms for coercing or luring women into prostitution, Chen argued, it was not possible "to curtail prostitution by punishing related activities." Chen was dissatisfied by the penalties meted out under SAPA:

> [F]or the prostitutes who willingly wallow in degeneration, a few days' confinement and criticism and education are of little consequence. . . . As for a fine of less than five thousand yuan, it is nothing. As a young prostitute by the name of Wang said, "I can make back tomorrow every penny they fine me today."

Chen went on to argue that the luring of women into prostitution was an external factor, whereas "the prostitutes' own will" was the "basis that determines the nature of their conduct." To aim legal penalties exclusively at pimps and madams, Chen insisted, was "putting the cart before the horse." Like the studies of "motivation" discussed in the previous chapter, Chen's argument took the psychologically complex individual, rather than economic forces or social classes, as the unit of causality and explanation.

Prostitution, in Chen's argument, was not a victimless crime; nor was the prostitute herself the victim. The victims were "China's socialist social morals and the people's physical and mental health," or more abstractly "the normal order of social administration." Crimes against "the normal order" were already punishable under chapter 6 of the criminal law, and Chen suggested that prostitution should be officially added to that category.

Implicit in this suggestion was the view that an end to prostitution should be tied to the larger modernizing project of strengthening the legal system, not to the old methods of education and mass campaigns. In the interests of legal precision, Chen argued for a definition of prostitution that involved five elements:

1. that the prostitute had sexual intercourse, and did not merely abscond with a customer's money (which would be fraud);
2. that the prostitute sold her own body and not someone else's (which would be procuring or keeping women for prostitution);
3. that the prostitute sold her body of her own free will (otherwise the legal liability would lie with the person who coerced her);
4. that the prostitute took an active role in soliciting customers;
5. that the prostitute was in business for money or other goods, not for other reasons.

All of these conditions could be read as the description of a woman in business for herself, performing certain acts of her own free will, actively planning her next business move, and trying to maximize her income. Yet although these were all entrepreneurial characteristics extolled by government authorities, Chen differentiated prostitution from other business activities when he characterized the prostitutes' motivation as criminal:

> The prostitutes know that their conduct will disrupt the order of social administration and corrupt society's morals, but because they love leisure and hate work and are greedy for material goods, and in order to obtain money, they enter into prostitution deliberately. . . . [T]he motive behind the crime of prostitution is sheer laziness, greed, and pursuit of an extravagant and degenerate lifestyle.

In September 1991, the National People's Congress issued a "Decision Strictly Forbidding Prostitution and Visiting Prostitutes," intended to supplement and amend the criminal law, which addressed many of Chen's criticisms. The new law increased the penalties for organizing, assisting, or coercing others into acts of prostitution, raising fines for these offenses to ten thousand yuan and increasing prison terms, with the possibility of a death sentence in certain cases involving coercion. It reiterated that both prostitution and visiting prostitutes were covered under article 30 of SAPA (with the penalties Chen had decried as inadequate—fifteen days, five thousand yuan, repentance, and so forth), but added that people found guilty of such violations could be sentenced to "centralized mandatory corrective legal and moral education as well as productive labor . . . for a period between six months and two years." Repeat offenders were to be sent for labor education and fined five thousand yuan. Medical examinations and treatment for sexually transmitted diseases were made compulsory. Prostitutes or customers who knew they were infected with sexually transmitted diseases but had commercial sexual contact anyway could be imprisoned for up to five years and fined up to five thousand yuan. The new law also stipulated stiff fines for hotel and entertainment facilities that permitted prostitution on their premises.[14]

The promulgation of this law served notice that prostitutes were to be held responsible for their own acts, not automatically regarded as minor offenders or victims of others. Prostitution began slowly to move into the category of crime, and more women were given "corrective education" terms of six months to two years. The law did little, however, to change the way state authorities dealt with enforcement: declaration of periodic crackdowns and campaigns (Guangdong and Shandong were particularly active in 1992), followed by the announcement of numbers arrested (and by a gradual reappearance of sex workers and customers) and then by sober official statements that the struggle to eliminate prostitution would be a long one.

Prostitution as Vice: Maoist Reprise

Even as government authorities turned to the legal system as a "modern" weapon in their fight against prostitution, they also relied on a more familiar form of social discipline: the campaign (*yundong*). Much favored by the late Mao Zedong, campaigns were clearly delineated periods of intense public activity in which the party and government mobilized their own organizations, which in turn mobilized the populace to achieve a particular end, rather than relying primarily on the daily operations of institutions like the courts and the police. Generally, campaigns were less successful in the reform period than they had been prior to Mao's death, both because the Chinese leadership was divided on the merits of particular campaigns and because the populace had grown increasingly weary and suspicious of mass mobilization in the years since the Cultural Revolution. The short-lived campaign against "spiritual pollution" in fall 1983, which targeted pornography and other Western imports, fizzled in a series of explanatory statements-cum-retractions by top Chinese leaders, although it left a rich legacy of pollution language that became part of everyday political discourse.[15] The much more protracted campaign against bourgeois liberalization, which began in 1987 and was reinvoked intermittently in the 1990s, was both vague in its goals and ambiguous in its effects.[16] In spite of their decreasing utility, however, campaigns retained a cachet with the party and government as a familiar way to effect social change. The result was a series of campaigns against prostitution with many of the rhetorical and organizational features that had characterized the Maoist period, but little of the mass political participation.

From the mid-1980s on, provincial and city governments combined public resolutions condemning prostitution with periodic sweeps of hotels and restaurants where sex workers were active. Detained by public security organs, prostitutes were subject to reeducation classes conducted by the Women's Federation and medical examinations administered by public-health personnel. Some observers were skeptical about the likely success of these efforts. "Whether this proven recipe from the 1950s for forbidding prostitution works in today's conditions remains to be seen," commented an overseas Chinese newspaper, adding that each sweep was followed by a brief decrease in the visibility of prostitution and then a rapid return to the status quo.[17]

By late 1989, local campaigns had been supplanted by a nationally coordinated effort. After trial runs in various localities, in mid-November 1989 the central government announced a concerted campaign against what it labeled the "Six Vices": prostitution (working as a prostitute or patronizing one), pornography, trafficking in women and children, using and dealing in narcotics, gambling, and profiting from superstition.[18] It is perhaps not coincidental that this quintessentially Maoist method was revived to combat prostitution in the autumn following the June 1989 crackdown on the popular movement. Perhaps the government hoped to draw on nostalgia for a simpler time, when the degree of national consensus was such that the population could be mobilized to achieve some common social goal. Perhaps this mobilization campaign was part of a larger move to reassert mechanisms of mutual surveillance that had fallen into partial disarray during the reform decade (as the leadership found out to its dismay when it tried to organize a full-scale purge after June 4). In any case, the language and methods of the campaign would have been familiar to any resident of Mao's China.[19]

The State Council initiated the campaign via a telephone conference with provincial authorities. Wang Fang, minister of public security, charged that the Six Vices had "seriously polluted our society, disturbed public order, and undermined the physical and mental health of vast numbers of people, especially the young people." The State Council called for all levels of government to "provide support in terms of funds, shelters, medical personnel, medicines, and equipment that are needed for sheltering and educating prostitutes, their patrons, and drug addicts, for taking forceful measures to help drug addicts, and for examining and treating venereal diseases."[20]

As the campaign got under way, political commentators stressed that eliminating the Six Vices was key to combating the pernicious effects of foreign influence on the party and the people. A *People's Daily* commentary linked the return of the "Six Evils" to a decline in the strength of party leadership:

[D]ue to the influence of the ideological trend of bourgeois liberalization, the revolutionary will of some Communist Party members has been waning. They did not dare criticize or resist disgusting social phenomena and did not dare carry out struggles against bad people and bad things. This is what those people who are trying to subvert and sabotage our country would like to see. It is also a vicious means used by people with ulterior motives to corrode our party, cadres, and socialist system.[21]

Even more directly accusatory was the comment by Shanghai's Public Security Bureau director, who said, "Wiping out the six vices is an important measure for intensifying socialist spiritual construction and a grave struggle against the inroads and infiltration of decadent capitalist ideology and the concept of peaceful evolution."[22]

Prostitution was thus firmly classified as one vice among many, all but one (feudal superstition) attributable to foreign, capitalist, bourgeois, revolution-eroding influences. It is perhaps not coincidental that a *People's Daily* columnist ran a story during this period that alleged that the student-movement leader Wuer Kaixi had visited prostitutes and then bragged about it.[23] In short, prostitution was yoked to a post–June 4 discourse on Maoist redemption from capitalist perdition via a mass campaign.

Almost simultaneously with the central government's announcement of the Six Vices campaign, provincial governments began to publicize their own operations. In Jiangxi the provincial party committee and the provincial government declared a four-month campaign against the vices and urged offenders to surrender voluntarily to public-security organs.[24] Harking back to venerable Maoist concepts, the province's deputy party secretary emphasized the importance of the mass line (relying on the masses to help formulate and endorse party policy, with the party holding final authority), and called for "arous[ing] the masses to wage total war against the six social evils."[25] Unlike the Jiangxi authorities, the Shanghai Public Security Bureau decided to disaggregate the vices, concentrating on prostitution and pornography before January 1, and moving on to gambling and superstition as the festival of the lunar New Year approached.[26] Guangdong overfulfilled its quota by declaring a campaign against seven vices rather than six.[27] Some provinces held press conferences to publicize the campaign; still others established special offices to supervise its progress.[28] Even the army was mobilized to take part; the deputy director of the Guangzhou military region announced an effort to prohibit prostitution at guest houses and hostels for army units, a tacit admission that sex workers were active in army-run enterprises.[29] Within several weeks, most cities and provinces had declared success in arresting hundreds, even thousands, of criminals. Since the vices were discussed as a group, it was often unclear exactly how many of the arrests were related to prostitution.[30] In many areas, particularly inland, it appeared that arrests for gambling and other offenses far outnumbered those for prostitution.[31] Two months after it began, the campaign virtually disappeared from the Chinese press,[32] to be replaced less than a year later by government pronouncements indicating that prostitution continued to grow along with other vices and serious crimes, and that none of these problems was amenable to quick solutions.[33]

But the campaign methods and terminology were periodically reinvigorated in the 1990s. In May 1991, government agencies that dealt with public security, commerce, public health, culture, and tourism began to coordinate efforts against prostitution, resulting in arrests of 29,315 people nationwide (of these, 10,655 were prostitutes.)[34] In April 1992, Shenzhen reopened a campaign against the "Seven Evils," coordinated by an office of the same title under the Public Security Bureau. By mid-June the head of the Seven Evils Office, Zhou Liqiang, was reporting that 935 prostitutes, 707 customers, and 105 pimps had been detained, and that 28 prostitution gangs had been exposed. Noting that almost 40 percent of the customers were from Hong Kong and Macao, Zhou announced that thenceforth all customers, including foreigners, would be detained for at least half a year of compulsory education, during which they would study the law and the government resolution on the Seven Evils, perform ordinary labor, and pay for their own food.[35] Beijing had a similar roundup in fall 1992, Guangdong repeated the threat to send foreign customers to labor camps in December, and Shanghai initiated a crackdown in spring and summer 1993.[36] In July 1993 an office of the party's central committee hosted a forum in Beijing on the fight against prostitution, reiterating the threat to jail both prostitutes and customers rather than fining them.[37] At the end of October 1993, the government announced yet another campaign that broadened the ban on gambling, pornography, and prostitution to include illegal dance halls and karaoke bars in which gambling and prostitution took place.[38] In the months preceding the opening of the 1995 United Nations World Conference on Women in Beijing, authorities arrested hundreds of people involved in prostitution; just prior to the conference, the head of propaganda for the city called for an intensified crackdown.[39] It appeared that forms of prostitution proliferated as quickly as did meetings denouncing them, requiring a constant campaign. As one source said, quoting an unidentified public-security official, prostitutes "are like garlic chives [*jiucai*]: you can cut off one shoot after another, but you simply cannot cut off the roots."[40]

As with the legal discussions, reports on the Six Vices campaign and its successors vacillated between representing women as victims (of traffickers) and victimizers (of social order), but in general the campaign focused less on prostitutes per se than on prostitution as one among many symptoms of social decay. The categorization of prostitution as a vice in this campaign meant that authorities approached it as an evil habit that could be eliminated by a combination of education and coercion. Yet as early as 1986, and increasingly in the 1990s, officials privately expressed their reservations about the formula of arrest sweeps, fines, detention, and reeducation. Some law-enforcement authorities suggested that since prostitution could not be eliminated, China should follow the example of some western European countries and set up red-light districts, in order to control the spread of prostitution and STDs.[41] Such suggestions, which were never publicly associated with the names of specific officials, drew periodic fire from opponents of legalization. In February 1993, for instance, a public-security official in the province of Hainan accused a "handful of people" of plotting to legalize prostitution as a means of attracting foreign funds and improving the economy. Noting indignantly that China had plenty of other qualities to attract foreigners, including "splendid natural scenery and shining cultural and man-made scenery," the official suggested that foreigners would come to China for business and tourism, rather than "to seek pleasures of the flesh and engage in pornographic activity."[42] In July 1993, the Beijing meeting sponsored by the central committee added its own denunciation of the argument that developing sex industries (*seqing hangye*) would be good for the service sector (*disan chanye*) and improve the investment climate.[43] Less than two months later, Beijing city officials accused party and state officials of paying verbal homage to banning prostitution while neglecting the actual work. Some cadres, it was said, even maintained that forbidding prostitution ruined the investment climate. In response, participants in the meeting launched an attack on the saying "Without prostitution there is no prosperity" (*wuchang bu xing, wuchang bu fu*)—an idea that apparently had considerable staying power in official quarters.[44] It was still being denounced in 1995, when a top official of the Women's Federation attacked cadres who took "a liberal view of prostitution."[45]

These participants in late twentieth-century debates about prostitution seemed utterly unaware of China's pre-1949 experiments with regulation, licensing, and abolition. Their referents lay not in their own history but in the cities of the "modernized" West. The only local history of regulation ever invoked in the 1980s and 1990s was the story of how prostitution was suppressed in the 1950s, a story celebrated in an outpouring of memoirs and other accounts that proliferated in the late 1980s, even as the practices of socialism were being discontinued.[46] As many people privately suggested, the successful 1950s campaign, with its mechanisms of comprehensive state intrusion and popular support, was unlikely to be repeated.

SCHOLARS AND SEX WORK

The increasing visibility of sex work during the reform period was accompanied by, indeed partly produced by, the emergence of professionals who took as their calling the articulation of social problems and solutions. This group included sociologists, legal scholars, criminologists, women's-studies researchers, social workers, and sexologists. Although they were located in established institutions such as universities and the Women's Federation, these scholars were defining themselves and their work under radically new conditions. Some were practitioners of disciplines that had long been discredited and suppressed as "bourgeois" by the government, and their analyses of prostitution took shape as they moved to rehabilitate and redefine their professions. Others, particularly women's-studies researchers and social workers who focused on gender relations, saw themselves as members of new professions whose legitimacy and function had not yet been defined in China. These analysts published their discussions of prostitution in a range of scholarly and popular journals. Although their perspectives were not uniform, as a group they departed in several respects from the formulations enunciated by state authorities. They tended to concern themselves more with questions of causality, attending both to the motivations of individual prostitutes and to larger social context. Virtually all of them shared the state characterization of prostitution as a problem, and they devoted a great deal of attention to proposing solutions. In establishing prostitutes as a legitimate object of social-scientific analysis, they simultaneously created themselves as legitimate social commentators. To say this is not to dismiss their writings as mere self-aggrandizement, but rather to direct attention to the nexus where knowledge about prostitution was produced. Scholarly commentators were not neutrally located observers; they were themselves situated in particular relationships of power and dependency.

The Search for Root Causes

As in the Republican era, most scholarly discussion of prostitution in the reform years was framed by the search for its causes, which were variously classified as psychological, sociosexual, or economic. Regardless of which type of explanation commentators emphasized (and most chose more than one), virtually all explanations pointed to the centrality of gender as a determinant of individual psychology, sexual behavior, and the differential effects of economic change. Even for analysts who were not explicitly engaged in the analysis of gender, this shared assumption about its importance showed that the grounds of social analysis had shifted in important ways from the Maoist emphasis on class.

Chapter 13 examined statements made by jailed prostitutes in which they voiced desires for money, material goods, social status, revenge, and pleasure. Statements like these led some scholars to conclude that prostitution was "caused," at least in part, by the psychological makeup of the prostitutes. This portrait of female motivation was part of a larger discourse on female criminality, one that argued that women turned to crime out of frustrated desires for material goods and love. In psychological studies of female criminals in China, the excessive desire for material goods was pathologized:

> As for women who believe in hedonism, because of various factors, they have not had the influence of a good education at home and school and a good social environment, and form a structure of bad individual psychological needs. Their desires to eat, drink, and have fun far exceed the limits of normal needs, and become separated from social reality and their actual individual situations, and they blindly seek pleasure. They are not satisfied with the ordinary standard of living of most people at present, and are extremely envious of the fashionable style current in society, and exert great effort to imitate it. They develop a special sort of insatiable desire for money and material goods. Relying on normal means, relying on the money earned from their labor, [they are] very far from being able to satisfy this special sort of insatiable desire. Therefore, the motive for crime gradually forms in their minds, and once they have the appropriate conditions, criminal activities will appear. . . . Some do not hesitate to sell their bodies for money.[47]

Psychology textbooks went on to assert that women who were initially forced or lured into sexual relations, and then abandoned, came to feel that they were damaged goods who could not face society and therefore might as well continue with illicit sexual activities. The explicit assumption about this trajectory was that women had

> a natural line of psychological defense against heterosexual relations, and relying on this . . . a woman has a strong sense of self-respect and dignity. But once that line of defense is pierced, she may lose her self-respect and sense of shame, lose her female psychological balance.

Aggravating this disruption of a woman's "natural defense," psychologists argued, were the ideas of sexual liberation and freedom associated with Western influences. Many women had come to believe in "glass-of-waterism" (*beishuizhuyi*), a term indicating that they regarded sexual intercourse as casually as they might contemplate drinking a glass of water.[48] (No motivating thirst for sex was implied here, however; female desire was not part of the discourse on rejection and revenge.) When prostitution was taken up as a social problem in the 1980s, it was assimilated to these categories of female criminality; prostitutes were seen as one group who had lost the "natural" psychological equilibrium particular to females.

Analyses that located causality at the level of individual psychology showed a curious tension over whether prostitutes were reformable. In a 1990 article entitled "Deep in the Heart of a Prostitute," for instance, the sociologist Ning Dong analyzed the attitudes of prostitutes in reformatories in the cities of Chengdu and Deyang.[49] Describing the enormous variety of ages, educational levels, physical attractiveness, and fees charged among the 139 women she studied, Ning stressed that virtually any woman could become a prostitute, provided that she wanted to do so. She thus attributed a degree of choice to the women. The question that interested Ning was why women became prostitutes. Noting that many of them were about seventeen years old, Ning attributed their choices partly to inexperience, which made it possible for them to "drift easily onto the wrong paths."[50] Ning also observed that all but one had had previous sexual encounters with men, adding that "[s]ince sexual relations are so casual, it is not at all difficult to wander onto the road of prostitution."[51]

Another motivation, in Ning's view, was that "they have bad habits of being fond of eating and averse to work and being afraid of difficulties and fatigue. . . . [E]ven if they have a job, they do not go to work. In the daytime they sit in the tea houses or go to restaurants; in the evenings they go to the dance halls, living a life of wanton extravagance."[52] If Ning's formulation posited laziness and a love of luxury, however, her examples also showed that women made shrewd economic assessments of their moneymaking possibilities. One woman rejected work in a brick factory (too hard) and as a babysitter in favor of earning twenty to thirty yuan per trick. A second abandoned a physically easy (but probably modest-paying) job as a telegraph operator for the much more remunerative work of sleeping with men for fifty yuan per encounter. She described this as "easy money, much better than regular work."[53] (A 1988 survey of women workers in business and manufacturing in Chengdu found that they earned an average of 138 yuan per month.)[54] Ning hypothesized that in their careers as prostitutes, women had seen men at their worst:

> As far as they are concerned, the entire world is nothing but a den of lechers, and the men lie in wait for them all the time and everywhere, and try every possible way—by lies, by force, or buying with money, or any sly trick—and exert every effort to possess them.[55]

Under these circumstances, the women figured, why not make money and assert control over these sexual transactions?

Each of the motivations Ning listed—inexperience, casual attitudes about sex, an aversion to work, a desire for money and control—were habits of thought that crusaders forty years earlier had seen as amenable to reform. Yet Ning stressed that prostitutes were deeply set in their ways, not easily altered by rescue and rehabilitation. Here again her explanations were primarily psychological rather than economic. Such women, she argued, were distinguished by their lack of shame, as illustrated by the following scene she witnessed in a detention center:

The women had just sat down to study when one woman stood up and started walking out. When an instructor asked her what she was doing, she said shamelessly, in a loud voice, "My . . . itches." And all the prostitutes in the room broke out in loud laughter. [Ellipsis in original.]⁵⁶

Ning concluded that whatever "positive results" the women gained from labor and classes in the detention centers were being undone by their informal bull sessions, where they "talked about the shamelessness of their customers, talked about the hypocrisy of men, exchanged their feelings about prostitution, and summed up the lessons they learned from being caught." In her view, women were so deeply marked by prostitution that they were unlikely to leave it. Unspoken in her analysis, but evident in her examples, was the economic calculation made by women who became prostitutes. As the authors of a sexological survey (patterned after the Kinsey Report) put it, "If one educates and reforms them, they feel that their 'dream of panning for gold' is being shattered."

Yet the sexologists, like Ning, were also making an implicit case for the intractability and gendered specificity of the human psyche. "[The prostitutes'] psychology is already seriously twisted," wrote the sexologists.

The sexual concepts of some of them have already degenerated to a thoroughly frightening degree. Their morals are sunken and lost, and they have thoroughly lost their sense of shame. Some feel that "he gives money, I give my body, both parties are willing, this is fair and rational." Some feel that "loosening the pants can replace a month of work" [*kuzi song yi song, dingdeshang zuo yige yue gong*], and is very advantageous; some feel that "if I don't reap some profit while I'm young and beautiful, I'm wasting my youth" [*buchen nianqing piaoliang shi lao yiba, duibuqi zhe qingchun nianhua*]. Some engage in prostitution with foreigners, get pregnant, and brag that this is "imported seed." And so forth. These deformed states of mind were not formed in a day or a night, and changing them will take a great deal of effort and time.⁵⁷

In spite of its weakly optimistic concluding note, this was a sobering and distinctly post-Maoist assessment of the limited malleability of human beings.

Other analyses combined individual psychology with a sociosexual approach, attributing prostitution to a destabilization of sexual mores induced by the reforms. The sociologist Zhang Yiquan saw one major difference between pre-1949 prostitution and the reform-era situation: whereas earlier prostitutes had been "forced into the profession . . . [t]oday, most prostitutes take up the profession voluntarily."⁵⁸ Zhang initially attributed the motivational difference to two factors: the desire of prostitutes to make money, and changing sexual attitudes that lessened the value of female chastity. Zhang's complete analysis, however, was more complex, even contradictory. On the one hand, Chinese society was experiencing a "removal of sexual prohibitions" that allowed "people's primitive sexual desire" to emerge. Paradoxically, this "primitive" sexual desire was shaped by such modern factors as "'newfangled' theories, movies, television, magazines, and other media that teach them about sex," as well as "modern technology that helped improve birth control drugs and methods." Just as psychologists portrayed prostitutes as individuals who had lost their equilibrium, Zhang saw Chinese society in its entirety as unbalanced by "a wave of ideas that overcorrected the traditional concepts." The result was the appearance of "ravenous carnal desire" in which "[w]omen who have overcome the psychological shadow cast by the social consequences can go after sexual pleasures without fear or worry."[59] Echoing earlier twentieth-century writing on the perils of the modern city, Zhang identified urban centers as the nodes of sexual arousal:

> The cities not only have the magnificence of modern civilization but also
> their filthy nooks and crannies. Beneath the cities' flourishing civilization
> and economic prosperity are a jumble of fish and dragons. Everything in the
> city no doubt appears "sexy" to those who are away from home. From the
> sexy clothing to the pornographic literature, from the couples kissing in
> public to the popularity of everything that is obscene, and from the cheerful
> bars to the decadent night life, they all stimulate the people's sexuality and
> heighten their sexual urges. And, like adding frost to snow, they further
> drive the already "sexually hungry" people who are away from home, and
> the prevalence of prostitution is inevitable.[60]

Other commentators noted the "anonymous and peripheral character" of the growing male transient population, whose long-term absence from home in such centers of stimulation might well lead them to patronize prostitutes.[61]

Although cities helped produce a climate of changing sexual behavior, Zhang believed that men and women experienced the climate differently. Women were still affected by a traditional double standard in morality, in which men had sexual privilege and could seek out prostitutes, whereas "one careless step can land a woman on the road of no return, and one wrong move can ruin her whole life."[62]

Both men and women were also affected by what Zhang called continuing flaws in the Chinese marriage system, where an estimated 60 percent of all marriages were based on economic considerations rather than love. Zhang argued that sexual satisfaction was impossible in loveless marriages, and that sexually frustrated men would seek out prostitutes.[63] Other analysts went further, saying that with the development of society, the primary purpose of sex had changed from the production of descendants to emotional and physical pleasure. They pointed to the loss of sexual interest within marriage, where sex is limited to one partner, and hypothesized that extramarital sex was a product of monogamous marriage. The result, they said, was that men turned to prostitutes for sexual satisfaction, while at least some prostitutes who had

lost hope in marriage sought the possibility of sexual satisfaction through prostitution.[64] "Many men like prostitutes. They are looking for a woman, not a
good worker. Many men have bad sex lives," commented the writer Lu
Xing'er.[65] In 1989–1990, a national sex survey modeled on the Kinsey Report
found that of 128 married prostitutes, less than a quarter called their marriages "harmonious" (though another 38 percent rated theirs as "passable").
Of the 105 who answered a question about sexual satisfaction within marriage,
only 6.7 percent were "very satisfied" (though another 42 percent were "satisfied"). These numbers were, in fact, somewhat lower than the rates of marital and sexual satisfaction reported by married women who were not prostitutes.[66] The factors predisposing men and women to exchange money for sex
were not all attributable to foreign influence, Zhang Yiquan and others implied; they were created by the interplay between "modern" practices, which
inflamed primitive desire, and "traditional" marriages, which frustrated it.[67]

Although many essayists were critical of Western sexual influences, using
words such as "corruption" and "corrosion" to describe them,[68] other commentators argued for a historically nuanced understanding of Western sexuality and its effects in China. In the West, argued Wang Xingjuan, the term
"sexual liberation" had developed during the European Renaissance as a
challenge to feudal theology and asceticism, and had had "a positive influence on social progress." In the 1960s and 1970s as well, "sexual liberation"
movements in Western countries had raised the status of women and attacked
traditional patriarchy. Yet "sexual liberation" in the West also possessed negative characteristics of extreme individualism and nihilism, leading to

> expressions of the rottenness of capitalist society: trial marriages, temporary
> marriages, serial mates, marriage clubs, and an extremely great quantity of
> extramarital sexual activity. In our country, owing to the influence of the
> power of old cultural traditions and habits, there has been a long-standing
> deep taboo about sexual questions, which are regarded as the root of all evil.
> This kind of avoidance of natural things . . . increases the attraction for
> them and for the most abnormal and stupid forms of them.[69]

Sexual liberation, then, was not intrinsically harmful. Its harm was created
when it interacted with a particular set of historical circumstances in China,
"destabilizing people's conception of sex" and leading to the production of
"obscene propaganda materials" that

> emphasize the extremes of sexual satisfaction, thoroughly splitting sexual
> activity off from marriage, reproduction, and love, taking sexual pleasure as
> the highest goal of sexual activity, holding that sexual problems are asocial,
> have no responsibility attached to them, and that the satisfaction of sexual
> desire exceeds the constraints of social norms. They give examples of all
> kinds of bad activities and activate and strengthen individual sexual desire.
> Many people have been led by obscene propaganda to sexual transgression.

For observers like Wang Xingjuan, the problem was not Western sexual liberation, or even "sexual knowledge that contains science, aesthetic pleasure, or usefulness for specialized research."[70] Sexologists, too, hailed the release of people "from the fetters of traditional life," which enabled them to seek "true love, satisfactory marriages, and healthy and harmonious sex lives." Yet with these new desires had come a series of problems: "early love" among middle school students, an increase in premarital and extramarital sex, sex crimes, prostitution, STDs, pornography, problems in birth-planning work, and chaos in sexual concepts, which mixed feudal, bourgeois, and "healthy rational" elements.[71]

In addition to psychological and sociosexual explanations, scholars also devoted considerable attention to economic explanations for prostitution, employing the language of supply, demand, and commodification. One important factor contributing to an increased supply of prostitutes, many analysts argued, was gender discrimination in work, housing, education, and other areas. Although the economic reforms provided women with new opportunities to get rich, many work units were unwilling to hire them, and they were the first ones laid off when an enterprise suffered losses.[72] Prostitutes told the social worker Chen Yiyun that women were discriminated against everywhere but in sex work.[73] Framing the question somewhat differently, some observers saw prostitution as part of a more general process by which female sexual attractiveness was commodified and sold. In an increasing variety of situations, beauty had become a job requirement for women, a means to attract business; women in the workplace became "ornaments for people's viewing enjoyment." An overseas Chinese newspaper, quoting a *New York Times* story, reported that at a 1993 Shanghai trade fair one enterprise had hired fifty beautifully made-up young women to dance with guests after a banquet. The same Chinese article noted that in the northern city of Luoyang, young women could be hired by the month for one thousand yuan, a sum known colloquially as a *cao* (water tank or wine vat).[74] (It may or may not be significant that *cao* is a homonym for "fuck.") Some accounts suggested that sexual intercourse was a job requirement for women in occupations other than sex work, and that hostesses and service workers were often told by their bosses that they would lose their jobs if they did not sleep with customers.[75] A Shenzhen secretary, describing the work culture in some of China's most coveted jobs for women, said flatly, "In Shenzhen, if a woman secretary has not slept with her manager, the manager is definitely impotent or gay."[76]

Explaining the new gendered, sexualized work environment of the reform era was a task taken up by sociologists and women's-studies scholars. China's low level of economic development, some of them argued, meant that although the nation was rich in labor power, the "quality" of individuals was relatively low, and that "in a society that takes males as the subject, actual gender inequality and gender discrimination in enterprises persist." Some of these "low-quality" individuals were young peasant women who had "a low literacy level and lacked modern scientific and technical knowledge or skill." Looking for work in the competitive environment of the city, most could find only menial or irregular jobs, and analysts saw them as inexperienced and vulnerable to the lure of sex work. For some who hated "the material and spiritual poverty of the countryside, selling sex was their shortcut to realizing their dream" of making money. In this they were joined by urban women who were driven by more subtle economic pressures.[77] Although overall living standards had improved during the reform period, Zhang Yiquan noted, some regions were getting rich more quickly than others. Women were not forced into prostitution by absolute poverty, as they had been before 1949. Rather, they were attracted to prostitution as a way out of *relative* poverty:

> People resort to different means to escape this kind of relative poverty. Some work hard physically and some rely on science and technology. But some women who love ease and hate work and are anxious to get rich may, under certain conditions, turn to prostitution to achieve their goal.[78]

Here prostitution was neither vice nor crime; it was a strategy women adopted to achieve certain economic and psychological ends. This, Wang Xingjuan believed, was "the reason that our country has both people selling sex in order to eke out a livelihood, as is the case in developing countries, and people selling sex in order to attain a better life, as is the case in developed countries."[79]

The demand for prostitution, these same commentators held, was likewise a product of the economic reforms and the commodification of sexual rights. "Generally, customers represent those who have funds that are not needed for life's necessities," wrote Wang Xingjuan. "They take money that might have been used in other types of consumption, and through visiting prostitutes transfer it into the hands of prostitutes, who then use it to support their families, for savings, marriage, leaving the country, or pleasure." She noted with dismay that prostitutes, far from experiencing their own commodification as demeaning, were enthusiastic participants in market activity:

> Some prostitutes thus regard it as "You go whoring [*piao*], I sell," all equal and rational. In coastal provinces and cities numerous incidents have occurred where customers have not paid enough money, and prostitutes have dragged them to the police station to lodge a complaint, trying to use the law to solve an "economic dispute."[80]

Social scientists vehemently contested this rendering of the prostitute/client relationship in terms of equal exchange. Constantly reiterated in their accounts was the argument that women came to this work out of lack—of money, training, opportunities, or psychological balance. Prostitutes were people unable to meet the new challenges of the reform period because of their "low quality" (physical weakness, insufficient brain power, lack of moral mettle). In these accounts, the only characteristics that prostitutes possessed in abundance were vanity and laziness. Even as they acknowledged that labor-market conditions confined most women to "low salaries and difficult work," scholars spoke of the move to prostitution in disparaging terms. For them it was an activity in which "one does not expend labor power yet achieves great riches," and was thus "attractive to a small number of very vain women."[81] In contrast, customers were characterized not by lack but by abundance: of money, mobility, and sexual opportunity. The different positionings of prostitute and customer were most evident, Wang Xingjuan argued, in that prostitutes were socially regarded always and only as prostitutes—as persons defined by a commercial sex act—whereas customers, as soon as they finished commercial sex, returned to other social positions, and could not be set apart as a kind of person.[82] Many scholars explained this asymmetry between prostitute and customer as the effect of gender discrimination, but their suggested solutions focused less on eliminating discrimination than on raising the "quality of the subject" through sustained social transformation.

The Search for Lasting Solutions

Scholars and other social commentators sought to establish themselves in the reform era as professionals with the training and insight to name social problems and propose authoritative solutions. Even those located at the margins of the state apparatus, such as researchers in the Women's Federation, saw themselves as somewhat independent of the party and government and thus in a position to influence state policy through public discussion. Although some of these new professionals felt that prostitution was an inevitable product of a specific historical stage,[83] they shared with state authorities the assumption that it was a social problem that required amelioration. They differed from government policy makers, however, in advocating long-term, expensive, broadly transformative solutions rather than short-term, focused ones.

Ultimately, these commentators argued, prostitution would disappear only after China achieved a high level of wealth and could provide its people with economic and social choices. In an echo of the repudiated egalitarian slogans of the Cultural Revolution, Wang Xingjuan sketched a vision of a prostitution-free future:

> When the differences between city and countryside, industry and agriculture, mental and manual labor have been eliminated, and where society has

extreme wealth, and people's cultural and knowledge level has been greatly raised, women will not have to sell themselves. . . . Particularly in relations with the opposite sex, when people have more choices, they can find love satisfaction with someone of the opposite sex from the same social stratum; then there will not be people patronizing prostitutes, nor women willing to be prostitutes. This is our social ideal.[84]

More concretely, Wang noted that "the economic value of sexual intercourse" was seriously incommensurate with the labor involved. Under these circumstances, "it is unavoidable that some women will take their own bodies as a commodity and exchange them for a relatively high economic value." Only by developing the economy, she said, could the value of female labor be raised.[85]

In the meantime, as China moved toward that level of development, scholars recommended that state and social-work efforts be directed at controlling the scope of prostitution and limiting its harm.[86] They advised correctional authorities to release most prostitutes after a short period of education, and to concentrate reform efforts on key offenders: recidivists, madams, and prostitutes who slept with foreigners. This last group was important because "selling sex to foreigners causes a loss to our national image and leads to the entry of every kind of STD including AIDS. It is also harmful to the protection of national secrets."[87] Prostitutes were doubly linked to the nation: a rise in China's economic fortunes would carry them up out of prostitution, but in the dangerous interlude before development was achieved, any breach of prostitutes' bodily integrity also imperiled the nation's physical health and political security.

Most of the institutional changes recommended by analysts were expensive and institutionally ambitious. Some wanted the establishment of a standing organization, funded with revenues from the state and from judicial fines, that would coordinate police, judicial, public-health, Women's Federation, and Communist Youth League efforts at education and prevention. They suggested that if the police and courts were allowed to keep the fines they collected rather than turning them over to other government organs, they would be able to spend them on improved facilities and working conditions for reform staff.[88] Funding was also urgently needed for detecting and treating STDs, and they recommended a broad target population for testing: not only detained prostitutes and customers, but also anyone who entered the country, applied for a job, married, or became pregnant.[89] They proposed measures to shield young people from inappropriate sexual knowledge, including a rating system for publications and a youth-protection law.[90]

Ultimately, like May Fourth reformers before them, social commentators placed their hope in education as both a means to economic development and a benefit to be derived from it. With education, families could be stabilized, individuals would make better marriage choices, and parents would raise their daughters properly. With education, prostitutes would learn to increase their self-respect and regulate themselves.[91] With education, the overall social environment would improve, and sexuality would be subordinated to the discipline of sexual science. Linking scientific sexual knowledge to the fate of the nation, the authors of the 1989–1990 nationwide sex survey claimed a venerable genealogy for their enterprise:

> Marx said that the degree of development of a branch of learning is contingent on the degree to which society needs it. Now, people increasingly recognize that society needs sexual science. From this we can see that it is all historically inevitable: the development of Chinese society is historically inevitable; the appearance of so many sexual problems during the course of developmental progress is historically inevitable; under these circumstances the opening up of sexual-science research is historically inevitable; conducting such a large-scale sex investigation in order to better carry out sexual-scientific research is also historically inevitable.[92]

Such knowledge, of course, was useful only if it was recirculated in the form of sex education, and here Kinsey's Chinese successors waxed poetic, quoting a writer named Yi Ni on the subject of prostitution:

> Ah, where is the sun? In a place where thinking takes place. Where is the cold? In a place where ignorance has long lodged. On the pallid earth the seeds of savagery and ignorance most easily send forth sprouts. Our society has neglected sex education, and therefore time has taken revenge on us, and will continue to take revenge on us! Because every time humanity neglects progress toward civilization, unavoidably there follows a historical retribution. This is not alarmist talk, much less a theory of predestination. Not to talk about sex, not to awaken and guide the sexual emotions of humanity, not to correctly guide people to seek the unity of spirit and flesh, not to guide and adjust the balance in the sex life between husbands and wives, will promote people seeking after primitive sexual desire, cause them merely to play with life's toys, especially the toys of sexual love, and thus to lose the civilized self.[93]

Here the *mission civilisatrice* was claimed by scholars and social scientists. Armed with education and scientific analysis, they would eliminate the conditions that enabled prostitution. In doing so, they would preserve and extend China's civilization, retooling it to fit the requirements of modernity. Although scholars devoted a great deal of attention to explaining the contemporary circumstances under which prostitution was produced, ultimately they classified it not as a feature of modernity, but as one of those practices holding China back from the circle of civilized nations. They inscribed it, as earlier generations had done, as a symptom of China's weakness, to which they held the cure.

REPORTAGE, TABLOID SEX, AND THE EROTIC IMAGINATION

More widely circulated than academic treatises were accounts of prostitution written for a general audience. These accounts appeared in two major genres of publication: reportage collections (in book and magazine format), and tabloid publications (in magazine and newspaper format). During the reform era, relaxed government controls and reduced government subsidies enabled the proliferation of newspapers and periodicals geared to the demands of an emerging mass market. I refer to this new genre as "tabloid" literature because that term most closely conveys its presentation of stories about crime and sex in a liberally illustrated format, as well as its blurring of fictional and nonfictional genres. Of the two genres, reportage appeared to be aimed at a somewhat more literate and intellectual audience, but the readership of the two probably overlapped. Each genre had its own conventions; with respect to prostitution, each advanced particular themes. Without more understanding of how these publications were circulated and consumed, it is not possible to map their effects on shared public understandings of prostitution. What can be said is that reportage and tabloid formulations of prostitution differed in important ways from both state and scholarly writings, and that in taking up prostitution as a new and important topic they increased its visibility and helped to shape the production of knowledge about it.

It was in the hybrid genre of reportage that the figure of the prostitute as victim received its most extended exposition. Reportage, a genre with roots in the exhortatory reporting of the Communist base areas, typically combined journalistic investigation, fictional techniques, and editorial commentary. The conventions of reportage allowed actual characters to utter imaginatively reconstructed dialogue, while the author freely inserted his or her own reactions and opinions. In the People's Republic of China, reportage has been used both to glorify the heroic exploits of workers inspired by "correct" state policies and to criticize, within limits, the implementation of such policies. During the reform era, the genre was widened to include muckraking social exposés in which state policy was only a minor feature. Pang Ruiyin's 1989 work on prostitution is one such piece.[94]

Pang was a full-time writer affiliated with a government-run cultural organization in Jiangsu. In 1986 he conducted extended interviews with seven prostitutes at a state prison farm, where they were serving sentences of reform through labor, a more serious penalty than reeducation. Pang reported that all of the women were from poor or disturbed families; none had serviced a foreign or high-class Chinese clientele, although one was arrested for attempting to flee to Macao in the company of traffickers from the Hong Kong underworld. In his preface Pang situated the women firmly as victims. Driven into prostitution by economic and social pressures, he argued, they were then further victimized by their lives as prostitutes: "Through difficult examination I have discovered that from the first day that they take up the profession of selling smiles, they lose the right to smile. . . . What kind of life is this?! Ah, reader, can you understand them?"[95] Pang invited the reader, presumed to be remote from these straitened circumstances, to accompany him on a journey through China's disorderly sectors.

Of the seven women Pang interviewed, several were described as desperately poor. Xilan, a thirty-six-year-old woman no taller than a nine-year-old, had been sent to the countryside with her widowed mother, three siblings, and child during the Cultural Revolution. (Her husband, a day laborer who had served a term in labor reform, did not accompany them and sent money when he felt like it.) When she returned to her city (possibly Nanjing) in 1974, she built a reed shack on a dike and joined the quasi-legal casual labor force, picking garbage, selling vegetables, collecting money for a street magician, pulling a cart, gambling, washing clothes, even selling her blood for sixteen yuan per cubic centimeter until she became too thin to qualify. Later she took a lover from among her laundry customers, and began to trade sexual services for goods:

> Other people say I used my good looks to seduce people, but actually, I'm not at all beautiful. If a man wants to touch [zhan] you, he doesn't care if you're good-looking or not. He has the demands of a male dog. As for me, I no longer worked to exhaustion in the wind and rain, and the money came fairly easily. I hooked up with one man and then another. One was from a city-owned company, one from the highway department, a driver, one from the housing office, a clothing-shop worker, a gardener, a vegetable seller. . . . Most of them lived in different places from their wives or were single. . . . I got continual benefits from this. You already know, I had been sent down [to the countryside] and was a "black household" [that is, had no city residence permit]. I used their ration cards to buy rice, their accounts to see the doctor. I got money, soap, laundry powder, a wooden bed frame with a rope-mesh bottom. I went with them to the movies, to hear storytelling, play cards. And in the deep of night I would take him, or him, into my always pitch-black shack.[96]

Although Xilan had been detained by the authorities numerous times, her language expressed the massive distance she felt from a life ordered by state regulation. She referred to all government organs as miaoli—literally, "in the temple" or "in the imperial court." In order to stay legal after her release, she said, she would need two things: a business license and a house. Otherwise, driven by economic need, "it is hard to guarantee that in the evening I won't run to the house of one of my lovers."[97] Economic pressure was a factor in almost all of these stories. Even the women who were not governed by serious privation had worked in onerous factory jobs that did not pay well, or had found it difficult to find work after being released from an initial stint of detention, and thus had been drawn to prostitution.

All but one of the women interviewed described being raised in troubled families marked by parents who variously died, disappeared, exhibited serious moral failings, or indulged their children excessively. Xilan's mother was a widow; Shaoshao's father divorced her mother and married a woman who cared little for her; Daxiu's mother pimped for her; Shuhong's parents loved her too much to restrain her trips to coffee shops and other dangerous places; Ximei learned from her mother and grandmother to dream of a man who would support her. A Ping hints darkly that her chronically ill father, abandoned by his wife, sexually approached his daughters:

> One cannot blame my father. He never brought women to the shack, and actually, what woman would hook up with him? But he was a man, after all, and gradually, at our young age, we came to know some things about men. . . . [M]y older sister later was sentenced to three years of labor education, and after that I also got into trouble. I don't know if that was part of the reason. . . . [98]

The marital liaisons entered into by these women were in various measures unhappy, unorthodox, or unsanctioned by the state. Xilan's ex-convict husband eventually divorced her. Shaoshao, too young to marry legally, lived with her boyfriend's family (where she did all their housework), got pregnant, had an abortion, and watched her boyfriend take up with other women and eventually throw her out. Daxiu shared her husband with her younger sister Xiaoxiu, and after her mother started pimping for her the husband sued for divorce so that he could legally marry Xiaoxiu. Shuhong sacrificed her savings and virginity to a no-good gambler, serving a jail term because she stole for him. Although she later had some success after opening a clothing store, she felt emotionally empty and was eventually induced by a madam to sleep with men for pay. A Ping quit prostitution at age sixteen to marry a tile worker, but left him for a second tile worker who paid the first one five hundred yuan for marital rights to her (no marriage license was involved). Ximei, whose husband was disabled and could not farm, took a series of lovers in return for presents and cash. When her husband objected she tried to divorce him; oddly, although they had never been legally married, the local authorities would not permit the divorce. Eventually he came to regard her liaisons as lucrative and became a "forked stick" (*chagar*), a man who depends on a prostitute for a living; he even negotiated prices with the customers. The layering of these details in story after story created the impression that much of Chinese society, both in rural areas and in poor urban districts, operated in a chaotic zone outside the reach of the state's legal and moral strictures.

When officialdom did make an appearance, however, it was not always a salutary one. Wu Ming, a former prostitute, left sex work and opened a restaurant without obtaining a health-department permit. Armed with cigarettes, liquor, and fruit, she went to see health-department official Kong, who was more interested in sex than these other blandishments. By sleeping with him on demand, she could run her restaurant without interference, although he still refused to give her a permit, perhaps to guarantee his continued access to her. Discovering that state cadres, not just individual entrepreneurs or businessmen, were fond of sex, she decided to seek out the head of the tax department as well, but was arrested in connection with her earlier work as a prostitute before she could do so. Kong tried to prevent her arrest, sending her frantic letters warning her not to reveal her relationship with him, and promised to compensate her for financial losses if she was convicted and sentenced. Wu Ming did not know what happened to him after her arrest, but Pang's account clearly implied that venal officials were frequent consumers of sexual services. Several of his interviewees referred to themselves as "marked people" (*zhe hao ren*) who were likely to get the worst of any encounter with officialdom.

In Pang's rendering, prostitutes were victims of political chaos, personal tragedy, economic upheaval, and an inconsistent and often corrupt state. He suggested one possibility of redemption: the relationship of the prostitutes to their children. Incarcerated, several of the women expressed their regret that they had set a bad example for their children or lost daily access to them, and Pang concluded one vignette with a heartbreaking account of Wu Ming's visit with her child. Conversely, it was in motherhood that Ximei, "like everyone who has been a mother, felt an enjoyment and satisfaction that was difficult to put into words."[99] Pang implied that the "natural" attachment of these women to their offspring might enable them to leave their victim status behind. This faith in the redemptive power of family ties was consonant with the formulations put forward by earlier generations of reformers, from the missionaries of the Door of Hope to the Communists of the 1950s.

Pang Ruiyin larded his account with lofty and educated statements, voicing his hope that just as Venus had been transformed over the centuries from a goddess of prostitution to an evil spirit to a spirit of love, so would prostitution itself be transformed.[100] Tabloid authors, who like reportage writers blended journalism and fiction, did not adopt such an edifying tone.

Tabloid literature was produced in some unexpected quarters. Law-enforcement newspapers, for instance, larded their didactic crime-fighting stories with gory descriptions of transgressions and retribution, while university and government presses, desperate for cash, published some of the most graphic descriptions of prostitution and its ancillary occupations.[101] It is therefore tempting simply to assert that publishers produced what sold, and that through this process sex and its embodiment, women, were commodified. Conceding this point about the economics of erotica, however, leaves us with more complex questions about the erotic economy. What sorts of writing about prostitution were served up as erotically appealing? How did these stories work? The following analysis draws mainly from Shang Xinren's 1993 tabloid magazine, *A Report from the Front Lines of Sweeping Away Pornography*, a rich example of this emergent genre that both typified and occasionally exceeded prevailing limits on explicitness.[102]

Although Shang uses the term "pornography," I employ it only very sparingly in the present discussion, and then only when it is introduced in a Chinese text. Even though the literal meaning of "pornography" in Greek is "writings about prostitutes," the various Chinese terms for pornography (*huangse, yinshu*) do not convey this sense (nor, for that matter, does it carry that connotation in contemporary English). In reform-era China "pornography," which along with prostitution was one of the Six Vices, was a term no less slippery than it was for the U.S. Supreme Court justice Potter Stewart ("I don't know what it is, but I know it when I see it"). It was, however, situated in an utterly different cultural matrix, where most representations of sexual desire and sexual acts were coded as foreign (usually Western) and entangled in a discussion about what China should take from the outside world in defining its own modernity. The types of materials most often denounced by the government as "pornography" were bootleg videotapes from the West and Hong Kong, privately circulated books that described or depicted sexual acts, and also—depending upon the political moment—works that in the West would be unproblematically classified as "erotica" or even "art." In the second decade of reform the category "pornography" was broadened somewhat to refer to any sexually explicit material, even if it had no foreign pedigree, but the boundaries of the sexually permissible continued to be constantly and fervently contested in ways inflected by the modernity debate. In late 1993, for instance, Chinese literary circles exploded in a controversy about Jia Pingao's potboiler novel *Fei du* (Defunct capital), in which the middle-aged male protagonist beds an endless variety of female partners (at least one of them a prostitute). The government banned the book, which served only to increase its sales in an increasingly unregulated literary market.[103] In this and other contretemps, most of the issues that animate and vex North American discussions about pornography—power, desire, gender positioning, erotica versus pornography, "vanilla" versus sadomasochistic sex, violence against women, the relationship of fantasy to action, and so on—were not featured.[104] Other issues, such as censorship, although important in China, operated quite differently in an environment innocent of First Amendment debates. Given these radically different contexts, which deserve a comparative explication of their own, it seems prudent to avoid a careless or commonsense use of "pornography" in analyzing texts about prostitution. In any case, as discussed later in this chapter, most tabloid texts about prostitution did not contain explicit descriptions of sexual acts.

Tabloid stories were highly formulaic in their narrative structure. As

Shang's title suggests, tabloid publications were often introduced by a title that established their law-abiding, anti-vice stance. The stories themselves were typically bracketed by utterances about seeking modernity, building the nation, and strengthening the legal system. In the opening passage of his report on prostitution, for instance, Shang referred to "the ugly phenomena of Western society—sex selling and whoring—[which] have also soundlessly slipped in through the nation's open door" in the course of the reforms, corrupting the social body of "the ancient nation with its five thousand years of civilization." In his closing passage, he invoked an antiprostitution statement by the Politburo Standing Committee member Qiao Shi and concluded with a call for better law enforcement and mass mobilization.[105] These bookend passages provided a context within which the stories were meant to be read, at least by government officials intent on expunging prurient content from the public realm. In framing his stories about prostitution as warnings and exhortations to improve society, it is possible that Shang intended to protect himself from accusations that he was purveying the very "pornography" he purported to criticize.

In between the opening and closing sheets, however, Shang's stories conveyed their cautionary message in another mode: by piling on details of physical violence done to prostitutes. He begins with three vignettes in quick succession. The first concerns a Miss Yang from a certain county seat, a woman with abnormally strong sexual desire (variously referred to as a physiological and a psychological disorder). Miss Yang becomes a prostitute in an attempt to satisfy this desire. When she criticizes a john for failing to satisfy her sexually, he shoves a liquor bottle into her vagina in a moment of drunken rage. Her injuries require surgery, she is subsequently detained by the authorities, and her husband divorces her. The second story describes a woman named Wei, dumped at the entrance of a hospital emergency room one night by two men who flee. A prostitute who had been working openly and without shame, Wei had told friends that she intended to make 100,000 yuan within a year. One night Wei encountered two sadists (*xing nüekuang*; literally, "sex cruelty maniacs") who wanted to enter her vaginally and anally at the same time; she agreed to do so in return for extra money, and ended up bleeding profusely with a ripped anus. The third vignette centers on an unemployed Shanghai woman named Qiu. Unable to attract customers because of her repulsive appearance, she is told by other prostitutes that she should "extend her strengths and avoid her weaknesses" (*yangchang biduan*). Qiu pulls out her two front teeth, which are damaged anyway, in order to provide "abnormal enjoyment [that is, fellatio] for a high price," and continues to work even after she develops venereal sores at the corners of her mouth.[106]

Explicit description in each of these cases is reserved not for sexual acts, but for the damage that ensues, twice through varieties of sexual battering and once through the spread of disease. Yang is portrayed as depraved because of the intensity of her desire for sex, which leads to catastrophe. Wei is portrayed as depraved because of the intensity of her desire for money and her lack of shame, which likewise lead to catastrophe. Qiu does not wait for a john to injure her; she knocks out her own teeth, leaving the reader with a description of a haglike, repulsive, yet active sex worker, relentlessly sucking the vitality of unwary customers into her diseased mouth. These vignettes rivet the reader not through their invocation of pleasure, but through descriptions of women's bodies whose literal boundaries are violated (each features a different mutilated orifice), even as the women violate boundaries of propriety and acceptable behavior. Embedded as well in the third vignette is a none-too-subtle warning that the nation's manly essence may be drawn off and poisoned by indulgence in paid sexual transactions.

Here it is important to return to Shang's opening passage about the nation's newly open door, which is apparently not merely window dressing intended to mollify the censors. This passage also focuses on a boundary that no longer successfully keeps things in their proper places:

> Opening wide the door of the nation, introducing foreign capital, techniques, and advanced management methods, quickening the progress of our nation's construction of modernization, has already become the common knowledge and activity of the entire party, nation, and people. But the ugly phenomena of Western society—sex selling and whoring—have also soundlessly slipped in through the nation's open door, and STDs, which had already been eliminated, have also once again seeped into people's lives. . . . [B]ecause of this the beautiful traditional virtues have begun to sink and be lost, to degenerate.[107]

Shang creates a resonance between the violation of corporeal and national boundaries. Foreign objects enter via unorthodox practices, bringing pain and disease; the penetrated entity (the woman, the nation) is blinded by desire and thus willingly complicit in her own violation; at the same time, the woman is figured as a danger to the bodily integrity and vital essence of the man/nation. Encapsulated in concentrated form (which is, after all, the original meaning of "tabloid") is the dual formulation of prostitute/nation as victim of (Western) incursions and prostitute as victimizer of the man/nation. This double anxiety is expressed through the textual deployment of the prostitute's body.[108]

After these opening anecdotes, which are apparently intended to simultaneously jar, titillate, and warn (and perhaps to convince the casual newsstand browser to buy), Shang abandons the theme of woman-as-victim and elaborates on the second scenario, in which men (and the modernization campaign) are corrupted, polluted, and cheated by sexually degraded women. Where such women are the victims of violence, they bring it on themselves. Men are positioned in several ways in these stories, all vulnerable and none very flattering. In a reprise of the Republican-era country-bumpkin motif, some are represented as neophytes unaware of the rules for obtaining sexual services. In his first time at a dance hall, for instance, Mou commits a number of social gaffes before he learns the correct procedures: first he must pay a ten-yuan introduction fee at the counter and pick the woman he wants. After they begin to dance, he must give the woman another ten yuan and she will dance closer. Ten-yuan increments buy him cheek to cheek, belly to belly, and pelvis to pelvis. The manager tells him that if he wants to procure additional services, the women will be willing; in fact, when they don't get such business, they become angry with the management, because if they do not earn outside income, the amount they make in an evening is not enough to buy a cup of coffee.[109] Apparently not much had changed in the taxi-dancing profession since the Republican period, but the writer does not dwell on the women's inadequate pay. Here their economic need is not the point; their willingness to sell sex is.

In addition to the sexually inexperienced rube, a second recurrent male figure is the morally upright and harassed government official or enterprise manager, an agent of modernization or a guardian of state purity, who is hindered in the performance of his job by disruptive prostitutes. In one story, a factory head and his assistant take a business trip to a coastal area. All night long prostitutes call them, charge into their rooms, help themselves to cigarettes, and announce that their services are very cheap, to the point where the angry factory head cannot sleep and changes hotels the next day. In another anecdote an official named Zhao, visiting a southern city, innocently wanders into what looks like a barbershop. Invited into the back room for a shampoo, he is startled when the female attendant proceeds to caress him and ask if he wants "special service." Suddenly realizing that this place is not a hair salon, he

> immediately used both hands to cover his shameful place, and said sternly, "I am a state cadre!" To his surprise, the woman, full of enthusiasm, replied, "Good, a leading cadre—we'll give you special treatment!" Then, unexpectedly, she leaped onto his body.

When Zhao tries to leave, the attendant insists that he pay a one-hundred-yuan "nestling fee" (*tui shen fei*), enforcing her demand with a menacing gang of toughs that suddenly appear.[110] Here we learn that prostitutes have no respect for social hierarchy or official position. The money and power of the new managerial class attract prostitutes rather than causing them to keep a respectful distance.

Not all men of authority in Shang's stories are as ethical as these two. The ones who succumb to the blandishments of prostitutes damage themselves and the nation. One factory head is arrested in Guangzhou for attempting to have sexual relations with a woman in a park at night. (The woman is from

Zhejiang, reinforcing the portrayal of Guangzhou as a magnet for prostitutes from around the country.) A second factory head is fined five thousand yuan for visiting prostitutes, but manages to manipulate his travel-expense report so that he can be reimbursed for the fine by claiming the money under other headings. His workers find out and are outraged, production goes down, but he remains the factory head.[111]

Shang provides an unusual glimpse of the difficulties facing law-enforcement agencies when they try to limit prostitution. Each work unit, he explains, signs a public-security contract in which it agrees to, among other stipulations, keep that unit free of prostitutes and their patrons. Once such a contract has been signed, the police do not patrol in the unit, leaving that duty to the unit's own security staff. In order to receive a public-order bonus, a unit must be, or appear to be, clean. Although the bonuses are not large, they affect the "face" of the leadership and the income of the employees. Therefore some work units act as "air-raid shelters" for prostitutes and their customers, rather than admitting that they have a problem and risking the bonus. By way of crudely symbolic illustration, Shang tells the story of a factory worker's son who brings prostitutes into his own father's office. Here prostitution sullies the "father's quarters"—that is, the nation, bringing economic ruination and injury to the modernization effort.[112] In extreme cases prostitution can also result in grievous bodily harm to the customer: one story depicts an aged couple going south to pick up the ashes of their thirty-seven-year-old son, tortured and murdered by an underworld character after he slept with a Russian woman who was being "kept" by a gangster.[113] Here the specter of national decay is closely linked to prostitution in the bodies of Russian sex workers, who are forced to seek their fortunes abroad after the Soviet Union collapses. At the same time, foreign influences are given a negative valence: it is the man's interest in "tasting foreign fruit" that leads to his death.

If the positions available to male characters in these narratives range from sexual neophyte to hapless, prurient, or venal official, prostitutes are portrayed as agents of pollution or swindling, regardless of where they are in the hierarchy of prostitution. Among the peasants and workers on a long-distance bus, for instance, we find a short, heavy-set woman wearing glass earrings and perfume. "This woman is surnamed Plum, a very beautiful name rich in poetic meaning, but from the time she boarded the bus she polluted the name—no! She began to do so a long time ago." Plum seats herself next to a thin, middle-aged man, rubs up against him "like a cat," and offers herself for ten yuan. She begins to fondle him, apparently with no result, for she is heard to ask accusingly, "Did you just go home to see your family?" In contrast to the homely woman on the crowded bus are the beautifully dressed sex workers with modern communications devices who arrive at roadside inns by taxi, fan out to the rooms, and leave when their business is finished; the author labels these as polluters of social morality.[114] Swindlers include the waitresses in hot-pot restaurants who charge unexpectedly high prices for a simple meal (consisting principally of bean sprouts and garlic shoots) and a massage.[115]

Shang's stories end as they began, with a series of violent bodily breaches. In addition to the customer who is tortured and murdered, we are told of a woman who dies from a dozen stab wounds when she encourages several violent customers to bid against one another for her services. We also learn of a compulsive gambler who sleeps with men to clear her gambling debts. In her final match she loses to three men after several days of nonstop gambling. Saying they have no energy to collect sexual services from her, they instead shove a carrot into her vagina and then doze off; she passes out and dies from loss of blood.[116]

What, one might well ask, is erotically pleasurable about these narratives, which are either pedantic recitations of official perfidy or crudely violent slasher stories? No more than a sentence is ever devoted to any particular caress, and nothing approaching sexual intercourse is ever described. It is possible that the violence is itself meant to be arousing, or that it is arousing to some readers even if this was not Shang's intent. Yet the narrative tone in such scenes is cold and clinical, and seems intended to shock rather than incite desire. The erotic economy here is organized not around explicit description but around what is not said. These stories titillate because they are each organized around a sexual encounter that is suggested rather than described. Mention of such encounters—as well as descriptions of the explicit violence that may accompany them—have been taboo in PRC-era writings, and the breaking of that taboo may well carry a powerful erotic charge, regardless of how banal or repulsive the stories may appear to a Western reader fresh from the wars about pornography. What is considered erotic, like what is considered female, is always locally and contextually fashioned. And yet there is something oddly recognizable to a North American reader in the luxuriant proliferation of brightly colored tabloid magazines, whose elliptically erotic stories lie between covers depicting skimpily dressed blondes blowing on saxophones and reclining bikini-clad brunettes with their hips thrust in the air. Ironically, although authors like Shang warn that prostitution is distracting men and women from the efforts to achieve modernity, tabloid writings about prostitution participate in the incitement to speak incessantly about sex that Foucault has called a particularly modern compulsion.[117]

Unvoiced Formulations: Prostitution and the Market for Female Labor

Much feminist debate over prostitution in North America and Europe in the 1970s and 1980s centered on a dispute over whether it was best understood as female sexual slavery (into which women were forced) or as sex work (which women chose from among a limited set of options as the most lucrative and/or liberatory income-producing activity available to them).[118] Neither of these positions appeared to hold much cachet in late twentieth-century China. As we have seen, in late twentieth-century China prostitutes were sometimes characterized as victims, but in general the public conversation assigned them much more agency than was assigned to their Republican-era predecessors. Yet in all of the public discussion about prostitution, virtually none of the state, scholarly, or popular interlocutors characterized it as work, or as a phenomenon shaped in part by labor-market conditions, even when the evidence they introduced might have lent itself to that type of analysis.

When Hainan Island's capital, Haikou, was emerging as a "vice capital," for instance, one Hong Kong reporter noted that the massive influx of people to the newly created Special Economic Zone on Hainan had created a serious unemployment problem. The population of Haikou had gone from 310,000 to 400,000 after the zone was established, with thirty to forty thousand people traveling between the mainland and Hainan each day. Most worked as vendors, earning about 150 yuan per month, but dancing girls (who, the article strongly implied, sold sexual services) could earn a monthly salary of 4,000 yuan—twenty times what they earned on the mainland. The article did not indicate whether this "salary" included income from sexual encounters with clients. Sex work was apparently more lucrative than any other option available to women, and paid better than many types of work open to men as well.[119]

Yet when the party secretary of Hainan province, Xu Shijie, took up the same topic four months later, he classified prostitution, together with gambling, as one of the "ugly social phenomena" brought about by the large influx of people, lack of police controls, and "decadent lifestyles [that] have made inroads into the province." He mentioned unemployment as a general problem predisposing people toward crime, but not as a factor inducing women in particular to work as prostitutes. Still less did he acknowledge that prostitution was a particularly lucrative line of work for women. His proposed solution matched the problem as he had defined it: "crack down on serious criminal activities, and exercise firmness in getting rid of various ugly phenomena. . . . [C]heck the blind inflow of population and tighten control over outside people coming into the province."[120]

Similarly, as we have seen, scholarly commentators acknowledged the lure of income and material goods as a major factor attracting women to prostitution. But in this rendering, prostitution was what women did *instead of work* in order to acquire these goods, usually because they had insufficient occupational, intellectual, or emotional skills to cope with the labor demands of the reform era.[121] Reportage and tabloid writers were too busy deploying prostitutes as figures of tragedy, depravity, and national menace to privilege labor as a category of analysis.

Why did China's state authorities and social scientists by and large find a labor-market framework uncongenial? Regulatory discourse in the 1990s centered on the task, in a rapidly changing reform economy, of devising new, "modern," but nonetheless stable work and family situations. In this way, the state argued, China could both modernize and resist the disruptions engendered by "bourgeois liberalization." In each of these cases modernity was seen as simultaneously displacing women (who were both victimized and set loose) and requiring that they be resituated (both protected and contained) with the help of strong state authority. At stake was the very control of what modernity looks like and means, as well as what "women" are and should be. In this formulation, just as in the Republican period, prostitution appeared as an interruption of stable work and family, rather than as a form of work that might, in fact, be helping to support many Chinese families.

Party and government leaders, as we have seen, were committed to an analytical framework organized around prostitution as vice and crime, as something that flourishes whenever foreign influence is permitted. In the 1950s, their forebears had devised an approach that identified prostitution with foreign vice and weak domestic government control, then removed the foreigners, strengthened the government, and eliminated prostitution. In the 1980s and 1990s, party and government policy welcomed foreigners and advocated reduced government control over many areas of Chinese life. The only element of the original approach that remained was the categorization of prostitution itself as vice—an approach that committed leaders to endless rounds of cleanup campaigns followed by periods of benign neglect and local payoffs. Within this framework, prostitutes were seen as either duped, depraved, or greedy—alternately victims and perpetrators of vice. As long as even a piece of the earlier "vice" framework remained in place, however, it was not possible for the state to classify prostitutes as workers, or to formulate policies directed at making other types of labor more competitive with sex work.

For China's new social scientists, who did so much to enliven the investigation of Chinese social life during the reform period, the issue was more complex. Unlike state authorities, they were not wedded to a disintegrating analytical framework (although they did have a love affair of sorts with Western social-science theory, which may or may not continue to serve their purposes). For many of them, "crime" appeared to be a particularly attractive topic of investigation, partly because the opportunities for new and better criminal activities made crime an expanding field, partly because any open discussion of social problems had for so long been restricted that their research was truly pioneering work. Labor, on the other hand, was an old and shopworn topic, exhaustively (even numbingly) discussed throughout the prereform period.

Likewise, social scientists who turned their attention to gender, often with an eye to combating growing gender inequalities, had an ambivalent attitude toward research on women's labor. On the one hand, they were extremely concerned about women's increasing exclusion from better-paying and high-prestige jobs, and many of them regarded with dismay the decision of some women to leave paid employment and return home. (The controversy around Tianjin's newly rich Daqiu Village, where village women withdrew in large numbers from the workforce, was the most hotly debated example of this trend.) This concern generated a substantial literature on the question of women's employment.[122] On the other hand, many of these scholars were in active retreat from a Maoist analytical framework that took employment as the sole criterion of women's liberation. As the sociologist Chen Yiyun put it in a 1989 forum on theories about women:

> During the early years of liberation, because of an inadequate educational foundation, emphasis was placed on employment of women. This not only surpassed the level of development of the productive forces, but also surpassed the awareness and capability of women themselves.[123]

Li Qiang of People's University, who made the most vehement statement on the insufficiency of an approach that stressed jobs for women, ended by advocating the Daqiu approach:

> In China, where the level of civilization has not reached a certain level, women are often considered liberated when a large number of women are employed and they play the role of men. Actually, this is another form of wrecking women. There are not many women who are doing intellectual work at a high level. Most women are still engaged in hard manual labor. This is precisely the reason why Chinese women look much older than their counterparts in developed countries. Therefore, we propose that ordinary women working in various trades have the right to go home to take care of their children when they are needed to raise them.[124]

Many of the theorists at this forum went on to argue that the key to women's liberation was education, not employment.[125] Li Ming of the Ministry of Civil Affairs put it most succinctly: "If the 'May Fourth' [1919] period was mainly for the liberation of 'feet' and the early years of the People's Republic of China were mainly for the liberation of 'hands,' then the women's liberation today is aimed at the liberation of 'brains.'"[126]

This dissatisfaction with a framework that analyzes women's status exclusively through the matrix of employment helped produce numerous new formulations for looking at gender inequality, focusing on female psychology, marriage, sexuality, and crime as well as on education. At the same time, however, the new intellectual stances on "the woman problem" made it highly unlikely that prostitution would be assimilated to a formulation that classified it as labor. Women's-studies researchers who were familiar with Western debates rejected the term "sex work" for another reason as well: they (not always accurately) understood Western "sex workers" to be legal, licensed providers of sex, and they (accurately) noted that this was not the situation in China.[127]

Nevertheless, although scholars did not regard prostitution itself as labor, and were much more likely to see it as a sign of women's unequal status and China's lack of modernity, some of them believed that only new labor-training policies would help curb the spread of prostitution. (Training programs, of course, were expensive, and it was unlikely that local governments would willingly do anything to increase the cost of running detention centers.) The nascent social-work profession may yet come to see prostitution, if not as a form of work, at least as an income-generating activity that looks more attractive than other available options.

By invoking a formulation that Chinese analysts do not find congenial, I do not argue that prostitution is "really" labor and that all Chinese commentators are operating under the cloud of false consciousness. My intention is rather to look at formulations people choose as well as the ones they foreclose, and ask why these choices are being made. Contemporary Western debates about prostitution are, after all, also a product of such choices, and deserve their own historical analysis. They are not a yardstick against which Chinese debates can be measured. As Chinese commentators make clear, their formulations of prostitution encompass questions of sexuality (male and female), disease, marriage markets, abduction, and local constructions of "modernity" as well as labor.

Nevertheless, if the subaltern voices of Chinese prostitutes could be heard more clearly outside of detention centers, it is possible that they would give more prominence to a labor framework than the people who regulate and study them do. The women in the disco on the thirtieth floor of Shanghai's Hongqiao Hotel, as they coolly approach customers and later negotiate prices, exhibit the kind of concentration and seriousness that one might associate with work. And, if the sexologist Pan Suiming is correct, prostitutes report that their occupation involves much of the drudgery, even alienation, often associated with work. Pan comments:

> Individual interviews with prostitutes . . . found that the majority of them describe their experience as "tiresome," "indifferent," "no alternative," "have to tolerate". . . . There is [a] popular joke today: the prostitute says to her customer, "Move your head, I am watching TV."[128]

More than any other Chinese scholar, Pan comes closest to a labor-market analysis of prostitution, again through a joke:

> A family of three were talking about prostitution. The husband said, "One act of a prostitute in *xx* city is worth my three years' salary!" The wife immediately responded, "Then, never visit a prostitute." The daughter unexpectedly said, "I should do this work."[129]

CHAPTER 15

History, Memory, and Nostalgia

Prostitution's "usable past," as created in the late twentieth century, had several dimensions. That most congruent with state interests was the publication of memoirs and historical narratives about the depredations of prostitution and the triumph of its eradication in the 1950s.[1] Largely celebratory of official success, they concentrated on the reform process, describing pre-1949 prostitution only in order to denounce its oppressive and shameful features. These accounts were soon supplemented and partly undermined by an official publishing project, taken up by many local organizations simultaneously, to write comprehensive accounts of Republican-era vice in their cities. The resulting volumes were generically entitled *Opium, Gambling, and Prostitution in Old [place name]*.[2] Although the editorial stance on these vices was unwaveringly disapproving, the books devoted much more space to describing the practices than to recounting their elimination, thus increasing their accessibility to contemporary imaginations.[3]

Focusing on the more distant past, scholars took up research on prostitution's long history in China. In 1988 Sun Guoqun published her *Secret History of Prostitution in Old Shanghai,* which concentrated on prostitution before 1919, quoting liberally from nineteenth- and early twentieth-century belles lettres and other sources devoted to appreciating courtesans. Her own introduction indicated a certain ambivalence about the subject: she gave her purpose for writing the book as "exposing this evil system," citing Engels on prostitution's connection to private property, but nonetheless opened with a compelling, almost seductive description of the colorful, lively sex-selling scene on Fuzhou Road in days gone by.[4] A 1990 volume by Wu Zhou, *A History of the Life of Chinese Prostitutes,* aimed at more comprehensive coverage, beginning in ancient times and proceeding through the first decade of the post-Mao reforms. Wu was interested in prostitution as an issue in the history of "traditional Chinese women's culture"—a conceptualization that reflected the reform-era development of women's studies in China and the growing assertion of women's-studies scholars that history, like the present, was gendered. Wu made an impassioned case for the importance of understanding history's impact on contemporary problems. The current appearance of prostitution in China, Wu argued, should not be seen as "foreign goods" or as a "new product" generated by the reforms, but rather as the reappearance of remnants of "prostitute culture" from the past, flourishing under particular historical conditions.[5]

This formulation at first appears to be a tired reiteration of the party's insistence that many Chinese social problems are "feudal remnants," an assertion that has come to seem increasingly absurd in the late twentieth century. Read somewhat differently, however, Wu's statement insists that history matters, and that only a serious investigation of the past will enable people to see (and, if they so wish, expunge) its traces in the present. The preface to Wu's book, by the senior scholar Ma Jigao, made an additional case for the importance of prostitution in China's cultural history. Ma acknowledged the contribution of early prostitutes to "our nation's ancient culture and art," deplored the expansion of unofficial prostitution in the early Qing, but asserted nonetheless that "the history of prostitution's emergence and development in China is obviously related to the particularities of Chinese social development, and also has a certain relationship to Chinese culture, especially Chinese literature and art," as well as to urban development. Of course, these positive aspects of historical prostitution were not to be confused with the present, when "prostitutes have already become a corrosive malignant tumor on society."[6] Here prostitution's past was salvaged and found to have some value, but was also clearly distinguished from its dangerous and degenerate present—a move that would have been familiar to any reader of the Republican period's literature of nostalgia.

An update to Wu Zhou's comprehensive survey is the 1995 volume by Shan Guangnai entitled *Chinese Prostitution—Past and Present,* written with the cooperation of the Chinese Academy of Social Sciences, as well as public-security organs and the Women's Federation.[7] Although the first 200 pages of this massive volume are devoted to historical material, and another 150 pages dutifully bring an account of Hong Kong and Taiwan prostitution into the present (thereby making the requisite nationalist point about what constitutes "China"), the heart of the book is its second half, which concentrates on prostitution in the PRC during the 1980s. Shan describes this methodology as that of "social science under the guidance of Marxism," arguing that since prostitution is a product of the system of private property, it is not produced by socialism itself, but rather by "seeds, soil, and climate" found in contemporary China.[8] "Seeds" include current social attitudes, many of which resemble those mentioned by reformers during Republican era: that it is more laughable to be poor than a prostitute; that people can afford to think about sexual desire when they are properly fed and clothed; that virginity is so highly valued that a woman who loses hers may feel herself to be worthless and become a prostitute; that women are playthings; and so forth. "Soil" comprises factors such as the gap between city and countryside, the persistence of poverty, a culture of poverty, and a male-centered society. "Climate" encompasses the move of rural people to the cities, the stimulation of the international environment, the inadequacy of social controls from the prereform period, and changes in the sexual concepts of Chinese over the previous ten or more years.[9] Shan's work is reminiscent of reform writings of the 1920s and 1930s in its use of social-science methods and its search for root causes. It participates as well in the conventions of late twentieth-century sexology, providing meticulous and technical depictions of sexual practices.[10]

A third type of account was the direct reprinting of pre-1949 sources about prostitution, part of a larger project to reissue books that had been banned, burned, or simply allowed to lapse from circulation before and during the Cultural Revolution. Among these was Wang Shunu's scholarly *History of Prostitution in China*, first published in 1935 and reprinted in 1988.[11] In its brief preface, the Shanghai publishing house that produced the reprint explained that it was reissuing specialized treatises published from the late Qing to 1949, books that had been influenced by the Western tradition of specialized research. Prostitution (which is never actually mentioned in this preface) thus assumed a place as a legitimate object of specialized study. Works of fiction were also reissued. By 1991, the Shanghai Ancient Books Publishing House had begun to reprint novels from the late nineteenth and early twentieth centuries that featured courtesans and/or social exposés of brothel life— classics such as *Dream of Shanghai Luxury* and Bi Yihong's *Hell on Earth*.[12] Billed as an attempt to circulate the works of authors whose techniques had not yet been influenced by modern Western theories of fiction, the series featured novels that had originally been serialized in late Qing and early Republican newspapers. The purpose, as the preface to *Dream of Shanghai Luxury* stated, was to help the reader "understand the Bund [Shanghai's avenue of imposing foreign buildings, here meant to invoke the entire semicolonial environment] and the people of Shanghai at that time, as well as to provide scholars and the relevant [government] departments with a type of material useful for researching old Shanghai."[13] The series preface praised these works for their realistic description of character types in old Shanghai: politicians, gamblers, foreigners, revolutionaries—and prostitutes and their customers. Even as it proceeded to denounce the "semifeudal, semicolonial" society of Shanghai, this framing established prostitutes—and their chroniclers in fiction—as serious historical actors.[14]

For those not inclined to read long novels in flowery semiclassical Chinese, tabloid magazines also began to re-create the world of the courtesan, who emerged from the dustbin of history with her virtues and her wiles intact. One story recounted the liaison of a courtesan named Yinxi with a man who eventually became a provincial governor under Qing rule. He was a profligate ne'er-do-well; she was the déclassé descendant of an official family that had lost everything in a robbery, forcing her into prostitution. Out of the savings she accumulated in the courtesan house, she produced a sum that he used to buy her out; the story also implied that she put up the money for him to purchase an official post. While he was off in Beijing she died suddenly, leaving him a box full of valuable jewelry and inspiring his resolve to move up the hierarchy of officialdom, where he proceeded to enjoy a successful career.[15] The loyal, capable, loving, and moneyed courtesan here was celebrated as the woman behind a distinguished man's rise to power. A second story in the same magazine recounted the exploits of a wily patron who outwitted the madam in a courtesan house by sleeping with every beautiful courtesan (twice) and charging all kinds of expenditures to his account, then disappearing. When police opened a fat wallet he had left with one of the courtesans for safekeeping, they found it full of white paper rather than banknotes. The story also made it clear that many of the women were lining their own pockets by charging expenses to his account.[16] The point of the story was not that courtesans were stupid, but that it required great ingenuity to outwit them; the author also reveled in lavish descriptions of wealth and free spending in the courtesan houses. Notably absent was any hint of condemnation.

Moving into politically more volatile territory, the 1994 film *Blush* (*Hong fen*), by the renowned woman director Li Shaohong,[17] offered an oblique comment on the limited success of the 1950s campaign to reform prostitutes. In the film's opening sequence, Qiuyi and Xiao'e, two Suzhou courtesans, are rounded up for reform. Disdainful of the entire process, Qiuyi stops to purchase a sweet potato, commenting that "even a condemned man gets a last meal." She escapes from the reform institute immediately upon arrival and goes to live with one of her customers, a gilded youth named Lao Pu. Xiao'e remains incarcerated. Frustrated by the hard work of bowing cotton in the institute factory, she tries unsuccessfully to hang herself.

In one of the film's most interesting moments, Xiao'e's political instructor urges her to tell her "classmates" that she attempted suicide because she was worn down by the oppression and exploitation of her past life as a prostitute. Without directly contradicting the instructor, Xiao'e makes it clear that it is not the past that troubles her: rather, she is afraid of the future, exhausted by the work, and uncomfortable because of blisters on her hands. Undaunted by Xiao'e's refusal to draw the proper political conclusions, the instructor then goes on to tearfully recount what is apparently her own story. She is the daughter of a prostitute who sacrificed to put her through university, yet it has taken her many years to get over her shame at her mother's occupation and to appreciate her efforts. Communist reformers are not pilloried or satirized in this account—in fact, the reform campaign is treated sympathetically—but it is clear that the attempt to impose a single narrative of oppression on a heterogeneous group of women is doomed to fail.

The remainder of the plot (which is based on a story by the popular young male writer Su Tong) is worthy of a first-class soap opera. Like Su Tong's story *Raise the Red Lantern,* which became a prize-winning film by Zhang Yimou, *Blush* contains enough inconsistencies and problems to annoy feminists, historians, and assorted other viewers. Qiuyi's liaison with Lao Pu during her stay in his family's house is incoherent: the two use each other mercilessly in an exchange of protection for sexual pleasure, then suddenly and inexplicably discover their undying love for each other long after the liaison has ended. By that time Qiuyi has left Lao Pu in a fit of pique, become a Buddhist nun, discovered she is pregnant with Lao Pu's child, miscarried, and married an older teahouse keeper whom she does not love. Meanwhile, Xiao'e is released from the reform institute, works briefly in a factory, quarrels with a woman who implies that she is still a prostitute, and marries Lao Pu. In the process she metamorphoses rapidly from petulant prostitute to sweet young worker and back. Xiao'e and Lao Pu are unhappy together; they fight continually about money, and Xiao'e exhibits what the reformers would undoubtedly call an unreconstructed courtesan's mentality, demanding material goods and throwing tantrums.

Tormented by guilt about Qiuyi's miscarriage and hoping to allay Xiao'e's complaints, Lao Pu embezzles a large sum of money from his factory, sends most of it to Qiuyi, and buys Xiao'e a week of luxurious living. He is caught and executed, but not before a tearful prison visit with Qiuyi. This episode appears to suggest that insatiable women, and guilt over liaisons with women, drive men to theft.

Ironically, the story calibrates female virtue on a scale that would have been familiar to Communist reformers: good women are good wives and mothers. In the film's concluding scene, the two women resume their friendship. Xiao'e, the reformed prostitute, having failed to become a good wife, now abandons her duties as a virtuous mother as well. She gives her child to Qiuyi and runs off with a northerner. Qiuyi, the unreformed prostitute, is full of maternal virtue. She renames the boy "New China" and raises him to adulthood. (It is unclear whether this is meant to be a sardonic comment on the unvirtuous ancestry of the Communist regime.) The Communists are given no credit for Qiuyi's virtue: she acts out of love for Lao Pu rather than out of values inculcated by a reform process that she avoided altogether. Nor is Xiao'e a Communist success story. A graduate of the reform program, she has survived with her love of indolence intact.

Ultimately, *Blush* is not a story about reform at all. Rather, the author and filmmaker regard the 1950s reform efforts as a safely distant treasure trove of long-ago times, to be mined for interesting dramatic material rather than contemporary political lessons. And the film's success—it won the Silver Bear award at the 1995 Berlin Film Festival—suggests that such material will find a receptive audience in the international artistic realm as well.

In these late twentieth-century reconstitutions of the past, prostitutes were multiply deployed: as figures in Republican China's interconnected social ills, as important historical figures who contributed to the nation's cultural heritage, as worthy subjects of elite male observation and writing, as exemplars of traditional female virtue, as sites of nostalgia and popular entertainment, as subjects incompletely reformed by the state. But perhaps something more was promised as well. As the editor's introduction to the reprint of *Hell on Earth* explained, "Through this book, longtime Shanghai residents can arouse their childhood memories; young people can see the bizarre and motley character of old Shanghai, and sense the health and prosperity of new Shanghai; social historians can find material they need; psychologists can rely on it to research the particular states of mind of the people who were active in those circles; linguists can make use of it to investigate changes in Shanghai dialect."[18] The reissue of courtesan novels was meant not only to facilitate research, but also to restimulate individual memories that might well have been buried under the state's master narrative of twentieth-century history. At the same time, although the introduction expressed the pious hope that young people would appreciate the contrast between the bad old days and the healthy present, the book itself aimed to make available to them a textured and colorful body of knowledge about the past, one that they might well use to fashion their own understandings of old Shanghai, of their own heritage, of their own Chineseness. Prostitutes were important figures in this reach for a new and improved past, making it likely that the meanings of prostitution will continue to be re-created and negotiated in China as elsewhere.

APPENDIX A

Tables

TABLE 1   Native Places of 118 Courtesans

Native Place	Number of Women	Percent of Total
Suzhou (or Gusu)	49*	41.5
Qinchuan (Changshu)	10	8.5
Yangzhou	7	5.9
Weichang (Yangzhou)	3	2.5
Siming (Ningbo)	5	4.2
Jiangxi	3 (1 Nanchang)	2.5
Wujiang	2	1.7
Hubei	2	1.7
Tianjin	1	.8
other	18	15.3
unclear	18	15.3
Total	118	100.0

* Of these, one says only "her mother was from Suzhou." Note the attempt to assert a Suzhou pedigree. Half of the women came from Suzhou or Changshu, the native place of high-class courtesans.

SOURCE: Huayu xiaozhu zhuren 1892: passim.

TABLE 2   Total Detentions Related to Prostitution
(Prostitutes, Customers, and Sometimes Pimps)*

Time Period	Number Detained	Total Arrests (%)	Source Number
1981–1991	580,000	100	1
1982	20,000+	3.4	2
1986	25,021	4.3	5
1987	68,091	11.7	5
1988	50,822	8.8	5
1989	110,000		3
1989	115,289	19.9	5
1990	146,000		3
1990	137,894	23.8	4
1991	210,000		2
1991	201,420	34.7	4
1992	242,428	—	4
1993 (Jan.–June)	104,624	—	4

* No effort has been made to choose among conflicting sets of figures, which vary significantly.

SOURCES: 1. "Security Ministry Cracks Down on Prostitution" (text). Beijing *Xinhua* in English (6 September 1991, 0847 GMT). *FBIS Daily Report—China*, 10 September 1991 (PrEx 7.10: FBIS-CHI-91-175), p. 31.

2. Pan Suiming 1993b: n.p.

3. "Gu Linfang on Drugs, Vice Sweeps" (text). Hong Kong *Tzu Ching*, 14 (5 November 1991), pp. 10–12. *FBIS Daily Report—China*, 25 November 1991 (PrEx 7.10: FBIS-CHI-91-227), p. 29.

4. *Shijie ribao* 1993: October 18.

5. "Situation Concerning the Investigation and Banning of Prostitution and Prostitute Patronization," submitted to 20th session of seventh NPC standing committee, printed June 18, 1991. Cited in "Document Studies Situation" (text). Hong Kong *Jiushi niandai* in Chinese (1 October 1991), 216, pp. 19–21. *FBIS Daily Report—China*, 9 October 1991 (PrEx 7.10: FBIS-CHI-91-196), pp. 28–30.

TABLE 3   Ages of Prostitutes in Selected
Reeducation Centers, 1989–1992

Year	Place	Number of Women	Under 20 (%)	21–25 (%)	26–30 (%)	31–35 (%)	Over 36 (%)
1989	not given	341	68	12.3	7.33	9.97*	2.3**
1989–90	9 places#	368	39.94	38.85	14.13	4.61	2.44
1992	Beijing	100	15***	56****	17	10	2
total		809	48.70	29.78	11.61	7.54	2.34

Suzhou, Shanghai, Chengdu, Mishan, Beijing, Qingdao, Nanjing, Xiamen, and Shenzhen. The survey included 2,136 men and women incarcerated for sexual crimes or misconduct. Forty-nine percent of this number were from Shanghai. Of the 2,136, 630 were women, of whom 385 were prostitutes (*maiyin funü*), 368 of whom gave their ages.

* age 30–40
** over age 41
*** under age 18
**** age 19–25
SOURCES: For 1989, Ye Po 1989: p. 8; and Wang Xingjuan 1990: p. 3.
For 1989–1990, derived from Liu Dalin et al. 1992: p. 716.
For 1992, Beijing shi Tiantang he laojiaosuo 1992?: pp. 1–2.

TABLE 4   Educational Level of Prostitutes in Selected
Reeducation Centers, 1988–1992

Year	Place	Number of Women	Illiterate (%)	Elementary (%)	Junior Middle (%)	Senior Middle (%)	University (%)*
1988	not given	not given	5	25	56	10	3
1989–1990	9 places	385	1.6	22.6	61	6	.3
1992a	Shenzhen	800	10	not given	75	12–13	2–3
1992b	Beijing	100		10	55	30	5

* "University" refers to postsecondary specialized training (*dazhuan*) as well as to university.
SOURCES: For 1988, Wang Xingjuan 1990: p. 2. Percentages refer to people who have attended school at a given level without necessarily graduating.
For 1989–1990, Liu Dalin et al. 1992: p. 717. For a list of locations, see table 3. Percentages refer to people who have completed school at a given level. The educational level of 8.6 percent of those surveyed was unclear.
For 1992a, Chen Yiyun 1992. Percentages refer to people who have attended or completed school at a given level.
For 1992b, Beijing shi Tiantang he laojiaosuo 1992?: p. 2. Percentages refer to people who have attended school at a given level without necessarily graduating.

TABLE 5   Occupations of Prostitutes in Selected
Reeducation Centers, 1989–1992

Occupation	Survey 1 (n=385) #	%	Survey 2 (n=100) #	%	Total #	%
Worker	56	14.5	14	14	70	14.43
Peasant	112	29.1	23	23	135	27.83
Service	28	7.3	31	31	59	12.16
Commerce	11	2.9	—	—	11	2.27
Teacher	3	.9	3	3	6	1.24
Medical	3	.9	3	3	6	1.24
Art/lit	2	.5	—	—	2	.41
Cadre	1	.3	—	—	1	.21
Clerk/bookkeeper	3	.8	1	1	4	.82
Military	1	.3	—	—	1	.21
Student	4	1.0	—	—	4	.82
Entrepreneur	35	9.1	7	7	42	8.66
Unemployed	102	26.5	18	18	120	24.74
Other	15	3.9	—	—	15	3.09
Unclear	9	2.3	—	—	9	1.85
Total	385	100.0	100	100	485	99.98

SOURCES: For Survey 1, Liu Dalin et al. 1992: p. 717. Prostitutes were from the nine locations listed in table 3.

For Survey 2, Beijing shi Tiantang he laojiaosuo 1992?: pp. 2–3.

TABLE 6   Motivations Reported
by Detained Prostitutes

Survey 1, Guangzhou (n=200)

Motivation	%
To make money	53
Were in business and suffered a theft, had no way to live	12
Livelihood difficulties	2
Unhappy home	10
Coerced	1.5
For pleasure	7
Influenced by pornographic publications	1.5
Had a clear goal	4.5
Other reasons (e.g., concern for self)	8.5

Survey 2, national (n=385)

Motivation	%
Money	50.1
Pursuit of happiness	11.9
Curiosity	11.4
Revenge	16.4
Other	3.9
Unclear	6.2

SOURCES: For Survey 1: Wang Xingjuan 1990: pp. 1–2.
For Survey 2: Liu Dalin et al. 1992: p. 719.

Poems

CHAPTER 2

靑蓮閣上野雞窠　　Qing lian ge shang ye ji ke
飛去飛來似織梭　　Fei qu fei lai si zhi suo
最是揚幫眞老臉　　Zui shi Yang bang zhen lao lian
做妹雙手把衣拖　　zuo mei shuang shou ba yi tuo

CHAPTER 3

鴇母驕人號本家　　Baomu jiaoren hao benjia
黃金不惜買嬌娃　　Huangjin buxi mai jiaowa
可憐十二三齡女　　Kelian shier san lingnü
演舞教歌到月斜　　Yanwu jiao ge dao yuexie

龜背難當代用肩　　Guibei nandang dai yong jian
時髦出局力能捐　　Shimao chuju lineng qian
虛心昨夜經期到　　Xuxin zuoye jingqi dao
點滴留心褲後前　　Diandi liuxin ku houqian

枇杷黃　　Pipa huang
娘姨忙　　Niangyi mang
小姐慌　　Xiaojie huang
大少藏　　Dashao cang
賑漂光　　Zhang piaoguang

POEMS BY LI PINGXIANG (李蘋香) CHAPTER 6

嘗製選菊詩

Chang zhi xuan ju shi

斜斜整整葉緣枝
一樣滋培有等差
縱帶容華終免俗
別操鑑賞任嘲痴
空羣駿足懸高價
絕代蛾眉壓衆孃
但惜東籬風骨冷
何人肯采未開時

xie xie zheng zheng ye yuan zhi
yi yang zipei you deng chai
zong dai rong hua zhong mian su
bie cao jian shang ren chao chi
kong qun jun zu xuan gao jia
jue dai e mei ya zhong chi
dan xi dong li feng gu leng
he ren ken cai wei kai shi

失貓詩

Shi mao shi

晝長貪臥亂書對
底事穿雲去不回
燈下漸看飢鼠出
花陰疑逐小虫來
深恩易背奴無行
飽食颺終將不才
恰笑主人癡太甚
臨風爲汝一徘徊

zhou chang tan wo luan shu dui
di shi chuan yun qu bu hui
deng xia jian kan ji shu chu
hua yin yi zhu xiao chong lai
shen en yi bei nu wu xing
bao shi yang zhong jiang bu cai
qia xiao zhu ren chi tai shen
lin feng wei ru yi pai huai

中秋詩

Zhong qiu shi

一年最好中秋月
強半都從病裡看
今夜酒杯浮瀲灩
誰家人影照團圓
近霜園果紛盈座
斫雪溪鱗乍上竿
寂寞閨中無伴侶
夜闌吟嘯繞花欄

yi nian zui hao zhong qiu yue
qiang ban dou cong bing li kan
jin ye jiu bei fu lian yan
shei jia ren ying zhao tuan yuan
jin shuang yuan guo fen ying zuo
zhuo xue xi lin zha shang gan
ji mo gui zhong wu ban lü
ye lan yin xiao rao hua lan

哭妹詩

Ku mei shi

芙蓉枯死菊衰零
十一年來一夢醒
苦向繡幃勤筆墨
角渠醫藥悟參苓
虛心善解雙親意
妙手常披一卷經
今日從頭頻憶惜
悽然寒月入疏欞

fu rong ku si ju shuai ling
shi yi nian lai yi meng xing
ku xiang xiu wei qin bi mo
jiao qu yi yao wu can ling
xu xin shan jie shuang qin yi
miao shou chang pi yi juan jing
jin ri cong tou pin yi xi
qi ran han yue ru shu ling

NOTES

ABBREVIATIONS

CMJ   *China Medical Journal* (prior to 1932)
       Chinese Medical Journal (1932 and later)
FBIS   Foreign Broadcast Information Service
JPRS   Joint Publications Research Service
MG   *Municipal Gazette*
NCH   *North-China Herald*
SMP   Shanghai Municipal Police
SVC   Special Vice Committee

CHAPTER 1: INTRODUCTION

1. Many of the ideas in this first chapter were published in earlier forms in Hershatter 1989; Hershatter 1991; Hershatter 1992a; Hershatter 1992b; Hershatter 1993; and Hershatter 1994.

2. Zeng Die 1935: p. 711.

3. See, for example, the very useful but interpretively limited work by Wang Shunu (1988).

4. Rosen 1982: p. 12.

5. White 1990: p. 10; see also Bernheimer 1989: p. 3.

6. Corbin 1990: p. xvii. Also see Corbin 1986.

7. Harsin 1985: p. xxiii.

8. Bernheimer 1989: p. 2. Bernheimer writes of literary and artistic portraits of prostitution in nineteenth-century France: "My argument is that the prostitute is ubiquitous in the novels and paintings of this period not only because of her prominence as a social phenomenon but, more important, because of her function in stimulating artistic strategies to control and dispel her fantasmatic threat to male mastery."

9. Rosen 1982: p. xiii; also see pp. 39–43. For similar arguments about nineteenth-century New York City, see Stansell 1987: p. 171.

10. On prostitution as labor, see, among others, White 1990: p. 12; Stansell 1987: p. 172; and Walkowitz 1980: pp. 9, 31.

11. See, for example, Rosen 1982: p. xiv.

12. Stansell 1987: p. 186; White 1990: pp. 2, 10–12, and passim.

13. See, in addition to the sources cited below, Mahood 1990: pp. 5–6.

14. See, for example, White 1990: pp. 17–18.

15. Rosen 1982: p. 47.

16. Walkowitz 1992.

17. Rosen 1982: p. 137. On the trafficking question, see pp. 112–35.

18. Stansell 1987: p. 192.

19. Walkowitz 1980: p. 31.

20. On France, and particularly the work of the public-health official Alexandre Parent-Duchâtelet, see Harsin 1985; Corbin 1990: pp. 3–111; and Gray 1992. On the Contagious Diseases Act in England (passed 1866, rescinded two decades later) and the fight for its repeal under the leadership of Josephine Butler, see Walkowitz 1980. On Scotland, see Mahood 1990. On Italy, see Gibson 1986. On Russia, see Bernstein 1995 and Engelstein 1992: pp. 74–75, 94, 84–92. On explanations of female sexual deviance in Russia, which both appropriated and rejected aspects of the European model of biologically determined sexual deviance, see Engelstein 1992: pp. 128–52.

21. Levine 1994. On a different set of colonial effects in Northern Sudan, see Spaulding and Beswick 1995.

22. On the effects of regulation, see, among others, Walkowitz 1980 and Harsin 1985.

23. Rosen 1982: pp. xii, 16, 33, 51–68, and passim. For other important recent studies of prostitution, see Otis 1985; Butler 1985; Rosen and Davidson 1977; and Gilfoyle 1992.

24. This book draws directly and indirectly on recent work about Shanghai history produced by many scholars. See, among others, Coble 1980; Fewsmith 1985; Fu 1993; Goodman 1995; Honig 1986; Honig 1992; Tahirih Lee 1995; Lu Hanchao 1995; Perry 1993; the essays in Wakeman and Yeh 1992; Wakeman 1995a; Wakeman 1995b; and Wasserstrom 1991. In a less scholarly vein, see Miller 1937, Pan 1984, and Sergeant 1991, as well as reminiscences cited throughout this book.

25. On the ideological work of gender, see Poovey 1988.

26. The term "upper-class prostitute" is used in this book synonymously with "courtesan," in contradistinction to "lower-class prostitute" or "streetwalker." Chapter 2 provides more refined classificatory schemes. Yet the hierarchies of class, as always, are inadequate to subsume crosscutting hierarchies of gender. "Class" here refers partly to the class status of the male clientele of these women. It is also meant to indicate that upper-class prostitutes commanded more income, and sometimes (not always) exercised more control over that income and the conditions of their labor, than did lower-class prostitutes. An "upper-class" prostitute, however, was not "upper class" in the same sense as her patrons, and was vulnerable to exploitation, abuse, social denigration, and reversals of fortune quite specific to her trade. See part 2, "Pleasures."

27. The term "mosquito press" was used in English; the Chinese term was *xiao bao* (small newspaper). See Link 1981: pp. 118–24. In this book I generally use the term "tabloid press," but the reader should not envision the Shanghai equivalent of

the *National Enquirer*; as indicated below, the tabloids were often highly literary in style, employing many novelists as regular contributors.

28. Sergeant (1991: p. 3) mentions that Shanghai itself was popularly known among foreign travelers as "the Whore of the Orient," an appellation that aptly suggests the foreign eroticization of pleasure, danger, mystery, degradation, and conquest in a Chinese venue. To my knowledge, this expression was not used by Chinese reformers, but their writings also made linkages of a less pleasurable sort between prostitution, modernity, and the Chinese nation.

29. For a discussion of the rise of the fiction press, see Link 1981: pp. 79–124. With respect to courtesan fiction, Stephen Cheng notes a change from portrayals of courtesans as devoted and loyal to representations of them in later courtesan novels as evil, greedy, lustful, and extortionist. He links this to the development of a group of commercial writers producing for a mass market: "It is doubtful that courtesans in the real world could have changed so much with the years; the change in their treatment can be more easily linked to the shift in both readership and authorship. The scholarly writers of old have given place to the crass commercial writers with a keen interest in the new market. The literati readers of the early period hungering for sentimental love stories have been replaced by new middle-class pleasure-seekers interested in the sensational." Cheng 1979: pp. 254–55.

30. Yeh (1992: p. 191) defines petty urbanites (*xiao shimin*) as "literate clerks and apprentices in trade, manufacturing, the professions and public and private service sectors." She also mentions elementary and normal-school teachers as a closely related but distinct group.

31. In late imperial writings, *jinü* was a neutral term that connoted prostitutes of all ranks. Ropp 1996. *Mingji* was used to refer to prominent courtesans. *Changji*, "prostitution," was found in medical literature from the sixteenth to the nineteenth century in conjunction with syphilis. By the 1920s, however, *jinü* appeared as a category of social problem. I am indebted to Ted Huters, Shu-mei Shih, and Frank Dikötter for sharing their philological expertise on this question. Also see Ko 1994: p. 253; and Hanyu da cidian bianji weiyuanhui 1989: vol. 4, pp. 295–96, 370.

32. For an eloquent demand that historians attend to discursive constructions of gender and their historical effects, see Scott 1988.

33. These are, of course, not entirely new concerns for historians, but they have been raised in particular ways by what Robert Berkhofer calls "the recent challenge to traditional history practice." See Berkhofer 1995: passim, but particularly chapter 1, for a summary of recent debates.

34. For a stunning discussion of nostalgia in imperial-era Chinese writings, and the genealogy of the term in European and American writings, see Kafalas 1995: chapter 2. He writes, "[N]ostalgia is not so much a way of keeping the past alive as it is a way of living amidst memory of what is irremediably lost." Rey Chow writes about the representation of prostitution in the 1987 Hong Kong film *Rouge*: "Nostalgia is . . . most acutely felt not as an attempt to return to the past as such, but as an effect of temporal dislocation—of something having been displaced in time. . . . But if its compressed images always convey a sense of loss and melancholy, nostalgia also worked by concealing and excluding the dirty and unpleasant elements of social hardships." Chow 1993: pp. 74–75.

On late imperial literati writings about courtesans, see Levy 1966; Ropp 1996; and

Li 1993. Levy, in a preface to his translation of Yu Huai's seventeenth-century memoir of the Nanjing courtesan district, argues that Yu Huai's nostalgia for his vanished youth and the defeated Ming dynasty found expression through his writings about courtesans (p. 5). Ropp argues that "courtesans in China could and often enough did become powerful symbols of morality and virtue," but that they "could not escape the taint of notoriety" (pp. 2–3; all page numbers for Ropp 1996 are from typescript, since the book was in press as of this writing). "In the early Qing period," he adds, "literati nostalgia for the now-lost glamour associated with late Ming courtesans is part of literati nostalgia and mourning for the fallen Ming dynasty" (p. 3). On seventeenth-century courtesan culture, see also Ko 1994: pp. 251–93.

35. On ethnocontext, see Berkhofer 1995: pp. 20–21.

36. Chi Zhicheng 1893: pp. 6, 8. Chi Zhicheng, a native of Rui'an in Zhejiang, was a secretary for the Taiwan *shunfu.*

37. Huang Renjing 1913; Wang Liaoweng 1922; Xin shijie baoshe 1918; Zhan Kai 1917; Banchisheng 1891.

38. For one among many examples of this usage, see Zhou Shoujuan 1928: vol. 1, p. 38.

39. See, for instance, the preface to Chan Qingshi 1884.

40. Chan Qingshi 1884: preface.

41. Qi Xia and Dan Ru 1917: vol. 1, n.p. [p. 34]. All page numbers in brackets were assigned by me.

42. Chan Qingshi 1884: preface. The practice of including numerous prefaces by various authors at the beginning of a work was particularly popular in the 1910s and early 1920s, according to Link (1981: p. 170).

43. On madams, see Li chuang wo dusheng 1905: *juan* 8, pp. 2–3. On customers and courtesans, see Zhou Shoujuan 1928: vol. 2, pp. 183–84. For a poetic enumeration of the sorrows of pheasant streetwalkers, expressed by a man using the pen name Master of the Green Idea Studio, see Zhou Shoujuan 1928: vol. 2, pp. 168–69.

44. Yang Guifei, a famously beautiful consort of a Tang emperor, was said to be the cause of a rebellion because the emperor neglected affairs of state to spend time with her and allowed her to install people of dubious loyalty in high office.

45. Zhou Shoujuan 1928: vol. 1, pp. 36–37. *Suiyuan Poetry Talks* [*Suiyuan shihua*] was written in the Qing by the poet Yuan Mei, whose honorific name (*hao*) was Suiyuan.

46. Zhou Shoujuan 1928: vol. 1, p. 48.

47. Some guidebooks initially appeared in serial form in the tabloid press. Wang Zhongxian n.d., for instance, originally appeared in *Shehui ribao* (Social news). Wang Zhongxian n.d.: introduction, n.p.

48. *Youxi bao* was founded in 1896 or 1897 and published until 1910; *Xiao bao* was founded in 1897. Sun Guoqun 1988a: p. 73; Link 1981: pp. 141–42. For a discussion of an essay in one of the earliest issues of *Youxi bao* that makes a case for informing readers about the national crisis via "playful" writings, see Meng Yue 1994: pp. 155 ff. For comprehensive surveys of the Shanghai tabloid press, see Yao Jiguang and Yu Yifen 1981; Zhu Junzhou 1988; and Ping Jinya 1986; for brief discussions, see Britton 1966: p. 96; and Lee and Nathan 1985: p. 374. Zhu Junzhou (1988: part 2, pp. 138–39) briefly treats tabloids of the 1920s devoted exclusively to courtesan news. In the career of Li Boyuan one can see the close linkage between entertainment fiction, writing about courtesans, and attention to national reform. Li was the editor of

a fiction magazine in Shanghai in 1903. In his 1901 novel *Panorama of Officialdom,* he criticized Chinese officials for failing "to resist the West effectively." Link 1981: pp. 134, 138–39, 143. "Castigatory novel" is Link's translation of a term coined by Lu Xun.

Link (1981: p. 142) argues that entertainment sheets like *Youxi bao* should not be lumped together with (presumably more substantial) tabloids like *Crystal,* discussed below. Yet in a retrospective treatment of the tabloids, the journalist and translator Bao Tianxiao does just that. Writing fifty years later, Bao described *Youxi bao* and others of its type in highly critical terms, as follows:

> And what was the content of these entertainment papers like? Fun, of course, was their core. Their first principle was not to speak of politics; they would hear nothing of "the great affairs of the nation" and things like that. What they carried was only gossip and rumor, anecdotes and overheard secrets—nothing that amounted to much. . . . Later on they got increasingly worse, writing exclusively about the affairs of prostitutes and actors. Sometimes they even confronted the brothels with a show of force, groundlessly extorting payoffs from them. For example: the high-class brothels of Shanghai collected their bills for banquet entertainment three times a year. If the entertainment papers had some reason to quarrel with a certain institution, they would start a rumor to the effect that such-and-such a courtesan was soon to be married. When this happened all of the male customers who had been showing up because of their special feelings for that lady would "float their accounts" ("floating an account" was professional jargon for failing a debt). Bao 1971: p. 445, translated in Link 1981: p. 142.

49. For the years of elections and a list of additional tabloids, see Sun Guoqun 1988a: pp. 73–74, 77.

50. *Jingbao,* Shanghai, 1919–1940. Link (1981: p. 119) calls *Crystal* "the premier example of the mosquito press for two decades." He gives its circulation in the 1920s as over ten thousand and describes its content as follows: "In addition to serialized fiction and irregular news, *Crystal* carried poetry and poetry games, a song and dance column, drama review, letters, a column called 'clever talk,' calligraphy, and advertisements" (p. 120). Zhu Junzhou (1988: part 1, p. 172) says that at its height the circulation of *Crystal* reached fifty thousand, surpassing other tabloids and topped only by the mainstream papers *Xinwen bao, Shenbao,* and *Shibao.* On the history of *Crystal* and its rivalry with other papers, see also Bao Tianxiao 1971: pp. 444–51; Lu Dafang 1980: pp. 63–67; Yao Jiguang and Yu Yifen 1981: pp. 225–33; and Zhu Junzhou 1988: part 1, pp. 171–72.

51. For one such list, printed serially, see *Jingbao* 1919: April 9, 15, 18, and 24; p. 3 in all cases. The headnote to the first installment said that the Shanghai telephone book listed brothels but not individual courtesans, and added that this was very inconvenient.

52. *Shenbao* 1919: May 10; *Jingbao* 1919: June 3, p. 3; June 12, p. 3. Also see chapter 6.

53. Li chuang wo dusheng 1905: *juan* 7, p. 6; Zhou Shoujuan 1928: vol. 2, p. 234; Wang Zhongxian n.d.: p. 92; Chunming shuju 1937: *zhiji,* p. 1.

54. "The Demi-monde of Shanghai" 1923: pp. 785–86. Li chuang wo dusheng 1905

(*juan* 6, pp. 13–14) defined a pheasant as "a person who appears to be a prostitute but also appears not to be one. She may have bound feet or big feet. She wears makeup and colorful clothing. At night they move around on Si malu [Fuzhou Road] near the teahouses and opium dens." Yu Muxia (1935: *shang*, p. 13) explained that pheasants (the birds) lived freely in the wild, possessed more beautiful plumage than domestic chickens, and went everywhere in search of food, just like prostitutes who traveled the streets and teahouses ceaselessly.

55. *Shenbao* 1919: November 12. Mainstream newspapers such as *Shenbao* and *Shibao* overlapped somewhat with tabloids such as *Crystal;* both published popular fiction. Link 1981: pp. 150–51 and passim. For a discussion of *Shenbao*'s literary section in the 1910s, which often mentioned brothels in the course of social satire, see Meng Yue 1994.

Five yuan, an amount paid frequently in fines by streetwalkers in the late 1910s and the 1920s, would have been a substantial amount for women working in other sectors. In 1919, women cotton-mill workers made .20 to .25 yuan per day. Perry 1993: p. 49. Women in eight different cotton mills surveyed in 1925 made between .20 and .40 yuan per day. Honig 1986: p. 179, table 6. From 1910 to 1934, the nominal wage of female textile workers in Shanghai crept slowly upward from .26 yuan per day to .46 yuan per day. Rawski 1989: pp. 301–2. In 1933, one Chinese yuan was approximately twenty-six U.S. cents. Rawski 1980: p. 157.

56. See, for instance, *Shenbao* 1920: May 11, May 13; and *Shibao* 1929: April 8, p. 7; April 12, p. 7; July 15, p. 7; and November 16, p. 7.

57. The phrase is David Strand's. Strand 1989: p. 66.

58. For a similar point about France since 1850, see Corbin 1990: p. viii.

59. Wang Liaoweng 1922: author's preface, pp. 1–4; Qi Xia and Dan Ru 1917: vol. 1, preface.

60. For examples of such copying, see the virtual reproduction of *juan* 6 of Banchisheng 1891 in Huayu xiaozhu zhuren 1892, and the use of Ge Yuanxu 1876: *juan* 2, pp. 34–36, in Li chuang wo dusheng 1905: *juan* 6, pp. 6–7. Pei Xibin 1905 appears to be an exact reprint of Li chuang wo dusheng 1905. Also see the extensive use of Wang Houzhe 1925, sometimes word for word, and of Wang Dingjiu 1932, in Sun Yusheng 1939.

61. Zhan Kai 1917: author's preface, dated 1907.

62. Wang Liaoweng 1922: author's preface, pp. 1–4.

63. Zhang Chunfan 1919: March 3, p. 3; March 24, p. 3; April 6, p. 3; May 6, p. 3.

64. Levenson 1972.

65. Sometimes the standard was not so unspoken. In Wang Liaoweng's comprehensive history of Shanghai courtesans, facing page 1 of the section containing pictures of famous courtesans was an advertisement for German-made pills reputed to cure a variety of illnesses having to do with pregnancy, childbirth, miscarriage, and difficult delivery. The advertisement featured a woman dressed in Western-style skirt, blouse, and high heels, clearly not a courtesan. Since so much of the advertisement was devoted to listing specifically female illnesses, one wonders about the audience for this book. Noncourtesan women? Courtesans? Men who might recommend the medicine to their wives?

At the end of the picture section, more than forty pages later, was an advertisement for a stationery and business-supply store, apparently directed at a literate audience, possibly businessmen. There were also advertisements for portraits, a transport company, a store for imported nylon and wool fabrics, amd a store that appeared to be giving away imported diamonds (perhaps rhinestones?) with every purchase of "scientific glasses." The dominance of advertisements for Western-style or imported goods side by side with this paean to nostalgia for courtesans is striking. Wang Liaoweng 1922: n.p.

66. Guha 1988: p. 35. Guha's approach to subaltern studies is one among many and cannot be taken as representative of the entire group. However, both because of his crucial role in defining and fostering this type of scholarship, and because his formulations raise particular problems, I single him out here. For recent appropriations and adaptations of the subaltern studies project from the perspectives of postcolonial criticism, Latin American history, and African history, see, respectively, Prakash 1994; Mallon 1994; and Cooper 1994.

67. On this process, see Anagnost forthcoming, chapter 1.

68. Hinton and Gordon 1984.

69. Although it should not be assumed that subversive voices can always be found, or that they are a required component in every historical situation, the attempt to locate and represent them has been enormously productive in the work of the Subaltern Studies Group.

70. Under such circumstances, what is a would-be people's historian to do? If one is lucky enough to interview someone whose prerevolutionary position fits the definition of a subaltern, as I was when investigating the pre-1949 working class of Tianjin (Hershatter 1986), one can try to interrupt the standard "speak bitterness" story so often heard in the formal political process with relentlessly detailed questions about specific local incidents and practices. I did this, and learned a great deal about food, friendships, menstruation, and other aspects of life conventionally regarded as subpolitical. My purpose was not to excavate a prediscursive reality, but to try to recapture the categories through which workers understood their own experience at the time. But the closer the questioning came to deliberate or collective acts of resistance, the more the official language crept back in. Nor were my questions necessarily helpful in locating a story that a subaltern might tell unprompted; my own line of questioning, after all, was no less situated than the discursive categories I was trying to disrupt.

71. Cao Manzhi 1986.

72. Spivak 1988b: p. 11.

73. Spivak 1988a: pp. 294, 308. Spivak's intellectual relationship to the Subaltern Studies Group is complex. She is not a historian or a member of the SSG, and she does not speak for them; yet no one has done more to publicize their project (albeit in her own terms) to a non-area-studies audience. Spivak simultaneously applauds their construction of and attention to subalterns, gently chides them for their insistence on "the determinate vigor and full autonomy" of the subaltern, and introduces a doubly subaltern position of a gendered colonial subject. Even the most energetic of excavators in the SSG do not argue that what they find in the historical record is a subaltern's autonomous and unmediated version of "what happened." An awareness that it is impossible to extricate any subaltern from a host of elite spokespersons is a subcurrent in much of the work of the group, as Spivak herself acknowledges.

74. Spivak 1988a: p. 287.

75. Spivak 1988a: p. 295.

76. Spivak 1988a: p. 296. Spivak's example is the practice of widow suicide, which the British mistakenly called sati (literally, "good wife"). What we hear in the records of nineteenth-century British moves against this practice, not to mention its inclusion today by white feminists in the catalog of timeless atrocities against women, is not the "voices" of women who threw themselves on the funeral pyres of their husbands, but rather the constitution "of the woman as *object* of protection from her own kind" (p. 299). Or, as Spivak acerbically puts it, "White men are saving brown women from brown men" (p. 296). "Between patriarchy and imperialism, subject-constitution and object-formation, the figure of the woman disappears, not into a pristine nothingness, but into a violent shuttling which is the displaced figuration of the 'third-world woman' caught between tradition and modernization" (p. 303).

77. Abu-Lughod (1990: p. 42) defines such romance as a tendency "to read all forms of resistance as signs of the ineffectiveness of systems of power and of the resilience and creativity of the human spirit in its refusal to be dominated." She suggests instead that "we should use resistance as a *diagnostic* of power," as something that has "been produced by power relations and cannot be seen as independent of them" (pp. 42, 47).

78. On the "virile" resistance of the full-scale peasant revolt, see O'Hanlon 1988: p. 223.

79. Other studies of prostitution that include or focus on Shanghai are Hō Aboku [Peng Amu] 1928; Pomerantz 1978; Gronewold 1984; Scherer 1981; Scherer 1986; Huebner 1988; Henriot 1992; Henriot 1994; Henriot 1995; Henriot 1996a; Henriot 1996b; Henriot forthcoming 1997. Wolfe 1980 provides explanations of terms having to do with prostitution and sexual activity more generally. Each of these works has different strengths. Pomerantz focuses on prostitution as an issue of concern to reformist intellectuals; Gronewold does an extensive survey of Western-language sources; Scherer, using mostly sources available in Taiwan, attempts to link marriage and prostitution in a single analytical framework, relating prostitution to Confucianism and Daoism. The forthcoming study of Shanghai prostitution by Christian Henriot is by far the most comprehensive of the group. His research was conducted at roughly the same time as my own, and I understand that his book, in press in France at this writing, deals far more comprehensively with nineteenth-century writings than does mine. It is my hope that his book will discuss the essays of Wang Tao (1828–1897) and the contribution of the illustrated magazine *Dian shi zhai huabao*. On Wang Tao, see Wang Tao 1934; Wang Tao 1929; and Huang Shiquan [Wang Tao] 1975; for a discussion of Wang Tao that does not include his extensive writings on courtesans, see Cohen 1974. On *Dian shi zhai huabao*, see Ye Xiaoqing 1991.

80. For a similar transgression in the study of nineteenth-century France, see Bernheimer 1989: p. 2 and passim.

81. According to a study by Stephen Cheng, the earliest and most famous courtesan novel about Shanghai was probably *Haishang hualie zhuan* (Flowers of Shanghai), by Han Bangqing (1856–1894), which first appeared in 1892 in a Qing literary magazine. The son of a Qing official, Han failed the civil-service examinations. He published poetry in Shanghai, had a long relationship with a courtesan, and died before the age of forty. Cheng 1979: pp. 24–30. Cheng (1979: pp. 176–77) translates

the introduction to the novel, which conveys a cautionary message not unlike those discussed in chapter 4 of the present study. It reads in part:

> The number of young men ruined and destroyed by journeys to the pleasure quarters is beyond counting; neither their fathers' and brothers' interdictions, nor their teachers' and friends' admonitions could stop them. . . . But once shown the true picture, they will feel like vomiting and dejected for their mistake, and they will all awaken and return to the right path. . . . So when the reader faces those more charming than Hsi-shih, he will realize that behind his back they are more spiteful than witches; when he perceives that today they are sweeter than the ideal wife, he will foresee that tomorrow they will be more venomous than snakes. For him the novel will be a warning bell, provoking him to reflect upon himself. It is for this reason that *Biographies of Flowers of Shanghai* has been written.

The novel has been reissued recently (Han Bangqing 1985); several chapters were translated into English in *Renditions* in 1982 (Han Bangqing 1982). For a complete plot summary, see Chen Sihe 1990: pp. 151–84. For an extended discussion from the perspective of literary history, see Cheng 1979: passim; Cheng 1982; Liu Ts'un-yan 1982: pp. 11–18; Chen Sihe 1990: pp. 140–50. For a brief evaluation, see Chen Dingshan 1967: p. 123. Herewith I give a partial catalog of fictional writing by the authors on whose nonfictional writings I rely, and who are frequently quoted in the chapters that follow.

Zhang Chunfan was the author of *Jiuwei gui* (The nine-tailed turtle), a courtesan novel first published in 1910 that featured himself as protagonist. See Zhang Chunfan 1917. For a searing critique of Zhang's inflated portrayal of his own skills in this novel, see Chen Dingshan 1967: p. 123. Cheng (1979: p. 232) calls the novel "sensationalistic and stereotyped." In 1919, Zhang published a series of articles in *Crystal* that nostalgically recalled the courtesan houses of twenty years earlier, discussing no one lower than the rank of *yao er* courtesan. See Zhang Chunfan 1919: passim. For further discussion of Zhang and his work, see Lu Dafang 1980: pp. 229–31.

Bi Yihong, the author of several short stories discussed briefly in chapter 10, also wrote the courtesan novel *Renjian diyu* (Hell on earth). Once a late Qing official in Beijing, and a minor revenue official in Zhejiang in the early Republican period, he spent the remainder of his life in Shanghai and was a close associate of Bao Tianxiao. Some of his popular fiction was published in *Shibao*. For Bao's reminiscence of Bi, see Bao Tianxiao 1990: vol. 3, pp. 591–617. Also see Bi Yihong 1922; Suoposheng and Bao Tianxiao 1991; Liu Ts'un-yan 1982: p. 34; Link 1981: pp. 148, 157; and the citations in chapter 10.

Sun Yusheng (1862 or 1863 to 1939?), was the author of a guidebook published in 1939 under the pseudonym Haishang Juewusheng. He also wrote *Haishang fanhua meng* (Dreams of glory in Shanghai), published in 1903, with a sequel in 1916. Like many of these authors, Sun was also a journalist; he edited *Xinwen bao* in 1891 and worked as an editor on *Shenbao* and other newspapers. Later he himself was sole publisher of three papers, apparently all tabloids: *Caifeng bao, Xiaolin bao,* and *Xin shijie bao.* He was the author of other novels as well. For brief biographical sketches, see Li Shengping 1989: p. 202; and Liu Ts'un-yan 1982: p. 12. Cheng (1979: pp. 231–50) gives *Haishang fanhua meng* a higher evaluation for its meticulous recording of prices (a characteristic also present in the 1939 guidebook) than for its literary qualities.

Zhou Shoujuan (1894–1968), a native of Suzhou, was a novelist, writer, teacher, translator (of Conan Doyle, among others), and editor at *Shenbao, Xinwen bao,* and *Libailiu* magazine. From 1920 to 1932 he was chief editor of *Shenbao*'s literary supplement, *Ziyou tan.* He also edited the monthly magazine *Violet* and contributed to the tabloid *Crystal* and the mainstream newspaper *Shibao.* Along with Bao Tianxiao, Zhou in the late Qing was one of the main practitioners of a form of translation that, in Link's words, used "Japanese translations of Western works for re-translation into Chinese, again classical. Users of this method frequently knew no Western language, and, just as often, knew little or no Japanese. . . . [A]ll that was sought was a gleaning of the essential plot of a story as a basis for telling one's own. For such purposes, a perusal of the *kanji* (Chinese characters) used in Japanese writing could suffice" (p. 136). Zhou Shoujuan was the author of the novel *Xin qiuhaitang* (New begonia). See Zhou Shoujuan n.d. In 1928 he published a two-volume work titled *Lao Shanghai sanshi nian jianwen lu* (A record of things seen by an old Shanghai hand in the last thirty years). In his preface he coyly denied authorship:

> "Unfortunately I have always shut my door and stayed at home, and not paid attention to things that don't directly concern me, so when people come to Shanghai from other places, and ask me about conditions here, I have nothing to say to them. And I know even less about stories of Shanghai's past. My old friend Chen Wuwo [literally, "Chen not me"] is more than ten years older than I, has worked in the journalism field for thirty years, and is really familiar with Shanghai's conditions. He has also collected many journals and books on the subject. Recently he has edited this "record of things seen by an old Shanghai hand in the last thirty years," divided into more than thirty topical sections. All of the myriad strange things that are found in Shanghai are in these 460-plus pages. Chen is truly an old Shanghai hand. We want to be one but cannot attain it." Zhou Shoujuan 1928: vol. 1, preface.

For a biographical sketch that makes no mention of Zhou Shoujuan's courtesan writings, see Li Shengping 1989: pp. 472–73; see also Liu Ts'un-yan 1982: pp. 31–32; Yao Jiguang and Yu Yifen 1981: p. 227; Link 1981: pp. 136, 138, 157, and passim; and Meng Yue 1994: p. 29.

Bao Tianxiao (1876–1973) was originally from Suzhou but spent most of his time after 1906 in Shanghai, where he was an editor of *Shibao* and four journals. His works include the castigatory novel *Shanghai chunqiu* (Shanghai annals). See Bao Tianxiao 1987. His two volumes of memoirs, published in Hong Kong in the 1970s, contain rich material on journalism as well as references to courtesan life. See Bao Tianxiao 1971, 1973, and 1990. On Bao, see Liu Ts'un-yan 1982: pp. 32–35; Link 1981: passim; and Bao Tianxiao 1987: pp. 1–18. According to Poshek Fu (1993: p. 138), after 1941 Bao wrote for the collaborationist press in occupied Shanghai in order to support his family.

According to Link (1981: pp. 164–65), many in this group of writers were closely connected. Bao Tianxiao was best man at Zhou Shoujuan's wedding; Bao also adopted one of Bi Yihong's children when Bi died young.

For a list of other courtesan novels, see Cheng 1979: pp. 251–52. For a discussion of courtesan novels as a subset of "middlebrow" fiction, see Liu Ts'un-yan 1982. Cheng (1979: p. 251) offers the following comment on changing readership for courtesan novels from the late nineteenth century to the 1920s: "The early novels appealed to literati interested in sentimental love stories like the traditional courtesan tales, whereas the later ones catered to shop-keepers, merchants and clerks who either frequent or are surreptitiously interested in the pleasure quarters. This shift in readership is reflected in the prose style, which changes from literary to colloquial. Furthermore, the quantity and quality of poetry in the novels also show a parallel decline." He argues that the new middle class, who he says were also the major clientele of tabloids like *Crystal*, which offered brothel gossip, read the new novels as guides to the brothels, and in the 1910s turned their attention to butterfly fiction. Cheng 1979: pp. 252–53.

82. On the history of scandal fiction in Shanghai, see Link 1981: passim. I have used mainly Qian Shengke 1933 and Chunming shuju 1937. The format of these collections was usually a series of short fictionalized tales divided into categories—for example, scandalous stories of women swindlers (*chaibaidang*)—under which were a number of shorter stories (the ruin of a student's reputation, a part-time prostitute [*bankai men*] meets a *chaibaidang*, and so forth). Other categories of women included students, concubines, doctors, nuns, child brides, servants, midwives, boatwomen, fruit sellers, kidnappers, part-time prostitutes, workers, newspaper sellers, flower sellers, witches, *changsan* courtesans, *yao er* courtesans, and pheasant streetwalkers. Women were prominently depicted as figures of danger in these cautionary tales.

83. See, in addition to the discussions cited elsewhere in this book, Yeh 1990 on intellectual uses of the courtesan trope; Liu Ts'un-yan 1982 on "middlebrow" fiction; Link 1981 on mandarin-duck and butterfly stories; and Chow 1991 on butterfly fiction as well as a critique of the analyses of Liu and Link.

84. On Beijing, see Morache 1869: pp. 123–32; Arlington and Lewisohn 1967: pp. 272–274; *Jingbao* 1919: May 9, p. 3; Chen Lianhen 1925: passim; Nakano Kōkan 1926; *Shenghuo zhoukan* 1930: 5, 40 (September 14), pp. 671–72; Beiping shehui diaochasuo bianzhi 1931: pp. 8, 19; Mai Qianzeng 1931; Woo 1982: pp. 6, 10–11; Jin Wenhua 1933: pp. 60–64; He Qiying 1934a: pp. 292–93; He Qiying 1934b: pp. 216–17; *Nüsheng* 1934: 2, 9 (February 10), p. 3; *Shizheng pinglun* 1934: 1 (June), pp. 107–8; 1935: 3, 18 (September 16), p. 16; 3, 19 (October 1), pp. 11–14; Beiping shi zhengfu mishuchu 1936: pp. 25, 73, 83; Ma Zhixiang 1935: pp. 24–28; Li Jiarui 1937: vol. 2, pp. 331, 334, 362, 364–65; 372–78; 381–82; 385–88; de Beauvoir 1958: pp. 41–42; and Li Jingwu 1967: pp. 84–87, 123–25.

85. On Guangzhou see Schlegel 1866; Schlegel 1894; Jones 1922; Mi Bi 1922; Oldt 1923; *Shenghuo zhoukan* 1933: 8, 47 (November 25), pp. 965, 967–68; Lao Xin 1934; *Renyan zhoukan* 1934: 1, 16 (May 26), pp. 325–26; *Funü yuebao* 1935: 1, 3 (April 1), pp. 40–41; *Funü gongming* 1935: 4, 11 (November 20), pp. 86–87; Lee 1936: pp. 95–96; and Liu Fujing and Wang Mingkun 1992.

86. On Tianjin, see Zhang Shou 1884: *juan zhong*, pp. 47–48; *Funü zazhi* 1923: 9, 7 (July 1), pp. 125–27; *Tianjin funü ribao* 1924: March 1, 2, 3, 4, 6 (thanks to Christina Gilmartin for this citation); [Tianjin] *Dagong bao* 1929: December 4, 5, 7; [Tianjin] *Dagong bao* 1930: August 26, October 2 (thanks to Manbun Kwan for this citation); *Tianjin tebieshi shehuiju* 1929: n.p.; Tianjin shi shehuiju 1930; *Shehui yuekan* 1930: n.p.; Song Yunpu 1931: p. 356; Wu Ao et al. 1931: n.p.; Wu Ao 1931: pp. 123, 156, 345;

Wang Da 1936: p. 118; Tianjin tebieshi gongshu 1939: p. 48; Tianjin tebieshi gong-shu 1940: p. 50; *Tianjin shi zhoukan* 1947: 1, 8 (February 1), p. 9; 2, 1 (March 8), p. 6; 2, 4 (March 29), p. 4; 2, 6 (April 12), pp. 10–11; 4, 9 (October 18), p. 14; and Li Ranshi 1963: pp. 205–6.

87. On Suzhou, see *Jingbao* 1929: May 27, p. 3; *Renyan zhoukan* 1935: 2, 42 (December 28), pp. 838–839; and *Shizheng pinglun* 1936: April 16, p. 31. On Xiamen, see *Shizheng pinglun* 1935: 3, 21 (November 1), pp. 18–20. On Chengdu, see Wen Shu 1981. On Kunming, see Xiao Su 1946. On Harbin, see Song Shisheng 1995.

CHAPTER 2: CLASSIFYING AND COUNTING

1. An abbreviated version of some of the material in this chapter first appeared in Hershatter 1989.

2. Sold prostitutes were commonly known as *taoren*, but one reformer account refers to them as *dujue de* (completely eradicated). Yi Feng 1933a: p. 40. Sale, pawning, and other arrangements are discussed in chapters 3 and 7; brief descriptions of arrangements among pheasants can be found in Huang Renjing 1913: p. 131; Wu Hanchi 1924: pp. 10–11; Wang Liaoweng 1922: p. 24; and Sun Yusheng 1939: p. 165.

3. "Free prostitutes" (*zijia shenti*) were of course preferable, wrote Wang Dingjiu of "salt-pork" prostitutes in 1932, "because the others are under the direction of the madam, and cannot decide based on their own likes and dislikes whether to receive a guest. They respond to the market every day, and are just as dangerous as pheasants. Free prostitutes, because their bodies are free, are a bit cleaner." Wang Dingjiu 1932: *Piao*, p. 27. Qian Shengke (1933: vol. 2, pp. 1–2), in his volume of scandal fiction, explains that among pheasants, hired women had two to four nights off per month, but that owned and pawned prostitutes received three to four guests every night with no time off unless they became seriously ill. Also see Wang Liaoweng 1922: p. 24; and Zhang Xinxin and Sang Ye 1987: p. 33. See chapters 3 and 7 for a detailed discussion of such arrangements.

4. See, for instance, Chi Zhicheng 1893: pp. 29–30; *Shenbao* 1916: July 8; *Shenbao* 1924: March 21; Xu Ke 1920: pp. 28–29; Wu Hanchi 1924: p. 12; *Shibao* 1929: July 18, p. 7; Chunming shuju 1937: *zhiji*, pp. 2–6; and Sun Yusheng 1939: p. 173.

5. Pheasants were on the seventeenth circle and flower-smoke prostitutes on the eighteenth and below. Sun Yusheng 1939: p. 172; for similar comments about salt-pork prostitutes, see p. 169. All of these types are described in more detail below.

6. Yu Wei 1948: pp. 12–13.

7. Chen Luwei 1938: p. 21.

8. Wang Dingjiu 1932: *Piao*, p. 51.

9. For lists far too detailed to include here, see, for instance, Huang Shiquan [Wang Tao] 1975: p. 199; Chi Zhicheng 1893: p. 25; *Jingbao* 1919: September 30, p. 3; Xu Ke 1920: pp. 18–20; Wang Liaoweng 1922: pp. 1–6; Hu Jifan 1930: *juan* 8, n.p.; Wu Jianren 1935: pp. 126–27; Liu Peiqian 1936: pp. 136–37; and Sun Yusheng 1939: pp. 2–4. Material on the geographical distribution of brothels culled from many sources has been plotted on a contemporary map of Shanghai by Dong Delun (1991: insert between p. 76 and p. 77). This map clearly shows the geographical segregation of brothels of different ranks.

10. *Jingbao* 1919: September 30, p. 3; Xu Ke 1920: pp. 20–21; Liu Peiqian 1936: 136–37; Sun Yusheng 1939: p. 3.

11. *Jingbao* 1919: September 30, p. 3; Xu Ke 1920: pp. 17–18; Wang Liaoweng 1922: pp. 141–42; Liu Peiqian 1936: pp. 136–37; Sun Yusheng 1939: p. 3.

12. Xu Ke 1920: p. 19; also see Xue Liyong 1988: pp. 154–55.

13. Wang Liaoweng 1922: pp. 141–42.

14. Qi Xia and Dan Ru 1917: vol. 1, n.p. [p. 71]; vol. 2, n.p. [p. 6].

15. Wang Liaoweng 1922: pp. 141–42.

16. Xu Ke 1920: p. 19.

17. Hu Jifan 1930: *juan* 8, n.p.; also see Tang Zhenchang 1989: p. 748.

18. Shanghai xintuo 1932: p. 8; also see Gamble 1921: chapter 5; and Wiley 1929: pp. 46–47.

19. These are *yao er* houses, discussed in more detail below. Huang Renjing 1913: p. 130; Xu Ke 1920: p. 25; Wang Liaoweng 1922: pp. 20–21; Wiley 1929: pp. 48, 65; and Hu Jifan 1930: *juan* 8, n.p.

20. On the movement of *yao er* houses, see Hu Jifan 1930: *juan* 8, n.p.; Yu Muxia 1935: *ji*, p. 35; Sun Yusheng 1939: p. 148; and Tu Shipin 1968: *xia*, p. 77. On *changsan* houses, see Tang Zhenchang 1989: p. 748. Throughout this discussion, the matching of prerevolutionary street names to their contemporary counterparts uses Tang Zhenchang 1989: pp. 1,028–73.

21. Xu Ke 1920: p. 18; also see Xue Liyong 1988: p. 153.

22. Xu Ke 1920: p. 20.

23. Shanghai xintuo 1932: p. 10.

24. Wakeman 1995b: p. 33; Shanghai xintuo 1932: p. 62.

25. Sun Yusheng 1939: p. 3.

26. Shanghai xintuo 1932: p. 8.

27. Sun Yusheng 1939: p. 4; also see *Jingbao* 1935: September 22, p. 3.

28. Henderson 1871: pp. 11–12. The French figures, reprinted by Henderson, date from 1869.

29. Gongyi shushe 1908: passim.

30. Ping Jinya 1988: p. 159. Ping refers to the Morals Correction Unit (*zhengsu ke*) of the Shanghai Municipal Council, but it was probably a police unit similar to that controlled by the Guomindang government in 1940s Shanghai (see chapters 8 and 11). The breakdown by ranks (see the next section of this chapter and chapter 3 for an explanation of each type) is as follows: 1,229 *changsan*, 505 *yao er*, 4,727 *zhiji*, 1,050 *huayan jian*, 250 Guangdong, and 30 *dingpeng*, for a total of 7,791. In addition, the survey found two thousand *changsan* attendants, *niangyi*, and *dajie*.

The survey did not include disguised or unlicensed prostitutes or those who worked in the French Concession. This set of statistics is reproduced or cited with slight variations in Chen Rongguang 1924: pp. 122–23; and in "The Demi-monde of Shanghai" 1923: p. 785.

31. Special Vice Committee 1920: p. 84. In a 1921 study of Beijing, Sidney Gamble found that 1 of every 258 residents was a licensed prostitute, whereas the figure in Shanghai was 1 in 137 residents. Gamble 1921: p. 247.

32. Wiley 1929: p. 45.

33. Yi Feng (1933a: p. 39) provides the following breakdown, purportedly collected sometime shortly before the 1920 ban on International Settlement prostitu-

tion: 1,200 *changsan,* 490 *yao er,* 24,850 *yeji* in the International Settlement and 12,311 in the French Concession, and 21,315 *huayan jian* and *dingpeng* (in both concessions).

34. Tang Youfeng 1931: p. 154; Yu Wei 1948: p. 11.

35. The 1927 figure is cited in Beijing shi gong'anju 1988 (p. 207), which does not give the original source. For the later figures see Yu Muxia 1935: *shang,* p. 30; Luo Qiong 1935: p. 37.

36. "The Prostitution Problem" 1937: pp. 7–8; similar, though not identical, figures are given by Ruo Wen (1938: pp. 8–9). The same articles reported fewer than eighteen hundred prostitutes in the French Concession, a figure that sounds like a serious undercount.

37. Yu Wei 1948: p. 10. In December 1946, the police chief told the mayor in an internal memo that the city had about forty thousand prostitutes. Shanghai shi dang-'an guan 1946–1949: file 1-10-246, p. 60.

38. Compare the highest estimates of 100,000 prostitutes to the number of female industrial workers in Shanghai in 1929: 173,432 women. The largest subgroup of these, 84,270, were employed in cotton spinning. Of 54,508 women workers counted in 1946, 35,306 were cotton spinners. Honig 1986: pp. 24–25.

39. In the mid-1930s, the various municipalities of Shanghai reported the following number of female residents: 863,585 females of all ages in the Chinese city (1935), 336,565 adult females in the International Settlement (1935), and 135,785 adult females in the French Concession (1936). Zou Yiren 1980: pp. 122–23. This yields an admittedly imprecise total of 1,335,935. If 100,000 of these were prostitutes, approximately one woman in thirteen was a prostitute—more if children and older women were excluded from the total.

In 1945–1947, the total number of females in the Shanghai population were given as follows: 1,532,985 in 1945; 1,680,461 in 1946; and 2,006,795 in 1947. Shanghai shi wenxian weiyuanhui 1948: pp. 14, 16, 18.

40. The total population of Greater Shanghai (including foreign settlements) changed from 1910 through 1947 as follows:

1910	1,185,859
1930	3,112,250
1945	3,370,230
1946	3,830,039
1947	4,494,390

SOURCES: For 1910 and 1930: Luo Zhiru 1932: p. 21, table 29. For 1945–1947: Shanghai shi wenxian weiyuanhui 1948: pp. 14, 16, 18. For a brief overview of changes in the city, see Honig 1986: pp. 9–40.

41. Luo Zhiru 1932: p. 27, table 43.

42. Available statistics on the occupational structure of Shanghai do not permit a complete portrait of the sexual division of labor. According to statistics collected by the municipal government of Greater Shanghai (that is, excluding the foreign settlements), Shanghai's population went from 1.7 million in 1930 to 1.8 million in 1931 to almost 1.6 million in 1932. Of these residents, about one-fifth were classified as industrial workers. Another one-fifth were in household service. The unemployed accounted for about 17 to 18 percent, farmers 11 percent, merchants 10 percent,

and laborers about 6 percent. Of the remainder, about 10 percent were apprentices, servants, or miscellaneous, and the rest worked in education, government, the military, communications, the police, and various professions. It is not clear where (if anywhere) prostitutes were registered in these statistics; nor is it clear how different the configuration of occupations was in the International Settlement and the French Concession. Shanghai Civic Association 1933: "Population," p. 5, table 6.

Only in industry do we have comprehensive information on the position of women. Most women industrial workers were employed in the textile industry. See Shanghai Civic Association 1933: "Labor," p. 1, table 1; Shanghai Bureau of Social Affairs 1929; and Shanghai shehuiju 1946, cited in Honig 1986: pp. 24–25.

43. Shanghai Civic Association 1933: "Population," p. 2, table 3; Shanghai shi wenxian weiyuanhui 1948: pp. 14, 16, 18.

44. Luo Zhiru 1932: p. 30.

45. The male-to-female ratio in the International Settlement moved steadily downward from 290 to 100 in 1870 to 156 to 100 in 1935. In the French Concession, the ratio was 217 to 100 in 1910 and 155 to 100 in 1936, although there were minor fluctuations in between. In 1945, 1946, and 1947 in the city as a whole, the ratios (including children) were 119.8 to 100, 127.9 to 100, and 123.9 to 100, respectively. Luo Zhiru 1932: p. 30, tables 49 and 51; Shanghai Civic Association 1933: "Population," p. 11, table 13; Zou Yiren 1980: pp. 122–25. A 1948 study, however, points out that in the central commercial districts the ratio was much more skewed, reaching highs of 250.7 in Huangpu, 201.1 in Laozha, and 153.2 in Zhabei. Chen Renbing 1948: p. 10. For a recapitulation of the argument that skewed sex ratios led to prostitution, see Henriques 1962: p. 268.

46. Banchisheng 1891: *juan* 1, p. 5. On official prostitutes, see Wang Shunu 1988: pp. 25–259; and Wu Zhou 1990: pp. 77–184. *Guanren* was often modified by "red" (*hong*) or "clear" (*qing*). A *hong guanren* was well-known and popular, a "hot" social item. Wu Hanchi 1924: p. 8. The term, used exclusively for courtesans who had had sexual relationships with customers, was occasionally modified to read "muddy" (*hun*) *guanren*. In contrast, a "clear" courtesan was a very young woman whose duties were limited to entertainment and did not include sex. Banchisheng 1891: *juan* 1, p. 5; Xue Liyong 1988: pp. 154–55.

47. "Demi-monde" 1923: p. 783; Zhang Chunfan 1919: March 6, p. 3; Wang Dingjiu 1932: *Piao*, pp. 1–2; Ping Jinya 1988: pp. 159–60; Xue Liyong 1988: p. 153. Xue Liyong (1988: p. 151) explains that these women were also known as *jiaoshu*, "proofreaders," a name that derived from the similarity of their performance to the work of proofreaders. Before printing was invented, most books were copied by hand. There were often mistakes, so one person would "sing" (read) the text, and the other would compare it to the copy. Because prostitutes carried on their business mostly by playing, singing, and storytelling, just like the two proofreaders, this term was used for them.

48. Wang Zhongxian n.d.: p. 30.

49. Li chuang wo dusheng 1905: *juan* 6, p. 6, indicates that the term *xiansheng* was also used for *huagu* (flower drum) performers.

50. "Demi-monde" 1923: p. 783; Lemière 1923: p. 127; Wiley 1929: p. 64. For details on the types of songs and stories they performed, and the protocol for ordering a performance, see Banchisheng 1891: *juan* 4, pp. 11–14; Li chuang wo

dusheng 1905: *juan* 6, p. 6; and Zhang Chunfan 1919: March 9, p. 3, and March 18, p. 3.

51. Lemière 1923: p. 127.

52. Chi Zhicheng 1893: pp. 9–11; Hu Jifan 1930: *juan* 8, n.p.; Sun Yusheng 1939: pp. 5–6; Tu Shipin 1968: *xia*, p. 76.

53. Zhang Chunfan 1932: August 16, p. 2; Hu Jifan 1930: *juan* 8, n.p.; Sun Yusheng 1939: p. 5.

54. "Demi-monde" 1923: p. 783; Zhang Chunfan 1919: March 6, p. 3; Wang Ding jiu 1932: *Piao*, pp. 1–2.

55. *Jingbao* 1919: October 3, p. 3; Sun Yusheng 1939: p. 7.

56. Arlington 1923: p. 317; this practice applied to *changsan* courtesans as well (see chapter 3).

57. Liu Peiqian 1936: p. 136; this story is repeated in Sun Yusheng 1939: p. 11. On the sale of voices rather than bodies, see Wang Ding jiu 1932: *Piao*, pp. 1–2.

58. Zhang Chunfan 1919: March 6, p. 3; "Demi-monde" 1923: p. 783; Zhang Chunfan 1932: August 16, p. 2; Tu Shipin 1968: *xia*, p. 76; Ping Jinya 1988: p. 160; Xue Liyong 1988: p. 152.

59. Wang Ding jiu 1932: *Piao*, pp. 1–2.

60. Zhang Chunfan 1919: March 6, p. 3; Xu Ke 1920: p. 22; Yu Wei 1948: p. 11. The comment on accessibility is from "Demi-monde" 1923: p. 784; see also Wiley 1929: p. 71.

61. Liu Peiqian 1936: p. 136; Tu Shipin 1968: *xia*, p. 76.

62. Sun Yusheng 1939: p. 11.

63. Zhang Chunfan 1932: August 16, p. 2.

64. Tu Shipin 1968: *xia*, p. 76; Xue Liyong 1988: pp. 155–56.

65. Henderson 1871: p. 14; Tu Shipin 1968: *xia*, p. 76.

66. In addition to the sources cited here and in the next four chapters, see also Datong tushushe n.d.: pp. 1–22.

67. Sun Yusheng 1939: p. 151.

68. "Demi-monde" 1923: pp. 783–85; Tu Shipin 1968: *xia*, p. 76; Wang Ding jiu 1932: *Piao*, pp. 1–2; Yu Wei 1948: p. 11; Liu Peiqian 1936: p. 136; Yi Feng 1933a: p. 39.

69. Zhang Chunfan 1932: August 16, p. 2; Sun Yusheng 1939: p. 8.

70. *Shenbao* 1941: November 2.

71. Sun Yusheng 1939: p. 5. In 1905, *ersan* courtesans charged two yuan for a plate of snacks and three yuan to attend guests in a public place. By 1919, it was said that they served drinks for two yuan and spent the night for three. Some sources date their disappearance as early as the late nineteenth century. Li chuang wo dusheng 1905: *juan* 6, p. 6; Zhang Chunfan 1919: March 9, p. 3; Xu Ke 1920: pp. 24–25; Hu Jifan 1930: *juan* 8, n.p.; Liu Peiqian 1936: p. 136; Tu Shipin 1968: *xia*, pp. 76–77.

72. Yu Wei 1948: p. 11; Tu Shipin 1968: *xia*, pp. 76–77; "Demi-monde" 1923: p. 785; Wiley 1929: p. 65; Tang Youfeng 1931: p. 152; Zhang Chunfan 1919: March 9, p. 3; Zhang Chunfan 1932: August 16, pp. 2–4; Yi Feng 1933a: p. 39; Sun Yusheng 1939: p. 149; Datong tushushe n.d.: pp. 23–29. Yu Muxia (1935: *ji*, pp. 34–35) reported that in the mid-1930s the price for spending the first night rose to eight yuan, with subsequent nights at five yuan.

73. Tu Shipin 1968: *xia*, p. 77.

74. Wang Zhongxian n.d.: p. 388.

75. Sun Yusheng 1939: pp. 150–51. On downward mobility from *changsan* to *yao er*, see also Wang Dingjiu 1932: *Piao*, p. 22.

76. Wang Liaoweng 1922: p. 23.

77. Trysting houses were reportedly first established by a woman named Baisha Pipa (White Sands Pipa), who rented a house in the American concession and put up a Private Residence sign, recruiting the concubines of officials to sleep with other men. The tradition was carried on by Xue Wenhua, a female descendant of the Qing official Xue Fucheng. It was said that Xue Wenhua had been dismissed from a famous girls' school for bad behavior and then went on to found and run more than ten luxuriously decorated trysting houses. One account adds a hint of political scandal to the story by reporting that Yuan Shikai intended to appoint her as the president of Beijing Women's Normal School in the early Republican period, but was dissuaded by the head of the education ministry. On the history of trysting places, see Chen Rongguang 1924: pp. 89–90; and Zhang Xunjiu 1934: vol. 2, pp. 64–73.

78. On the operation of trysting houses, see Ma Yongsheng 1930: *juan* 2, p. 9; *Shenbao* 1880, October 28; Huang Shiquan [Wang Tao] 1975: p. 178; Huang Renjing 1913: pp. 127–28, 132–33; *Shenbao* 1915, February 7, May 15; *Jingbao* 1920: April 27, p. 2; "Demi-monde" 1923: pp. 788–89; Qian Shengke 1933: vol. 2, pp. 11–22; and Datong tushushe n.d.: pp. 45–50.

79. Chen Rongguang 1924: pp. 89–90; Qian Shengke 1933: vol. 2, pp. 13–16.

80. Chen Rongguang 1924: pp. 89–90; Zhang Xunjiu 1934: vol. 2, pp. 64–73. Yu Muxia (1935: *shang*, pp. 58–59) comments that big hotels relied on local people rather than travelers for their business; such patrons rented rooms in order to gamble, summon courtesans, smoke opium, or have sexual liaisons.

81. For statements linking the two types of houses of prostitution, see Huang Renjing 1913: p. 132; Wu Hanchi 1924: p. 17; Wang Liaoweng 1922: pp. 21–22; and Zhang Xunjiu 1934: vol. 2, pp. 64–73. One account referred to the trysting houses as the "larval form" of the salt-pork shops. Wang Dingjiu 1932: *Piao*, p. 25.

82. Wang Dingjiu 1932: *Piao*, p. 25; Liu Peiqian 1936: p. 136.

83. Yu Muxia 1935: *shang*, p. 14.

84. Yu Muxia 1935: *ji*, p. 36.

85. Wang Dingjiu 1932: *Piao*, p. 26; parts of this description are reproduced verbatim in Liu Peiqian 1936: p. 136.

86. Wang Dingjiu 1932: *Piao*, pp. 27–28; Yu Muxia 1935: *shang*, p. 14 and *ji*, p. 40; Sun Yusheng 1939: p. 168.

87. Yu Muxia 1935: *shang*, p. 32.

88. Wang Zhongxian n.d.: p. 23.

89. Wang Zhongxian n.d.: p. 24.

90. Tu Shipin 1968: *xia*, p. 77; Yi Feng 1933a: p. 40. Highly placed government officials were said to frequent the more elaborate facilities, while the prostitutes included "the concubines of government officials, misses, dance stars, social stars, movie stars, pretty daughters from simple families, socially prominent young women, and women students." Yi Feng 1933a: p. 40. Unwary customers, however, ran the risk of being deceived by women masquerading as daughters of high-class families, with prices to match. One guidebook asserted that respectable women no longer frequented houses of assignation, and that customers should not allow themselves to

be defrauded. Women with in-laws and husbands, the author explained, dressed modestly and wore little makeup, so that their excursions outside the home would not arouse the suspicions of their family members. They could easily be distinguished from the salt-pork prostitutes. Wang Dingjiu 1932: *Piao*, pp. 26–27.

91. Sun Liqi et al. 1986; Zhang Xinxin and Sang Ye 1987: p. 32.

92. Yi Feng 1933a: p. 40.

93. Yi Feng (1933a: p. 40) says that the salt-pork houses began in 1920.

94. For detailed listings of locations, see Wang Dingjiu 1932: *Piao*, p. 25; Yu Muxia 1935: *shang*, 14; Sun Yusheng 1939: pp. 167–68; and Tu Shipin 1968: *xia*, 77.

95. Wang Zhongxian n.d.: p. 24.

96. "Demi-monde" 1923: p. 786; see also Datong tushushe n.d.: pp. 31–37.

97. For customers as hunters, see Li chuang wo dusheng 1905: *juan* 6, pp. 13–14, and *juan* 7, p. 6. Zhang Chunfan (1932: August 16, p. 4) explained that the term *yeji* was originally used by the women themselves to refer to their customers, because if a *yeji* saw a person on the street paying attention to her, she would approach and seize him just like somebody catching a pheasant. Ironically, he adds, society came to see the women as pheasants, and customers considered themselves to be the hunters.

98. Streets mentioned as major sites of pheasant activity included Fuzhou, Hankou, Nanjing, Yunnan, Guangxi, Zhejiang, Ningbo, Guizhou, and Laohe Roads; Chujia, Touji, Dongxin, Baxian, and Zhujia bridges; the area of the Great World Amusement Hall in the French Concession; and the back of the Sincere Company. See Li chuang wo dusheng 1905: *juan* 6, p. 13–14; Xu Ke 1920: p. 27; Huang Renjing 1913: p. 131; Qi Xia and Dan Ru 1917: vol. 1, n.p. [p. 2]; Wang Dingjiu 1932: *Piao*, p. 48; Yu Muxia 1935: *shang*, p. 24; and Sun Yusheng 1939: p. 165.

99. Huang Renjing 1913: pp. 130–31; Wang Dingjiu 1932: *Piao*, p. 48. A late Qing poem evoked their frenetic activity:

> On top of the Qing Lian Ge [a teahouse] is a pheasant nest.
> They fly back and forth like the shuttlecock on a loom.
> The most shameless are the ones from Yangzhou.
> The middlemen pull people's clothes with both hands.

Li chuang wo dusheng 1905: *juan* 7, p. 7; see appendix B for Chinese text.

See also Huang Shiquan [Wang Tao] 1975: pp. 184–85.

100. Li chuang wo dusheng 1905: *juan* 7, p. 6. For later warnings to rural visitors, see Wang Dingjiu 1932: *Piao*, pp. 49–50; and Wang Zhongxian n.d.: pp. 60, 93.

101. Tang Youfeng 1931: pp. 152–53.

102. Wang Zhongxian n.d.: p. 422. Also see Yu Muxia 1935: *shang*, p. 24.

103. Wang Zhongxian n.d.: p. 595.

104. Wang Dingjiu 1932: *Piao*, p. 49. Similar prices are given for an earlier period by Xu Ke (1920: p. 28), who says that the fee dropped if it was late at night and guests were scarce. Also see Liu Peiqian 1936: p. 136; and Sun Yusheng 1939: pp. 164–65.

105. Yu Muxia 1935: *shang*, p. 27; Qian Shengke 1933: vol. 2, pp. 22–24; Wu Hanchi 1924: p. 11; Xu Ke 1920: p. 29; Wang Liaoweng 1922: p. 24; "Demi-monde" 1923: p. 786.

106. Qian Shengke 1933: vol. 2, p. 3.

107. Liu Peiqian 1936: p. 136.

108. Wiley 1929: p. 66.

109. Of five hundred prostitutes surveyed in 1948, almost half had begun work between the ages of fifteen and nineteen; the largest group was between the ages of twenty and twenty-four at the time the interviews were conducted. Yu Wei 1948: p. 11. For prostitutes of all ranks, increasing age brought the risk of descent down the hierarchy. As one guidebook author commented about *yao er* courtesans, "After age thirty, how good can their business be? People who live by prostitution have their bodies ruined. . . . Ten years of it and they are past their prime, old and decayed, sallow and full of ailments." Sun Yusheng 1939: p. 149.

110. Xu Ke 1920: pp. 27–28; Wu Hanchi 1924: p. 10; Yu Muxia 1935: *ji*, p. 36.

111. Sun Yusheng 1939: p. 164.

112. *Shibao* 1936: February 27, p. 5; Wang Zhongxian n.d.: p. 93; Tu Shipin 1968: *xia*, p. 77; Chen Dingshan 1967: p. 20.

113. Hauser 1940: pp. 268–69.

114. "Demi-monde" 1923: p. 786. See also Hong Ya 1933: p. 6; and Sun Yusheng 1939: p. 166.

115. Wang Zhongxian n.d.: p. 93.

116. Yu Wei 1948: p. 13.

117. Luo Qiong 1935: p. 36. For a recent reiteration of this kind of account, see Zhang Xinxin and Sang Ye 1987: p. 32. The Chinese original of this particular story is found in Zhang Xinxin and Sang Ye 1985: pp. 13–17.

118. Yu Wei 1948: p. 13; "Demi-monde" 1923: p. 786.

119. See, for example, *Shibao* 1929: July 22, p. 7. Also see chapter 8.

120. Tang Youfeng 1931: pp. 152–53. For descriptions of pheasants written by scholars in the 1980s, see Xue Liyong 1988: pp. 156–57; and Ping Jinya 1988: p. 165.

121. Sun Yusheng 1939: p. 166.

122. Yu Muxia 1935: *shang*, p. 24.

123. For general descriptions of *huayan jian*, see Yu Muxia 1935: *ji*, p. 49; Liu Peiqian 1936: p. 136; and Sun Yusheng 1939: pp. 169–70.

124. For spatial mapping of *huayan jian*, see Huang Renjing 1913: p. 131; Xu Ke 1920: p. 30; Wang Dingjiu 1932: *Piao*, p. 50; Wang Zhongxian n.d.: pp. 115–16; Yu Muxia 1935: *ji*, p. 49; and Sun Yusheng 1939: pp. 171–72.

125. Chi Zhicheng 1893: p. 28; also see Huang Shiquan [Wang Tao] 1975: p. 178; and Li chuang wo dusheng 1905: *juan* 6, p. 6. Xu Ke (1920: pp. 29–30) notes that customers who stayed the whole night in the late nineteenth century were expected to pay a dollar. For other comments on *huayan jian* clientele, see Huang Renjing 1913: p. 131; Wang Dingjiu 1932: *Piao*, p. 50; and Yu Muxia 1935: *ji*, p. 50. Strings of copper cash were used for small payments, particularly among the lower classes; ideally, one thousand cash (in strings of ten) were equal to one silver tael. In 1889 China began to mint dollar (yuan) coins, although they did not immediately supplant cash and taels. For intricacies and variations in this system, see King 1969: pp. 31–33, 40–42. Ten dimes (jiao) equalled one yuan.

126. Sun Yusheng 1939: p. 173.

127. Yu Muxia 1935: *ji*, p. 50.

128. Wang Dingjiu 1932: *Piao*, p. 50; Sun Yusheng 1939: pp. 169–74. The de-

scription, which is of conditions at the turn of the century, is from Wang Zhongxian n.d.: p. 116.

129. Sun Yusheng 1939: p. 173.

130. Wang Zhongxian n.d.: p. 116.

131. "Demi-monde" 1923: p. 787; Zhang Chunfan 1932: August 16, p. 4. For slightly different information on fees, see Xu Ke 1920: p. 30; Yu Muxia 1935: *ji*, p. 49; Wang Zhongxian n.d.: p. 117; and Sun Yusheng 1939: pp. 170–71.

132. The 1933 date is from Tu Shipin 1968: *xia*, p. 77. The Qing government undertook an anti-opium drive in the years immediately prior to its 1911 demise, closing all opium dens in 1909. This campaign was continued by Yuan Shikai in the 1910s. Opium use continued to flourish in areas controlled by foreigners and warlords. The government of Jiang Jieshi (Chiang Kai-shek) made intermittent and localized attempts to ban opium in the 1930s. Spence 1990: pp. 256–57, 285, 288; Shangwu yinshuguan bianjisuo 1926: *juan* 2, p. 43. The effects of any of these campaigns on Shanghai is not clear. Ping Jinya (1988: p. 162) says that in the late Qing, *huayan jian* moved from Chinese-controlled areas of Shanghai to the foreign concessions in order to circumvent the Qing ban. On the other hand, Li chuang wo dusheng (1905: *juan* 6, pp. 13–14) notes that in about 1904 the British and French police forbade women attendants to light opium pipes because of the deleterious effect on public morals. Xu Ke (1920: p. 30) mentions that opium was banned and *huayan jian* business discontinued (sometime prior to 1920), but "Demi-monde" (1923: p. 787) finds more than one thousand such prostitutes in 1918 Shanghai. For evidence that the name continued after opium was banned, see Yu Muxia 1935: *ji*, p. 50. Ping Jinya (1988: pp. 162–63) argues that the *huayan jian* became just another form of unlicensed brothel by the early twentieth century. For fines levied on prostitutes and madams in other types of brothels in the International Settlement, see chapter 8.

133. Ping Jinya 1988: p. 163.

134. Wang Dingjiu 1932: *Piao*, p. 51.

135. Xu Ke 1920: p. 30; "Demi-monde" 1923: p. 787; Wang Dingjiu 1932: *Piao*, p. 51.

136. Xu Ke 1930: p. 30; Wang Dingjiu 1932: *Piao*, p. 51. Wu Hanchi (1924: p. 12) defines a "nail" as the fee for spending the night. By the mid-1930s, one guidebook reported that nail sheds were no longer found in Shanghai. Wang Zhongxian n.d.: p. 115.

137. For a discussion of a League of Nations conference in Bandung in February 1937, at which "white slavery" in India, China, Japan, and Manchuria was discussed, and which also touched on the domestic traffic in women in China, see the press clippings in SMP 1937: Box 63, Document 7779. On a case of white-slave trafficking in Russian women, conducted by Russian traffickers, see SMP 1939: D9577(c), December 8. Five Russian women, aged seventeen to twenty-two, were transported from Harbin to Shanghai by a male Russian named Tirinin under a contract to sell them "as brides or otherwise." The women ended up in a combination massage parlor–brothel run by a Russian woman.

138. Foreign prostitutes in Shanghai are the subject of a vast literature. See, for instance, Tang Youfeng 1931: pp. 153–54; Yi Feng 1933a: p. 41; Champly 1934: passim; De Leeuw 1933: pp. 114–45; Crad 1940: pp. 134–45 (an account based heavily

on De Leeuw); Hauser 1940: p. 267; Tu Shipin 1968: *xia,* p. 77; and, for a modern summary, O'Callaghan 1968: pp. 11–12; and Chou 1971: pp. 104–5, 112–13.

139. On the term "paradise of adventurers," see Miller 1937: pp. 7–10. For a colorful description of the American madam Gracie Gale, her establishment, and her women in the early twentieth century, see Finch 1953: p. 37. Finch comments: "What Ming was to porcelain and the Rolls Royce to cars, the American girl was to commercial vice in Shanghai. She was the quintessence of desire, the ideal of nocturnal pleasure, the irresistible reason why a man should mortgage his pay check for months to come."

140. De Leeuw 1933: p. 121. Scott Road was in the Hongkou district. See also Crad 1940: pp. 134–45, cribbed almost entirely from De Leeuw, which elaborates on the disgust felt by the author at seeing nonwhite men make sexual advances to white women.

141. De Leeuw 1933: p. 138.

142. Li chuang wo dusheng 1905: *juan* 2, p. 10. The same description appears in Huang Shiquan [Wang Tao] 1975: p. 190.

143. Wang Dingjiu 1932: *Piao,* p. 41; *Shenbao* 1941: November 3.

144. *Chinese Recorder* 1905: pp. 307–8.

145. Finch (1953: p. 48) comments that because of White Russian competition, "American houses could not compete and the American girl vanished from The Line as the buffalo vanished from the great plains of the West." Pal (1963: pp. 20–21) discusses a League of Nations report on the subject (the date is not given) that reads in part, "[T]he appearance of white women in such disgraceful capacity as that of prostitutes among the natives of the lowest class, *affects very deeply the prestige of the Western nations in the Orient*" (emphasis in original); also see pp. 85–86 for a colorful description of the brawls and police corruption entailed in this sector of the trade.

146. Champly 1934: pp. 188–89.

147. Tang Youfeng 1931: p. 153; Hauser 1940: p. 267. O'Callaghan (1968: p. 12) quotes a 1932 League of Nations report as saying that traffickers were bringing many of these women from Harbin to cities like Beijing, Tianjin, Qufu, Shanghai, and Hankou. The League report continues:

> "The attractions which these places have in the imagination of Harbin girls makes it very easy for traffickers to obtain control of their victim by persuasion and deceit. . . . She is then helpless to protest, she is in a strange place, she can make no proposal for the repayment of the money advanced, she sees no hope of finding the easy position which she imagined would be hers for the seeking. Moreover, she has left to the agent all the arrangements regarding her papers of identity and her permit to travel, without which no Russian can move about in China, and these documents are in his possession. She is entirely ignorant concerning the measures she can take to oppose the demands of the trafficker, and she feels she can do nothing but submit."

148. *North-China Herald* 1923: September 1, p. 618.

149. These men apparently received a small fee from the customers and a percentage from the prostitutes. Tang Youfeng 1931: p. 153; Wang Dingjiu 1932: *Piao,* p. 40; Yu Muxia 1935: *ji,* pp. 33–34.

150. Wang Dingjiu 1932: *Piao*, p. 41; *Shenbao* 1941: November 3. For other discussions of Russian prostitutes, see Kisch 1935: pp. 110–20; Peters 1937: pp. 210–11; Datong tushushe n.d.: pp. 42–43; Xu Chi et al. 1942: pp. 86–91; Wan Molin 1973: pp. 37–39; and Sergeant 1991: pp. 51–54, 60–66. For a heated defense of the honor of Russian women in China, see the leftist journal *China Weekly Review* 1935: 72, 12 (May 18), pp. 375–76, where it is argued that Russian women in Shanghai got a reputation as prostitutes because they "are more conspicuous in the cabarets, hence they receive most of the credit, or rather discredit, for the other profession."

151. On the location of Japanese brothels, see Yu Muxia 1935: *shang*, pp. 26, 38–39, *ji*, p. 46; and Tu Shipin 1968: *xia*, p. 77.

152. The description is from Guan Keshou zhai ban 1884: p. 16; the comparison to courtesans is made in *Jingbao* 1919: December 12, p. 2; and Wang Dingjiu 1932: *Piao*, p. 42. See also Datong tushushe n.d.: pp. 43–44.

153. On sexual availability, see Guan Keshou zhai ban 1884: p. 16; and Yu Muxia 1935: *shang*, p. 26. On second jobs, see Tang Youfeng 1931: p. 153; and Yu Muxia 1935: *shang*, p. 26. On street solicitors, see Yu Muxia 1935: *ji*, p. 47.

154. *Jingbao* 1919: December 12, p. 2.

155. Yu Muxia 1935: *ji*, p. 46.

156. Wang Dingjiu 1932: *Piao*, pp. 42–43.

157. See, for instance, Huayu xiaozhu zhuren 1892, which lists the native places of 118 courtesans. For a detailed breakdown, see table 1 in appendix A.

158. Wiley 1929: pp. 52–53.

159. Wiley 1929: pp. 66–67.

160. Lemière 1923: p. 133.

161. Huang Renjing 1913: p. 127; Morris 1916: p. 756; Lemière 1923: p. 133; Yi Feng 1933a: pp. 39–40; Wiley 1929: p. 53; Yu Muxia 1935: *shang*, p. 12. Within the upper echelons of prostitution were further regional fissures, such as recurrent rivalries between courtesans from Changshou and Wuxi. *Jingbao* 1919: September 15, p. 3; Zhang Chunfan 1932: August 16, p. 3.

162. Tang Zhenchang 1989: p. 748.

163. Chi Zhicheng 1893: p. 25; Huang Renjing 1913: p. 128; Zhou Shoujuan 1928: vol. 1, p. 35; Zhang Chunfan 1932: August 16, p. 3; Tu Shipin 1968: *xia*, pp. 76–77; Yu Wei 1948: p. 11; Xue Liyong 1988: p. 151.

164. Sun Liqi et al. 1986.

165. Yi Feng 1933a: pp. 39–40; Yu Muxia 1935: *shang*, p. 12; Tang Zhenchang 1989: p. 748. The short-lived *ersan* group of courtesans were said to be mostly from Shanghai.

166. Xu Ke 1920: p. 30; Yi Feng 1933a: p. 39; Yu Muxia 1935: *shang*, p. 12.

167. *Shibao* 1929: April 6, p. 7.

168. Honig 1992: passim. On prostitutes of Subei origin in Shanghai, see especially pp. 56, 65, and 67. Whether or not low-class prostitutes were actually from Subei, they were widely thought to be Subei natives precisely *because* of their low-class status.

169. Lemière 1923: p. 133.

170. For explanations of terminology, decoration, and performance, see Banchisheng 1891: *juan* 4, p. 15; Li chuang wo dusheng 1905: *juan* 6, p. 7; Xu Ke 1920: p. 31; Wu Hanchi 1924: pp. 13–14; and Yu Muxia 1935: *shang*, p. 23. On the locations of Cantonese brothels and their move from the International Settlement to North

Sichuan Road, see Hu Jifan 1930: *juan* 8, n.p.; Wang Dingjiu 1932: *Piao*, p. 36; Yu Muxia 1935: *shang*, p. 23; and Sun Yusheng 1939: p. 160. See also Datong tushushe n.d.: pp. 39–40.

171. Xu Ke 1920: p. 31; Wang Dingjiu 1932: *Piao*, p. 36.

172. Wang Dingjiu 1932: *Piao*, p. 37.

173. Wang Dingjiu 1932: *Piao*, p. 36; Yu Muxia 1935: *shang*, p. 23.

174. *Jingbao* 1919: October 30, p. 3; Yu Muxia 1935: *ji*, p. 44; Sun Yusheng 1939: p. 161; Datong tushushe n.d.: p. 40.

175. Yu Muxia 1935: *ji*, p. 45; Sun Yusheng 1939: p. 162. The disparaging comments about food and music are from Wang Dingjiu 1932: *Piao*, pp. 35, 37.

176. Yi Feng 1933a: pp. 39–40.

177. Chi Zhicheng 1893: p. 27.

178. Li chuang wo dusheng 1905: *juan* 2, pp. 10–11; Xu Ke 1920: p. 31.

179. On the location of these brothels, see Xu Ke 1920: p. 32; "Demi-monde" 1923: p. 787; Hu Jifan 1930: *juan* 8, n.p.; Wang Dingjiu 1932: *Piao*, p. 37; Yu Muxia 1935: *shang*, p. 16; Sun Yusheng 1939: p. 160; and Datong tushushe n.d.: pp. 40–42.

180. Yu Muxia 1935: *shang*, p. 17.

181. Wang Dingjiu 1932: *Piao*, p. 38.

182. Xu Ke 1920: pp. 31–32; Tu Shipin 1968: *xia*, p. 77.

183. Li chuang wo dusheng 1905: *juan* 2, p. 10–11; Xu Ke 1920: p. 31. One guidebook observes that when Hong Kong was first opened as a port in the mid–nineteenth century, no prostitutes would consort with foreigners because the women were frightened by their bizarre appearance. The women who poled sampans became familiar with the foreigners from navigating around their steamships, learned a smattering of foreign languages, and took up servicing foreigners as an occupation. Yu Muxia 1935: *shang*, p. 17. On the ability of these women to speak foreign languages, see also Tang Youfeng 1931: p. 153. As the foreign trade in Shanghai grew, groups of these East Guangdong women moved there as well to capture the expanding market in sailors. Xu Ke 1920: p. 31.

184. Chi Zhicheng 1893: p. 27.

185. Guidebooks in the 1930s indicated that increased numbers of saltwater sisters and the resultant competition among them had led them to broaden their clientele to include Chinese. Wang Dingjiu 1932: *Piao*, p. 38; Sun Yusheng 1939: p. 157.

186. Henderson 1871: p. 16.

187. "Demi-monde" 1923: p. 788.

188. On the inspection of saltwater sisters, see SVC 1920: pp. 83–84; Zhou Shoujuan 1928: vol. 1, p. 3; Hu Jifan 1930: *juan* 8, n.p.; Wang Dingjiu 1932: *Piao*, p. 39; and Yu Muxia 1935: *shang*, p. 16.

189. Tang Youfeng 1931: p. 153.

190. Wang Dingjiu 1932: *Piao*, pp. 38–39.

191. In at least one respect, however, foreign ways were considered superior. Some commentators suggested that foreign government officials in Shanghai took more initiative than their Chinese counterparts in protecting their own populations by inspecting prostitutes for disease, and that the inspection requirement should be extended to women who serviced a domestic clientele as well. Hu Jifan 1930: *juan* 8, n.p.

192. Cheng 1979: 199–203. The latter were described (p. 203) as follows:

They carried their heads stiffly, with a loose braid of hair hanging behind. They wore round green patches beside their eyes and a quivering red woolen ball at the back of their head. More surprising still, their cheeks were bright red as though they just had been slapped. Their waists were stiff as though they had been bent with torture. Their sleeves flopped like pigs' ears. Their shoes kicking about were hard like turtle shells.

193. Chen Dingshan 1967: pp. 20–21.

194. See, for example, Yu Muxia 1935: *shang*, p. 30. On *sichang*, see also Datong tushushe n.d.: pp. 51–56.

195. Tang Youfeng 1931: p. 154; Chunming shuju 1937: p. 1.

196. "Shanghai de teshu zhiye" 1946: p. 13.

197. Xu Chi et al. 1942: p. 57.

198. Yu Muxia 1935: *shang*, p. 33.

199. Shanghai xintuo 1932: p. 62; Yu Muxia 1935: *ji*, p. 53; Shen Xiao 1938: p. 25.

200. Lü He 1934: pp. 99–107.

201. Xu Chi et al. 1942: p. 61.

202. Lü He 1934: pp. 103, 106–7; Shen Xiao 1938: p. 25; Yu Muxia 1935: pp. 52–53.

203. Lü He 1934: pp. 90–96; *Shenbao* 1941: November 2.

204. Lü He 1934: p. 102; Xu Chi et al. 1942: p. 60.

205. Shen Xiao 1938: pp. 24–25.

206. Mo Ruoqiang 1930: pp. 1–4; Wang Dingjiu 1932: *Wan*, pp. 9–11, 16; Datong tushushe n.d.: pp. 65–71.

207. Wang Dingjiu 1932: *Wan*, p. 12; *Jingbao* 1935: September 29, p. 3; *Jingbao* 1939: November 5, p. 6. Some of the guidebook literature drew parallels between taxi dancers and courtesans, advising customers on how to win the favor of particularly popular or beautiful women, and noting that the dance-hall proprietors were planning a contest for the most popular taxi dancer in the tradition of elections held for courtesans (see chapter 6). Wang Dingjiu 1932: *Wan*, pp. 11–17. On taxi dancers during the Japanese occupation, see Minfeng bianjisuo 1945: pp. 10–11.

208. Xiao Jianqing 1937: pp. 88–89. In a 1928 report on dance cafés, an International Settlement detective named Mr. Quayle commented: "The frequenters of these places are mostly Chinese and comprise persons in all walks of life, the majority however being young rich Chinese who are having their fling. I have personally visited these places and have found them conducted in a very orderly manner in fact better than most of the cafes run by foreigners and having Russian dancing partners." SMP 1928: Reel 4, D1249.

209. For accounts of taxi dancers in such situations, see *Jingbao* 1935: September 26, p. 2; "Prostitution Problem" 1937: pp. 8–9; Yi Xiao 1938: pp. 14–15; Yi Xiao 1939: p. 28; and Yuan Shike et al. 1949: p. 22. For anti-Japanese sentiment among taxi dancers in 1937–1938, see Zhu Zuotong and Mei Yi 1939: part 3, pp. 188–89; for the experiences of four dancers who volunteered for relief work in the wake of the Japanese invasion, see part 4, pp. 163–65.

210. *Jingbao* 1939: November 6, p. 6.

211. Lü He 1934: p. 107.

212. Wang Dingjiu 1932: *Wan*, pp. 3–6.

213. Wang Dingjiu 1932: *Wan*, pp. 6–7.

214. Yu Muxia 1935: *shang*, pp. 34–35. Also see Datong tushushe n.d.: pp. 57–59; and Yuan Shike et al. 1949: pp. 2–3.

215. Wang Dingjiu 1932: *Wan*, p. 8.

216. Xiao Jianqing 1937: p. 90.

217. *Shenbao* 1941: November 2.

218. Qian Gucheng 1938: p. 16.

219. Before World War II, massage parlors in the French Concession, but not in the International Settlement, were licensed and supervised by the police. The postwar Guomindang government briefly closed them down in 1946; the police opposed reopening them because they continued to hire women as attendants. See chapter 11 and "Prostitution Problem" 1937: p. 8; Ruo Wen 1938: p. 9; and [Shanghai] *Dagong bao* 1946: March 5, p. 3.

220. For early descriptions of guide agencies see *Jingbao* 1935: September 23; *Jingbao* 1935: October 11, p. 3; "Prostitution Problem" 1937: p. 8; and Ruo Wen 1938: p. 9. Chen Dingshan (1967: vol. 2, p. 63) recalls their inception date as around 1937.

221. Xu Chi et al. 1942: p. 64.

222. *Jingbao* 1935: September 23, p.3, and October 11, p. 3; Xiao Jianqing 1937: p. 91. For a similar denunciation, see *Shenbao* 1941: November 2.

223. "Prostitution Problem" 1937: p. 8; Ruo Wen 1938: p. 9.

224. Xu Chi et al. 1942: pp. 61–65 (quotation from p. 63); "Shanghai de teshu zhiye" 1946: p. 13.

225. Wang Zhongxian n.d.: p. 23. For similar definitions, see Wang Dingjiu 1932: *Piao*, p. 30; and Yu Muxia 1935: *shang*, p. 32.

226. Tang Youfeng 1931: p. 153.

227. Sun Yusheng 1939: pp. 162–63.

228. Wang Dingjiu 1932: *Piao*, p. 30. Immediately following this helpful advice, Wang offers a bizarre recipe for getting rid of an unwanted *tangpai*. He suggests purchasing some "Holland powder" at a pharmacy and sneaking it into her drink. "If a *tangpai* eats it she will not be able to control herself, and will produce a big series of farts. She will not be able to hide herself" and will have to leave and no longer bother you. Furthermore, he continues, a man who bears a grudge against a *tangpai* can send a friend to slip the Holland powder into her beverage: "She will fart and it will stink, and everyone in the vicinity will cover their noses. She will be so ashamed . . . that her face will turn red, and you can stand on the side and clap and cheer, in order to vent your hatred." Wang Dingjiu 1932: *Piao*, p. 33.

229. Yu Muxia 1935: *ji*, pp. 43, 45–46.

230. Wang Dingjiu 1932: *Piao*, p. 47; Yu Muxia 1935: *ji*, pp. 50–52.

231. "Shanghai de teshu zhiye" 1946: p. 13.

232. SMP: Box 116, N-1366 and Reel 25, D7042.

233. SMP: Reel 25, D7042.

234. The jewelry-shop and guide-agency striptease numbers were reported in an article in *Tanxing huabao* (Flexibility pictorial) on August 26, 1939. The Hawaiian number was advertised in *Ju shijie, Zhengbao, Huibao, Hollywood Bao, Shengbao, Huabao,* and *Crystal (Jingbao)*, all mosquito papers, as well as in *Da wanbao,* on August 15, 1939, and in *Xibao, Taose xinwenbao, Shunbao,* and *Luobinhan* (Robin Hood) on the following day. For publication details, see SMP: Box 116, N-1366 and Reel 25, D7042.

235. For instance, A. L. Teodoro, the publisher of *Crystal* (*Jingbao*), was tried in the U.S. Court for China, on April 23, 1940, on four counts of publishing "indecent, obscene and lascivious articles." He pleaded guilty, was fined ten U.S. dollars by Judge Milton J. Helmick, and was given a term of ten months to be served in Manila, suspended for five years while he remained on parole. According to an article on the same date in the *Shanghai Evening Post and Mercury,* Teodoro had been warned on November 14, 1939, to cease "publishing articles of lewd and indecent nature." He subsequently allowed such articles to appear on February 17, 18, and 22, 1940. An article characterized as "relatively indecent" by the Shanghai police was published on April 15, 1940, and they were originally considering bringing this up as evidence. Subsequently, in April 1940, Teodoro ceased his connection with the paper, and the Chinese publishers Chow Tien-lai, Woo Chih-ts [sic], Chang Ziang-sun, and Woo Tsung-chi came forward to reregister the paper under their names. The new publishers were warned that the certificate would be withdrawn if objectionable articles were published. SMP: Box 71, D8149-C-484; and Box 73, D-8149. For a similar set of 1939 complaints against the tabloid *Wei [Hui] bao,* see SMP: Box 71, D8149-C-505.

236. A 1949 article on traveling floor shows that specialized in intercourse between dogs and teenage girls, for instance, commented with dismay that viewing such a show cost more than visiting a *changsan* courtesan house. Yuan Shike et al. 1949: p. 6. For allegations that disguised prostitution flourished in conjunction with gambling houses in occupied Shanghai, see Minfeng bianjisuo 1945: p. 6.

237. Yu Muxia 1935: *shang,* p. 42, *ji,* pp. 41–43. On male prostitution, see also Wang Dingjiu 1932: *Piao,* pp. 44–46; Qian Shengke 1933: vol. 3; Yu Muxia 1935: *shang,* p. 30; and Matignon 1936: pp. 270–76. A 1988 study of Shanghai prostitution published in the PRC comments of male prostitutes that they "were completely stripped of their rights and character as males. A man is not like a man, a woman is not like a woman—it makes one sick." Ping Jinya 1988: p. 165. Male prostitution is not addressed in the present study because it is invoked far less frequently than female prostitution, and is portrayed as entailing a different set of pleasures and problems. It deserves its own study.

238. Wang Zhongxian n.d.: pp. 253–54.

239. For a fuller discussion of Shanghai prostitutes and the language of commodification, see Hershatter 1991.

240. Mapping the changes in twentieth-century urban elites themselves is a subject alluded to but not directly investigated in this book. Many useful approaches to the topic are presented in Esherick and Rankin 1990: passim; for comments on the fusing of merchant and gentry elites in Shanghai, see p. 20.

CHAPTER 3: RULES OF THE HOUSE

1. For a discussion of the production of persons via ritualized behavior in a very different context, see Zito 1993.

2. Courtesan houses in Shanghai were founded and run by a variety of investors. In some cases, the musicians who accompanied courtesans at their performances organized brothels, securing a house and the necessary permits to open it. Such establishments might employ their own house musicians, who were paid directly from

performance fees collected from each table of banquet guests after a courtesan sang. For one such case, see Wang Liaoweng 1922: pp. 12–13. More often, though, the brothel organizers were women.

3. See, for instance, SMP: Box 41, D5300, which contains materials on licensed brothels in the French Concession in 1933–1934. Much of the material summarizes license applications from the French Concession's *Bulletin municipal.* The names and addresses of the women requesting the licenses are given.

4. Chou 1971: p. 57.

5. Sun Yusheng 1939: p. 23; for the term applied to a courtesan, see Wu Hanchi 1924: p. 10.

6. Wu Hanchi 1924: p. 6.

7. For the former, see Sun Yusheng 1939: p. 19; for the latter, Cheng 1979: p. 48. One source suggests that *benjia* owned their own rooms whereas *zhuzheng* rented space. *Jingbao* 1919: November 15, p. 3.

8. Sun Yusheng 1939: p. 19; also see Wiley 1929: p. 59.

9. *Jingbao* 1919: March 27, p. 2.

10. Wu Hanchi 1924: p. 6; Sun Yusheng 1939: pp. 31–32; Zhu Zuojia 1964: p. 82.

11. For a quasi-fictional account of cooperation between the madam of a large brothel and the manager of an inn, see Chunming shuju 1937: *changsan,* pp. 34–36.

12. Sun Yusheng 1939: p. 19; see also Zhonghua tushu jicheng 1925: vol. 3, pp. 81–85.

13. Wiley 1929: p. 44.

14. Courtesan houses, even those of the "great hall" variety, were usually small. A list of 127 such houses published in 1925 (selected by the guidebook author because they had telephones) showed that 86 percent of them had four or fewer courtesans, and 68 percent of all courtesans lived in houses of this size. A quarter of all courtesans lived in one- or two-courtesan establishments (which together accounted for almost half of all houses). Larger houses were somewhat more common in the French Concession and the Chinese-controlled areas than in the International Settlement, but even the largest house listed had only twelve courtesans. The actual working population of a courtesan house, however, was often much larger: it included the madam, attendants, maids, male servants, bookkeepers, and children. Wang Houzhe 1925: n.p.

15. *Jingbao* 1919: November 15, p. 3; for a brief description of the types of spaces rented, see Sun Yusheng 1939: pp. 20–21.

16. Wang Liaoweng 1922: pp. 13–14; Sun Yusheng 1939: pp. 20–21. The lower-ranking *yao er* brothels were apparently a variation on this type. A secondary landlord would invite madams, each with several courtesans and a maid, to rent a room. The number of rooms in the brothel might range from twenty to fifty. Sun Yusheng 1939: pp. 148–49.

17. Sun Yusheng 1939: pp. 20–21. For a recent scholarly account of financial arrangements that attributes less control to madams and more to "owners" (*laoban*) with hoodlum connections, see Ping Jinya 1988: p. 160. As is usual with post-1949 sources, Ping characterizes the courtesan/madam relationship as one of exploitation: courtesans who could not give their quota of banquets had to sleep with guests to fulfill their financial quotas, or else borrow at usurious rates and be insulted and beaten by the madam and hoodlums.

18. Wang Liaoweng 1922: pp. 13–14.

19. Banchisheng 1891, *juan* 1, pp. 10–11; Sun Yusheng 1939: p. 21.

20. Wang Houzhe 1925: n.p.

21. *Jingbao* 1919: October 10, p. 6; October 18, p. 3; October 24, p. 3. The first reads, in part: "The sign Shanshan recently appeared in Qinghe Fang Yan Malu. This is the sign for Qiu Shui of Hexin Fang, lane number two. Miao Lian of Huile Li San Nong has transferred from Fuzhi Li. Her telephone number is 3076. This prostitute is the most enthusiastic about national affairs. Zhong Qing of Xin Qingfang Yi Nong is now called Qing E. She now hangs out her sign at lane number two. She now owns her own body [*zijia shenti*]."

22. *Jingbao* 1919: April 9, 15, 18, 24, p. 3; June 24, p. 2; June 27, 30, p. 3; July 3, p. 3.

23. *Jingbao* 1929: May 3, p. 3; also see Liu Peiqian 1936: p. 137.

24. Wiley 1929: p. 50.

25. Sun Yusheng 1939: pp. 22, 31.

26. This sum was called "shoe-and-sock money" (*xiewa qian*). In 1922 the courtesan's go-between could expect a fee of ten yuan, while the madam's go-between received one or two yuan. Wang Liaoweng 1922: p. 14. In the late Qing period it was customary for the hiring madam to seal the season's contract by providing the courtesan with a meal, although this practice had disappeared by the 1930s. Sun Yusheng 1939: p. 14.

27. Sun Yusheng 1939: p. 32.

28. Banchisheng 1891: *juan* 2, p. 17.

29. Lemière 1923: p. 131.

30. An 1891 glossary referred to this type of courtesan by the respectful term "guest master" (*keshi*) or the more neutral term "employee" (*huoji*). Banchisheng 1891: *juan* 1, p. 4. Several late Qing sources comment that the madam would lend a courtesan several hundred yuan when she arrived so that she could buy clothing and jewelry. She was expected to return the money when she left. This money was called *daidang*. Good courtesans could command large *daidang* sums, but the very best courtesans had enough personal resources that they did not need *daidang* at all. Banchisheng 1891: *juan* 2, pp. 16–17; Li chuang wo dusheng 1905: *juan* 6, p. 6.

31. Sun Yusheng 1939: p. 23. Sun notes that some *xiansheng* who had many regular customers divided the profits with the madam according to a preset formula, with the *xiansheng* receiving 10 to 20 percent. This was probably in addition to the season's fee, since otherwise it would not have been a very profitable arrangement for the courtesan.

32. Sun Yusheng 1939: p. 30; Wang Liaoweng 1922: pp. 15–16.

33. Zhou Shoujuan 1928: vol. 1, p. 49. *Jingbao* (1919: December 27, p. 3) has an account of a madam deciding not to keep a courtesan for the following season after squabbling with her about how many banquets she should host.

34. Wu Hanchi 1924: p. 6.

35. An alternative term for *taozhu* in one source was *fuxiong*–literally, "father brother"–which sounded, the source explained, like *wuxiong*, "definitely fierce," in an indirect reference to their cruelty. This term may also indicate that some *taozhu* were male. On *taozhu* and *fuxiong*, see Banchisheng 1891: *juan* 1, pp. 4–5. Banchisheng (1891: *juan* 3, pp. 12–13) talks about professionals who raised *taoren* for sale to brothels. On *taoren* (also known as *taoren shenti*, "sold body"), see Banchisheng 1891: *juan*

1, p. 6; Wu Hanchi 1924: p. 8; and Lemière 1923: p. 131. See chapter 7 for alternative definitions of *fuxiong* and *wuxiong* as traffickers.

36. Huang Renjing 1913: p. 130.

37. In 1871 Henderson wrote: "Brothel-keepers almost constantly invest money in the purchase of female children, bringing them up in their houses with a view to ultimate gain by their prostitution. In some of the larger establishments I have counted five or six, of from two or three to fifteen years of age, at which last period they are usually considered ready to engage in the regular business of the brothel." Henderson 1871: pp. 5–6. An 1892 guidebook to 118 courtesans included 19 (16 percent) who were aged fifteen or younger. Huayu 1892: passim. By the early twentieth century the International Settlement had made it illegal for girls under sixteen to reside in houses of prostitution, a provision that was often flouted (see chapters 8 and 11). Lemière 1923: p. 134. In July 1924, a commission on child labor appointed by the Shanghai Municipal Council found it likely, "from the evidence given before it, that many slave children are employed in native brothels and trained to prostitution. Such sale of female children, although undoubtedly contrary to Chinese law, does not appear to be interfered with in any way by those charged with the administration of justice. It is true, however, that in cases where actual cruelty is proved the International Mixed Court at Shanghai will order children to be taken away from the custody of the persons concerned." *CMJ* 1924: 38.11 (November), p. 925. On trafficking more generally, see chapter 7.

38. Henderson 1871: p. 6.

39. For accounts of Li Shanshan's dramatic life and death, see Wang Liaoweng 1922; 35–39; and Chen Rongguang 1924: pp. 109–10. For an embellishment in historical romance style, see Zhang Xunjiu 1934: vol. 2, 33–50.

40. Ma Yongsheng 1930: *juan* 3, p. 16; see appendix B for Chinese text. The same poem is quoted in Qi Xia and Dan Ru 1917: vol. 1, n.p. [p. 5]. Ma Yongsheng 1930 appears to be a reprint of Ge Yuanxu 1876, with punctuation and Japanese pronunciation added.

41. Sun Yusheng 1939: p. 24.

42. Zhang Chunfan 1919: March 21, p. 3; Wu Hanchi 1924: p. 6.

43. Xu Ke 1920: p. 22.

44. Zhang Chunfan 1919: March 21, p. 3.

45. Sun Yusheng 1939: p. 24.

46. On ironworking apprentices, see Hershatter 1986: pp. 101–9.

47. Wolf and Huang 1980: pp. 82–93, 230–31, and passim.

48. Bao Lin, the article reported, was kind to her mother and insisted that the customers respect her. Several weeks later, Sao Muma wrote to the tabloid to set the record straight. She was only thirty-four, she said, not thirty-eight. She insisted that Bao Lin had not intervened with her customers to secure courteous treatment for her, and that she would not have accepted such an intervention. Furthermore, Sao Muma complained, ever since *Crystal* had described her as flirtatious and attractive, Bao Lin's many customers demanded that Sao Muma accompany her on calls, tiring her out. "You are responsible for this," she scolded the newspaper. *Jingbao* 1924: June 24, p. 3; July 12, p. 3.

49. *Jingbao* 1919: December 21, p. 3.

50. For a critique of the term "fictive kinship," see Weston 1991.

51. For definitions of *dajie*, see Banchisheng 1891: *juan* 1, p. 7; Li chuang wo dusheng 1905: *juan* 6, p. 6; and Wu Hanchi 1924: p. 8. On *ajie*, see Sun Yusheng 1939: pp. 23–26, 119–21. On *genju*, see Wu Hanchi 1924: p. 6; and Sun Yusheng 1939: p. 23. On *zuoshou*, see Zhang Chunfan 1919: March 24, p. 3; Wang Liaoweng 1922: pp. 14–15; and Yu Muxia 1935: *ji*, p. 38. Huang Renjing (1913: p. 129) says that the term *zuoshou* referred more generally to male and female servants who invested in a brothel; and Wang Liaoweng (1922: pp. 14–15) also suggests that most *zuoshou* were investors (see also my note 60 below).

52. Sun Yusheng 1939: pp. 22–23.

53. Sun Yusheng 1939: pp. 25–26.

54. On income sharing, see Chunming shuju 1937: *changsan*, pp. 21–22; on shared customers, see pp. 26–28.

55. Banchisheng 1891: *juan* 1, p. 7.

56. Sun Yusheng 1939: pp. 25–26.

57. Li chuang wo dusheng 1905: *juan* 6, p. 6; Qi Xia and Dan Ru 1917: vol. 2, n.p. [p. 34].

58. Banchisheng 1891, *juan* 1, p. 6; *juan* 2, p. 10.

59. Xu Ke 1920: p. 21.

60. For descriptions of *daidang*, see Huang Renjing 1913: p. 129; Lemière 1923: p. 132; Wu Hanchi 1924: p. 6; and Zhou Shoujuan 1928: vol. 1, pp. 37–38.

61. *Jingbao* 1919: August 30, p. 3.

62. Sun Yusheng 1939: p. 27.

63. Zhou Shoujuan 1928: vol. 1, pp. 37–38.

64. Huang Renjing 1913: pp. 129–30.

65. Signing themselves "A Group of Shanghai Niangyi and Dajie Who Have Suffered Harm," a group of servants placed an advertisement in a local paper in the early twentieth century, saying that they had lost their savings when a badly managed bank folded and the banker left town. They threatened to report the malfeasance to a government official, emphasizing that they depended on these savings. Zhou Shoujuan 1928: vol. 2, p. 79. This advertisement is one of several reprinted by Zhou that first appeared twenty years earlier.

66. Chunming shuju 1937: *changsan*, pp. 16–17.

67. Qi Xia and Dan Ru 1917: vol. 2, n.p. [p. 34].

68. For a characterization of *dajie* as more pleasant, see Qi Xia and Dan Ru 1917: vol. 2, n.p. [p. 34]; for a criticism of language, see Zhou Shoujuan 1928: vol. 2, p. 185.

69. Xu Ke 1920: p. 22.

70. Ma Yongsheng 1930: *juan* 2, p. 8.

71. Chunming shuju 1937: *changsan*, pp. 24–26.

72. Banchisheng 1891, *juan* 1, p. 7; Wang Liaoweng 1922: p. 14.

73. Banchisheng 1891, *juan* 1, p. 7; Li chuang wo dusheng 1905: *juan* 6, p. 6; Qi Xia and Dan Ru 1917: vol. 1, n.p. [p. 66]; Zhang Chunfan 1919: March 21, p. 3; Wu Hanchi 1924: p. 6.

74. Zhang Chunfan 1919: March 21, p. 3.

75. Qi Xia and Dan Ru 1917: vol. 1, n.p. [p. 66].

76. Wang Zhongxian n.d.: p. 584.

77. Xu Ke 1920: p. 23.

78. Tu Shipin 1968: *xia*, p. 76. Zhou Shoujuan tells the following story: Once a customer saw a *xiangbang* carrying a young girl of ten on his shoulder on Si Malu. He laughed, saying, "This is *renshang ren* [person on a person/person above people]." An old man beside him said, "For this class of little girls, learning how to sing is a very difficult thing. I don't know how many lashes of the whip have forced them to the point where they can go out and earn money. They are an example to people of the saying that if you don't eat bitterness within bitterness, it is hard to be a person above people [*buchi kuzhong ku, nan wei renshang ren*]." Zhou Shoujuan 1928: vol. 1, p. 43.

79. *Xiao xiansheng yeye mo guitou.* Wang Liaoweng 1922: p. 150.

80. Li chuang wo dusheng 1905: *juan* 7, p. 7; see appendix B for Chinese text.

81. Different sources report, respectively, that shoulder transport was later banned by police order, or that it fell into disuse when hired rickshaws (*baoche*) became common. Wiley 1929: p. 50; Tu Shipin 1968: *xia*, p. 76.

82. Wang Zhongxian n.d.: pp. 34–35.

83. Banchisheng 1891, *juan* 1, p. 12; Li chuang wo dusheng 1905: *juan* 6, p. 6; Zhang Chunfan 1919: March 18, p. 3; Wu Hanchi 1924: p. 8; Yu Muxia 1935: *ji*, 38; Sun Yusheng 1939: pp. 54, 65–66. Upon spending the night with a new customer, a courtesan was also supposed to give a sum of money to the male and female servants. A 1922 source said that the amount had recently risen from twelve to sixteen yuan to thirty to forty yuan, an amount high enough to drive many courtesans to spend the night with customers in hotels instead. Wang Liaoweng 1922: p. 15. Government regulation also played a role in this move to hotels.

84. Sun Yusheng 1939: pp. 9, 53–54, 66.

85. Wu Hanchi 1924: p. 8. This custom was known as *song yinpen*, "sending a silver platter." Merely proffering congratulations, the same source said, would net the *niangyi* and *xiangbang* two to three yuan apiece.

86. Zhou Shoujuan 1928: vol. 2, p. 78.

87. Sun Yusheng 1939: pp. 53–55.

88. Wiley 1929: p. 74.

89. Banchisheng 1891: *juan* 3, pp. 11–12; *juan* 4, p. 9.

90. Banchisheng 1891: *juan* 4, p. 6.

91. Lemière 1923: p. 127.

92. Banchisheng 1891: *juan* 4, p. 5.

93. See, for example, *Shenbao* 1916: March 2, March 5; and *Shenbao* 1918: March 13, April 19, September 20.

94. *Shenbao* 1922: April 18.

95. For cases of clothing theft, see *Shenbao* 1917: May 9, December 24.

96. *Shenbao* 1920: March 28; *Shenbao* 1920: April 11.

97. For a piece of scandal fiction about this kind of situation, see Chunming shuju 1937: *changsan*, pp. 23–24.

98. *Shibao* 1929: May 20, p. 7. Jewelry and suicide were also entangled in a 1920 case when Xu Di, a prominent Shanghai courtesan, was robbed of her diamonds and other jewelry in Hankou. Reports appeared in every newspaper that she had committed suicide, but several days later she was spotted by one of her customers at a Shanghai tailor shop. Xu Di explained to the customer that she had fainted, not died. She added that she found it advantageous for the general public to think she was

dead at that juncture, because after she was robbed she had told the police she suspected a Mr. Tian. When it turned out that Tian was innocent, he began proceedings to sue Xu Di for damaging his reputation. To avoid trouble, Xu had secretly moved back to Shanghai, using the rumors of her death as a cover. *Jingbao* 1920: June 21, p. 3. Clearly the robbery of courtesans was a publicly discussed event.

99. At least one author did bemoan the fact that prostitutes were becoming the trendsetters for ordinary women, wondering whether this meant that social and moral standards were coming to favor the spread of prostitution. Zhang Chunfan 1919: March 24, p. 3; April 6, p. 3. This series of articles describes the situation at the turn of the century. Wiley (1929: p. 74) comments, "Since seduction is her trade her dress sets her off from other women. Her rich apparel of brilliant silk makes her much better dressed than any class of women save the very rich. On the streets she is the object of attention for those who wish to see the new styles in feminine dress especially in cities like Shanghai." For an article purporting to be instructions to courtesans on the importance of dressing to attract attention, see Zhonghua tushu jicheng 1925: vol. 3, pp. 67–68.

100. Banchisheng 1891: *juan* 3, p. 11. According to Perry Link, by the first years of the Republican period, pictures of courtesans routinely adorned magazines such as *Funü shibao* (Women's times) and *Nüzi shijie* (Women's world). Citing Bao Tianxiao 1971: p. 360, Link comments, "Because photography was a new fad, women from the entertainment quarter could be induced to pose for no reimbursement beyond the promise of a copy of the photograph for themselves." Link 1981: p. 146.

101. Qi Xia and Dan Ru 1917: vols. 1–2, passim. The preface to this book is dated 1915, but many of the capsule biographies of courtesans describe events at the turn of the century. It is not clear when the photographs were taken.

102. Li chuang wo dusheng 1905: *juan* 6, p. 14.

103. *Jingbao* 1919: March 15, p. 3.

104. Qi Xia and Dan Ru 1917: vol. 1, n.p. [p. 18].

105. Qi Xia and Dan Ru 1917: vol. 1, n.p. [p. 62].

106. *Jingbao* 1929: March 24, p. 3.

107. Arlington 1923: pp. 317–19.

108. *Jingbao* 1919: December 30, p. 3.

109. *Jingbao* 1919: March 12, p. 3.

110. *Jingbao* 1919 October 15, p. 3.

111. *Jingbao* 1929: April 18, p. 3; *Jingbao* 1935: October 10, p. 3.

112. *Jingbao* 1919: December 6, p. 3.

113. *Jingbao* 1919: March 6, p. 3.

114. *Jingbao* 1919: March 12, p. 3.

115. Qi Xia and Dan Ru 1917: vol. 2, n.p. [p. 73].

116. Qi Xia and Dan Ru 1917: vol. 2, n.p. [p. 73].

117. Henderson 1871: p. 13; Sun Yusheng 1939: p. 29. Sun says that upstairs rooms were more luxurious and less vulnerable to peeping or disturbances from the street.

118. Henderson 1871: p. 12.

119. Chi Zhicheng 1893: p. 26.

120. Banchisheng 1891: *juan* 4, pp. 7–9. On wallpaper, see *juan* 1, pp. 9–10; and Sun Yusheng 1939: pp. 13–14.

121. Banchisheng 1891: *juan* 1, p. 10.

122. Banchisheng 1891: *juan* 1, p. 10; *Shenbao* 1917: December 9; *Shenbao* 1918: October 30. In the latter case, the madam claimed that the customers were angry that she had pressed them to pay their outstanding bill.

123. Banchisheng 1891: *juan* 1, pp. 7–11.

124. Sun Yusheng 1939: pp. 51–52.

125. For descriptions of the daily routines of courtesans, see Henderson 1871: p. 14; Qi Xia and Dan Ru 1917: vol. 1, n.p. [p. 42]; Zhang Chunfan 1919: May 6, p. 3; and Sun Yusheng 1939: pp. 144–45.

126. McAleavy 1959: p. 193.

127. Although *ju* literally translates as "party" or "act," the sense of the occasion is more accurately conveyed by the term "call."

128. By the 1920s, printed tickets had replaced the handwritten type. The description of call procedures that follows, unless otherwise indicated, draws on the following sources: Li chuang wo dusheng 1905: *juan* 6, p. 6; Xu Ke 1920: p. 23; Wang Liaoweng 1922: p. 11; Wu Hanchi 1924: p. 7; Yu Muxia 1935: *shang*, p. 16; Liu Peiqian 1936: p. 137; and Sun Yusheng 1939: pp. 22–23, 29–30.

129. Banchisheng 1891: *juan* 3, p. 9; Chi Zhicheng 1893: p. 12.

130. Banchisheng 1891: *juan* 4, p. 9; Wang Zhongxian n.d.: p. 34.

131. Lemière 1923: p. 131; Xu Ke 1920: p. 23.

132. Wang Liaoweng 1922: p. 131.

133. Li chuang wo dusheng 1905: *juan* 7, p. 7.

134. Yu Muxia 1935: *shang*, pp. 22–23.

135. Pal 1963: p. 118; also see pp. 172–73.

136. Banchisheng 1891: *juan* 4, p. 9; Sun Yusheng 1939: pp. 29–30.

137. A 1917 source says that virgin prostitutes charged only one yuan per call. Qi Xia and Dan Ru 1917: vol. 2, n.p. [p. 9].

138. Lemière 1923: p. 131. On falling fees, see Xu Ke 1920: p. 23; Liu Peiqian 1936: p. 137; and Sun Yusheng 1939: p. 11.

139. In Chinese, *lanwu changsan ban yao er.* For discussion of this phrase, see Wang Zhongxian n.d.: p. 32; and Yu Muxia 1935: *shang*, p. 12. On price increases in the 1930s, see Yu Muxia 1935: *ji*, pp. 34–35.

140. Sun Yusheng 1939: pp. 12, 39.

141. Liu Peiqian 1936: p. 137; Sun Yusheng 1939: pp. 22–23.

142. Wu Hanchi 1924: p. 7.

143. Sun Yusheng 1939: p. 98.

144. Wang Houzhe 1925: n.p. This was also called *jieju*, "to borrow a party." Banchisheng 1891, *juan* 1, p. 13. The quotation is from Sun Yusheng 1939: p. 39.

145. Wang Dingjiu 1932: *Piao*, p. 2; Sun Yusheng 1939: p. 40.

146. Liu Peiqian 1936: p. 137.

147. Sun Yusheng 1939: p. 99.

148. Sun Yusheng 1939: p. 98.

149. Sun Yusheng 1939: pp. 35–37.

150. Qi Xia and Dan Ru 1917: vol. 1, n.p. [p. 47].

151. Banchisheng 1891: *juan* 1, pp. 13–14. On "dawn calls," see also Wu Hanchi 1924: p. 9.

152. Banchisheng 1891: *juan* 3, pp. 8–9; Chi Zhicheng 1893: p. 18. The discussion of non-Chinese garb is from Li chuang wo dusheng 1905: *juan* 6, p. 14. This

practice was replaced by automobile rides in the twentieth century. See, for instance, Yu Muxia 1935: *shang*, pp. 61–62.

153. Banchisheng 1891: *juan* 2, p. 5; Wu Hanchi 1924: p. 7; Wang Dingjiu 1932: *Piao*, p. 3; Liu Peiqian 1936: p. 137; Sun Yusheng 1939: p. 99.

154. Sun Yusheng 1939: p. 40.

155. Sun Yusheng 1939: p. 34.

156. *Yao er* and other lower-ranking houses where services were more clearly commodified, in contrast, offered tea-drinking encounters but required payment of one yuan on the spot. Wang Dingjiu 1932: *Piao*, p. 3; Liu Peiqian 1936: p. 137.

157. Sun Yusheng 1939: p. 100.

158. Wang Dingjiu 1932: *Piao*, p. 3; Sun Yusheng 1939: p. 100. Here and elsewhere, Sun appears to have adopted sections of Wang's text almost verbatim.

159. Sun Yusheng 1939: p. 101.

160. Sun Yusheng 1939: p. 40.

161. Wu Hanchi 1924: p. 7; Wang Dingjiu 1932: *Piao*, p. 3; Sun Yusheng 1939: p. 101.

162. Qi Xia and Dan Ru 1917: vol. 2, n.p. [p. 60].

163. Banchisheng 1891: *juan* 2, pp. 3–5. On two guests drinking tea, see Zhang Chunfan 1919: March 21, p. 3; Zhang is describing the situation twenty years earlier.

164. Wang Zhongxian n.d.: p. 32; Yu Muxia 1935: *ji*, p. 39; Sun Yusheng 1939: pp. 153–55 (the quotation is from p. 154).

165. The cost of a banquet is given in various sources as follows: thirteen yuan per table in about 1908 (Zhou Shoujuan 1928: vol. 2, p. 78); fifteen yuan per table in 1917 (Qi Xia and Dan Ru 1917: vol. 2, n.p. [p. 58]); ten silver yuan and five yuan in tips in 1920 (Xu Ke 1920: p. 23); ten foreign dollars (*yangyuan*) plus substantial tips in 1925 (Wang Houzhe 1925: n.p.); twelve yuan for tips alone in 1939, and double that amount on holidays (Sun Yusheng 1939: p. 59). It is not clear whether this "table charge" included the cost of the food. Wang Liaoweng comments that previously (exactly when is unclear) the cost of a table had been twelve yuan, plus eight yuan for food and four yuan for tips; by 1922 he gives the cost of dishes as ten yuan and the cost of tips as five to six yuan (Wang Liaoweng 1922: pp. 17–18). For general figures on costs, see Cheng 1979: pp. 50–52. For stories probably dating to the turn of the century about particularly wealthy and profligate guests, see Wu Jianren 1935: pp. 127–28.

166. Banchisheng 1891: *juan* 2, p. 7; Li chuang wo dusheng 1905: *juan* 6, p. 6; Wu Hanchi 1924: p. 8.

167. Zhang Chunfan 1919: May 3, p. 3; *Jingbao* 1919: October 10, p. 6; Wu Hanchi 1924: p. 8. A banquet with no gambling was known as "barefoot wine" (*chijiao jiu*); the host was usually someone from out of town who did not have many friends to invite, but who was responding to courtesan requests that he host a gathering. Yu Muxia 1935: *ji*, p. 39; Sun Yusheng 1939: p. 66.

168. Sun Yusheng 1939: p. 42.

169. Wu Hanchi 1924: p. 7; Yu Muxia 1935: *shang*, p. 16, and *ji*, p. 38.

170. Sun Yusheng 1939: pp. 42–43.

171. Wang Dingjiu 1932: *Piao*, p. 3.

172. Banchisheng 1891: *juan* 1, p. 12; Sun Yusheng 1939: p. 65.

173. Sun Yusheng 1939: p. 12. Liu Peiqian (1936: p. 137) suggests that the minimum expenditure was "more than ten" *huatou*, or more than 120 yuan.

174. Liu Peiqian 1936: p. 137; Sun Yusheng 1939: pp. 43, 104–5. Some of the proceeds went to pay the "flower tax" (*na hua shui*), which was apparently collected as a tax on gambling, not on prostitution per se. Sun Yusheng 1939: p. 43.

175. On this system and its changes over time, see Wu Hanchi 1924: p. 8; Yu Muxia 1935: *shang*, pp. 17–19; and Sun Yusheng 1939: pp. 12–13, 44. Yu Muxia explains that the tokens had patterns carved on all sides, and the prostitute's name in the middle. They could be redeemed for two hundred cash at the brothel that issued them. Later they became collector's items, so the brothels were forced to keep minting them, which was a nuisance. In the mid-1920s, the owner of a cigarette shop near one brothel printed a paper version, slightly larger than the paper money then in circulation. Brothels bought them in advance at a 5 to 7 percent discount. They were convenient in two ways: the brothel got a discount, and at same time could avoid the labor of paying out money to the bearers. When the bearers got the tickets they would go to the shop that printed them and get reimbursed there. As for the cigarette shops, they benefited from the fact that brothels purchased these in bulk, but drivers redeemed them piecemeal.

176. Banchisheng 1891: *juan* 2, pp. 15–16.

177. The musicians were dispatched by a guild, which at its height had a membership of 520. Their profession declined after the Municipal Council began a campaign to close brothels in the 1920s. Wang Liaoweng 1922: p. 174.

178. Banchisheng 1891: *juan* 2, pp. 15–16, 8–9; *juan* 3, pp. 5, 7.

179. Wang Dingjiu 1932: *Piao*, p. 4; Sun Yusheng 1939: pp. 58–59; Wang Liaoweng 1922: p. 14.

180. Sun Yusheng 1939: p. 103.

181. Liu Peiqian 1936: p. 137.

182. Sun Yusheng 1939: p. 105.

183. Sun Yusheng 1939: pp. 41–42. For an earlier observation about the increasing size and rising cost of banquets, see Wang Liaoweng 1922: p. 16.

184. Wang Dingjiu 1932: *Piao*, p. 4.

185. Sun Yusheng 1939: p. 103.

186. Houses sometimes gave small discounts on the charges for calls, but they never discounted the food bill, since their own suppliers had been waiting several months for payment. Xu Ke 1920: p. 22; Wang Houzhe 1925: n.p.; Sun Yusheng 1939: pp. 61–62.

187. Xu Ke 1920: p. 22. For other explanations of *piaozhang*, see Banchisheng 1891: *juan* 2, p. 11; Li chuang wo dusheng 1905: *juan* 6, p. 6; and Wu Hanchi 1924: p. 9.

188. Qi Xia and Dan Ru 1917: vol. 1, n.p. [p. 24]; see appendix B for Chinese text.

189. Banchisheng 1891: *juan* 2, p. 11.

190. Zhou Shoujuan 1928: vol. 2, pp. 77–78. The names of the maids signing the two notices are not identical.

191. Zhou Shoujuan 1928: vol. 1, p. 50.

192. Sun Yusheng 1939: p. 63.

193. Sun Yusheng 1939: p. 66.

194. Wang Liaoweng 1922: p. 15; Wu Hanchi 1924: p. 9.

195. Sun Yusheng 1939: p. 63.

196. For a lengthy description of how shares were paid out, see Sun Yusheng 1939: pp. 27–29.

197. Sun Yusheng 1939: p. 15.

198. Banchisheng 1891: *juan* 2, p. 7. On *shao lutou* and associated rituals, see Banchisheng 1891: *juan* 2, pp. 5–7; Li chuang wo dusheng 1905: *juan* 6, p. 6; Qi Xia and Dan Ru 1917: vol. 1, n.p. [p. 36]; Xu Ke 1920: p. 24; Wang Liaoweng 1922: p. 16; Wu Hanchi 1924: p. 10; and Chen Rongguang 1924: pp. 85–86. On the continuing obligation of guests to spend money on such occasions, see Wang Houzhe 1925: n.p.; and Sun Yusheng 1939: p. 118.

199. Banchisheng 1891: *juan* 3, pp. 1–2; Wang Liaoweng 1922: pp. 18–20; Wu Hanchi 1924: p. 9; Wang Houzhe 1925: n.p.; Sun Yusheng 1939: pp. 56–57; Liu Peiqian 1936: p. 138.

200. Charges for the fruit plate ranged from ten yuan in 1924 to as much as forty in 1936. For discussions of this custom see Li chuang wo dusheng 1905: *juan* 6, p. 6; Zhang Chunfan 1919: March 12, p. 3; Wu Hanchi 1924: p. 9; Wang Houzhe 1925: n.p.; Sun Yusheng 1939: pp. 9–10, 66; and Liu Peiqian 1936: p. 138. On "lords of the sixteenth," see Liu Peiqian 1936: p. 138.

201. Zhang Chunfan 1919: March 12, p. 3; Hu Jifan 1930: *juan* 8, n.p.; Wang Zhongxian n.d.: pp. 31–32, 387–90; Sun Yusheng 1939: pp. 157–58.

202. Banchisheng 1891: *juan* 3, p. 12.

203. Before the brothels moved into the concessions, favorite destinations included the Wu Shen Tang in Xin Beimen Nei and the Shixiang Gongmiao in Hongqiao. Later the Hong Miao on Nanjing Road in the International Settlement became the most popular place of worship. Chen Rongguang 1924: pp. 85–86. A 1917 source mentions the Longhua Si in the south of Shanghai, and a 1939 guidebook lists Bao An Si temple, the city temple, the God of Wealth Hall, and the Jiangshao Gongsuo as additional sites. Qi Xia and Dan Ru 1917: vol. 2, n.p. [p. 31]; Sun Yusheng 1939: p. 16.

204. Qi Xia and Dan Ru 1917: vol. 2, n.p. [p. 42].

205. Yu Muxia 1935: *shang*, pp. 40–41. Also see Chen Rongguang 1924: pp. 85–86; and Sun Yusheng 1939: p. 16. Like courtesan houses, pheasant brothels had distinctive rituals dedicated to improving the business of individual prostitutes. When a long-absent patron (known as a "cold-footed customer") reappeared at the brothel, the pheasant would wait until he was asleep, then burn paper money in front of his bed to smoke his socks and shoes in order to make him into a "hot-footed customer." If a guest quarreled with the prostitute or refused to pay her, she might wave a dirty broom behind his back and above his head, or use a kitchen knife to chop the threshold when he was leaving, or burn white paper in front and back of him, or light a firecracker to frighten him. This was called "driving out the poor devil." Alternatively, she would wait until he left and burn paper money to smoke the room, the bed, and the chair on which he had sat. When business did not go well, pheasants reportedly asked male servants in the brothel to strip from the waist down and walk around the brothel holding a burning painted image of the Buddha. On burning incense, see Wu Hanchi 1924: p. 11; Wang Liaoweng 1922: p. 25; and Qian Shengke 1933: vol. 2, p. 4. On cold-footed customers, see Wang Liaoweng 1922: p. 24; and Qian Shengke 1933: vol. 2, p. 4. Wu Hanchi (1924: p. 11) calls them cold-headed customers. On chopping in the vicinity of troublesome guests, see Qian Shengke 1933: vol. 2, p. 8.

On smoking them out, see Wang Liaoweng 1922: p. 2; and Qian Shengke 1933: vol. 2, p. 3. On half-naked servants burning images of the Buddha, see Wu Hanchi 1924: p. 11; and Wang Liaoweng 1922: pp. 24–25.

206. Banchisheng 1891: *juan* 3, pp. 14–15.

207. Banchisheng 1891: *juan* 4, pp. 2–3; Sun Yusheng 1939: p. 70.

208. Sun Yusheng 1939: p. 37. A 1919 source insisted, in contrast, that a visiting courtesan was required to urinate as soon as she arrived at another house. *Jingbao* 1919: November 21, p. 3. Sun (p. 70) comments that a customer also was not permitted to urinate immediately upon arrival.

209. *Jingbao* 1919: November 21, p. 3; Wang Houzhe 1925: n.p.; Sun Yusheng 1939: pp. 69–71.

CHAPTER 4: AFFAIRS OF THE HEART

1. Wiley 1929: p. 61.

2. Wiley 1929: p. 31.

3. L. S. Gannet, "Young China Marries," *Harpers,* May 1927, cited in Wiley 1929: p. 31.

4. Wei 1930: pp. 13, 15.

5. Lemière 1923: p. 127.

6. Banchisheng 1891: *juan* 2, p. 1.

7. One guidebook notes, however, that guests sometimes used the opportunity to establish a liaison with a courtesan without paying the required tips. "Dry beds" fell into disuse with the rise of the hotel industry and the passage of regulations forbidding customers to spend the night in International Settlement brothels. Sun Yusheng 1939: p. 53.

8. Banchisheng 1891: *juan* 2, p. 2.

9. In the late nineteenth century, the two categories of courtesans were also known as "clear" and "muddy" (see chapter 2). Banchisheng 1891: *juan* 1, p. 5. Also see Wu Hanchi 1924: p. 7. Wu adds that in Beijing, virgin courtesans were called *zhuo mianr,* "tabletops," and nonvirgins were *kang mianr,* "bed tops."

10. Sun Liqi et al. 1986; see also below.

11. Banchisheng 1891: *juan* 2, p. 2.

12. Banchisheng 1891: *juan* 3, p. 13.

13. Lemière 1923: pp. 133–34.

14. Sun Liqi et al. 1986; "Demi-monde" 1923: p. 785.

15. Sun Liqi et al. 1986.

16. Qi Xia and Dan Ru 1917: vol. 1, n.p. [p. 5].

17. Lin Biyao 1922: part 1, p. 5.

18. Banchisheng 1891: *juan* 1, p. 5.

19. Wiley 1929: p. 72.

20. Zhang Chunfan 1932: September 1, pp. 2–3.

21. Zhang Chunfan 1932: September 1, p. 3; see also Wu Hanchi 1924: p. 6.

22. Sun Yusheng 1939: p. 116.

23. A gossip item originally printed in a 1919 tabloid concerned one customer who abandoned his desire to "light the big candles" when the madam told him he

would have to pay in advance with one hundred *huatou* of entertaining, or about 1,200 yuan. *Jingbao* 1939: October 31, p. 5 (this is a reprint of an article that originally appeared twenty years earlier).

24. Sun Yusheng 1939: p. 48; also see Zhang Chunfan 1932: September 1, pp. 1–2.

25. Sun Yusheng 1939: p. 48.

26. Yu Muxia 1935: *shang*, p. 20; Zhang Chunfan 1932: September 1, pp. 1–2.

27. Sun Yusheng 1939: pp. 48, 111. This elaborate procedure was presented in stark contrast to the immediate sexual availability of virgin courtesans in the lower-ranking *yao er* houses. Both pawning and purchase were mentioned more often in descriptions of *yao er* houses than among the higher-ranking *changsan* courtesans; one source stated that fewer than one in ten *yao er* was "free." Sun Yusheng 1939: p. 149. The prevalence of pawning and sale was linked to a portrayal of cruel, exploitative madams and vulnerable, sexually accessible *yao er* courtesans, in pronounced contrast to the *changsan* descriptions. Frequency of sexual activity became a marker of relatively low status in the hierarchy of prostitution. As soon as a *yao er* madam paid several hundred yuan to a poor family from Suzhou or Hangzhou, she acquired control over their daughter for a period of one to four years. The parents remained unaware that their daughter, in the cautionary language of one guidebook, had "descended into hell to be the object of excessive lust." After acquiring a pawned prostitute, a madam's first act would be to sell her virginity to one of the guests (attracted by the young courtesan like a "mad swarm of romantic butterflies"), then force her to have nightly sexual relations. A pawned prostitute in a *yao er* house had to follow a madam's directions or else suffer beatings and mistreatment, "and if the girl has anger in her stomach, she can only fart it out." All fees went to the madam; the *yao er* courtesan could not even expect regular tips from guests who had already paid a great deal for spending the night. One guidebook author compared the situation of sold courtesans to that of criminals serving a life sentence, and likened pawned prostitutes to criminals serving a shorter term. Sun Yusheng 1939: pp. 151–52. For another use of the prisoner metaphor and similar allegations of physical abuse, see Huang Renjing 1913: p. 130. Huang was a Christian; his discussion of brothels is laced with colorful cautionary language.

28. Wang Dingjiu 1932: *Piao*, p. 8.

29. Wang Zhongxian n.d.: pp. 12, 11.

30. Wang Zhongxian n.d.: p. 11.

31. Sun Yusheng 1939: p. 112.

32. Yu Muxia 1935: *ji*, pp. 39–40. The actual age of courtesans at any given point in Shanghai's history eludes sociological precision. One 1892 catalog of courtesans mentions the age of 118 different women, with the following result: 16 percent were fifteen or younger, 39 percent were sixteen to eighteen, 18 percent were nineteen or twenty, 7 percent were twenty-one to twenty-five, and the ages of 20 percent were unclear. Huayu 1992: passim.

33. Sun Yusheng 1939: p. 111; Yu Muxia 1935: *shang*, p. 20; Bao Tianxiao 1973: p. 159.

34. Sun Yusheng 1939: p. 111. On classical antecedents of this belief, see Furth 1994: passim.

35. For an instruction to courtesans on how to limit customer access and thus increase their desirability, see Zhonghua tushu jicheng 1925: vol. 3, pp. 72–73.

36. *Jingbao* 1929: April 24, p. 3.

37. Banchisheng 1891: *juan* 1, pp. 15–16.

38. For a case where a wild man, referred to as a "black cyclone," propositioned two courtesans in succession, see *Jingbao* 1919: December 21, p. 3. One courtesan was reportedly terrified, the other irritated; both left his room abruptly.

39. For accounts of *changsan* working a "double day," all dating from 1919, see *Jingbao* 1919: December 9, p. 3; *Jingbao* 1939: October 29, p. 5; and *Jingbao* 1939: October 31, p. 5. The latter two are nostalgic reprints of twenty-year-old gossip items.

40. Qi Xia and Dan Ru 1917: vol. 1, n.p. [p. 40].

41. Banchisheng 1891: *juan* 2, p. 11.

42. The poem continues, "This money is like a petal carried away by the water—canceled with a stroke of the pen." The Chinese phrase is *luohua liushui,* possibly a play on words, since *luoshui* (literally, "to get into the water") also means "to have sexual relations with a courtesan."

43. Xu Ke 1920: pp. 92–93.

44. Chunming shuju 1937: *changsan,* pp. 36–37. This particular phrase (*jie er ai qiao, bao er ai chao*) comes at the end of a scandal story in which a madam forces a virgin prostitute to sleep with an ugly old Cantonese merchant rather than the Suzhou youth she prefers. Region as well as good looks are hierarchized here.

45. Sun Yusheng 1939: p. 106.

46. Sun Yusheng 1939: pp. 24–25.

47. Sun Yusheng 1939: p. 118; see also Wang Houzhe 1925: n.p.

48. Zhang Chunfan 1932: September 1, pp. 3. Here he appears to be describing events about forty years earlier.

49. Tu Shipin 1968: *xia,* p. 76. For almost identical language, see Liu Peiqian 1936: p. 136.

50. Wang Dingjiu 1932: *Piao,* p. 6.

51. Sun Yusheng 1939: pp. 88–89.

52. Lü He 1934: pp. 103–5.

53. See, for example, Huayu xiaozhu zhuren 1892: *juan* 1.

54. Banchisheng 1891: *juan* 3, pp. 16, 13.

55. *Jingbao* 1919: September 30, p. 3.

56. Banchisheng 1891: *juan* 3, p. 14; Banchisheng 1891: *juan* 4, p. 4.

57. Yu Muxia 1935: *ji,* pp. 40–41.

58. See, for instance, Li Yu 1990; and *Jin Ping Mei* 1994. These are both Ming dynasty literary works. On the Qing, see Byron 1987.

59. Banchisheng 1891: *juan* 3, pp. 14–15. The exact phrase is *fangzhong miaojue,* "clever bedchamber formulas." The few women who possess such skills are praised by others as *hao chuangmian* (good at bed).

60. Qi Xia and Dan Ru 1917: vol. 2, n.p. [p. 56]. Geng Jingzhong was one of the leaders of the War of the Three Feudatories (1673–1681).

61. See, for example, Qi Xia and Dan Ru 1917: vol. 1, n.p. [p.70], vol. 2, n.p. [p. 2]; Wang Dingjiu 1932: *Piao,* p. 6; Wang Zhongxian n.d.: p. 12; Yu Muxia 1935, *shang,* p. 15; and Sun Yusheng 1939: pp. 44–47, 85–89, 93–94, 105–9.

62. For one such admonition, see Sun Yusheng 1939: pp. 87–88; also see p. 86.

63. Yu Muxia 1935: *shang,* p. 15.

64. Sun Yusheng 1939: p. 138.

65. Sun Yusheng 1939: pp. 93–94. Here the phrase "eyes on the ceiling" is meant figuratively; compare the much cruder description in chapter 14 of a bored present-day prostitute who tells her customer, "Move your head—I am watching TV."

66. Sun Yusheng 1939: p. 94. On the persistently low status of Jiangbei (Subei) people in Shanghai, see chapter 2 and Honig 1992: passim.

67. Sun Yusheng 1939: pp. 25–26, 46–47, 107, 119–22.

68. Sun Yusheng 1939: pp. 114–15.

69. *Jingbao* 1919: December 21, p. 3; Xu Ke 1920: p. 24; Sun Yusheng 1939: pp. 45–46, 105–6.

70. Sun Yusheng 1939: pp. 7–8, 46, 106–7.

71. Wang Zhongxian n.d.: pp. 28–29.

72. Wang Zhongxian n.d.: p. 29.

73. Zhou Shoujuan 1928: vol. 1, p. 35.

74. *Jingbao* 1919: March 3, p. 3.

75. Banchisheng 1891: *juan* 3, p. 8; *Jingbao* 1919: December 18, p. 3; Qi Xia and Dan Ru 1917: vol. 1, n.p. [p. 60].

76. Zhou Shoujuan 1928: vol. 1, p. 36.

77. *Jingbao* 1919: December 18, p. 3.

78. Banchisheng 1891: *juan* 3, p. 8.

79. Qi Xia and Dan Ru 1917: vol. 2, n.p. [p. 11]; Zhou Shoujuan 1928: vol. 1, p. 35.

80. The list is reprinted in Wang Liaoweng 1922: pp. 137–40.

81. The list is reprinted in Chen Rongguang 1924: pp. 123–28.

82. Zhou Shoujuan 1928: vol. 1, p. 175.

83. Sun Yusheng 1939: pp. 22, 135. For definitions of "raising a small devil," see Wang Zhongxian n.d.: pp. 254–55; Yu Muxia 1935: *shang*, p. 16; and Sun Yusheng 1939: pp. 146–47. For an account of how the courtesan Ping Guo pawned her own possessions to clear the gambling debts of the opera singer Bao Lian, see *Jingbao* 1919: October 6, p. 3.

84. *Jingbao* 1919: November 30, p. 3.

85. Zhou Shoujuan 1928: vol. 1, pp. 156–57.

86. Wang Zhongxian n.d.: p. 254.

87. Wang Zhongxian n.d.: p. 254; Sun Yusheng 1939: pp. 146–147. For a slightly different explanation of "small devils," see Yu Muxia 1935: *shang*, pp. 96–98.

88. *Jingbao* 1939: October 29, p. 5.

89. Wang Zhongxian n.d.: pp. 148–50.

90. Wu Jianren 1935: pp. 109–10.

91. These passages appear in Xu Ke 1920: p. 115; and in Chen Rongguang 1924: p. 122.

92. On jealousy and quarrels, see Xu Ke 1920: p. 115; Chen Rongguang 1924: p. 122; Zhonghua tushu jicheng 1925: vol. 4, pp. 65–70; and Yu Muxia 1935: *shang*, p. 43. Yu added a bit of physiognomy, commenting, "Their faces must be very white and their eyes very dark. Those who are good at reading complexions can tell them at a glance."

93. Chen Rongguang 1924: p. 122.

94. Wang Zhongxian n.d.: pp. 148–50. In a different context unconnected to prostitution, a 1935 guidebook advertised dildos, both domestic and imported, known

colloquially as "Mr. Horn" (*jiao xiansheng*) or "women's pleasure machine." Banned by the government, they were sold in stores that specialized in funeral goods, if the purchaser asked for them by their code name, "Happily Raise It High." Yu Muxia 1935: *shang*, p. 67.

95. Xu Ke 1920: p. 94.

96. Tian Xiao 1922a: pp. 1–12.

97. Zhou Shoujuan 1928: vol. 1, pp. 42–43.

98. See, for instance, Qi Xia and Dan Ru 1917: vol. 2, n.p. [p. 21]; and Zhou Shoujuan 1928: vol. 1, pp. 41–42.

99. Wiley 1929: p. 76. Commonly used terms included "to marry someone" (*shiren*), "to be given in marriage" (*jia*), and "to take in marriage" (*qu*). For this reason, the term "marriage" is used to describe concubine arrangements in the discussion that follows, with due attention to differences in status between principal wife and concubine. On prostitution and concubinage in Hong Kong, see Jaschok 1988.

100. Henderson 1871: p. 10. He added that the male children of such unions were forbidden to compete in the exams, but he doubted that this rule was observed. Candidates for the exams were required to produce proof that their families had not been "contaminated" by such activity for three generations. It is not at all clear, in spite of Henderson's comments, that these prohibitions were still in force in the late nineteenth century. See Mann 1997.

101. Lemière 1923: p. 132.

102. Wei 1930: p. 14; *Shibao* 1929: July 31, p. 7. In 1871, Edward Henderson noted that many foreigners in Shanghai also hired mistresses by the month from courtesan houses, adding huffily, "I suppose the intimate relations in which these women stand to foreigners may to some extent improve their mentally degraded condition—the peculiar position they occupy most certainly does not lower it—but I have myself seen little to justify the conclusion that such improvement is often well marked." Henderson 1871: p. 16.

103. See, for instance, *Jingbao* 1919: December 9, p. 3.

104. See Qi Xia and Dan Ru 1917: vol. 1, n.p. [p. 70], for the story of a businessman who married the courtesan Xie Lijuan because otherwise her schedule would have been too crowded for her to have sexual relations with him.

105. For stories in which a body price was paid, see, among others, *Jingbao* 1919: March 6, p. 3; October 18, p. 3; October 24, p. 3. The middle-class clients who frequented *yao er* houses were less likely than *changsan* patrons to be able to afford to buy them out as concubines. Sun Yusheng 1939: pp. 152–53.

106. Edward Henderson, a public-health official in the International Settlement, in 1871 reported two cases where officials had paid seven thousand and eight thousand taels for Shanghai courtesans. Henderson 1871: p. 10.

107. Banchisheng 1891: *juan* 2, pp. 13–14.

108. See, for instance, Chunming shuju 1937: *changsan*, pp. 31–33.

109. The phrase derived from *xun hua wen liu*, "to seek out flowers and ask after willows," which meant "to frequent courtesans."

110. Li chuang wo dusheng 1905: *juan* 8, pp. 2–3. Special thanks to Wang Xiangyun and Ko-wu Huang for help with this translation; any remaining gaffes are my own.

111. *Jingbao* 1919: November 18, p. 3; for other descriptions of courtesan debt, see *Jingbao* 1919: December 24, p. 3; and Zhou Shoujuan 1928: vol. 1, p. 38.

112. *Jingbao* 1919: August 9, p. 2.

113. Wu Hanchi 1924: p. 9; Zhonghua tushu jicheng 1925: vol. 3, pp. 77–78.

114. See, for instance, *Jingbao* 1919: March 6, p. 3.

115. *Jingbao* 1919: September 21, p. 3. An additional nine marriages were announced in *Jingbao* 1919: October 18, p. 3.

116. Qi Xia and Dan Ru 1917: vol. 2, n.p. [pp. 22–23]; also see *Jingbao* 1919: October 24, p. 3; *Jingbao* 1919: December 9, p. 3; and Zhonghua tushu jicheng 1925: vol. 3, pp. 77–78.

117. Lemière 1923: p. 133. Zhonghua tushu jicheng 1925: vol. 3, p. 78, contains a piece of popular writing purportedly directed at courtesans, advising them either to collect property and flee the marriage or to provoke their husband to let them go by picking fights, sleeping with other men, and inciting the sons of the family to do immoral things and the wives and daughters to lose their chastity.

118. *Jingbao* 1919: September 12, p. 3. On other rumors about her destination, see *Jingbao* 1919: November 3, p. 3. On Kui's tough but honest character, see Xin shijie baoshe 1918: n.p. Wang Liaoweng (1922: pp. 68–69) has a brief biography of Kui that stresses her extremely independent character and fondness for dressing in men's clothing. Wang suggests that her affection for opera singers was behind her breakup with Huang, who was a merchant.

119. *Jingbao* 1929: April 6, p. 3. For other accounts of divorces, see the biographies of Gui Di, Miao Yuege, and Hua Yuanchun in Qi Xia and Dan Ru 1917, vol. 1, n.p. [pp. 1, 9], vol. 2, n.p. [p. 3]; also see *Jingbao* 1919: December 21, p. 3; and Wang Liaoweng 1922: pp. 154–55. For two pieces of fiction revolving around the lives of prostitutes after marriage, see U. U. 1922 and Zhuo Dai 1922.

120. On Bao Qin's short-lived marriage, stormy departure, and subsequent liaisons, see *Jingbao* 1919: September 21, p. 3; September 27, p. 3; October 10, p. 6; October 18, p. 3; October 24, p. 3; November 3, p. 3; December 24, p. 3; *Jingbao* 1929: February 24, p. 3; March 12, p. 3; and Wang Liaoweng 1922: p. 70.

121. Wang Liaoweng 1922: p. 70.

122. *Jingbao* 1929: February 3, p. 3; *Jingbao* 1929: February 27, p. 3; *Jingbao* 1929: March 30, p. 3.

123. The term most frequently used for "divorce" in these accounts was *xiatang*, "to go down from the hall," rather than *lihun*, "to leave the marriage." No sources indicate whether formal legal procedures were involved in such divorces, and no stories of financial negotiations between concubines and their husbands mention the courts or other legal authorities. Kathryn Bernhardt (1994, pp. 210–12) argues that Republican-period law gave concubines increasing protection, making it easier for them to leave concubinage but more difficult for the family head to expel them. (The law did not call this procedure "divorce," since it did not regard concubinage as marriage.) Since courtesans and lower-ranking prostitutes did go to court on other matters (see part 3), it seems that if Shanghai courtesan-concubines had made frequent use of this legal protection, it would have left more of a paper trail.

124. See, for instance, *Jingbao* 1919: October 24, p. 3; and *Jingbao* 1919: December 21, p. 3.

125. *Jingbao* 1929: February 21, p. 3.

CHAPTER 5: TRICKS OF THE TRADE

1. Banchisheng 1891: preface.
2. Sun Yusheng 1939: p. 2.
3. Sun Yusheng 1939: cover.
4. Sun Yusheng 1939: pp. 3–4. For another example of a cautionary message preceding pages of detailed description, see Wang Dingjiu 1932: *Piao*, pp. 1–2.
5. A 1932 guide noted that clothing was considered especially important in Shanghai, even more important than character, especially in the brothels. Guests were advised to dress beautifully, but not too excessively, lest the madams regard them as swindlers. Western suits were regarded very favorably. Wang Dingjiu 1932: *Piao*, p. 17.
6. On the dangers of unwarranted assumptions of intimacy, see Sun Yusheng 1939: pp. 134–37.
7. For examples of this kind of writing, see Wang Dingjiu 1932: *Piao*, p. 2; Sun Yusheng 1939: pp. 8, 18, 33; and *Jingbao* 1919: November 30, p. 3. Sun Yusheng compared the situation of bumpkins in the brothels to a famous episode in the Qing novel *Dream of the Red Chamber* where Granny Liu, a poor and distant relative, first enters the grand residence of the Jia family.
8. The term derived originally from the Suzhou-area custom of naming a child with a character containing the wood radical if his fortune (based on the presence of the elements gold, wood, water, fire, and earth) lacked wood. Later, any ignorant country person became known as *amulin*. Wang Zhongxian n.d.: pp. 583–84. On courtesans despising "bumpkins," see also Wang Dingjiu 1932: *Piao*, p. 6.
9. For definitions and examples of *wensheng*, see Wu Hanchi 1924: p. 7; Zhonghua tushu jicheng 1925: vol. 3, p. 69; *Jingbao* 1929: May 9, p. 3; Wang Dingjiu 1932: *Piao*, pp. 11, 13; Lü He 1934: p. 104; and Sun Yusheng 1939: pp. 69, 124, 131, 135.
10. Wang Dingjiu 1932: *Piao*, p. 11.
11. Wang Dingjiu 1932: *Piao*, p. 13.
12. Sun Yusheng 1939: p. 135.
13. *Jingbao* 1919: December 27, p. 3.
14. Wang Dingjiu 1932: *Piao*, p. 11; Sun Yusheng 1939: pp. 135–36, 139; Wu Hanchi 1924: pp. 6, 10.
15. Wang Dingjiu 1932: *Piao*, pp. 12–13. For more egregious fictional stories of customer-swindlers, whose tricks ranged from various deceptions to outright theft, see Qian Shengke 1933: vol. 4, part 1, pp. 12 and 16, and part 2, pp. 4–5.
16. Sun Yusheng 1939: p. 131.
17. *Jingbao* 1919: November 30, p. 3.
18. Wang Dingjiu 1932: *Piao*, pp. 16–17, 23.
19. Sun Yusheng 1939: pp. 94–95. On the danger of younger customers behaving wildly and damaging the reputation of older ones, see *Jingbao* 1919: December 12, p. 3.
20. Zhou Shoujuan 1928: vol. 2, pp. 71–75.
21. Wang Houzhe 1925: n.p.; Sun Yusheng 1939: p. 50.
22. Zhang Chunfan 1932: September 1, pp. 2–3.
23. Sun Yusheng 1939: p. 50.

24. Wang Zhongxian n.d.: p. 12.

25. Wang Zhongxian n.d.: p. 12; Sun Yusheng 1939: p. 113.

26. Sun Yusheng 1939: p. 49.

27. Sun Yusheng 1939: pp. 49, 113.

28. Zhang Chunfan 1932: September 1, p. 2.

29. Sun Yusheng 1939: pp. 49, 112.

30. Wang Houzhe 1925: n.p. Some stories about courtesans, even virgin courtesans, portray them as having some choice of customers and the option of using the legal system to protect that choice. See, for instance, *Shibao* 1929: July 10, p. 7.

31. *Jingbao* 1919: December 30, p. 3.

32. For examples of this kind of nostalgia, see Wang Dingjiu 1932: *Piao,* p. 8; Wang Zhongxian n.d.: pp. 30–31; and Sun Yusheng 1939: p. 48.

33. Yu Muxia 1935: *shang,* pp. 20–21; *ji,* pp. 30–32.

34. Wang Dingjiu 1932: *Piao,* p. 8.

35. Sun Yusheng 1939: p. 47.

36. Chunming shuju 1937: *changsan,* pp. 6–8.

37. Sun Liqi et al. 1986.

38. Zhang Xinxin and Sang Ye 1987: p. 32.

39. For a piece of writing purporting to be instructions to courtesans about how to steal a desirable customer from a rival, see Zhonghua tushu jicheng 1925: vol. 3, p. 72.

40. Sun Yusheng 1939: pp. 36–37.

41. See, for instance, *Jingbao* 1919: September 27, p. 3; October 24, p. 3; December 24, p. 3.

42. Banchisheng 1891: *juan* 2, p. 11.

43. Yu Muxia 1935: *shang,* p. 15; Sun Yusheng 1939: pp. 36–37, 60, 147.

44. Sun Yusheng 1939: pp. 132–33.

45. *Jingbao* 1919: October 15, p. 3.

46. Banchisheng 1891: *juan* 1, pp. 14–15.

47. For an account of one such case dating from the late Qing, see Wang Liaoweng 1922: pp. 123–25.

48. Yu Muxia 1935: *shang,* p. 16, *ji,* p. 35; Wang Zhongxian n.d.: pp. 43–45.

49. Other tiles had racy nicknames such as "large buttocks," "male genitals," and "female genitals." Wang Zhongxian n.d.: p. 44.

50. Wang Zhongxian n.d.: p. 44.

51. Wang Zhongxian n.d.: p. 45.

52. On "eating vinegar" in the courtesan houses, see Sun Yusheng 1939: pp. 36, 131–32.

53. *Shenbao* 1875: January 23.

54. On rich versus very rich, see *Jingbao* 1919: August 12, p. 3, and August 15, p. 3. On Hua Yunyu, see *Jingbao* 1919: July 18, p. 3. On Gao Yayun, see *Jingbao* 1919: September 9, p. 3.

55. Wang Zhongxian n.d.: p. 45.

56. Banchisheng 1891: *juan* 3, p. 15.

57. Wu Hanchi 1924: pp. 9, 13; Wang Houzhe 1925: n.p.; Ping Jinya 1988: p. 160; Shuliu shanfang 1919: March 18, p. 3.

58. Li chuang wo dusheng 1905: *juan* 6, p. 6; Zhang Chunfan 1919: March 18, p.

3; Xu Ke 1920: p. 22; Zhonghua tushu jicheng 1925: vol. 3, pp. 74–75; Yu Muxia 1935: *ji*, p. 39.

59. Zhang Chunfan 1919: March 18, p. 3; Wu Hanchi 1924: pp. 9, 13; Wang Houzhe 1925: n.p.; Yu Muxia 1935: *ji*, p. 39; Ping Jinya 1988: p. 160.

60. On "pouring rice soup," see Zhonghua tushu jicheng 1925: vol. 3, p. 74; Wang Houzhe 1925: n.p.; *Jingbao* 1939: October 29, p. 5; Sun Yusheng 1939: pp. 130–31; and Yu Muxia 1935: *shang*, p. 16.

61. Wang Zhongxian n.d.: p. 42. On the importance of flattery, also see Zhonghua tushu jicheng 1925: vol. 3, pp. 66–67, 75.

62. Qi Xia and Dan Ru 1917: vol. 1, n.p. [p. 56].

63. Sun Yusheng 1939: pp. 68–69; Wang Houzhe 1925: n.p.

64. Wu Hanchi 1924: p. 10.

65. Wang Liaoweng 1922: p. 135. A variation of these definitions was offered in Qi Xia and Dan Ru 1917: vol. 1, n.p. [p. 55]: those who could be taken in after one attempt were called orange customers; after two attempts, walnut customers; and those who could not be tricked at all were called stone customers. These definitions were reproduced in Zhou Shoujuan 1928: vol. 1, pp. 51–52.

66. Yu Muxia 1935: *ji*, pp. 48–49. This theme had currency before the 1930s. Xu Ke's 1920 collection, describing mid-nineteenth-century conditions, stated that "often the nature of smoke flowers [prostitutes] is to be fond of being a wild duck and ashamed of being a domesticated chicken. Therefore seldom is there one who refuses guests and closes the gate." Xu Ke 1920: p. 18.

67. *Jingbao* 1935: October 25, n.p. (p. 3?).

68. Sun Yusheng 1939: p. 130.

69. For examples of this kind of argument, see *Jingbao* 1919: July 12, p. 3; Zhonghua tushu jicheng 1925: vol. 3, pp. 70–72; and Sun Yusheng 1939: pp. 90–91.

70. Lü He 1934: pp. 103–4.

71. Chunming shuju 1937: *changsan*, pp. 2–3, 5–6, 38–40. On similar exploits by a *yao er* courtesan, see Chunming shuju 1937: *yao er*, pp. 4–5.

72. On white-pigeon scams, see Ma Yongsheng 1930: *juan* 2, p. 8; Huang Renjing 1913: pp. 176–77; "Demi-monde" 1923: p. 787.

73. Wang Zhongxian n.d.: pp. 5–6, 9.

74. For examples of fairy-jump stories, see Qian Shengke 1933: vol. 1, pp. 19–24; and Chunming shuju 1937: *bankai men*, pp. 5–10.

75. Wang Zhongxian n.d.: pp. 5–6.

76. Chunming shuju 1937: *bankai men*, pp. 5–16. As noted in chapter 2, *bankai men* was a more general term for women who did not at first glance appear to be prostitutes. Not all of them were involved in scams, and the scams in which they participated were not limited to the "fairy jump." Chunming shuju (1937: pp. 1–5), for instance, tells of a woman who poses as a young upper-class mother, complete with baby, wet nurse, and a husband away from home twenty days a month. She lures a passerby into an affair and allows him to pay all the household expenses. He arrives one day to find that the woman has disappeared, leaving a For Rent sign on the door. For similar stories classified under *tangpai*, see Chunming shuju 1937: *tangpai*, pp. 1–4.

77. For a discussion of imposture in the context of early post-Mao China, see Anagnost forthcoming: chapter 2.

78. Qian Shengke 1933: vol. 2, pp. 7–8. The quotation is from Chunming shuju 1937: *zhiji*, pp. 13–15.

79. Qian Shengke 1933: vol. 1, pp. 24–26; Chunming shuju 1937: *bankai men*, pp. 10–12.

80. Chunming shuju 1937: *bankai men*, pp. 5–6, 10–12.

81. Chunming shuju 1937: *nü chaibaidang*, pp. 8–10.

CHAPTER 6: CAREERS

1. Wang Liaoweng 1922: p. 65; Chen Rongguang 1924: pp. 97–98.

2. Wang Liaoweng 1922: pp. 74–76; *Jingbao* 1919: July 15, p. 3.

3. A guidebook published in 1892 said that she was twenty-three years old, which would mean that she was born in 1869. In 1919 *Crystal* gave her age as fifty-four, which would mean an 1865 birth date. *Jingbao* 1919: August 3, p. 3.

4. For Yunjian, see Huayu 1892: *juan* 1, n.p. For Songjiang, see Qi Xia and Dan Ru 1917: vol. 1, n.p. [p. 43]; and Xu Ke 1920: p. 105. For Zhang Lian Tang, see Wang Liaoweng 1922: p. 50.

5. Wang Liaoweng 1922: p. 50.

6. Except where otherwise noted, this account is based on Wang Liaoweng 1922: pp. 50–56. For embellished versions of some of these events, see Chen Dingshan 1967: pp. 9–10.

7. Many of the stories from this point until Lin's second sojourn in Tianjin (see below) are also found in Wu Jianren 1935: pp. 103–6.

8. The term for "donation," *bushi*, is usually used in the context of Buddhism to refer to donations of money to a religious charity.

9. Qi Xia and Dan Ru (1917: vol. 2, n.p. [p. 75]) complain that rather than heeding the warnings contained in the novel, many people, including courtesans, became obsessed by the plot and characters.

10. Wang Liaoweng 1922: pp. 50–51.

11. Xu Ke 1920: p. 106. The expression "taking a bath" was said to have originated with Lin Daiyu.

12. Wu Jianren 1935: pp. 104–5. This version also says that the match broke up when Huang's father threatened to have them both arrested.

13. For an alternative account of this relationship, which has Lin Daiyu forgetting about Li and enjoying a luxurious life in the Wang household, see Chen Dingshan 1967: vol. 1, p. 40.

14. Xia Zhengnong (1979: vol. 2, p. 2,901) gives his dates as 1855–1925. For a more detailed account of his career and numerous sexual liaisons, see Chen Dingshan 1967: vol. 1, pp. 339–41.

15. For another account of this marriage, which stresses the venality of a go-between who lied to Qiu and Lin about each other, see Zhou Shoujuan 1928: vol. 1, p. 177.

16. Wang Liaoweng 1922: p. 52. According to Chen Dingshan (1967: vol. 2, pp. 13–14), she connived her way into the official's presence by sending in her calling card, which labeled her a scholar of the Hanlin Imperial Academy.

17. Xu Ke 1920: p. 105; also see Chen Rongguang 1924: pp. 105–6. For a historical-romance version, see Zhang Xunjiu 1934: vol. 1, pp. 65–66.

18. Zhou Shoujuan 1928: vol. 1, p. 77–78; see also Qi Xia and Dan Ru 1917: vol. 2, n.p. [pp. 44–45].

19. Zhou Shoujuan 1928: vol. 1, p. 58–59.

20. Lu Lanfen, like Lin Daiyu, was one of the four famous courtesans collectively known as Four Guardian Spirits (see the account elsewhere in this chapter). On Lu, see Xu Ke 1920: p. 106; Chen Rongguang 1924: pp. 107–8; Zhou Shoujuan 1928: vol. 1, pp. 177–78; Zhang Xunjiu 1934: vol. 1, pp. 49–52; and Ping Jinya 1988: p. 167.

21. Chen Dingshan 1967: vol. 2, pp. 10–11.

22. Zhou Shoujuan 1928: vol. 1, pp. 149–52.

23. This was not the only account of Lin Daiyu's conflicts with other courtesans. For an account of a fight with a courtesan improbably named Huolu Laoer (Heating Stove Old Two), see *Jingbao* 1919: July 21, p. 3. Also see the discussion of the Four Guardian Spirits later in this chapter.

24. Zhou Shoujuan 1928: vol. 1, pp. 173–74.

25. Wang Liaoweng 1922: p. 53. For another account of her relationship with Long, see Chen Dingshan 1967: vol. 2, p. 14.

26. For a sketch of Tang Hualong's career, see Xia Zhengnong 1979: vol. 2, p. 2,042.

27. *Jingbao* 1919: July 21, p. 3; *Jingbao* 1920: January 27, p. 2; *Jingbao* 1919: August 27, p. 3.

28. Wang Liaoweng 1922: p. 53; *Jingbao* 1919: April 27, p. 3.

29. *Jingbao* 1920: February 6, p. 2.

30. *Jingbao* 1919: December 9, p. 3; *Jingbao* 1919: December 15, p. 3. For another story about her reemergence as a courtesan in 1918, see Yu Muxia 1935: *xia*, p. 5. For an account by a Japanese traveller of Lin Daiyu's appearance on call when she was about fifty-eight, see Akutagawa 1977–78. My thanks to Joshua Fogel for calling my attention to this reference, which he has translated.

31. *Jingbao* 1919: September 21, p. 3.

32. Wang Liaoweng 1922: pp. 175–78.

33. This would have been in 1925. Ping Jinya 1988: p. 167.

34. Cuo Zong, for instance, was the daughter of a bankrupt rice merchant; Fan Caixia was the daughter of a bankrupt medicine dealer. Wang Xiaobao decided to sell herself to a courtesan house in order to pay for her father's burial. Wang Xiulan, sold into a courtesan house when her father went bankrupt, reportedly still maintained her chastity, just like the daughter of a good family. On Cuo Zong, see Qi Xia and Dan Ru 1917: vol. 1, n.p. [p. 5]. On Fan Caixia, see Zhan Kai 1917: *juan* 3, pp. 33–34; Qi Xia and Dan Ru 1917: vol. 1, n.p. [p. 7]; and Wang Liaoweng 1922: pp. 63–64. (Fan was not represented as an utter paragon of virtue; Qi Xia and Dan Ru [1917] say that she was once imprisoned for mistreating her maids.) On Wang Xiaobao, see Qi Xia and Dan Ru 1917: vol. 2, n.p. [p. 68]. On Wang Xiulan, see Huayu 1892: *juan* 1, p. 2; and Zhan Kai 1917: *juan* 2, pp. 16–17.

35. *Jingbao* 1919: August 15, p. 3.

36. *Jingbao* 1919: November 15, p. 3.

37. *Jingbao* 1919: March 3, p. 3; August 27, p. 3.

38. Qi Xia and Dan Ru 1917: vol. 2, n.p. [pp. 12–13].

39. Qi Xia and Dan Ru 1917: vol. 2, n.p. [pp. 13–13]; Zhou Shoujuan 1928: vol. 1, p. 181.

40. Lemière 1923: p. 130.

41. Zhou Shoujuan 1928: vol. 1, p. 182.

42. Zhou Shoujuan 1928: vol. 1, p. 183.

43. Lemière 1923: 130; Zhou Shoujuan 1928: vol. 1, p. 182; Wu Jianren 1935: p. 107.

44. Ping Jinya 1988: p. 168.

45. Qi Xia and Dan Ru 1917: vol. 2, n.p. [p. 32]. This source gives her age as twenty-five in 1917, which would put her birth date in about 1892. Wang Liaoweng (1922: p. 62), however, says that she was married in 1906, after a career as a courtesan, so 1892 is probably too late a date for her birth. It is likely that the information in the Qi Xia collection, although published in 1917, actually dates from the early twentieth century. On Li's life story, see also Wu Jianren 1935: pp. 101–2.

46. Qi Xia and Dan Ru 1917: vol. 2, n.p. [p. 32].

47. Wu Jianren 1935: p. 101.

48. Wang Liaoweng 1922: p. 61; Wu Jianren 1935: p. 102. On her father's Confucian learning, see Qi Xia and Dan Ru 1917: vol. 2, n.p. [p. 32]. Chen Dingshan (1967: vol. 2, pp. 102–3) says that her father tried to pass the civil-service examinations for ten years, but failed and became a merchant.

49. Qi Xia and Dan Ru 1917: vol. 2, n.p. [p. 33].

50. A historical-romance version of Li's story gives her husband's name as Liu Ziren. Zhang Xunjiu 1934: vol. 2, p. 74.

51. Pan's given name is included in the historical romance by Zhang Xunjiu. Zhang Xunjiu 1934: vol. 2, p. 74.

52. Wang Liaoweng 1922: p. 61. According to Chen Dingshan (1967: vol. 2, pp. 102–3), Huang became pregnant by Pan. Her mother became frightened and took her to Hangzhou to pray. When they reached Hangzhou, the mother bought a coffin and tried to force her daughter into suicide, but Huang and Pan convinced the mother to fill the coffin with tiles and stones instead and to put it in the Xiao temple. They then sent a telegram to the Liu family reporting that Huang had died.

53. Chen Dingshan 1967: vol. 2, pp. 102–3.

54. Qi Xia and Dan Ru 1917: vol. 2, n.p. [pp. 32–33]; Chen Dingshan 1967: vol. 2, pp. 102–4.

55. Chen Dingshan 1967: vol. 2, pp. 102–4.

56. The texts of all four poems appear in Qi Xia and Dan Ru 1917: vol. 2, n.p. [p. 33]; and in Wang Liaoweng 1922: p. 62. Max Ko-wu Huang provided invaluable assistance with the translations that follow; any remaining infelicities are my own.

57. Tao Yuanming was an official and poet of the eastern Jin, whose dates are given as 365 (or 372 or 376) to 467.

58. See appendix B for the Chinese text of this poem.

59. See appendix B for the Chinese text of this poem.

60. See appendix B for the Chinese text of this poem.

61. See appendix B for the Chinese text of this poem.

62. The historical-romance version of this story gives his name as Song Jingbo. Zhang Xunjiu 1934: vol. 2, p. 78.

63. Chen Dingshan (1967: vol. 2, pp. 102–4) says that the family patriarch was a Hanlin academician, and that it was he who became infuriated by Li's relationship with the grandson. Other accounts say that it was the patriarch's wife who summoned

her. A version of this incident that did not mention Li Pingxiang's name circulated in 1930s scandal fiction. It involved a "half-open door" (*bankai men*) named Zhang rather than a courtesan. Zhang had an affair with a youth and later also with a middle-aged man. One night, the youth put his fan on the table and forgot to take it. Zhang did not notice. When the older man came and saw the fan, he recognized it as one he had painted. When he inquired, Zhang said it belonged to her husband. He secretly substituted another fan for it. The following day the youth came and found his father's fan on the table. Zhang told him, too, that it was her husband's. The youth took the fan away, and from that time on the two men did not visit Zhang anymore. Chunming shuju 1937: *bankai men*, pp. 16–18.

64. Zhang Xunjiu 1934: vol. 2, p. 79.

65. Chen Dingshan (1967: vol. 2, pp. 102–4) says that Pan went back to Li Pingxiang's first husband, Liu, told him that she had not really died and that she had become a courtesan, and convinced him to join Pan in suing her in order to get her money. According to this account, the official who adjudicated the case took pity on Li and protected her. He forbade her to be a prostitute, ordered Pan caned, and dismissed Liu.

66. Wang Liaoweng 1922: pp. 61–62. This date is debatable. Chen Dingshan (1967: vol. 2, p. 102) has her still working as a Shanghai courtesan in 1908–1909.

67. *Jingbao* 1929: April 3, p. 3; April 30, p. 3; May 3, p. 3; May 6, p. 3.

68. Walkowitz 1992.

69. These biographical details about Lian Ying, unless otherwise noted, come from Xin shijie baoshe 1918: n.p.; Wang Liaoweng 1922: p. 67; *Jingbao* 1919: October 21, p. 3; December 6, p. 3; and *Jingbao* 1920: August 18, p. 3.

70. The ceremony and Lian Ying's resumption of courtesan life were announced in the "Chronology of Important Flower World Events of 1919," *Jingbao* 1920: January 1, p. 7.

71. Except where otherwise noted, this account of the murder and subsequent trial is based on Wang Liaoweng 1922: pp. 161–73; *NCH* 1920: June 26, p. 797; August 14, p. 437; August 21, p. 515; September 18, p. 751; and Chen Dingshan 1967: vol. 1, pp. 65–69. Liang Hongying (1991) retells the story in semifictional form with retrospectively invented dialogue; this account focuses on Yan rather than Lian Ying.

72. *Shenbao* 1920: June 28.

73. *Jingbao* 1920: June 21, p. 3.

74. *Jingbao* 1920: June 21, p. 3.

75. *Shenbao* 1920: June 21, July 9.

76. Chen Dingshan 1967: vol. 1, pp. 65–69. A 1991 account gives the date of execution as November 23, 1920. Liang Hongying 1991: p. 155.

77. Wang Liaoweng 1922: p. 162.

78. *NCH* 1920: June 26, p. 797.

79. *Jingbao* 1929: March 30, p. 3.

80. Chen Dingshan 1967: vol. 1, pp. 65–69. For details on the making of the movie, see Liang Hongying 1991: pp. 183–84; on the play and movie, see Yu Muxia 1935: *ji*, pp. 135–37.

81. Accounts of the elections are found in Chan Qingshi 1884: passim; Ping Jinya 1988: pp. 166–67; Chen Rongguang 1924, pp. 90–95; Huayu xiaozhu zhuren 1892: *juan* 1, p. 2; Qi Xia and Dan Ru 1917: vol. 1, n.p. [p. 69], vol. 2, n.p. [p. 39]; Yu Muxia 1935,

ji, pp. 37–38; Zhou Shoujuan 1928: vol. 2, pp. 2–4, 38–51; Xu Ke 1928: pp. 1–4; and Sun Guoqun 1988a: pp. 71–78. In 1888, Wang Tao commented, "Shanghai is a prosperous city. Yesterday I went to Furong Cheng [Hibiscus City] and saw the 1888 summer flower roll, on which there were sixteen people." Wang Tao 1934: *juan* 7, p. 125.

82. Xu Ke 1920: p. 1.

83. For a general account of these elections, see Sun Guoqun 1988a: pp. 71–78.

84. The population of courtesans from the turn of the century through the late 1910s was usually given as two to three thousand, though the editor of one tabloid was said to have commented that Shanghai courtesans were as numerous as the sands of the Ganges. This same editor put the odds of being selected at one in ten, a figure that apparently included women who received lesser titles. See Zhou Shoujuan 1928: vol. 2, pp. 2–4, 15, 20–23. For the odds of passing various levels in the imperial civil-service examinations, see Miyazaki 1981: pp. 121–22.

85. Zhou Shoujuan 1928: vol. 2, pp. 32–36, 38–51; Ping Jinya 1988: p. 166.

86. Zhou Shoujuan 1928: vol. 2, pp. 1–2.

87. Zhou Shoujuan 1928: vol. 2, pp. 17–18.

88. Xu Ke 1920: pp. 2–4; Li chuang wo dusheng 1905: *juan* 6, p. 4–5; Zhou Shoujuan 1928: vol. 2, pp. 8–13. The most elaborated example of this genre, dating from the 1917 election, is Xin shijie baoshe 1918, a book containing biographies and photographs of thirty-three women.

89. For reprints of several such letters, see Zhou Shoujuan 1928: vol. 2, pp. 5–7, 25–27, 36–37.

90. Zhou Shoujuan 1928: vol. 2, pp. 15–16.

91. Xin shijie baoshe 1918: p. 2.

92. Qi Xia and Dan Ru 1917: vol. 1, n.p. [p. 69]. Zhou Shoujuan (1928: vol. 1, pp. 50–51) retells an anecdote from the 1897 elections, when nervous courtesans awaiting the results first heard that a woman named Sibao had been elected *zhuangyuan*. Wang Sibao of Puqing Li, Jin Sibao of Shangren Li, Hong Sibao of Baihua Li, and Zuo Sibao of Qinghe Li each were busy congratulating themselves when the newspaper arrived with the news that the winner was Zhang Sibao of Xi Huifang.

93. See, for instance, *Jingbao* 1920: January 1, p. 7.

94. *Jingbao* 1919: August 9, p. 3; Sun Guoqun 1988a: p. 72.

95. Xu Ke 1928: p. 1; see also Qi Xia and Dan Ru 1917: vol. 2, n.p. [p. 39].

96. Zhou Shoujuan 1928: vol. 1, pp. 72–74.

97. *Jingbao* 1919: October 15, p. 3; December 27, p. 3.

98. Zhou Shoujuan 1928: vol. 2, pp. 27–28.

99. Wang Liaoweng 1922: pp. 79–82; Zhou Shoujuan 1928: vol. 2, p. 1; also see Sun Guoqun 1988a: p. 74. The list of sponsoring tabloids is from Ping Jinya 1988: pp. 166–67.

100. Zhou Shoujuan 1928; vol. 2, pp. 3, 8. For a similar set of comparisons at the end of the Ming dynasty, see Carlitz 1994.

101. Xin shijie baoshe 1918: n.p.

102. On the New Culture Movement see, among many other works, Chow 1960; Grieder 1970; Schwarcz 1986; and Goldman 1977.

103. Wang Liaoweng 1922: p. 98; also reprinted in Sun Guoqun 1988a: p. 78.

104. On 1917, see Xin shijie baoshe 1918: n.p.; on 1918, see Sun Guoqun 1988a: p. 75. In the 1917 story, the son of the governor of Canton bought more than twenty

thousand election tickets and filled them all out in the name of Ju Di. The next day he died of a sudden illness. Elected vice president, a grieving Ju Di was helped to meet her public, her election story blending seamlessly into an account of true love. By early 1919, however, *Crystal* reported that she had eloped with the son of a wealthy businessman. *Jingbao* 1919: March 6, p. 3.

105. *Jingbao* 1919: October 3, 6, 12, 15, December 27; p. 3 in all cases.

106. Sun Guoqun 1988a: p. 76.

107. Yu Muxia 1935: *ji*, pp. 37–38; Wang Liaoweng 1922: p. 95; Sun Guoqun 1988a: p. 75.

108. Sun Guoqun 1988a: p. 76.

109. Sun Guoqun 1988a: p. 76.

110. See, for instance, Xu Ke 1920: pp. 2–4; Wang Liaoweng 1922: pp. 86–98; and Chen Rongguang 1924: pp. 90–95.

111. On business cooperation, see *Jingbao* 1919: April 27, p. 3; *Jingbao* 1929: April 9, p. 3; and *Jingbao* 1935: September 27, p. 3.

112. On sworn sisterhood, which was colloquially known as "exchanging hand-kerchiefs," see Wu Hanchi 1924: p. 9.

113. Wang Liaoweng 1922: 151–52; also see Qi Xia and Dan Ru 1917: vol. 2, n.p. [p. 62].

114. Qi Xia and Dan Ru 1917: vol. 1, n.p. [p. 58].

115. Zhang Shuyu was sometimes said to be from Suzhou (the native place claimed by most famous courtesans), but most reports agree that she was from the less ex-alted region of Jiangbei, north of the Yangzi River. She was said to be unremarkable in appearance and mediocre at socializing and singing, fond of actors and drivers (including some of Lin Daiyu's castoffs), willing to sleep with diseased customers, and generally licentious. When she had a son whose paternity was uncertain, people called him Little Zhu Lu, after the surnames of the two men who were her lovers at the time. In spite of this unsavory reputation, which placed her clearly in the ranks of "bad girls," she attracted the favor of Li Meisun, a close relative of Li Hongzhang. (Li Meisun hosted a massive and very expensive banquet on her behalf, a favor to her that backfired, since her regular customers assumed that she was about to be-come his concubine and stopped visiting her.) When Li was called to Beijing, her business collapsed. In the last years of the Qing, Zhang Shuyu married a man from Beijing and later traveled in the United States with him. On Zhang Shuyu's native place, see Chan Qinshi 1884: *juan* 2, p. 12; Wang Liaoweng 1922: p. 57; Zhou Shou-juan 1928: vol. 1, p. 180; and Ping Jinya 1988: p. 167. On Jiangbei people in Shang-hai, see Honig 1992: passim. On her singing, see Zhou Shoujuan 1928: vol. 1, pp. 178–79. On her relationships with Li Meisun, see Wang Liaoweng 1922: p. 58; and Zhang Xunjiu 1934: vol. 1, pp. 49–64. An alternative version of this story in Chen Dingshan 1967 (vol. 2, pp. 12–13) suggests that Li Meisun hosted this banquet to embarrass Zhang for not valuing her guests sufficiently. Li left her with most of the bill unpaid, returned to Nanjing, spread rumors that he was coming back to take her as a concubine, and ruined her business. For other stories about Zhang Shuyu, see Wang Liaoweng 1922: 57–58; Zhou Shoujuan 1928: vol. 1, pp. 156–57, 178–80, vol. 2, pp. 75–76; and Zhang Xunjiu 1934: vol. 1, 52–53, 55–61.

116. Lu Lanfen, Lin Daiyu's occasional rival in love, was originally from Suzhou. Courtesan collectanea most often tell three stories about her: that she appeared in

a book by a Western scholar as an example of a Chinese beauty; that guests came to congratulate her on her birthday in formal official dress, and were greeted by her five-year-old son wearing an official hat and gown; and that when she died, one of her lovers published an obituary notice that referred to her as "my late wife, the noblewoman." Another account mentions that she used her earnings as a courtesan to enable her brother to attend school, and later helped to find him a job and a wife. See Xu Ke 1920: p. 106; Chen Rongguang 1924: pp. 107–8; Zhou Shoujuan 1928: vol. 1, pp. 177–78; Zhang Xunjiu 1934: vol. 1, pp. 49–52; Ping Jinya 1988: p. 167; Wu Jianren 1935: p. 107; and Chen Dingshan 1967: vol. 2, pp. 10–11.

117. For sources that name these four, see *Jingbao* 1920: May 27, p. 3; Wang Liaoweng 1922: frontispiece; Lemière 1923: p. 130; and Zhou Shoujuan 1928: vol. 1, p. 34. For a completely different set of women, see Zhan Kai 1917: *juan* 3, pp. 26–29. For a summary of an argument by Bao Tianxiao that Jin Xiaobao was thirteen or fourteen years younger than the others and was not one of the Guardians, see Ping Jinya 1988: 167–68. For anecdotes about each of the four, see also Chen Dingshan 1967: vol. 2, pp. 9–14.

118. Several accounts suggest that the Guardians were elected or appointed in a tabloid ritual much like that for the flower roll. Wang Liaoweng 1922: pp. 82–85; Sun Guoqun 1988a: pp. 74–75; Ping Jinya 1988: p. 166.

119. For accounts of the fund-raising drive, see Zhou Shoujuan 1928: vol. 1, pp. 122–23, 148–49. For fund-raising letters written on behalf of the Guardians, see Zhou Shoujuan 1928: vol. 1, pp. 125–28. For the full text of the men's fund-raising notice, full of nostalgia for departed courtesans, see Zhou Shoujuan 1928: vol. 1, pp. 123–24.

120. Zhou Shoujuan 1928: vol. 1, p. 137.

121. On late Qing and early Republican reforms by and for women, which focused on the elimination of footbinding and women's education, see Beahan 1976. On p. 364 she writes: "It was the link feminist writers drew between the improvement in conditions for women and the interests of a strong nation that gained public support for women's education and an end to footbinding. Nationalism also served as the vehicle for the acquisition of a legitimate public role for women."

122. On Lanqiao Bieshu, see Zhan Kai 1917: *juan* 1, pp. 1–3; and Qi Xia and Dan Ru 1917: vol. 1, n.p. [pp. 19–20]. On the rights-recovery movement, see Spence 1990: pp. 252–53. Charlotte Beahan explains that in the 1907 movement to oppose a British loan that would finance the Shanghai-Ningbo railroad line, women were active in raising funds to buy railroad stock. Prostitutes were also exhorted to join. A courtesan handbill that originally appeared in *Zhongguo ribao* on November 29, 1907, read: "Attention! On the Su-Hang railroad matter, the Foreign Ministry is pressing to make foreign loans, but once our railroad rights are gone the pulse of life will be exhausted. All our sisters must form a group, for we cannot abandon our rights. One who is not a citizen is one who is not eagerly sincere about this matter of railroad protection. To plan for today, we need only each to extend our mental force to the limit and resolutely buy stock, so there will be a meeting on the nineteenth at two in the afternoon at the Suqing temple to sell shares in the hopes that we will soon be on the point of good fortune in this." Beahan 1976: pp. 283–86. The text of the handbill is translated by Beahan from Bao Jialin 1974: p. 2.

123. Except where otherwise noted, this account is based upon Wang Liaoweng 1922: pp. 43, 156–57.

124. Wang Liaoweng 1922: p. 151.

125. For a brief biography that characterizes Zhu as "lascivious," see Zhan Kai 1917: *juan* 1, pp. 10–11.

126. Wang Liaoweng 1922: p. 158; *Jingbao* 1919: September 21, p. 3. For an allegation that sponsorship of projects such as cemeteries and schools was basically a way to garner publicity and advance one's career, similar to dressing stylishly and attending the theater, see Zhonghua tushu jicheng 1925: vol. 3, pp. 73–74.

127. The most celebrated instance of courtesan entanglement with national political events is the story of Sai Jinhua, the courtesan credited with saving Beijing from the worst depredations of the Eight-Nation Expedition in the wake of the Boxer uprising. I have not taken up Sai Jinhua's story in this book for several reasons. Although she was a Shanghai courtesan, the most famous episodes of her career took place in Europe and Beijing rather than Shanghai. She was the subject of novels, plays, and poetry, in which her status as a courtesan was deployed in ways far too complex to be summarized here, and these in turn have given rise to studies in literary criticism that explore representations of her in fascinating and subtle detail. In short, she not only deserves, but has already inspired, several books devoted just to her. I offer here only a brief summary of her life story as told in courtesan collectanea, as well as a guide to some of the works written about her.

Sai Jinhua, also known as Fu Caiyun and Cao Menglan, originally from Suzhou, was born in 1874. Her father died when she was young. After an early career as a virgin courtesan, at age thirteen she became the concubine of Hong Wenqing, who had won the first place (*zhuangyuan*) in the imperial examinations. She accompanied him on a diplomatic mission to Europe, where she reportedly met Queen Victoria and had an affair with a German military officer named Count Waldersee. (In true "bad girl" form, she is also said to have had an affair with her husband's servant.) After the death of Hong Wenqing, who was several decades her senior, in 1893, she worked as a courtesan in Shanghai, Tianjin, and Beijing. In Beijing she either began or renewed her affair with Waldersee, and is credited with influencing him to moderate the harsh treatment of Beijing residents during the post-Boxer foreign occupation. In 1908 she mistreated one of the young courtesans who worked for her, driving the young woman to suicide. She was banished to her hometown. Both before and after this time, in Shanghai and Beijing, she had numerous liaisons with opera singers, a railroad official, and a member of the National Assembly. In 1935 *Crystal* reported that she was penniless; in 1936 she died and was buried in Beijing. Information and anecdotes about her life can be found in, among other places, Xu Ke 1920: pp. 118–19; Wang Liaoweng 1922: pp. 59–61; Zhou Shoujuan 1928: vol. 1, pp. 169–72; Wu Jianren 1935: pp. 102–3; Jin Xian 1935: pp. 73–80; *Renyan zhoukan* 1.50 (1935), p. 1,028; *Jingbao* 1935: October 31, p. 3; Bi 1936, p. 12; *Funü gongming* 1936: 5.12 (December 20), p. 27; *Funü yuebao* 1937: January 10, p. 19; McAleavy 1959a: pp. 193–99; McAleavy 1959b, passim; and Chen Dingshan 1967: pp. 79–80.

Sai Jinhua's life was the subject of Zeng Pu's 1905 novel *Niehai hua* (Flower in a sea of evil); see Zeng Pu 1979. Catherine Yeh (1990) has argued that in this novel, the courtesan trope is deployed in a sophisticated critique of late Qing intellectuals, with the courtesan both mirroring ineffective literati behavior and mocking it by behaving more boldly than intellectuals did. She also discusses the leftist writer Xia Yan's 1936 play *Sai Jinhua* (Xia Yan 1984), which she calls "another scathing self-portrait of the Chinese intellectual with all his low moral fibre and political ineptitude." Jon Kowallis (1995) offers a masterful translation and subtle reading of the classical-language prose poem *Caiyun qu* (Song of the rainbow cloud), comprising two parts composed in 1899 and 1904. Kowallis takes a more laudatory view of Sai Jinhua's role as a "cross-cultural courtesan" in a chaotic time. He also mentions a Taiwanese film and television series concentrating on her exploits. In the 1980s and 1990s Sai Jinhua was resurrected as a patriotic heroine in books and articles published in the People's Republic of China and Taiwan, which generally take a positive attitude toward her intervention with Waldersee. See *Zhongwai funü*, 5 (1985), pp. 20–22; Wu 1985; Bei 1991; and Huo 1991.

128. Wang Liaoweng 1922: p. 158; for other letters see also pp. 158–59.

129. *Jingbao* 1919: April 30, p. 3.

130. On May Fourth activities in the courtesan houses, see *Shenbao* 1919: May 10; and *Jingbao* 1919: May 12, p. 3; June 9, p. 3; June 12, p. 3; June 18, p. 3; July 15, p. 3.

131. *Jingbao* 1919: June 3, p. 3. There are no records dating from this period about Shanghai courtesans organizing to improve their own working conditions. In Nanjing, however, courtesans distributed leaflets encouraging their fellows to refuse to make calls at the Nanjing Hotel, where the management was barring courtesans from the main entrance and charging them a fee even when they earned no money from calls. *Jingbao* 1919: September 30, p. 2.

132. *Jingbao* 1919: November 18, p. 3.

133. *Jingbao* 1919: December 15, p. 3.

134. Zhu Zuotong and Mei Yi 1939: part 3, pp. 61–62.

135. For a discussion of the practice and poetics of speaking bitterness, see Anagnost forthcoming: chapter 1.

136. Zhang Xinxin and Sang Ye 1987: p. 32; Luo Qiong 1935: p. 36.

137. Yang Jiezeng 1986; Sun Liqi et al. 1986. This particular piece of oral folklore is buttressed by the fact that the PRC government later undertook research on the effectiveness of tadpoles as an oral contraceptive. The formula under study, as reported to the National People's Congress in 1956, was as follows:

> Fresh tadpoles coming out in the spring should be washed clean in cold boiled water, and swallowed whole three or four days after menstruation. If a woman swallows fourteen live tadpoles on the first day and ten more on the following day, she will not conceive for five years. If contraception is still required after that, she can repeat the formula twice, and be forever sterile. Cited in Tien 1973: p. 249.

The research results were discouraging, however. In one Zhejiang study, women swallowed live tadpoles on two successive days shortly after their periods. Within four months, 43 percent of the women became pregnant, while medical authorities worried that the consumption of tadpoles may have exposed them to parasitic diseases. In 1958, tadpoles were "officially declared to have no contraceptive value." Tien 1973: p. 250.

Methods of birth control used by men never appear in conjunction with descriptions of prostitution. A 1935 description of a condom (*guitou tao*) presents it as an instrument for enhancing male sexual pleasure, much like the penis ring (*yin tuozi*) of Ximen Qing in the novel *Golden Lotus*. Yu Muxia 1935: *shang*, p. 66.

138. Although it was apparently not forbidden under Ming and Qing laws, in the

final years of the nineteenth century and again in the early Republican Criminal Code (articles 332–338) it was illegal for a woman to procure an abortion or for someone else to procure one for her. Kotenev 1968: pp. 417–18; *CMJ* 1928: 42.1 (January), pp. 12–13. A 1926 letter from J. Preston Maxwell, a professor of obstetrics and gynecology at Peking Union Medical College, to a medical-missionary journal published in China states that "criminal abortion" was common in large cities, frequently resulting in pelvic inflammation or death from sepsis. The writer continued, "Besides numbers of drugs sold as abortifacients, I have known of the use of a chopstick, of a portion of root used as a tent, and of a tampon containing some drug whose nature I was unable to ascertain. In addition there are regular spots where the uterus may be needled through the abdominal wall during the early months, for the purpose of producing abortion. . . . And I am afraid that the practice of criminal abortion is on the increase." *CMJ* 1926: 40.2 (February), p. 182. In a 1928 report, Maxwell listed three prescriptions used to induce abortion in the first five months:

I.

14 pc. Cantharides
2 pc. ladybugs
1.5 gms native calomel
5.6 gms scale of pangolin
5.6 gms horse-leech
1.9 gms horse-fly
1.9 gms cast skin of cicada (mixed together, powdered, drunk dissolved in millet wine)

II.

11.2 gms of each of following: root of smallage, root of red peony, Tibetan saffron, peach kernels, sappan wood, xylosma ramemosa, dianthus superbus, achryanthes bidentata, root of ginger-like plant sanleng, root of ginger-like plant mulewort, dried varnish-tree wood. Boiled with water, liquid mixed with musk and yellow wine, with possible addition of rhubarb.

III.

3.7 gms musk
11.2 gms powdered gourd-like plant root
11.2 gms powdered thorns of shittah-tree
1 large white stick of native union root
The first three ingredients are ground with the fourth to make a thick paste, which is placed in a silk bag tied to a thread and inserted into the vagina for one week. [In one case Maxwell saw, use of this tampon resulted in an abortion, but the woman was left with adhesions, fibrous tissue blocking the vagina, and dysmenorrhea.]

CMJ 1928: 42.1 (January), pp. 16–19.

139. Yu and Wong 1949: p. 235; Yu Wei 1948: p. 13.
140. Sun Liqi et al. 1986.
141. *Jingbao* 1919: September 3, p. 3.

142. *Jingbao* 1939: October 31, p. 5. This is a reprint of a 1919 item.

143. Wang Liaoweng 1922: pp. 35–39; Chen Rongguang 1924: pp. 109–110; Zhang Xunjiu 1934: vol. 2, pp. 33–48.

144. See *Jingbao* 1919: April 24, p. 3, for the story of an aging courtesan whose son graduated from middle school.

145. Wang Liaoweng 1922: pp. 183–84; *Shibao* 1929: September 4, p. 7.

146. On Weng's early riches, see Zhan Kai 1917: *juan* 1, pp. 16–19; on her fame and arrogance as a performer in 1899, see Zhou Shoujuan 1928: vol. 1, pp. 58–59; on her descent into vagrancy, see Yu Muxia 1935: *ji*, pp. 56–57.

These themes carried over into social-science investigation as well. A Japanese study of prostitution in Shanghai, much quoted by Chinese reformers in the 1930s, said that Shanghai prostitutes came to one of three ends. The lucky ones became wives or concubines of well-off men, or bought an illegitimate child, educated him or her, and lived off the proceeds. Those of middling good fortune became madams, married poor peasants or coolies, or became women workers or servants. The unluckiest ones moved down in the hierarchy to flower-smoke rooms or nail sheds, suffered or died from complications of venereal disease, or became beggars. The author found that 2.5 to 3 percent of those he surveyed came to a good end, 45.5 to 46 percent to a middling end, and 41.5 to 42 percent to a bad end. A Mu, *Shina kenkyu*, p. 18, cited in Yi Feng 1933b: pp. 33–34. For the original Japanese text, see Hō Aboku 1928: pp. 747–48.

147. On Hu Baoyu, see, among others, Wu Jianren 1935: pp. 120–26; Chen Rongguang 1924: pp. 116–17, 120; Wang Liaoweng 1922: pp. 31–35; Zhang Chunfan 1919: May 6, p. 3; *Jingbao* 1919: October 3, p. 3; and Xu Ke 1920: pp. 123–26.

148. On nostalgia centered on Hu Baoyu and others of her generation, see, for instance, Zhang Chunfan 1919: May 6, p. 3; on ephemerality and Weng Meiqian, see Yu Muxia 1935: *ji*, p. 56.

CHAPTER 7: TRAFFICKING

1. An abbreviated version of the arguments in this chapter first appeared in Hershatter 1992c. For an example of a victim story, see Chen Luwei 1938: p. 21.

2. Women were not the only victims. Many of the reports about kidnapping in Shanghai concerned children who were abducted. See, for instance, *Shenbao* 1875: January 14, April 7, April 16; *Shenbao* 1915: May 16; *Shenbao* 1916: March 18, July 28, August 16; *Shenbao* 1917: May 15, May 16, June 20, November 3; *Shenbao* 1918: March 14, April 20, September 18; *Shenbao* 1921: February 16; and *Shenbao* 1925: December 30. The frequency of child abductions helped to generate a cautionary literature directed at parents, which was somewhat distinct from that directed at potential women victims. Parents were advised, for instance, to help their children memorize their home address, to supervise them in crowded places, not to buy the children of others as servants, to handle any case of a lost child through relief organizations (so that yet another kidnapper could not claim the child), to report lost children to the police, to search the docks in case a lost child had been spirited away to an outgoing vessel by kidnappers, and to use the services of the Anti-Kidnapping Society (*Furu jiujihui*). Huang Renjing 1913: pp. 174–76.

3. Wong 1920: p. 632. Huang Renjing (1913: pp. 179–80) warned his readers not to let children, wives, or daughters go alone to the theater or storytelling houses, and to report harassment of family members to the police.

4. *Shenbao* 1920: November 7.

5. Huang Renjing 1913: p. 171.

6. Huang Renjing 1913: p. 171; on female servants from Subei collaborating with kidnappers, see Xu Huifang and Liu Qingyu 1932: pp. 75, 78. As explained in chapter 2, "Subei" is a geographically imprecise but socially significant term for people in Shanghai whose native place was north of the Yangzi River and south of the Huai River. Subei people were said to predominate in the dirtiest, worst-paid, and least respectable trades in Shanghai. Honig 1989: passim; Honig 1992: passim.

7. *Shibao* 1929: July 19, p. 7.

8. *Shibao* 1929: October 20, p. 7, and August 21, p. 7.

9. For sales to the northeastern provinces of women kidnapped in Shanghai, see, for instance, *Shenbao* 1916: March 23, July 3; *Shenbao* 1918: March 3; *Shenbao* 1921: January 1, April 4, July 18; and *Shibao* 1929: July 11, p. 7. Other destinations mentioned in 1910s, 1920s, and 1930s news reports included Guangdong (*Shenbao* 1916: March 22); Qingdao (*Shenbao* 1916: March 26); Fujian (*Shenbao* 1916: April 6; *Shenbao* 1931: January 22, January 30); Beijing (*Shenbao* 1916: July 19); Tianjin (*Shenbao* 1931: March 24); Japan (*Shenbao* 1917: June 28); and Hong Kong (*Shenbao* 1917: November 15).

10. Huang Renjing 1913: p. 171; Gamewell 1916: p. 210.

11. Hauser 1940: p. 268.

12. For cases where the kidnap victim was a married woman, see *Shenbao* 1915: January 27, February 2; *Shenbao* 1916: April 7; *Shenbao* 1918: March 13 (both mother and daughter were abducted), April 30, September 4, October 9, October 16 (another mother-daughter abduction); and *Shenbao* 1923: May 18.

13. Qian Shengke 1933: vol. 2, p. 1.

14. *Zhongguo jiuji furu zonghui*; literally, "Chinese Society for the Salvation of Women and Children." The records are contained in Shanghai shi dang'an guan 1920s and 1930s: file number Q113-1-14.

Guidebooks and newspapers reported on the ongoing work of the Chinese Anti-Kidnapping Society. Established in 1912 by about thirty Chinese men and supported at least in part by private donations and fund-raising events (such as teas, chrysanthemum exhibits, and raffles) among the Shanghai elite, it had an office on Sijing Road, and hired detectives to search out kidnappers who were traveling by train or ship. By 1918 the detectives had acquired their own steamboat in order to better pursue kidnappers operating on ships in Shanghai, and routinely stopped ships in order to search them for kidnappers and victims. The society publicized its work by writing to local newspapers, describing the ruses used by kidnappers. It advertised in Chinese newspapers, and published photographs and descriptions of children it had rescued, so that their parents could identify them. As its operation became known, women who were working in brothels against their will wrote to the society asking for help. When the society could not locate the origins of kidnapped women or children rescued in Shanghai, it housed them in an old temple that had been converted to a group home, where it also ran a primary school. In 1916 the society reported that since its founding it had helped more than one thousand kidnapped women and children, sending about 60 percent back to their homes and housing the remaining 40 percent. In 1917 the director was Zhu Baosan, whose son was peripherally involved in the Lian Ying murder case (see chapter 6); his annual report for 1917 listed 230 women and children rescued for the year, and a total of 1,349 since 1912. (Of the 230 rescued in 1917, 90 were taken back by their families, 62 were sent back to their hometowns, 15 had died of disease, 5 had gotten married, and 12 children had been adopted.) (A report in *China Critic* (1937: April 1, p. 11) listed the much higher figure of 10,233 women and children rescued by the society from 1913 to 1917.) The society established branches in many other cities that were common destinations of traffickers transporting women from Shanghai, including Changchun, Shenyang, Dalian, Tianjin, and Hankou. In 1935, a report on trafficking in *Trans-Pacific* commented that "[t]he Chinese Anti-Kidnapping Society has done a lot to make the export of children from Shanghai to the South unsafe." "Traffic in Women" 1935: p. 16.

On the institutional operations of the Anti-Kidnapping Society, see Huang Renjing 1913: pp. 175–76; Gamewell 1916: pp. 210–12; *Shenbao* 1916: April 24, August 15; *Shenbao* 1917: May 25, May 27, June 11, November 10, November 11, December 3, December 22, December 24; *Shenbao* 1918: September 7, September 22, October 3; "Traffic in Women" 1935: p. 16; *China Critic* 1937: April 1, p. 13; and Chen Dingshan 1967: p. 142.

Goodman (1995: pp. 254–55) suggests that Ningbo sojourners played an active part in the founding and functioning of the society in Shanghai, and that in an expression of native-place rivalry they routinely searched ships full of Guangdong provincials going home, ostensibly looking for kidnap victims but managing to make off with the belongings of the travelers in the process. Her sources on these conflicts date from 1914 and 1917.

For reports of cases in which the society successfully apprehended kidnappers, sometimes with the aid of the police, see *Shenbao* 1916: July 12, July 15, July 20, August 2; *Shenbao* 1917: June 22; *Shenbao* 1921: February 12, May 6, May 9, May 14; *Shenbao* 1922: July 11; and *Shenbao* 1925: April 6, June 17, November 1, November 22, December 12.

For reports of women or their relatives and friends seeking out help from the society, see *Shenbao* 1917: June 3; *Shenbao* 1918: April 16; *Shenbao* 1920: November 26; *Shenbao* 1921: May 13; and *Shenbao* 1923: February 24.

15. This case entered the Shanghai records of the Anti-Kidnapping Society because the Association of Sojourners in Hankou from Seven Counties in Shaoxing asked its (probably bigger and more powerful) Shanghai branch for help in resolving the case. For other cases in which native-place associations tried to help locate kidnap victims, see *Shenbao* 1915: February 27; *Shenbao* 1923: October 10; and Goodman 1995: p. 249.

16. Gamewell (1916: p. 210) states that kidnapping was one of the most common crimes in Shanghai, and that most of the kidnappers were women. Reports that mentioned that the kidnapper or trafficker was female include *Shenbao* 1915: February 2; *Shenbao* 1916: March 6, March 21, April 10, April 30, July 11; *Shenbao* 1917: May 22, June 13; *Shenbao* 1918: April 7, April 20, April 24; and *Shenbao* 1925: December 31.

17. Yen 1934–35: pp. 302–3.

18. Ge Yuanxu 1876: *juan* 2, pp. 34–36; reprinted in Li chuang wo dusheng 1905:

juan 6, p. 6, and also in Qi Xia and Dan Ru 1917: vol. 1, n.p. [p. 73]. These sources note that because the *fuxiong* often mistreated women and others who offended them, they became known as *wuxiong*, "definitely fierce."

19. Huang Renjing 1913: pp. 172–73; *Shenbao* 1916: July 30; *Shenbao* 1921: May 5, May 7, June 30; *Shenbao* 1923: May 9; *Shibao* 1929: October 14, p. 7; Tang Youfeng 1931: p. 481.

20. See, for example, *Shibao* 1936: March 7, p. 5, in which Wang Suzhen, whose case is discussed below, agreed to visit a lake in Hangzhou with two neighbors; they sold her to a Shanghai brothel instead. "Traffic in Women" 1935 (p. 15) stated that sometimes young women were "persuaded to travel to Shanghai to pick up the easy jobs that are going. Once there they soon learn that there are no vacancies, and then those who have misled them point out an easy way of making a living until a post is obtainable."

21. *Shibao* 1929: April 6, p. 7. Subei, the economically hard-pressed area north of Shanghai, seemed to be a locale where women were frequently kidnapped or sold to traffickers. See, for instance, *Shenbao* 1915: May 13, May 21.

22. Huang Renjing 1913: pp. 172–73.

23. "Prostitution Problem" 1937: p. 13.

24. The connection of Qing Bang and Hong Bang members to the brothels is indisputable, but many of the details remain murky. According to Hu Zhusheng (1979: p. 109), unemployed boatmen in the late Qing moved into managing smuggling operations, brothels, and gambling dens. Some also went to work as patrolmen in the International Settlement, linking police and criminal interests. For a general assertion that Green Gang boss Du Yuesheng was in control of "gambling, prostitution, blackmail, and other vices and rackets" in Shanghai, see Sues 1944: p. 69; for his connections with the French Concession police, as well as similar gangster-police relations in the International Settlement, see Pal 1963: p. 19. Du Yuesheng was reportedly adopted by a madam and possibly introduced into the Green Gang by her; see Zhu Zijia 1964: p. 82. At least two of his concubines also came from brothels. On his connection with the courtesan Han Xiang, see Chen Dingshan 1967: pp. 135–39; Fan Shaozeng 1986: p. 209; and Yu Yongfu 1986: p. 272. On the former courtesan who became the wife of the gang boss Zhang Xiaolin, see Yu Yunjiu 1986: p. 348. For an examination of the Green Gang relationship with the French Concession authorities, which deals mainly with the narcotics trade and anti-Communist activity but also details Green Gang control of the French Concession and International Settlement detective squads, see Martin 1992: passim; on Green Gang connections with the Guomindang in Shanghai during the Nanjing Decade, see Martin 1995. For an account of the scope of gang activities, see Zhu Xuefan 1986: passim, especially the essay by Xue Gengxin. Xue Gengxin argues (p. 98) that a Chinese policeman in the French Concession who was a disciple of Du Yuesheng, and who enjoyed the backing of a French Concession policeman named Volenti, was in charge of trafficking in the French Concession, and that because of this backing no one dared interfere with the sale of young women into and out of French Concession brothels. For a news report that two men involved in the abduction and sale of women from Shanghai to Harbin were Green Gang members, see *Shenbao* 1922: July 5, July 8, July 16.

25. For cases of resale that moved women in and out of such markets, see *Shenbao* 1916: March 29, July 27; *Shenbao* 1922: October 22; and *Shenbao* 1923: January 16, May 12, October 31.

26. Huang Renjing 1913: p. 171.

27. Ma Yongsheng 1930: *juan* 2, p. 9. This work is a reprint of Ge Yuanxu 1876.

28. Wang Liaoweng 1922: pp. 23–24.

29. Huang Renjing 1913: p. 171.

30. Qian Shengke 1933: vol. 2, p. 1.

31. Wang Liaoweng 1922: pp. 23–24.

32. "Prostitution Problem" 1937: p. 7.

33. Chunming shuju 1937: *nüguaizi*, pp. 1–25.

34. Chunming shuju 1937: *nüguaizi*, pp. 1–6, 13–15, 21–25.

35. The Qing code provisions, as discussed in chapter 8, prohibited more activities associated with prostitution, but also did not ban it directly. In the Republican period, individual cities sometimes undertook to ban prostitution, usually with the result that prostitutes moved to neighboring cities. See chapter 11.

36. Kotenev 1968: pp. 413–14. The Provisional Criminal Code of 1912 contained similar language in articles 240 and 242. Stauffer 1922: p. 397; Wiley 1929: p. 81. Police files dating from 1946 cite article 231 of the criminal code on "offending public morality" (*fanghai fenghua*) as follows: "[A]ttempting to make a profit by luring or keeping women of respectable families to have sexual relations with others will carry a sentence of three years or less, along with a fine of five hundred yuan or less. People who attempt to make a profit by causing people to engage in obscene activities are the same. Those who commit the above two crimes as a regular routine will be sentenced to five years or less and be fined one thousand yuan or less." The year of this version of the criminal code is not given. Shanghai shi dang'an guan 1946: file 011-4-162, case 9, p. 30.

37. Shanghai Municipal Council Legal Department 1935: pp. 86–88. "Traffic in Women" 1935 (p. 15) gives the following explanation: chapter 25, articles 313–315 of the Criminal Code dealt with kidnapping. Article 313 outlawed bringing "another into a state of slavery." Article 314 outlawed taking people out of China fraudulently. Article 315 outlawed: (1) abducting a female for purposes of marriage; (2) abducting a female "for lucrative purposes, or with intent that an indecent act may be committed against her or that carnal knowledge may be had of her" (and mandated sentences of three to ten years and fines of up to one thousand yuan); and (3) transporting an abducted person out of China (five years to life). Perhaps acknowledging the central role of parents in these sales, a topic that is discussed later in this chapter, decisions of the Chinese Supreme Court modified this provision to say that "a parent selling a child for purposes of adoption and without knowledge of possible immoral purposes among those who are buying the child, is guilty of no offense."

38. British Foreign Office Records. London: Her Majesty's Public Record Office. FO671–500, 6703/30/46, cited in Wakeman 1995a: p. 345, n37.

39. League of Nations 1924–1946: Document C.164.M.40., p. 21.

40. For instance, Edward Henderson, Public Health Officer for the International Settlement, wrote in 1871: "[A]lthough such transactions are strictly speaking illegal, they are in reality matters of everyday occurrence, constituting a trade which engages considerable capital, and which is never, save under peculiarly aggravated circumstances, interfered with by the native magistrates." Henderson 1871: p. 5. Also see chapter 3.

41. Kotenev 1968: p. 295.

42. Local regulations took precedence over Chinese and international law. "Prostitution Problem" 1937: p. 7.

43. Other crimes included extortion, murder, burglary, and robbery. The total number of solved cases was 2,759; the total number of criminals, 5,189. *Shanghai tebieshi gong'anju yewu baogao* 1929: chart, n.p.

44. For the number of people charged annually from 1912 to 1924, see Kotenev 1968: pp. 315–16. For 1925, see *SMC Report 1925*, pp. 42–3; 56–7. For 1926, see *SMC Report 1926*, pp. 41–2, 55–6. The numbers refer to those charged with trafficking in women and children. For the 1934 numbers of people charged with trafficking in and abducting women, see "Traffic in Women" 1935: p. 15. The Chinese population of the International Settlement was estimated to be 488,055 in 1910; 620,401 in 1915; 759,839 in 1920; and 810,279 in 1925. See *NCH* 1925: December 12, p. 482.

For estimated numbers of prostitutes, see chapter 2.

In a 1932 survey of 359 women convicts in three jails in Shanghai (in the International Settlement, the French Concession, and the Chinese city), 71 (about one-fifth) were serving sentences for abduction (*guaipian*) and another 29 (8 percent) for kidnapping (*bangpiao*). In other words, more than a quarter of all female convicts imprisoned in the city at that time had been convicted of trafficking. Xu Huifang and Liu Qingyu 1932: p. 76.

45. League of Nations 1924–1946: pp. 5–6.

46. According to a 1937 report, the relevant laws on trafficking in the International Settlement were Bylaw no. 36 and article 43 of Police Punishments for Violation of Morals. In the French Concession, the relevant laws were Consular Ordinance no. 183 and the provisions of chapter 16 (221 and subsequent articles) and chapter 17 (237 and subsequent articles) of the Chinese Criminal Code, which was applied by Chinese courts in the concession. "Prostitution Problem" 1937: p. 7. After World War II, the Shanghai municipal government issued regulations prohibiting inducing others to become prostitutes in order to make a profit, or having sexual relations with people for profit. It is unclear how these regulations squared with the municipal government's elaborate schemes to license brothels and prostitutes. The relevant police regulations were 64 and 65. Shanghai shi dang'an guan [Shanghai Municipal Archives] 1946–1948: file 011–4–163, "Qudi jiyuan an" [Cases of banning brothels], case 4.

47. Gamewell (1916: pp. 25–26) notes that among the inmates of the Woman's Prison in the International Settlement were female kidnappers who were serving sentences of eight to ten years at the longest.

48. *Shenbao* 1916: March 6, March 10, April 1, July 20, August 1, August 8, August 11, August 23, August 24; *Shenbao* 1917: November 14, November 28; *Shenbao* 1918: April 19, September 7, October 24; *Shenbao* 1919: May 11, July 17; *Shenbao* 1920: July 11, September 5, November 7; *Shenbao* 1921: February 17, February 19, May 28; *Shenbao* 1922: July 28, October 30; *Shenbao* 1923: January 13, January 15, February 4; *Shenbao* 1925: April 26, November 19, December 28.

49. *Shenbao* 1920: May 11 and May 13. For other stories of escape from kidnappers, see *Shenbao* 1916: July 2, July 9; and *Shenbao* 1919: February 25.

50. *Shibao* 1929: April 6, p. 7. In another case, a Shanghai woman abducted to Fengtian worked as a prostitute there for two years, won her freedom, returned to Shanghai, saw her kidnapper on the street, and had him arrested. *Shibao* 1929: October 14, p. 7.

51. See, for example, *Shenbao* 1919: July 17; and *Shenbao* 1920: September 5.

52. On mothers, see *Shenbao* 1920: January 21; *Shenbao* 1922: October 19; and *Shenbao* 1925: December 1. On aunts, see *Shenbao* 1919: July 17. On great-aunts, see *Shenbao* 1925: June 25. On uncles, see *Shenbao* 1918: April 6; and *Shenbao* 1925: December 16. On sisters, see *Shenbao* 1916: April 27; and *Shenbao* 1920: June 1. On brothers, see *Shenbao* 1925: June 29. On fathers, see *Shenbao* 1918: March 13; *Shenbao* 1920: November 20; *Shenbao* 1923: October 19; and *Shenbao* 1925: November 10. On husbands, see *Shenbao* 1921: February 22; *Shenbao* 1923: May 4, May 8; and *Shenbao* 1925: June 18.

53. See, for instance, *Shenbao* 1925: November 18, December 9. For a case where Gaoyou officials responded to a family complaint about abduction, see *Shenbao* 1920: November 22; for involvement of Haimen officials, see *Shenbao* 1925: April 3.

54. Most of the cases reported in *Shenbao* were handled by the Mixed Court in the International Settlement.

55. *Shenbao* 1880: October 29.

56. *Shibao* 1936: March 7, p. 5; for a case in which a father discovered his daughter soliciting at an amusement hall and reported it to the police, see *Shibao* 1929: June 10, p. 7; for the case mentioned earlier in which a woman was kidnapped by monks, and later was found soliciting on the street by a male relative who informed the police, see *Shibao* 1929: Oct. 20, p. 7.

57. *Shibao* 1929: November 25, p. 7.

58. *Shibao* 1929: July 15, p. 7. For a similar case involving a flower-smoke-room prostitute, see *Shenbao* 1915: June 9.

59. See, among many others, *Shenbao* 1921: February 19.

60. See, for instance, *Shenbao* 1918: April 2.

61. Henderson 1871: p. 9; Huang Renjing 1913, pp. 176–77. The explanation of the term is from "Demi-monde" 1923: p. 787.

62. See, for example, the case of Sun Fengying as reported in *Shibao* 1929: April 19, p. 7. For a case of sale (but not abduction) where a woman testified that she was selling sex in order to clear her mother's funeral debt, see *Shenbao* 1923: January 12.

63. For statements that kidnappings were a minority of trafficking cases, see "Prostitution Problem" 1937: p. 7; and *Shenbao* 1941: November 1.

64. On sale by parents, see *Shenbao* 1918: March 3; and *Shenbao* 1920: February 11. On fathers, see *Shenbao* 1915: May 7; *Shenbao* 1922: July 3; and *Shibao* 1929: July 18, p. 7. On mothers, see *Shenbao* 1915: May 20, May 31, June 12; *Shenbao* 1916: April 29; *Shenbao* 1917: May 22, June 30; and *Shenbao* 1918: September 19. On stepfathers, see *Shenbao* 1875: January 16. On foster mothers, see *Shibao* 1936: March 24, p. 2. On foster fathers, see *Shenbao* 1918: September 11. On mothers' lovers, see *Shenbao* 1915: January 1; *Shenbao* 1916: April 11; *Shenbao* 1917: December 27; and *Shenbao* 1922: July 11. On aunts, see *Shenbao* 1920: November 25. On uncles, see *Shenbao* 1916: July 12; *Shenbao* 1917: November 7; and *Shenbao* 1919: January 8. On future mothers-in-law, see *Shenbao* 1915: June 30. On mothers-in-law, see *Shenbao* 1917: November 21; *Shenbao* 1919: June 27 (this case also involved the father-in-law); and *Shenbao* 1921: January 5. On husbands selling principal wives, see *Shenbao* 1915: January 1; *Shenbao* 1917: December 9, December 24; *Shenbao* 1919: December 24, December 25; *Shenbao* 1920: June 9; *Shenbao* 1922: July 11; *Shibao* 1929: September 20, p. 7; and *Shibao* 1936: March 22, p. 4. On a husband selling a concubine, see *Shenbao* 1918: October 12. On a sister-in-law, see *Shenbao* 1915: February 26. On lovers, see *Shenbao* 1920: November 25; and

Shenbao 1923: October 23. On a friend, see *Shenbao* 1917: May 31. On acquaintances from the same native place, see *Shenbao* 1921: June 29; and *Shibao* 1929: March 2, p. 7.

65. *Shenbao* 1916: April 11; *Shenbao* 1915: February 26; *Shenbao* 1920: January 21; *Shenbao* 1921: June 29; *Shibao* 1929: March 2, p. 7. For other cases (not necessarily involving fellow townspeople) where women were promised jobs as maids or factory workers and then sold to brothels, see *Shenbao* 1916: July 17; *Shenbao* 1922: July 1; and *Shenbao* 1923: May 30.

66. *Shenbao* 1917: December 27.

67. See, for instance, *Shibao* 1929: July 18, p. 7; *Shenbao* 1915: May 31; and *Shenbao* 1917; May 22.

68. See, for example, *Shenbao* 1916: August 3; *Shenbao* 1921: May 17; and *Shenbao* 1923: October 23. In the 1916 case, the woman was sold to a brothel in Yingkou, rescued by a welfare organization, and returned to Shanghai, whereupon her husband declined to take her back and asked for a divorce.

69. *Shenbao* 1917: June 30.

70. *Shenbao* 1917: November 21.

71. *Shenbao* 1917: December 9.

72. In an 1880 case, a woman went to live with her brother after her husband threatened to sell her to a brothel; the woman and her brother later went to the French court to ask that the husband be ordered to stop harassing her. *Shenbao* 1880: July 4. On a husband accusing a wife of selling their daughter, see *Shenbao* 1917: December 17. For complaints brought by a woman's sister against her brother-in-law, see *Shenbao* 1920: March 19, March 26. For the sale of a child bride by her mother-in-law, with a complaint brought by the girl's mother, see *Shenbao* 1922: April 14.

73. For a woman granted a divorce, see *Shenbao* 1920: March 19, March 26. For the Mixed Court judgment returning a woman to her husband after he had sold her to a pheasant brothel (a charge he denied), see *Shenbao* 1919: December 25. For a woman's return to her husband (after he had sold her, and after the court had ordered him to return the purchase price to the brothel!), see *Shenbao* 1921: June 15. For a woman remanded to the Door of Hope, see *Shenbao* 1920: May 7.

74. *Shenbao* 1923: January 11.

75. *Shibao* 1929: June 17, p. 7.

76. In a 1923 case, for instance, a woman came to court to claim her sister on behalf of her mother; the judge said that the mother had to appear in person. Natal family claims on women were not automatically assured by the courts. *Shenbao* 1923: January 17. In another case, a Mr. Weng reported to the police that a girl whom he had bought from a merchant had escaped. The police found that she was staying with her father, so they arrested both of them. The girl's father said that he had borrowed thirty yuan from Mr. Weng and had no money to return, so he sold his daughter to Mr. Weng. But, he added, Mr. Weng mistreated his daughter and planned to sell her to a brothel, so the girl escaped. The verdict: Mr. Weng was fined fifty yuan, and the girl was sent to the Door of Hope. In this case, the court was apparently prepared initially to defend Weng's right to the girl he had purchased. The family then strengthened their claim to her by saying that Weng had planned to sell her to a brothel. Perhaps because of the first sale, the court was reluctant to return the girl to her natal family. *Shenbao* 1923: May 4.

In a 1923 Mixed Court case reported by the *North-China Herald*, a thirteen-year-old girl was found in a brothel by Subinspector Moore, and was arrested along with the brothel keeper. She spent about a month in the Door of Hope. A fifty-five-year-old woman claiming to be her mother made an application through the lawyer Mr. L. K. Kentwell for the return of the daughter. She argued that her daughter (the writer was clearly skeptical about the relationship, given the age gap) had been kidnapped and brought to Shanghai and placed in a brothel without her knowledge. The mother said that she planned to take the daughter back home and teach her to sew and make shoes. The girl asked to stay in the Door of Hope but wanted to see her mother too; the normal rule was for visitors to be allowed once a year, since there were two hundred inmates. The court ordered that the mother be allowed to visit once a quarter. *North-China Herald* 1923: November 3, p. 349.

77. Cited in O'Callaghan 1968: p. 13. For a report in a Chinese women's magazine on the findings of this commission, see "Shijie fanmai funü zhi diaocha" 1933.

78. Shanghai shi dang'an guan 1946–1948: file 011-4-163, case 4, documents 2-6.

79. Cao Manzhi, a Communist official whose work in eliminating prostitution is discussed in chapter 12, suggests that many of the women felt filial obligations to the dead as well:

> Another concept that was especially strong—about 80 percent of them had it—was that all prostitutes were atoning for crimes committed in a previous life, and at the same time atoning for the crimes of their deceased fathers and mothers. So some prostitutes would work for several years, be permitted to return home, and would sweep the graves of their parents, crying out, "Baba, Mama, I have already worked for ten years, and probably still have five years in which I can atone for all my crimes." Because after five more years she would no longer be able to entertain customers. The idea was, "I can face my parents. When you were alive I was not able to be thoroughly filial, but after your death I am atoning for the crimes of the whole family."

Cao Manzhi 1986.

80. Yu Wei 1948: p. 12.

81. Yu Wei and Amos Wong 1949: p. 237. Yu and Wong added: "Our social workers failed to find any outstanding psychological abnormalities among the prostitutes. They are not antisocial though they have no special desire to leave the life they are leading. Only 10% love and care for their guests while 67% have no special feelings towards them, their sole aim and purpose being to make money to support themselves, their children and homes."

82. These figures are derived from Yang Jiezeng and He Wannan 1988: p. 61.

83. For the operation of these networks in the Shanghai cotton mills, see Honig 1986: chapters 3 and 4.

84. Shanghai shi dang'an guan n.d.: file 011-4-162; Huang Yunqiu and Wang Dingfei 1986.

85. *Shenbao* 1941: November 1.

86. Le Jiayu and Xu Chongli 1986.

87. Yu Wei 1948: p. 11.

88. Yu Wei and Amos Wong 1949: p. 237.

89. Huang Yunqiu and Wang Dingfei 1986.

90. Shanghai shi dang'an guan 1946–1948: file 011–4–163, case 19.

91. Shanghai shi dang'an guan 1946–1948: file 011–4–163, case 19.

92. This contract is from Canton, but the author claimed to have seen similar contracts for Shanghai. Henderson 1871: pp. 8–9.

93. *Shenbao* 1920: March 19, March 26.

94. This was the nature of the cases cited in the earlier discussion on trafficking, when families used the courts to reclaim daughters and wives who had been sold without their knowledge.

95. *Shibao* 1929: April 12, p. 7.

96. *Shibao* 1936: March 22, p. 4.

97. "Demi-monde" (1923: p. 785) suggests that most of the *changsan* class of courtesans in the 1920s comprised pawned women, although whether they were pawned by themselves or others is ambiguous. But see chapter 3; most other sources that deal with courtesans mention pawning infrequently. For an estimate (in a work of popular fiction) that half of all *yao er* prostitutes were pawned, see Chunming shuju 1937: *yao er*, pp. 2–3. Most prostitutes in the low-class nail-shed and flower-smoke-room brothels were said to be pawned. Huang Renjing 1913: p. 132.

98. See, for example, Hershatter 1986: pp. 183–84.

99. Henderson 1871: p. 7.

100. Yi Feng 1933a: pp. 40–41; Huang Renjing 1913: p. 131.

101. Wang Liaoweng 1922: p. 24; Henderson 1871: p. 7.

102. Sun Yusheng 1939: p. 165; *Shibao* 1929: July 10, p. 7.

103. *Shenbao* 1920: November 3; *Shibao* 1929: May 29, p. 7; also see "Prostitution Problem" 1937: p. 8.

104. The investigation was undertaken by the Industrial and Social Division of the International Settlement, at the behest of the Shanghai Municipal Council. It included a study of 176 slave girls, 72 girls who had "been sold or mortgaged into a life of prostitution," and 27 contract laborers in industrial enterprises. The report noted similarity among all of these types. Hinder 1944: p. 117.

105. See, for instance, *Shenbao* 1920: June 17, June 25, July 28, December 14.

106. See, for instance, *Shenbao* 1920: December 14; and *Shenbao* 1922: October 19, December 22.

107. Sun Yusheng 1939: p. 165.

108. *Shenbao* 1917: November 29. For a case of a father who pawned his daughter to a madam but took the madam to court for reselling the girl to a brothel, see *Shenbao* 1880: October 27.

109. *Shenbao* 1920: October 4, October 10.

110. *Jingbao* 1924: July 18, p. 3.

111. Lu Wei 1938: pp. 14–15.

112. *Shibao* 1929: September 20, p. 7.

113. See, for instance, Zhou Shoujuan 1928: pp. 181–183; Wang Liaoweng 1922: pp. 63–64; Zhan Kai 1917: *juan* 2, pp. 16–17; and *Jingbao* 1919: August 27, p. 3.

114. See, for instance, Wang Liaoweng 1922: pp. 61–62. For a case of a courtesan who had been hired/adopted out to a more experienced courtesan, but whose parents had to be consulted about the price when a customer planned to buy her out as a concubine, see *Jingbao* 1919: December 12, p. 3.

115. *Jingbao* 1919: August 27, p. 3.

116. Shanghai shi dang'an guan 1946–1948: file 011-4-163, case 12.

117. Shanghai shi dang'an guan 1946–1948: file 011-4-163, case 2.

118. For details of this campaign, see chapter 11 and Hershatter 1992b: passim.

119. Chinese Christian writers used the same argument. Huang Renjing (1913: p. 133) stated that most brothels were places where women were lured or kidnapped, and that therefore all civilized countries prohibited brothels. He advocated that China join the ranks of brothel prohibitors, thereby linking abolition to membership in the community of civilized nations. See chapter 10 for further development of this point.

120. *NCH* 1923: January 13, p. 103.

121. *NCH* 1924: February 2, p. 179.

122. On the arrangement of marriages by the Anti-Kidnapping Society, see *Shenbao* 1917: December 24; and *Shenbao* 1925: December 7. On the Door of Hope, see *Shenbao* 1923: October 31; and chapter 10. On Chinese police regulations for finding mates for women in welfare organizations, see *Shanghai tebieshi gong'anju yewu baogao* 1929: pp. 105–6; and chapter 10.

CHAPTER 8: LAW AND DISORDER

1. The Qing Code contained the following provisions applicable to trafficking and prostitution. Material in parentheses is interlinear commentary in the edition used in the Jones translation. Corresponding pages in the Staunton translation are also given.

"Article 113. Marrying Musicians as Wives or Concubines. Every (civil or military) official (or) clerk who takes a musician (a prostitute) to be a wife or concubine will be punished with 60 strokes of the heavy bamboo. Moreover, the marriage is dissolved. (She will be returned to her family. She will not be returned to her work as a musician. The wedding presents will be forfeit to the government.) If the son or son's son of an official (who will inherit a title) takes [a musician] in marriage, the punishment is the same. . . . " Jones 1994: p. 132 (also see Staunton 1966: p. 118).

"Article 275. Kidnapping persons and selling the person kidnapped." This article provides penalties for people who kidnap and sell honorable persons as slaves, or use the pretext of adopting a child from an honorable family to sell it, or kidnap another's slaves, or kidnap their own relatives. Penalties were also stipulated for brokers and buyers who knew the circumstances under which the person was sold. Jones 1994: pp. 257–259 (also see Staunton 1966: pp. 290–293).

"Article 374. An official or clerk who sleeps with a prostitute.

"1. Every (civil or military) official or clerk who sleeps with a prostitute will receive 60 strokes of the heavy bamboo. (Also use this law to punish embracing and drinking wine with prostitutes.) A go-between [will receive] the same penalty reduced one degree.

"2. If the son or son's son of an official ([who has] a title which is inheritable) sleeps with a prostitute, the penalty will be the same." Jones 1994: pp. 352–353 (also see Staunton 1966: p. 410).

"Article 375. To Buy a Person of Honourable Condition as a Prostitute. Every singer, actor, or musician who buys the son or daughter of a person of honourable condition to be a singer or actor, or takes [a girl from an honourable family] in marriage as a wife or concubine, or adopts a person [from an honourable family] as son or daughter, will receive 100 strokes of the heavy bamboo. If he knows the circumstances, the one who sells in marriage will receive the same penalty [as the one who buys]. The go-between will receive the same penalty reduced one degree. The presents will be forfeit to the government. The boy or girl will be returned to his or her clan." Jones 1994: p. 353 (also see Staunton 1966: p. 410).

According to a 1920 reformer's article, Qing law also penalized those who gave shelter to prostitutes, lived on the earnings of prostitution, or permitted brothels to exist within their jurisdictions. It also forbade brothel-keeping. Full excerpts from his article, which unfortunately do not refer to specific articles in the Qing Code, are as follows.

"1. Any official, civil or military, who frequents a brothel shall be liable to be flogged with the bamboo, the number of strokes not to exceed sixty. To send for girls during a banquet shall be deemed evidence of guilt within the meaning of this act. Sons of officials committing same offence shall be dealt with accordingly. The procurer shall be liable to 50 strokes of the bamboo.

"2. Any prostitute, actor, or singer who buys children from a decent family with the object of training them to follow the same professions or who adopts such as their own children, or who takes a respectable girl for wife or concubine, shall be liable to a sentence of 100 strokes of the bamboo. Any persons who knowingly sell or give their children in marriage to this class of people shall be similarly punished. The dowry and bargain money shall be confiscated and the children ordered to return to their own families. The procurer shall be liable to 90 strokes of the bamboo.

"3. Any person who takes a girl from a respectable family as a concubine, or adopted daughter, or under other names, but abets or compels her to have carnal knowledge with any person, shall be liable to be cangued at his own door for a term of one month;

"Whoever procures any girl from a respectable family to become a common prostitute shall be liable to be cangued for three months, flogged 100 strokes, and banished for three years;

"Whoever sells a girl with knowledge that she will be used for immoral purposes shall be liable to similar punishments. The middleman shall be liable to be flogged and the girl shall be restored to her parents.

"4. A soldier, servant or other person in government employ, who keeps or shelters a prostitute, temporarily and for a short time, shall be liable to be cangued for three months and flogged 100 strokes; one who keeps or shelters a prostitute, continuously and for a long time, shall be liable to be flogged 100 strokes and banished for three years for the first offence, and to be flogged 100 strokes and banished for 3,000 li (1,000 miles) on a second conviction. Any person of this class, who lives on the earnings of prostitution, shall be deemed guilty of violating the law and shall be punished in proportion to the amount of goods or money received; or if he knowingly permits prostitution to exist in the neighborhood, he shall be liable to 80 strokes of the bamboo. If the official in charge of the district fails to discover such offences within his jurisdiction, he shall be liable to be censored and punished.

"5. Any person who keeps or assists in the management of a brothel shall be punished according to law; or a landlord, who knowingly lets his premises to be used as a brothel shall be liable to be flogged 80 strokes and banished for two years for the

first offence; and given 100 strokes and exiled for three years on a second conviction, in addition to confiscation of the house; and whoever permits a brothel-keeper
to be his neighbour shall be liable to 80 strokes of the bamboo." Wong 1920: pp.
633–634.

The 1912 Provisional Criminal Code, cited in chapter 7, replaced flogging with
imprisonment and fines. Stauffer 1922: p. 397.

Sommer (1994: pp. 58–59, 301) points out that until the Yongzheng reign of
the Qing (1723–1736), prostitutes were associated with legally debased (*jian*) hereditary groups. "The purpose of law up through the early Qing, then, was not to ban
prostitution—on the contrary, that business was regulated and taxed—but rather to
maintain the fiction of a fixed boundary between the debased species defined by prostitution, and the common people. . . . " (p. 301). Commoner men could sleep with
prostitutes, although officials were penalized for doing so. When these hereditary
groups were emancipated from their debased status, "the law continued to treat people engaged in such work as a debased group" (p. 59), and to treat prostitution as
criminal conduct (p. 326). For an extended discussion of the legal status of prostitutes from the Yuan through the Qing dynasties, see Sommer 1994: pp. 292–357. He
argues that although the legal codes never stated clearly whether prostitution was legal or illegal, examination of actual legal cases indicates that "prostitution, like all
sexual promiscuity, was illegal for commoner women, constituting the crime of 'illicit sex'" (p. 294). Here the issue was not "the payment of money for sex," but rather
illicit sex of any kind which violated "the sexual monopoly of one husband as the key
to patriarchal stability." (p. 295).

On the Qing and Republican codes, see also Henriot 1988: pp. 67–69.

2. Wang Qisheng 1993: pp. 11, 17. Under sex crimes, the Provisional Criminal
Code of 1912 included adultery, bigamy, enticement, and indecency. The 1928 Criminal Law of the Republic of China used the term "sex crime" mainly to refer to harming morals, marriage, and the family. Wang Qisheng 1993: p. 12. Wang argues that
the 1912 law was stricter than the 1927 law in regulating women's sexuality. For instance, it enabled girls as young as twelve to be charged wth adultery, whereas the
1928 code raised the age to sixteen and classified as rape any sexual act involving a
girl younger than sixteen.

3. Xu Huifang and Liu Qingyu 1932: pp. 73–87. The study was based on interviews with women prisoners and examination of prison records in Shanghai. The authors estimated that at any given time there were between three hundred and four
hundred female convicts in Shanghai. As noted in chapter 7, more than a quarter of
all female convicts included in this survey were imprisoned for trafficking. Of the
thirty-four women (9.5 percent of the total) serving time for sex crimes (*xingyu de
zui*), sixteen had been convicted of adultery (*jianfei*), eleven of enticement (*heyou*),
three of aggressive enticement (*lüeyou*), two of harming marriage, and one each of
harming the moral atmosphere and of escape. One lawyer told the investigators that
sex crimes were actually the dominant type of crime committed by Shanghai female
criminals, but since most of them did not pass through the courts, they appeared as
a relatively small percentage of the total. This was probably a reference to the fact
that solicitation offenses were handled directly by the police; see discussion later in
this chapter. According to the investigators, most female sex criminals were married
women from Subei who had left their husbands in the countryside, come to Shang-

hai in search of factory work, and been induced to commit these crimes by a combination of material and sexual temptations.

4. Stauffer 1922: p. 396. Stauffer (p. 397) does note that the Police Offense Law of December 1915 made it an offense to be an unlicensed prostitute, but the scope and rates of licensing were apparently locally set. For rates and procedures in Beijing in the 1910s, see Gamble 1921: pp. 246–49, 479–80.

Of seventy-one Chinese cities surveyed in 1922, 49 percent reported some variety of tax on prostitution, with five classes of prostitutes subject to taxation in Shanghai. Stauffer 1922: p. 396. Yu Muxia (1935: *shang*, p. 29) specifies that five types of houses were licensed and taxed: *changsan, yao er*, pheasants, salt-pork shops, and opium prostitutes. Wang Dingjiu (1932: "Piao," p. 25) also discusses the licensing and taxation of salt-pork shops. Yi Feng (1933a: p. 40) gives the following description of a salt-pork-shop licensing procedure. When one of these places opened, it purchased a general license (*da zhaohui*) for forty-five yuan. After being granted this license it obtained twelve "small licenses" (*xiao zhaohui*). There was no extra charge for these, but when the brothel owners issued them to the prostitutes they paid four yuan apiece for them. Prostitutes were then required to go with the brothel owners to the police station to have a physical exam and be photographed. Each woman was asked her reasons for wishing to become a prostitute, and was then given permission to begin work. Sun Yusheng (1939: pp. 26–27) gives the licensing fees for *changsan* houses as thirty to forty yuan per season, payable the day the brothel opened. Fees for salt-pork and other types of houses are given as thirty silver taels a month, which included the charge for twelve "small licenses."

5. *CMJ* 1924: 38.1 (January), supplement, p. 11.

6. Kotenev 1968: p. 574.

7. Kotenev 1968: p. 574.

8. *CMJ* 1924: 38.1 (January), supplement, p. 15.

9. On fines levied on prostitutes for operating without a license, see *Shenbao* 1919: November 28; *Shenbao* 1921: May 16, June 4; *Shenbao* 1922: April 10, April 29, July 4, July 24, July 31; *Shenbao* 1923: January 8, February 10; *Shenbao* 1924: November 2; and *Shenbao* 1925: April 12, November 9.

On fines levied on madams or other brothel owners for operating brothels without a license, see *Shenbao* 1920: October 8, October 16, October 30; *Shenbao* 1922: July 1, July 3, July 18, July 31, December 13; *Shenbao* 1923: January 20, February 22, and February 28 (a Russian madam); *Shenbao* 1924: April 4, April 11; and *Shenbao* 1925: April 27 (a male brothel owner), June 8 (landlord allowing tenant to operate brothel).

On fines levied on madams for allowing unlicensed prostitutes to work in their brothels, see *Shenbao* 1920: December 12; *Shenbao* 1921: May 27; *Shenbao* 1923: February 2, February 25, May 5, May 7, May 31; and *Shenbao* 1925: December 18.

On fines levied on madams for changing the prostitutes licensed in their brothels (during the period when some were still licensed) without reporting changes to the police, see *Shenbao* 1921: January 1, May 15; and *Shenbao* 1923: October 21.

On fines levied on licensed prostitutes (during the period when some were still licensed) for hiring unlicensed prostitutes to sell sex under their names, see *Shenbao* 1922: December 3. On fines levied on licensed prostitutes for allowing unlicensed prostitutes to sell sex in their rooms, see *Shenbao* 1923: January 29.

Since prostitutes in the French Concession were required to obtain licenses during this period, operating without a license was an offense there as well. *Shenbao* 1924: April 9.

10. In 1929 *Shibao* reported that the police station on Gedeng Road had received a letter complaining of an unlicensed pheasant brothel on a lane off of Fujian Road. The letter writer mentioned that prostitutes went out every evening to solicit, disturbing the neighbors, and requested that they be arrested and tried. The policemen asked for help from the Laozha police station from detective Guo Akui, who specialized in investigating brothels. At 7 A.M. the foreign constable and several Chinese patrolmen raided the brothel and found that it had two stories and more than twenty rooms, some exclusively devoted to sexual activity. They led the customers out (although it is not clear if they arrested them) and arrested the madam, a Jiangbei woman named Chen née Shen; ten prostitutes; and a male servant—twenty-one people in all. The provisional court judge sentenced the madam to a fine of one hundred yuan or thirty days' detention, the prostitutes to sixty yuan apiece or twenty days, and eight other men and women (it is not clear who they were; perhaps some were customers) to twenty yuan or seven days. *Shibao* 1929: June 17, p. 7; also see *Shibao* 1936: April 15, p. 5. The letter of complaint from neighbors became a common genre by the 1940s; see Chapter 11.

11. The numbers of licenses issued from 1936 through 1940 were as follows:

1936	697
1937	558
1938	585
1939	1,155
1940	1,325

In addition to the quarterly tax on brothels, singing girls (*genü*) were charged a quarterly tax of twenty-four yuan. *Annual Report of the Shanghai Municipal Council* 1940: pp. 299, 307, 295, cited in Sun Guoqun 1988a: p. 112. It is not clear how the total revenue figures were calculated by the Municipal Council, since 1,325 brothels paying 48 yuan every three months should have yielded the much higher total of 254,400 yuan.

12. *Shenbao* 1941: November 1. In 1919, the French Concession police issued a decree that each brothel must purchase a license for the price of ten taels; a 1923 rule required all madams to bring their prostitutes to the police stations to be photographed. *Shenbao* 1919: September 19; *Shenbao* 1923: January 18.

13. After the application was published in the *Bulletin municipal* and processed by the Commission for Classified Establishments, it would be submitted to the Municipal Administration Council. If the council approved the application, a brothel could then pay the stipulated license fees and taxes and open for operation. Brothels were to be open for inspection by government officials or police at any time. For the full text of the regulations, and a list of Category C establishments, see SMP 1928: D4165, August 28.

14. For details of these applications, see SMP 1933–1934: Box 41, D5300.

15. *Shibao* 1936: January 5, pp. 1, 3.

16. So were violations of the regulation against selling opium in a brothel or providing opium implements to customers. On opium violations, see *Shenbao* 1919: December 12; *Shenbao* 1920: January 11; *Shenbao* 1921: January 4, May 4, June 26; *Shen-*

bao 1922: July 14, July 22, July 24, October 15; *Shenbao* 1923: October 1, October 11, October 20; *Shenbao* 1924: December 7; and *Shenbao* 1925: April 1, November 12, December 7, December 30.

The International Settlement and French Concession police kept suspected foreign prostitutes and madams under particularly close surveillance, accumulating detailed dossiers on some of them. In 1928, foreign police detectives submitted to the Shanghai Municipal Police a list of observations of cabarets, cafés, and bars in the Hongkou district that were frequented by Japanese and Eurasian dancers who took customers back to their homes for sexual purposes. Detective J. Haranoff commented of the St. Georges Café, owned by a German: "The dancing girls, employed in this café at that time, were nearly all prostitutes, and while no actual prostitution was ever committed on the premises, arrangements were made by visitors to the café, whereby they met the girls on their leaving the premises and escorted them to their homes, chiefly in Avenue Joffre, for the purpose of sexual intercourse." See SMP 1928: May 17, D1249; and SMP 1928: June 12, D1249 (the quotation is from the latter).

Some of the dossiers provide glimpses into the lives of the European women who operated brothels in Shanghai. The 1935 file on a Polish woman named Pola Gray, for instance, noted that she had American, Russian, German, and Portuguese prostitutes working for her; she first operated a brothel in the French Concession, later one in the International Settlement. Although her file indicates that the house did not entertain Chinese customers, it also contains a translation of an article by a Chinese, from a Chinese newspaper, about the pleasures of a visit to this house. The article begins, "Many Chinese love to taste the pleasures that can be procured with foreign women." SMP 1935: Box 50, D6459.

In 1937, the following announcement in the *Shanghai Evening Post and Mercury* attracted the attention of the International Settlement police: "Miss Paulette, who previously was at 617 Embankment Building, wishes to inform her friends that her new residence is 233 Race Course Rd., Apt. 12, Tel 37965." In her dossier, a Special Branch memo explained that "Miss Paulette Goubert, French, about 30 years of age, is a woman of uncertain morals; she arrived in Shanghai about 18 months ago. According to our information, she stayed in Singapore and Hongkong for several months prior to coming to Shanghai. This woman is very well educated and on several occasions has boasted that she has studied medicine. She possesses a perfect knowledge of English." In Shanghai she frequented the company of European prostitutes and brothel keepers, used the Embankment Road house as "a house of assignation," had to leave her flat because of Sino-Japanese hostilities (hence the address change), and was suspected by the police of using her new house as a brothel. SMP: Box 79, Doc. 8245; the documents in this file mostly date from December 1937.

For other cases, see SMP 1939: Box 97, D9466, October 9 (on Eugenie Yakovlevna Shkolnikovna); SMP 1939: Reel 4, D1249, November 29 (on Vera Gorskaya, a.k.a. Vera Smith); and SMP 1939: Box 98, D9577(c), December 8 (on trafficking in Russians and a Russian madam named Maria Poluhova-Morosenko).

17. From 1912 to 1920, from several hundred to more than a thousand prostitutes each year were charged in the Mixed Court with breaching municipal bylaws, although the bylaw they were breaching was not specified. In 1920, with the campaign to license brothels and then progressively withdraw the licenses, brothels began to be cited as well for the breach of municipal regulations. See chapter 11.

18. When the Zhabei district was temporarily under Japanese control in 1932, gambling dens, opium, and prostitutes were readily available, and plans were made to license brothels in return for a monthly fee. SMP 1932: D-3445, April 27; D-3445, May 2.

19. Duban Shanghai shizheng gongshu mishuchu 1938: 7 (August), pp. 96–98. After the Japanese occupied the foreign-controlled areas of Shanghai in December 1941, they issued an amended version of the 1898 licensing bylaw. Brothels were still included among legally licensed establishments, and massage houses were added to the list. SMP 1942: Box 71, D8149-F13, August 4. The full scope of social changes in the world of prostitution during the Japanese occupation deserves further exploration. Poshek Fu writes of the serious economic crisis in the concession areas of Shanghai from 1939 to 1941, exacerbated by a Japanese economic blockade and serious inflation. He argues that "serious social polarization" resulted, along with "a mood of hedonism" that sent people flocking to the city's amusement halls, brothels, and gambling dens. After the Japanese occupied the concessions the day after Pearl Harbor, the city underwent almost four years of "political suppression, extreme economic deprivation, rampant political corruption, and fin-de-siècle decadence." Poshek Fu 1993: pp. 46–48, 56. For worsening inflation figures and economic conditions after Pearl Harbor, see Poshek Fu 1993: pp. 123–25. Fu writes that during this period, "the few parvenus who had made quick fortunes in speculation indulged themselves in a decadent life of luxury. Casinos, high-priced restaurants, high-class brothels, and opium dens opened everywhere" (p. 125).

Fu also discusses the literary deployment of the figure of the sing-song girl as a symbolic resister in the writing of Wang Tongzhao. See Poshek Fu 1993: pp. 64–65; for the courtesan as epitome of loyalty in a wartime play by A Ying, see pp. 90–91; for a discussion of Japanese promotion of Shanghai tabloids that specialized in discussions of nightlife and pornography, but whose ulterior political purpose was to promote armistice with Japan, see pp. 114–15.

20. Shanghai shi dang'an guan 1945: File 1–62–44, pp. 3–4. The statement about lifting the ban was made by the Guomindang government police chief in 1945; I have been unable to corroborate it with records from the occupation period. Exactly how the lifting of the ban differs from the licensing approach in place through 1941 is unclear.

The same Guomindang police chief included in an internal memo a set of licensing statistics from the occupation period (exact year unclear). The statistics showed 799 *shuyu*, 2,742 guides, 1,327 prostitutes, and 385 masseuses, for a total of 5,253 women. Guide-agency employees outnumbered brothel prostitutes by more than two to one, but it is unclear whether this reflected a change in the overall organization of the sex trades or merely the relative rate of licensing compliance in the two types of establishments. Shanghai shi dang'anguan 1945: File 1–62–44, p. 6.

21. The complex and ever-changing organization of the Shanghai police is described in Wakeman 1995a. For descriptions of the Chinese-controlled police in the late Qing, see pp. 16–23. In 1913 this police force came under provincial control, and after 1927 under the control of the Shanghai Garrison Command (pp. 23–24). In the late 1920s, this Public Security Bureau took on partial responsibility for public-health questions such as tuberculosis, garbage-can repair, public toilets, and the cleanliness of public swimming pools and baths. Wakeman argues (1995a: p. 85) that

the Public Security Bureau cast its larger social mission "in medical terms, as though the police were white-smocked doctors warding off pathological infections. Opium and gambling were frequently described as 'contagions' (*ran*) emanating from the International Settlement and transmitted to the masses via the commercial classes. The job of the police was to 'ban and prohibit opium and gambling' from entering their jurisdiction, much as they tried to quarantine infectious disease in their capacity as public health officials." During the Nanjing Decade the police developed a plan to register births, deaths, marriages, and people moving in and out of households, as well as all guests in hotels and lodging houses.

In 1931, Richard Feetham lamented the lack of coordination among the three police forces: "The areas, policed by the Settlement, the French Concession and the Chinese Police Forces form one definite urban area with no natural boundaries. The boundaries are merely streets, and sometimes pass through the interiors of houses. Factors which affect the crime situation in one area may be centred in another area over which the area which suffers has no control. Criminal gangs, living in and taking refuge in one area, may operate in another area, and the work of crime prevention by surveillance and police intelligence work becomes well nigh impossible. While the police forces do cooperate wth each other to the best of their ability in the circumstances, full cooperation is impossible because of fundamental differences in ideas of police administration. Prevalence of crime in one area is not likely to give cause for anxiety to the police of another area; in fact, there is no exchange of information between the three authorities in connection with the general state of crime. There is no central police control, without which there can be no coordination, no common policy, and little check on the evils that cause the crime situation in Shanghai as a whole." Feetham 1931: vol. 1, p. 159.

22. Shangwu yinshuguan bianjisuo 1926: *juan* 2, p. 27.

23. Shangwu yinshuguan bianjisuo 1926: *juan* 2, pp. 35–36.

24. Most of the court cases mentioned in this chapter, as well as in chapter 7, were heard in the Mixed Court in the International Settlement. I was not able to examine original court records of these cases, and have relied on accounts in the local mainstream press, which sometimes (but not always) reproduced testimony verbatim. The Mixed Court was established in 1864. It brought a Chinese magistrate into the International Settlement, where he sat jointly with a foreign assessor in cases involving Chinese and foreigners. In cases involving only Chinese, the Chinese magistrate alone presided. The scope of foreign control over this system was bitterly contested in the 1905 Mixed Court riots, when a dispute erupted between Chinese and Western authorities over where to incarcerate a Guangdong widow accused of trafficking. The dispute led many Chinese organizations to condemn foreign actions as an insult to Chinese sovereignty, and to declare a general strike. In the ensuing mêlée, crowds of angry Chinese attacked the International Settlement town hall and police stations.

After the 1911 revolution the consular body took over the court and brought the Chinese magistrates under their control, making the court utterly independent of the Chinese judicial system. In 1927 this situation was partly redressed when the Mixed Court was replaced by a Provisional Court, with appointment and payment of judges under the control of the Jiangsu provincial government. Once again Chinese judges adjudicated Chinese cases alone, and even in cases involving foreigners the role of a foreign deputy was made advisory. The Mixed Court in the French Concession followed a similar course of development. In 1930, even this deputy judge system was abolished, and the Provisional Court was replaced by a district court and an appeals court. In 1931, the Chinese government nullified the new rules under which both Mixed Courts had operated, bringing the foreign-controlled areas under the Chinese civil and criminal codes.

In the years prior to 1927 the Mixed Court was in charge of, among many other things, enforcing government regulations on licensing, in which capacity it encountered many brothels, madams, and prostitutes. It also enforced the "land regulations and byelaws, the ordinances, proclamations, and notifications of the municipal council and the Provisional Criminal Code" of the Republic of China, although the assessors sometimes departed from this code to impose additional penalties (Stephens 1992: p. 86). Private suits were also heard there. Its judgments were enforced by the Shanghai Municipal Police, which was under the jurisdiction of the International Settlement government.

The history of the Mixed Court is summarized in Wakeman 1995a: pp. 70–71, 340, n72. Also see Kotenev 1968: passim; Hoh 1928: pp. 162–64; Feetham 1931: vol. 1, pp. 45, 47–49, 99–100, 171–80; and Stephens 1992. On the 1905 Mixed Court riot, see Kotenev 1968: pp. 126–31; Xi Dichen 1933; and Goodman 1995: pp. 187–95.

25. "Shanghai policemen also had at their disposal an elaborate code of administrative laws . . . and police regulations that they were authorized to enforce and prosecute entirely on their own," writes Frederic Wakeman. Penalties for breaching police regulations were set under this administrative law. Wakeman 1995a: p. 91.

26. In the International Settlement, the Chinese courts had jurisdiction over cases which fell under the purview of this law. Responsibility for enforcing regulations on "the management and banning of prostitution" lay with the customs correction unit (*zheng su gu*) of the police department's second section (*ke*). The outer inspectorate of the police was responsible for, among other things, punishing police employees who took bribes from unlicensed sellers of sex. Patrolmen could be fired for protecting prostitution or failing to report it. Shanghai tebieshi gong'anju yewu jiyao 1928: pp. 18, 29, 53.

27. Shanghai Municipal Police: Box 106, D6810. Law of penalties for breaches of police regulations promulgated by the Nationalist government on July 21, 1928, translated into English and annotated by R. T. Bryan, Jr. The translation is dated December 17, 1934. The file also includes an earlier version of the law dated November 7, 1915, translated November 30, 1925, in which the text of articles 43 and 45 are identical. The law was national in scope, with special arrangements for enforcement in Shanghai's multigovernment environment.

28. Shanghai tebieshi gong'anju yewu jiyao 1928: p. 72. Similar regulations were in force in the foreign concessions during the 1920s. See chapter 11 on the movement of prostitution into hotels after the 1920 abolition campaign in the International Settlement.

29. *Funü gongming* 1936: 5, 11 (November 20), p. 22. In the late 1920s and 1930s the Public Security Bureau heard thousands of cases involving breaches of police regulations each year. Wakeman argues that "[t]his quasi-independent judicial authority gave the Shanghai Chinese police force unusual power to regulate social mores." Wakeman 1995a: p. 92. On p. 91 he writes, "Between July 1927 and June 1928, 4,652

adjudicated trials for breaking administrative laws were judged (*panjue*) entirely by the PSB proper, often within twenty-four hours of the misdemeanor." *Shanghai tebieshi gong'anju yewu jiyao, Minguo shiliu nian ba yue zhi shiqi nian qi yue, jishi*, p. 50., cited in Wakeman 1995a: p. 350 n114. In 1930–1931, the police handled 4,844 cases. Wakeman 1995a: p. 350, n114. But in 1929–1930, the number was 38,147 cases. *Shanghai shi gong'anju yewu baogao* [Shanghai Municipality Public Security Bureau report of affairs], vol. 3 (July 1929–June 1930), p. 107, cited in Wakeman 1995a: pp. 92, 350, n166. There were forty-five police regulations altogether, most of them not involving prostitution.

30. Wakeman 1995a: pp. 165, 377, n3. At the end of 1930 the total number was 5,033, of which 4,286 were actual police. *Shanghai shi gong'anju yewu baogao*, vol. 4, table following p. 56, cited in Wakeman 1995a: p. 377. This meant that there was approximately one policeman for every 390 residents of the Chinese-controlled areas. Derived from population figures in Luo Zhiru 1932: p. 21, table 29.

This was not the total number of policemen in the city as a whole. The International Settlement had a police force of 4,879, of whom 3,477 were Chinese. Of the Chinese, 2,936 were constables and another 227 detective constables. Feetham 1931: p. 157. This meant one constable or detective for every 319 residents. Derived from population figures in Luo Zhiru 1932: p. 21, table 29. In 1931, Richard Feetham noted that police work in the International Settlement was hampered by a lack of Chinese officers: "The lack of a sufficient number of Chinese in the more senior ranks is a disadvantage, as proper liaison with the Chinese public, a proper control over the lower ranks in the Chinese branch, and an effective measure of crime detection is not possible unless the Foreign officers are assisted by a sufficient number of Chinese of good social standing, good education and proper training in the higher ranks." Feetham 1931: vol. 1, p. 158.

31. Henriot (1993: pp. 120–21) notes that in 1928, 71 percent of Shanghai policemen were natives of these northern provinces, while only 18 percent were of local origin. He explains that both poverty in the northern provinces, and the fact that the police force had been assembled under an earlier administration by northern warlords, accounted for this high percentage of northerners, and that the Nationalist authorities continued the practice of recruiting former soldiers from the northern armies to be policemen.

32. Henriot (1993: p. 126) writes: "[T]he persons appointed to the directorship of the Public Security Bureau were active military officers commanding units of loyal men. Each director therefore brought in not just his closest associates but also a host of officers and soldiers who fanned out into the Shanghai police forces and left with their patron when he was transferred to another job." Each PSB director also recruited policemen from his own geographic area (p. 128). Henriot concludes (p. 129) that municipal staff in every department were ignorant of local conditions and uncommitted to reform projects, adding, "Such commitment was especially weak among the police, who were notoriously corrupt and who saw a succession of chief officials file past at every level. No one could claim to lead a police force whose chiefs—from the central office to the police stations, not to mention the departments responsible for surveillance and discipline—were constantly being replaced."

33. During some periods, this may have been true in the foreign settlements as well. Hauser (1940: p. 269) comments: "The International Police did not take them

[the prostitutes] very seriously. They were rounded up, at regular intervals, had to spend a night at the station, and got away with a trifling fine that was paid by their keepers: they could start in again the next evening. Nor did the police interfere with those hundreds of 'girl guide agencies' that were scattered all over town and that had become an integral part of Shanghai's million-dollar vice industry."

34. Wakeman 1995a: p. 167. Henriot (1993: pp. 144, 148) notes, however, that expenditures on the PSB accounted for at least 30 percent of the municipal budget during the Nanjing decade, and that the government's motivation in providing such generous funding was that it was determined to suppress political agitation, particularly by the Communists. He sees "the upkeep of excessive police forces" as a major factor leading to the municipal budget deficit (pp. 166–67). In a policing environment dominated by such concerns, it is likely that licensing and soliciting violations by prostitutes and brothels were a low priority. For a survey of attempts by the Guomindang government to regulate social mores and leisure activities in Shanghai from 1927 to 1949, see Wakeman 1995b.

35. Street solicitation was apparently not a feature of prostitution in every city in China. Among seventy-one cities included in a 1922 Christian survey of "commercialized vice," Shanghai was said to have a particularly "unenviable reputation in this regard." Stauffer 1922: p. 396.

Most news reports concerned offenders in the International Settlement and the French Concession. The number of women charged with this offense in the Mixed Court reached a high of 1,234 in 1917, but from 1912 to 1924 the figure was typically a half to a third of that number. Kotenev 1968: p. 315.

36. For news reports of pheasants soliciting, see *Shenbao* 1915: May 24, June 3, June 14, June 18; *Shenbao* 1916: March 20, April 24, April 25, July 24, July 31; *Shenbao* 1917: June 7, June 11, November 12, November 19, November 26, December 11, December 27; *Shenbao* 1918: March 3, March 7, March 18, April 1, April 2, April 8, September 8, September 16, September 23, September 28, October 8, October 12; *Shenbao* 1919: March 14, April 7, April 21, July 15, July 17, July 18, July 27, July 29, August 19, September 1, October 21, November 10, November 12, December 24, December 27; *Shenbao* 1920: May 17, July 26, August 23, November 29; *Shenbao* 1921: February 21, May 16; *Shenbao* 1922: April 3, April 24, December 23; *Shenbao* 1923: May 7; and *Shibao* 1929: July 22, p. 7.

On opium prostitutes soliciting, see *Shenbao* 1915: June 14; and *Shenbao* 1919: April 11.

For news reports of Cantonese streetwalkers, see *Shenbao* 1916: August 19; *Shenbao* 1917: November 16; *Shenbao* 1918: September 2, September 18, October 6; *Shenbao* 1919: January 15, March 20, November 20; and *Shenbao* 1922: July 3, July 31.

On Russian prostitutes, see *Shenbao* 1925: April 12.

37. On women jumping bail, see *Shenbao* 1918: October 8; *Shenbao* 1919: March 14; and *Shenbao* 1920: December 18. On detention in place of a fine, see *Shenbao* 1919: November 18.

38. *Shenbao* 1915: May 14, June 12, June 14; *Shenbao* 1917: June 22, June 26, November 24; *Shenbao* 1918: March 22, April 25; *Shenbao* 1919: April 11; *Shenbao* 1921: January 24, June 2, June 17; *Shenbao* 1922: December 16; and *Shenbao* 1923: February 24. On madams serving one to two weeks of detention, see *Shenbao* 1920: December 10; on a madam sentenced to four months, see *Shenbao* 1923: October 22.

39. *Shenbao* 1917: November 12.
40. *Municipal Gazette* 1930: March 21, p. 80.
41. *Renyan zhoukan* 1934: 1, 4 (March 10), p. 74. For a description of the same phenomenon in Guangzhou, see *Shenghuo zhoukan* 1933, 8, 47 (November 25), pp. 965, 967–68. The author of this article argues that unlicensed prostitutes had an advantage over licensed prostitutes during this period, since they could cut their prices and be flexible about where and how they conducted business in order to maximize the possibility of making ends meet. They also, of course, had no tax liability.
42. *Funü gongming* 1934: 3, 12 (December), p. 54; Yu Muxia 1935: *shang*, pp. 24–25.
43. *Shenbao* 1941: October 31.
44. Chief Xuan wrote to four of his busiest branch stations in September 1946:

> Eliminating prostitutes engaged in street soliciting has been strictly ordered many times by this department; this is a matter of record. We have discovered that your implementation of this order has not been thorough. The busy streets in the districts under your control are still full of prostitutes when evening comes, aggressively soliciting customers. The local police ignore this. This not only looks bad, but destroys the reputation of the police. We order each branch station to respect all previous orders, to strictly order the police under your command to truly eliminate prostitution. Do not continue to ignore this order and to make the same mistake.

Shanghai shi dang'anguan 1946–1948: File 001–4–170.

The memos to subordinates are dated July 31, August 7, and September 24, 1946 (from which the quotation is drawn). The report on detained prostitutes is dated August 13, 1946.

45. Shanghai shi dang'anguan 1946–1948: File 001–4–170. See, for example, the memos of February 17, 1947, and January 26, 1948.
46. On married prostitutes soliciting, see *Shenbao* 1919: November 17; and *Shibao* 1929: August 26, p. 7.
47. On fights, see *Shibao* 1929: June 27, p. 7. On bribes, see *Shenbao* 1925: April 29.
48. Peters 1937: pp. 205–8.
49. *Jingbao* 1935: October 5, p. 3.
50. Tian Xiao [Bao Tianxiao?] 1922b: pp. 1–5.
51. For a collection of these voices and arguments, see Pheterson 1989: passim; and McClintock 1993.
52. Shanghai shi dang'anguan 1946–1948: File 001–4–170. The letter dates from April 20 of either 1946 or 1947.
53. Shanghai shi dang'anguan 1946–1948: File 001–4–170. The report dates from July 31, 1946.
54. *Jingbao* 1935: October 5, p. 3. For stories of Suzhou prostitutes filling out license application forms with similar language, see *Shizheng pinglun* 1936: April 16, p. 31.
55. Stauffer 1922: p. 396.
56. In the Chinese city, this was apparently a condition under which brothels obtained their licenses. Sun Yusheng 1939: p. 27.
57. Annual totals from 1912 to 1924 of cases heard before the Mixed Court in

which Chinese were accused of allowing children under sixteen in brothels are given in Kotenev 1968: p. 314.

58. On girls being remanded to relatives, see *Shenbao* 1916: March 5; *Shenbao* 1919: October 15; *Shenbao* 1920: October 20, December 8, December 31; *Shenbao* 1921: January 1, May 11; *Shenbao* 1923: February 7, October 3; *Shenbao* 1925: April 22.

On girls sent to the Door of Hope, see *Shenbao* 1916: March 3, March 5, April 26; *Shenbao* 1919: April 30; *Shenbao* 1920: October 14, October 23, November 2, November 3, November 29, December 2, December 5, December 21, December 24; *Shenbao* 1921: May 10; *Shenbao* 1924: December 7; and *Shenbao* 1925: April 17.

59. On fines, see *Shenbao* 1916: March 3, March 5, April 26; *Shenbao* 1918: October 18; *Shenbao* 1919: April 2, April 30, May 7, July 30, October 15; *Shenbao* 1920: October 20, November 3, December 5, December 21, December 31; *Shenbao* 1921: January 1, January 11, February 12, May 1, May 10, May 11, June 10, June 19; *Shenbao* 1923: February 7; and *Shenbao* 1925: April 16, April 22, December 30. For a hundred-yuan fine (where the madam was both keeping young girls and selling opium), see *Shenbao* 1925: April 1.

On jail sentences, see *Shenbao* 1919: July 18; and *Shenbao* 1920: October 14, October 23, November 2. In 1925, after brothels had been made illegal in the International Settlement, a madam named Zhang née Wu was sentenced to serve six months in jail and then be expelled from the Settlement for running an illegal brothel in which she kept, and regularly beat, several young girls. *Shenbao* 1925: April 17.

60. *Shenbao* 1915: January 6, January 13. For other cases of brothels keeping young girls to train them to perform songs from plays, see *Shenbao* 1919: July 25, July 30; and *Shenbao* 1920: December 31.

61. *Shenbao* 1920: December 8. For other cases where the madams retained lawyers, see *Shenbao* 1919: May 7; and *Shenbao* 1920: December 21.

62. *Shenbao* 1919: October 15.

63. In one case, a brothel servant let her twelve-year-old daughter, who had already been engaged at the age of three and who apparently lived with her in-laws, stay overnight with her in the pheasant brothel where she worked. In court, the mother asked for permission to return her daughter to her in-laws. *Shenbao* 1919: February 19. In another, a ten-year-old had been purchased by a brothel servant who let her stay overnight in the establishment. *Shenbao* 1920: October 14. For other cases of servants allowing their daughters to stay at their places of work, see *Shenbao* 1920: October 24, December 2.

64. *Shenbao* 1919: April 30. In this case the court turned the daughter, and three other girls from the same brothel, over to the Door of Hope. On a mother ordered to close her brothel, see *Shenbao* 1920: October 1. On daughters who visited their mothers who were madams, where the madams were fined but given their daughters back, see *Shenbao* 1925: April 16. On a madam who claimed that the girl in question was her mother's adopted daughter, who lived in the house next door, see *Shenbao* 1921: January 6.

65. On unsuccessful custody claims, see *Shenbao* 1918: October 18; and *Shenbao* 1921: January 11, June 10. On the successful custody claim, see *Shenbao* 1921: June 19, June 26.

66. *Shenbao* 1917: November 9.

67. *Shenbao* 1916: March 27; *Shenbao* 1921: January 10.

68. *Shenbao* 1918: April 17; *Shenbao* 1919: October 24; *Shenbao* 1920: September

6. Also see *Shenbao* 1919: September 21 for the story of a man sentenced to nine months in prison for beating a prostitute in a Cantonese brothel in Shanghai and stealing her jewelry. For a case of customers arrested for brawling in an opium brothel, see *Shenbao* 1917: November 23.

69. *Shenbao* 1880: October 11.

70. In 1922, for instance, a madam from Hankou found one of her missing prostitutes in Shanghai, and the police arrested both the prostitute and her customer Mr. Chen, charging the latter with abduction. The prostitute told the police that she did not want to sell sex, so she had fled to Shanghai with Mr. Chen and both of them had gotten jobs there in a cigarette factory. *Shenbao* 1922: December 17, December 18. A few weeks later a Nanjing madam located one of her prostitutes who had fled to Shanghai with a customer, been abandoned by him, and gone to work in a Shanghai pheasant brothel. When the prostitute refused to return to Nanjing with the madam, and the two quarreled publicly, the police arrested both of them, sending the prostitute to the Door of Hope and fining her new Shanghai madam for employing her without a license. *Shenbao* 1922: December 27.

71. *Shibao* 1936: April 9, p. 5.

72. See, for instance, *Shenbao* 1920: September 5, October 8.

73. This was not a successful intervention: the madam and her husband were jailed, and the prostitute was freed. *Shenbao* 1920: November 27.

74. *Shibao* 1936: March 25, p. 5.

75. On brothel props in courtesan houses, see Sun Yusheng 1939: pp. 31–33. Sun complained that powerful props made prostitutes into "monopoly goods" and intimidated other guests. On props and counterfeit trademarks in pheasant houses, see Wang Liaoweng 1922: p. 24; Wu Hanchi 1924: p. 11; and Qian Shengke 1933: vol. 2, p. 3. On hoodlums who become lovers of madams and protected brothels, see Huang Renjing 1913: p. 180. On the case of a rascal hired to protect a Cantonese brothel, see *Shenbao* 1880: July 25.

76. Qian Shengke 1933: vol. 2, p. 3.

77. *Jingbao* 1924: April 24, p. 3. Martin (1992: pp. 273–74) says that Huang Jinrong, who was simultaneously a gang boss and a detective in the French Concession police, "either protected or controlled all of the opium *hongs*, gambling joints, and brothels in the French Concession."

78. Wu Hanchi 1924: p. 6.

79. *Shibao* 1929: September 30, p. 7.

80. On cups of tea, see Banchisheng 1891: *juan* 2, pp. 3–4. On police and detectives as protectors of trysting places, see Wu Hanchi 1924: p. 17. On a Chinese policeman in the International Settlement who was the lover of a madam—and who was arrested for purchasing a young rural woman for her—see *Shenbao* 1915: May 21.

81. Kotenev 1968: p. 295.

82. Banchisheng 1891: *juan* 2, p. 14; *Shenbao* 1880: July 4; Huang Shiquan 1975: p. 198. The woman in the 1880 case was seeking permission to marry (*congliang*).

83. In this case, having removed the madam from a position of control over Wang, the courts and welfare workers installed themselves instead. The Western female director of the Door of Hope denied Wu's request to marry Wang Yueying. Wu hired a lawyer and went to court, where a judge ruled that he could marry Wang after she spent a month confined in a relief organization. Unwilling to wait, the couple mar-

ried immediately, for which act the court fined Wu five hundred yuan but permitted him to keep his new wife. *Shenbao* 1917: May 10, May 25, June 27, June 29.

84. *Shenbao* 1921: February 3.

85. Bao Tianxiao 1973: pp. 105–10.

86. *Jingbao* 1929: February 18, p. 3; April 15, p. 3; March 15, p. 3. This last suit against an adoptive mother was not unique. In 1929, another prostitute fled her own mother, who had forced her to engage in prostitution, and engaged a lawyer to petition the Provisional Court to order the mother not to interfere with her freedom. *Shibao* 1929: May 23, p. 7.

87. *Shibao* 1929: April 8, p. 7.

88. *Shenbao* 1875: April 26, April 27.

89. *Shenbao* 1916: March 19; *Shenbao* 1919: May 5.

90. *Shenbao* 1917: November 7; *Shibao* 1929: April 8, April 12, July 15, November 16; p. 7 in all cases.

91. For cases of battering in pheasant brothels, see *Shenbao* 1920: January 29, November 6; *Shenbao* 1923: January 31; *Shenbao* 1924: March 21; and *Shibao* 1936: February 10, p. 4. For flower-smoke rooms, see *Shenbao* 1915: May 7, May 9; and *Shenbao* 1916: July 8. For a case in a courtesan house (called a *shuyu* in the news report), see *Shibao* 1929: November 16, p. 7. For cases in which the type of brothel was not specified, see *Shenbao* 1918: March 13, April 4, September 25; *Shenbao* 1922: April 24, December 4, December 6; *Shenbao* 1923: May 18, May 24; and *Shibao* 1929: July 6, p. 7. For a case of torture by a male brothel owner or servant, see *Shenbao* 1918: March 26.

92. Chunming shuju 1937: *zhiji*, pp. 2–6. For a similar story in which a prostitute was beaten with bamboo and stabbed with a hairpin by her madam, see Qian Shengke 1933: vol. 2, pp. 10–11.

93. *Shibao* 1929: May 29, p. 7.

94. See, for instance, *Shenbao* 1917: May 11 and May 13, for the story of a fifteen-year-old sold to a brothel by her father-in-law and mistreated by her madam. She fled with a customer, and both were picked up by the police. The customer was sentenced to a year in prison for abduction, and the girl was sent to a philanthropic organization, after which her family in Hunan was supposed to be notified to come get her.

95. *Shenbao* 1918: March 28; *Shenbao* 1921: May 3; and *Shenbao* 1923: January 23. For the suspected case of murder, see *Shenbao* 1918: September 12, September 13, October 23.

96. *Shibao* 1929: July 31, p. 7.

97. *Shenbao* 1919: October 10, November 10, November 28; *Shenbao* 1925: June 3; *Shibao* 1936: May 5, p. 5. For the robbery of a U.S. sailor in a Cantonese brothel, see *Shenbao* 1923: May 8. Foreign prostitutes in Shanghai apparently engaged in theft as well. SMP (Box 69, D8059, "Crime Diaries") reports the arrest of a Russian prostitute, Marie Feoktistova, for stealing $145 from an American sailor. The report, dated September 11, 1939, comments: "Upon being interrogated regarding the reported amount of U.S. $145.00 stolen she denied that this amount was correct however she did admit that since the theft she has bought a $55.00 wrist watch, redeemed property from pawnshops to the value of $33.00, paid 2 months house rent in advance and further having bought a quantity of new gramophone records. The female when questioned could produce no proof that the above transactions had been done with her own money."

98. *Shenbao* 1916: April 7.

99. *Shibao* 1929: February 23.

100. Lu Wei 1938: pp. 14–15.

101. *Shenbao* 1915: January 4, January 29; *Shenbao* 1916: July 6; *Shenbao* 1919: September 11.

102. *Shenbao* 1920: November 16; *Shenbao* 1922: December 3, December 12.

103. See cases cited in chapter 3. See also *Shenbao* 1875: April 29; *Shenbao* 1917: May 10; *Shenbao* 1918: September 14, September 24, September 28; *Shenbao* 1919: January 15; *Shenbao* 1923: October 14; *Shibao* 1928: January 28, p. 6; and *Shibao* 1929: December 10, p. 7.

104. *Shenbao* 1919: May 18; *Shenbao* 1916: April 22; *Shenbao* 1918: March 4; *Shenbao* 1920: August 9.

105. *Shibao* 1929: Dec. 27, p. 7.

106. *Shenbao* 1917: December 9.

CHAPTER 9: DISEASE

1. "Venereal" disease, although it eventually came to mean disease transmitted by sexual means, derives its name from the Greek goddess Venus, and in Victorian parlance carried connotations of lust and lasciviousness. This may be why it has been discarded in recent years in favor of the coolly scientific term "sexually transmitted disease." The Chinese terms are no less freighted: *hualiu bing*, or "flower and willows" disease, is a clear reference to prostitutes (a classical phrase for frequenting brothels was "seeking the flowers and asking after the willows"). Probably the closest equivalent to the sanitized term STD is *xingbing*, sex diseases, which is used in some Republican and most contemporary writings. The Chinese names for particular STDs are a veritable riot of colorful description, cataloged in 1918 by K. C. Wong. For syphilis: strawberry sore, Canton sore, heavenly vesicles sore, fruit sore, cotton sore, nutmeg sore, rotten strawberry sore, strawberry pea, strawberry pox, strawberry poison, climatic sore, evil sore, collection of poison, strawberry leak, strawberry wind, goose web wind, strawberry scurf, leaky foot wind. Genital chancres were known by various names, including lower sore, open sore, jealousy sore, eaten away sore, fighting semen sore, candlestick chancre, turned up sleeve chancre, eaten away chancre, itchy chancre, spiral grooved chancre. Buboes were called fish mouth, transverse groin chancre, genital poison, cancerous sore, and transverse swelling. Gonorrhea was known as, among other terms, lymph turbid, white discharge, and white and turbid. K. C. Wong, "Notes on Chinese Medicine," *CMJ* 1918: 32.4, pp. 351–53. In this chapter, I have used the terms "venereal disease" and "sexually transmitted disease" interchangeably, since the former, although out of fashion, is predominant in the English-language sources I consulted.

2. Wong and Wu 1936: p. 255.

3. Henderson 1871: pp. 3–4. Macpherson (1987: p. 224) gives Henderson a somewhat different reading, saying that he places blame for STDs more on transient sailors than on prostitutes.

4. Henderson 1871: pp. 3, 16, 21, 27–28, and passim. On p. 27, he commented that venereal disease among natives also posed a threat to foreigners when they selected possibly infected Chinese wet-nurses for their infants.

5. Gordon 1884: p. 146. In 1869, Henderson himself attempted to inspect brothels in the Hongkou section. He wrote: "These houses were for the most part dark, dirty and unfurnished, and all that were visited were alike destitute of appliances necessary for those ablutions which, according to many, form the best preventative against disease." He was unable to conduct thorough physical examinations because of "the prejudices of the women, the absence in many cases of the necessary light, and in all of the necessary privacy." *CMJ* 1924: 38.1 (January), supplement, pp. 1–2; see pp. 3–8 for a detailed discussion of the failure of inspection efforts before 1877; also see Macpherson 1987: pp. 219–35. For a brief account of inspection efforts during this period, see also Henriot 1988: pp. 73–76.

6. The most detailed account of the lock hospital's history is found in Macpherson 1987: pp. 213–58. Macpherson places the lock-hospital debates in Shanghai within the context of discussions in Britain and France during the same period, particularly the Contagious Diseases Act of 1866 in Britain. Macpherson emphasizes the lack of resources allocated for the Shanghai hospital's operation, as well as the role of top British Navy officials in promoting the hospital. Macpherson's conclusion (p. 250) is that the system of inspections was "restricted in scope, partial in application, and highly discriminatory."

7. *CMJ* 1924: 38.1 (January), supplement, pp. 8–11. The French Council agreed to cooperate in these efforts. Henderson also noted that foreign prostitutes would be difficult to examine because the government lacked the necessary authority. Henderson 1871: p. 28.

In the French Concession, the police were in charge of inspecting brothels and examining inmates, but in the 1870s the French Concession had no lock hospital. Nor did prostitutes from the French Concession use the International Settlement lock hospital. Macpherson 1987: pp. 230, 243.

8. Special Vice Committee 1920: pp. 83–84.

9. *CMJ* 1924: 38.1 (January), supplement, pp. 13–15. Macpherson (1987: pp. 250–55) explains Henderson's response as a reaction not only to the actual operation of the Shanghai hospital, but also to the "evisceration" and effective repeal of the Contagious Diseases Act in the 1880s. At the new facility, Macpherson adds, treatment was limited "to prostitutes who when arrested were discovered to be infected, and to those who presented themselves at the Isolation Hospital" (p. 257).

10. *CMJ* 1924: 38.1 (January), supplement, p. 3.

11. Special Vice Committee 1920: p. 83.

12. It was discontinued by vote of the 1920 Annual Ratepayer's Meeting in the International Settlement. Stauffer 1922: p. 397.

In the French Concession, where brothels remained licensed (see chapter 11), physical examinations could be required by the police at any time. On September 30, 1932, the French consul general, James Meyrier, issued the following regulation

"Regarding Article XIII of the Municipal Regulation of Organization

Have ordered and order that which follows:

1. Brothel keepers are forbidden to employ or receive women having any contagious disease.

2. The Director of the Police Services may, at any time, oblige women in brothels to submit to a medical examination.

3. The licenses of women found to be suffering from a contagious disease will immediately be withdrawn and a Police fine of from $5.00 to $50.00 for each sick woman will be inflicted on the tenant of the house. In the case of repetition of the offence the establishment may be closed by the Police at the decision of the Consul-General of France." Shanghai Municipal Police 1932: September 30, File D4165.

13. *Municipal Gazette* 1921: February 3, pp. 35–36.

14. *Municipal Gazette* 1921: May 26, p. 196; *CMJ* 1923: 37.3–4 (March-April), p. 343; 37.9 (September), p. 794.

15. The clinic was founded in 1922. For reports of its founding, see *NCH* 1923: October 6, p. 63; October 20, p. 151. The 469 patients examined in 1926 offered the following account of how they became infected:

By Chinese prostitutes	64%
By Russian prostitutes	27%
By Japanese prostitutes	5%
By other nationalities	4%

SMC Report 1926: pp. 195–96.

Henriot (1992: p. 108) summarizes by year the number of cases treated by this clinic from 1923 to 1940.

16. Henriot (1992) provides a meticulous survey of the articles on venereal disease in this journal. As he points out, the journal began in 1905 as the *China Missionary Medical Journal,* published by the China Missionary Medical Association, which was founded in 1886. It became a bimonthly in 1905, then a monthly in 1923, changing its name to *China Medical Journal.* Meanwhile, the emergent Western-trained Chinese medical community in 1915 set up a National Medical Association, which published the *National Medical Journal of China.* The two journals merged in 1932 under the name *Chinese Medical Journal.*

17. Henriot 1992: p. 104. Also see chapter 11. The 1920 initiative was undertaken by foreigners in Shanghai, the 1928 initiative by the national government in Nanjing. Both failed.

18. Percentage of patients with syphilis ranged from 1.18 percent in a 1933–1934 study of 2,367 female patients to 53.3 percent in a 1916–1917 study of 120 patients taking a Wasserman test. For reports on nine different studies, see *CMJ* 1917: 31.1 (January), pp. 48–50; *CMJ* 1917: 31.6 (November), p. 567; *CMJ* 1924: 38.1 (January), supplement, pp. 19–20; *CMJ* 1924: 38.1 (January), supplement, p. 21 (for further commentary on this study see *CMJ* 1927: 41.1 [January], p. 29); and *CMJ* 1935: 49 (October), p. 1,125.

19. Most of their studies were confined to one city or province; some surveyed all patients in a single hospital, others all the patients who had undergone blood tests, still others a particular occupational group. A survey by Christian Henriot of venereal-disease studies published between 1917 and 1932 states that they found syphilitics constituting anywhere between 3.3 and 50.9 percent of patients tested, depending upon the type of study and the target population. Henriot 1992: pp. 106–7.

20. *CMJ* 1935: 49 (October), p. 1,126.

21. Yu Wei 1947: p. 17.

22. *CMJ* 1927: 41.1 (January), p. 30. Dr. L. F. Heimburger commented in a study of two thousand syphilis cases in Shandong: "There is no doubt that syphilis is rapidly spreading throughout China. With war and the constant migration of soldiers the spread is hastened." *CMJ* 1927: 41.6 (June), p. 542. Describing syphilis among Chinese soldiers in Swatow (Shantou), Guangdong, in 1928 Drs. Daniel Lai and Sucheng Wang Lai elaborated on the connection between soldiers and prostitutes, after finding that 22 percent of 310 wounded soldiers had syphilis: "Since the Revolution of 1911, China has had a continuous civil war and each new outbreak tends to increase the number of newly-recruited soldiers and the movements of troops. At present, among the nations of the world, she is said to have the largest standing army, reaching the mark of two million men. Moreover, prostitution is legalized in the Chinese cities and many local governments derive much money through the Prostitution Bureau (*huajuan ju*) without medical supervision of the prostitutes. Browning in England did Wassermann tests on 104 prostitutes, and found 100% positives, and if this is also true in China, then prostitution is the biggest factor in increasing syphilitics among Chinese soldiers." *CMJ* 1928: 42.8 (August), pp. 559, 561. See also Henriot 1992: pp. 109–10.

High rates of infection dated from the nineteenth century. An 1864 report on the health of the police force referred to venereal disease as the most prevalent disease among police. In 1870, Police Surgeon Henderson found that among thirty-seven foreigners on the police force, 541 days had been lost to disease, 205 of these on account of venereal disease. Army health reports in 1862 and 1863 (in 1862 European troops occupied Shanghai) showed 234.2 cases of venereal disease per 1,000 men (1862) and 221.1 per 1,000 men (1864) among soldiers stationed in Shanghai and Dagu (Tianjin). Henderson 1871: pp. 22–23.

23. Henderson 1871: p. 26; Henriot 1992: p. 110.

24. For studies giving the incidence of STDs in prostitutes in various cities, see *CMJ* 1927: 41.6 (June), p. 544; *CMJ* 1930: 44.6 (June), p. 561; Mai Qianzeng 1931; [Shanghai] *Dagong bao* 1946: March 7; *CMJ* 1948: 64, pp. 389–90; *CMJ* 1948: 66, pp. 312–18; and Yu Wei 1948: p. 13.

25. Wong 1920: p. 632.

26. *CMJ* 1928: 42.7 (July), p. 547.

27. *Shenbao* 1941: October 31–November 3. This series of articles was translated by Ke Chun from the *China Press* (*Dalubao*), a foreign-language newspaper in Shanghai; the name of the original author is not given.

28. Yu Wei 1948: pp. 11, 13.

29. "Chinese native practitioners have been using mercury by mouth or inhalation for centuries. Metallic mercury and crude calomel are given in huge doses. One patient stated that he had taken 3 ounces (Chinese) of metallic mercury in a single dose. . . . Fumigations with burning calomel and metallic mercury are frequent procedures for introducing mercury in the body." *CMJ* 1927: 41.6 (June), p. 548. See also Gordon 1884 (pp. 144–45), which describes treatments in use for two thousand years as follows: calomel, cinnabar, and realgar were used. Then prescriptions were given to counter the "poison of the calomel." Mercury was used in fumigations and vapor mercurial baths. Lead and mercury were fumed together with mace, cinnabar, and other substances. All ingredients were pulverized, wrapped in paper, formed into a wick, and put into a lamp. The patient was to drink cold water while inhaling fumes from this vapor bath.

30. Heath 1925: p. 280.

31. *CMJ* 1919: 33.6 (November), pp. 551–52; Dikötter 1995: p. 135. Henriot (1992: p. 100) explains that salvarsan was invented in 1910 by a German doctor, and that the first blood test for syphilis was invented in 1906.

32. *CMJ* 1937: 51 (June), p. 1045.

33. Henriot 1992: p. 100.

34. In 1946, *Dagong bao* reported that a municipal-government clinic would need more than 1 million yuan to purchase enough penicillin to treat the city's prostitutes for syphilis. A neosalvarsan treatment, which required sixty weeks (rather than a week for penicillin), would cost sixty thousand yuan per prostitute. [Shanghai] *Dagong bao* 1946: March 7; Yu Wei 1947: p. 18. Also see chapter 11. It should be noted that this was a time of hyperinflation; if Shanghai's cost-of-living index for 1937 was set at 100, then in January 1946 it would have been 89,924; in January 1947, 1,145,000; and in January 1948, 11,293,000. King 1968: p. 161.

35. *CMJ* 1926: 40.1 (January), pp. 131–35; *CMJ* 1928: 42.7 (July), pp. 546–48.

36. Zhou Shoujuan 1928: vol. 2, p. 82.

37. Huang 1988: passim. On p. 183 he cites three examples: *Shenbao* 1913: September 28; *Shenbao* 1916: October 16; and *Shenbao* 1922: May 8. For advertisements about cures for gonorrhea, see also *Shibao* 1936: passim. For an assertion that venereal-disease hospitals were mainly out for profit, see Datong tushushe n.d.: pp. 161–62.

38. Tang Youfeng 1931: pp. 154–55.

39. In a study of "syphilophobia" in 1930s Beijing, Hugh Shapiro has noted that "by the 1930s, anxieties regarding sexually transmitted infection were so prevalent, that it became common practice following intercourse to seek prophylactic 'injections,' even in the absence of any concrete indication." Shapiro 1994: p. 1.

40. Dikötter 1995: pp. 136–37.

41. *CMJ* 1924: 38.1 (January), supplement, pp. 16–17, 26–29; *Municipal Gazette* 1924: January 17, pp. 15–16. For a similar argument see *North-China Herald* 1923: January 13, p. 102; and *Municipal Gazette* 1924: March 27, p. 114.

42. *CMJ* 1918: 32.5, p. 450.

43. *CMJ* 1919: 33.4, p. 333.

44. Heath 1925: p. 283. Implicit in Heath's analysis was a recognition of the low status of women, which was coupled with a wide-ranging argument for the suppression of sexuality: "Where so large an emphasis was placed on sex indulgence, masturbation became a large factor in the youth of both sexes. One of the serious problems in boarding schools for boys or girls is the amount of auto-eroticism, masturbation, and homosexual abuse found. Parents early teach their children the habit (to stop their crying), and it is difficult to cope with an abuse whose indulgence elicits no shame."

45. K. C. Wong, "Notes on Chinese Medicine," *CMJ* 1918: 32.4, pp. 349–53; Wong and Wu 1936: pp. 109–12. Also see *CMJ* 1927: 41.1 (January), p. 28.

46. Dikötter 1995: pp. 130–31.

47. Wong 1920: p. 633.

48. *CMJ* 1924: 38.6 (June), pp. 488–89.

49. Henriot (1992: p. 115) notes that until the early 1920s, articles by Western and Western-trained doctors "quite surprisingly, did not mention the issue of prostitution at all. They contented themselves with a strictly medical approach which was

aimed at assessing the diffusion of syphilis among the population." On p. 112 he comments on "a growing secularization process" in physician writings about STDs after 1924.

50. *CMJ* 1927: 41.1 (January), p. 35.

51. *CMJ* 1937: 51 (June), p. 1,044.

52. Banchisheng 1891: *juan* 4, p. 2; *juan* 3, pp. 14–15.

53. Wang Zhongxian n.d.: pp. 34–35.

54. See, for instance, Chunming shuju 1937: *changsan*, pp. 13–16.

55. Sun Yusheng 1939: pp. 109–11. The warning about harm to the body, money, and reputation is an almost verbatim borrowing from Wang Houzhe 1925 (n.p.).

56. Sun Yusheng 1939: p. 159.

57. See, for example, Wang Dingjiu 1932: *Piao*, p. 27; and Sun Yusheng 1939: pp. 165, 169–71.

58. See, for example, *Shenbao* 1919: May 7; and *Shenbao* 1920: January 29, April 26, May 17, September 5.

59. Qian Shengke 1933: vol. 2, p. 8.

60. Wang Zhongxian n.d.: p. 60; Chunming shuju 1937: *zhiji*, pp. 1–2.

61. Wang Dingjiu 1932: p. 25.

62. Wang Dingjiu 1932: *Piao*, pp. 31–32, 50; Chunming shuju 1937: *zhiji*, pp. 15–16.

63. Sun Yusheng 1939: pp. 170–71. For earlier warnings, see Banchisheng 1891: *juan* 3, p. 15; Li chuang wo dusheng 1905: *juan* 6, p. 6; and Yu Muxia 1935: *ji*, 49.

64. Wu Hanchi 1924: p. 12.

65. *Jingbao* 1919: April 18, p. 2.

66. Wang Dingjiu 1932: *Piao*, p. 51.

67. Wang Dingjiu 1932: *Piao*, pp. 41–43.

68. Wang Dingjiu 1932: *Piao*, p. 39. For a similar warning, see Sun Yusheng 1939: p. 157.

69. Zhou Shoujuan 1928: vol. 1, p. 3; Yu Muxia 1935: *shang*, 16.

70. Wang Dingjiu 1932: *Piao*, p. 39.

71. Hu Jifan 1930: n.p.

72. Xiao Jianqing 1937b: pp. 89–90.

73. Wang Dingjiu 1932: *Wan*, 8. For a foreign version of such warnings, see *China Weekly Review* 1930: June 14, p. 57.

74. Newspaper articles ventured similar judgments. A death notice in the 1931 *Shenbao*, for instance, attributed a silversmith's demise to syphilis contracted when a "weakness in his character" sent him repeatedly to prostitutes. *Shenbao* 1931: March 4.

75. Dikötter 1995: pp. 124, 129–30. For a summary of Chinese medical writings about venereal disease from the 1630s to the 1830s, see Dikötter 1995: p. 127. Chinese reformers pointed out that venereal disease transmitted by prostitutes harmed European nations as well, citing statistics on infection from France, Germany, Prussia, and Japan. Jiang Jingsan 1925: pp. 772–73.

76. Fan Shouyuan, *Qingnian weisheng jianghua* [Guide to youth hygiene] (Shanghai: Zhengzhong shuju, 1947), p. 44, cited in Dikötter 1995: p. 134.

77. Chen Fangzhi 1935: pp. 48–53.

78. Lin Chongwu 1936: p. 221. On the emergence of race as a prominent category of analysis during this period, see Dikötter 1992.

79. Although, of course, the Western powers were themselves seen as the source of syphilitic infection. Dikötter writes: "Syphilis was interpreted as a cause of 'racial decline': the idea of degeneracy, encompassed in the powerful myth of hereditary syphilis, was debunked in Europe in the aftermath of the First World War, but a combination of nationalist rhetoric and social hygiene contributed to the perpetuation of such notions in China well into the 1940s. . . . Syphilis was a disease of 'modernity', a symbol of the decline of civilization thought to be confined to the great metropolises of the coast." Dikötter 1995: pp. 130, 132.

80. This was the case with Lin Chongwu 1936. For other arguments, see chapters 10 and 11.

81. Shan 1933: p. 30.

82. *Shenbao* 1941: November 1, p. 3.

83. Mu Hua 1936: p. 24.

84. Mu Hua 1936: p. 26.

CHAPTER 10: REFORMERS

1. Various aspects of this theme are developed in quite different ways in Beahan 1975; Beahan 1976; Johnson 1983; Stacey 1983; Gilmartin 1989; Gilmartin 1995; Gipoulon 1989-1990; and Edwards 1994.

2. Wang Shuhuai 1994: p. 33 and passim. Kang mentions the danger of being sold into prostitution as part of the bitterness of being a slave girl; he does not link prostitution to the status of all women. On Kang's utopian thought, see also Spence 1982: pp. 64-73; and Beahan 1976: pp. 86-95.

3. Beahan 1976: p. 122. On Liang's views about women, his personal marriage history, and his growing conservatism on gender questions, see Zhang Mingyuan 1994: passim. For his argument that women were "a vast but neglected pool of human energy which could be directed toward national goals," and arguments linking footbinding, inferior mothering, and national weakness, see Witke 1970: pp. 8, 26, 31.

4. Beahan 1976: pp. 133-53. On the anti-footbinding movement, see also Drucker 1981 and Tao 1994.

It should be noted that not all reform-minded intellectuals of the late Qing saw prostitution as emblematic of national weakness. Li Boyuan, for example, who is briefly discussed in chapter 1, was both the author of a late Qing "castigatory novel" criticizing official weakness with respect to the foreigners and the editor of a major tabloid that organized a series of "flower-roll elections." For him and others like him, courtesans were apparently part of a Chinese cultural practice worth celebrating. On Li, see Link 1981: pp. 134, 138, 139, 143.

5. Zarrow 1990: p. 101.

6. Zarrow 1988; Zarrow 1990: p. 133. Zarrow writes: "Like Liang Qichao, He Zhen saw dependency as the problem, but she saw different causes at work: not male dominance alone but also the unequal distribution of wealth." Zarrow 1990: p. 131. For a more cursory treatment of He Zhen, see Dirlik 1991: pp. 103-4.

7. Zarrow 1990: pp. 131-35.

8. For further development of this theme, see Zarrow 1990: pp. 130-55.

9. For instance, *Shenbao* (1915: May 11) ran the following item: "Negotiations be-

tween China and Japan are extremely urgent now, but in Beijing there are some unconscious people still visiting prostitutes and engaging in gambling. How shameful they are!" And after listing which government emissary was visiting which Shanghai courtesan, the tabloid *Crystal* concluded, "How much they have done about negotiating for peace goes without saying." *Jingbao* 1919: November 24, p. 3.

10. Beahan 1976: p. 318.

11. Zarrow 1990: pp. 189–92.

12. On this use of *Jinde hui*, see *Shenbao* 1919: April 9.

13. Huang Renjing 1913: pp. 134–35.

14. *Chinese Recorder* 1920: August, pp. 579–80.

15. Bu Minghui, M.D., of the Shanghai Moral Welfare League, writing in *Shenbao* 1919: May 19.

16. Bu Minghui in *Shenbao* 1919: May 17, May 19.

17. Wong 1920: p. 630.

18. Wong 1920: p. 631; *CMJ* 1924: 38.6 (June), p. 488.

19. Wong 1920: p. 631. Garon (1993) makes the argument that the Japanese state at this time regarded prostitution as a form of filial behavior by young women. He sees a gendered division of labor in which upholding traditional values such as filiality was the duty of women, and performing modernizing tasks such as building a navy was the duty of men.

20. As a 1920 editorial in a journal published by the China Medical Missionary Association commented, eliminating prostitution would require recognizing that "only the redeeming power of Christianity is capable of coping effectively with the social evil in all its ramifications." *CMJ* 1920: pp. 635–36.

21. For studies of the May Fourth Movement see, among others, Chow 1960; Schwarcz 1986; Spence 1982: pp. 154–87; and Dirlik 1991: pp. 148–96. In PRC historiography, 1919 is taken as the dividing line between "modern" and "contemporary" history. In literary history, as Chow (1991: p. 35) argues, it is regarded "a historic watershed between the old and the new Chinas."

22. See, for instance, Lu Qiuxin 1920. Earlier, the anarchist He Zhen had also linked prostitution and concubinage as types of class-based sexual exploitation. Zarrow 1990: p. 141.

23. Li Dazhao 1919: pp. 347–49.

24. Se Lu 1920: p. 1; Yan Dunyi 1923: p. 29; Se Lu 1920: p. 2; Qiao Feng 1923: p. 6.

25. Yan Dunyi 1923: p. 28.

26. Gongchang 1924: p. 586.

27. Se Lu 1920: pp. 1–2. Although they were not always cited, readers will recognize ideas voiced earlier by Lewis Henry Morgan, Friedrich Engels, and many others.

28. Se Lu 1920: p. 1; Jiang Jingsan 1925: p. 774; Qiao Feng 1923: p. 6.

29. Jiang Jingsan 1925: p. 774.

30. Jiang Jingsan 1925: p. 775.

31. Se Lu 1923: p. 3.

32. Se Lu 1920: pp. 3–8; Zhu Zhenxin 1923: p. 9; Chu Hui 1927: p. 13; Huang Shi 1928.

33. Zhu Zhenxin 1923: p. 9.

34. Se Lu 1923: p. 3; Zhu Zhenxin 1923: p. 9.

35. *Funü zazhi* 1923: 9.3 (March 3), pp. 25–41; 1925: 11, 7, pp. 1,156–65.

36. Se Lu 1923: pp. 3–4. If chaste women throughout Chinese history had been raised in poor conditions, one author asserted, many of them would probably have been prostitutes. Tun Min 1923: p. 20.

37. Tun Min 1923: p. 19.

38. Se Lu 1920: pp. 8, 2. But Chen Dezheng (1923: p. 16) notes that men who went to prostitutes were not necessarily the poorest of the poor. The latter group had to meet minimum human needs for food and clothing before they could think about satisfying their sexual desire.

39. Qiao Feng 1923: p. 8; Jiang Jingsan 1925: p. 776.

40. Qiao Feng 1923: p. 8.

41. Zhu Zhenxin 1923: p. 10.

42. Chen Dezheng 1923: p. 13; Chu Hui 1927: p. 14.

43. Chen Dezheng 1923: pp. 13–14.

44. Chen Dezheng 1923: p. 13; Jiang Jingsan 1925: p. 777.

45. Chen Dezheng 1923: p. 13.

46. Chen Dezheng 1923: p. 14; Jiang Jingsan 1925: p. 777.

47. Zhu Zhenxin 1923: pp. 9, 11. Bebel's argument was summarized by Zhu Zhenxin as follows: under capitalism, women are not easily economically independent because men and women are not equal; women lack educational opportunities and men occupy most types of employment. Most women depend on men, while women without protection are forced by economics to become prostitutes, servants, or workers. Of these options, prostitution is the most "peaceful, happy, and comfortable." Zhu Zhenxin 1923: p. 11; for a similar statement, see Chu Hui 1927: p. 14. Western experts who were frequently cited on the inability of women to be economically independent included Havelock Ellis (see Qiao Feng 1923: p. 7; Chen Dezheng 1923: p. 18; and Chu Hui 1927: pp. 13–14) and Abraham Flexner (see Qiao Feng 1923: p. 7; and Chu Hui 1927: p. 14).

48. Zhu Zhenxin 1923: p. 9.

49. Chen Dezheng 1923: p. 16; for a similar argument, see also Jiang Jingsan 1925: p. 779.

50. Dai Qiu 1923: pp. 22–24; see also Huang Shi 1927: pp. 800–801.

51. Huang Shi 1927: p. 801.

52. Jiang Jingsan 1925: pp. 773, 775–776, 779.

53. Gongchang 1924: pp. 586–87.

54. Gongchang 1924: p. 586.

55. Chu Hui 1927: p. 13.

56. Tun Min 1923: pp. 20–21. Less common suggestions assigned women more blame for prostitution and more responsibility for preventing it. One argument held that women were easily moved by extravagant desires for clothing and jewelry, leading to loss of chastity and prostitution. The same author commented that Chinese wives should put more effort into treating their husbands with affection so that they would not be driven to the company of prostitutes. Zhong Yan 1927: pp. 17–18.

57. You Xiongyi 1923: p. 44. For additional arguments against licensing, see Se Lu 1923: p. 4; Zhu Zhenxin 1923: p. 12; Gongchang 1924: pp. 586–87; and Tian Di et al. 1924: pp. 1,264–72.

58. Hu Huaichen 1920: pp. 9–10; Se Lu 1923: p. 4; Tun Min 1923: p. 21; Qiao

Feng 1923: p. 8; Yan Dunyi 1923: p. 29; Chu Hui 1927: pp. 15–16; Zhong Yan 1927: pp. 18–19; Huang Shi 1927: pp. 796–99, 805.

59. Se Lu 1920: pp. 2, 8; Qiao Feng 1923: p. 8.

60. Li Sanwu 1920: pp. 350–58.

61. Ping Jinya 1988: p. 170. This suggestion was made in a 1988 article by Ping Jinya. Ping's censorious tone is typical of much 1980s writing on pre-1949 prostitution, but Ping himself was no Party functionary. Rather, Poshek Fu tells us, he was "a famous tabloid writer and publisher of pirate editions" in the 1930s and 1940s. Poshek Fu 1993: p. 62. For a complete table of contents of the special issue of *Xin ren*, which does indeed much resemble a guidebook, see Zhonggong zhongyang 1978: vol. 2, part 2, pp. 869–70.

62. *Shenbao* 1920: November 10. A similar article in the tabloid *Crystal* argued that military governors and prostitutes were equally difficult to abolish, because neither group had alternative means of making a living. *Jingbao* 1920: November 15, p. 2.

The theme of the evil madam, also discussed in chapter 8, was not a new theme in writings about prostitution. For a literary denunciation of madams published in 1905, written in the style of a Tang-dynasty declaration attacking Empress Wu Zetian, see Li chuang wo dusheng 1905: *juan* 8, pp. 2–3. That declaration, too, calls for the abolition of prostitution via the elimination of madams. What is new in the 1920 editorial is the broadening of the context to encompass the welfare of the populace as a whole.

63. *Jingbao* 1920: March 27, p. 2. A reader wrote in reply to the proposed lifelong ban on marriage for prostitutes that such a measure would not be humanitarian. Courtesans, he pointed out, did not become wives; they became concubines, with little power in the family compared with that of the principal wife. Many returned to the brothels because they found the status of concubine too difficult. *Jingbao* 1920: March 30, p. 2. Also see *Jingbao* 1921: January 1, p. 2. For further elaboration of this point, see chapter 4.

64. *Jingbao* 1920: March 27, p. 2. For exactly this type of declaration that prostitutes were "forced by life" and ill-treated, see *Jingbao* 1920: November 20, p. 2.

Not everyone who wrote for *Jingbao* in this period was supportive of the ban on prostitution. A 1924 article by a man signing himself Old Man Dan said that feminists in Hunan who attempted to ban prostitution were ugly women who could not appreciate the pleasures of makeup, jokes, riding in cars, going to operas, and checking in to big hotels. Prostitutes were women of noble character, he said, and there was no reason to ban them. *Jingbao* 1924: June 21, p. 2.

65. *Shenbao* 1919: April 9.

66. *Jingbao* 1919: June 9, p. 3. For a similar denunciation deriding the high status of Shanghai courtesans as undeserved and indicative of social disorder, see *Jingbao* 1920: June 12, p. 2.

67. For an analysis of this readership, see Link 1981: pp. 189–95. Link suggests that although many May Fourth writers attacked the type of literature published in the fiction magazines, their "efflorescence" in 1921–1922 "was in part a result of the larger aspects of the May Fourth literary movement which asserted the patriotism, and respectability, of fiction writing." Link 1981: p. 91. For a further discussion of "mandarin duck and butterfly" fiction in the context of May Fourth literature, where "May Fourth" is used as a sign of the modern, see Chow 1991: pp. 34–83.

68. Bi Yihong was both a fiction writer and a news editor, exemplifying the move-

ment across genres that makes it unwise to disregard fiction as a source for the history of prostitution. He wrote for *Shibao* in the 1910s, and had a long liaison with a courtesan, which formed the basis for his novel *Renjian diyu* (Hell on earth), serialized daily in *Shenbao* in 1923–1924. The novel, completed by Bao Tianxiao after Bi Yihong's death, is set in a *changsan* courtesan house. According to Chen Dingshan, Bi Yihong was a bit of a prankster who once stole the clothes of a friend who was spending the night with a courtesan, then sent him a note telling him his wife had arrived from Songjiang, forcing him to take a rickshaw home in his underwear. On Bi Yihong, see Link 1981: pp. 115, 117, 174–75; Chen Dingshan 1967: pp. 123–126; and the 1990 preface by Chen Zhengshu to the reissue of *Renjian diyu* (Suoposheng and Bao Tianxiao 1990: *shang*, pp. 1–4).

69. Link 1981: p. 174.

70. Bi Yihong 1922; Qiu xingfu 1922a; Lin Biyao 1922; Qiu xingfu 1922b; Xu Jinfu 1922.

71. Link 1981: p. 176.

72. Link 1981: pp. 175–76; for the original story, see Bi Yihong 1922.

73. The author was He Haiming, "a revolutionary general who had held an independent Nanking for about a month (1913) during the campaign against Yuan Shih-k'ai." Liu Ts'un-yan 1982: p. 31. According to Perry Link, He was "a revolutionary journalist and soldier before 1911," and after the failed "Second Revolution" of 1913 he fled to Japan. After his return "he retired from politics and the military to devote himself to writing amusement fiction, especially stories about prostitutes." Link 1981: p. 160.

74. Qiu xingfu zhaiju 1922a.

75. Lin Biyao 1922.

76. For a similar autobiographical account from 1938, see Zhu Zuotong and Mei Yi 1939: part 4, pp. 165–67. The author of this piece, a *changsan* courtesan named Yuyu Fengzian, is herself the daughter of a *changsan* courtesan. She blames Japanese imperialism and male perfidy in equal parts for her suffering, commenting of courtesans, "Although one cannot say that we sell our flesh, we undoubtedly sell our souls." Her description of the atmosphere at a courtesan banquet is particularly graphic; she describes the fetid odor of the room in the August heat and the revolting smell of liquor on the breath of patrons who try to steal kisses.

77. Xu Yasheng 1930 (much of this article was lifted without attribution in Qian Yiwei 1937); Zhi Shan 1933: pp. 9–10; Zhu Meiyu 1933: p. 36; Yi Feng 1933b: p. 31; Sun Changshu 1933: pp. 30–31.

78. Tang Guozhen 1932: pp. 17–18. Tang felt that men exhausted from visiting prostitutes began to use stimulants such as opium, heroin, and liquor to revive themselves and became incurably ill, or were distracted by sexual desire from paying attention to the development of society.

79. For example, on prostitution in Greece and Rome, in Christianity, and in the Crusades, see Yi Feng 1933a: pp. 32–33, Hong Hua 1935; and Ye Derong 1936: p. 32. On prostitution in modern Paris, Brussels, London, the United States, Italy, Russia, Japan, and Germany, see Song Xian 1930; Yi Feng 1933a: p. 33, 36–37; Hong Hua 1935; Wang Yiren 1935; Ye Derong 1936: p. 34; Tang Guozhen 1932: p. 17; and Shen Lihong 1932: part 2, pp. 23–24. On prostitution in ancient China, see Yi Feng 1933a: pp. 34–35; and Zhu Meiyu 1933: pp. 29–35.

80. Mu Hua 1936: p. 22. The proximate cause of Mu's polemic was decisions by

the police in Suzhou and Wuxi to permit licensed prostitution (p. 21). Mu gives no attribution for the quotation about poverty, but appears to be quoting Bebel.

81. Mu Hua 1936: p. 22.

82. Mu Hua 1936: p. 23.

83. Mu Hua 1936: p. 25.

84. Mu Hua 1936: pp. 24–26. For a similar clarion call asking women to become conscious, recognize their own power, and join the struggle for their own liberation and that of all humankind, see Qian Gucheng 1938: p. 16. In his assertion that prostitution causes social decay, Mu Hua draws on Wang Shunu 1935: pp. 340–42. Wang quotes various Qing sources to the effect that prostitution provided a livelihood to many poor people, then denounces those who would apply this argument to the twentieth century.

85. Guo Chongjie 1936: p. 24. Wang Shunu makes a similar universalizing argument about the connection of prostitution to social disorder. Thieves in London and Paris, he says, sometimes testify that they turned to stealing because they had squandered their fortunes by visiting prostitutes. Wang Shunu 1935: p. 341.

86. Or mangled versions thereof. In one account, "unlicensed prostitution" was rendered as "Anu lice Dea Prastitution." Ye Derong 1936: p. 33. Bebel was still prominent: see, for instance, Shen Lihong 1932: part 1, pp. 31–32, 35; Hong Hua 1935; and Li Jingxi 1935: p. 93.

87. See Guo Chongjie 1936: pp. 23–28; and Lin Chongwu 1936: pp. 215–223. More than a decade later, in 1948, Yu Wei and Amos Wong made a similar linkage between marriage and prostitution by arguing that a more permissive divorce law should be passed "so that unhappy marriages may be given a chance of readjustment, instead of seeking an escape in prostitution." Yu and Wong 1949: p. 248.

Unlike many other reform authors, Guo felt that all prostitution should be licensed rather than banned, at least until women acquired the necessary knowledge and skills to make a living independently. For a similar argument, see Lin Chongwu 1936: pp. 221–23.

About Ellen Key's influence on an earlier May Fourth generation of writers, Roxane Witke writes: "After 1919, largely under the influence of the Swedish feminist Ellen Key, May Fourth writings on the topics of love, romantic love and sexual relations became somewhat depersonalized and systematized under the current European term 'free love,' which translated into Chinese as lien-ai tzu-yu [lian'ai ziyou]. . . . The Chinese term is perhaps distorted less in translation as 'freedom to love.'" Key's thought was selected and interpreted for a Chinese audience by the writer Qin Lu. Witke continues, "The stage of her argument which won the greatest support among May Fourth liberals was that love must be the basis of marriage (naturally monogamous), and that only love is sufficient to make marriage moral." Key also argued "that men and women have separate abilities which should be expressed in separate spheres of activity" and that women become complete through motherhood. Witke 1970: pp. 140–43. The articles she cites are Qin Lu 1921 and Qin Lu 1920. For an example of Ellen Key's writing on marriage, see Key 1911.

88. Song Xian 1930; Yi Feng 1933a: p. 37; Sun Changshu 1933: p. 30; He Jiwei 1933: p. 24; Shao Xiangyi 1934: p. 2. On prostitutes coming from the ranks of the proletariat in Europe and the United States, see Yi Feng 1933b: p. 26. On the economic reasons that men postponed marriage and visited prostitutes, see Jing Xiangding 1934: p. 884; Sun Changshu 1933: p. 31; and Fang Long 1935: p. 31.

89. On proper production skills, see Xu Yasheng 1930; Qian Yiwei 1937; and Ye Derong 1936. A particularly elaborate scheme was offered in 1932 by Tang Guozhen, in which social workers would staff factories where prostitutes were to spend half their time in work and half in study. Tang proposed that each woman be detained for two to three years, and that the local government find jobs for graduates in factories, shops, companies, and so forth. This program anticipated in almost every respect the Communist reform campaign of the 1950s. Tang Guozhen 1932: p. 19. On a broad range of legal, educational, and welfare measures for women, as well as sexual freedom, see Yi Wen 1933: pp. 20–21. See also Lin Chongwu 1936: pp. 221–23.

90. Lin Chongwu 1936: p. 221.

91. Guo Chongjie 1936: p. 27.

92. Lin Chongwu 1936: p. 222.

93. Lin Chongwu 1936: passim. Lin's argument is more than a trifle incoherent; the defense of Confucian virtues is preceded by an attack on the "three obediences" and "four virtues" as a means by which men enslaved women (p. 215).

94. She Ying 1933: p. 1.

95. Shan 1934: p. 35.

96. She Ying 1933: p. 2.

97. Jizhe 1933: p. 75.

98. Shan 1934: p. 35.

99. She Ying 1933: p. 3. For other arguments against lifting the ban, see Guo Zhen 1933: p. 16; Wei Yu 1933; and Wu Ming 1933.

100. Suo Fei 1933.

101. Fang Long 1935: p. 32.

102. Luo Tianwen 1934: p. 258.

103. The exact calculation went as follows: according a Japanese study of prostitution in Shanghai, if Shanghai was estimated to have 30,000 prostitutes, of which 1,200 were *changsan* courtesans, and each one made five calls a night, at one yuan per call, this was five yuan per prostitute. If each spent the night with a customer, and/or drank with them, she garnered twelve yuan per occasion. *Yao er* courtesans numbered 500, and if each spent each night with a guest, she took in eight yuan. Pheasants and others numbered 28,400, and if each slept with one customer a night, at five yuan, then the totals were: *changsan* call fees (1,200 x 5 yuan): 6,000 yuan; *changsan* banquet fees et al. (1,200 x 12 yuan): 14,400 yuan; *yao er* fees (500 x 8 yuan): 4,000 yuan; fees from pheasants and others (28,400 x 5 yuan): 142,000 yuan—for a daily total of 166,400 yuan; monthly, 4,992,000; yearly, 60,736,000. A Mu, *Shina kenkyu*, 18, cited in Yi Feng 1933b: pp. 32–33. For the original, see Hō Aboku [Peng Amu] 1928: pp. 745–46.

104. Tang Guozhen 1932: p. 17.

105. Zhu Meiyu 1933: p. 29.

106. Cao Gongqi 1934: p. 854.

107. Cao Gongqi 1934; Su Ming 1936; Ye Derong 1936. Some authors disagreed with this diagnosis. Wang Yiren (1935, p. 1,024) pointed out that prostitution existed in a number of very different environments—including Tang and Song China, Europe (particularly Paris) and America, and Japan throughout the Meiji period and into the present—and that therefore it was not merely the result of the bankruptcy of the village economy. The same argument was made by Kuang Jianping (1934: p. 866). For a Marxist analysis arguing that prostitutes were more exploited than ordi-

nary laborers, and that the world depression had increased their numbers and depressed their income, see Luo Qiong 1935. Luo went on to become a top-ranking functionary in the Women's Federation after 1949.

108. Cao Gongqi 1934; Shao Yuancheng 1936; Sui Zhi 1936: p. 968.

109. Qiebei jinü 1936: 2, 2, (February 16), pp. 30–32; Tan Fengyang 1934. For a summary of the debate over solutions, see Yao Shaomei 1935. Yong He in 1933 called on "[us] intellectual women" to go among the lower strata of women, raise their consciousness, lead them to join the struggle against imperialism and Japan, to oppose warlord war and excessive taxation. Only this would push the government to be able to do something constructive for women, allowing them to have work, food, and equality with men in education and health. At that time, prostitution would naturally disappear. Yong He 1933: p. 28.

110. Yi Feng 1933b: pp. 36–37; Yong He 1933: pp. 24, 26–27; Zhang Jialiang 1934; Zhang Hequn 1935; Shao Yuancheng 1936; Jing Zhi 1936; Lin Chongwu 1936: p. 221. For a precursor to such accounts, see Se Lu 1920: p. 2.

111. Changji 1934; Sun Changshu 1933: p. 32.

112. Yi Feng 1933b: p. 37.

113. Zhou Shixian 1934.

114. Jing Zhi 1936.

115. *Yinku* can also refer to female genitalia, a particularly salient association in this context. Many thanks to Richard van Glahn for pointing this out.

116. Bi Yao 1938: pp. 10–11. For similar declarations by the playwright and resister Li Jianwu, see Poshek Fu 1993: p. 86; for Fu's suggestion that collaboration itself was often portrayed as licentiousness or obscenity, see p. 89. Fu also details the move of the collaborationist government of Wang Jingwei into Shanghai tabloid publishing in 1940, where coverage of "social scandals, nightly guides, and pornography" was deployed to cover up the political intent of collaboration. Poshek Fu 1993: pp. 114–55.

117. Poshek Fu 1993: p. 64.

118. Carlitz 1994.

119. Poshek Fu 1993: pp. 90–91.

120. Cited in Poshek Fu 1993: p. 145.

121. Lin Chongwu 1936: p. 223. One feature of Lin's program that was not adopted by the Communists was the suggestion that customers should be detained and charged with seduction and rape.

122. Aside from the Door of Hope, two other institutions are mentioned less frequently in the press: the Xin Puyutang, which appeared to operate in 1915–1917; and the Cishan Tuan, which appears in reports from 1917 to 1922. Prostitutes were apparently sent to these places by the police when they asked for help. On the Xin Puyutang, see *Shenbao* 1915: January 5, January 20; *Shenbao* 1916: August 18; and *Shenbao* 1917: December 11; as well as the stories of disturbances cited below. On the Cishan tuan, see *Shenbao* 1917: December 22; *Shenbao* 1918: March 3, September 7, October 7; *Shenbao* 1919: May 12, June 3; and *Shenbao* 1922: December 20. For a critical survey of Shanghai reform institutions in 1929, which concludes that most of them were underfunded and dirty, see Wu Ruohua 1929. On rescue missions in the American West, some of which sought to rescue Chinese prostitutes in San Francisco, see Pascoe 1990.

123. The Door of Hope is the subject of a 1995 Columbia University dissertation by Sue Gronewold (Gronewold 1995). For spirited tributes by contemporaries to the work of this institution, see Morris 1916; Harding 1917; and Dennett 1918: p. 664.

124. Darwent 1920: p. 154; Gamewell 1916; p. 190.

125. Harding 1917: p. 5.

126. Gamewell 1916: pp. 190–91. The regulation on posting the Receiving Home's address is reproduced in Li chuang wo dusheng 1905: *juan* 7, p. 4.

127. Darwent 1920: p. 154. In 1927, the Shanghai Municipal Council made a grant of four thousand taels to the Door of Hope. *Municipal Gazette* 1927: 20, 1060 (January 21), p. 19.

An institution known as the Door of Hope existed in Beijing in 1921 as well, but there it was run by the police department. According to Sidney Gamble, women were referred there by police if they had been forced into prostitution, were badly treated, wanted to leave prostitution, or had no place to go. Once confined, they were not permitted to leave the Beijing establishment unless they were married. Their photographs were hung outside the gate to aid passersby in choosing one as a spouse. The Beijing Door of Hope was supported by tax money, marriage subscriptions from men who married inmates, special subscriptions, rent, and police funds. Inmates learned Chinese, moral teachings, arithmetic, art, cooking, drawing, calisthenics, and music, and also did industrial work. Women who violated regulations were subject to a variety of punishments, including "the learning of moral maxims or old and wise sayings, small demerits, large demerits, sitting with the face to the wall for from one to three hours, being deprived of vegetables for one meal." Gamble 1921: pp. 249, 260–62, 480–85. Harding (1917: p. 6) mentions the existence of a Chinese-run Door of Hope in Tianjin, and Wiley (1929: pp. 97–98) notes that the police also founded Doors of Hope in Suzhou and Canton.

128. For women sent to the Door of Hope by police or the courts, see, among others: *Shenbao* 1915: January 6, January 10; *Shenbao* 1916: March 30, April 14, April 23, July 24, August 10; *Shenbao* 1917: November 13, December 23, December 26; *Shenbao* 1918: March 8, March 22, April 3, April 19, April 24, September 17, October 25; *Shenbao* 1919: January 1, February 16, June 21, July 4, July 9, August 13, October 24; *Shenbao* 1920: February 11, May 17; *Shenbao* 1921: January 11, February 14; and *Shibao* 1929: February 23, p. 7; July 15, p. 7. For women sent there by Door of Hope workers, see *Shenbao* 1922: July 26.

For prostitutes turning themselves in to the Door of Hope, see *Shenbao* 1915: May 3, June 4; *Shenbao* 1917: June 7, December 21; *Shenbao* 1918: March 13, March 25, April 15; *Shenbao* 1919: May 7, July 17, July 25, November 19, December 17; *Shenbao* 1920: March 26, March 27, April 26, July 24, October 26; *Shenbao* 1921: June 9, June 27, June 28; *Shenbao* 1922: April 8, April 29, July 3, July 16, October 11, October 18, December 16, December 26; *Shenbao* 1923: May 2, May 3, May 14, May 18, May 19, May 21; and *Shenbao* 1925: April 29, December 15, December 27.

From 1913 to 1924, between twenty-four and fifty women went to the Mixed Court each year seeking Door of Hope protection. Kotenev 1925: pp. 315–16.

129. Gamewell 1916: p. 192. A 1920 report in the Chinese women's magazine *Funü zazhi* said that men who wished to marry Door of Hope residents paid 105 yuan. Of this, 30 went to the Door of Hope and the remaining 75 were used by the intended

wife to buy clothes and other goods. No woman was forced to marry. *Funü zazhi* 1920: 5.8, pp. 2–4.

130. Darwent 1920: p. 155.

131. SMP 1932 (Box 112, MIS 8, p. 3) shows fifty-one women remanded to the Door of Hope in 1932.

132. Hu Huaichen 1920: pp. 8–9.

133. *North-China Herald* 1922: September 2, p. 643. Although it is not made explicit in this editorial, the author may have been talking about foreign prostitutes, since he goes on to advocate that the women be shipped elsewhere to make "a new start in a new land."

134. For trouble in the Door of Hope, see *Shenbao* 1916; August 17; *Shenbao* 1918: October 17; *Shenbao* 1920: December 29; and *Shenbao* 1922: December 29. For trouble in the Xin Puyutang, see *Shenbao* 1915: January 5 (tunnel digging); and *Shenbao* 1916: March 8, March 19 (arson and yelling).

135. Liao Guofang 1929: pp. 34–35. Liao was writing from a girls' school in Jiangxi for a journal published in Shanghai.

136. Chen Luwei 1938: pp. 21–22. Reform-minded foreigners, even while vigorously arguing the need for stronger trafficking laws and rescue work, admitted, "It is true that many of the girls and women engaged in the profession have developed a peculiar psychology which makes them particularly antagonistic toward any attempt to change their mode of life." *China Critic* 1937: p. 7.

CHAPTER 11: REGULATORS

1. For briefer treatments of some of these campaigns, see Henriot 1988: pp. 76–87; and Hershatter 1992b: passim.

2. Not all Chinese were impressed by the depth of Euro-American concern. In a 1892 publication, a Chinese writer lampooned the foreign governments in Shanghai for regulating trivial matters such as the number of people allowed in a horse carriage, the cleanliness of chauffeurs, and the obligation of hotels not to throw sick or dead customers into the street while ignoring a list of serious problems that included brothels, trafficking, and madams. Huang Shiquan [Wang Tao] 1975: pp. 200–201.

3. Jamieson 1870: p. 211. Jamieson, however, did not believe that abolition was feasible: "[A] ttempts to abolish this form of vice can never prove successful, and therefore . . . rational men will direct their energies towards limiting the extent and lessening the severity of the inevitable effects." As a remedy, he pointed to the Contagious Diseases Act in England, "an act most limited in its operation, most cumbrous in its provisions, and most clumsy in its working." Yet, he felt, it had helped to diminish prostitution and disease. In one of the earliest statements of the regulationist approach, he concluded: "In plain English, every prostitute, whether foreign or native, plying her trade within the limits of the settlements at Shanghai ought to be registered, taxed, and periodically examined."

4. *CMJ* 1924: 38.1 (January), supplement, p. 11.

5. Jamieson 1870: p. 211.

6. *NCH* 1917: November 3, p. 259; also see *CMJ*, especially 1917–1930.

7. It is not clear whether the incidence of sexually transmitted diseases in Shanghai was increasing during this time, or whether increased awareness of disease and increased panic fed discussions about a coming epidemic. Statistics in the *CMJ* (1924: 38.1 [January], supplement, p. 19) on cases treated at the General Hospital show no clear rise (1910–1914: 599 cases; 1915–1919: 507 cases; 1920–1922: 591 cases). The same statistics show an actual decline in cases of sexually transmitted diseases as a percentage of all patients treated at the hospital between 1910 and 1914 (7.5 percent) and between 1915 and 1919 (6.6 percent), when the debate intensified. The percentage rose to 8.2 percent for the period 1920–1922.

8. SVC 1920: pp. 83–84. This report found that the number of brothels rose from 463 in 1871 to 633 in 1920, an increase of more than one-third, while the number of known prostitutes almost tripled, jumping from 1,612 to 4,575. Estimated figures for the French Concession pushed the totals still higher. Of course, as chapter 2 indicated, such statistics say as much about intensified attention to counting and classifying as they do about rising numbers.

9. For contemporary statements of their social agenda see, for example, Dennett 1918: pp. 657–64; and "Child Labour in China" 1924: pp. 923–29.

10. Gamewell 1916: p. 48.

11. *NCH* 1916: December 16, p. 571.

12. *NCH* 1917: September 8, pp. 557–58. This condemnation of prostitutes continued throughout the 1920s campaign. A 1922 letter to the *North-China Herald*, for instance, called them "a community of parasites whose lewd vocation is the downfall of many many men and boys in this town. . . . One may be willing to admit that the evil will always be with us, but that is no reason why its sirens should by [*sic*] lauded as martyrs to a system." *NCH* 1922: September 9, p. 741.

13. *NCH* 1917: September 15, p. 614. Rebutting this argument, another letter to the editor replied: "Everyone knows that hiding a festering place is not curing it. Every just man knows that removing a mud heap from his own front door to the door of his neighbour is not cleaning up a city. . . . Society had never condemned men for it [frequenting houses of prostitution], the public has endorsed it, the city authorities get revenue from it, so 'Pride's Purge' would better touch on something more vital than hiding evil if he wants response." *NCH* 1917: September 22, p. 675.

A similar denunciation of the proximity of courtesan houses to churches was printed, oddly enough, in the Chinese tabloid press in 1919. Noting that singing and playing music were not permitted at certain hours in brothels located near mosques, one author observed that no such restrictions applied to brothels near a Christian church and a private girls' school in San Malu. "Do Christians not respect their religion as much as the Moslems?" the article asked. "If they do, why do they not ask the concession police for help to clean up their area?" *Jingbao* 1919: November 24, p. 3.

14. *NCH* 1917: November 3, p. 289.

15. *NCH* 1918: December 21, p. 748.

16. *NCH* 1917: February 10, p. 284. Like other activists on this issue, White was dissatisfied with what she saw as the passive approach of the Shanghai Municipal Council. She remarked that the council's attitude could be summed up in the phrase "Don't shoot the pianist: he's doing his best." For similar assertions of female superiority by other women, see *NCH* 1919: April 12, p. 101, and July 5, p. 49. Festina

Lente's letter of April 12 read in part: "Essentially the whole problem is one for women to solve—men are too clumsy and dull-witted in such matters—and we may hope that in the near future well-educated and progressive Chinese women will take a strong, active interest in the misfortunes of this large class."

17. *NCH* 1918: February 9, p. 325.

18. *NCH* 1918: May 25, p. 469, and December 14, p. 644; Wiley 1929: pp. 94–96. Finch (1953: pp. 46–48) asserts, somewhat implausibly, that the American madam Gracie Gale was a principal target of this campaign. For details of a nearly contemporaneous campaign in Guangzhou, see Mi Bi 1922; *Shenbao* 1922: April 8; *CMJ* 1923: 37.1 (January), p. 105; and Oldt 1923. The activity in Guangzhou was part of a Purity Campaign sponsored by the Guangzhou YMCA that began in September 1921, conducted largely through public meetings, parades, and petitions to the city government to ban prostitution. The mayor pronounced himself receptive, albeit worried about the loss of income provided by taxes on prostitution, which reportedly amounted to one-quarter of all municipal revenues. He was also concerned about the costs of welfare work and the projected increase in unlicensed prostitution. Meanwhile, an overseas Chinese student in Vietnam wrote in 1922 to the magazine *Funü zazhi*, complaining that prostitutes banned in Canton had moved their operations to Vietnam. "Feichang yundong" 1922. Another writer in the same magazine criticized the Christian approach of the Canton campaign, commenting that the reformers were motivated by pity, charity, and a desire to save individual prostitutes, rather than by a more thoroughgoing approach to social reform. Se Lu 1923: p. 4. For a 1923 campaign in Tianjin whose organizers (grandly titled the Tianjin Student Comrade Association, Women's Rights Division) promised to learn from the mistakes of Shanghai and Guangdong, see *Funü zazhi* 1923: 9.7 (July 1), pp. 125–27.

19. *NCH* 1918: December 21, p. 748; but see the letter in *NCH* 1916: August 19, p. 358, which says, "The opinion has been expressed that, until the evils of a European nature have been remedied, any preachment against these native haunts could be very appropriately met with the retort 'Physician heal thyself.'"

20. *NCH* 1919: April 5, p. 7; Kotenev 1925: p. 574. For the full text of this bylaw, see chapter 8.

21. *NCH* 1919: April 12, p. 114.

22. *NCH* 1918: December 14, p. 645.

23. *NCH* 1918: December 21, p. 748.

24. *NCH* 1919: April 12, p. 115.

25. *NCH* 1919: April 5, p. 7.

26. *NCH* 1918: December 14, p. 645.

27. *NCH* 1919: April 5, p. 45; *CMJ* 1924: 38.1 (January), supplement, p. 15.

28. The Special Vice Committee (SVC), as it was called, had nine members: three appointed by the SMC, three by the Moral Welfare Committee, and three by the first six. In the course of its existence the Vice Committee held twenty-two meetings, examined twenty-five witnesses, consulted municipal records, and solicited Chinese views through the Chinese General Chamber of Commerce. SVC 1920: p. 83.

29. *NCH* 1919: July 5, pp. 48–49.

30. As detailed in chapter 8, all these regulations were already in force.

31. SVC 1920: pp. 84–86. For contemporary commentary in praise of this report, see *Millard's Review* 1920: pp. 207–10.

32. For instance, it recommended that health officials take on increased responsibility for the treatment of venereal disease, as well as for education and record keeping. It approved the idea of funding the Door of Hope, and the enforcement of laws against soliciting, indecent advertisements, and sale of alcohol in unlicensed premises. As with prostitution itself, however, the SMC felt that licensing rather than suppression was the practical approach to alcohol consumption in brothels. Finally, the SMC maintained that the medical examination of prostitutes should continue. *MG* 1920: April 1, p. 124.

33. *MG* 1920: April 9, p. 164. Supporters of the SMC approach apparently were not well prepared for this meeting. Several years later, when debate over the policy broke out again, the *North-China Herald* would note that the 1920 vote was taken "when the room contained practically nobody but those who were for that vote, in defiance of the urgently expressed opinion of the Council." *NCH* 1922: August 26, p. 571.

34. *Shenbao* 1920: July 2.

35. *MG* 1920: May 13, pp. 192–93; on ineligible courtesan houses, see *Shenbao* 1920: July 2.

36. One such letter, signed by ten people, commented: "We view with alarm the unprecedented growth of prostitution within the foreign settlement during the last few years, and believe that stringent action should at once be taken in order to check it." A similar letter was signed by the Kiangsu (Jiangsu) Education Association, the Shanghai Education Association, the National Vocational Education Association, the Overseas Chinese Association, the Western Returned Students' Union of Shanghai, the World's Chinese Students' Federation, and the Shanghai Chinese YMCA. *NCH* 1920: April 10, p. 85.

37. In the future, mused the author, when concubinage was abolished, perhaps prostitutes would become "common wives" (*gong qi*) under socialism. *Jingbao* 1920: March 27, p. 2.

38. *Jingbao* 1920: June 15, p. 2.

39. *MG* 1920: July 8, p. 259.

40. *MG* 1920: July 8, pp. 259–60.

41. In Shanghai dialect, "Tse ma keu, pe ma sang" (*Zhi mai kou, bu mai shen*). Lemière 1923: p. 128.

Not everyone agreed that the sing-song girls were a breed apart. The Christian missionary Milton Stauffer commented in 1922: "The question is often raised as to the actual status of the 'Sing Song Girl' or the first-class prostitute. This class of prostitutes are entertainers as well as prostitutes, and the fees they get are the highest. But Chinese public opinion always classes them with the prostitutes. They raised little objection in the International Settlement of Shanghai to being registered as prostitutes under recent Municipal rulings. In the Chinese Government regulations for supervision of brothels they are definitely included as the first of the four grades of prostitutes to be supervised." Stauffer 1922: p. 396.

42. *MG* 1920: July 8, pp. 259–60; this letter is also reprinted in Lemière 1923: pp. 128–29.

43. *NCH* 1923: April 14, p. 115.

44. *NCH* 1923: April 21, p. 176.

45. *MG* 1920: July 8, p. 260.

46. In at least one case, news reporters incorporated the licensing controversy

into their breezy reporting about the social life of courtesans. A 1924 English-language caption in the *Shanghai Times* read: "Queen of the Singsong girls. Miss Chingyu is Queen of the Shanghai singsong girls by virtue of her election as "president of the Flower Circle" at Wing On's roof garden. She is a native of Soochow, the city through centuries famous for its pretty girls, but even her charm and beauty have not saved her from the controlling hand of municipal licensing." Cited in *Jingbao* 1924: June 21, p. 2. This election was apparently a latter-day descendant of the flower-roll elections described in chapter 6, which were discontinued after 1920.

47. *Shenbao* 1920: October 4, October 8, October 30, November 19, November 24, December 12, December 13.

48. *Shenbao* 1921: January 25, May 26.

49. On the French Concession see *Shenbao* 1920: July 2; and Wang Liaoweng 1922: p. 13. On Zhabei, see *Jingbao* 1920: March 27, p. 2.

50. Wang Liaoweng 1922: p. 214.

51. *Shenbao* 1920: May 31.

52. Wang Liaoweng 1922: p. 23.

53. Peters 1937: p. 208.

54. *MG* 1920: December 23, p. 434. The drawing, commented the *North-China Herald,* was accomplished with only one slight hitch: "After three numbers had been drawn, something went wrong with the drum, and instead of the fourth number tinkling into the receiver, the whole 881 tumbled out. The only thing to be done . . . was to begin the draw *de novo.*" *NCH* 1920: December 25, p. 876.

55. *MG* 1921: December 15, p. 407; *MG* 1923: December 13, p. 435. For a list of brothels closed in the first drawing see Wang Liaoweng 1922: pp. 186–96; for the second drawing, see pp. 196–204. Wang (pp. 204–14) states that before the 1922 drawing, the International Settlement had 124 courtesan houses and 401 courtesans remaining, while the French Concession had 2 courtesan houses and 16 courtesans. The two concessions combined had 7 *yao er* houses with 83 prostitutes, for a total of 500 courtesans in the two concessions. In 1922, *Shenbao* reported that the third drawing, held on December 5, involved 343 brothels. One-third of them, or 114, were selected to close by April 1, 1923. This group included 56 *changsan* houses and 2 *yao er* houses. The remainder were pheasant, Cantonese, and flower-smoke houses. *Shenbao* 1922: December 4, December 6, December 18.

56. *MG* 1924: April 3, p. 138.

57. See, for example, *NCH* 1921: March 26, pp. 813–14.

58. *MG* 1922: April 13, p. 120.

59. *MG* 1922: June 22, p. 223.

60. *NCH* 1922: August 26, p. 571.

61. *NCH* 1922: August 26, p. 574.

62. *Shenbao* 1922: December 8. This was not the last venture of the league into social work. In 1923 it proposed the establishment of another facility in addition to the Door of Hope, to be called the Mixed Court Home, where women charged with street soliciting would be sent. "Every month there come before the Court some thirty or more cases of girls charged with soliciting on the streets. . . . A small fine is usually inflicted, which is paid by the brothel keeper, and the girl goes back to the unwholesome life," wrote Isaac Mason in putting forward the proposal. He added that the police department had approved, and the Mixed Court magistrate had encour-

aged, the formation of such a home, to which women could be sent for a few days in lieu of a fine, and where they could be detained while waiting for a hearing. "[I]t is hoped that some of them will catch a vision of a better life during such a respite. Those who wish to take advantage of the chance will be helped in every way possible to make a fresh start, and to become good members of society," wrote Mason. Chinese and foreign women were to manage the home, which would employ a Chinese matron. *NCH* 1923: May 19, pp. 468–69. The Mixed Court Home was opened in September 1923, and by January 1924 it had taken in fifty-one girls, all for short periods. *NCH* 1924: January 19, p. 98. It lasted for about a year, took in more than one hundred women and girls, and received five hundred taels from the Municipal Council, but it ultimately had to close for lack of funds. *NCH* 1925: February 7, p. 224.

63. *North China Daily News* 1921: January 24, in SMP: Box 103, D3572.

64. *NCH* 1923: January 6, pp. 32–33. For the 1885 controversy over "maiden tribute" in London, whose language and categories were echoed in the discussion among foreigners in Shanghai, see Walkowitz 1992: pp. 81–134.

65. *NCH* 1923: January 13, p. 103.

66. Hu Jifan 1930: *juan* 8, n. p.; Yi Feng 1933a: p. 40. On the move of *yao er* brothels, see Yu Muxia 1935: *ji*, pp. 34–35.

67. *China Weekly Review* 1927: August 20, p. 8. Some courtesan houses did so as soon as the first drawing of licenses was completed, so that they would not have to pay seasonal rent past the time when they were legal, or attempt to collect customer debts after they had closed. *Shenbao* 1921: January 4. In an attempt to make it easier to inspect brothels, the International Settlement police issued an order in January 1921 that courtesan houses were not to follow their usual custom of changing location at the Spring Festival. The moves, which took place as often as three times per year, gave the houses an excuse to invite their customers to visit them. *Shenbao* 1921: January 24. On brothels moving in spite of the police decree, see *Shenbao* 1921: February 11. On seasonal courtesan-house accounting practices, see chapter 3.

68. Guo Chongjie 1936: p. 26.

69. *NCH* 1924: January 19, p. 98.

70. *NCH* 1924: March 15, p. 408.

71. Finch 1953: p. 11.

72. *MG* 1924: March 6, pp. 92–93.

73. *NCH* 1924: February 9, p. 218.

74. *NCH* 1924: October 18, p. 115.

75. *NCH* 1924: January 19, p. 98; *NCH* 1923: October 20, p. 187.

76. The author of this article went on to argue that although thorough elimination of prostitution would require both economic and moral reform, and was extremely difficult to achieve, this was no reason to dispense with short-term measures like the 1920 ban. With licensed prostitution, the article said, trafficking was more convenient, madams could openly mistreat their prostitutes, young people became more easily misled, and disease was more easily spread. *Funü zazhi* 1924: 10.7 (July), pp. 1,067–68. For a tabloid commentary also condemning the relicensing, see *Jingbao* 1924: April 30, p. 2.

77. These regulations are from Shangwu yinshuguan 1926: *juan* 2, p. 46.

The age limit of fifteen was specified in *MG* (1925: March 26, p. 107) as calculated by foreign reckoning, which would correspond to the age limit of sixteen by

Chinese reckoning that is described in chapter 8. I have not been able to locate the earliest codification of the provision about young girls in brothels, but news reports about establishments fined for violating it date from at least 1915. See chapter 8.

For revisions to the 1924 regulations that further tightened several of the requirements, see *MG* 1925: March 26, p. 107; *MG* 1926: November 19, p. 377; and *MG* 1929: August 9, p. 325.

78. Licensing-revenue data for 1920–1926 are given in *Shanghai Municipal Council Report and Budget* 1925: pp. 43A–44A; and *Shanghai Municipal Council Report and Budget* 1926: p. 412.

79. *Shenbao* 1924: December 1; *Shenbao* 1925: April 13.

80. For examples of these violations, see *Shenbao* 1922: December 11; *Shenbao* 1923: May 13, October 31; and *Shenbao* 1925: April 19, November 16, December 7, December 21, December 27.

81. *NCH* 1923: April 28, p. 270.

82. Shanghai tebieshi zhengfu mishuchu 1928: *juan* 1, p. 76A. On the move of prostitution to hotels, see also *Renyan zhoukan* 1934: 1.4 (March 10), p. 74.

83. The figures for the two types of cases heard by the Mixed Court from 1912 to 1924 are given in Kotenev 1968: pp. 315–16. For 1925–1926, see *Shanghai Municipal Council Report* 1925: pp. 42–43, 56–57; and *Shanghai Municipal Council Report* 1926: pp. 41–42, 55–56.

In 1932, ninety-eight brothels (ninety-seven of them Chinese) and 1,262 prostitutes (1,250 of them Chinese) were charged with breach of municipal bylaws and regulations. SMP: Box 112, MIS 8 (1932).

84. *CMJ* 1924: 38.1 (January), supplement, pp. 16–17, 26–29; *MG* 1924: January 17, pp. 15–16; also see *NCH* 1923: January 13, p. 102; and *MG* 1924: March 27, p. 114.

85. *NCH* 1923: October 20, p. 187.

86. *NCH* 1924: February 2, p. 179. In his 1931 report on Shanghai municipal governance prepared for the SMC, the South African jurist R. C. Feetham noted that the campaign had been a failure. He wrote, "The problem as to how to secure effective control of an evil which cannot be eliminated remains unsolved, and, under the law as it at present stands, the decision against continuance of any licensing system has imposed on the police an extremely difficult task. Police efforts are at present limited to taking measures to confine prostitutes within certain areas, and to keeping some check on soliciting in the streets. Special demands made on the Police in recent years by the general crime situation have, however, made it difficult for the Commissioner to spare sufficient men for such work." Feetham 1931: vol. 2, pp. 89–90.

87. *Renyan zhoukan* 1934: 1.10 (April 21), p. 203; Beijing shi gong'anju 1988: p. 209; *Jingbao* 1929: May 3, p. 3; May 27, p. 3. In many other cities, licensed prostitution remained legal. See, for instance, Beiping shehui diaocha suo 1931: p. 8 for a graph indicating that in 1930 the city of Beiping collected about seventy thousand yuan in prostitution taxes (*jijuan*). In Guangzhou, the authorities in 1935 made a three-year plan for a ban on prostitution. They proposed to begin by registering prostitutes in order to determine their exact number, then persuade them to marry or find another job. They intended to provide welfare facilities for the remainder, drawing lots to eliminate licensed prostitutes in the same manner that had proved ineffective in Shang-

hai. The city and provincial tax burden on Guangdong prostitutes was relatively heavy. *Funü yuebao* 1935: 1.3 (April 1), pp. 40–41; *Funü gongming* 1935: 4.11 (November 20), pp. 86–87; Lee 1936: pp. 95–96; and Lin Chongwu 1936: pp. 219–20.

88. *Jingbao* 1929: May 3, p. 3; May 18, p. 3.

89. *Funü gongming* 1934: 3.12 (December), p. 54; Sun Yusheng 1939: p. 3.

90. See, for instance, *Jingbao* 1929: March 21, p. 3; and May 21, p. 3.

91. *Jingbao* 1929: February 15, p. 3; February 21, p. 3; March 12, p. 2; March 24, p. 3; April 21, p. 3; May 24, p. 3. Many aspects of this episode remain obscure. The February 15 article names the manager of the stamp-tax office as Guan Jiongzhi, whom Stephens (1992: pp. 49, 52) identifies as the senior Chinese magistrate of the Mixed Court from 1911 to 1927. It seems unlikely that such a distinguished former official would move on to stamp-tax collection, but if the collection scheme did have his sponsorship, it indicates a much closer degree of cooperation with International Settlement authorities than the *Jingbao* accounts suggest.

92. Arguments about the ban were summarized in chapter 10. The announcement about lifting the ban was made in 1933, but the ban was actually scheduled to be lifted in 1934, and some reports had it still under discussion in 1935. After the ban was lifted, prostitution was to be confined to a designated area and limited to women aged sixteen or over (older women of some unspecified age were also to be banned). The women were to undergo health inspections. Cao Juren 1933; *Renyan zhoukan* 1934: 1.4 (March 10), p. 74; *Nüsheng* 1933: 2.4 (November 25), p. 1; *Funü gongming* 1935: 4.9 (September 20), p. 59.

The most ingenious rollback argument came from a Nanjing police official, who in January 1935 at a public talk on the subject indicated that since men in Nanjing outnumbered women by more than 100,000, and these men felt sexual frustration, prostitution in Nanjing was inevitable. This caused a commentator in a women's magazine to wonder why male prostitutes had not appeared to ease the sexual frustration of surplus women in Germany and France after World War I, and to ask the police who was attending to all the sexually frustrated wives the surplus men in Nanjing had left at home. *Funü gongming* 1935: 4.2 (February 20), pp. 32–33.

For an argument using the Nanjing ban to argue that prostitution could not be eliminated under China's prevailing social system, see Li Shanhu 1933. For letters, telegrams, and news conferences by women's groups who protested lifting the ban, see *Funü gongming* 1933: 2.5 (May), pp. 40–44.

On licensed prostitution in Suzhou after the ban was lifted, see *Shizheng pinglun* 1936: April 16, p. 31.

93. For details on the administration of Shanghai by the Guomindang during this period, see Pepper 1978: pp. 17–24, 27–28, 33–35, and 121–28.

94. Shanghai shi mishuchu 1945: 1.5 (December 15), pp. 11–12; Shanghai shi dang'an guan 1945: file 1-62-44, p. 3.

95. Shanghai shi dang'an guan 1945: file 1-62-44, p. 3.

96. The draft regulations are in Shanghai shi dang'an guan 1945: file 1-62-44, pp. 7–10. The published version, dated December 11, 1946 (more than a year after the draft regulations were proposed), is in Shanghai shi jingchaju fagui huibian 1947 (pp. 20–21).

97. Shanghai shi dang'an guan 1945: file 1-62-44, pp. 25–26.

98. [Shanghai] *Dagong bao* 1946: January 21.

99. Shanghai shi dang'an guan 1945: file 1-62-44, p. 3. In practice, the government eventually began to license four classes of brothel: *changsan* and *yao er* houses, salt-pork shops, and pheasant houses. Yu Wei 1948: p. 11.

100. Shanghai shi dang'an guan 1945: file 1-62-44, pp. 3–4.

101. Shanghai shi dang'an guan 1946–1947: file 6-9-666, p. 5.

102. Shanghai shi dang'an guan 1946–1947: file 6-9-666, pp. 17–18.

103. Shanghai shi dang'an guan 1946–1947: file 6-9-666, p. 8.

104. Shanghai shi dang'an guan 1946–1947: file 1-10-246, pp. 16–17.

105. Shanghai shi dang'an guan 1946–1947: file 1-10-246, p. 32.

106. Shanghai shi dang'an guan 1946–1947: file 6-9-666, p. 5. In October the mayor received a letter from one Yang Hongkui, of the Lixin jiating gongyeshe (Beautiful New Household Industry Society), volunteering to help teach embroidery skills to detained prostitutes in order to end prostitution, which "ruins the social atmosphere and destroys the nation's people. The damage done is greater than that caused by beasts of prey or flood." Yang was willing to hire the women to do embroidery work. The mayor referred his letter to the Social Affairs Bureau, but nothing conclusive ever came of his proposal. Shanghai shi dang'an guan 1946–1947: file 1-10-246, pp. 25–27, 47–48.

107. For such complaints, see Shanghai shi dang'an guan 1946–1949: file 011-4-163, cases 9, 12, 14, 15; and Shanghai shi dang'an guan 1946: file 011-4-162, case 3.

108. In addition to the cases cited later, see also Shanghai shi dang'an guan 1946–1949: file 011-4-163, cases 1, 3, 4, 11, and 14; and Shanghai shi dang'an guan 1946: file 011-4-162, cases 6, 7, and 8.

109. Shanghai shi dang'an guan 1946: file 011-4-162, case 5.

110. The repeated allegations of bribery set off an internal police investigation, which eventually cleared the police officers of charges that they had behaved improperly. The brothel owner and his prostitutes were fined, but the investigators concluded that they had violated only police regulations, not the criminal code, since there seemed to be no force involved and the women were former guide-agency employees who "did not seem to be from respectable families." About the brothel owner who had hid under the bed, the police log concluded, "Although Cai Wenyuan is operating an unlicensed brothel and this is against the law and deserves punishment, he is blind and has no job, and so his activities can be forgiven." Shanghai shi dang'an guan 1946: file 011-4-163, case 9.

111. Shanghai shi dang'an guan 1946–1947: file 1-10-246, p. 49.

112. Shanghai shi dang'an guan 1946–1949: file 011-4-163, case 2. See also Shanghai shi dang'an guan 1946–1949: file 011-4-163, case 3.

113. Shanghai shi dang'an guan 1946–1949: file 011-4-163, case 15.

114. Shanghai shi dang'an guan 1946–1949: file 011-4-163, cases 13 and 16.

115. Shanghai shi dang'an guan 1946–1949: file 011-4-163, cases 17 and 9. The writer of the second letter went on to complain that the local patrolmen were corrupt and in the pay of the brothel owners. See also case 18.

116. Shanghai shi dang'an guan 1946–1949: file 011-4-163, case 10.

117. Materials on the rise and fall of these organizations are in Shanghai shi dang'an guan 1945–1947: file 011-4-260, passim. The [Shanghai] *Dagong bao* (1946: February 7) reported that the owners of 347 brothels had petitioned the city government for permission to organize a "weaving flower girl fellowship society" (*zhi*

hua nü lianyi she), to act as a guild organization for *shuyu* and all other licensed prostitutes. The authorities agreed to consider the request. It is not clear if this was the same group.

After 1949, Hui Genquan was pilloried in the press as a "counterrevolutionary tyrant" who was responsible for smothering and nailing into a coffin a prostitute named Xiao Mei. For an account of his crime (but not his ultimate fate) see *Jiefang ribao* 1951: November 23.

118. [Shanghai] *Dagong bao* 1946: February 21, March 7. The size of the group was not given. The organization administering these examinations was the Shanghai Institute for the Prevention and Treatment of Sexually Transmitted Diseases; it is not clear whether this was a predecessor of the organization described later, founded at the end of 1946.

119. Shanghai shi dang'an guan 1946–1947: file 6-9-666, p. 8; Shanghai shi dang'an guan 1946–1947: file 1-10-246, p. 21.

120. Shanghai shi dang'an guan 1946–1947: file 1-10-246, p. 64. Xu Chongli, formerly a doctor at the Institute for the Prevention and Treatment of Sexually Transmitted Diseases, recalls that many prostitutes took just enough injections so that their blood tested negative for STDs, and then returned to work. Le Jiayu and Xu Chongli 1986.

121. [Shanghai] *Dagong bao* 1946: March 14.

122. Shanghai shi dang'an guan 1946–1947: file 1-10-246, p. 68.

123. Numbers of women inspected are given in Yu Wei 1947: p. 18.

124. Yu Wei 1947: p. 18.

125. These figures are from combined statistics for 1946 and 1947. For the combined statistics, see Yu Wei 1947: p. 17; for a breakdown by year and infection, as well as a critique of medical methods, see Yu Wei 1948: pp. 11–13.

126. Le Jiayu and Xu Chongli 1986.

127. Shanghai shi dang'an guan 1948: file 011-4-171, passim. Altogether the file contains thirteen of these orders. Eleven are from the Laozha district, one is from Xincheng, and one is from Tilan Qiao.

128. Yu Wei 1947: p. 18.

129. Shanghai shi dang'an guan 1946–1947: file 1-10-246, pp. 60–61, 70, 72.

130. For examples of this type of complaint and the government response, see Shanghai shi dang'an guan 1946–1947: file 1-10-246, pp. 76–80 and 99–101.

131. *Shizheng pinglun* 1946: 8.9 (November 1), pp. 42–43. The facility was called the Shanghai Municipal Relief Division Women's Education and Training Institute [Shanghai shi jiuji yuan funü jiaoyang suo]. For its articles of organization, see Shanghai shi jiuji yuan 1947.

132. Shanghai ertong 1948: p. 44; Chen Renbing 1948: pp. 154–55.

133. Shanghai shi dang'an guan 1946–1947: file 6-9-666, pp. 9–10.

134. Shanghai shi dang'an guan 1946–1947: file 1-10-246, pp. 86, 90.

135. Shanghai shi dang'an guan 1946–1947: file 1-10-246, pp. 92–95, 96, 98.

136. Shanghai shi dang'an guan 1946–1947: file 1-10-246, p. 60; Shanghai shi dang'an guan 1946–1947: file 6-9-666, p. 9. According to a 1948 survey, at the end of 1946 there were about eight thousand registered prostitutes, and by the end of 1947 the number had shrunk to somewhat more than three thousand, while the number of unlicensed prostitutes continued to increase. Yu Wei 1948: p. 10.

137. *Shanghai jingcha* 1948: 2.5 (January), p. 71. The police department had also prepared special residence registration cards for dancers, prostitutes, vagrants, and others, giving each person's name, address, aliases, regular movements, and activities. How widely these cards were distributed and used is unclear. *Shanghai jingcha* 1948: 2.5 (January), p. 31. An article in the following issue on establishments and people requiring special police investigation and management included both brothel keeping and prostitution among its list of improper occupations. (Singing girls and dancers were included as well.) Prostitutes were portrayed as harmful to public health and morality, apt to extort money from their customers and try to operate without licenses. Yet they also required police surveillance in case they were victims of trafficking or ill-treatment. Additionally, they were considered potentially useful as sources of intelligence for the police. With training, the article said, they could let the police know who was carrying concealed weapons or had suspicious scars. *Shanghai jingcha* 1948: 2.6 (February), pp. 35–39.

138. *Shanghai jingcha* 1948: 2.5 (January), p. 46. The totals given on the chart on this page are incorrect and have been recalculated. In 1948, the head of the Morals Correction Unit of the Shanghai police said in an interview that most new prostitutes were coming from the countryside. *Jia* 1948: 25 (January), p. 24.

139. *Shanghai jingcha* 1948: 2.7 (March), pp. 73–74.

140. Shanghai shi dang'an guan 1946–1947: file 1-10-246, pp. 90, 87. In April 1948 the police increased their arrests of unlicensed prostitutes and opened up registration, and as of June 1948 they had registered ten thousand prostitutes. Yu Wei 1948: p. 10.

141. Shanghai shi dang'an guan 1946–1947: file 1-10-246, pp. 106–8.

142. Le Jiayu and Xu Chongli 1986.

143. Shanghai shi zhengfu mishuchu 1945: 1.3 (December 9), p. 11.

144. Draft regulations for these groups were sent by police chief Xuan Tiewu to Mayor Qian on November 24, 1945. Shanghai shi dang'an guan 1945: file 1-62-44, pp. 42–52. The final regulations for dancers, dated January 8, 1946, were published in Shanghai shi jingchaju fagui huibian 1947 (pp. 19–20). Regulations for bar and coffee-shop dancers are on pp. 21–22.

145. Shanghai shi dang'an guan 1945: file 1-62-44, pp. 29–30.

146. [Shanghai] *Dagong bao* 1946: January 5.

147. [Shanghai] *Dagong bao* 1946: January 5, p. 3, March 5, p. 3; Tu Shipin 1968: *xia*, p. 77.

148. "Shanghai de teshu zhiye" 1946: p. 13.

149. [Shanghai] *Dagong bao* 1946: March 5, p. 3.

150. [Shanghai] *Dagong bao* 1946: February 7. But see also June 21 for similar numbers.

151. [Shanghai] *Dagong bao* 1946: August 8, p. 4.

152. Except where otherwise noted, this account is based upon Liu Huanong 1948: pp. 40–47; and Fan Xipin 1979: pp. 190–99.

153. *Xiandai funü* (1948: 11.2 (February 1), p. 3) estimated that the ban would affect more than four thousand dancers and several tens of thousands of other employees. Fan Xipin (1979: pp. 190–91), however, offers a more modest estimate of more than two thousand employees, including more than eight hundred licensed taxi dancers.

154. *Xiandai funü* 1948: 11.2 (February 1), p. 3. For a letter written by (or in the

voice of) a taxi dancer who could not find alternative means of support, see p. 18 of the same issue.

155. *Jia* 1947: 23 (December), p. 422.

156. Liu Huanong 1948: pp. 44–47. The Dance Hall Employees Union was under the leadership of the Three People's Principles Youth Corps. For a memoir of this riot written by a local official of the youth corps, see Fan Xipin 1979: pp. 190–99.

CHAPTER 12: REVOLUTIONARIES

1. An abbreviated version of this chapter was first published in Hershatter 1992b. Cao Manzhi was vice-chair of the Political Takeover Committee of the Shanghai Military Management Group (*Shanghai junguan hui zhengwu jieguanhui fuzhuren*), vice-secretary of the People's Government and head of the Civil Administration Bureau (*Minzheng ju*). He was primarily responsible for the 1950s reform campaign, from taking in (*shourong*) prostitutes to curing their sexually transmitted diseases to providing job training. He called the reform of prostitutes "the most complex and difficult" of the problems involved in the takeover of Shanghai. Cao Manzhi, "Introduction," in Yang He 1988: pp. 1–2. Unless otherwise noted, all subsequent references to Cao Manzhi's activities are based on interviews with him conducted in Shanghai on November 10 and 20, 1986.

2. Yang Jiezeng and He Wannan 1988: pp. 28–30.

3. Xi'an, Nantong, Qingdao, and Wuhan took up similar campaigns at about the same time as Shanghai. For details on some of these cities, see Yang Jiezeng and He Wannan 1988: pp. 22–24. On Beijing, see also Hsiao Kan 1950 and Beijing shi gong'anju 1988.

4. [Shanghai] *Jiefang ribao* 1951: November 23.

5. [Shanghai] *Dagong bao* 1950: June 11, p. 4.

6. [Shanghai] *Jiefang ribao* 1951: November 23.

7. [Shanghai] *Jiefang ribao* 1951: November 23; [Shanghai] *Dagong bao* 1951: November 27, p. 1.

8. Yang Xiuqin and Xu Huiqing 1986.

9. Yang Jiezeng 1986.

10. Yang Xiuqin and Xu Huiqing 1986; Yang Jiezeng and He Wannan 1988: pp. 34–36.

11. Yang Xiuqin and Xu Huiqing 1986.

12. Yang Xiuqin and Xu Huiqing 1986.

13. Huang Shi 1986.

14. *Xinwen ribao* 1951: November 27, p. 1; [Shanghai] *Jiefang ribao* 1951: November 27, p. 1; [Shanghai] *Dagong bao* 1951: November 27, p. 1.

15. Yang Xiuqin and Xu Huiqing 1986.

16. See, for example, [Shanghai] *Dagong bao* 1951: November 26, p. 6, and December 14, p. 4; *Xinwen ribao* 1951: November 25, p. 4, and November 27, p. 4; and Hsiao Wen 1957: pp. 24–27. For stories retold in the 1980s that detail torture and other abuses, see He Wannan 1984: pp. 20–22.

17. [Shanghai] *Dagong bao* 1951: November 27, p. 1; *Xinwen ribao* 1951: November 27, p. 4.

18. Yu Wei 1948: p. 12.
19. Yu and Wong 1949: p. 237.
20. Yang Jiezeng 1986. Cao Manzhi 1986 recalls:

We took them to the receiving station, and people lined up on both sides of the street to look, all thinking, "Why is the CCP being so unreasonable?" (These people didn't know that the women were prostitutes.) "How can they arbitrarily seize people and load them into cars, car after car? They're sending them to the suburbs. The CCP is seizing women and selling them." Rumors flew. The next day we quickly got on the radio and broadcast the fact that we were taking in prostitutes. . . . At that time many people made unfounded charges about us, and the common people cursed us: "The CCP are bastards. Your People's Liberation Army is so disciplined, how could you be seizing women? The CCP members have no wives, the CCP hasn't brought wives with them into the city. When foreign troops invaded China they all brought brothels with them. The CCP has no army prostitutes, so they are seizing women everywhere to be army prostitutes for them."

21. Cao Manzhi 1986.
22. [Shanghai] *Dagong bao* 1951: November 27, p. 1.
23. Yang Xiuqin and Xu Huiqing 1986.
24. Cao Manzhi 1986.
25. Yang Jiezeng 1986. In addition to other accounts of the reform process cited in this chapter, see Cusack 1958: pp. 237–59; Lu Feiyun and Zhang Zhongru 1983; and A Zhao 1984.
26. For an account of the national project to eliminate sexually transmitted diseases in the PRC, see Cohen et al. 1993. Mass screening of the population for syphilis was conducted in some former treaty-port cities, including Shanghai. Public-health workers asked people, among other questions, whether they had had sexual relations with prostitutes or worked as prostitutes. Cohen et al. point out that "Western civilization and capitalism" were identified as the culprit in spreading STDs, and that the elimination of such diseases was characterized as patriotic.
27. He Wannan 1984: p. 21.
28. [Shanghai] *Dagong bao* 1951: November 30, p. 4; Yang Xiuqin and Xu Huiqing 1986.
29. Shanghai shi minzheng ju 1959: p. 3; He Wannan 1984: p. 21. This was a considerable sum. Approximately seven thousand women passed through the institute prior to its closure in 1958. If half of these (thirty-five hundred) suffered from sexually transmitted diseases, then the government spent an average of 51 yuan to cure each one. By way of crude comparison, in 1952 the per capita gross domestic product was 126 yuan. King 1968: p. 181.
30. Le Jiayu and Xu Chongli 1986; Yang Jiezeng 1986.
31. Cao Manzhi in Yang Jiezeng and He Wannan 1988: pp. iii–iv; Le Jiayu and Xu Chongli 1986.
32. Cao Manzhi 1986; Yang Jiezeng 1986.
33. *Xinwen ribao* 1952: August 22, p. 4; Shanghai shi minzheng ju 1959: p. 2.
34. Shanghai shi minzheng ju 1959: p. 2.
35. Yang Xiuqin and Xu Huiqing 1986.

36. [Shanghai] *Dagong bao* 1951: December 14, p. 4. Like most of the claims for the success of ideological work made in the official press, this one should be read cautiously. Yang Jiezeng, the woman in charge of the institute, commented in the 1986 interview, "At the beginning . . . they made themselves blind and deaf and didn't want to listen. We would show them movies and they wouldn't watch." Yang Jiezeng 1986.

Sometime after the campaign to eliminate prostitution, a Shanghai film studio portrayed the campaign in *Rebirth of a Daughter of Smoke and Flowers*. Ku Liang 1969: p. 7.

37. Statistics on 7,513 woman who passed through the institute indicate that 673 were from Shanghai, 2,627 from various parts of Jiangsu province, 2,379 from Zhejiang, and the remainder from other provinces. Minzheng ju n.d.

38. Honig 1986: passim.

39. Yang Xiuqin and Xu Huiqing 1986. This account is necessarily based on the recollections of reformers rather than subjects. It is certainly possible that former prostitutes would recall native-place and status alliances differently.

40. Huang Shi, who was in charge of the criminal division of the police during this period, comments that the most powerful people in the brothels were not the madams, but male owners who had powerful gang connections. Owners received prison sentences; some of those who had also collaborated with the Japanese or committed other "counterrevolutionary crimes" were executed. Madams were generally put under surveillance by residents' security committees. Huang Shi 1986.

41. Yang Jiezeng 1986; He Wannan 1984: p. 20.

42. Yang Jiezeng 1986.

43. *Xinwen ribao* 1952: August 22, p. 4.

44. *Xinwen ribao* 1952: August 22, p. 4; Yang Jiezeng 1986.

45. Shanghai shi minzheng ju 1959: pp. 2–3.

46. Yang Xiuqin and Xu Huiqing 1986.

47. He Wannan 1984: p. 22.

48. Shanghai shi minzheng ju 1959: p. 3.

49. Huang Yunqiu and Wang Dingfei 1986. For a description of their daily routine, see [Shanghai] *Dagong bao* 1951: November 30, p. 4.

50. Yang Jiezeng 1986.

51. Every surviving Chinese source that speaks of this reform process is, of course, heavily invested in declaring its success. A chilling contrast to this enthusiasm is found in the account by one Peter Schmid, a German who visited the institute in 1958. He refers to Yang Jiezeng, the chief administrator of the institute, as "anti-eroticism personified: with a face like a spider, without even a spark of that maternal kindness which, surely, one might have expected from some one in her position. Frigid to the bone, she had borne no children and had left her husband, to devote herself to this task—the reeducation of fallen girls." Schmid implies that Yang took a malicious pleasure in being given control over beautiful women. His description (Schmid 1958: pp. 110–11) of the institute reads in part:

The institution was almost indistinguishable from a prison—with its grey walls, the red star over the gate, its hermetic seclusion from the outside world and only twice-monthly visits by relatives. . . . In the courtyard a board proudly proclaimed the aims of the institution in big Chinese letters: 'We are fighting against the degradation of womanhood and are striving for the creation of a new human being.'

> But when I set out hopefully in search of the 'new human being' I found nothing but the mixture as before: production targets as the supreme revealed truth, flags, portraits of Mao. Nowhere a flower, a bird, or anything that might have rekindled something like real gentleness in the downtrodden souls. I made no secret to Mrs. Yang of my opinion of her inhuman institution. In the workshops the former prostitutes were sitting behind their machines as tightly packed together as sardines, knitting socks and gloves. Packed just as tightly, the night shift were dozing through the afternoon in their dormitories. 'Six months,' was Mrs. Yang's reply to my question of how long on an average the girls spent in this satanic mill.

This description is as enmeshed in a story of anticommunist dehumanization as the Chinese official accounts are in tales of humane nation building. In spite of their contrasting evaluations of the reform enterprise, however, the two types of stories share a set of assumptions about reaching women by appealing to their "natural" womanly qualities. For Schmid, these inhered in gentleness, the love of beauty, and a sexuality that was not "frigid to the bone"; for the Chinese reformers, they inhered in women's reinsertion into families as daughters, wives, and mothers.

52. Yang Jiezeng and He Wannan 1988: pp. 49–50.

53. Cao Manzhi 1986. He adds with evident pride, "Some of our cadres had a lot of experience, particularly those in the underground party. Some could pull in fifty or sixty prostitutes a night. They worked the Great World all night long."

54. Yang Xiuqin and Xu Huiqing 1986.

55. Yang Xiuqin and Xu Huiqing 1986. Taxi dancers, who had successfully resisted Guomindang efforts to ban them, were called together by the Communist government and told that they would first be licensed and then found alternative employment. Cao Manzhi states that this problem was solved within about two weeks, the main impediment being the difficulty of calling the dancers together and lecturing to a room of heavily perfumed women:

> We decided to close the dance halls because sometimes they couldn't be separated from prostitutes and from the rotten atmosphere of the corrupt society. And sometimes some dancers sold sex. Besides, the dance halls were all under the absolute control of the Green Gang and the Red Gang, because they owed a lot of money. . . .
>
> I held a big meeting at Da Guangming. The place was full of dancers; there wasn't an empty seat. I made two long reports to the dancers so all of them came. Though they were a little better [than prostitutes], still the perfume that they used, if it was one person at home or two, you could tolerate it, but you couldn't stay in a room with the smell of more than three people, and with more than a thousand of them in one room listening to a report, every one wearing perfume, you were doing well if you didn't vomit when you entered the room. . . .
>
> Later the ones with a higher cultural level became typists or clerks. The rest usually became workers. Their income was not as high as before, and there were complaints about this. They were definitely not very happy, because as dancers they had more income and ate better.

Cao Manzhi 1986.

56. Huang Yunqiu and Wang Dingfei 1986.

57. Yang Jiezeng 1986.

58. Yang Xiuqin and Xu Huiqing 1986.

59. Yang Xiuqin and Xu Huiqing 1986; also see Shanghai shi minzheng ju 1959: p. 4. Yang Jiezeng (1986) estimates that altogether more than nine hundred women were sent to Xinjiang.

The decision to send women outside of Shanghai was not entirely uncontroversial among the Shanghai populace. Cao Manzhi recalls that when a plan was floated to send some of the women to northern Jiangsu (Subei),

> another rumor started, saying that we were sending them to the northern part of the Soviet Union [*Sulian*], to Siberia—"Subei." That it was forty below zero there, and that people would die of the cold as soon as they went. They said that there were no people in that part of the Soviet Union, that they needed a group of Chinese to open up the wilderness. They said that they would all die on the road.

Cao Manzhi 1986.

60. Yang Jiezeng 1986.

61. Yang Jiezeng 1986.

62. A film showing in Shanghai in 1995, *The Unwelcome Lady* (*Hong cheng* in Chinese; the English title is not a direct translation) deals with persistent gossip about a reformed prostitute in Xi'an. The woman and her husband are tormented by the neighbors for three decades. In the 1980s, the man finally leaves his wife and she commits suicide; his remorseful return is too late. Unwise as it would be to conclude anything about the treatment of reformed prostitutes from their representation in this story, the film nevertheless suggests that the reintegration of these women into local society provides possibilities for dramatic tension. I am grateful to Kathleen Erwin for sending me a plot summary of this film.

63. Yang Jiezeng and He Wannan 1988: p. 124. Of these, 858 had been licensed prostitutes and 6,655 unlicensed prostitutes. Minzheng ju n.d.

64. When the first group of prostitutes was taken in in November 1951, *Xinwen ribao* reported that neighbors came out to watch the Public Security Bureau seal up the brothels, commenting that now the noise, drinking, and quarreling that had marred the neighborhood peace would come to an end. *Xinwen ribao* 1951: November 27, p. 4; see also [Shanghai] *Dagong bao* 1951: November 27, p. 1. For letters to the editor from the residents' committee and housewives' association of Huile Li, as well as from other urban residents supporting the roundup, see [Shanghai] *Dagong bao* 1951: November 26, p. 6. This orchestrated outpouring of support obviously says little about any ambivalence residents may have experienced at the move of the state into highly efficient and localized control.

65. On the policing of households and work in the People's Republic of China, see Dutton 1992: pp. 187–245.

66. On this effort see Stacey 1984: pp. 203–47.

67. Johnson 1983.

68. Evans 1991; Evans 1995.

69. A version of this paragraph appeared in Hershatter 1996: p. 87.

CHAPTER 13: NAMING

1. Schoenhals 1992: chapter 1; quoted passages are from pp. 1–2.

2. For instance, in August 1965 it was considered correct to say that socialist society contained classes (*you jieji de shehui*) but not that it was a class society (*jieji shehui*). Schoenhals 1992: p. 7.

3. Gao Xiaoxian and Du Li 1993.

4. Wang Xingjuan 1993b.

5. But see also a 1927 article in which Huang Shi argued for a distinction between the "prostitution system" (*changji zhidu*), referring to licensed prostitution, and the broader "sex-selling system" (*maiyin zhidu*), which encompassed the far larger number of unlicensed and part-time prostitutes as well. Huang Shi 1927: pp. 796–98.

6. Tyler 1993. In a February 1992 speech, Deng stated that this decision was one of his "biggest mistakes."

7. Burns 1985; Southerland 1985; Gargan 1988; Ignatius and Leung 1989; Sun 1992.

8. Gargan 1988: p. 4. The degree of similarity across accounts leads to a suspicion that these reporters were all reading the same background sources, hiring the same local informants, or even just reading one another's dispatches. Compare Gargan's account to one Lena Sun published more than three years later: "Before socialist morality became creed, prostitutes thrived in China's port cities. Shanghai was infamous for its brothels in the 1930s and '40s. After the Communist takeover in 1949, the eradication of social evils such as prostitution became a priority. Brothels were closed; thousands of prostitutes were sent to reeducation camps. For decades, officials claimed that prostitution and venereal disease had disappeared from the mainland." Sun 1992.

9. Sun 1992.

10. Burns 1985: p. 12; Southerland 1985: p. A20. Chen Yun, age eighty, was chair of the party's Discipline Inspection Commission. Deng Liqun was in charge of party propaganda work. Deng Xiaoping was a member of the Standing Committee of the Politburo and chair of the Military Affairs Commission. The reform policies, which were proposed piecemeal and implemented unevenly, included the establishment of a contract system in agriculture, attempts to make industry more accountable for profits and losses, the ceding of increased fiscal and planning authority to local governments, the development of individual enterprises, the elimination of some state subsidies, a loosening of restrictions on migration, and increased foreign investment and trade.

11. Ku Liang 1969: pp. 8–10.

12. Yan Ping 1977: pp. 11–17.

13. Yan Ping 1977: pp. 11–13.

14. For a brief discussion of prostitution by a Chinese scholar writing in English, see Ruan Fangfu 1991: pp. 73–84.

15. For general descriptions of the sex trades, based on Chinese news reports and written for overseas Chinese, see *Huaqiao ribao* 1986: March 1; and *Shijie ribao* 1993: October 18.

16. "Security Ministry Cracks Down on Prostitution" (text). Beijing *Xinhua* in English (6 September 1991, 0847 GMT). *FBIS Daily Report—China,* 10 September 1991 (PrEx 7.10: FBIS-CHI-91-175), p. 31.

17. *China News Digest* 1994: February 26. Another way of assessing the number is to look at one antiprostitution campaign in Shenzhen from April 1 to June 15, 1992, in the course of which 1,747 people were detained. Of these, 53.5 percent were prostitutes, 40.5 percent were customers, and 6 percent were pimps. See *Shijie ribao* 1992: July 6, p. 13. If we take the lower possible total of people arrested from 1986 to mid-1993 (940,300; this figure is derived from appendix A, table 2) and apply this same formula to it, it suggests that something like 503,061 arrests were made of prostitutes in a seven-and-a-half-year period. Even assuming that some women were detained more than once, this was still in the range of half a million women.

18. Wang Xingjuan 1990: p. 5.

19. The size, instability, and employment of the urban floating population was of particular concern to Chinese officials and scholars. Surveys of Shanghai, Beijing, and Hangzhou found that "on an average day in 1986, the transient population of Shanghai was 1.834 million, which accounted for 25.1 percent of a total population of 7.102 million; in Beijing it was 1 million, or 17.6 percent of a total population of 5.967 million; in Hangzhou it was 250,000, or 20.1 percent of a total population of 1.2 million. In 1977, before reform and opening up, the transient populations in Shanghai, Beijing, and Hangzhou were 600,000, 500,000, and 86,200, respectively." Zhou Weixin, "An Analysis of Criminal Activities in China's Urban Areas," *Shehui* 5.20 (May 1988), pp. 12–16, translated in JPRS-CAR-88-047 (19 August 1988), pp. 44–48; statistics are from p. 44. See also Li and Hu 1991; Chai 1990; Pan 1991; Solinger 1991; Solinger 1992; and Honig 1993. On young girls (aged fifteen or younger) in the floating population, a small number of whom engaged in prostitution, see Tong 1993.

20. See the Chinese studies cited in Solinger 1991: p. 11, nn. 60–63.

21. Gao Xiaoxian and Du Li 1993.

22. Detailed reports on Guangzhou and environs date from late 1985. One example is *Huaqiao ribao* 1986: March 1–3. Prostitution reportedly became more obvious and visible in Shanghai in 1989 and 1990. Lu Xing'er 1993b.

23. Ignatius and Leung 1989.

24. Chen Yiyun 1992; Lu Xing'er 1993b.

25. "NPC Examines Prostitution, Countermeasures" (text). Hong Kong *Jiushi niandai* in Chinese (1 October 1991), no. 216, pp. 11–13. *FBIS Daily Report—China*, 9 October 1991 (PrEx 7.10: FBIS-CHI-91-196), pp. 27–28.

26. On the army hotel, see Ignatius and Leung 1989: p. A23; and Ignatius and Leung 1990?: p. A11. On the Women's Federation guest house, see Kristof 1993. On Shanghai brothels, see Malhotra 1994 and Buruma 1996: p. 48.

27. Personal observation, Shanghai, June 26, 1993. For a colorful description of similar activities in several bars, private clubs, and brothels, see Malhotra 1994.

28. Lague 1993.

29. But they were not utterly absent. In 1992, an overseas Chinese newspaper reported that three Hong Kong businesspeople had been arrested for attempting to run a nightclub-cum-brothel in a county of Shenzhen. Detained along with the managers were twenty-eight "house ladies" (*gongguan xiaojie*) who had been trained to solicit customers for the Fuli Tanghuang nightclub, drink with them, and sell them high-priced liquor. A house rule also required that each new "house lady" sleep with a guest for one thousand yuan on her first day of work, dividing the money with the nightclub. A spokesperson for the police said that these arrangements were mod-

eled on those in Hong Kong nightclubs. *Shijie ribao* 1992: July 6, p. 13. For the emergence of brothels with official sponsorship in Shanghai, see Malhotra 1994.

30. Wang Xingjuan 1990: pp. 5–6.

31. Lu Xing'er 1993b: n.p.; Chen Yiyun 1992; personal conversations, Hongqiao Hotel, Shanghai, June 26, 1993; Lee 1995.

32. Ignatius and Leung 1989: p. A1.

33. *Huaqiao ribao* 1986: March 1–2. Statistics for 1988 based on interviews with 483 customers and 10 pimps detained by the Shenzhen public security bureau found that 43.1 percent were from Hong Kong, 43 percent were from Shenzhen and the rest of Guangdong, and the remainder were from other provinces. Their occupations were classified as follows:

Driver	37.3%
Employee, contractor, or *getihu*	34.5%
Cadre	16.1%
No proper occupation	12.1%

Wang Xingjuan 1990: pp. 3–4.

On arrests of high-ranking cadres in Sichuan, see also *Shijie ribao* 1993: October 18. In Yiyang, Hunan, in 1992, government agencies made arrests of twenty-eight johns within a week, and discovered that half of them were retirees older than fifty. Of this sample of fourteen, two were widowers; the rest had wives. Most were first offenders. The news report commented that the men found life lonely after retirement and were looking for stimulation. One prosperous sixty-seven-year-old who felt that life after retirement was uninteresting struck up an acquaintance with prostitutes on his street, inviting them in to "melt the soul" at about 10 A.M. each day, after his children left for work. *Shijie ribao* 1992: July 28, p. 13.

34. Lu Xing'er 1993b.

35. One such case involved exchange students at Fudan University in Shanghai, who were hired through the school to work at a Guangdong karaoke bar during school vacations. The students discovered that the bar managers expected them to sleep with staff and customers. Fudan spokespersons denied any knowledge of this arrangement. The article concluded, "Russians and eastern Europeans have flocked to China since the fall of Communism in their countries to engage in trade or work as waitresses. Some of the women have become prostitutes in a nation where white women are sometimes seen as being more attractive and having looser morals than Chinese women." Charlene Fu 1993. In mid-June, nine Russian women were expelled by authorities from Chengdu, where they had been hired by companies and restaurants some months earlier. Although their offense was ostensibly failing to register with the police, the implication was clearly that they were working as prostitutes. "Nine Russian Women" 1993. On teenaged prostitution in Shanghai, see *China News Digest* 1994: March 22.

36. Gao Xiaoxian and Du Li 1993.

37. Lu Xing'er 1993b. The development of a moneyed class of Chinese businessmen also facilitated the emergence of "kept women" who were classified as sex-selling women by the authorities. In a narrative of one incarcerated woman, a Shanghai nurse named Daqin, the writer Lu Xing'er explains that Daqin met a company

manager from the southern province of Hainan at an amusement center. (Like Guangzhou and other southern locales, Hainan here connotes vice and greed.) He invited her to accompany him to Suzhou and rented a taxi to take them there, paying 360 yuan. Daqin reflected that in a month of work, half of it on night shift, she could make only 300 yuan, and her attraction for him intensified when she accompanied him to meet powerful city leaders in Suzhou. Telling her that after his wife she was number one, he sent considerable sums of money to her every month after he returned to Hainan. Although Daqin had a boyfriend who earned about 700 yuan a month in a joint venture, she concluded that her monthly income combined with his would have been only 1000 yuan, "not enough to buy a skirt," and so she broke off with him. She did not love the Hainan manager, but felt that he was concerned about her. She enjoyed being able to take a taxi after work and invite her friends out for meals, basking in their envy. (This same indefatigable man reportedly also supported another mistress in Shanghai, this one a prostitute he had met in southern China.) Lu Xing'er 1993a: pp. 23–25.

38. Wang Xingjuan 1990: p. 4.

39. "Official Journal Cited on Cases of Prostitution" (text). Hong Kong AFP in English (16 January 1989 at 935 GMT). *FBIS Daily Report—China*, 17 January 1989 (PrEx 7.10: FBIS-CHI-89–010), pp. 34–35; Sun 1992; A Qiao 1993: 53–55.

40. "Shandong Holds Forum on Eliminating Prostitution" (text). Jinan Shandong People's Radio Network in Mandarin (3 August 1992, 2300 GMT). *FBIS Daily Report—China*, 5 August 1992 (PrEx 7.10: FBIS-CHI-92-151), p. 50.

41. A Qiao 1993: p. 53.

42. A Qiao 1993: pp. 53–55.

43. A Qiao 1993: p. 55.

44. *Xi'an fazhi bao* 1993: 486, July 2, p. 2.

45. Gargan 1988: p. 4.

46. Ye Po 1989: p. 8; Wang Xingjuan 1990. Pimps sometimes became bail bondsmen as well: at the Guangzhou train station, two foreign reporters interviewed a Shanghainese pimp named Feng who had gone to Guangzhou with two women he had known since childhood. The three stayed in a hotel, where liaisons with customers were arranged by hotel staff. Feng was interviewed just after the two women were detained by police; he was on his way back to Shanghai to collect money for payoffs so that "his girls" could go back to work. Ignatius and Leung 1990?: p. 11.

47. For a report on the latter type of case originally reported in *Xiamen ribao*, see *Shijie ribao* 1992: July 31, p. 11.

48. Sun 1992; Malhotra 1994.

49. Lu Xing'er 1993b. As the next footnote indicates, Shanghai did execute two pimps in 1990.

50. "Last year [1988?] in Canton alone, 15 pimps were executed," the *Asian Wall Street Journal* reported in 1990. Ignatius and Leung 1989: p. A23. Many such cases appear to have involved pimping in combination with rape, physical coercion, or other offenses. On the execution of two pimps who robbed and injured customers, see "Guangzhou, Shanghai Crack Down on Crime, Vice" (text). Hong Kong AFP in English (4 June 1992, 1247 GMT). *FBIS Daily Report—China*, 5 June 1992 (PrEx 7.10: FBIS-CHI-92-109), pp. 25–26. On 1990 Shanghai, see "Two Pimps Executed in Shanghai Municipality" (text). Shanghai City Service in Mandarin (30 November

1990, 2300 GMT). *FBIS Daily Report—China,* 3 December 1990 (PrEx 7.10: FBIS-CHI-90–232), p. 47. On the execution of a Beijing pimp who had physically coerced women into prostitution and also murdered a man, see "Beijing Court Orders Execution of Repeat Offender" (text). *Beijing ribao* in Chinese (18 November 1990), p. 1. *FBIS Daily Report—China,* 20 December 1990 (PrEx 7.10: FBIS-CHI-90–245), pp. 69–70.

51. Wang Xingjuan 1990: p. 5. Apparently sex-selling groups, with or without pimps, were on the rise; a survey of one hundred prostitutes undergoing labor education in Beijing found that twenty-eight of them had been in associations of two or more who engaged in mutual help, introduced customers to one another, and hired themselves out for group sexual activities. Beijing shi Tiantang he laojiaosuo 1992?: p. 3. One survey suggested that rural women did not merely drift into urban prostitution, but formed "specialized households" that earned a major portion of family income through selling sex, sometimes coming to the city in groups of sisters and sisters-in-law, mothers and daughters, or husbands and wives. Liu Dalin et al. 1992: p. 717; Wang Xingjuan 1990: p. 5; Wang Xingjuan 1992a: p. 426.

52. In 1991, a Shanghai woman named Zhang Yuzhen was sentenced to seven years' imprisonment for such an offense. "Shanghai Courts Set Verdicts on Obscenity Charges" (text). Shanghai *Wenhui bao* in Chinese (15 January 1991), p. 2. *FBIS Daily Report—China,* 24 January 1991 (PrEx 7.10: FBIS-CHI-91–016), pp. 47–48.

53. Southerland 1985: p. A20; *Huaqiao ribao* 1986: March 1.

54. Wen Wei 1990: pp. 21–22.

55. See, for instance, *Huaqiao ribao* 1986: March 3.

56. The Beijing Reeducation Center for Prostitutes, founded in 1986 in the northern outskirts of Beijing, by September 1991 had housed (altogether) 427 prostitutes. "Reeducation Center for Prostitutes Profiled" (text). Beijing *Xinhua* in English (5 September 1991, 1356 GMT). Translation by the Foreign Broadcast Information Service. *FBIS Daily Report—China,* 6 September 1991 (PrEx 7.10: FBIS-CHI-91–173), pp. 38–39.

57. For instance, when the Beijing shi Tiantang he laojiaosuo was founded in September 1989, of 96 female inmates (*laojiao renyuan*), 22 (22.9 percent) had sold sex. By August 1991, when inmates were separated out by offense for purposes of reeducation, 108 of 171 female inmates (63.2 percent) were prostitutes, an increase of 40.3 percent. Beijing shi Tiantang he laojiaosuo 1992?: p. 1. According to a 1987 Shanghai investigation of several reform institutions for women and youth, within three years the number of women taken in for prostitution offenses had increased almost fivefold. Of the 2,136 male and female sex offenders investigated in Liu Dalin's national survey, 385 were *maiyin funü,* making up 61.1 percent of all women who committed sexual crimes or misconduct. Liu Dalin et al. 1992: p. 716.

58. "Security Ministry Cracks Down on Prostitution" (text). Beijing Xinhua in English (6 September 1991, 0847 GMT). *FBIS Daily Report—China,* 10 September 1991 (PrEx 7.10: FBIS-CHI-91–175), p. 31. It is not clear when most of these were opened. In March 1988 Yu Lei, the vice-chief of the Ministry for Public Security, reported that the country had sixty-eight receiving centers for women who were selling sex (*maiyin funü shourongsuo*) and reform centers (*gaizao zhongxin*). Wang Xingjuan 1992a: p. 420.

59. Wang Xingjuan 1992b. The Guangzhou facility was built in the mid-1980s by the local government at a cost of 6 million yuan. *Huaqiao ribao* 1986: March 3. The Beijing *Funü jiaoyangsuo* was founded in October 1988, and held four hundred to

five hundred people. Wang Xing juan 1992b. The *Funü jiaoyangsuo* in Shanghai was founded in the early 1990s under the authority of the Public Security Bureau. In 1993 it held more than eight hundred women, most of them low-class prostitutes, serving one-year to two-year sentences. Lu Xing'er 1993b: n.p. Of one hundred prostitutes in the Beijing Tiantang he laojiaosuo, ninety were incarcerated for the first time, nine for the second time, one for the third time. Beijing shi Tiantang he laojiaosuo 1992?: p. 2. In one Guangzhou reform institute studied by Wang Xing juan, 98 percent of those locked up were first offenders. Wang Xing juan 1990: p. 7.

60. Beijing shi Tiantang he laojiaosuo 1992?: p. 1.

61. Beijing shi Tiantang he laojiaosuo 1992?: pp. 8–9.

62. Beijing shi Tiantang he laojiaosuo 1992?: p. 9; for a reportage piece that also asserts that incarcerated women have a bad influence on each other and engage in lesbian sex, see Pang Ruiyin et al. 1989: p. 65.

63. Wang Xing juan 1990: p. 7.

64. Wang Xing juan 1993.

65. Wang Xing juan 1990: pp. 7–8. On the make-work nature of reform labor, see also Chen Yiyun 1993.

66. One study notes that the protection measures to keep staff from catching STDs were not effective; in other sources, police are also mentioned as prone to infection. It is not clear which STD or means of transmission is being discussed here, or even whether staff understood how STDs were transmitted. Wang Xing juan 1990: p. 8.

67. Wang Xing juan 1990: p. 7; Wang Xing juan 1992b; Lu Xing'er 1993b.

68. According to a 1985 Shanghai investigation, among female sexual offenders (including but not limited to those arrested for prostitution), 25 to 30 percent became repeat offenders. Liu Dalin et al. 1992: p. 742. When the Guangdong provincial justice bureau (*sifating*) did a follow-up investigation in 1988 of 1,133 female labor-education inmates who had been released for more than three years, it was found that 23.9 percent had a good performance (*biaoxian hao*), 36.4 percent had an ordinary (*yiban*) performance, 14.5 percent had an inadequate (*cha*) performance, 14.5 percent had returned to illegal activities, and 8.4 percent were criminals. Wang Xing juan 1990: p. 7.

69. Lu Xing'er 1993b.

70. Beijing shi Tiantang he laojiaosuo 1992?: p. 2.

71. Gao Xiaoxian and Du Li 1993; Lu Xing'er 1993b.

72. Chen Yiyun 1992.

73. "Party Members Expelled for Pimping for Foreigners" (text). Beijing *Renmin ribao* in Chinese (9 July 1989), p. 4. *FBIS Daily Report—China*, 17 July 1989 (PrEx 7.10: FBIS-CHI-89-135), p. 31; "Laws Punished on Cadres Involved in Prostitution" (text). Beijing *Xinhua* in English (7 December 1989, 0908 GMT). *FBIS Daily Report—China*, 7 December 1989 (PrEx 7.10: FBIS-CHI-89-234), p. 13; "Guangxi Charges 300 Cadres with Six Vices" (text). Beijing *Zhongguo xinwen she* (25 January 1990, 1317 GMT). *FBIS Daily Report—China*, 26 January 1990 (PrEx 7.10: FBIS-CHI-90-018), p. 44; "Former Official Jailed for 'Indecent Behavior'" (text). Hong Kong *Zhongguo tongxun she* in Chinese (24 January 1992, 1213 GMT). *FBIS Daily Report—China*, 27 January 1992 (PrEx 7.10: FBIS-CHI-92-017), p. 58.

74. Beijing shi Tiantang he laojiaosuo 1992?: p. 2; the national figure is derived from Liu Dalin et al. 1992: p. 719.

75. Ye Po 1989: p. 8; Wang Xingjuan 1990: p. 3.

76. In a survey of incarcerated prostitutes in Guangdong, the sociologist Chen Yiyun found that 50 percent were from broken or unhappy or neglectful homes, and thus wanted to leave home. Chen Yiyun 1992. Wang Xingjuan (1992b) also mentioned divorce, adding that many of the women had been raped as children or adolescents. A survey by Feng Tianyun in 1988 investigated 205 women incarcerated for sexual crimes and misconduct (not just prostitution) in the Shanghai shi laojiao jiaoyangsuo. Of the 123 young women aged thirteen to twenty, she found that 23.9 percent had been sexually victimized (*xing shanghai*) and had "therefore taken the road of violating the law and committing crimes." One need not accept the causality in order to take note of the high reported rates of sexual abuse, a topic not normally mentioned in the Chinese press. Feng Tianyun, *Shehui* 1990: no. 7, cited in Liu Dalin et al. 1992: p. 632.

77. Beijing shi Tiantang he laojiaosuo 1992?: p. 2; Liu Dalin et al. 1992: p. 719.

78. Of the survey's larger sample of 385 prostitutes (not all of whom reported their age at first offense), ever-married women made up 31.4 percent. Liu Dalin et al. 1992: p. 719. I use the smaller sample here because it focuses on women who began work as prostitutes *after* they were married.

79. Lu Xing'er 1993b; Chen Yiyun 1992.

80. Wang Xingjuan 1990: pp. 2–3.

81. Beijing shi Tiantang he laojiaosuo 1992?: p. 2.

82. Ye Po 1989: p. 8.

83. These numbers are consistent with a 1989 study of ninety-two inmates in a Guangzhou reeducation center, which was not included in appendix A, table 5, because it did not provide subtotals in different job categories. Of the ninety-two women, 56.5 percent had jobs as workers, salespersons, service workers, nurses, accountants, individual entrepreneurs, and temporary workers. Workers (presumably in manufacturing jobs) made up 40.4 percent of those employed, or about 23 percent of the total. Ye Po 1989: p. 7.

84. Shang Xinren 1993: pp. 32–33.

85. Their top ten places of origin were Shanghai, Sichuan, Hubei, Liaoning, Guangxi, Fujian, Jiangsu, Jilin, and Henan. Wang Xingjuan 1990: p. 2. This finding is consistent with an earlier figure reported in an overseas Chinese newspaper. Of 524 prostitutes arrested in late 1985 or early 1986, almost two-thirds (340) came from outside Guangzhou. Most were from Hunan, a fact the article attributed to the disasters brought about there by "leftist" policies at the provincial level. Following this were Guangxi, Sichuan, Shanghai, Beijing, and Liaoning. *Huaqiao ribao* 1986: March 1–2.

86. Wang Xingjuan 1990: pp. 4–5.

87. On Liaoning women, see Chen Yiyun 1992; on Xinjiang women, see *Huaqiao ribao* 1986: March 1.

88. Wang Xingjuan 1992b.

89. Huang Jiaxin and Ye Min, "Why Do These People Whore?", *Shehui*, no. 82 (20 November 1991), pp. 35–37, translated in JPRS-CAR-92-007 (18 February 1992), pp. 41–43. The statistic is from p. 42 of the translation.

90. Ignatius and Leung 1990?: p. 11.

91. "'Social Report' Examines AIDS Epidemic" (text). Beijing *Renmin gong'an bao*

in Chinese (22 January 1991), p. 4. *FBIS Daily Report—China,* 28 February 1991 (PrEx 7.10: FBIS-CHI-91-040), p. 20.

92. *Jiankang bao* 1989: November 21; cited in Wang Xingjuan 1992a: pp. 420–21.

93. Sun 1992. This statistic may actually refer to 1990; in that year, China's sixteen STD monitoring stations reported 44,117 cases, and cases in major urban centers in the first half of 1991 were said to have fallen 30 percent as the result of government efforts. "Cases of Sexually Transmitted Disease Decrease" (text). Beijing Xinhua in English (6 September 1991, 1220 GMT). *FBIS Daily Report—China,* 9 September 1991 (PrEx 7.10: FBIS-CHI-91-174), p. 41. In Beijing, where the first case was discovered in 1982, there were 1,098 reported cases by the end of 1988, and authorities were estimating that the actual number was almost double that. Wen Wei 1990: p. 21.

94. *Shijie ribao* 1993: October 18. For an estimate from the same year stating that 830,000 Chinese had contracted an STD since 1980, see *Renmin ribao* 1993: December 1; cited in Cohen et al. 1993: n.p.

95. Personal observation, June 1993.

96. Wen Wei 1990: pp. 21–22. It was reported in 1991 that gonorrhea accounted for about 60 percent of all reported cases, and syphilis 1.2 percent. "Cases of Sexually Transmitted Disease Decrease" (text). Beijing Xinhua in English (6 September 1991, 1220 GMT). *FBIS Daily Report—China,* 9 September 1991 (PrEx 7.10: FBIS-CHI-91-174), p. 41.

97. Chen Yiyun 1992. The two prostitutes were in Guangdong and Sichuan. More than 700 of the HIV cases were associated with the Yunnan drug trade, where it was estimated that 82 percent of drug users were HIV positive. These numbers had grown rapidly since the end of 1990, when there were 493 reported cases of HIV and 6 cases of AIDS; by November 1991 the numbers were 607 and 8, respectively; by mid-1992 they were 705 and 8. "Cases of Sexually Transmitted Disease Decrease" (text). Beijing Xinhua in English (6 September 1991, 1220 GMT). *FBIS Daily Report—China,* 9 September 1991 (PrEx 7.10: FBIS-CHI-91-174), p. 41; "Health Official on AIDS Statistics, Measures." (text). Beijing Xinhua in English (30 November 1991, 1357 GMT). *FBIS Daily Report—China,* 5 December 1991 (PrEx 7.10: FBIS-CHI-91-234), p. 27; and "705 Cases of HIV-Infected Persons Discovered" (text). Beijing Zhongguo xinwen she in English (10 Jun 1992, 1404 GMT). *FBIS Daily Report—China,* 12 June 1992 (PrEx 7.10: FBIS-CHI-92-114), pp. 22–23). On AIDS transmission, see also "AIDS Cases Increase in Guangdong" (text). Hong Kong *Wen wei bao* in Chinese (25 July 1991), p. 4. *FBIS Daily Report—China,* 25 July 1991 (PrEx 7.10: FBIS-CHI-91-143), pp. 51–52. Figures for 1993 are from the *China News Digest* 1993: December 2; for 1994, from *China News Digest* 1994: September 23. The latter report adds: "Of the 1,535 people who have tested positive for the AIDS virus in China, 66 percent are intravenous drug users, 16 percent are foreigners, and 9.4 percent are Chinese who became infected while working overseas, mainly in Africa, according to government statistics." On the estimate of carriers by the China AIDS Network, see *China News Digest* 1994: December 2.

Cohen et al. (1993) write: "HIV disease has been concentrated in the southern border province of Yunnan, where IV drug use has been a problem. While China has formulated AIDS prevention policies, the Chinese people are being led to believe that HIV is a disease of foreigners, and there is little public STD education."

98. Wen Wei 1990: p. 21. In 1994, the National Quarantine Authorities were run-

ning health stations at the Beijing and Shanghai airports for the mandatory HIV testing of Chinese citizens returning from abroad, as well as some foreign students studying in China. Foreigners were required to pay 120 yuan for the test. *China News Digest* 1994: March 22.

99. Chen Yehong, "On Prostitution and the Application of Criminal Law" (text). Wuhan *Huazhong shifan daxue xuebao,* 6 (1 December 1990), pp. 35–40. Translated in JPRS-CAR-91-005 (31 January 1991), pp. 65–70. Quotation is from p. 68 of the translation..

100. Lu Xing'er 1993b.

101. *Huaqiao ribao* 1986: March 1. The 40 percent figure is from "Cases of Sexually Transmitted Disease Decrease" (text). Beijing Xinhua in English (6 September 1991, 1220 GMT). *FBIS Daily Report—China,* 9 September 1991 (PrEx 7.10: FBIS-CHI-91-174), p. 41. The size of the first Beijing sample, of women arrested in 1988, was seventy, of whom fifty-nine were infected. Wen Wei 1990: p. 22. Sixty-five of the second group of one hundred incarcerated women had an STD. Beijing shi Tiantang he laojiaosuo 1992?: p. 3. The Guangzhou estimate is from Chen Yiyun 1992.

102. Chen Yiyun 1992; Wang Xingjuan 1990: p. 8.

103. For a mid-1994 report published under the auspices of the State Council, calling for more AIDS education, see *China News Digest* 1994: July 6. In late 1994 Zhang Konglai, an epidemiologist and founder of the China AIDS Network, cited promiscuity, prostitution, and ignorance as reasons that China might soon face a crisis of HIV infection. He recommended that high school and college students be taught about AIDS transmission and that workers be trained to masturbate rather than patronizing brothels while working abroad. *China News Digest* 1994: December 2.

104. See Wang Xingjuan 1990.

105. Liu Dalin et al. 1992: pp. 833–34.

106. Liu Dalin et al. 1992: pp. 718–19.

107. "Lun jinü" [On prostitution], *Shehui* 1989: no. 6; cited in Wang Xingjuan 1992a: p. 423.

108. Wang Xingjuan 1992b.

109. Beijing shi Tiantang he laojiaosuo 1992?: p. 3.

110. Beijing shi Tiantang he laojiaosuo 1992?: p. 4. For a similar story about a retail clerk who began soliciting hotel guests after work, see Ye Po 1989: p. 7.

111. Beijing shi Tiantang he laojiaosuo 1992?: p. 4.

112. Ye Po 1989: p. 7.

113. Lu Xing'er 1993b.

114. Wang Xingjuan estimates that women made up 70 percent of those laid off from factory jobs in the late 1980s and early 1990s. Wang Xingjuan 1993a. On discrimination against women in hiring, see Honig and Hershatter 1988, pp. 243–50, 264–65; on the problem of women's employment, see many of the essays in Li Xiaojiang and Tan Shen 1991.

115. Chen Yiyun 1992.

116. Lu Xing'er 1993b: n.p.

117. For such liaisons between men from Hong Kong and women in southern China, see Nora Lee 1995.

118. Gao Xiaoxian and Du Li 1993.

119. Lu Xing'er 1993b: n.p.

120. Wang Xingjuan 1990: p. 3; Lu Xing'er 1993b.

121. Lu Xing'er 1993a: pp. 20–23.

122. On youth and beauty as capital, see Wang Xingjuan 1992b; on capital-accumulation strategies, see Gao Xiaoxian and Du Li 1993; and Lu Xing'er 1993b.

123. *Huaqiao ribao* 1986: March 1.

124. Wang Xingjuan 1992b.

125. Beijing shi Tiantang he laojiaosuo 1992?: pp. 4–5.

126. See, for instance, Lu Xing'er 1993a: pp. 18–20.

127. Liu Dalin et al. 1992: p. 725.

128. Wang Xingjuan 1992b.

129. *Huaqiao ribao* 1986: March 3.

130. Beijing shi Tiantang he laojiaosuo 1992?: p. 6.

131. A Qiao 1993: pp. 55–57.

132. Liu Dalin et al. 1992: pp. 725–26.

133. Wang Zheng 1993: p. 161. Others also mention this "anywhere but here" attitude among prostitutes. Lu Xing'er, another fiction writer and essayist, reports that prostitutes ask her why they should get married and have a home and children, a project that entails a great deal of work, the possibility of beatings, and other problems. Rather, "[t]hey want pleasure. They want to marry a foreigner and go far away." Lu Xing'er 1993b.

134. A Qiao 1993: p. 58.

CHAPTER 14: EXPLAINING

1. "Situation Concerning the Investigation and Banning of Prostitution and Prostitute Patronization," submitted to 20th session of seventh NPC standing committee, printed June 18, 1991, cited in "Document Studies Situation" (text). Hong Kong *Jiushi niandai* in Chinese (1 October 1991), no. 216, pp. 19–21. *FBIS Daily Report—China*, 9 October 1991 (PrEx 7.10: FBIS-CHI-91-196), pp. 28–30.

2. For instance, the Guangdong provincial people's standing committee issued a resolution on December 25, 1985, on "launching broad and deep comprehensive administration of social order," whose first and outstanding content was to emphasize the strict ban on prostitution and visiting prostitutes. *Huaqiao ribao* 1986: March 3. Also in 1985, a member of the Shenzhen city committee stated to a reporter that opening casinos or brothels in Shenzhen did "not conform with the principle of our socialist system," and indicated that casinos and brothels would be banned. "Casinos, Brothels Prohibited in Shenzhen" (text). Hong Kong *Xinwan bao* in Chinese (27 June 1985), p. 1. *FBIS Daily Report—China*, 11 July 1985 (PrEx 7.10: FBIS-CHI-85-133), pp. W11–12.

3. Cohen 1988: pp. 102–3. Article 140, which is in a category of laws regarding "crimes of infringing upon the rights of the person and the democratic rights of citizens," reads in full: "Whoever forces women into prostitution is to be sentenced to not less than three years and not more than ten years of fixed-term imprisonment." It is situated between a law on rape and one on abduction and sale of people. Article 169, in the category of "crimes of disrupting the order of social administration," states in full: "Whoever, for the purpose of reaping profits, lures women into prosti-

tution or shelters them in prostitution, is to be sentenced to not more than five years of fixed-term imprisonment, criminal detention, or control; when the circumstances are serious, the sentence is to be not less than five years of fixed-term imprisonment, and the offender may in addition be sentenced to a fine or confiscation of property." It is situated between a law on gambling and one on pornographic books and pictures. Article 79 reads: "A crime that is not expressly stipulated in the Special Provisions of this law may be determined and punished according to the most closely analogous article of the Special Provisions of this law, but the matter shall be submitted to the Supreme People's Court for approval." *Criminal Law* 1984: pp. 47, 50, 54, 58, 32. Although Cohen says that prostitution can be prosecuted under this principle of analogy, none of the materials I have examined for this book mentions such a case.

4. Cohen 1988: pp. 102–4. The specific instance analyzed by Cohen concerns the application to foreigners of the SAPA provision on relations with a prostitute. For a discussion of some features of the 1957 SAPA, see Cohen 1968: pp. 200–237.

5. Cohen 1988: p. 106.

6. In June 1987, the Guangdong Provincial People's Congress promulgated a provincial regulation banning prostitution. While singling out "those luring, allowing, and forcing women to engage in prostitution" for criminal punishment, it was much less strict with pimps and prostitutes. Pimps could be detained for fifteen days or sentenced to reform through labor (presumably for repeat offenders); they could also be fined five thousand yuan. Prostitutes were to be detained fifteen days, fined five thousand yuan or sentenced to reform through labor, and "ordered to write a statement of repentance." Examination and treatment for sexually transmitted diseases was compulsory, with detainees to pay their own medical costs. "Guangdong Regulation Bans Prostitution" (text). Guangzhou *Nanfang ribao* in Chinese (20 June 1987), p. 1, translated in JPRS-CAR-87-038 (25 August 1987), pp. 93–94. In November 1988, Hainan province passed a virtually identical regulation. Significantly, one of the articles on the new rules noted that five thousand yuan was less than two months' salary for a masseuse. Fak Cheuk-wan, "Dealing with ''Vice Capital' Label" (text). Hong Kong *Hongkong Standard* in English (15 November 1988), p. 7. *FBIS Daily Report—China,* 17 November 1988 (PrEx 7.10: FBIS-CHI-88-222), pp. 60–61. Regulations for Shaanxi, passed in December 1989, contained similar provisions. Shaanxi sheng 1992: pp. 126–28. For national regulations on hotels passed in November 1987, see Cohen 1988: p. 104, note 16.

7. See Honig and Hershatter 1988: pp. 289–91. The most powerful and comprehensive exposé of the abduction and sale of women in reform-era China is Xie Zhihong and Jia Lusheng 1989.

8. See, for instance, "Beijing Court Orders Execution of Repeat Offender" (text). *Beijing Ribao* (18 November 1990), p. 1. *FBIS Daily Report—China,* 20 December 1990 (PrEx 7.10: FBIS-CHI-90-245), pp. 69–70.

9. An early campaign against both abductions and those who induced women to become prostitutes was announced in Sichuan in 1982. *Shijie ribao* 1982: December 31, p. 3. Also see "Qiao Shi, Others at Meeting on Sale of Women" (text). Beijing Television Service in Mandarin (18 December 1990, 1100 GMT). *FBIS Daily Report— China,* 19 December 1990 (PrEx 7.10: FBIS-CHI-90-244), p. 13.

10. *Shijie ribao* 1993: September 9, p. A11; "Young Mainlanders Procured for Prostitution" (text). Hong Kong *Ming bao* in Chinese, 27 July 1989, p. 9. Translation by

the Joint Publications Research Service. JPRS-CAR-89-103 (17 October 1989), pp. 66–67. See also Wang Xing juan 1990: p. 6.

11. "Law Protecting Women's Rights, Interests." Beijing Xinhua Domestic Service in Chinese (7 April 1992, 0414 GMT). *FBIS Daily Report—China*, 14 April 1992 (PrEx 7.10: FBIS-CHI-92-072-S), pp. 17–21. Quotations from p. 19. For the Chinese text, see Guan Tao et al. 1992: p. 193.

12. Guan Tao et al. 1988: pp. 120, 127–29.

13. Chen Yehong, "On Prostitution and the Application of Criminal Law" (text). [Wuhan] *Huazhong Shifan Daxue xuebao* 6 (1 December 1990), pp. 35–40. Translated in JPRS-CAR-91-005 (31 January 1991), pp. 65–70. For another summary of this type of argument, see Wang Xing juan 1992a: pp. 432–34.

14. "Decision on Prostitution" (text). Beijing Xinhua Domestic Service in Chinese (4 September 1991, GMT 2020). *FBIS Daily Report—China*, 5 September 1991 (PrEx 7.10: FBIS-CHI-91-172), pp. 28–30. By the summer of 1993, hotel regulations placed in guest rooms routinely forbade prostitution on the premises, along with activities such as drug dealing, smuggling, gambling, fighting, and circulating salacious books. See, for instance, "Service Guide Book," Xi'an Hotel, Xi'an; and "Service Directory," Peace Hotel, Shanghai. For a discussion of the Decision on Prostitution, see Yang Xiaobing 1991: pp. 27–29.

15. By the early 1990s, it was commonplace to see in government documents statements to the effect that, for instance, "worship of money has polluted the social environment," or inadequately managed hotels and amusement places "pollute the social atmosphere." Beijing shi Tiantang he laojiaosuo 1992?: pp. 6–7.

16. For a brief discussion of the vagueness of this campaign, as well as its entanglement with local jealousies and fears in Chinese work units, see Link 1992: pp. 177–78, 245.

17. *Huaqiao ribao* 1986: March 3. For accounts of arrest sweeps in Guangdong, see *Huaqiao ribao* 1986: March 1–3. The *Beijing Review* reported in 1991 that China had conducted a three-year campaign from 1983 to 1986 to arrest criminals who "forced, seduced and solicited women for prostitution." Yang Xiaobing 1991: p. 27.

18. Chang Hong, "Security Minister Condemns 'Six Social Vices'" (text). Beijing *China Daily* in English (14 November 1989), p. 1. *FBIS Daily Report—China*, 16 November 1989 (PrEx 7.10: FBIS-CHI-89-220), p. 17; "Wang Fang Announces Prostitution Crackdown" (text). Beijing Xinhua in English (13 November 1989). *FBIS Daily Report—China*, 21 November 1989 (PrEx 7.10: FBIS-CHI-89-223), pp. 25–26.

19. In fact, the *South China Morning Post* commented, "[a]nalysts say the way the 'Six Evils' campaign was implemented is reminiscent of the mass movements launched by the late Chairman Mao Tsetung to 'purify the spirit' of the people." Willy Wo-lap Lam, "Beijing Roots Out 'Unorthodox Party Members'" (text). Hong Kong *South China Morning Post* in English (27 November 1989, p. 9). *FBIS Daily Report—China*, 22 November 1989 (PrEx 7.10: FBIS-CHI-89-228), p. 45.

20. "State Council Calls for Eliminating 'Six Evils'" (text). Beijing Domestic Service in Mandarin (13 November 1989, 1030 GMT). *FBIS Daily Report—China*, 22 November 1989 (PrEx 7.10: FBIS-CHI-89-224), pp. 30–31.

21. "Commentator's Article Condemns 'Six Vices' (text). Beijing *Renmin ribao* in Chinese (15 November 1989), p. 1. *FBIS Daily Report—China*, 30 November 1989 (PrEx 7.10: FBIS-CHI-89-229), p. 21.

22. "Shanghai Prepares Campaign against Six Vices" (text). Shanghai City Service in Mandarin (9 November 1989, 1000 GMT). *FBIS Daily Report—China*, 7 December 1989 (PrEx 7.10: FBIS-CHI-89-234), pp. 41–42.

23. "*Renmin Ribao* Answers Reader's Criticism" (text). Beijing *Renmin ribao* in Chinese (31 December 1989), p. 3. *FBIS Daily Report—China*, 8 January 1990 (PrEx 7.10: FBIS-CHI-90-005), p. 18.

24. "Jiangxi Begins Operation Against Six 'Scourges'" (text). Beijing Xinhua Domestic Service in Chinese (13 November 1989, 1130 GMT). *FBIS Daily Report—China*, 21 November 1989 (PrEx 7.10: FBIS-CHI-89-223), p. 45.

25. "Jiangxi Meeting Discussing 'Social Evils'" (text). Nanchang Jiangxi Provincial Service in Mandarin (11 November 1989, 1100 GMT). *FBIS Daily Report—China*, 29 November 1989 (PrEx 7.10: FBIS-CHI-89-228), pp. 35–36.

26. "Shanghai's Prostitution, Drug Campaign Outlined" (text). Beijing Xinhua in English (15 November 1989, 0914 GMT). *FBIS Daily Report—China*, 22 November 1989 (PrEx 7.10: FBIS-CHI-89-224), p. 58.

27. "Guangdong Sentences Thirty-one Criminals to Death" (excerpt). Guangzhou Guangdong Provincial Service in Mandarin (11 January 1990, 1000 GMT). *FBIS Daily Report—China*, 12 January 1990 (PrEx 7.10: FBIS-CHI-90-009), p. 38. According to a 1992 article, Guangzhou's Seven Evils were prostitution, sex (*seqing;* possibly a reference to pornography), gambling, drugs, trafficking in women and children, feudal superstition, and underworld activities (*hei shehui*)—the last not listed in other locales. *Shijie ribao* 1992: July 6, p. 13.

28. "Hunan Advances against 'Six Vices'" (text). Changsha Hunan Provincial Service in Mandarin (19 November 1989; 2300 GMT). *FBIS Daily Report—China*, 30 November 1989 (PrEx 7.10: FBIS-CHI-89-229), p. 54; "Shaanxi Mobilizes against 'Six Vices'" (text). Xi'an Shaanxi Provincial Service in Mandarin (19 November 1989, 0030 GMT). *FBIS Daily Report—China*, 30 November 1989) (PrEx 7.10: FBIS-CHI-89-229), pp. 69–70.

29. "Guangdong Military Official Condemns Prostitution" (text). Guangzhou Guangdong Provincial Service in Mandarin (18 November 1989, 0040 GMT). *FBIS Daily Report—China*, 30 November 1989 (PrEx 7.10: FBIS-CHI-89-229), p. 46.

30. See, among others, "Jiangxi County Cracks Down on 'Six Vices'" (text). Nanchang Jiangxi Provincial Service in Mandarin (20 November 1989, 1100 GMT). *FBIS Daily Report—China*, 30 November 1989 (PrEx 7.10: FBIS-CHI-89-229), p. 43; "Fujian Launches Campaign against 'Six Vices'" (text). Fujian Provincial Service in Mandarin (19 November 1989, 1100 GMT). *FBIS Daily Report—China*, 1 December 1989 (PrEx 7.10: FBIS-CHI-89-230), p. 30; "Tianjin 'Victories' against 'Six Vices' Reported" (text). Tianjin City Service in Mandarin (21 November 1989, 1000 GMT). *FBIS Daily Report—China*, 1 December 1989 (PrEx 7.10: FBIS-CHI-89-230), p. 42; "Heilongjiang Clamps Down on 'Six Vices' (text). Harbin Heilongjiang Provincial Service in Mandarin (22 November 1989, 2200 GMT). *FBIS Daily Report—China*, 30 November 1989 (PrEx 7.10: FBIS-CHI-89-229), p. 62; "Beijing Mayor Calls for Crackdown on Six Vices" (text). Beijing Xinhua in English (23 November 1989, 0851 GMT). *FBIS Daily Report—China*, 13 December 1989 (PrEx 7.10: FBIS-CHI-89-238), p. 61; "Nationwide Crackdown on Six Vices Yields Results" (text). Beijing Television Service in Mandarin (7 December 1989, 1100 GMT). *FBIS Daily Report—China*, 15 December 1989 (PrEx 7.10: FBIS-CHI-89-240), p. 28; "Anhui Governor Calls for Eliminating Six Vices" (text). An-

hui Provincial Service in Mandarin (11 December 1989, 1100 GMT). *FBIS Daily Report—China*, 20 December 1989 (PrEx 7.10: FBIS-CHI-89-243), pp. 28–29; "Hainan Launches Operation against Six Vices" (text). Haikou Hainan Provincial Service in Mandarin (15 December 1989, 2300 GMT). *FBIS Daily Report—China*, 20 December 1989 (PrEx 7.10: FBIS-CHI-89-243), p. 33.

31. In Ningxia, for instance, 1,300 gamblers were arrested, as were 148 prostitutes and their clients. Many of the prostitutes were said to be "castaways from the neighboring provinces of Shaanxi and Gansu." Among the inns that lost their licenses for permitting prostitution was the guest house of the Yinchuan Canning Factory. "Ningxia Cracks Down on Six Vices" (text). Yinchuan *Ningxia Ribao* in Chinese (12 December 1989), p. 1. *FBIS Daily Report—China*, 10 January 1990 (PrEx 7.10: FBIS-CHI-90-007), p. 64–65.

32. Nevertheless, the *Beijing Review* reported in 1991 that another campaign against prostitution had been launched in May 1990. It left few written traces. Yang Xiaobing 1991: p. 27.

33. See, for examples, "Guangdong Faces 'Grim' Law, Order Situation" (text). Hong Kong *Ta Kung Pao* in Chinese (7 September 1990), p. 2. *FBIS Daily Report—China*, 18 September 1990 (PrEx 7.10: FBIS-CHI-90-181), p. 43; "Qiao Shi Promises Continuing Crackdown on Crime" (text). Beijing Xinhua in English (22 October 1990, 0835 GMT). *FBIS Daily Report—China*, 23 October 1990 (PrEx 7.10: FBIS-CHI-90-205), p. 23.

34. Yang Xiaobing 1991: p. 28.

35. *Shijie ribao* 1992: July 6, p. 13; see also *China News Digest* 1992: December 4.

36. Chen Yiyun 1992; *China News Digest* 1992: December 5; Walker 1993; *Shijie ribao* 1993: July 31, p. A13.

37. *Shijie ribao* 1993: July 31, p. A13.

38. *China News Digest* 1993: October 29.

39. *China News Digest* 1995: August 8. In July, State Councillor Luo Gan called for strict enforcement of laws against prostitution, as well as stricter regulation of karaoke bars, dance halls, and public sauna baths. "Luo Gan on Fighting Prostitution, Pornography." Beijing Xinhua in English (21 July 1995, 1608 GMT). *FBIS Daily Report—China*, 24 July 1995 (PrEx 7.10: FBIS-CHI-95-141), p. 16.

40. A Qiao 1993: p. 53.

41. *Huaqiao ribao* 1986: March 3.

42. *China News Digest* 1993: February 20.

43. *Shijie ribao* 1993: July 31, p. A13.

44. *Shijie ribao* 1993: September 9. For a similar attack by Politburo members in 1994, see *Shijie ribao* 1994: January 10.

45. Daniel Kwan, "Speaker Berates Cadres' Liberal View of Prostitution" (text), Hong Kong *South China Morning Post* in English (11 March 1995), p. 6. *FBIS Daily Report—China*, 13 March 1995 (PrEx 7.10: FBIS-CHI-95-048), pp. 63–64.

46. See, for instance, Yang and He 1988 and Beijing shi gong'anju 1988.

47. Ren Ping'an and Zhao Yanbing 1987: pp. 167–68.

48. Ren Ping'an and Zhao Yanbing 1987: pp. 171, 184–85. Although they do not explain the term, it dates from a reported conversation between Aleksandra Kollontai and Lenin, in which she said that sexual relations should be like drinking a glass of water, and he asked her in reply who would want to drink from a dirty glass. I am grateful to Marilyn Young for this reference.

49. Ning Dong 1990;, excerpts translated in JPRS-CAR-90-055 (26 July 1990), pp. 88–90.

50. Ning Dong 1990: translation, p. 89.

51. Ning Dong 1990: translation, p. 89.

52. Ning Dong 1990: translation, p. 89.

53. Ning Dong 1990: translation, p. 89.

54. Zhonghua quanguo 1991: p. 323.

55. Ning Dong 1990: translation, p. 90.

56. Ning Dong 1990: translation, p. 89.

57. Liu Dalin et al. 1992: p. 727.

58. Zhang Yiquan, "The Social Background of Prostitution," *Shehui*, no. 68 (20 October 1990), pp. 38–40, translated in JPRS-CAR-91-005 (31 January 1991), pp. 62–65. Quotation is from p. 62. For a far more vehement statement of the distinction between pre- and post-1949 prostitutes, see Chen Yehong 1990: p. 68.

59. Zhang Yiquan 1990: p. 62.

60. Zhang Yiquan 1990: p. 65.

61. Wang Xingjuan 1992a: pp. 429–30.

62. Zhang Yiquan 1990: p. 63.

63. Zhang Yiquan 1990: p. 64.

64. Wang Xingjuan 1992a: p. 428.

65. Lu Xing'er 1993b: n.p.

66. Liu Dalin et al. 1992: p. 720. It would be interesting to compare these results more closely with those of married women who were not prostitutes, but unfortunately that group was given a slightly different set of answers to choose from. Fifty-nine percent of urban wives (n=4,215) and 65.2 percent of rural wives (n=1,087) declared themselves "satisfied" with their marriages. Among urban wives (n=3,870), 17.1 percent were "very satisfied" and 41.8 percent were "relatively satisfied" with their marital sex lives. Among rural wives (n=1,083), 30.4 percent reported that they were "very satisfied" with marital sex and 33.3 percent that they were "relatively satisfied." Liu Dalin et al. 1992: pp. 289, 435. One need hardly note that "satisfaction" is a slippery category and that all of these numbers quantify without elucidating much. It is particularly interesting that the sexologist authors of the report themselves cautioned against attributing too much significance to the marital sex lives of prostitutes, arguing that "[t]he problems that exist in their sex lives are not ones of sexual desire but of emotion; the centripetal force of their marital relations, family and marriage." Liu Dalin et al. 1992: p. 721.

67. For a slightly different version of this argument, voiced in an overseas Chinese newspaper, see Xiong Zhongxie and Sun Yun 1993: p. 2. Xiong and Sun shared Zhang's emphasis on transformed female attitudes toward sex: "A new phenomenon among young unmarried women is that they have more sexual freedom and new concepts compared with women in the past. They no longer feel that sex must be initiated by the man or that sex is for the amusement of men." On the other hand, Xiong and Sun argued that the opening up of society in the Deng Xiaoping era caused the gradual restoration of China's traditional patriarchal society, and that prostitution, pornographic literature, and the traffic in women fell under the rubric of resurgent patriarchy. At the same time, they also faulted the importation of Western advertising for creating a Chinese advertising industry that is "a disguised sex industry, urg-

ing women to use their own bodies as capital to achieve the goal of earning money." Here, as in Zhang's analysis, both "traditional patriarchy" and "Western modernity" came in for their share of blame.

68. Zhang Yiquan 1990: p. 62; see also "Huangse chongji boxiade qingshaonian xing fanzui," *Qing shaonian fanzui wenti* 1 (1990), cited in Wang Xingjuan 1992a: pp. 423–24.

69. Wang Xingjuan 1992a: p. 425.

70. Wang Xingjuan 1992a: p. 424. For a further elaboration of Wang Xingjuan's views on prostitution, see Ma Li 1991.

71. Liu Dalin et al. 1992: pp. 11–13.

72. These arguments are developed in many sources; for a brief summary, see Xiong and Sun 1993: p. 2.

73. Chen Yiyun 1992.

74. Xiong and Sun 1993: p. 2.

75. Wang Xingjuan 1992a: p. 426.

76. Mo Ming (anon.) 1993.

77. Wang Xingjuan 1992a: pp. 421–22. On the "low quality of the subject," a ubiquitous phrase in the discussion of many reform-era social problems, also see p. 425.

78. Zhang Yiquan 1990: p. 63.

79. Wang Xingjuan 1992a: pp. 422–23.

80. Wang Xingjuan 1992a: p. 423.

81. Wang Xingjuan 1992a: p. 427.

82. Wang Xingjuan 1992a: p. 434.

83. For an interesting exposition of this point, see Wang Xingjuan 1992a: p. 427. The two articles by her that are cited in this section summarize an extensive survey of the social-science literature on prostitution.

84. Wang Xingjuan 1990: p. 6.

85. Wang Xingjuan 1992a: p. 437.

86. Wang Xingjuan 1990: pp. 6–7.

87. Wang Xingjuan 1990: pp. 9–10; Wang Xingjuan 1992a: p. 438.

88. Wang Xingjuan 1990: p. 10; Wang Xingjuan 1992a: pp. 439–40.

89. Wang Xingjuan 1990: p. 10.

90. Wang Xingjuan 1990: p. 11; Wang Xingjuan 1992a: p. 437.

91. Wang Xingjuan 1990: p. 11; Wang Xingjuan 1992a: pp. 439, 437.

92. Liu Dalin et al. 1992: p. 13.

93. Yi Ni, *Yangguangxia de sikao* [Reflections in sunlight] (Zhongguo wenlian chuban gongsi, 1988), pp. 116–17, quoted in Liu Dalin et al. 1992: pp. 727–28.

94. Pang Ruiyin et al. 1989a, 1989b. This is a series of essays by different authors, bound in a single volume. Pang's essay on prostitution gives the book its title. There are two editions of the same book, published under different titles in Hong Kong (1989a) and Taiwan (1989b). Although I have not seen an edition published on the Chinese mainland, I suspect that the material has been published there as well, because it conforms to all the conventions of representing prostitution that characterize PRC reportage. All page numbers given here are from the Hong Kong edition.

95. Pang Ruiyin et al. 1989a: p. 3.

96. Pang Ruiyin et al. 1989a: pp. 6–7.

97. Pang Ruiyin et al. 1989a: pp. 1–8.

98. Pang Ruiyin et al. 1989a: p. 48.

99. Pang Ruiyin et al. 1989a: p. 54.

100. Pang Ruiyin et al. 1989a: pp. 66–67.

101. For an example of the former, see *Xi'an fazhi bao* 1993: 486 (July 2), p. 2; examples of the latter include Shang Xinren 1993, published by Sichuan University Press; Yan Ji 1992, published by the Beijing Normal University; and Yang Quan 1993a and 1993b, published by the Inner Mongolia Cultural Publishing Company.

102. Shang Xinren 1993.

103. Kaye 1993: pp. 40–41.

104. For a useful summary of these issues, see Williams 1989: pp. 1–33.

105. Shang Xinren 1993: pp. 24, 36–37.

106. Shang Xinren 1993: pp. 24–25.

107. Shang Xinren 1993: p. 24.

108. The anxiety about the exposed female/national body is also a frequent theme in overseas Chinese publications. In a 1986 issue of *Shibao zhoukan*, for instance, we find a full-page spread inaccurately titled "Night Shanghai," with the subtitle "Why Do Mainland University Students Let Japanese Take Nude Pictures?" It is illustrated with four photographs: (1) a naked woman apparently standing on the deck of a boat in Guangdong, her face artfully turned away so it is not exposed, her genital area in shadow (caption: "A woman attendant in the Guangzhou Hotel temporarily serves as model for a Japanese"); (2) a snapshot of a fully clothed woman smiling into the camera (caption: "Fang Min is a student at Shanghai Art Institute, and also lets Japanese take nude pictures"); (3) a woman under a sign for Huangpu Road at night (caption: "A young woman obstructing the road [*zujie*] on Guangzhou's Huangpu Road"); (4) a naked woman on a bed holding bikini underwear up to her genital area, surrounded by piles of other underwear (caption: "Japanese give large quantities of cheap underwear to mainland prostitutes"). The overall caption reads, "Japanese who are anxious to use sex to subdue others [*rezhong xing zhengfu de Riben ren*] recently have once again pushed their battlefield onto the Chinese mainland. They not only seek out prostitutes to take naked pictures, but even seek women students in art departments. Why do [these women] wish to let Japanese hunt for photographic shots?" Note the echo by Chinese in diaspora of nationalist anxieties expressed during the Japanese occupation about the Japanese using sex to conquer China. *Shibao zhoukan* 1986: April 20–26, p. 96.

109. Shang Xinren 1993: p. 25.

110. Shang Xinren 1993: p. 26.

111. Shang Xinren 1993: pp. 27–28.

112. Shang Xinren 1993: pp. 28–29.

113. Shang Xinren 1993: pp. 35–36.

114. Shang Xinren 1993: pp. 26–27.

115. Shang Xinren 1993: pp. 25–26.

116. Shang Xinren 1993: pp. 33–35.

117. Foucault 1980: pp. 17–35.

118. This debate is far too complex to be summarized here. For expositions of the "sexual slavery" position, see Barry 1979 and Barry et al. 1984. On prostitution as sex work, see Delacoste and Alexander 1987; Pheterson 1989; and McClintock 1992: pp. 87–95.

119. Fak Cheuk-wan, "Unemployment Problem Increasing" (text). Hong Kong *Hongkong Standard* in English (16 November 1988), p. 6. *FBIS Daily Report—China*, 17 November 1988 (PrEx 7.10: FBIS-CHI-88-222), pp. 62–63.

120. "Hainan Secretary on Social Order 'Pressure'" (text). Beijing Zhongguo xin-wen she in Chinese (27 March 1989, 0845 GMT). *FBIS Daily Report—China*, 29 March 1989 (PrEx 7.10: FBIS-CHI-89-059), pp. 57–58.

121. See, for instance, Wang Xingjuan 1992a: pp. 425–26.

122. See, for example, Liu Bohong 1992.

123. "Reform and Opening Up to the Outside World and a New Train of Thought on the Women's Liberation Movement—Notes on the Symposium on Theories Concerning Women" (text). Beijing *Qiushi* in Chinese, 5 (1 March 1989), pp. 42–45. Translated in JPRS-CAR-89-049 (19 May 1989), 36–40. Quotation is from pp. 39–40.

124. "Reform and Opening Up" 1989: p. 38.

125. Among those expressing this argument were Chen Yiyun, Dai Qing, and Jin Nan. "Reform and Opening Up" 1989: pp. 38–40.

126. "Reform and Opening Up" 1989: p. 37.

127. Wang Xingjuan 1993b. As noted in chapter 13, this was also one explanation a researcher gave for using the term *maiyin funü* (woman who sells sex) rather than *jinü* (prostitute).

128. Pan Suiming, "Decipher the Myth of Prostitution" (text). Shanghai *Shehui* in Chinese, 87 (20 April 1992), pp. 25–26. Translated in JPRS-CAR-92-044 (24 June 1992), pp. 55–56. Quotation is from p. 55.

129. Pan Suiming, "Decipher the Myth," p. 55.

CHAPTER 15: HISTORY, MEMORY, AND NOSTALGIA

1. See, for instance, Zhou Yinjun et al. 1980; Zhou Yinjun et al. 1981; Hua Min 1986; Zhu Tianze 1988; Yang and He 1988; and Beijing shi gong'anju 1988.

2. See, for example, Shanghai shi wenshi guan 1988; and Liu Fujing and Wang Mingkun 1992. The Shanghai volume was reprinted in a Hong Kong edition by the Zhongyuan chubanshe in 1989.

3. The same combination of denunciation and attention to detail was a feature of the biographical novel *Courtesan-House Hatred* by Kang Suzhen, a woman who had been a prostitute in Chengdu, Baoji, and Lanzhou before she was purchased by a general's secretary. Kang Suzhen 1988.

4. Sun Guoqun 1988a: pp. 1–3 of preface. Briefer treatments of the same time period are found in Wu Guifang 1980 and Tang Weikang et al. 1987: pp. 261–74.

5. Wu Zhou 1990: p. 420. Wu used the term *nüxing*, sometimes translated into English as "essential woman," rather than the term *funü*, which was used in the Maoist period and after to signify "woman as state subject." For further discussion of these terms, see Barlow 1994.

6. Wu Zhou 1990: preface (by Ma Jigao), pp. 1–4. This preface touts the book as a new and improved successor to the 1935 study by Wang Shunu mentioned below.

7. Shan Guangnai 1995. This very rich source was published just as my own volume was going to press; hence the cursory treatment of it here.

8. Shan Guangnai 1995: pp. 2–3.

9. Shan Guangnai 1995: pp. 537–78.

10. Shan Guangnai 1995: pp. 515–23.

11. Wang Shunu 1988.

12. Haishang soushisheng 1991; Suoposheng and Bao Tianxiao 1991.

13. Haishang soushisheng 1991: p. 3 of second preface.

14. Haishang soushisheng 1991: p. 2 of first preface.

15. Yang Quan 1993b: pp. 32–34.

16. Yang Quan 1993a: pp. 26–28.

17. Li Shaohong 1994.

18. Suoposheng and Bao Tianxiao 1991: p. 4 of second preface. A similar rationale was put forward by Lan Xiang in a 1990 collection of stories about wealthy persons (most with gang connections) in Shanghai, based on oral interviews with old Shanghai residents. For stories about prostitutes and accounts of female hoodlums, including madams, see Lan Xiang 1990: pp. 235–73.

GLOSSARY OF CHINESE CHARACTERS

A Jin　阿金

A Mu　阿母

A Zhen　阿珍

A Zhu　阿珠

Ai Wen　愛溫

Baisha Pipa　白沙批杷

Ban Gu　班固

Banyue　半月

Bao Lin　寶琳

Bao Qin　寶琴

Baxian Qiao　八仙橋

Beili　北里

Bi Yao　碧瑤

Bi Yihong　畢倚虹

Cao Gongqi　曹公奇

Cao Manzhi　曹漫之

Cao Menglan　曹夢蘭

Cao Xueqin　曹雪芹

Chang E　嫦娥

Chen Abao　陳阿寶

Chen Daiyu　陳黛玉

Chen Dezheng　陳德徵

Chen Dingshan　陳定山

Chen Lianbao　陳連寶

Chen Xiaofeng　陳小鳳

Chen Ying　陳英

Chen Yiyun　陳一韻

Chi Zhicheng　池志澂

Cishan tuan　慈善團

Dagong bao　大公報

Dagou Qiao　打狗橋

Duan Fang　端方

Er Lanzi　二蘭子

Fang Long　房龍

Fang Rishan　方日珊

Fei Du　廢都

Fu Caiyun　傅彩雲

Funü gongming　婦女共鳴

Funü laodong jiaoyangsuo　婦女勞
動教養所

Funü zazhi　婦女雜誌

Furu jiujihui　婦孺救濟會

Gao Yayun　高雅雲

Geng Jingzhong　耿精忠

Gong Fangzi　龔芳子

Gongshang ju　工商局

Gu Er　顧二

Guo Chongjie　郭崇階

Hao Guan　好冠

He Haiming　何海鳴

He Zhen　何震

Hei er Chen Jitai　黑兒陳吉太

Hong Bang　紅幫

Hong Fen　紅粉

Hong Nainai　洪奶奶

Hong Wenqing　洪文卿

Hu Baoyu　胡寶玉

Hua Yue Ge　花月閣

Hua Yunyu　花雲玉

Huang Jingyi　黃靜儀

Huang Renjing　黃人鏡

Huang Xiubo　黃秀伯

Huang Youpeng　黃又鵬

Huayang delüfeng　華洋德律風

Huazhong shifan daxue xuebao　華中師範大學學報

Hui Genquan　惠根泉

Huile Li　會樂里

Huiran Laojiu　惠然老九

Jian Bing　鑑冰

Jiang Jieshi　蔣介石

Jiaxing　嘉興

Jidu jiao furen jiaofeng hui　基督教婦人矯風會

Jiejie meimei zhanqilai　姐姐妹妹站起來

Jin de hui　進德會

Jin Hanxiang　金含香

Jin Qiaolin　金巧林

Jin Shuyu　金書玉

Jin Xiaobao　金小寶

Jin Yin Lou　金銀樓

Jinbao　金寶

Jing Zhi　敬芷

Jiuwei gui　九尾龜

Kang Youwei　康有爲

Kui Qingyun Laowu　葵青雲老五

Lan Yunge　蘭雲閣

Lanqiao Bieshu　藍橋別墅

Lao Wang Ji　老王記

Leizu　雷祖

Li Bai　李白

Li Boyuan　李伯元

Li Chunlai　李春來

Li Dazhao　李大釗

Li Hongzhang　李鴻章

Li Jinlian　李金蓮

Li Ping　黎平

Li Pingxiang　李蘋香

Li Qingzhao　李清照

Li Sanwu　李三無

Li Shanshan　李珊珊

Li Shaohong　李少紅

Li Yunshu　李雲書

Lian Ying　蓮英

Liang Caihua　梁彩花

Liang Deyu　梁德餘

Liang Qichao　梁啓超

Liao Guofang　廖國芳

Lin Biyao　林碧瑤

Lin Chongwu　林崇武

Lin Daiyu　林黛玉

Liu Ziren　劉子仁

Long Xiaoyun　龍小雲

Lou Shi　陋室

Lu Lanfen　陸蘭芬

Lu Xing'er　陸星兒

Luo Tianwen　羅天問

Luopeng Ajin　落蓬阿金

Luosong tangzi　羅宋堂子

Ma Ruizhen　馬瑞珍

Malishi　馬立師

Meng Yuesheng　夢月生

Minzheng ju　民政局

Mu Hua　木華

Nian Nian Hong　年年紅

Ning Dong　寧東

Pan　潘

Pan Qingyuan　潘青園

Pang Ruiyin　龐瑞垠

Qi liu suo　棲流所

Qimei　企妹

Qing Bang　青幫

Qinglou jinhuatuan　青樓進化團

Qinglou jiuguo tuan　青樓救國團

Qinglou jiujituan　青樓救濟團

Sao Muma　騷姆媽

Shan Guangnai　單光鼐

Shang Xinren　商欣仁

Shanghai chunqiu　上海春秋

Shanghai junguan hui zhengwu jie-
    guanhui fuzhuren　上海軍管會
    政務接管會副主任

Shanghai shi huanü lianyihui　上海
    市花女聯誼會

Shao Meiting　邵美亭

Shen Yanchuan　深硯傳

Shenbao　申報

Shibao　時報

Shoutou mazi　壽頭麻子

Shuang Fu Tang　雙富堂

Si malu　四馬路

Sida jingang　四大金剛

Sima Qian　司馬遷

Song Jingbo　宋靜波

Songjiang　松江

Su Tong　蘇童

Su Yuanyuan　蘇媛媛

Suiyuan shihua　隨園詩話

Sun Guoqun　孫國群

Sun Yusheng　孫玉聲

Suo Fei　所非

Suzhen　素珍

Tang Guozhen　唐國楨

Tang Hualong　湯化龍

Tang Xiaolong　唐小龍

Tao Yuanming　陶淵明

Ti Hongguan　題紅館

Tianma shan　天馬山

Tianyun ge shi　天韻閣詩

Tilan Qiao　提籃橋

Wang Anyi　王安憶

Wang Asan　王阿三

Wang Changfa　王長發

Wang Hengfang　王蘅舫

Wang Lancui　王蘭翠

Wang Lianying　王蓮英

Wang Liaoweng　汪了翁

Wang Shunu　王書奴

Wang Suzhen　王素貞

Wang Xingjuan　王行娟

Wang Yiting　王一亭

Wang Yiyong   王一庸

Wang Yuanruo   汪淵若

Wang Yueying   王月英

Wendi laosi   文第老四

Weng Meiqian   翁梅倩

Wenming shuju   文明書局

Wu Chunfang   吳春芳

Wu Jianren   吳研人

Wu Jintang   吳錦堂

Wu Zetian   武則天

Wu Zhou   武舟

Xiao bao   笑報

Xiao dong men   小東門

Xiao Huayuan   小花園

Xiao Jinling   小金鈴

Xiao Lin Daiyu   小林黛玉

Xiao Linglong   小玲瓏

Xiao Linglong laoqi   小玲瓏老七

Xie Shanbao   謝珊寶

Xie Wenyi   謝文漪

Ximen Qing   西門慶

Xin Beimen   新北門

Xin puyutang   新普育堂

Xin ren   新人

Xu Chongli   徐崇禮

Xu Dingyi   徐定義

Xu Jingye   徐敬業

Xu Ke   徐珂

Xu Shaoqian   許少謙

Xuan Tiewu   宣鐵吾

Xue Wenhua   薛文華

Yan Ruisheng   閻瑞生

Yang Er   楊二

Yang Guifei   楊貴妃

Yang Jiezeng   楊潔曾

Yang Xiuqin   楊秀琴

Yi Feng   乙楓

Yi Ni   伊妮

Yi Shifu   易實甫

Yong'an (Wing On)   永安

Youxi bao   游戲報

Yu Shuping   俞叔平

Yunjian   雲間

Zang Chunge   藏春閣

Zeng Guozhu   曾國柱

Zhan Kai   詹塏

Zhang Chunfan   張春帆

Zhang Lian Tang   章練塘

Zhang Manjun   張曼君

Zhang Shuyu   張書玉

Zhang Sibao   張四寶

Zhang Xiuying   張秀英

Zhang Yimou   張藝謀

Zhang Yuehua   張月華

Zhang Zibi   張子芯

Zhao Xiuying   趙秀英

Zhen Zhuhua   珍珠花

Zhendan (daxue)   震旦 (大學)

Zheng Mantuo   鄭曼陀

Zheng Shuwen   鄭叔問

Zhihua nü lianyishe   織花女聯誼社

Zhongguo jiuji furu zonghui   中國
    救濟婦孺總會

Zhonghua xinbao   中華新報

Zhou Shixian   周時賢

Zhou Shoujuan   周瘦鵑

Zhu Bangsheng   朱榜生

Zhu Baosan   朱葆三

Zhu Meiyu　朱美予

Zhu Ruchun　祝如椿

Zhu Xiaofang　朱小芳

Zhu Yajia　祝雅嘉

Zi　姊

Zui Chun　醉春

TERMS

ai chengmen　挨城門

ajie　阿姐

amulin　阿木林

anchang　暗娼

bai huajiu　擺花酒

bai mayi　白螞蟻

bai taimian　擺臺面

baiban duisha　白板對煞

ban kaimen　半開門

bang　幫

bang dakuan　傍大款

bangpiao　綁票

bangyan　榜眼

bao fangjian　包房間

bao shenti　包身體

bao zhu　鴇主

baochang fengchen ziweide banlao
　　xuniang　飽嘗風塵滋味的半老
　　徐娘

baofu　鴇父

baomu　鴇母

baozhang　包帳

beitou feng　被頭風

benjia　本家

bianxing　變性

biao fangjian　裱房間

bing fangjian　併房間

bing fangjian　病房間

bolibei　玻璃杯

boxiang menjing　白相門徑

boxiang ren　白相人

buchen nianqing piaoliang shi lao
　　yiba, duibuqi zhe qingchun
　　nianhua　不趁年輕漂亮時撈一
　　把, 對不起這青春年華

bugui　不軌

bujie jinshi　不櫛進士

cai jun nan yibai　採俊男一百

chaibaidang　拆白黨

changji zhidu　娼妓制度

changmen chengtou　娼門撐頭

changsan　長三

chao xiaohuo　抄小貨

chi jiao jiu　赤腳酒

chi tangzi fan　吃堂子飯

chi zifan tuan　喫粢飯團

chu tangchai　出堂差

chuji　雛妓

chuju　出局

ci shi　詞史

congliang　從良

cuican　摧殘

da changhu　大場戶

da chawei　打茶圍

da fangjian　打房間

da qiaozi　搭殼子

da xiansheng　大先生

da zhaohui　大照會

dadi niangyi 打底娘姨

daidang 帶擋

daidang niangyi 帶擋娘姨

daijiao 代轎

dajie 大姐

danda wangwei 膽大妄爲

dayang ju 打樣局

dian da lazhu 點大蠟燭

dianshi 典史

diao fangjian 調房間

diaotou 調頭

ding shao 釘梢

dingpeng 釘棚

disan chanye 第三產業

diuren 丟人

duizhang 隊長

duoduo guaishi 咄咄怪事

en xianghao 恩相好

er san 二三

fang baige 放白鴿

fangjian 房間

fangming saodi 芳名掃地

fangzhong miaojue 房中妙訣

fei yin duo hun 飛茵墮溷

furen 夫人

fuxiong 父兄

gai paitou 戲牌頭

gan xianghao 乾相好

genju 跟局

genü 歌女

gezi peng 鴿子棚

gong qi 共妻

gonggong zhi wu 公共之物

gongsuo 公所

gongwu 公務

gongwu zhengtang 公務正堂

goulan 勾欄

guai 怪

guaipian 拐騙

guan fangjian 關房間

guancha 觀察

guanfu 官府

guangfu 光復

guanji 官妓

guanren 官人

gudao 孤島

gui guazi 龜瓜子

guinu 龜奴

guitou tao 龜頭套

guniang 姑娘

guomen ju 過門局

hao chuangmian 好床面

heyou 和誘

hua fan wei jian 化繁爲簡

hua guniang 花姑娘

hua ling wei zheng 化零爲整

hua si wei gong 化私爲公

huabang 花榜

huangse 黃色

huangse xinwen zhi bizu 黃色
新聞之鼻祖

huangtou qian 黃頭錢

huatou 花頭

huawu zongli 花務總理

huayan jian 花煙間

huhua lüshi 護花律師

huoji 夥計

huyu 淴浴

ji juan　妓捐

ji se er zhi xuyao pin　急色兒之需要品

jia　嫁

jia jiao　家教

jian　賤

jian fei　奸非

jian xiansheng　尖先生

jianwu　奸污

jiao　角

jiao tangchai　叫堂差

jiao xiansheng　角先生

jiao yicha　叫移茶

jiaoju　叫局

jiaoshu　校書

jiaoyang suo　教養所

jie er ai qiao, bao er ai chao　姐兒愛俏, 鴇兒愛鈔

jie fangjian　借房間

jie gan pu　借乾舖

jiejie meimei ku　姐姐妹妹哭

jiemei xiaozu　姐妹小組

jinü　妓女

jiucai　韭菜

jun　君

jupiao　局票

kai bao　開苞

kai fangjian　開房間

kai guopan　開果盤

kaipao　開砲

kan futou　砍斧頭

kaoshan　靠山

ke　科

keshi　客師

koutou　叩頭

kuai　塊

kurou ji　苦肉計

kuzi song yi song, dingdeshang zuo yige yue gong　褲子松一松, 頂得上做一個月工

la pitiaoke　拉皮條客

laji mache　垃圾馬車

lanwu changsan ban yao er　濫污長三板幺二

lao yingxiong　老英雄

laoban　老板

laobanniang　老板娘

laobao　老鴇

laodong jiaoyang　勞動教養

laoshi　老師

li chai　釐差

lian di dong　連底凍

lian'ai ziyou　戀愛自由

lihun　離婚

ling fangjian　領房間

liu su　留宿

luangao liangxing guanxi　亂搞兩性關係

lüe you　略誘

luo xianghao　落相好

luo zhangfang　落帳房

luohua liushui　落花流水

luoshui　落水

ma wang　馬王

mada　馬達

mafang　馬房

maiyin　賣淫

maiyin funü　賣淫婦女

maiyin zhidu　賣淫制度

majiang　麻將

mei shaonian, pianpian zhuoshi jia gongzi　美少年, 翩翩濁世佳公子

mingji　名妓

minzu　民族

mo jingzi　磨鏡子

niangyi　娘姨

niaojin　嬲金

penghe　碰和

piao　嫖

piao nüren　嫖女人

piaosu anchang　嫖宿暗娼

piaozhang　漂帳

pin xizi　姘戲子

pipa　琵琶

po liang wei chang　迫良爲娼

pogua　破瓜

pu fangjian　舖房間

pu fangjian zhe　舖房間者

qianze xiaoshuo　譴責小說

qianzhang　捐賬

qiao bianzi　翹辮子

qing　清

qing guanren　清官人

qipao　旗袍

qu　娶

qunfang yizhong　群芳義塚

ren yao　人妖

renge　人格

renminbi　人民幣

renshen ziyou　人身自由

saniao pusa　撒尿菩薩

sao fangjian　掃房間

sao laji　掃垃圾

saosao　嫂嫂

seqing hangye　色情行業

seqing xingwei　色情行爲

shao leng zao　燒冷灶

shao lutou　燒路頭

shenghuo　生活

shewai　涉外

shi ji　詩妓

shi jiaozi　世腳子

shi ren　適人

shi xianghao　澀相好

shi yanhuo　食煙火

shi zimei　十姊妹

shiniang　師娘

shisan dan　十三旦

shitou　石頭

shourong　收容

shourong jiaoyu suo　收容教育所

shouyin　手淫

shulong　梳櫳

shulou　書樓

shuofa　說法

shushi　書史

shuyu　書寓

si wozi　私窩子

sichang　私娼

sifa bu　司法部

sihui furan　死恢復燃

taiji　台基

tan fenpi　攤粉皮

tangbai　淌白

tangpai　淌排

tanhua　探花

tao ren　討人

tao zhu　討主

teng fangjian　騰房間

tiao cao　跳槽

tiaozi　條子

tijiao　提轎, 踢腳

tongxing ai　同性愛

tongxing lian　同性戀

tou kaibao　偷開苞

tuanhuo　團伙

waichang　外場

wensheng　瘟生

wuchang bu xing, wuchang bu fu
　無娼不興, 無娼不富

wugui　烏龜

wuxiong　務凶

xia jiao　下腳

xia tang　下堂

xian ren tiao　仙人跳

xiancheng　縣承

xiangbang　相幫

xiangdao she　向導社

xiangde chuan, kandepo, fangdeluo
　想得穿, 看得破, 放得落

xiange liyi　弦歌禮義

xianrou zhuang　鹹肉莊

xiansheng　先生

xianshui mei　鹹水妹

xiao bailian　小白臉

xiao benjia　小本家

xiao bocai　小菠菜

xiao fangzi　小房子

xiao xiansheng　小先生

xiao zhaohui　小照會

xiaojie　小姐

xin dang　新黨

xing nüekuang　性虐狂

xing wuran　性污染

xingde jineng zhi shangpinhua　性
　的機能之商品化

xingyu de zui　性欲的罪

xingzheng yuan　行政院

xinren weiji　信任危機

xizao　洗澡

xueyuan　學員

yang xiaogui　養小鬼

yangchang biduan　揚長避短

yangnü　養女

yanhuo　煙火

yao er　幺二

yaotan　搖攤

yeji　野雞

yeji dawang　野雞大王

yichang　异常

yida huatou　一打花頭

yin　淫

yin ku　陰窟

yin tuozi　銀托子

yinshu　淫書

yinwu　淫務

yinye　淫業

yipao zhuyi　一砲主義

yitai longzhong　意態龍種

yuan　圓

yuejie zhulu　越界築路

yundong　運動

zaiye dang　在野黨

zhai　齋

zhaohui　照會

zheng su gu　正俗股

zhenge xiaohun　眞個銷魂

zhengtang　正堂

zhi mai kou bu mai shen　只賣口不
　賣身

zhiji　雉雞

zhong zhuangyuan　中狀元

zhu yexiang　住夜廂

zhuan niantou　轉念頭

zhuang le hong　撞了紅

zhuangyuan　狀元

zhuanju　轉局

zhujia　住家

zhujia yeji　住家野雞

zhuo　濁

zhuo mianr　桌面兒

zhuzheng　主政

zishen　自身

zuo baozhang　做包帳

zuo huatou　做花頭

zuoshou　做手

zuoyou liangtang　左右兩堂

BIBLIOGRAPHY

A Qiao. 1993. "Lubian heidianli de maixiao nü" [Smile-selling women (prostitutes) in roadside brigand inns]. *Hehua dian* 28: 52–59.

A Zhao. 1984. "Shanghai gaizao changji shi" [A history of the reform of Shanghai prostitutes]. *Jiushi niandai* 4: 8.

Abu-Lughod, Lila. 1990. "The Romance of Resistance: Tracing Transformations of Power through Bedouin Women." *American Ethnologist* 17.1 (February): 41–55.

Akutagawa Ryūnosuke. 1977–78. "Shanhai yūki" [Travelogue of Shanghai]. In Akutagawa Ryūnosuke zenshū [Collected works of Akutagawa Ryūnosuke]. Tokyo: Iwanami shoten, vol. 5, 3–59.

Anagnost, Ann. Forthcoming. *National Past-times: Narrative, Writing, and History in Modern China*. Durham, N.C.: Duke University Press.

Arlington, L. C. 1923. "The Chinese Female Names." *China Journal of Science and Arts* 1.4: 316–25.

Arlington, L. C., and William Lewisohn. 1967 (1935). *In Search of Old Peking*. New York: Paragon Book Reprint Corporation.

Ballhatchet, Kenneth. 1980. *Race, Sex, and Class under the Raj: Imperial Attitudes and Policies and Their Critics, 1793–1905*. New York: St. Martin's Press.

Banchisheng [Half-Crazy One; pseud.]. 1891. *Haishang yeyou beilan* [A complete look at Shanghai philandering]. N.p. 4 *juan*.

Bao Jialin. 1974. "Xinhai shiqi de funü sixiang: 1898–1911" [Women's thought in the 1911 era: 1898–1911]. *Zhonghua xuebao* 1: 1–22.

Bao Tianxiao. 1971. *Chuanying Lou huiyi lu* [Reminiscences of Bracelet Shadow Tower]. Hong Kong: Dahua chubanshe.

———. 1973. *Chuanying Lou huiyi lu xubian* [Continuation of reminiscences of Bracelet Shadow Tower]. Hong Kong: Dahua chubanshe.

———. 1987 (1925). *Shanghai chunqiu* [Shanghai annals]. Guangxi: Guangxi lijiang chubanshe. 2 vols.

———. 1990. *Chuanying Lou huiyi lu* [Reminiscences of Bracelet Shadow Tower]. Ed.

Zhang Yufa and Zhang Ruide. Zhongguo xiandai zizhuan congshu no. 2. Taipei: Longwen chubanshe gufen youxian gongsi. 3 vols.

Barlow, Tani E. 1994. "Politics and Protocols of *Funü*: (Un)Making National Woman." In Christina Gilmartin, Gail Hershatter, Lisa Rofel, and Tyrene White, eds. *Engendering China: Women, Culture, and the State.* Cambridge, Mass.: Harvard University Press, 339–59.

Barry, Kathleen. 1979. *Female Sexual Slavery.* New York and London: New York University Press.

Barry, Kathleen, Charlotte Bunch, and Shirley Castley, eds. 1984. *International Feminism: Networking against Female Sexual Slavery.* New York: International Women's Tribune Centre.

Beahan, Charlotte L. 1975. "Feminism and Nationalism in the Chinese Women's Press, 1902–1911." *Modern China* 1.4 (October): 379–416.

———. 1976. "The Women's Movement and Nationalism in Late Ch'ing China." Ph.D. dissertation, Columbia University.

Bei Hai. 1991. *Sai Jinhua.* Bei Shi: Haifeng chubanshe youxian gongsi.

Beijing shi gong'anju, ed. 1988. *Beijing fengbi jiyuan jishi* [A record of the Beijing brothel closings]. Beijing: Zhongguo heping chubanshe.

Beijing shi Tiantang he laojiaosuo. 1992? "Guanyu 100 ming nü laojiao renyuan rusuo qian maiyin qingkuang de diaocha" [Investigation on the conditions under which one hundred women sold sex prior to their entry into the labor education institute]. Jiaoyu gaizao maiyin nü laojiao renyuan gongzuo zuotanhui canyue cailiao zhi jiu [Reference material item no. 9 for the forum on the work of educating and reforming women sex sellers who are in labor education facilities]. Unpublished paper.

Beiping shehui diaochasuo bianzhi. 1931. *Beiping shehui gaikuang tongji tu* [A statistical survey of Beiping society]. Beiping: Beiping shehui diaochasuo.

Beiping shi zhengfu mishuchu diyike tongji qu bian. 1936. *Beiping shi tongji lanyao* [Essential Beiping statistics]. Beiping: Beiping shi zhengfu mishuchu diyike bian zuan gu.

Berkhofer, Robert F., Jr. 1995. *Beyond the Great Story: History as Text and Discourse.* Cambridge, Mass.: Harvard University Press.

Bernhardt, Kathryn. 1994. "Women and the Law: Divorce in the Republican Period." In Kathryn Bernhardt and Philip C. C. Huang, eds. *Civil Law in Qing and Republican China.* Stanford, Calif.: Stanford University Press, 187–214.

Bernheimer, Charles. 1989. *Figures of Ill Repute: Representing Prostitution in Nineteenth-Century France.* Cambridge, Mass.: Harvard University Press.

Bernstein, Laurie. 1995. *Sonia's Daughters: Prostitutes and Their Regulation in Imperial Russia.* Berkeley and Los Angeles: University of California Press.

Bi Bi. 1936. "You gong zuguo de Sai Jinhua" [Sai Jinhua, who made a contribution to the motherland]. *Funü yuebao* 2.11 (December 10): 12.

Bi Yao. 1938. "Gudao de huiyinzhe" [Those who invite adultery on the lonely island]. *Shanghai funü* 1.8 (August 5): 10–11.

Bi Yihong. 1922. "Beili ying'er" [Infant of the northern lanes]. *Banyue* 1.18 (May): 1–15.

Britton, Roswell S. 1966 (1933). *The Chinese Periodical Press, 1800–1912.* Taipei (Shanghai): Ch'eng-wen Publishing Co. (Kelly and Walsh).

Burns, John F. 1985. "Prostitution Is Back, and Peking Isn't Happy." *New York Times* (October 6): 12.

Buruma, Ian 1996. "The 21st Century Starts Here." *New York Times Magazine* (February 18): 28–35, 47–48, 54, 58.

Butler, Anne M. 1985. *Daughters of Joy, Sisters of Misery: Prostitutes in the American West, 1865–1890.* Urbana and Chicago: University of Illinois Press.

Byron, John. 1987. *Portrait of a Chinese Paradise: Erotica and Sexual Customs of the Late Qing.* London: Quartet Books.

Cao Gongqi. 1934. "Changji wenti zhi genben jiuzhi" [A fundamental remedy for the prostitution problem]. *Renyan zhoukan* 1.41 (November 24): 854–55.

Cao Juren. 1933. "Changjin" [Prostitution ban]. *Shenbao ziyou tan* (June 22).

Cao Manzhi. 1986. Interview by author with former head of the Shanghai Civil Administration Bureau.

Carlitz, Katherine. 1994. "Desire, Danger, and the Body: Stories of Women's Virtue in Late Ming China." In Christina Gilmartin, Gail Hershatter, Lisa Rofel, and Tyrene White, eds. *Engendering China: Women, Culture, and the State.* Cambridge, Mass.: Harvard University Press, 101–24.

Chai Junyong. 1990. "Liudong renkou: Chengshi guanli de yi da kunrao" [The floating population: A major challenge for city management]. *Shehui* 10 (October): 8.

Champly, Henry. 1934. *The Road to Shanghai: White Slave Traffic in Asia.* Trans. Warre B. Wells. London: John Long, Ltd.

Chan Qingshi [Attendant Who Repents Emotion; pseud.]. 1884. *Haishang chunfang pu* [An album of Shanghai ladies]. Shanghai: Shenbao guan. 4 *juan.*

"Changji wenti de zhengjie" [The crux of the prostitution problem]. 1934. *Nüsheng* 2.16 (May 25): 4.

Chen Dezheng. 1923. "Maiyin shiye zhi jingji de yuanyin" [The economic reasons for the enterprise of selling sex]. *Funü zazhi* 9.3: 13–18.

Chen Dingshan. 1967. *Chunshen jiuwen* [Hearsay from Chun Shen]. Taipei (?): Chenguang yuekan she. 2 vols.

Chen Fangzhi. 1935. "Tantan kepa de hualiu bing" [Talk about frightening venereal disease]. *Funü shenghuo* 1.4 (October 1): 48–53.

Chen Lianhen. 1925. *Jinghua chunmeng lu* [Record of spring dreams in the national capital]. Shanghai: Guangyi shuju.

Chen Luwei. 1938. "Shourong jinü de jingguo" [The process of taking in prostitutes]. *Shanghai funü* 1.1 (April): 21–22.

Chen Renbing. 1948. *Youguan Shanghai ertong fuli de shehui diaocha* [A social investigation concerning the welfare of Shanghai children]. Shanghai: Shanghai ertong fuli zujinhui.

Chen Rongguang [Chen Boxi]. 1924. *Lao Shanghai* [Old Shanghai hand]. Shanghai: Taidong tushuju.

Chen Sihe, ed. 1990. *Wenxue zhong de jinü xingxiang* [The image of the prostitute in literature]. Beijing: Renmin ribao chubanshe.

Chen Yehong. 1991. "On Prostitution and the Application of Criminal Law." [Wuhan] *Huazhong Shifan Daxue xuebao* 6 (1990): 35–40. Translated in JPRS-CAR-91-005 (31 January 1991): 65–70.

Chen Yiyun. 1992 and 1993. Interview by author. Beijing.

Cheng, Stephen. 1979. "Flowers of Shanghai and the Late-Ch'ing Courtesan Novel." Ph.D. dissertation, Harvard University.

——. 1982. "*Sing-song Girls of Shanghai* and Its Narrative Methods." *Renditions* 17–18: 111–36.

Chi Zhicheng. 1893. "Huyou mengying" [Dream images of Shanghai travels]. Ed. Hu Zhusheng. Unpublished paper. Photocopy of edited version of unpublished manuscript (*chaoben*) in Wenzhou museum.

"Child Labour in China." 1924. *China Medical Journal* 38.11 (November): 923–29.

China Medical Missionary Association. 1909–1930. *China Medical Journal* 23–44. Shanghai: Presbyterian Mission.

China News Digest. 1992–. On-line journal available via Internet and Bitnet.

China Weekly Review. Shanghai. 1927–1935.

Chinese Medical Journal. 1932–. Peiping: Chinese Medical Association.

Chinese Recorder. 1920.

Chinese Recorder and Missionary Journal. 1905.

Chou, Eric. 1971. *The Dragon and the Phoenix: Love, Sex, and the Chinese.* London: Michael Joseph, Ltd.

Chow, Rey. 1991. *Woman and Chinese Modernity: The Politics of Reading between East and West.* Minnesota and Oxford: University of Minnesota Press.

——. 1993. "A Souvenir of Love." *Modern Chinese Literature* 7 (fall): 59–78.

Chow, Tse-tsung. 1960. *The May Fourth Movement: Intellectual Revolution in Modern China.* Cambridge, Mass.: Harvard University Press.

Chu Hui. 1927. "Guanyu feichang shijian de taolun: (yi) Tantan feichang de wenti" [A discussion concerning the matter of abolishing prostitution: (1.) Talking about the problem of abolishing prostitution]. *Funü zazhi* 13.12: 12–17.

Chunming shuju, ed. 1937. *Shanghai heimu yiqian zhong* [One thousand scandalous stories of Shanghai]. Shanghai: Shanghai shuju.

Coble, Parks. 1980. *The Shanghai Capitalists and the Nationalist Government, 1927–1937.* Cambridge, Mass.: Council on East Asian Studies, Harvard University; distributed by Harvard University Press.

Cohen, Jerome Alan. 1968. *The Criminal Process in the People's Republic of China, 1949–1963.* Cambridge, Mass.: Harvard University Press.

——. 1988. "Sex, Chinese Law and the Foreigner." *Hong Kong Law Journal* 18.1: 102–10.

Cohen, Myron S., Gail E. Henderson, Pat Aiello, and Zheng Heyi. 1993. "Successful Eradication of Sexually Transmitted Diseases in the People's Republic of China: Implications for the 21st Century." Paper presented at the tenth international meeting of the International Society for Sexually Transmitted Disease Research, Helsinki, Finland.

Cohen, Paul A. 1974. *Between Tradition and Modernity: Wang T'ao and Reform in Late Ch'ing China.* Cambridge, Mass.: Harvard University Press.

Cooper, Frederick. 1994. "Conflict and Connection: Rethinking Colonial African History." *American Historical Review* 99 (December): 1,516–45.

Corbin, Alain. 1986. "Commercial Sexuality in Nineteenth-Century France: A System of Images and Regulations." *Representations* 14 (spring): 209–17.

——. 1990. *Women for Hire: Prostitution and Sexuality in France after 1850.* Cambridge, Mass.: Harvard University Press.

Crad, Joseph. 1940. *Traders in Women: A Comprehensive Survey of "White Slavery."* London: John Long, Ltd.

The Criminal Law and the Criminal Procedure Law of the People's Republic of China. 1984. Beijing: Foreign Languages Press.

Cusack, Dymphna. 1985 (1958). *Chinese Women Speak.* London: Century Hutchinson, Ltd.

Dai Qiu. 1923. "Maiyin de dongji" [The motivation for selling sex]. *Funü zazhi* 9.3: 22–24.

Darwent, C. E. 1920. *Shanghai: A Handbook for Travellers and Residents.* Shanghai: Kelly and Walsh, Ltd.

Datong tushushe, ed. n.d. *Shanghai shenmi zhinan* [Guide to the mysteries of Shanghai]. Shanghai: Datong tushu she.

de Beauvoir, Simone. 1958. *The Long March.* Cleveland: World Publishing Company.

De Leeuw, Hendrick. 1933. *Cities of Sin.* New York: Harrison Smith and Robert Haas.

Delacoste, Frederique, and Priscilla Alexander, eds. 1987. *Sex Work: Writings by Women in the Sex Industry.* Pittsburgh: Cleis.

"The Demi-monde of Shanghai." 1923. *China Medical Journal* 37: 782–88.

Dennett, Tyler. 1918. "New Codes for Old." *Asia* (August): 657–64.

Dikötter, Frank. 1992. *The Discourse of Race in Modern China.* Stanford, Calif.: Stanford University Press.

———. 1995. *Sex, Culture, and Modernity in Early Republican China.* Honolulu: University of Hawaii Press.

Dirlik, Arif. 1991. *Anarchism in the Chinese Revolution.* Berkeley and Los Angeles: University of California Press.

Dong Delun. 1991. "Shanghai changji zhi yanjiu" [Research on Shanghai prostitution]. Master's thesis, Donghai University.

Drucker, Alison R. 1981. "The Influence of Western Women on the Anti-Footbinding Movement, 1840–1911." In Richard W. Guisso and Stanley Johannesen, eds. *Women in China: Current Directions in Historical Scholarship.* New York: Philo, 179–99.

Duban Shanghai shizheng gongshu mishuchu. 1938. *Shi gongbao* 7 (August): 96–98.

Dutton, Michael. 1992. *Policing and Punishment in China: From Patriarchy to "the People."* Cambridge: Cambridge University Press.

"Editorial." 1920. *China Medical Journal* 34.6 (November): 635–37.

Edwards, Louise. 1994. "Chin Sung-ts'en's *A Tocsin for Women*: The Dextrous Merger of Radicalism and Conservatism in Feminism of the Early Twentieth Century." *Jindai Zhongguo funü shi yanjiu* 2 (June): 117–40.

Engelstein, Laura. 1992. *The Keys to Happiness: Sex and the Search for Modernity in Fin-de-Siècle Russia.* Ithaca and London: Cornell University Press.

Esherick, Joseph W., and Mary Backus Rankin, eds. 1990. *Chinese Local Elites and Patterns of Dominance.* Berkeley and Los Angeles: University of California Press.

Evans, Harriet. 1991. "The Official Construction of Female Sexuality and Gender in the People's Republic of China, 1949–1959." Ph.D. dissertation, University of London.

———. 1995. "Defining Difference: The 'Scientific' Construction of Sexuality and Gender in the People's Republic of China." *Signs* 20.2 (winter): 357–95.

Fan Shaozeng. 1986. "Guanyu Du Yuesheng" [About Du Yuesheng]. Oral history. As told to Shen Zui. In Zhu Xuefan, ed. *Jiu Shanghai de banghui* [The gangs of Old Shanghai]. Shanghai: Shanghai renmin chubanshe, 195–247.

Fang Long. 1935. "Cong piaoji shuodao xianfu liangfu" [From visiting prostitutes to a discussion of good husbands and loving fathers]. *Funü gongming* 4.11 (November 20): 30–34.

Feetham, R. C. 1931. *Report to the Shanghai Municipal Council.* Shanghai: North-China Daily News and Herald, Ltd. 3 vols.

"Feichang yundong" [The movement to abolish prostitution]. 1922. *Funü zazhi* 8.11: 118–19.

Fewsmith, Joseph. 1985. *Party, State and Local Elites in Republican China: Merchant Organizations and Politics in Shanghai, 1890–1930.* Honolulu: University of Hawaii Press.

Finch, Percy. 1953. *Shanghai and Beyond.* New York: Scribner's.

Foreign Broadcast Information Service. 1982–1995. *FBIS Daily Report—China.* Washington, D.C.: Government Printing Office.

Foucault, Michel. 1980. *The History of Sexuality.* Vol. 1, *An Introduction.* New York: Vintage.

Fu, Charlene L. 1993. "Foreign Students in China Accuse Fudan of Wrongdoing." Associated Press (February 4), electronically reprinted in *China News Digest* (February 8).

Fu, Poshek. 1993. *Passivity, Resistance, and Collaboration: Intellectual Choices in Occupied Shanghai, 1937–1945.* Stanford, Calif.: Stanford University Press.

Funü gongming [Women's sympathetic understanding]. 1930s.

Funü yuebao [Women's monthly]. 1935.

Funü zazhi [Ladies' journal]. 1915–1931. Vols. 1–17. Shanghai: Commercial Press, Ltd.

Furth, Charlotte. 1994. "Rethinking Van Gulik: Sexuality and Reproduction in Traditional Chinese Medicine." In Christina Gilmartin, Gail Hershatter, Lisa Rofel, and Tyrene White, eds. *Engendering China: Women, Culture, and the State.* Cambridge, Mass.: Harvard University Press, 125–46.

Gamble, Sidney. 1921. *Peking.* New York: George H. Doran Co.

Gamewell, Mary Ninde. 1916. *The Gateway to China: Pictures of Shanghai.* New York: Fleming H. Revell Co.

Gao Xiaoxian and Du Li. 1993. Interview by author. Xi'an.

Gargan, Edward. 1988. "Newest Economics Revives the Oldest Profession." *New York Times,* September 17, p. 4.

Garon, Sheldon. 1993. "The World's Oldest Debate? Prostitution and the State in Imperial Japan, 1900–1945." *American Historical Review* 98.3 (June): 710–33.

Ge Yuanxu. 1876. *Huyou zaji* [Miscellaneous records of Shanghai travels]. N.p.

Gibson, Mary. 1986. *Prostitution and the State in Italy, 1860–1915.* New Brunswick, N.J., and London: Rutgers University Press.

Gilfoyle, Timothy J. 1992. *City of Eros: New York City, Prostitution, and the Commercialization of Sex, 1820–1920.* New York and London: W. W. Norton and Co.

Gilmartin, Christina. 1989. "Gender, Politics, and Patriarchy in China: The Experiences of Early Women Communists, 1920–27." In Sonia Kruks, Rayna Rapp, and Marilyn B. Young, eds. *Promissory Notes: Women in the Transition to Socialism.* New York: Monthly Review Press, 82–105.

———. 1995. *Engendering the Chinese Revolution: Radical Women, Communist Politics, and Mass Movements in the 1920s.* Berkeley and Los Angeles: University of California Press.

Gipoulon, Catherine. 1989–1990. "The Emergence of Women in Politics in China, 1898–1927." *Chinese Studies in History* (winter): 46–67.

Goldman, Merle, ed. 1977. *Modern Chinese Literature in the May Fourth Era.* Cambridge, Mass.: Harvard University Press.

"Gongchang shi liang zhiduma" [Is licensed prostitution a good system?]. 1924. *Funü zazhi* 10.4: 586–87.

Gongyi shushe, ed. 1908. *Hujiang seyi zhinan* [Guide to the beauty and art of Shanghai]. Shanghai: Gongyi shushe.

Goodman, Bryna. 1995. *The Native Place and the City: Immigrant Consciousness and Organization in Shanghai, 1853–1927.* Berkeley and Los Angeles: University of California Press.

Gordon, C. A., comp. 1884. *An Epitome of the Reports of the Medical Officers to the Chinese Imperial Maritime Customs Service from 1871 to 1882.* Inspectorate General of Customs for China. London: Baillière, Tindall, and Cox.

Gray, Francine du Plessix. 1992. "Splendor and Miseries." *New York Review of Books* 16 (July): 31–35.

Grieder, Jerome. 1970. *Hu Shih and the Chinese Renaissance: Liberalism in the Chinese Revolution, 1917–1937.* Cambridge, Mass.: Harvard University Press.

Gronewold, Sue. 1984. *Beautiful Merchandise: Prostitution in China, 1840–1936.* New York: Haworth Press.

———. 1995. "Encountering Hope: The Door of Hope Mission in Shanghai and Taipei." Ph.D. dissertation, Columbia University.

Guan Keshou zhai ban. 1884. *Shenjiang jingsheng tushuo* [Pictures and descriptions of Shanghai's famous places]. Shanghai: Rou yun guan.

Guan Tao, Wu Changzhen, Wang Deyi, and Yang Dawen. 1992. *"Funü quanyi baozhang fa" jiben zhishi* [Basic knowlege about the Law Protecting Women's Rights and Interests]. Beijing: Zhongguo funü chubanshe.

Guha, Ranajit. 1988. "Preface." In Ranajit Guha and Gayatri Chakravorty Spivak, eds. *Selected Subaltern Studies.* New York and Oxford: Oxford University Press, pp. 35–36.

Guo Chongjie. 1936. "Lun suqing changji" [On ridding the country of prostitution]. *Shehui banyue kan* 1.6 (November): 23–28.

Guo Zhen. 1933. "Duiyu jingshi changji wenti de jiantao" [A review of the question of prostitution in the capital]. *Funü gongming* 2.5 (May): 13–16.

Haishang Soushisheng [One Who Pillows Himself on a Rock and Lets Water Wash over Him; pseud.]. 1991. *Haishang fanhua meng* [Dream of Shanghai luxury]. Shanghai tan yu Shanghai ren congshu [Series 2]. Shanghai: Shanghai guji chubanshe. 4 vols.

Han Bangqing [Han Pang-ch'ing]. 1982. "Sing-Song Girls of Shanghai." Translation of first two chapters of *Haishang hualie zhuan.* Trans. Eileen Chang. *Renditions* 17–18: 95–110.

———. 1985 (1894). *Haishang hualie zhuan* [Flowers of Shanghai]. Beijing: Renmin wenxue chubanshe.

Hanyu da cidian bianji weiyuanhui. 1989. *Hanyu da cidian* [Comprehensive dictionary of Chinese]. Shanghai: Hanyu da cidian chubanshe.

Harding, Gardner L. 1917. "The Door of Hope." *World Outlook* (February): 5–6.

Harsin, Jill. 1985. *Policing Prostitution in Nineteenth-Century Paris.* Princeton, N.J.: Princeton University Press.

Hauser, Ernest O. 1940. *Shanghai: City for Sale.* New York: Harcourt, Brace and Co.

He Jiwei. 1933. "Cong 'shi' 'se' wenti tandao qudi sichang banfa" [Talking about eliminating unlicensed prostitution from the angle of "food" and "sex"]. *Nüzi yuekan* 1.10 (December 15): 23–27.

He Qiying. 1934a."Beiping de yutang" [The public baths of Beiping]. *Shanghai zhoubao* 3.11 (February 8): 216–17.

———. 1934b. "Beiping de genü" [The singing girls of Beiping]. *Shanghai zhoubao* 3.15 (March 8): 292–93.

He Wannan. 1984. "Dangwu digou hua dangnian" [Speaking of the times when we cleaned up the dirt]. *Minzhu yu fazhi* 1 (January): 19–23.

Heath, Frances J. 1925. "Venereal Diseases in Relation to Prostitution in China." *Social Pathology* 1.6: 278–84.

Henderson, Edward. 1871. *A Report on Prostitution in Shanghai*. Shanghai: North-China Herald Office.

Henriot, Christian. 1988. "Prostitution et 'Police des Moeurs' à Shanghai aux XIXe–XXe siècles." In Christian Henriot, ed. *La femme en Asie orientale*. Centre Rhonalpin de Recherche sur l'Extrême-Orient Contemporain. Lyon: Université Jean Moulin Lyon II, 64–93.

———. 1992. "Medicine, VD and Prostitution in Pre-Revolutionary China." *Social History of Medicine* 5.1 (April): 95–120.

———. 1993. *Shanghai 1927–1937: Municipal Power, Locality, and Modernization*. Trans. Noël Castelino. Berkeley and Los Angeles: University of California Press.

Henriot, Christian. 1994. "Chinese Courtesans in Late Qing and Early Republican Shanghai (1849–1925)." *East Asian History* 8 (December): 33–52.

———. 1995. "'La Fermeture': The Abolition of Prostitution in Shanghai, 1949–1958." *China Quarterly*, 142 (June): 467–86.

———. 1996a. "'From A Throne of Glory to a Seat of Ignominy'": Shanghai Prostitution Revisited (1849–1949)." *Modern China* 22.2 (April): 132–63.

———. 1996b. *Belles de Shanghai: Prostitution et sexualité en Chine aux XIXe–XXe siècles*. Paris: CNRS-Editions.

———. Forthcoming 1997. *Shanghai Ladies of the Night: Prostitution and Sexuality in Nineteenth- and Twentieth-Century China*. New York: Cambridge University Press.

Henriques, Fernando. 1962. *Prostitution and Society*. London: MacGibbon and Kee.

Hershatter, Gail. 1986. *The Workers of Tianjin*. Stanford, Calif.: Stanford University Press.

———. 1989. "The Hierarchy of Shanghai Prostitution, 1919–1949." *Modern China* 15.4 (October): 463–97.

———. 1991. "Prostitution and the Market in Women in Early Twentieth-Century Shanghai." In Rubie S. Watson and Patricia Buckley Ebrey, eds. *Marriage and Inequality in Chinese Society*. Berkeley and Los Angeles: University of California Press, 256–85.

———. 1992a. "Courtesans and Streetwalkers: The Changing Discourses on Shanghai Prostitution, 1890–1949" *Journal of the History of Sexuality* 3.2 (October): 245–69.

———. 1992b. "Regulating Sex in Shanghai: The Reform of Prostitution in 1920 and 1951." In Frederic Wakeman, Jr., and Wen-hsin Yeh, eds. *Shanghai Sojourners*. China Research Monograph no. 40. Berkeley: University of California Institute of East Asian Studies, 147–86.

———. 1992c. "Sex Work and Social Order: Prostitutes, Their Families, and the State in Twentieth-Century Shanghai." In *Family Process and Political Process in Modern Chinese History*. Taipei: Academia Sinica, vol. 2, 1,083–1,124.

————. 1993. "The Subaltern Talks Back: Reflections on Subaltern Theory and Chinese History." *positions: east asia cultures critique* 1.1 (spring): 103–30.

————. 1994. "Modernizing Sex, Sexing Modernity: Prostitution in Early Twentieth-Century Shanghai." In Christina Gilmartin, Gail Hershatter, Lisa Rofel, and Tyrene White, eds. *Engendering China: Women, Culture, and the State.* Cambridge, Mass.: Harvard University Press, 147–74.

————. 1996. "Sexing Modern China." In Gail Hershatter, Emily Honig, Jonathan N. Lipman, and Randall Stross, eds. *Remapping China: Fissures in Historical Terrain.* Stanford, Calif.: Stanford University Press, 77–93.

Hinder, Eleanor M. 1944. *Life and Labour in Shanghai.* New York: Institute of Pacific Relations.

Hinton, Carma, and Richard Gordon, directors. 1984. *Small Happiness: Women of a Chinese Village.* Long Bow Group.

Hō Aboku [Peng Amu]. 1928. "Shanhai no baishōfu" [Shanghai prostitutes]. *Shina kenkyu* 18 (December): 731–51.

Hoh, Chieh-shiang. 1928. "The Shanghai Provisional Court: Its Past, Present and Future." *China Weekly Review* (October 10): 162–65, 193.

Hong Hua. 1935. "Beibei'er lun changji" [Bebel discusses prostitution]. *Choumou yuekan* 2.3–4 (November 25; December 15): 32–34; 70–73.

Hong Ya. 1933. "Shanghai Aiduoyalu zhi ye" [Night on Shanghai's Avenue Edward VI]. *Funü xunkan* 17.25 (September 10): 4–6.

Honig, Emily. 1986. *Sisters and Strangers: Women in the Shanghai Cotton Mills, 1919–1949.* Stanford, Calif.: Stanford University Press.

————. 1992. *Creating Chinese Ethnicity: Subei People in Shanghai, 1850–1980.* New Haven, Conn.: Yale University Press.

————. 1993. "Regional Identity, Labor, and Ethnicity in Contemporary China." Paper presented at the conference "East Asian Labor in Comparative Perspective," Lake Tahoe, Calif.

Honig, Emily, and Gail Hershatter. 1988. *Personal Voices: Chinese Women in the 1980s.* Stanford, Calif.: Stanford University Press.

Hsiao Kan. 1950. "The Return to Daylight: The Reformation of Peking Prostitutes." *People's China* 1.12 (March 16): 22–26.

Hsiao Wen. 1957. "Shanghai Prostitutes Begin Their Lives Anew." *Women of China* 2: 24–27.

Hu Huaichen. 1920. "Feichang wenti" [The question of abolishing prostitution]. *Funü zazhi* 6.6: 7–11.

Hu Jifan. 1930. *Shanghai xiaozhi* [Small records of Shanghai]. Shanghai: Chuanjing tang shudian.

Hu Zhusheng. 1979. "Qing Bang shi chutan" [A preliminary exploration of the Green Gang]. *Lishi xue jikan* 3: 102–20.

Hua Min [pseud. for Liu Xiuming]. 1986. "Jixing shehui zhong de beican shijie" [A miserable world in the midst of an abnormal society]. *Renmin jingcha* 10 (October): 33–35.

Huang Ko-wu. 1988. "Cong Shenbao yiyao guanggao kan minchu Shanghai de yiliao wenhua yu shehui shenghuo, 1912–1926" [Looking at early Republican Shanghai medical culture and social life through the medical advertisements in *Shenbao, 1912–1926*]. *Zhongyang yanjiuyuan jindaishi yanjiusuo jikan* 17, part 2 (December): 141–94.

Huang Renjing. 1913. *Huren baojian* [Precious mirror of Shanghai; English title: *What the Chinese in Shanghai Ought to Know*]. Shanghai: Huamei shuju [Methodist Publishing House].

Huang Shi. 1927. "Feichang yundong" [The movement to abolish prostitution]. *Xin nüxing* 2.8 (August 1): 795–805.

———. 1928. "Changji zhidu de chuxing" [Early forms of the system of prostitution]. *Xin nüxing* 3.10 (October 1): 1,147–57.

Huang Shi. 1986. Interview by author with retired official of the Shanghai Public Security Bureau. Shanghai.

Huang Shiquan [Huang Xiexun; pseud. for Wang Tao]. 1975 (1892). *Songnan mengying lu* [Record of Songnan dream shadows]. In Wang Xiqi, comp. *Xiaofang huzhai yudi congchao* [Collected writings on geography from Small Square Pot Studio]. Taipei: Xuesheng shuju, vol. 9.

Huang Yunqiu and Wang Dingfei. 1986. Interview by author with former staff members of the Shanghai Women's Labor Training Institute. Shanghai.

Huaqiao ribao. 1986.

Huayu xiaozhu zhuren. 1892. *Haishang qinglou tuji* [Records and drawings of Shanghai houses of prostitution]. N.p. 6 *juan*.

Huebner, John. 1988. "A Note on Prostitution in Shanghai during the 1910s." *American Asian Review* 6.3 (fall): 93–99.

Huo Bilie. 1991. *Sai Jinhua zhuan* [Biography of Sai Jinhua]. Taipei: Guoji wenhua shiye youxian gongsi.

Ignatius, Adi, and Julia Leung. 1989. "What the Revolution in China Wiped Out, Reform Brought Back." *Wall Street Journal* (November 15): A1, A23.

———. 1990? "For Ah Hong, Prostitution Proves a Lucrative Field." *Asian Wall Street Journal* (January?): 1, 11.

Jamieson, R. Alex. 1870. "Memorandum on the Sanitary Condition of the Yang-King-Pang and Hongque Settlements at Shanghai (September 23, 1869)." *North-China Herald* (March 22): 211.

Jaschok, Maria. 1988. *Concubines and Bondservants: The Social History of a Chinese Custom.* London: Zed Books, Ltd.

Jia [Home]. 1947–1948.

Jiang Jingsan. 1925. "Xiandai wenming yu maiyin wenti" [Modern civilization and the prostitution problem]. *Funü zazhi* 11.5: 772–79.

Jiefang ribao. 1950s. Shanghai.

Jin Ping Mei. 1994. Trans. David Roy. Chicago: University of Chicago Press.

Jin Wenhua, ed. 1933. *Beiping youlan zhinan* [Guide to touring Beiping]. Beiping: Zhonghua yinshu ju.

Jin Xian. 1935. *Xiangyan jinghua* [Essence of fragrant dazzling beauty]. Shanghai: Xinmin shuju.

Jing Xiangding. 1934. "Maiyin de xuyao zhi poushi" [A dissection of the necessity for prostitution]. *Renyan zhoukan* 1.43 (December 8): 884–85.

Jing Zhi. 1936. "Sulian changji gailiangsuo canguanji" [Record of a visit to a prostitute reform institute in the Soviet Union]. *Funü shenghuo* 3.5 (September 16): 23–25.

Jingbao [Crystal]. 1919–1939. Shanghai.

Jizhe [Reporter; pseud.]. 1933. "Changji wenti yu Zhongwai yulun" [The problem of prostitution and public opinion in China and abroad]. *Funü gongming* 2.6 (June): 74–76.

Johnson, Kay Ann. 1983. *Women, the Family and Peasant Revolution in China.* Chicago: University of Chicago Press.

Joint Publications Research Service. 1987–1992. Washington, D.C.: Government Printing Office.

Jones, T. K. 1922. "The Canton Purity Campaign." *Chinese Recorder* (May): 341–44.

Jones, William C., trans. 1994. *The Great Qing Code.* Tianquan Cheng and Yongling Jiang, assts. Oxford: Clarendon Press.

Kafalas, Philip. 1995. "Nostalgia and the Reading of the Late Ming Essay: Zhang Dai's *Tao'an Mengyi.*" Ph.D. dissertation, Stanford University.

Kang Suzhen. 1988. *Qinglou hen* [Courtesan-house hatred]. Ed. Yan Nian. Harbin: Heilongjiang renmin chubanshe.

Kaye, Lincoln. 1993. "Reining in Erotica: China Bans Bestseller in New Crackdown." *Far Eastern Economic Review* (November 18): 40–41.

Key, Ellen. 1911. *The Morality of Woman and Other Essays.* Trans. Mamah Bouton Brothwick. Chicago: Ralph Fletcher Seymour Co.

King, Frank H. H. 1969. *A Concise Economic History of Modern China, 1940–1961.* New York: Praeger.

Kisch, Egon Erwin. 1935. *La Chine secrète.* Trans. Jeanne Stern. Paris: Gallimard.

Ko, Dorothy. 1994. *Teachers of the Inner Chambers: Women and Culture in Seventeenth-Century China.* Stanford, Calif.: Stanford University Press.

Kotenev, Anatol M. 1968 (1925). *Shanghai: Its Mixed Court and Council.* Taipei (Shanghai): Ch'eng-wen Publishing Co. (North-China Daily News and Herald, Ltd.).

Kowallis, Jon. Forthcoming. "Depravity's Rainbow: Fan Zengxiang's *Caiyun qu* and the Legend of Sai Jin Hua, Cross-Cultural Courtesan of the Late Qing." In Li Huayuan Mowry, ed., *Stories and Songs.* Hanover, N.H.: University Press of New England.

Kristof, Nicholas. 1993. "China Sees 'Market-Leninism' as Way to Future." *New York Times* (September 6): 1, 5.

Ku Liang [Gu Liang]. 1969. "Mainland Prostitutes under Chinese Communist Rule." *Xingdao ribao* [Hong Kong] (December 8–10):4. Translated in JPRS(?) 5292-CSO: 3577-D: 7–12.

Kuang Jianping. 1934. "Yanli jujinxia zhi changji wenti" [The prostitution problem under conditions of strictly being taken into custody]. *Renyan zhoukan* 1.42 (December 1): 866–67.

Lague, David. 1993. Article in *The Weekend Australian Review* (April 4). Electronically reprinted in *China News Digest Books and Journals Review* (April 11).

Lan Xiang, ed. 1990. *Shanghai tan daheng zhuanji* [Biographical sketches of prosperous persons on the Shanghai Bund]. Shanghai: Shanghai wenyi chubanshe.

Lao Xin. 1934. "Guangzhou de mangji" [The blind prostitutes of Guangzhou]. *Renyan zhoukan* 1.45 (December 22): 927.

Le Jiayu and Xu Chongli. 1986. Interview by author. Shanghai.

League of Nations. 1924–1946. *Summary of Annual Reports Received from Governments Relating to Traffic in Women and Children.* Geneva. Document C.164.M.40.

Lee, Edward Bing-shuey. 1936. *Modern Canton.* Shanghai: The Mercury.

Lee, Leo, and Andrew J. Nathan. 1985. "The Beginnings of Mass Culture: Journalism and Fiction in the Late Ch'ing and Beyond." In David Johnson, Andrew J. Nathan, and Evelyn S. Rawski, eds. *Popular Culture in Late Imperial China*. Berkeley and Los Angeles: University of California Press, 360–95.

Lee, Nora. 1995. "Duplicitous Liaisons." *Far Eastern Economic Review* (April 20): 64–65.

Lee, Tahirih V. 1995. "Coping with Shanghai: Means to Survival and Success in the Early Twentieth Century—A Symposium." *Journal of Asian Studies* 54.1 (February): 3–18.

Lemière, J. Em. 1923. "The Sing-Song Girl: From a Throne of Glory to a Seat of Ignominy." *China Journal of Science and Arts* 1.2 (March): 126–34.

Levenson, Joseph. 1972. *Confucian China and Its Modern Fate*. Berkeley and Los Angeles: University of California Press.

Levine, Philippa. 1994. "Venereal Disease, Prostitution, and the Politics of Empire: The Case of British India." *Journal of the History of Sexuality* 4.4 (April): 579–602.

Levy, Howard. 1966. Preface to *A Feast of Mist and Flowers: The Gay Quarters of Nanking at the End of the Ming*, by Yu Huai. Trans. Howard Levy. Yokohama, Japan. Unpublished typescript.

Li, Wai-yee. 1993. "The Late-Ming Courtesan: Invention of a Cultural Ideal." Paper presented at the conference "Women and Literature in Ming-Qing China," Yale University.

Li chuang wo dusheng. 1905. *Huitu Shanghai zaji* [Miscellaneous Shanghai notes, illustrated]. Shanghai wenbao shuju shi yingben. 8 *juan*.

Li Dazhao [pseud.: Chang]. 1981 (1919). "Feichang wenti" [The question of abolishing prostitution]. *Meizhou pinglun* 19 (April 27, 1919). Reprinted in Zhonghua quanguo funü lianhehui funü yundong lishi yanjiushi, eds. *Wusi shiqi funü wenti wenxuan* [Selected documents on the woman question in the May Fourth era]. Beijing: Sanlian shudian, 1981, 347–49.

Li Jiarui, ed. 1937. *Beiping fengsu leizhi* [Catalog of Beiping customs]. Guoli zhongyang yanjiuyuan lishi yuyan yanjiusuo zhuankan. Shanghai: Guowu yinshuguan. 2 vols.

Li Jingwu. 1967. *Beiping fengtu zhi* [Life in old Beiping]. Taipei: Zhongguo wenhua xueyuan fengsu yanjiusuo.

Li Jingxi. 1935. "Maiyin zai falüshang de maodun yu tiaohe" [Contradictions and compromise about prostitution in the law]. *Liudong xuebao* 1.1 (July 1): 88–96.

Li Mengbai and Hu Xin. 1991. *Liudong renkou dui dachengshi fazhan de yingxiang ji duice* [The influence of the floating population on the development of large cities and measures to deal with it]. Beijing: Jingji ribao chubanshe.

Li Ranshi. 1963. "Jiu Tianjin de hunhunr" [The *hunhunr* of old Tianjin]. *Wenshi ziliao* 47 (January): 187–209.

Li Sanwu. 1920. "Feichang yundong guanjian" [My humble opinion on the movement to abolish prostitution]. *Funü zazhi* 6.8: 7–16.

Li Shanhu. 1933. "Nanjing changji kaijin wenti" [The question of lifting the ban on Nanjing prostitution]. *Nüzi yuekan* 1.9 (November 15): 20–29.

Li Shaohong, director. 1994. *Hong fen* [Blush]. Based on a story by Su Tong. Beijing Film Studio.

Li Shengping, ed. 1989. *Zhongguo jinxiandai renming da cidian* [Biographical dictionary of persons in modern China]. Beijing: Zhongguo guoji guangbo chubanshe.

Li Xiaojiang and Tan Shen, eds. 1991. *Zhongguo funü fenceng yanjiu* [Research on stratification among Chinese women]. "Zhishi funü" jicong. Zhengzhou: Henan renmin chubanshe.

Li Yu. 1990. *The Carnal Prayer Mat*. Trans. Patrick Hanan. New York: Ballantine Books.

Liang Hongying. 1991. "Yan Ruisheng yousha jinü an" [The case of Yan Ruisheng luring a prostitute to destruction]. In Xin Zhi and Xiao Ming, eds. *Jiu Shanghai shehui baitai* [One hundred shapes of old Shanghai society]. Shanghai: Shanghai renmin chubanshe, 155–84.

Liao Guofang. 1929. "Bude jiefang de funü" [Women who have not achieved liberation]. *Funü zazhi* 15.2: 33–35.

Lin Biyao. 1922. "Changmen zhi nü" [Daughter of the brothels]. Oral history. As told to Yao Min'ai. *Banyue* 1.18 (May): 1–5; 1.19 (June): 1–8.

Lin Chongwu. 1936. "Changji wenti zhi yanjiu" [Research on the prostitution problem]. *Minzhong jikan* 2.2 (June): 215–23.

Link, Perry, 1981. *Mandarin Ducks and Butterflies: Popular Fiction in Early Twentieth-Century Chinese Cities*. Berkeley and Los Angeles: University of California Press.

———. 1992. *Evening Chats in Beijing*. New York: W. W. Norton.

Liu Bohong. 1992. "Guanyu nüxing jiuye wenti zongshu" [A summary of the women's employment question]. In Liu Xiaocong, Xiong Yumei, and Qu Wen, eds., *Zhongguo funü lilun yanjiu shinian* [Ten years of research on Chinese women's theory]. Beijing: Zhongguo funü chubanshe, 310–57.

Liu Dalin et al. 1992. *Zhongguo dangdai xing wenhua: Zhongguo liangwan li 'xing wenming' diaocha baogao* (English title: *Sexual Behaviour in Modern China: A Report of the Nationwide 'Sex Civilisation' Survey on 20,000 Subjects in China*). Shanghai: Sanlian shudian.

Liu Fujing and Wang Mingkun. 1992. *Jiu Guangdong yanduchang* [Opium, gambling, and prostitution in old Guangdong]. Hong Kong: Zhonghua shuju.

Liu Huanong. 1948. "Jinwu qianhou" [The whole story of the ban on dancing]. *Shehui yuekan* 3.2 (February 5): 40–47.

Liu Peiqian. 1936. *Da Shanghai zhinan* [Guide to greater Shanghai]. Shanghai: Zhonghua shuju.

Liu Ts'un-yan. 1982. "Introduction: 'Middlebrow' in Perspective." *Renditions* 17–18: 1–40.

Lu, Hanchao. 1995. "Away from Nanking Road: Small Stores and Neighborhood Life in Modern Shanghai." *Journal of Asian Studies* 54.1 (February): 93–123.

Lu Dafang. 1980. *Shanghai tan yijiulu* [Remembering the Old Shanghai Bund]. Taipei: Shijie shuju.

Lu Feiyun and Zhang Zhongru. 1983. "Shanghai jiefang chuqi de jinü gaizao gongzuo" [The work of reforming prostitutes in the early period of Liberation in Shanghai]. In Shanghai shehuixue xuehui, ed. *Shehui xue wenji* [Collection of writings on sociology]. N.p., 121–36.

Lü He. 1934. *Zhongguo funü xiezhen* [Portraits of Chinese women]. Shenghuo congshu zhiyi. Shanghai: Guangyi shuju.

Lu Qiuxin. 1920. "Xiaomie 'qie' he 'ji' liangge zi" [Eliminate the two words "concubine" and "prostitute"]. *Xin funü* 1.1 (January 1).

Lu Wei [pseud. for Chen Luwei]. 1938. "Tiaochu huokeng yihou: Jinü Ma Ruizhen zishu" [After jumping out of the fiery pit: An account in her own words by the prostitute Ma Ruizhen]. *Shanghai funü* 1.12 (October): 14–15.

Lu Xing'er. 1993a. "'Meng' de xilie—funü jiaoyangsuo caifang lu" ["Dream" series—record of a visit to the women's education institute]. *Dongfang jian* 1.1 (January): 18–25.

———. 1993b. Interview by author. Shanghai.

Luo Qiong. 1935. "Changji zai Zhongguo" [Prostitution in China]. *Funü shenghuo* 1.6 (December 1): 34–40.

Luo Tianwen. 1934. "Changji wenti" [The prostitution problem]. *Maodun* 2.5 (January 1): 256–58.

Luo Zhiru. 1932. *Tongji biao zhong zhi Shanghai* [Shanghai in statistical charts]. Nanjing: Guoli zhongyang yanjiu yuan.

Ma Li. 1991. "Burang lishi chou'e xianxiang fuhuo" [Do not allow the rebirth of ugly phenomena from history]. *Minzhu yu fazhi* 1: 32–34.

Ma Yongsheng. 1930 (1876). *Shanghai fanchangji* [Record of Shanghai's prosperity]. Japan: n.p. 3 *juan*.

Ma Zhixiang. 1935. *Beiping lüxing zhinan* [Guide to travel in Beiping]. Beiping: Jingji xinwen she.

MacPherson, Kerrie L. 1987. *A Wilderness of Marshes: The Origins of Public Health in Shanghai, 1843–1893*. New York and Oxford: Oxford University Press.

Mahood, Linda. 1990. *The Magdalenes: Prostitution in the Nineteenth Century*. London and New York: Routledge.

Mai Qianzeng. 1931. "Beiping changji diaocha" [An investigation of prostitution in Beiping]. *Shehui xuejie* 5 (June): 105–46.

Malhotra, Angelina. 1994. "Prostitution, Triads and Corruption—Shanghai's Dark Side." *Asia, Inc.* (February): 32–39. Electronically reprinted in *China News Digest Books and Journals Review* (March 20).

Mallon, Florencia. 1994. "The Promise and Dilemma of Subaltern Studies: Perspectives from Latin American History." *American Historical Review* 99.5 (December): 1,491–515.

Mann, Susan. 1997. *Women in Eighteenth-Century China: Gender and Culture in the Lower Yangzi Region, 1683–1839*. Stanford, Calif.: Stanford University Press.

Martin, Brian G. 1992. "'The Pact with the Devil': The Relationship Between the Green Gang and the Shanghai French Concession Authorities, 1925–1935." In Frederic Wakeman, Jr., and Wen-hsin Yeh, eds. *Shanghai Sojourners*. China Research Monograph no. 40. Berkeley: University of California Institute of East Asian Studies, 266–304.

———. 1995. "The Green Gang and the Guomindang State: Du Yuesheng and the Politics of Shanghai, 1927–1937." *Journal of Asian Studies* 54.1 (February): 64–91.

Matignon, Jean-Jacques. 1936. *La Chine hermétique: Superstitions, crime et misère*. Paris: Librairie Orientaliste Paul Geuthner.

McAleavy, Henry. 1959a. "Sai-chin-hua (1874–1936): The Fortunes of a Chinese Singing-Girl." *History Today* 7 (March): 191–99.

———, trans. 1959b (1935). *That Chinese Woman: The Life of Sai-Chin-Hua*, by Zui Xu [Drunken Whiskers; pseud.]. Translation of *Sai Jinhua zhuan* [Biography of Sai Jinhua]. New York: Thomas Crowell Co.

McClintock, Anne. 1992. "Screwing the System: Sexwork, Race, and the Law." *Boundary 2* 19.2: 70–95.

———. 1993. "Sex Workers and Sex Work: Introduction." *Social Text* 37 (winter): 1–10.

Meng Yue. 1994. "A Playful Discourse, Its Site, and Its Social Subject: Shen Bao's *Ziyou Tan* 1911–1917." Unpublished paper.

Mi Bi. 1922. "Guangzhou de feichang yundong" [The movement to abolish prostitution in Guangzhou]. *Funü zazhi* 8.7: 44–46.

Miller, G. E. [pseud.]. 1937. *Shanghai, the Paradise of Adventurers.* New York: Orsay Publishing House.

Minfeng bianjisuo, ed. 1945. *Feng Shanghai* [Crazed Shanghai]. Shanghai: Minfeng chubanshe.

Minzheng ju [Civil Administration Department]. N.d. *Funü laodong jiaoyangsuo* [Women's Labor Training Institute]. Shanghai. Unpublished report.

Miyazaki, Ichisada. 1981. *China's Examination Hell.* New Haven, Conn.: Yale University Press.

Mo Ming [Anon.]. 1993. "Yige Shenzhen nümishu de dubai" [Soliloquy of a woman secretary in Shenzhen]. *Shijie zhoukan* (14 November): S-7.

Mo Ruoqiang. 1930. "Tiaowu chang di cunfei wenti" [The problem of keeping or discarding dance halls]. *Shehui yuekan* 2.3 (September): 1–4.

Morache, G. 1869. *Pékin et ses habitants: Étude d'hygiène.* Paris: n.p.

Morris, M. C. 1916. "Chinese Daughters of the Night." *Missionary Review* 39 (October): 753–62.

Mu Hua. 1936. "Gongchang zhidu de bihai qiji lunju de huangmiu" [The harm of the licensed prostitution system and the absurdity of its grounds of argument]. *Nüzi yuekan* 4.4 (April): 21–26.

Municipal Gazette. 1920–30. Shanghai.

Nakano Kōkan. 1926. *Shina no baishō* [Chinese prostitution]. Shina Pekin: Shina fūbutsu kenkyukai.

"Nine Russian Women Told to Leave." 1993. *China Daily* (June 24): 3.

Ning Dong. 1990. "Zai maiyin funü de xinling shenchu" [Deep in the heart of a prostitute]. *Shehui* 5 (May): 12–14.

North-China Herald. 1869–1871, 1916–1925. Shanghai.

Nüsheng [Woman's voice]. 1934.

O'Callaghan, Sean. 1968. *The Yellow Slave Trade: A Survey of the Traffic in Women and Children in the East.* London: Anthony Blond.

O'Hanlon, Rosalind. 1988. "Recovering the Subject: Subaltern Studies and Histories of Resistance in Colonial South Asia." *Modern Asian Studies* 22.1: 189–224.

Oldt, F. 1923. "Purity Campaign, Canton." *China Medical Journal* 37.9 (September): 776–82.

Otis, Leah L. 1985. *Prostitution in Medieval Society: The History of an Urban Institution in Languedoc.* Chicago: University of Chicago Press.

Pal, John. 1963. *Shanghai Saga.* London: Jarrolds.

Pan, Ling. 1984. *Old Shanghai: Gangsters in Paradise.* Hong Kong, Singapore, Kuala Lumpur: Heinemann Asia.

Pan Li. 1991. "Nongcun liudong renkou de diyuan juji xiaoyin he diyuan liansuo xiaoying" [The effect of the geographic concentration of the rural floating population and its geographic chain reaction]. *Shehui* 6 (June): 24–25.

Pan Suiming. 1993a. "Changing Sexual Behavior in China and Its Gender Issues." Paper presented at the first conference of the North American Chinese Sociologists' Association, "Gender Issues in Contemporary Chinese Societies," Miami Beach, July 1.

———. 1993b. "A Sex Revolution in Current China." Unpublished paper.

Pang Ruiyin et al. 1989a. *Zhongguo changji xinsheng dai* [A new generation of Chinese prostitutes]. Dalu shehui wenti jishi. Hong Kong: Kaiyi wenhua shiye gongsi.

————. 1989b. *Zhongguo chenlun nü* [China's fallen women]. Dalu shehui wenti jishi. Taipei: Fengyun shidai chuban gongsi.

Pascoe, Peggy. 1990. *Relations of Rescue: The Search for Female Moral Authority in the American West, 1874–1939.* New York and Oxford: Oxford University Press.

Pei Xibin. 1905. *Huitu yeyou Shanghai zaji* [Miscellaneous records of drawings of philandering in Shanghai]. N.p.: Wenbin shuju.

Pepper, Suzanne. 1978. *Civil War in China: The Political Struggle, 1945–1949.* Berkeley and Los Angeles: University of California Press.

Perry, Elizabeth J. 1993. *Shanghai on Strike: The Politics of Chinese Labor.* Stanford, Calif.: Stanford University Press.

Peters, E. W. 1937. *Shanghai Policeman.* Ed. Hugh Barnes. London: Rich and Cowan Ltd.

Pheterson, Gail, ed. 1989. *A Vindication of the Rights of Whores.* Seattle: Seal Press.

Ping Jinya. 1986. "Shanghai xiaobao shiliao" [Historical materials on Shanghai tabloids]. In Shanghai shi wenshiguan. Shanghai shi renmin zhengfu canshi shi, Wenshi ziliao gongzuo weiyuanhui, eds. *Shanghai difang shi ziliao* [Material on Shanghai local history]. Shanghai: Shanghai shehui kexue yuan chubanshe, vol. 5, 70–86.

————. 1988. "Jiu Shanghai de changji" [Prostitution in old Shanghai]. In Shanghai shi wenshiguan, ed. *Jiu Shanghai de yanduchang* [Opium, gambling, and prostitution in old Shanghai]. Shanghai: Baijia chubanshe, 159–171.

Pomerantz, Linda. 1978. "Prostitution as a Social Issue in Republican China." Unpublished paper.

Poovey, Mary. 1988. *Uneven Developments: The Ideological Work of Gender in Mid-Victorian England.* Chicago: University of Chicago Press.

Prakash, Gyan. 1994. "Subaltern Studies as Postcolonial Criticism." *American Historical Review* 99.5 (December): 1,475–90.

"The Prostitution Problem in Shanghai." 1937. *China Critic* 17.1 (April): 7–9.

Qi Xia and Dan Ru, eds. 1917 (1915). *Haishang hua yinglu* [A record in images of Shanghai flowers]. Revised edition. Shanghai: Zhongguo tushuguan. 3 vols.

Qian Gucheng. 1938. "Tan anmo nülang" [About massage girls]. *Shanghai funü* 1.5 (June 20): 16.

Qian Shengke, ed. 1933. *Shanghai heimu huibian* [A collection of scandalous stories of Shanghai]. Shanghai: Shanghai zhentan yanjiu hui. 4 vols.

Qian Yiwei. 1937. "Changji de chansheng ji qi jiuji" [The emergence of prostitution and its relief]. *Funü yuebao* 3.2 (February 19): 8–14.

Qiao Feng. 1923. "Feichang de genben wenti" [The fundamental problem of abolishing prostitution]. *Funü zazhi* 9.3: 6–8.

"Qiebei jinü nügai yu shiye funü wang hechu qu?" [Where can concubines, slave girls, prostitutes, women beggars, and unemployed women go?]. 1936. *Funü shenghuo* 2.2 (February 16): 30–32.

Qin Lu. 1920. "Jindai sixiangjia de xingyuguan he lian'ai" [Modern thinkers' views on sex and love]. *Funü zazhi* 6.10.

————. 1921. "Ai-lun-k'ai nüshi yu qi sixiang" [Ms. Ellen Key and her thought]. *Funü zazhi* 7.7.

Qiu xingfu zhai zhu [pseud. for He Haiming]. 1922a. "Changmen zhi zi" [Son of the brothels]. *Banyue* 1.14 (March): 1–15.

———. 1922b. "Changmen zhi mu" [Mother of the brothels]. *Banyue* 1.22 (July): 1–15.

Rawski, Thomas G. 1980. *China's Transition to Industrialism.* Ann Arbor: University of Michigan Press.

———. 1989. *Economic Growth in Prewar China.* Berkeley and Los Angeles: University of California Press.

Ren Ping'an and Zhao Yanbing. 1987. *Funü xinlixue* [Female psychology]. Shenyang: Liaoning daxue chubanshe.

Renyan zhoukan [Public opinion weekly]. 1934–1936.

Ropp, Paul S. 1996. "Ambiguous Images of Courtesan Culture in Late Imperial China." In Kang-i Sun Chang and Ellen Widmer, eds. *Writing Chinese Women.* Stanford, Calif.: Stanford University Press.

Rosen, Ruth. 1982. *The Lost Sisterhood: Prostitution in America, 1900–1918.* Baltimore and London: Johns Hopkins University Press.

Rosen, Ruth, and Sue Davidson, eds. 1977. *The Maimie Papers.* Old Westbury, N.Y.: Feminist Press.

Ruan, Fang Fu. 1991. *Sex in China: Studies in Sexology in Chinese Culture.* New York and London: Plenum.

Ruo Wen. 1938. "Shanghai de maiyinzhe" [The prostitutes of Shanghai]. *Shanghai funü* 2.4 (December 5): 29–30.

Scherer, Renate. 1981. "Das System der chinesichen Prostitution dargestellt am Beispiel Shanghais in der Zeit von 1840 bis 1949." Ph.D. dissertation, Free University of Berlin.

———. 1986. *Das System der chinesichen Prostitution dargestellt am Beispiel Shanghais in der Zeit von 1840 bis 1949.* Berlin: Papyrus-Druck.

Schlegel, G. 1866. *Ietsover de prostitutie in China.* Batavia: Transactions of the Batavian Society of Arts and Sciences.

———. 1894. "A Canton Flowerboat." *International Archives of Ethnography* 7: 1–9.

Schmid, Peter. 1958. *The New Face of China.* Trans. E. Osers. London: George G. Harrap and Company, Ltd.

Schoenhals, Michael. 1992. *Doing Things with Words in Chinese Politics: Five Studies.* China Research Monograph no. 41. Berkeley: University of California Institute of East Asian Studies.

Schwarcz, Vera. 1986. *The Chinese Enlightenment: Intellectuals and the Legacy of the May Fourth Movement of 1919.* Berkeley and Los Angeles: University of California Press.

Scott, Joan Wallach. 1988. *Gender and the Politics of History.* New York: Columbia University Press.

Se Lu. 1920. "Changji zhidu shikao" [A historical investigation of the prostitution system]. *Funü zazhi* 6.9: 1–8.

———. 1923. "Shijie renlei de chiru" [A disgrace to the people of the world]. *Funü zazhi* 9.3: 2–5.

———. 1938. "Bubai" [Filler]. *Shanghai funü* 1.1 (April): 22.

Sergeant, Harriet. 1991. *Shanghai.* London: Jonathan Cape.

Service Directory. 1993. Shanghai: Peace Hotel.

Service Guide Book. 1933. Xi'an: Xi'an Hotel.

Shaanxi sheng renmin daibiao dahui fazhi weiyuan hui, ed. 1992. *Shaanxi sheng difangxing fagui huibian 1980–1992* [A compilation of local laws and regulations for

Shaanxi province 1980–1992]. Xi'an: Shaanxi sheng renda fazhi weiyuan hui ban-gongshi.

Shan. 1933. "Wo duiyu Hangzhou jianyan jinü zhi ganxiang" [My feeling about the examination of Hangzhou prostitutes]. *Funü gongming* 2.12 (December): 30.

———. 1934. "Guanyu changji de yijian yishi" [An opinion about prostitution]. *Funü gongming* 3.7 (July): 34–37.

Shan Guangnai. 1995. *Zhongguo changji—guoqu he xianzai* [Chinese prostitution—past and present]. Beijing: Falü chubanshe.

Shang Xinren, ed. 1993. "Laizi daji maiyin piaochang qianxian de shilu" [True records from the front lines of the battle against sex selling and whoring]. In *Laizi saohuang qianxiande baogao* [A report from the front lines of sweeping away pornography]. Chengdu: Sichuan daxue chubanshe, 24–37. Published in popular-magazine format.

Shanghai Bureau of Social Affairs. 1929. *Wages and Hours of Labor, Greater Shanghai, 1929.* Shanghai.

Shanghai Civic Association. 1933. *Shanghai Statistics* [Chinese title: *Shanghai shi tongji*]. Shanghai.

[Shanghai] *Dagong bao.* 1946–1948.

"Shanghai de teshu zhiye" [The special occupations of Shanghai]. 1946. *Shanghai shiri* 2 (30 June): 13.

Shanghai ertong fuli zujinhui yanjiu diaocha zu. 1948. *Shanghai shi shehui fuli jiguan yaolan* [A look at Shanghai social welfare organizations]. Shanghai ertong fuli zujinhui diaocha congshu no. 2. Shanghai: Shanghai ertong fuli zujinhui.

Shanghai jingcha [Shanghai police]. 1948. Shanghai.

Shanghai Municipal Council Legal Department, trans. 1935. *The Chinese Criminal Code and Special Criminal and Administrative Laws.* Shanghai: Commercial Press.

Shanghai Municipal Council Report and Budget. 1877–. Shanghai: Kelly and Walsh.

Shanghai Municipal Police. Shanghai Municipal Police Files, 1894–1947 (formerly Security Classified Investigation Files, 1916–1947). National Archives: Record Group 263 (Central Intelligence Agency).

Shanghai shi dang'an guan [Shanghai Municipal Archives]. 1945. Police regulations on prostitutes, dancing girls, singing girls, and hostesses. File 1-62-44.

———. 1945–1947. *Jinü tuanti zuzhi an* [Cases of the organization of prostitute groups]. File 011-4-260.

———. 1946. *Chajin sichang an* [Cases of investigating and forbidding unlicensed prostitution]. File 011-4-162.

———. 1946–1947. Bureau of Social Affairs documents on dealing with prostitutes. File 6-9-666.

———. 1946–1948. *Qudi jinü lake an* [Cases of banning solicitation by prostitutes]. File 001-4-170.

———. 1946–1948. *Qudi jiyuan an* [Cases of banning brothels]. File 011-4-163.

———. 1946–1949. City government documents on prostitution. File 1-10-246.

———. 1948. *Jinü buzhao guiding jianyan shenti anjian* [Cases of prostitutes failing to have physical examinations in violation of regulations]. File 011-4-171.

———. Zhongguo jiuji furu zonghui [Chinese Society for the Salvation of Women and Children]. 1920s and 1930s. *Shimin guanyu funü haitong bei youguai pianmai he nüedai qingjiu yuanzhu jiuji wenti de shu* [Letters from urban residents on the problem of aiding, helping, and saving women and children who have been kidnapped, tricked, sold, and ill-treated]. File Q-113-1-14.

Shanghai shi jingcha ju, ed. 1947. *Shanghai shi jingcha ju fagui huibian* [A collection of laws and regulations of the Shanghai Police Department]. Shanghai: Shanghai shi jingcha ju, vol. 1.

"Shanghai shi jiuji yuan funü jiaoyangsuo zuzhi guicheng" [Rules and regulations of the Shanghai Relief Institute and Women's Training Institute]. 1947. *Shehui yuekan* 2.2 (February 5): 69–70.

Shanghai shi minzheng ju. 1959. *Shanghai shi youmin, jinü gaizao gongzuo* [The work of reforming vagrants and prostitutes]. N.p. (October).

Shanghai shi wenshi guan, ed. 1988. *Jiu Shanghai de yanduchang* [Opium, gambling, and prostitution in old Shanghai]. Shanghai: Baijia chubanshe.

Shanghai shi wenxian weiyuanhui. 1948. *Shanghai renkou zhilüe* [Brief record of the Shanghai population]. Shanghai: Shanghai shi wenxian weiyuanhui.

Shanghai shi zhengfu mishuchu. 1945. *Shanghai shi zhengfu gongbao* [Shanghai municipal government gazette]. Shanghai: Shanghai shi zhengfu mishuchu.

Shanghai tebieshi gong'anju yewu baogao, minguo shiqi nian qi yue zhi shiba nian liu yue [Report on the affairs of the Shanghai Special Municipality Public Security Bureau from July 1928 to June 1929]. 1929. Shanghai: Shanghai tebieshi gong'anju, vol. 2.

Shanghai tebieshi gong'anju yewu jiyao, Minguo shiliu nian ba yue zhi shiqi nian qi yue. 1928. [Summary of the affairs of the Shanghai Special Municipality Public Security Bureau from August 1927 to July 1928]. Shanghai: Shanghai tebieshi gong'anju.

Shanghai tebieshi zhengfu mishuchu. 1928. *Shanghai tebieshi zhengfa guihui bian chuji* [A preliminary edition of the rules and statutes for Shanghai Special Municipality]. Shanghai: Shanghai tebieshi zhengfu mishuchu (September). 2 juan.

Shanghai xintuo gufen youxian gongsi bianjibu. 1932. *Shanghai fengtu zaji* [Notes on the natural conditions and social customs of Shanghai]. Shanghai: Shanghai xintuo gufen youxian gongsi.

Shangwu yinshuguan bianjisuo. 1926. *Shanghai zhinan* [English title: *Guide to Shanghai: A Chinese Directory of the Port.*] 22nd edition (1st edition published 1909). Shanghai: Shangwu yinshuguan.

Shao Xiangyi. 1934. "Wo duiyu changji kaijin wenti de yijian" [My opinion on the problem of lifting the ban on prostitution. *Yishi gonglun* 2.5 (December 16): 1–4.

Shao Yuancheng. 1936. "Qieshi (?) jinchang" [Really (?) ban prostitution]. *Renyan zhoukan* 2.45 (January 18): 886–87.

Shapiro, Hugh. 1994. "Syphilophobia in 1930s Peking." Paper presented at the annual meeting of the Association for Asian Studies, Boston.

She Ying. 1933. "Xiaomie changji zhi genben fangfa" [The fundamental method of exterminating prostitution]. *Funü gongming* 2.5 (May): 1–6.

Shehui yuekan [Social monthly]. 1930. Tianjin.

Shen Lihong. 1932. "Maiyin yu shehui yinguo" [Prostitution and social causality]. *Funü gongming* 1.11–12 (November 15, December 15): 31–36 (November), 23–29 (December).

Shen Xiao. 1938. "Zhanhou Shanghai nüzhaodai de shenghuo" [The life of Shanghai hostesses since the war began]. *Shanghai funü* 2.2 (November 5): 24–25.

Shenbao. 1875–1941. Shanghai.

Shenghuo zhoukan [Life weekly]. 1933.

Shibao. 1928–1936. Shanghai.

Shibao zhoukan [Times weekly magazine]. 1986.

"Shijie fanmai funü zhi diaocha" [An investigation of the worldwide traffic in women]. 1933. *Funü gongming* 2.5 (May): 46–47.

Shijie ribao. 1982, 1992–1995.

Shizheng pinglun [Municipal administration commentary]. 1934–1936.

Solinger, Dorothy. 1991. "China's Transients and the State: A Form of Civil Society?" USC Seminar Series no. 1. *Hong Kong Institute of Asia-Pacific Studies:* 1–46.

———. 1992. "The Floating Population in the Cities: Chances for Assimilation?" Paper presented at the Woodrow Wilson Center's "Urban China" conference, Washington, D.C.

Sommer, Matthew Harvey. 1994. "Sex, Law, and Society in Late Imperial China." Ph.D. dissertation, University of California at Los Angeles.

Song Shisheng. 1995. "The Brothels of Harbin in the Old Society." In Søren Clausen and Stig Thøgersen, eds. *The Making of a Chinese City: History and Historiography in Harbin.* Armonk, N.Y., and London: M. E. Sharpe, 103–8.

Song Xian. 1930. "Changji wenti" [The problem of prostitution]. *Shehui yuekan* 2.1 (July): 1–7.

Song Yunpu. 1931. *Tianjin zhilüe* [An outline record of Tianjin]. Tianjin: Tianjin xiecheng yinshua ju.

Southerland, Daniel. 1985. "Prostitution Returns, Chinese Officials Say." *Washington Post* (October 7): A20.

Spaulding, Jay, and Stephanie Beswick. 1995. "Sex, Bondage, and the Market: The Emergence of Prostitution in Northern Sudan, 1750–1950." *Journal of the History of Sexuality* 5.4 (April): 512–34.

Special Vice Committee. 1920. "Vice Conditions in Shanghai." *Municipal Gazette* 13.681 (March 19): 83–86.

Spence, Jonathan D. 1982. *The Gate of Heavenly Peace.* Harmondsworth and New York: Penguin Books.

———. 1990. *The Search for Modern China.* New York: W. W. Norton.

Spivak, Gayatri Chakravorty. 1988a. "Can the Subaltern Speak?" In Cary Nelson and Lawrence Grossberg, eds. *Marxism and the Interpretation of Culture.* Urbana and Chicago: University of Illinois Press, 271–313.

———. 1988b. "Subaltern Studies: Deconstructing Historiography." In Ranajit Guha and Gayatri Chakravorty Spivak, eds. *Selected Subaltern Studies.* New York and Oxford: Oxford University Press, 3–32.

Stacey, Judith. 1983. *Patriarchy and Socialist Revolution in China.* Berkeley and Los Angeles: University of California Press.

Stansell, Christine. 1987. *City of Women: Sex and Class in New York, 1789–1860.* Urbana and Chicago: University of Illinois Press.

Stauffer, Milton Theobald, ed. 1922. *The Christian Occupation of China.* Shanghai: China Continuation Committee.

Staunton, George Thomas, trans. 1966 (1810). *Da Tsing Leu Lee.* Taipei: Ch'eng-wen Publishing Co.

Stephens, Thomas B. 1992. *Order and Discipline in China: The Shanghai Mixed Court 1911–27.* Seattle and London: University of Washington Press.

Strand, David. 1989. *Rickshaw Beijing: City People and Politics in the 1920s*. Berkeley and Los Angeles: University of California Press.

Su Ming. 1936. "Changji wenti" [The problem of prostitution]. *Nüzi yuekan* 4.10 (October 1): 11–14.

Sues, Ilona Ralf. 1944. *Shark's Fins and Millet*. Boston: Little, Brown and Company.

Sui Zhi. 1936. "Jinxu beinu jinchang yu nongcun funü de maimai wenti" [Banning the keeping of servants and prostitution and the problem of the traffic in village women]. *Renyan zhoukan* 2.49 (February 15): 967–68.

Sun, Lena. 1992. "Prostitution Thriving Again in China." *Washington Post* (March 12).

Sun Changshu. 1933. "Changji zhidu yu shehui jingji zuzhi" [The prostitution system and the organization of the social economy]. *Nüzi yuekan* 1.6 (August 15): 29–32.

Sun Guoqun. 1988a. *Jiu Shanghai changji mishi* [The secret history of prostitution in old Shanghai]. Henan: Henan renmin chubanshe.

———. 1988b. "Lun jiu Shanghai changji zhidu de fazhan jieduan he tedian" [On the stages of development and characteristics of the prostitution system in old Shanghai]. Paper prepared for the "Conference on Shanghai History," Shanghai Academy of Social Sciences, Shanghai, September.

Sun Liqi, Yu Huiqing, Yuan Xiangmei, Zhang Peihua, and Cao Zhuxian. 1986. Interview by author with former residents of Shanghai's brothel districts.

Sun Yusheng [pseud.: Haishang Juewusheng]. 1939. *Jinü de shenghuo* [The life of prostitutes]. Shanghai: Chunming shudian.

Suo Fei [pseud.]. 1933. "Maiyin jiuguo lun" [On saving the nation through prostitution]. *Funü gongming* 2.5 (May): 39–42.

Suoposheng [Lingering One; pseud. for Bi Yihong] and Bao Tianxiao. 1991. *Renjian diyu* [Hell on earth]. Shanghai tan yu Shanghai ren congshu [Series 2]. Shanghai: Shanghai guji chubanshe. 2 vols.

Tan Fengyang. 1934. "Changji wenti yu jingji zhidu" [The prostitution problem and the economic system]. *Renyan zhoukan* 1.44 (December 15): 905–6.

Tang Guozhen. 1932. "Ruhe jiejue changji wenti" [How to solve the prostitution problem]. *Funü gongming* 1.3–4 (June 15): 17–21.

Tang Weikang, Zhu Dalu, and Du Li, eds. 1987. *Shanghai yishi* [Shanghai anecdotes]. Shanghai: Shanghai wenhua chubanshe.

Tang Youfeng. 1931. *Xin Shanghai* [New Shanghai]. Shanghai: Shanghai yinshuguan.

Tang Zhenchang, ed. 1989. *Shanghai shi* [History of Shanghai]. Shen Hengchun, assoc. ed. Shanghai: Shanghai renmin chubanshe.

Tao, Chia-lin Pao. 1994. "The Anti-footbinding Movement in Late Ch'ing China: Indigenous Development and Western Influence." *Jindai Zhongguo funü shi yanjiu* 2 (June): 141–78.

Tian Di et al. 1924. "Sichang yu gongchang de libi" [The advantages and disadvantages of unlicensed and licensed prostitution]. *Funü zazhi* 10.8: 1,264–72.

Tian Xiao [Bao Tianxiao?]. 1922a. "Ji zhi jiezao" [Prostitute's honor]. *Xingqi* 21: 1–12.

Tian Xiao. [Bao Tianxiao?] 1922b. "Jietou de nüzi" [Woman of the street]. *Xingqi* 46: 1–5.

[Tianjin] *Dagong bao*. 1929–1930.

Tianjin funü ribao [Tianjin women's daily]. 1924.

Tianjin shi shehuiju [Tianjin Bureau of Social Affairs]. 1930. *Tianjinshi jihu jinü diaocha baogao* [Report on an investigation of Tianjin brothels and prostitutes]. Tianjin: Tianjin shi shehuiju.

Tianjin shi zhoukan [Tianjin weekly]. 1947. Tianjin.

Tianjin tebieshi gongshu shehuiju disanke. 1939. *Shehui tongji yuekan* 1.2: 48.

———. 1940. *Shehui tongji yuekan* 1.3: 50.

Tianjin tebieshi shehuiju yi zhounian gongzuo zong baogao, 1928–1929 [Report on the work of the Tianjin Municipal Bureau of Social Affairs during the first year, 1928–1929]. 1929. Tianjin: Shehuiju.

Tien, H. Yuan. 1973. *China's Population Struggle*. Columbus, Ohio: Ohio State University Press.

Tong Xin. 1993. "Burong hushi de liulang shaonü" [Vagrant girls will not brook neglect]. *Funü yanjiu luncong* 2: 25–29.

"Traffic in Women Problem for China." 1935. *Trans-Pacific* 23 (March 28): 15–16.

Tu Shipin, ed. 1968 (1948). *Shanghai chunqiu* [Shanghai annals]. Hong Kong: Zhongguo tushu bianyiguan.

Tun Min. 1923. "Changji he zhenjie" [Prostitution and chastity]. *Funü zazhi* 9.3: 18–21.

Tyler, Patrick E. 1993. "Economic Focus in Shanghai: Catching Up." *New York Times* (December 22): A1, A6.

"The Vice Committee Proposal." 1920. *Millard's Review of the Far East* (April 3): 207–10.

U. U. 1922. "Jinü jiahou de xin" [The heart of a prostitute after marriage]. *Xingqi* 28: 1–11.

Wakeman, Frederic, Jr. 1995a. *Policing Shanghai 1927–1937*. Berkeley and Los Angeles: University of California Press.

———. 1995b. "Licensing Leisure: The Chinese Nationalists' Attempt to Regulate Shanghai, 1927–49." *Journal of Asian Studies* 54.1 (February): 19–42.

Wakeman, Frederic, Jr., and Wen-hsin Yeh. 1992. *Shanghai Sojourners*. Berkeley: University of California Institute of East Asian Studies.

Walker, Tony. 1993. "Open Wide for a Dose of Ideology." *Sydney Morning Herald* (April 19). Electronically reprinted in *China News Digest* (April 20).

Walkowitz, Judith R. 1980. *Prostitution and Victorian Society: Women, Class, and the State*. Cambridge: Cambridge University Press.

———. 1992. *City of Dreadful Delight: Narratives of Sexual Danger in Late-Victorian London*. Chicago: University of Chicago Press.

Wan Molin. 1973. *Hushang wangshi* [Shanghai bygones]. Taipei: Zhongwai tushu chubanshe.

Wang Da. 1936. "Tianjin zhi gongye" [The industry of Tianjin]. *Shiye bu yuekan* 1.1 (April): 109–218.

Wang Dingjiu. 1932. *Shanghai menjing* [Key to Shanghai]. [Shanghai]: Zhongyang shudian.

Wang Houzhe. 1925. *Shanghai baojian* [Precious mirror of Shanghai]. Shanghai: Shijie shuju.

Wang Liaoweng. 1922. *Shanghai liushinian huajie shi* [A sixty-year history of the Shanghai flower world]. Shanghai: Shixin shuju.

Wang Qisheng. 1993. "Minguo chunian de nüxing fanzui, 1914–1936" [Female crime in the early years of the Republic, 1914–1936]. *Jindai Zhongguo funü shi yanjiu* 1 (June): 5–18.

Wang Shuhuai. 1994. "Kang Youwei dui nüxing ji hunyin de taidu" [The attitude of

Kang Youwei toward women and marriage]. *Jindai Zhongguo funü shi yanjiu* 2 (June): 27–49.

Wang Shunu. 1988 (1935). *Zhongguo changji shi* [History of prostitution in China]. Shanghai: Sanlian (Shenghuo shudian).

Wang Tao. 1929 (1878). *Haizou yeyou lu* [Record of keeping company with courtesans in Shanghai]. *Juan* 6 of *Yanshi shi er zhong: Biji xiaoshuo* [Twelve colorful histories: Belles lettres and novels]. Shanghai: Hanwen yuanshu si.

———. 1934 (1914). *Songbin suohua* [Tales of trivia from the banks of the Wusong]. Shanghai: Xin wenhua shushe. 12 *juan.*

Wang Xingjuan. 1990. "Dangqian maiyin piaochang de tedian, qushi ji duice" [Current characteristics, tendencies, and countermeasures concerning sex sellers and customers]. Unpublished paper.

———. 1992a. "Guanyu maiyin piaochang wenti de yanjiu" [Concerning research on the problem of selling sex and visiting prostitutes]. In Liu Xiaocong, Xiong Yumei, and Qu Wen, eds. *Zhongguo funü lilun yanjiu shinian* [Ten years of research on Chinese women's theory]. Beijing: Zhongguo funü chubanshe, 420–41.

———. 1992b. Interview by author. Beijing.

———. 1993a. Interview by author. Beijing.

———. 1993b. Personal communication with author.

Wang Yiren. 1935. "Feichang de chulu zai nali" [Where is the road to abolishing prostitution?]. *Renyan zhoukan* 1.50 (January 26): 1,024–26.

Wang Zheng. 1993. "Three Interviews: Wang Anyi, Zhu Lin, Dai Qing." In Tani E. Barlow, ed. *Gender Politics in Modern China.* Durham, N.C., and London: Duke University Press, 159–208.

Wang Zhongxian. n.d. (1935) *Shanghai suyu tushuo* [An illustrated dictionary of Shanghai slang]. Shanghai: Shanghai shehui chubanshe, 1935; reprint, Hong Kong: Shenzhou tushu gongsi, 1978 (?).

Wasserstrom, Jeffrey N. 1991. *Student Protests in Twentieth-Century China: The View from Shanghai.* Stanford, Calif.: Stanford University Press.

Wei, W. Lock. 1930. "Sing-Song Girls." *Mentor* 18 (July): 12–15, 50.

Wei Yu. 1933. "Gongchang zhidu kexing ma" [Can the system of licensed prostitution work?]. *Funü gongming* 2.5 (May): 33–36.

Wen Shu. 1981. "Jiefang qian Rongcheng jinü de beican shijie" [The miserable world of prostitutes in Chengdu before Liberation]. *Longmen zhen* 2: 24–29.

Wen Wei. 1990. "Xingbing zai Beijing manyan burong hushi" [The spread of sexually transmitted diseases in Beijing does not brook neglect]. *Funü yanjiu* 1: 21–22.

Weston, Kath. 1991. *Families We Choose: Lesbians, Gays, Kinship.* New York: Columbia University Press.

White, Luise. 1990. *The Comforts of Home: Prostitution in Colonial Nairobi.* Chicago: University of Chicago Press.

Wiley, James Hundley. 1929. "A Study of Chinese Prostitution." M.A. thesis, University of Chicago.

Williams, Linda. 1989. *Hard Core: Power, Pleasure, and the "Frenzy of the Visible."* Berkeley and Los Angeles: University of California Press.

Witke, Roxane Heater. 1970. "Transformation of Attitudes towards Women during the May Fourth Era of Modern China." Ph.D. dissertation. University of California at Berkeley.

Wolf, Arthur P., and Chieh-shan Huang. 1980. *Marriage and Adoption in China, 1845–1945*. Stanford, Calif.: Stanford University Press.

Wolfe, Barnard. 1980. *The Daily Life of a Chinese Courtesan Climbing up a Tricky Ladder, with A Chinese Courtesan's Dictionary*. Hong Kong: Learner's Bookstore.

Wong, K. C. 1920. "The Social Evil in China." *China Medical Journal* 34.6 (November): 630–34.

Wong, K. Chimin, and Lien-teh Wu. 1936. *History of Chinese Medicine*. Tientsin: Tientsin Press, Ltd.

Woo, Toh. 1982 (1931). *An Analysis of 2,330 Case Work Records of the Social Service Department, Peiping Union Medical College*. Bulletins of the Social Research Department 1928–1933, vol. 5. In the series *China during the Interregnum 1911–1949*, ed. Ramon H. Myers. New York and London: Garland Press.

Wu Ao. 1931. *Tianjin shi fangshaye diaocha baogao* [Report on an investigation of the Tianjin spinning industry]. Tianjin: Tianjin shi shehuiju.

Wu Ao et al. 1931. *Tianjinshi shehuiju tongji huikan* [Collected statistics of the Tianjin Municipal Bureau of Social Affairs]. Tianjin: Tianjin shi shehuiju.

Wu Deduo, comp. 1985. *Sai Jinhua benshi* [Source material on Sai Jinhua]. Changsha: Yuelu shushe.

Wu Guifang. 1980. "Jindai Shanghai de 'shili yangchang' pian" [Pieces about the "ten-li foreign market" of modern Shanghai]. *Shehui kexue* 2: 115–23.

Wu Hanchi, ed. 1924. *Quanguo gejie qiekou da cidian* [National dictionary of secret language from all walks of life]. Shanghai: Donglu tushu gongsi.

Wu Jianren. 1935. *Wo foshanren biji* [Brief sketches by a man of Foshan]. Shanghai: Dada tushu gongying she.

Wu Ming [No Name; pseud.]. 1933. "Kaifang changjin zhi liyou anzai?" [Where is the reason for lifting the ban on prostitution?]. *Funü gongming* 2.5 (May): 37.

Wu Ruohua. 1929. "Shanghai funü jiuji shiye yingyou de gaige" [The reforms that should happen in the undertaking of rescuing Shanghai women]. *Shehui yuekan* 1.2 (February): 1–8.

Wu Zhou. 1990. *Zhongguo jinü shenghuo shi* [A history of the life of Chinese prostitutes]. Changsha: Hunan wenyi chubanshe.

Xi Dichen. 1933. "Danao gongtang an" [The Mixed Court riot]. *Shanghai shi tongzhiguan qikan* 1.2 (September): 407–40.

Xia Yan. 1984 (1936). *Sai Jinhua*. Beijing (Shanghai): Zhongguo xiju chubanshe (Shenghuo shudian).

Xia Zhengnong, ed. 1979. *Cihai* [Sea of words]. Shanghai: Shanghai cishu chubanshe. 3 vols.

Xi'an fazhi bao [Xi'an legal news]. 1993.

Xiandai funü [Contemporary woman]. 1948.

Xiao Jianqing. 1936. *Manhua Shanghai* [Cartoons of Shanghai]. Shanghai: Shanghai jingwei shuju.

———. 1937. *Shanghai xiangdao* [Guide to Shanghai]. Shanghai: Shanghai jingwei shuju.

Xiao Su. 1946. "Changji shenghuo ku" [A prostitute's life is bitter]. *Jia* 9 (October): 31.

Xie Zhihong and Jia Lusheng. 1989. *Gulao de zui'e* [Ancient crime]. Zhejiang: Zhejiang wenyi chubanshe.

Xin shijie baoshe. 1918. *Huaguo baimei tu* [Pictures of the hundred beauties of flow-erland]. Shanghai: Shengsheng meishu gongsi.

Xinwen ribao. 1950s. Shanghai.

Xiong Zhongxie and Sun Yun. 1993. "Funü xing jiefang, diwei da xiajiang" [Women's sexual liberation (has caused a) great decline in their status]. *Xinwen ziyou daobao* (February 19): 2.

Xu Chi et al. 1942. *Shanghai zhongsheng xiang* [A photo of all the living things of Shang-hai]. Shanghai: Xin Zhongguo baoshe.

Xu Huifang and Liu Qingyu. 1932. "Shanghai nüxing fan de shehui fenxi" [A social analysis of female crime in Shanghai]. *Dalu zazhi* 1.4 (October): 71–92.

Xu Jinfu. 1922. "Changmen zhi fu" [Father of the brothels]. *Banyue* 2.3: 1–7.

Xu Ke. 1920. *Qingbai leichao* [Qing unofficial reference book]. Shanghai: Shangwu yinshuguan.

Xu Yasheng. 1930. "Chang ji yu shehui" [Prostitution and society]. *Funü zazhi* 16.6: 16–27.

Xue Gengxin. 1986. "Wo jiechuguo de Shanghai banghui renwu" [Shanghai gang-sters I have known]. In Zhu Xuefan, ed. *Jiu Shanghai de banghui* [The gangs of old Shanghai]. Shanghai: Shanghai renmin chubanshe, 87–107.

Xue Liyong. 1988. "Mingqing shiqi de Shanghai chang ji" [Prostitution in Shanghai in the Ming and Qing period]. In Shanghai shi wenshi guan, ed. *Jiu Shanghai de yanduchang* [Opium, gambling, and prostitution in old Shanghai]. Shanghai: Bai-jia chubanshe, 150–58.

Yan Dunyi. 1923. "Feichang wenti de zhongyao" [The importance of abolishing pros-titution]. *Funü zazhi* 9.5: 28–29.

Yan Ji. 1992. *Jingcheng wunü qun* [Crowds of taxi dancers in the capital city]. Beijing: Beijing shifan daxue chubanshe.

Yan Ping. 1977. "Guangdong jinü gaikuang" [A survey of Guangdong prostitutes]. *Beidou* [Hong Kong] 3 (August 1): 11–18.

Yang Jiezeng. 1986. Interview by author with head of the Shanghai Women's Labor Training Institute from 1952 to 1958.

Yang Jiezeng and He Wannan, eds. 1988. *Shanghai chang ji gaizao shihua* [A history of the reform of Shanghai prostitutes]. Shanghai: Shanghai sanlian shudian.

Yang Quan, ed. 1993b. "Jinü peiyang de zongdu" [The provincial governor trained by a prostitute]. *Jiu Zhongguo jixing jiating jishi* [Records of abnormal households in old China] (June): 32–34. Nei Menggu wenhua chubanshe.

———. 1993a. "Piaoke, yuanlai shi pianzi" [It turns out that the john was a swindler]. *Jiu Zhongguo jixing jiating jishi* [Records of abnormal households in old China] (June): 26–28. Nei Menggu wenhua chubanshe.

Yang Xiaobing. 1991. "China Launches Anti-Prostitution Campaign." *Beijing Review* 34.50 (December 16–22): 27–29.

Yang Xiuqin and Xu Huiqing. 1986. Interview by author with former workers at the Shanghai Women's Labor Training Institute. Shanghai.

Yao Jiguang and Yu Yifen. 1981. "Shanghai de xiaobao" [The mosquito press of Shang-hai]. *Xinwen yanjiu ziliao congkan* 3–4 (*zong* 9–10): 223–44 (3); 245–91 (4).

Yao Shaomei. 1935. "Chang ji wenti de zong jianyue" [A general review of the pros-titution question]. *Renyan zhoukan* 2.9 (March 30): 167–68.

Ye Derong. 1936. "Zhongguo changji wenti de tantao" [An investigation of the problem of prostitution in China]. *Nüzi yuekan* 4.11 (November): 30–41.

Ye Po. 1989. "Maiyin: huangse de qianliu" [Sex-selling: The pornographic undercurrent]. *Funü yanjiu* 6: 7–8.

Ye Xiaoqing. 1991. "Popular Culture in Shanghai 1884–1898." Ph.D. dissertation, Australian National University.

Yeh, Catherine. 1990. "The Intellectual as the Courtesan: A Trope in Twentieth-Century Chinese Literature." Conference paper presented at Harvard University.

Yeh, Wen-hsin. 1992. "Progressive Journalism and Shanghai's Petty Urbanites." In Frederic Wakeman, Jr., and Wen-hsin Yeh, eds. *Shanghai Sojourners*. Berkeley: University of California Institute of East Asian Studies, 186–238.

Yen, Ching-yueh. 1934–1935. "Crime in Relation to Social Change in China." *American Journal of Sociology* 40.3.

Yi Feng. 1933a. "Changji wenti yanjiu" [Research on the problem of prostitution]. *Funü gongming* 2.2 (February): 31–44.

———. 1933b. "Changji wenti yanjiu, ji" [Research on the problem of prostitution, continued]. *Funü gongming* 2.3 (March): 25–37.

Yi Wen. 1933. "Changji kaijin wenti zhi wojian" [My opinion on the problem of lifting the ban on prostitution]. *Funü gongming* 2.4 (April): 18–21.

Yi Xiao. 1938. "Shenghuo zishu: Wunü Wei Xueshu yu Yang Minshi" [My life in my own words: Taxi dancers Wei Xueshu and Yang Minshi]. *Shanghai funü* 1.2 (May): 14–15.

———. 1939. "Yige wunü de laixin" [Letter from a taxi dancer]. *Shanghai funü* 3.2 (May): 28.

Yong He. 1933. "Jinchang wenti yu zhengge funü yundong" [The problem of banning prostitution and the women's movement as a whole]. *Funü gongming* 2.5 (May): 23–28.

You Xiongyi. 1923. "Changji zhi weisheng de qudi" [The health ban on prostitution]. *Funü zazhi* 9.3: 42–44.

Yu Muxia. 1935. *Shanghai linzhao* [Shanghai tidbits]. Shanghai: Shanghai hubaoguan chubanbu. 3 vols.: *shang, xia, ji.*

Yu Wei. 1947. "Jinchang yu xingbing fangzhi" [Banning prostitution and the prevention and cure of sexually transmitted diseases]. *Shizheng pinglun* 9.9–10 (October 15): 17–18, 45.

———. 1948. "Shanghai changji wubaige an diaocha" [An investigation of five hundred cases of prostitution in Shanghai]. *Shizheng pinglun* 10.10 (October 15): 10–14.

Yu Wei and Amos Wong. 1949. "A Study of 500 Prostitutes in Shanghai." *International Journal of Sexology* 2.4 (May): 234–38.

Yu Yongfu. 1986. "Wo suo zhidao de Du Yuesheng" [The Du Yuesheng I knew]. In Zhu Xuefan, ed. *Jiu Shanghai de banghui* [The gangs of old Shanghai]. Shanghai: Shanghai renmin chubanshe, 268–83.

Yu Yunjiu. 1986. "Wo suo zhidao de Zhang Xiaolin" [The Zhang Xiaolin I knew]. In Zhu Xuefan, ed. *Jiu Shanghai de banghui* [The gangs of old Shanghai]. Shanghai: Shanghai renmin chubanshe, 347–49.

Yuan Shike et al. 1949. *Shanghai fengqing* [Shanghai romance]. N.p.: Lantian shubao zazhi she.

Zarrow, Peter. 1990. *Anarchism and Chinese Political Culture.* New York: Columbia University Press.

———. 1988. "He Zhen and Anarcho-Feminism in China." *Journal of Asian Studies* 47.4 (November): 796–813.

Zeng Die. 1935. "Guanyu changji diaocha" [An investigation about prostitution]. *Renyan zhoukan* 2.36 (November 16): 710–11.

Zeng Pu. 1979. *Niehai hua* [Flowers in a sea of evil]. Shanghai: Shanghai guji chubanshe.

Zhan Kai. 1917 (1914). *Rouxiang yunshi* [A history of the charm of the gentle village]. Author's preface dated 1907. Shanghai: Wenyi xiaoqian suo. 3 *juan.*

Zhang Chunfan [pseud.: Shuliu Shanfang]. 1917. *Huitu jiuwei gui* [Illustrated nine-tailed turtle]. Shanghai: Jicheng shuju.

———. 1919. "Shanghai qinglou zhi jinxi guan" [A look at Shanghai brothels present and past]. *Jingbao*, March 3, 6, 9, 12, 15, 18, 21, 24, 30; April 6, 12, 27; May 6; p. 3 in all cases.

———. 1932. "Haishang qinglou yange ji" [A record of the evolution of Shanghai houses of prostitution]. *Wansui zazhi* 1.2–9 (August 16–December 1).

Zhang Hequn. 1935. "Sulian feichang zhi yifa" [The Soviet Union method for abolishing prostitution]." *Renyan zhoukan* 1.50 (January 26): 1,026–27.

Zhang Jialiang. 1934. "Jinchang de genben banfa" [A fundamental method of banning prostitution]. *Zhongguo shehui* 1.1 (July 15): 54–56.

Zhang Mingyuan. 1994. "Liang Qichao de liangxing guan: Lun chuantong dui zhishifenzi de yueshu" [Liang Qichao's view of the two sexes: The restraint of tradition on intellectuals]. *Jindai Zhongguo funü shi yanjiu* 2 (June): 51–64.

Zhang Shou. 1884. *Jinmen zaji* [Tianjin miscellany]. Tianjin: N.p.

Zhang Xinxin and Sang Ye. 1985. "Beijing ren" [Beijing people]. *Zuojia*, no. 1: 1–17.

———. 1987. *Chinese Lives: An Oral History of Contemporary China.* Ed. and trans. W. J. F. Jenner and Delia Davin. New York: Pantheon Books.

Zhang Xunjiu. 1934. *Shanghai lishi yanyi* [Historical romance of Shanghai]. Shanghai: Danan shuju. 2 vols.

Zhang Yiquan. 1990. "The Social Background of Prostitution." *Shehui* 68 (October 20): 38–40. Translated in JPRS-CAR-91-005 (January 31, 1991), pp. 62–65.

Zhi Shan. 1933. "Changji wenti de yanjiu yu shoudu kaijin" [Research on the question of prostitution and the lifting of the ban in the capital]. *Funü gongming* 2.5 (May): 7–12.

Zhong Yan. 1927. "Feichang shijian de wojian" [My view on the business of abolishing prostitution]. *Funü zazhi* 13.12: 17–19.

Zhonggong zhongyang Makesi Engesi Lienin Sidalin zhuzuo bianziju yanjiushi, eds. 1978. *Wusi shiqi qikan jieshao* [An introduction to the magazines of the May Fourth era]. Shenyang: Shenguo dushu xinzhi sanlian shudian, 2 vols.

Zhonghua quanguo funü lianhehui funü yanjiusuo, Shaanxi sheng funü lianhehui yanjiu shi, ed. 1991. *Zhongguo funü tongji ziliao 1949–1989* [Statistics on Chinese women, 1949–1989]. Beijing: Zhongguo tongji chubanshe.

Zhonghua tushu jicheng bianji suo. 1925 (1918). *Shanghai funü nie jingtai* [The evil dressing table of Shanghai women]. Shanghai: Zhonghua tushu jicheng gongsi.

Zhongwai funü [Chinese and foreign women]. 1985.

Zhou Shixian. 1934. "Changji de zaocheng" [The formation of prostitution]. *Renyan zhoukan* 1.45 (December 22): 939.

Zhou Shoujuan. 1928. *Lao Shanghai sanshi nian jianwen lu* [A record of things seen by an old Shanghai hand in the last thirty years]. Shanghai: Dadong shuju, 2 vols.

————. n.d. (1940s?). *Xin qiuhaitang* [New begonia]. Hong Kong: Dawen shuju.

Zhou Yinjun, Yang Jiezeng, and Xue Suzhen. 1980. "Yige jinü de xuelei shi" [A prostitute's history of blood and tears]. *Qingnian yidai*, no. 6: 31–32.

————. 1981. "Xin shehui ba gui biancheng ren" [The new society turns ghosts into people]. *Shehui* 1 (October): 46–51.

Zhu Junzhou. 1988. "Shanghai xiaobao de lishi yange" [The historical evolution of the Shanghai mosquito press]. *Xinwen yanjiu ziliao* 42–44 (June, September, December): 163–77 (June), 137–53 (September), 210–20 (December).

Zhu Meiyu. 1933. "Zhongguo changji wenti zhi yanjiu" [Research on the problem of prostitution in China]. *Funü gongming* 2.10 (October): 28–40.

Zhu Tianze. 1988. "Jinri Huile Li" [Huile Li today]. *Renmin ribao* [overseas edition], April 20.

Zhu Xuefan, ed. 1986. *Jiu Shanghai de banghui* [The gangs of old Shanghai]. Shanghai: Shanghai renmin chubanshe.

Zhu Zhenxin. 1923. "Lun changji wenti" [On the problem of prostitution]. *Funü zazhi* 9.3: 9–12.

Zhu Zijia [pseud. for Jin Qiongbai]. 1964. *Huangpu jiang de zhuolang* [Muddy waves of the Huangpu River]. Hong Kong: Wuxingji shubao she.

Zhu Zuotong and Mei Yi, eds. 1939. *Shanghai yiri* [One day in Shanghai]. Shanghai: Hwa Mei Publishing Co., H. P. Mills, Publisher. 4 parts.

Zhuo Dai. 1922. "Jinü jiahou de xin" [The heart of a prostitute after marriage]. *Xingqi* 38: 1–9.

Zito, Angela. 1993. "Ritualizing *Li*: Implications for Studying Power and Gender." *positions: east asia cultures critique* 1.2 (fall): 321–48.

Zou Yiren. 1980. *Jiu Shanghai renkou bianqian de yanjiu* [Research on changes in the population of old Shanghai]. Shanghai: Shanghai renmin chubanshe.

INDEX

A Mu, 221
A Zhen, 258–259
A Zhu, 259–260
abolition, 3, 6, 19, 181, 200–201, 240–241,
    271; campaigns of 1920s, 246, 271–287;
    campaigns of 1930s, 246; debates about,
    253, 272–287, 322, 504n. 3; 1928 at-
    tempt, 287–288; in 1950s, 30, 32, 65,
    267, 303, 304–324, 367, 393, 396–397;
    recommended by foreigners, 229; as
    ultimate goal in 1940s, 288–289, 295
abortion, 175, 316, 348, 463n. 138
Abu-Lughod, Lila, 27
adoption, 75, 85, 176; by courtesans, 143
Ah Hong, 335, 345, 347, 348
AIDS, 348–350, 377, 527n. 97, 528n. 103
Aiwen, 84
ajie, 77
amusement halls, 38, 59; licensing and, 301
anarchism, 247; critique of capitalism in, 247
anchang. See prostitutes, secret
Asian Wall Street Journal, 348
Association of Shanghai Shuyu, 299
Augustine, Saint, 263
"ax chop," 137

"bad girls," 143–152, 164; characteristics
    of, 144; class and, 145; sexuality and,
    144–145
Bai Zhongxi, 124
Ban Gu, 21
bankai men. See "half-open doors"

banquets, 55, 93, 94–96, 106, 115, 125,
    129–130, 134, 135; ceremony and,
    95–96; *changsan* and, 43; cost of, 81,
    442n. 165; courtesan house income
    and, 94; courtesans and, 14; customers
    and, 94, 104, 107; madams and, 72;
    shuyu and, 42; terminology of, 94–95,
    442n. 167
Bao Lin, 76, 437n. 48
Bao Qin, 122–124
bao shenti. See pawning
Bao Tianxiao, 30, 217, 416n. 81
baofu, 71
baomu, 71
baozhang, 197
Beahan, Charlotte, 247
Bebel, August, 253, 260–261, 497n. 47
Beili, 15, 146
benjia, 71
Berkhofer, Robert, 13
Bi Yao, 266
Bi Yihong, 30, 257–258, 395, 416n. 81,
    498n. 68
"bitter-meat stratagem," 137
"blockhead," 129–130, 451n. 8
Blue Bridge Villa, 171
"body price," 120, 122, 124
bolibei. See tea hostesses
Boxers, 147, 173
boxiang ren, 71
"breaking the melon," 107, 133
"brothel prop," 71, 487n. 75

577

Compositor: Integrated Composition Systems
Text 10/12 Baskerville
Display: Baskerville
Printer: Thomson-Shore, Inc.
Binder: Thomson-Shore, Inc.